RPG II WITH BUSINESS APPLICATIONS

Stanley E. Myers

Professor
Norwalk State Technical College
Norwalk, Connecticut

Reston Publishing Company, Inc.
A Prentice-Hall Company
Reston, Virginia

Library of Congress Cataloging in Publication Data

Myers, Stanley E., 1926–
    RPG II with business applications.

    Includes index.
    1. RPG (Computer program language)
2. Business—Data processing. I. Title.
HF5548.5.R2M928   001.6'424   79-10458
ISBN 0-8359-6303-9

© 1979 by Reston Publishing Company, Inc.
A Prentice-Hall Company
Reston, Virginia 22090

10 9 8 7 6 5 4 3 2

Printed in the United States of America

To my wife, Mona,
my daughter, Kathy,
and grandsons,
Christopher and Terrence.

CONTENTS

PREFACE

This book is a revised and updated edition of *RPG: With Business and Accounting Applications*. Advantages of this text over the previous edition include:

1. Students are able to write, compile, and execute their first programs after completing Chapter 2.

2. Every important feature of the RPG II Computer language is supported by "error-free" computer executed programs supplemented by line by line discussions.

3. Hundreds of figures are used throughout the text to explain the Where and

4. Questions, Exercises, and Laboratory Assignments are included for every chapter. Questions are designed for recall of chapter material. Exercises require that chapter concepts be entered on coding forms. At least two lab assignments (some chapters have seven) that range in difficulty from the simple to complex support the practical approach to the learning of the RPG II language.

5. Comprehensive coverage of Sequential, Indexed-Sequential, Direct, and Addrout disk files is presented in separate chapters.

6. An exhaustive discussion of the coding and concepts related to arrays is presented in a separate chapter.

7. A general building block approach is used for the subject matter that ranges from the simple to complex.

8. Emphasis is placed on the importance of data and how it affects processing and end results.

Specifically, the text follows a sequence of subject matter discussed in the following paragraphs.

In order to familiarize the student with the world of data processing, Chapter 1 introduces basic computer concepts. The overall configuration of a computer system, including input and output devices and media, is discussed. An example RPG II program with resulting output is illustrated.

Chapter 2 leaves the total computer environment and introduces specifics about one subset of study, the RPG II programming language. The sequence of steps usually followed for the completion of an RPG II source program, which includes an analysis of the problem, design of input and output requirements, formatting, coding, keypunching, compilation, debugging, and program execution, are explained. Completion of this chapter will provide the student with enough knowledge to write his or her first RPG II program.

Chapter 3 further develops the student's knowledge of RPG II coding rules with an introduction of report headings common to most printed reports. Also presented is the editing of numeric fields by edit codes and words. At this point in the text students are able to write any card input and printer output program without calculations.

RPG II calculation coding is presented in Chapter 4 with emphasis on the mathematical operations including addition, subtraction, multiplication, division, move remainder, and square root. In addition, Resulting and Field Indicator concepts and usage is explained.

Programs presented in the text and assigned as exercises and lab work have only used one record type in a data file. Chapter 5 introduces *Multiple Record File* concepts along with sequence checking of data records, and the MOVE operations.

RPG II has often been considered the language ideally suited for the printing of reports. Chapter 6 illustrates the power of this language for this purpose and details the logic and coding fundamentals associated with *group reports*. Additional control over printed output is provided by the SETON and SETOF operations and Fetch Overflow. The Z-ADD and Z-SUB operation are also introduced in this chapter.

Chapter 7 introduces coding techniques for the Compare (COMP) operation, which gives the computer the power to make a decision based upon the condition of a test for high, low, or equal. Also presented in this chapter are two important features of any computer language; the ability to instruct a computer to Branch and/or Loop within a set of instructions.

The Exception (EXCPT) operation is presented in Chapter 8 which adds a new dimension to the RPG II language. The EXCPT operation code instructs control to leave calculations, go to output, and then return control back to calculations. Also discussed is page overflow control with EXCPT (exception) output.

Chapter 9 introduces disk file concepts and the creation (loading), processing, and addition to Sequentially Organized disk files. Blocking of data records and Packed Decimal Format are other important subjects discussed in this chapter.

Chapter 10 discusses the processing of files by the Matching Record technique. This often confusing RPG II concept is simplified by a listing of the processing rules associated with Matching Records. The processing and updating of data files by this method supports the learning of this important concept.

The creation, sequential processing, addition, limits processing, random processing, and the updating of Indexed-Sequential (ISAM) disk files is presented in Chapter 11. This very important disk file organization method is emphasized through a sequence of computer executed programs supporting every ISAM concept.

Chapter 12 introduces Direct and Addrout disk file concepts. Efficiency is an important consideration in the processing of data files and Direct and Addrout files often offer advantages not found with sequential or indexed-sequential organization methods.

Chapter 13 presents a comprehensive discussion of RPG II Table Concepts. Emphasis is placed on the alternative ways of organizing table data and the time in which tables are loaded in the program cycle.

An extensive Chapter 14 details the RPG II coding rules for array processing. A comparison of tables to arrays is presented and supported by a discussion of when a table or an array should be used for the application.

Additional RPG II features including Internal Subroutines, the *PLACE word, the DEBUG operation, Look Ahead Feature, the FORCE operation, and the DSPLY operation are presented in Chapter 15. Some of these concepts may be introduced after Chapter 5. For example, the DEBUG operation could be useful in debugging any program using extensive calculations. The use of Internal Subroutines could also be used in programs to increase efficiency.

This text may serve as the foundation for further study of the RPG II programming language for any computer system. Even though RPG II is compatible with any manufacturer's RPG II compiler, there are usually minor differences in a specific manufacturer's software. Consequently, the text is not intended to be the only source of specific information concerning all aspects of the language and the respective manufacturer's language and programmer's manuals should be referred to in order to compensate for any minor differences.

ACKNOWLEDGMENTS

I would like to extend special thanks to Robert Avery for his guidance and constructive criticism in revising this book.

In addition, I offer my appreciation to Diana Cooper, Lorraine Farrell, and Carolyn Henderson for their help in the keypunching, compilation, and execution of many computer programs in this text.

Furthermore, I want to express my appreciation to my wife, Mona, for her patience and understanding of the time I have devoted to this book in lieu of family activities.

1
BASIC DATA
PROCESSING CONCEPTS

ELEMENTS OF A COMPUTER SYSTEM

The fastest method for the handling, manipulating, and storing of *instructions* and *data* is by electronic data processing with the aid of a computer. There are three basic elements involved with computer usage: input, processing, and output. Input includes the entering of instructions and/or data into the central processing unit through an input hardware unit. Processing stores the instructions and uses them to manipulate the incoming data into the required output. The output may be in the form of a printed report, displayed on a cathode ray tube, punched into cards, or stored in magnetic characters on a disk, tape, drum, cell, or diskette unit.

Figure 1-1 shows the three elements relating to the actual hardware of a computer installation.

An examination of Figure 1-1 will show that the input element for this installation is a card reader; the processing element, the processor or CPU; and the output, a printer. Obviously, the basic elements of electronic data processing with the aid of a computer are related to functional hardware devices. The sequence of steps involved in the usage of this installation would be as follows:

1. Data cards would be loaded into the card reader. The information contained in the cards might be the source document information

1

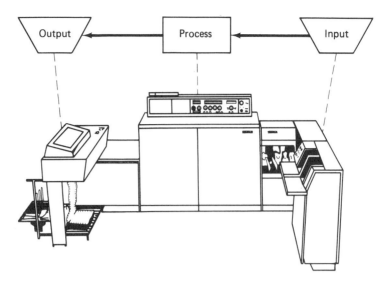

Fig. 1-1.   Hardware elements of a computer installation.

related to a business, commercial, engineering, or scientific transaction, application, or problem.

2. The data would be processed by the Central Processing Unit (CPU) by instructions (program) read in previously and stored before the data was read.

3. If the instructions were error free, the output, in the form of a report or answer, would be obtained on the printer.

In addition to card readers and printers there are many other types of equipment used as input and output hardware. Some of the other devices include the magnetic disk drive, magnetic tape drive, terminals, paper tape drive, magnetic drum unit, data cells, magnetic diskette drive, and a card punch. Figure 1-2 shows which hardware units may be used as input devices and those used for output. Notice that many of the hardware devices may be used for both input and output.

An input/output device popular today is the terminal illustrated in Figure 1-3. Notice that it consists of a television-type cathode ray tube and a typewriter keyboard. Some terminal units do not have the display tube but include a carriage for paper similar to a typewriter. Because terminals are connected to a central computer by telephone lines, a major advantage is that the user does not have to physically be at the computer site.

Also, because of the multiprogramming features of many computer frames which allow the computer to process more than one program at a time, more than one user may utilize the computer simultaneously by the installation of many terminals connected to one computer. The installation illustrated in

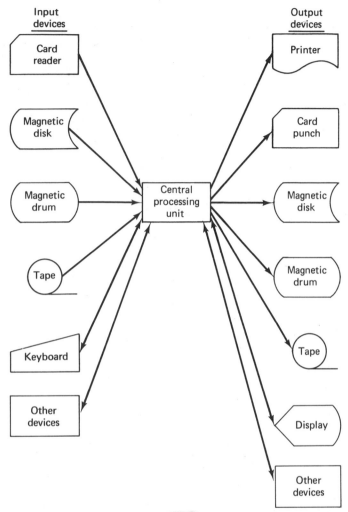

Fig. 1-2. Input/Output Hardware Units

Figure 1-1 is commonly called the typical *batch system* which limits the computer's usage to one user at a time. Because of the speed of the CPU, which is much faster than any input/output device, it is usually waiting for work. Multiprogramming features and terminals have enabled users to utilize the *wait time* of the CPU and take better advantage of its processing potential at reduced costs.

Because of the spectrum of devices on the market today and their individual unique features it is not within the scope of this book to cover each hardware unit in detail. The book will, however, place the greatest emphasis on computer systems using card and disk input and printed and disk output.

Fig. 1-3. Cathode Ray Tube Terminal

A discussion of punch card designs is presented in the following paragraphs. Punch cards are used to enter and store data information related to a transaction and program instructions that inform the computer to process the data in the required way.

HOLLERITH CARD

The two punch card designs in common use today are the Hollerith card and the IBM System/3 card. A Hollerith card that has not been punched is shown in Figure 1-4. Notice that it is a rectangular-shaped card with 80 vertical columns and 12 horizontal rows. The top of the card is referred to as the 12 edge and the bottom of the card as the nine edge. The left side of the card is numbered the one column and the extreme right the 80 column. Because of the design no more than 80 characters may be punched on any one card.

Figure 1-4 also shows a Hollerith card with all the arabic numbers, English alphabet, and popular special characters punched on one card. Observe that each number, 0 through 9, has only one punch per vertical column. A zero will be represented by a punch in the zero row; a one by a punch in the one row; and so on. However, two punches per column are necessary for alphabetic characters: a zone punch and a digit punch. The card shows the zone punching area that includes two undefined rows, the 12 row and 11 row, along with the zero row. Consequently, there are three rows, 12, 11, and zero, that are referred to as zone punches. With a zone punch there must be a digit punch to make an alphabetic character. Notice that the letter A has a zone punch in the 12 row and a digit punch in the one row; a K has a zone punch in the 11 row and a digit punch in the two row. By examining the figure the student can readily see the combination of punches needed to represent a letter. Furthermore, special characters have their own combination of punches that

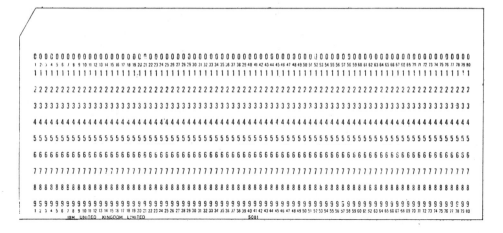

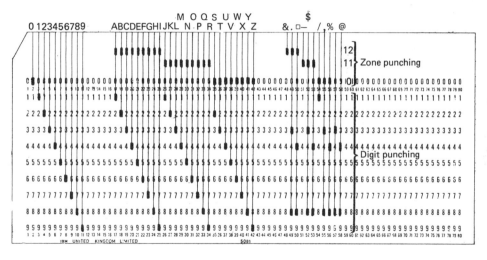

Fig. 1-4.   The Hollerith card.

may require three punches per column, as can be seen in the figure.

A card may be divided into fields, one or more columns assigned to a data item, according to the needs of the user. For example, if a field were to be assigned for the calendar years, as 1978, no less than four card columns could be assigned to this information. The field could be anywhere on the card—the first four columns, the middle four, the last four, or any four the programmer selected. A card field may be only one column in length or the entire 80 column width of the Hollerith card.

Besides punching rectangular holes in punch cards a keypunch machine may be purchased or rented that prints on the top line, above the 12 row, what is punched in each column. This worthwhile feature is called interpreting and enables anyone to visually check for mistakes or determine what is punched in the card at a glance. The beginning student is encouraged to use a keypunch with this feature if possible.

SYSTEM/3 CARD

Figure 1-5 shows the System/3 card. The area indicated as the print area is used only for interpreting what is punched in the lower two-thirds of the card. Also, the punch portion is divided into three 32-column tiers giving a total of 96 columns of available information per card or 16 more than the Hollerith card previously discussed. Because all the tiers are identical in design it is necessary to examine the format of only one tier to see the typical design. Figure 1-5 explodes a tier so the reader may study the design. Observe that there are six rows per tier with each of the rows labeled B, A, 8, 4, 2, 1. The B

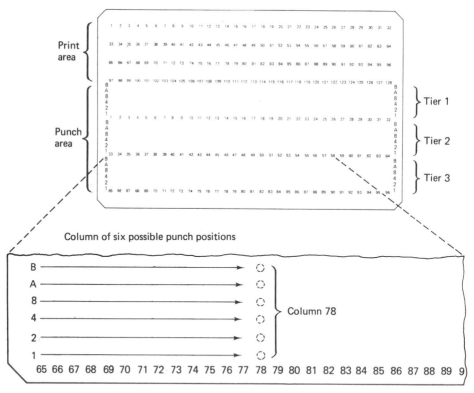

Source: International Business Machines Corporation, Data Processing Division, *IBM System/3 Card System Introduction,* Number C21-7505-0 (White Plains, New York, 1970), pp. 10-12.

Fig. 1-5.   System/3 card design.

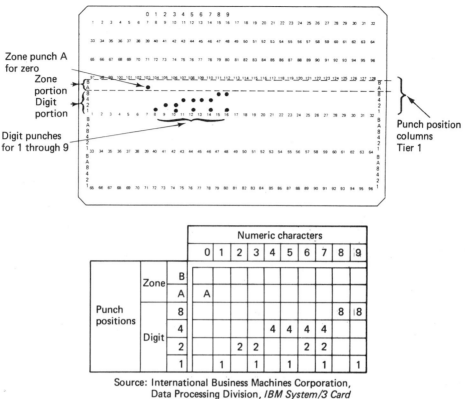

Fig. 1-6.   System/3 card and chart showing number punches.

			Numeric characters										
			0	1	2	3	4	5	6	7	8	9
Punch positions	Zone	B										
		A	A										
	Digit	8									8	8
		4					4	4	4	4		
		2			2	2			2	2		
		1		1		1		1		1		1

Source: International Business Machines Corporation,
Data Processing Division, *IBM System/3 Card
System Introduction.* Number C21-7505-0
(White Plains, New York, 1970), pp. 14-15.

and A rows of each tier are referred to as the zone portion and rows 8, 4, 2, and 1 the digit portion of the tier. Furthermore, the first tier has columns numbered 1 through 32, the second tier contains columns 33 to 64, and the last tier columns 65 through 96, giving 32 available columns per tier or 96 for the System/3 card.

A card punched with all of the arabic numbers is shown in Figure 1-6. A punch in the A row or zone portion of a tier in any card column as seen in the figure will always represent the number 0. The chart also illustrated in Fig. 1-6 shows all of the possible punch combinations for the numbers 0 through 9. Notice that many of the numbers require more than one punch per card column. For example, the number 7 requires punches in rows 4, 2, and 1 of the same card column in the digit portion of a tier.

In Figure 1-7 a card is shown with the alphabetic characters T, O, and M punched. An examination of this card will indicate that letters have at least one zone punch in B or A and one or more digit punches. Figure 1-7 further shows

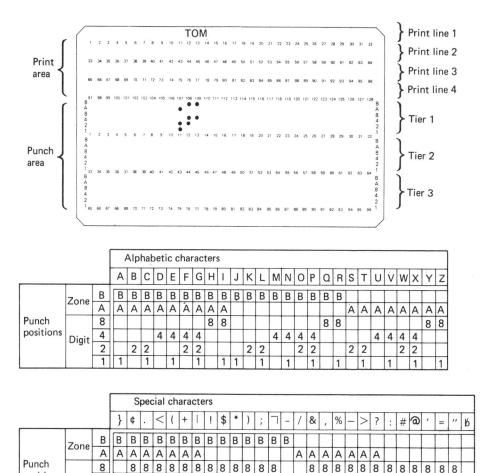

Source: International Business Machines Corporation,
Data Processing Division, *IBM System/3 Card
System Introduction,* Number C21-7505-0
(White Plains, New York, 1970), pp. 15-16.

Fig. 1-7. System/3 card and chart showing alphabetic and special character punch combinations.

the punch combinations for all the letters of the English alphabet. The letter A, for example, requires a punch in rows B and A of the zone portion and a punch in row 1 of the digit portion of one of the tiers. Again, every letter needs at least one zone punch with some digit punch or punches. A chart is also shown in Figure 1-7 for the punch codes of special characters that are commonly used in data processing. Although both the Hollerith and System/3 cards have been explained, a student does not need to memorize the punching codes but should only be familiar with the principles of this important input media.

CARD READERS

A schematic of a card reader/punch unit showing the basic features common on this type of input device is illustrated in Figure 1-8. This hardware component is designated by the manufacturer as the IBM 1442 card read /punch unit. Hollerith cards, in order to be read, are placed face down nine edge first in the hopper labeled A as indicated in the figure. After a read button is pushed the cards are read one at a time automatically until the stack is exhausted. Processed cards are placed in stacker 1, labeled B in the example. The programmer or operator has the option of returning the cards to stacker 2, labeled C, if needed, by a simple code in his instructions to the computer.

The operating speeds of card readers vary according to manufacturer and model. The unit illustrated has a maximum reader speed of 400 cards per minute and a maximum punch speed of 160 columns per second. A student must realize that all equipment does not look or, in fact, operate the same. Familiarity with the operating characteristics of the available equipment will be necessary.

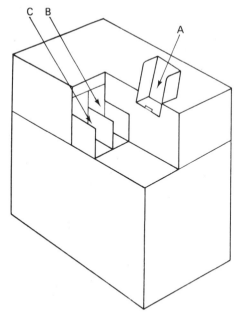

Source: International Business Machines Corporation, Data Processing Division, *IBM 1130 RPG Coding,* Book 1, Number R29-0276-0 (White Plains, New York, 1970), p. 234.

Fig. 1-8. IBM 1442 Reader/Punch Unit.

PROCESSING

The second element of data processing is processing. The process unit of any computer is called the CPU or Central Processing Unit. Figure 1-9 shows a diagram for a computer system including the input, CPU, and output. The CPU consists of three basic sections: memory, control, and arithmetic. A computer's memory is the construction of a string of ferro-magnetic cores or donuts called binary digits. When characters, digits, letters, or special characters are read they are converted to a binary code for storage purposes. Computer memories are, therefore, organized into many storage positions, and the size of a computer is determined by the number of available storage positions in its system.

A computer's memory may perform two functions. First, it may contain characters from the data being processed at the moment. For example, information read in from an input device such as a card reader is first placed in storage and then processed later. When processing is complete the results are transmitted to an output device such as a printer. Each record (punch card in a card system) of the file is processed in this manner until the entire card file is read.

The second function of a computer's memory involves the storage of a computer program or a set of sequential instructions. A program enables the computer to process the data records of a file in some specific way. RPG programs, which are sets of instructions which the student will learn to write by studying this text, are stored accordingly.

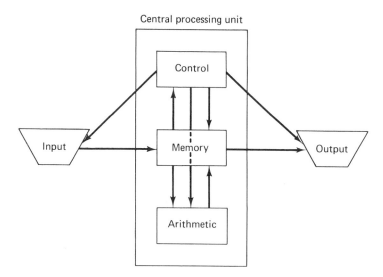

Fig. 1-9. Components of a computer system.

Furthermore, a computer system may have primary and secondary memory. Primary memory is that which is an integral part of the computer system. Secondary memory is extra memory that is peripheral to the main unit. Typical examples of secondary memory are a disk unit, magnetic tape unit, data cell unit, or any other piece of equipment developed for a certain computer. Secondary memory units are used when an increase of storage capacity is necessary.

CONTROL UNIT

The Control Unit literally takes the computer by the hand and instructs it on what to do and when. All the necessary steps to be performed must be translated into executable instructions. After a series of instructions, called a program, is read into the storage area of a computer, the instructions are available for execution by the control unit. Included in all computer systems is a set of instructions that will let the control unit break away from its sequence of instructions and go to some other memory position. This technique is called branching and is considered one of the major features that has made the computer a practical, useful tool. The Control Unit coordinates all operations which are called by programmed instructions, including all input and output (I/O) commands to devices.

ARITHMETIC UNIT

Addition, Subtraction, Division, Multiplication, Compare, and Logical Decisions, such as whether a number is zero, negative, or positive, all may be performed by the arithmetic unit. Consequently, complex calculations are possible by some combination of these operations.

Data stored in memory is transmitted to the arithmetic unit where calculations are performed and answers or results are placed in memory in an assigned storage position. Processing speeds of the CPU depend on the model and generation of the computer and range from milliseconds (thousandths of a second) to picoseconds (trillionths of a second). Hence, these phenomenal speeds have, of course, made complex problem solving both practical and possible.

OUTPUT

After the input of data and subsequent processing, the results must be made available to an output device of some type. Results may be printed, punched into cards, or stored magnetically on disk or tape, or on any other available output device. The user's needs will specify the type of equipment needed. In the introductory chapters of this text only the printer will be considered as an output device. However, in later chapters other methods of storing results will be discussed.

COMPUTER OPERATION

The steps involved in electronic data processing are similar to manual processing or the paper and pencil method. Readable information must be provided for input and the knowledge of arithmetic functions applied to solve problems. Intermediate results are placed on workpapers which can be compared with the storage of a computer. Final results or answers are the output.

A brief explanation of the internal operation of a computer should provide the student with an insight into the processes involved. As previously mentioned, the brain of a computer is the control unit. This unit can search, locate, and collect information from a computer's memory. Furthermore, a very unique feature of the unit is that when data is retrieved from memory the information at that location in storage is not destroyed but remains there for future use if so desired. This all-important feature is called the *nondestructive* readout process.

A storage location may contain data, numbers, or instructions for a program in operation. During operation the control unit calls in instructions from storage and interprets and executes them so that in turn they may cause another computer component to operate.

In order for the computer to distinguish between the types of information stored in memory a specific set of instructions must be followed. The series of instructions is known as a program and must be able to interpret and execute data and instructions stored in memory. The program must be written in a form that is easy for the programmer to use and for the computer to understand. In order to facilitate this conversation between man and computer, many types of programming languages have been created.

COMPUTER LANGUAGES

Languages have been developed to enable men to communicate with each other. With the development of the computer a practical method had to be created to provide a communication link between man and this formidable tool he had perfected.

The first computer language developed and used was a low–level language commonly known as machine language. It consists of only two words: a "1" and "0". A combination of these two words may represent a piece of information. Because of the choice of only "1" or "0", programming in machine language involves writing a combination of these two words. For example, if a programmer wanted to add the contents of two storage areas together an instruction such as 0101101000010000000000000111000 would have to be written. Obviously, the ability to communicate with a computer would be difficult if not impossible for the average human being.

The difficulty of writing computer programs in machine language caused users to find a more efficient and simpler way of utilizing the computer's potential. Consequently, computer languages, such as ALGOL, APL, BAL, BASIC, COBOL, FORTRAN, PL-1, and RPG II, were developed and thereby provided an easier communication link between man and the computer. Individuals could now write in a form they readily understood and the computer, through a software package called a compiler (or translator) could translate the symbolic language (RPG II) into machine language, the only form it understands.

RPG II (Report Program Generator) has become a widely used high-level symbolic language because of its simplicity and ease of learning. The RPG II language is an updated version of RPG I which has incorporated many new features which have made it more powerful and flexible for accounting and business applications.

An RPG II source program, written by a programmer, with the input data punched into cards and the printed report it generated is illustrated in Figure 1-10. The rules and details of writing this RPG II source program will be discussed in Chapter 2; however, a few important points should be noted when examining the figure.

First, notice the area named *source program*. This is what you (the programmer) have written according to the coding rules of the RPG II language on preprinted coding forms. The filled-in forms are used to keypunch the source program onto punch cards. Then the source program cards are loaded into the hopper of the card reader and processed by the computer. If there are no errors in your program the RPG II compiler will have translated it into machine language (object code) and stored it temporarily in the computer.

This stored program (now in object code) is the instructions you have told the computer to perform on the input data. The punched data cards (Figure 1-10) are then loaded into the hopper of the card reader and processed by following the stored instructions your source program, now in object code, has ordered the computer to execute. The final result is the printed report illustrated in Figure 1-10.

The following chapters of this book will present and explain the coding rules and techniques necessary for writing practical and efficient RPG II source programs for numerous accounting and business applications.

Data File:

502SALARIES EXPENSE   EXPENSE
501REPAIRS EXPENSE   EXPENSE
500GAS & OIL EXPENSE   EXPENSE
400COMMISSIONS EARNED   REVENUE
302JOHN SMITH,WITHDRAWALS   OWNER'S EQUITY
301JOHN SMITH,CAPITAL   OWNER'S EQUITY
211MORTGAGE PAYABLE   LONG-TERM LIABILITY
201ACCOUNTS PAYABLE   CURRENT LIABILITY
110AUTOMOBILE   FIXED ASSET
104PREPAID RENT   CURRENT ASSET
103NOTES RECEIVABLE   CURRENT ASSET
102ACCOUNTS RECEIVABLE   CURRENT ASSET
101CASH   CURRENT ASSET

Source Program Listing by the Computer:

```
DOS - RPGII          JOB - SAMPLE     03/21/78        PROGRAM - RPGOBJ

    0001    01 020  FCARDS   IP  F  80  80      MFCM1  SYSIPT         LEDGER
    0002    01 030  FREPORT  O   F 132 132      PRINTERSYSLST         LEDGER
    0003    02 010  ICARDS   SM  01                                  LEDGER
    0004    02 020  I                              1   3 ACTNO        LEDGER
    0005    02 030  I                              4  30 NAME         LEDGER
    0006    02 040  I                             31  50 TYPE         LEDGER
    0007    03 020  OREPORT  D 2      01                              LEDGER
    0008    03 030  O                       ACTNO      5             LEDGER
    0009    03 040  O                       NAME      41             LEDGER
    0010    03 050  O                       TYPE      68             LEDGER

          END OF SOURCE
```

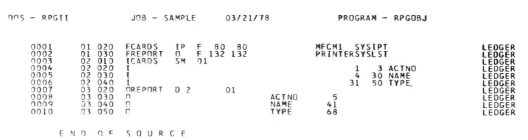

Fig. 1-10. Illustrated data file, source program listing, and printed output.

14

Printed Output Result:

101	CASH	CURRENT ASSET
102	ACCOUNTS RECEIVABLE	CURRENT ASSET
103	NOTES RECEIVABLE	CURRENT ASSET
104	PREPAID RENT	CURRENT ASSET
110	AUTOMOBILE	FIXED ASSET
201	ACCOUNTS PAYABLE	CURRENT LIABILITY
211	MORTGAGE PAYABLE	LONG-TERM LIABILITY
301	JOHN SMITH,CAPITAL	OWNER'S EQUITY
302	JOHN SMITH,WITHDRAWALS	OWNER'S EQUITY
400	COMMISSIONS EARNED	REVENUE
500	GAS & OIL EXPENSE	EXPENSE
501	REPAIRS EXPENSE	EXPENSE
502	SALARIES EXPENSE	EXPENSE

Fig. 1-10.   (continued)

QUESTIONS AND EXERCISES

1. Name the three basic elements of a computer system.
2. What is the function of each element?
3. Name five input devices.
4. Name five output devices.
5. What devices may be used for both input and output?
6. What device permits more than one user to use the computer at a time?
7. What is multiprogramming? Name a major advantage of this feature.
8. Describe the design of a Hollerith punch card.
9. Take a Hollerith punch card and mark the appropriate rows to indicate the ones that would be punched to spell the word *accounting*.
10. How many punch columns are available on a System/3 card? How many tiers?
11. What are the names of the rows common to the tiers of the System/3 card? Which are the zone rows? The digit rows?
12. Take a System/3 card and mark the correct rows so if punched it would represent the word REPORTS 1972.
13. What is meant by the word *interpreting*?
14. The part of the card reader device where punch cards are loaded is called the _____.
15. The part of the card reader that receives the processed cards is called the _____.
16. Another name for the processing unit of a computer is the _____.
17. Name the parts of the unit to which question 11 refers. In your own words, explain each function.
18. What is the name given to the feature of a computer's memory that does not destroy the contents already there after processing it?
19. What are picoseconds?
20. RPG is a _____ language.
21. Machine language contains how many words? Name them.
22. What are some of the functions that the arithmetic unit of the processor performs?
23. What is branching?
24. Name three popular computer languages.
25. What is a source program? Who writes it?
26. What is the function of a compiler (translator)?
27. What is object code?

LABORATORY ASSIGNMENTS

LABORATORY ASSIGNMENT 1-1:
RECORDING OF DATA ON RECORDS

You may have a card keypunch, data terminal, key-to-disk recorder, or key-to-tape recorder on the system available to you. In any case you must become familiar with the unit you will be using.

After the instructor gives you directions on the use of the machine, record the following data according to the locations indicated.

Name of company	positions 1–25
Street address	positions 26–50
City	positions 55–70
State	positions 71–72
Zip	positions 73–77

Data You Are To Record:

Name of company	Street address	City	State	Zip
SIKORSKY AIRCRAFT INC.	RIVER ROAD	STRATFORD	CT	06497
AVCO CORPORATION	SOUTH MAIN STREET	STRATFORD	CT	06497
COLUMBIA PICTURES, INC.	BOX 999	HOLLYWOOD	CA	90000
your name here	. . . . your address here			

2
INTRODUCTION
TO RPG II

PRELIMINARY PLANNING

Before an RPG II source program is written, preliminary planning steps must be considered. Specifically initial planning must consider first, the type and size of the data to be used as input; second, the design of the output; and third, the RPG II source program coding logic needed to process the data in the manner to obtain the required output.

DESIGN OF INPUT RECORDS

The planning and design of the input data to be entered on punch cards requires an understanding of general card terms such as file, record, field, and column. Figure 2-1 illustrates and explains the four concepts common to punch card terminology.

A data file may contain any number of physical records related to the same transaction. In fact a data file may only be one record long or may contain thousands of records. Examples of typical data files would be payroll information for the employees of a company, the deposit or withdrawal information for depositors' checking accounts, or the general ledger account information for a company. A data file may contain more than one *record type*;

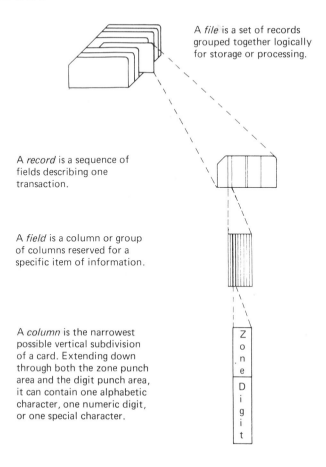

A *file* is a set of records grouped together logically for storage or processing.

A *record* is a sequence of fields describing one transaction.

A *field* is a column or group of columns reserved for a specific item of information.

A *column* is the narrowest possible vertical subdivision of a card. Extending down through both the zone punch area and the digit punch area, it can contain one alphabetic character, one numeric digit, or one special character.

Source: International Business Machines Corporation, Data Processing Division, *IBM 1130 RPG Coding,* Book 1, Number R29-0276-0 (White Plains, New York, 1970), p. iv.

Fig. 2-1. Punch card terminology.

however, for the purpose of simplicity this concept will be reserved for a later chapter.

Items to consider when input is designed as the data base for an RPG II program include a determination of field sizes; the type of fields, whether numeric, alphabetic, or alphanumeric; and the number of fields needed in each record to meet the data requirements. When determining the size of any field the maximum possible practical size must be provided or important information could be lost in processing and the ultimate output.

A useful tool to facilitate data punch card layout is illustrated in Figure 2-2. This card layout form is designed for the Hollerith card; however, other forms are available for the System/3 card as well as disk, etc. Notice that a maximum of six data card designs could be planned on the form with each record containing its own logical information.

Figure 2-2 also shows the relationship of a data base source information to the card layout form and how the form is used as the tool to punch data cards. In the example illustrated the source information is the general ledger of a small proprietorship. After the maximum size of the Account Number, Account Name, and Account Type fields is determined these fields are formatted on the layout form by drawing a vertical line to indicate the boundaries of each field. The name of each field is written within the field as shown. Note that the fields in a record do not have to be next to each other but may use any available consecutive columns on the form.

The size of the Account Number field was determined to be three characters in length; consequently, columns 1–3 are reserved for this field information. Account Name field has been given a size of 27 characters (columns 4–30) which is larger than the longest account name in the ledger. The programmer has provided for any new account names that may be longer than those presently used. The Account Type field has been assigned 20 characters in the reserved columns 31–50. Note that this field information was not included in the general ledger data base, but was given to the programmer by an accountant or systems analyst.

Also illustrated in Figure 2-2 is the relationship between the card layout form and an interpreted punched data card. There are several important concepts to understand before keypunching data cards. First, all alphabetic and alphanumeric data information must be punched *left-justified* in its respective assigned field. This means that the first character of the data item must begin in the first column of the field assigned to that variable.

An examination of Figure 2-2 will show that the number 1 is punched in column 1, the first position of the Account Number field; the letter C in column 4, the first position of the Account Name field; and C in column 31, the first position of the Account Type field. Furthermore, notice that columns 8 through 30 are not used for this data in the Account Name field. The field size assigned to Account Name is 27 characters long (columns 4–30) and if the variable data information is smaller than the maximum field size any unused *low-order* (right-hand) columns would be blank. The data entry CASH is only four characters long which leaves 23 unused positions in the assigned field.

On the other hand, numeric data used in input must be *right-justified* in the assigned columns of the field. This means that the lowest digit of the number must be punched in the last column of the respective field. Any unused *high-order* (left-hand) positions may remain blank or be filled in with zeros. Either method is acceptable in RPG II. The details of punching numeric data

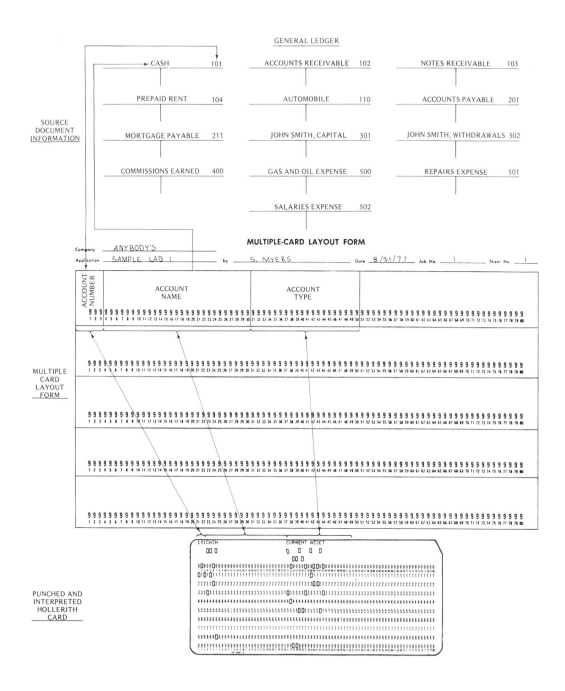

Fig. 2-2. Relationship of source document information, card layout form and punched data card.

into cards will be discussed in Chapter 3. Because calculations are not to be performed on Account Number data it may be considered alphanumeric and not numeric even though it contains all numbers.

Now that the data input requirements have been planned we are ready to discuss the format and design of the printed output for the introductory RPG II source program presented in this chapter.

PRINTED OUTPUT DESIGN

Supplemental to the design of input data before RPG II source program coding is attempted is the design of the printed output. A convenient tool used for printed output design is the Printer Spacing Chart. The comprehensive discussion of this chart is reserved for Chapter 3; however, a partial chart is illustrated in Figure 2-3 that shows the output design for the introductory RPG II source program.

Examine Figure 2-3 and locate the large numbers 0, 1, 2, and the small numbers that range from one to nine in the first field and zero to nine in the remaining fields. These represent individual print positions that permit easy location and reference of printed characters, spaces, and fields. For example, print position 42 would be found within the large number four field under the two column. The typical maximum widths of line printers are 100, 120, 132, and 144 print positions, with 132 the most common. Incidentally, line printers do not print like a typewriter, but print all the characters and/or spaces in one line simultaneously, whether there is one character on the line or the full width of the printer is used.

Figure 2-3 also illustrates how the Printer Spacing Chart is related to actual computer printed output. Locate print positions 03 to 05, 15 to 41, and 49 to 68. These represent the variable data fields that were established when input was designed and formatted. The Xs within each field represent the characters and spaces that are contained within the printed input data field. Xs are the standard characters used on Printer Spacing Charts to represent variable data fields.

Again remember that the *size of the variable data fields on the Printer Spacing Chart was determined by the input design*. The fields should not be any larger or smaller than the input data field. In a later chapter, however, you will learn that another source of output field sizes are determined in Calculations.

Furthermore, notice that the output variable data field locations *are not* related to the position of the data in the input data records. Figure 2-3 indicates that the Account Number data will be punched in columns 1 to 3; Account Name, columns 4 to 30; and Account Type, columns 31 to 50. Output, however, shows that the Account Number field is to be printed in print positions 3 to 5; Account Name, 15 to 41; and Account Type 49 to 68. In other words, there is no relationship between the location of the variable data in the input record to the respective data location on output. Output fields may be

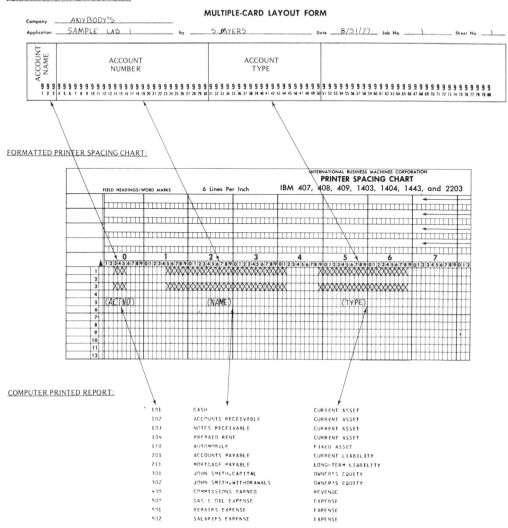

Fig. 2-3. Relationship of Card Layout Form (input design) to the Printer Spacing Chart (output design) and printed report.

printed in any available print positions and in any field order. However, as was indicated before, the input and output sizes for the same variable data field must be exactly the same.

Refer to Figure 2-3 and notice that there are two rows of Xs with a blank line between them. This is the usual way to indicate line spacing on the Printer Spacing Chart. It *does not*, however, indicate that only two data lines are to be printed, but informs the programmer that all printed lines (in this example) are to be *double spaced* whether there are only two lines or thousands of lines in the report. If there was no blank line between the rows of Xs the output should be single spaced; if two blank lines, triple spaced; and so forth.

The letters enclosed in parenthesis, (ACTNO), (NAME), and (TYPE), represent the variable field names assigned to data fields and are only used for reference. Variable field names used in RPG II source programs are limited to a maximum of six characters. Consequently many full data names must be abbreviated accordingly. Names enclosed in parenthesis on a Printer Spacing Chart are not to be construed as headings, but as names of variable data fields used in the program. The report shown in Figure 2-3 has no headings. In Chapter 3 you will learn how report headings are formatted and identified on the chart.

THE RPG II LANGUAGE

Having learned to evaluate, plan, and define card data input and format printed output, the student is now ready to learn RPG II coding rules and techniques which are used to command the computer to process input data based upon a set of instructions. The computer is instructed to perform certain functions by a source program written in a computer language. In this text all programs to provide the computer with a set of instructions will be written in RPG II.

The coding of programs written in RPG II requires the use of standard coding forms. Because all source program entries must be in a predetermined location it is impossible to code in RPG II without them. You should make no attempt to memorize the format of each form, but have them available when coding or debugging a program.

Functions involved in processing an RPG II program include:

1. Program generation

2. Program execution

Refer to Figure 2-4 and examine the sequence of operations included for program generation and execution times. The steps defined in Figure 2-4 relate to source programs entered on punch cards; however, other input media, such as disk, tape, diskettes, etc., may be used to store source programs. For example, there are key-to-disk and key-to-tape devices available that completely eliminate the need for punch cards for source programs and data.

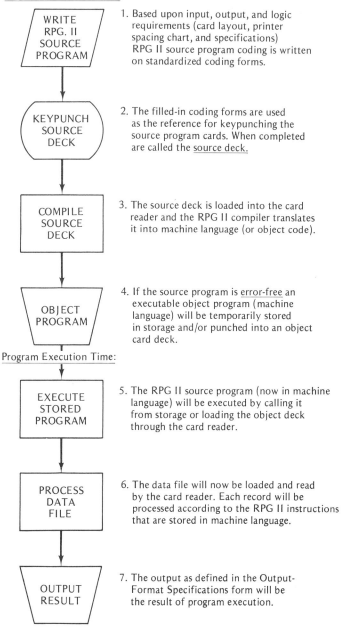

Program Generation Time:

WRITE RPG. II SOURCE PROGRAM

1. Based upon input, output, and logic requirements (card layout, printer spacing chart, and specifications) RPG II source program coding is written on standardized coding forms.

KEYPUNCH SOURCE DECK

2. The filled-in coding forms are used as the reference for keypunching the source program cards. When completed are called the source deck.

COMPILE SOURCE DECK

3. The source deck is loaded into the card reader and the RPG II compiler translates it into machine language (or object code).

OBJECT PROGRAM

4. If the source program is error-free an executable object program (machine language) will be temporarily stored in storage and/or punched into an object card deck.

Program Execution Time:

EXECUTE STORED PROGRAM

5. The RPG II source program (now in machine language) will be executed by calling it from storage or loading the object deck through the card reader.

PROCESS DATA FILE

6. The data file will now be loaded and read by the card reader. Each record will be processed according to the RPG II instructions that are stored in machine language.

OUTPUT RESULT

7. The output as defined in the Output-Format Specifications form will be the result of program execution.

Fig. 2-4. Program compilation and execution steps.

RPG CODING FORMS

The five commonly used RPG II coding forms are shown in Figure 2-5. They include the File Description Specifications, Extension and Line Counter Specifications, Input Specifications, Calculation Specifications, and Output-Format Specifications.

The function of each form is broadly defined below:

1. File Description Specifications—Describes input, output, table files, etc. used in a source program. The type of system hardware used for input and output is also defined on this form.

2. Extension and Line Counter Specifications—Defines table, array, and disk processing information. The Line Counter section is used to control line spacing.

3. Input Specifications—Defines the record types including size, names, and field types within each record in the input files used in the source program.

4. Calculation Specifications—All arithmetic operations, table lookup, array lookup, etc. are entered on this form.

5. Output-Format Specifications—The coding needed to obtain the required output is entered on this form. Output may be in the form of a printed report or creation of a disk file, etc.

An easy way to remember the forms is to take the first letter of each, which includes F, E, I, C, O and combine them to make the word FEICO. This suggested memory aid also represents the *compilation order* when the RPG II source program is processed. The compilation order refers to the order in which the source program cards must be placed in the source deck to permit execution of the program.

File Description, Input, and Output-Format Specifications forms are introduced in this chapter; Calculation Specifications in Chapter 4; and Extension and Line Counter Specification form in Chapter 11.

An examination of Figure 2-5 will indicate that certain areas are identical to each form. Figure 2-6 illustrates the features common to the forms with an explanation of the identifying numbers given below.

1. Every form provides spaces for date, program name, and the programmer's name. This information is *not punched* in the source program, but appears only for documentation purposes.

2. The punching instruction area of the forms is significant because it will enable the keypunch operator to distinguish between confusing alphabetic and numeric characters. For example, it may be difficult to differentiate between a zero and the letter O, an S and a 5, a Z and a 2, and an i and a 1 unless some information is given to identify each

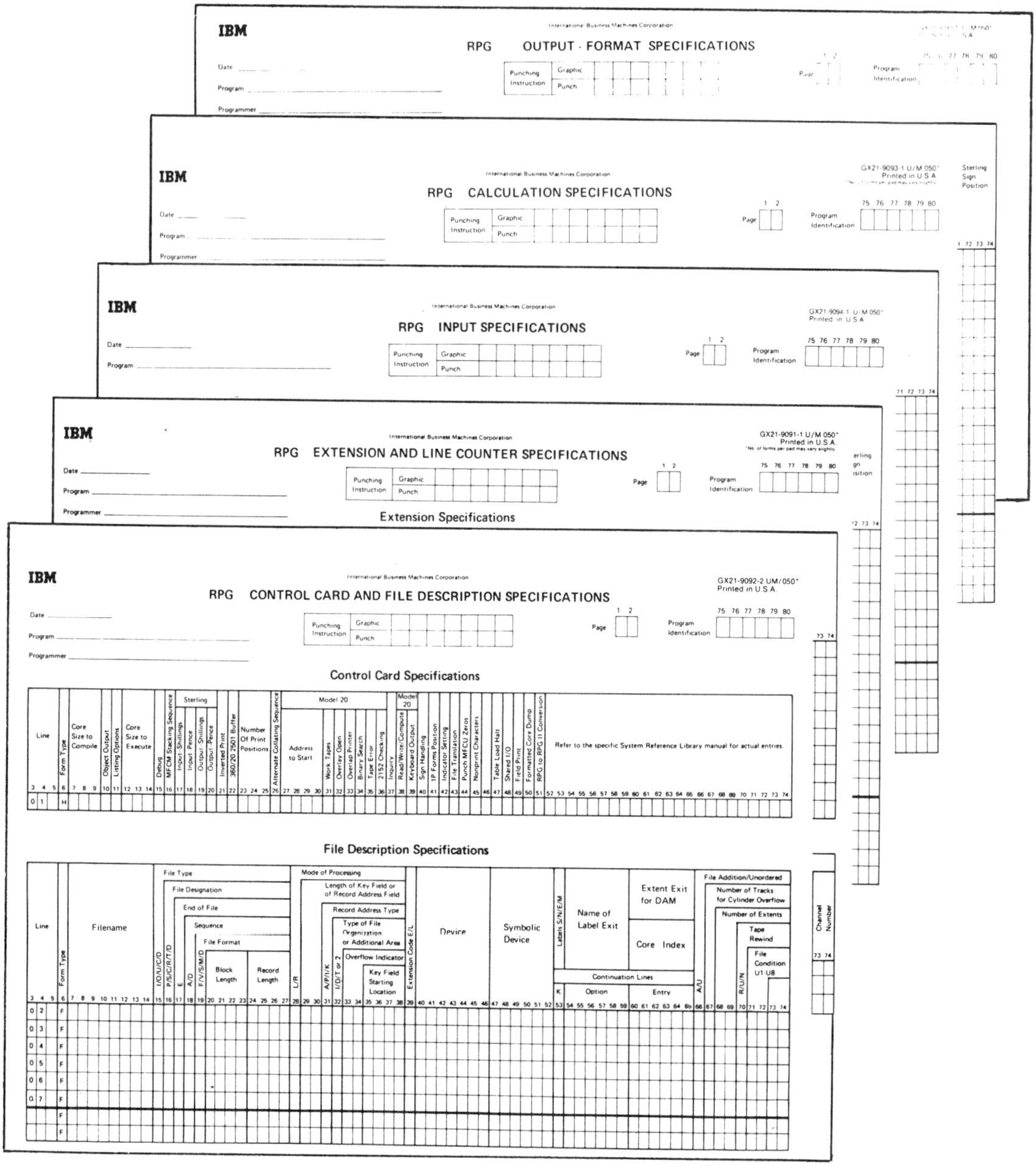

Fig. 2-5.   RPG II specification forms.

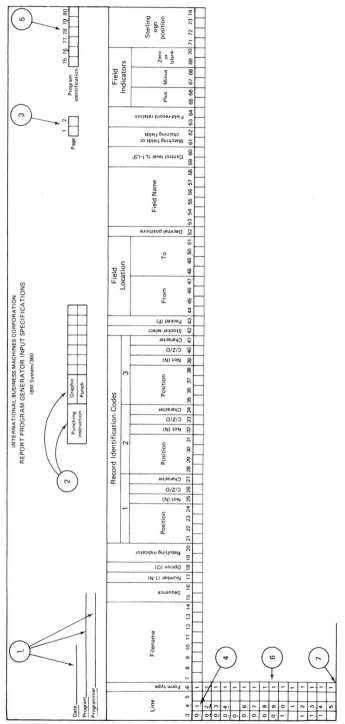

Fig. 2-6. Features common to all RPG II coding forms.

29

character. The letters or characters are printed in the Graphic boxes and the letter N would be printed in the Punch box directly under the character if it represented a number or the letter A if it was alphabetic. Look at Figure 2-7 and notice how the troublesome characters are identified in the punching instruction area. *Remember, however, that this information is not punched into any cards.*

3. The two boxes represent the first two columns of a punch card to assign a page number to each coding sheet. Obviously, the page numbers may only range from 01 to 99, which should be more than sufficient. Also, because cards in an RPG program are in the FEICO order, page number 01 would be the first page of the File Description Specifications forms and, of course, the first page of any RPG program. All of the following forms would be numbered in an ascending order to the last Output-Format Specifications form. The page number is punched in the first two columns of every punch card in the source deck. RPG programs will execute without this entry. However, it is a great help in debugging a program and is invaluable for the sorting of a deck into proper order in the event it is dropped or mishandled. We should establish good programming habits now and use page numbers in all of the programs.

4. Another feature that is common to all forms is line number. The extreme left hand side of the form illustrated in Figure 2-6 has the word Line entered. Note the numbers 3, 4, and 5 above their respective columns as these represent the card columns of a punch card. Also, the entry under these numbers is the number 01 and a blank. This is the first line of this coding sheet with each line representing a separate punch card. The line number is used in conjunction with the page number mentioned previously. For example, if the number 01010 was punched in the first five columns of a punch card it would indicate that this was page one and line one of the first coding sheet for the program. The blank in column 5 is for adding lines of coding that were left out during initial coding but discovered later. Up to nine additional lines may be added between each line on the coding sheet and still maintain an ascending sequence. Line numbering may be ignored and the program will still execute, but a great deal of time may be saved if the entry is made on all cards of a source program.

5. The six boxes represent card columns 75, 76, 77, 78, 79, and 80, which are used for program identification. When many programs are being used in a company some appropriate abbreviated name should be used for identification. *It is a useful documentation feature, but not required* and if not used the columns would be blank in our RPG source program deck.

6. An entry *must* be made in column 6 of every card in an RPG II source program. Letters are preprinted on all the forms (column 6) to

designate the appropriate entry for the card type. For example, Fs represent File Description cards; an E, Extension and Line Counter Specifications; an I, Input Specification cards; a C, Calculation Specifications, and an O, for Output-Format Specifications. These entries must be keypunched in the corresponding cards in order for the program to compile and execute. *Any source program card missing the necessary entry in column 6 will cause the program to cancel.*

7. The File Description Specifications form has the first seven lines prenumbered and a heavy line separating these from lines that are not numbered. Coding should only be entered on the numbered lines reserving the lines not numbered for any additional entries that may be needed after a coding sheet is completed. This eliminates rewriting a coding sheet and any "in between" entries can be made after the cards are punched. Again this procedure does not have to be followed as it is only a convenience that may help in general program writing.

RPG II SOURCE PROGRAM CODING

Before RPG II source program coding is discussed the reader must understand that all of the columns contained in the forms are not used in any one program. In fact, many columns have a special purpose and are practically never used.

Figure 2-7 illustrates the completed coding forms for the introductory program discussed in this chapter. Notice that only three forms are used—the minimum number of form types required for any RPG II program. The File Description, Input, and Output-Format Specifications must be used in any program; however, Extension and Line Counter Specifications, and Calculations are not required and are used only when needed. Usually, however, calculations are part of most source programs and the form is more than often included. Calculation Specifications coding will be discussed in Chapter 4.

An examination of the *source deck* (Figure 2-8) will indicate every filled in line on the coding forms (illustrated in Figure 2-7) requires a separate punch card. Notice that the first card is the Control Card, with the H in column 6, followed by the F, I, O compilation order of any RPG II program. Any errors in keypunching the source deck or incorrect coding logic may cause the program to cancel and prevent compilation. Errors that cancel a program are usually called *terminal errors* and must be corrected before the program can be successfully compiled. Other errors may only be *warnings* and not prevent compilation; however, these errors should be examined to insure that incorrect final results will not be included on output. The process of correcting errors in a program is called *debugging*. A convenient *Debugging Template*, available for RPG II source programs, will be discussed later in this chapter.

A detailed discussion of the File Description, Input, and Output-Format Specifications coding entries will be presented in the following pages of this chapter.

International Business Machines Corporation

GX21-9092-2 UM/050*
Printed in U.S.A.

RPG   CONTROL CARD AND FILE DESCRIPTION SPECIFICATIONS

Date 8/31/77
Program SAMPLE PROGRAM - NO. 1
Programmer S. MYERS

| Punching Instruction | Graphic | Ø O I Z 2 S |
| | Punch | N A A N A N A |

Page Ø1   Program Identification LEDGER

Control Card Specifications

Line	Form Type		Refer to the specific System Reference Library manual for actual entries.
0 1 Ø	H	X	SAMPLE PROGRAM NUMBER 1-READ A RECORD AND PRINT WITH NO HEADINGS

File Description Specifications

Line	Form Type	Filename	I/O/U/C/D	P/S/C/R/T/D	A/D	F/V/S/M/D	Block Length	Record Length	L/R	Device	Symbolic Device	
0 2 Ø	F	CARDS	I P		F	8 Ø	8 Ø		MFCM1	SYSIPT	
0 3 Ø	F	REPORT	O		F	1 3 2	1 3 2		PRINTER	SYSLST	

International Business Machines Corporation

GX21-9094-1 U/M 050*
Printed in U.S.A.

RPG   INPUT SPECIFICATIONS

Date 8/31/77
Program SAMPLE PROGRAM - NO. 1
Programmer S. MYERS

| Punching Instruction | Graphic | Ø O I Z 2 S |
| | Punch | N A A N A N A |

Page Ø2   Program Identification LEDGER

Line	Form Type	Filename	Sequence	Number (1-N)	Option (O)	Record Identifying Indicator or **	Position (1)	Not (N)	C/Z/D	Character	Position (2)	Not (N)	C/Z/D	Character	Position (3)	Not (N)	C/Z/D	Character	P = Packed/B = Binary	From	To	Decimal Positions	Field Name	Control Level (L1-L9)	Matching Fields or Chaining Fields	Field Record Relation	Plus	Minus	Zero or Blank	Sterling Sign Position
0 1 Ø	I	CARDS	A A			Ø1																								
0 2 Ø	I																			1	3		ACTNO							
0 3 Ø	I																			4	3 Ø		NAME							
0 4 Ø	I																			3 1	5 Ø		TYPE							

International Business Machines Corporation

GX21-9090-1 U/M 050*
Printed in U.S.A.

RPG   OUTPUT - FORMAT SPECIFICATIONS

Date 8/31/77
Program SAMPLE PROGRAM - NO. 1
Programmer S. MYERS

| Punching Instruction | Graphic | Ø O I Z 2 S |
| | Punch | N A A N A N A |

Page Ø3   Program Identification LEDGER

Edit Codes

	Commas	Zero Balances to Print	No Sign	CR	-	X = Remove Plus Sign
	Yes	Yes	1	A	J	Y = Date Field Edit
	Yes	No	2	B	K	Z = Zero Suppress
	No	Yes	3	C	L	
	No	No	4	D	M	

Line	Form Type	Type (H/D/T/E)	Stacker Select/Fetch Overflow (F)	Space After	Space Before	Skip After	Skip Before	Output Indicators And Not	And Not	Not	Field Name	Edit Codes	Blank After (B)	End Position in Output Record	P = Packed/B = Binary	Constant or Edit Word	Sterling Sign Position
0 1 Ø	O	REPORT	D	2				Ø1									
0 2 Ø	O																
0 3 Ø	O										ACTNO			5			
0 4 Ø	O										NAME			4 1			
0 5 Ø	O										TYPE			6 8			

Fig. 2-7.   RPG II sample program written on specification forms.

Source Deck

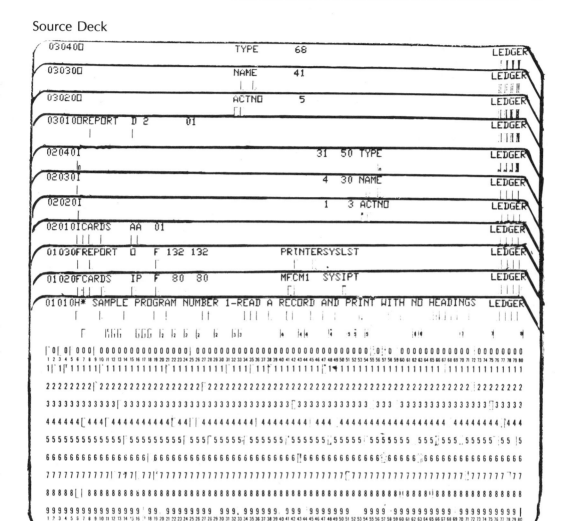

Fig. 2-8. RPG II sample source program keypunched on cards and arranged in compilation order.

CONTROL CARD AND FILE DESCRIPTION SPECIFICATIONS

Control Card Specifications

Examine Figure 2-7 and notice the Control Card and File Description Specifications sheet is a combined form. The top, or Control Card section, represents the first card that may precede the RPG II source program deck. The only required entry on this card is the H in column 6 unless one of the options detailed in the fields and columns is needed. Whether this card is used before your source program (actual source program begins with the first F card) depends on the requirements of the program; Control Card options required; and/or the computer system.

For example, an IBM 370 DOS/VS system does not require the H card unless one of the options is desired. On the other hand, IBM 1130 and System/3 computers do need this card for RPG programs. Note: this card will not be included in subsequent sample programs in this text unless a specific option is needed because all programs are compiled and executed on an IBM 370/115 DOS/VS system which does not require its use.

A re-examination of the Control Card section (Figure 2-7) will indicate that an asterisk is entered in column 7 immediately following the H. *This is how all comments are entered in RPG II source programs.* The use of comments is encouraged for documentation purposes and may be entered on any form by punching the appropriate letter in column 6 (F, E, I, C, O) and an asterisk in column 7. There is no limit on the number of comments used in a program and anything may be punched in the remaining columns of the card.

File Description Specifications

Refer to Figure 2-9 and notice the relationship of the various entries defined in the File Description Specifications coding form to actual input and output items used in the sample program.

Before commencing with any discussion of the columns and fields in RPG II coding forms the reader should understand that only the areas needed for the sample program presented in this chapter will be discussed now. Other fields and their uses are introduced throughout the text as more complex programs are presented. An explanation of the rules for coding fields in the File Description Specifications-form for the introductory program will be discussed in the following paragraphs.

Filename (Columns 7–14). At least one input data file and one output file must be specified on this coding sheet. Notice in Figure 2-9 the input file is named CARDS and the output REPORT. Any *programmer-supplied* names could have been used here, but the names used should be as meaningful as possible. For example, a file name A1234 would not signify the type of file to anyone except the programmer; however, the name SALES would be explanatory.

The input file, CARDS, represents the data file that contains the records to be processed by the source program. The output file, REPORT, represents the printed report containing the information from the processed input data.

Purpose of this form:

1) Name files
2) Indicate type of file
3) Designate files as Primary or Secondary.
4) Indicate record lengths for files
5) Tell computer devices (hardware) the particular file will be read or written

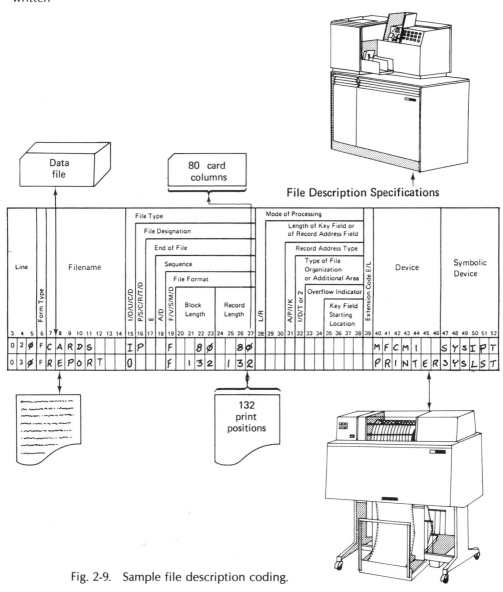

Fig. 2-9. Sample file description coding.

The following rules must be followed when creating file names:

1. A file name may contain no more than eight alphanumeric characters.

2. The first character of the file name must be alphabetic and entered left-justified in the respective field beginning in column 7.

3. Any character other than the first may be a number.

4. No imbedded blanks may be used in the file name.

5. No special characters may be used in the file name.

Figure 2-10 shows examples of file names with an explanation of why the entry is correct or incorrect.

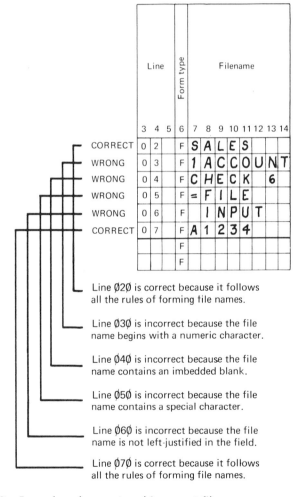

Line Ø2Ø is correct because it follows all the rules of forming file names.

Line Ø3Ø is incorrect because the file name begins with a numeric character.

Line Ø4Ø is incorrect because the file name contains an imbedded blank.

Line Ø5Ø is incorrect because the file name contains a special character.

Line Ø6Ø is incorrect because the file name is not left-justified in the field.

Line Ø7Ø is correct because it follows all the rules of forming file names.

Fig. 2-10. Examples of correct and incorrect file names.

File Type (Column 15). The letters printed in the heading of this one column field indicate the following file types:

I	Input file	C	Combined file
O	Output file	D	Display file
U	Update file		

Only card input and printer output files will be discussed now, reserving the explanation of other types for later chapters. Examine Figure 2-9 and notice the letter I is entered in column 15 for the input file CARD. This entry indicates the file is an input file which contains data from some input device. The letter O entered in column 15 for the REPORT file indicates the file is output.

At least one input and output file must be used for every RPG II program. However, more than one input and/or output may be included to meet processing requirements. These are called *multifile* programs and will be presented in a subsequent chapter.

File Designation (Column 16). The letters indicated in this field represent the following file types:

P	Primary file	R	Record address file
S	Secondary file	C	Chained file
T	Table file	D	Demand file

Only primary and secondary files will be reviewed now. The other file types will be explained as needed in later chapters.

The letters P and S are used only with input files and *never* with any output files. When only one input file is specified in a program, a P, meaning primary file, must be entered in column 16. Look at Figure 2-9 and observe that a P is entered in column 16 for the input file (CARD) designating it as the primary file.

If more than one input file is to be processed in a program, any other input files must have an S, for secondary, entered in this field. Also, when several files are specified, the primary file is processed first. As will be learned later, this feature is important when processing sequentially organized files using the matching record technique.

An examination of Figure 2-9 will indicate the output file (REPORT) does not contain an entry in column 16. This is in accordance with the rule that output files (O in column 15) must not contain an entry in column 16.

File Format (Column 19). An F is always entered in this column for card input and printer output files. The letter indicates that the records in the file all have the same length. Maximum record lengths for the Hollerith card are 80 and the System/3 type card, 96. The output for printed records would be the number of print positions assigned to the output file. Every printed line would have the same number of available positions. Sometimes in order to save room on multi-record magnetic tape files a V may be used to indicate the records are a variable length.

Block Length (Columns 20–23)
Record Length (Columns 24–27)

Because card input and printed output are used for the sample program the block and record lengths are identical. Either the block or record length entry must be *right-justified* in their respective fields (Figure 2-9). If a Hollerith card was used for the data cards the entry in these fields would be a maximum of 80. On the other hand, if a System/3 type data card was used the maximum entry would be 96. Less than the maximum width of the cards may be used; however, any columns outside the record or block lengths mentioned would not be read.

Refer to Figure 2-9 again and notice that the entry for the output file is 132 for both record and block lengths. This represents the maximum width of the printer used for this program. Depending on the requirements of the program's output, smaller lengths may be assigned. Note, however, that the maximum size of the block and record lengths is limited by the input/output devices used on the computer system.

Most computer systems do not require an entry in the block length field for card input and printer output files, but IBM 370 DOS systems do. If the block length entry was left out only a warning error would be indicated on your source listing and the program would not terminate as the computer would assume the same size as the entry made in the record length field. The blocking length field will be discussed in greater detail in the chapter on disk file processing.

All computer systems using RPG II require that the record length field be used.

Device (Columns 40–46). Examine Figure 2-9 and notice the entry in this field for the input file (CARDS) is MFCM1 and the entry for the output file (REPORT) is PRINTER. These entries represent the manufacturer-supplied code name for input/output hardware used on a computer system. Notice that they are left-justified in this field.

All programs in this text are compiled and executed on an IBM 370/115 DOS/VS system with a 2560 model card reader/punch/interpreter unit and a model 3203, 600 lines per minute line printer. There are many other input/output devices available for this system and the manufacturer's code name for each, of course, will be unique. In addition to IBM other companies make excellent computers and have developed their own hardware codes. Appendix I lists some of the device names common to other manufacturers of computer systems.

Symbolic Device (Columns 47–52). As can be seen from Figure 2-9, SYSIPT is assigned to the input data file (CARDS) and SYSLST is assigned to the output printer file (REPORT). Symbolic device assignments are unique to IBM 360 (except model 20) and 370 computer systems.

Symbolic device entries assign a symbolic unit to a physical device. They permit the interchangeability of devices on a system that has several units of the same hardware type. For example, assume a system had two 3203s attached to it. An assignment could be made to the one being used without regard to the actual unit. Otherwise, the RPG II program would have to be changed to access the specific printer.

Symbolic device assignments are also needed for disk and magnetic tape file processing on an IBM 360 or 370 system.

INPUT SPECIFICATIONS

Normally, after coding the File Description Specifications form, the Input Specifications should be coded. Figure 2-11 illustrates the standard Input Specifications form that is used to describe all input records of a file. Notice that the form is divided into two different sections: Record Identification (columns 7–42) and Field Description (columns 43–74).

Observe that these terms are not printed on the form but are only mentioned in order to separate the function of each major area. Record Identification entries are used to identify the file, card types that the file contains, and the order in which the card types should appear.

Every input file that was specified in the File Description Specifications form must have its records defined on this form. Also, when more than one input file is specified, the file listed first is the first to be processed.

The Field Description section describes the field sizes, types, relationships, and variable names of the punch card fields. Incidentally, variable names of the punch card fields should be an abbreviated expression of the field names defined on the card layout form. A very important RPG rule to remember is that Record Identification entries and Field Description entries cannot be entered on the same line. Consequently, when coding a line on the form, entries may only be made through column 42 and any coding beyond that must be entered on another line. Keep in mind that each line of all the forms represents one punch card and any incorrect entries on a coding sheet may result in the improper punching of the RPG source program punch cards.

Some of the commonly used fields in the Input Specifications form are described in Figure 2-11. Except for the decimal position field (column 52), the fields shown are the minimum that must be used for Input Specifications coding for any RPG II source program. Notice that the letter I is preprinted in column 6 on every line of this form. The letter must be punched into every input source card or the program will cancel. All of the fields used for the program presented in this chapter will be explained in the following text.

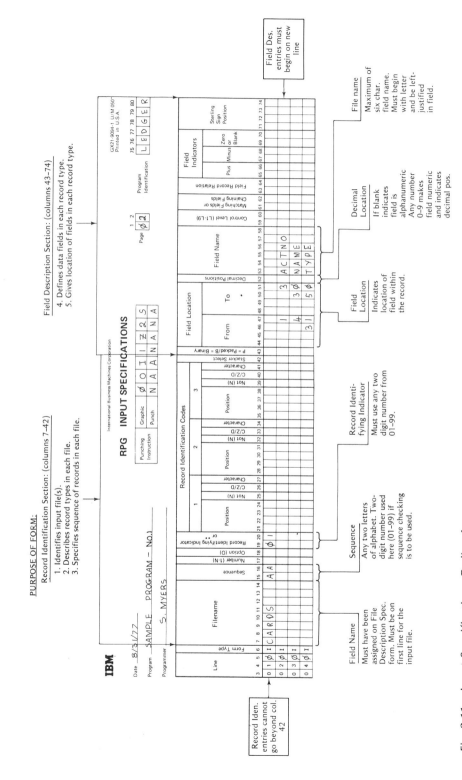

Fig. 2-11. Input Specifications Coding form.

40

Input Specifications Coding For
Introductory Program

The required Input Specifications coding for the introductory program is illustrated in Figure 2-11. These entries represent the minimum that must be used on this form. A file name, sequence, record-identifying indicator, and the field location and field name, for at least one field, must be used. Each field used will be explained in detail in the following paragraphs. As an area is discussed the reader should refer to Figure 2-11 to determine how the entry and description relate to each other.

File name (Columns 7–14). All input file names are entered left-justified in this field and must be spelled exactly the same as the corresponding input file described in the File Description Specifications form. If the spelling of the file name on the two coding forms differed, many errors would result.

An examination of Figure 2-11 indicates the file name CARDS is left-justified in this field. Also, notice the file name is entered on the *first line* only and is *not repeated* for every line on this form. The Filename entry is contained in the Record Identification portion of this form (Figure 2-11) and coding cannot extend beyond column 42.

Sequence (Columns 15 and 16). A two character entry must be placed in these columns for every record type in a file. Depending on the requirements of the program, the entry may be either two alphabetic or two numeric characters. Any combination of two letters of the alphabet should be used when:

1. the file only has one record type, or,
2. the input records are not in a predetermined sequence, or
3. processing is not to be ended when any input records are out of sequence, or
4. the specific record type is not part of a predetermined sequence.

On the other hand, a two-number entry should be made when:

1. a file contains more than one card type within a card group, and
2. the RPG program is to check that all card types are present and that their sequence, in the respective group, is correct.

A combination of entries may be made for the record of a file. For example, some records of a file may be sequence checked and others may not.

Look at Figure 2-11 and notice the letters AA are entered in this field. Any two letters of the alphabet (in any order) may be used here because there is only one record type in this file. However, when multirecord files are discussed (Chapter 5) sequence checking may be required and numbers would be used instead of letters.

Record Identifying Indicator (Columns 19 and 20). Every *record type* in a file must be assigned a unique two-digit code (01-99). The number you decide to use here is the *numeric name* you have given that record type. The number used for a record type is determined by the programmer. These indicators are turned *on* and *off* during the *processing of data* by the RPG II object program. The rules concerning this important entry are as follows:

1. A unique two-digit code that may be any two numbers from 01 to 99 must be assigned to each record type in the file.

2. The indicators do not have to be in sequential order, but may be assigned in any order.

3. Only one Record Identifying Indicator may be on at a time. When one is turned on for a particular record type the others are turned off automatically by the RPG compiler (translator).

Record Identifying Indicators are punched only in the cards for the RPG source program (not in data cards) in order to permit control of calculations and output.

For example, a calculation function could be conditioned so that it would only be performed when a certain Record Identifying Indicator is on; or the contents of some record or result of calculation may be controlled by an indicator. When a particular record type is read the indicator assigned to that record in the Input Specifications form is automatically turned on. After the data record is processed (reads the last output instruction) the indicator is then turned off. If the next record read is the same type, the same indicator will be turned back on until the data records are all processed.

Figure 2-11 shows the number 01 entered in columns 19 and 20. This is the indicator the programmer has assigned to the one record type in the file (CARDS). Any number could have been used here and the number used is strictly programmer preference.

Every time a data card is read the 01 indicator will turn on which allows the control or conditioning, of any calculations and/or output. The introductory lab contains 13 data cards in its input file. Consequently, this indicator will turn on and off 13 times during the processing cycle. If there were 10,000 cards it would be turned on and off 10,000 times.

A thorough understanding of indicators is a prerequisite to logical and efficient RPG II programming. As more complex programs are introduced in later chapters other indicators will be presented and their logic and usage discussed.

Field Location (Columns 44–51). The field location section of the Input Specifications form must be entered on a different line which, of course, also means another punch card when the RPG source program is keypunched. Notice that this area is divided into two separate fields: the FROM field (columns 44–47) and the TO field (columns 48–51). The FROM field represents the beginning column or high order position of the respective field, and the TO field indicates the last, or low order, position of the field. Consequently, 44 would be the high order position and 47 the low order. There are four RPG coding rules for making entries in these fields:

1. There must be a numeric entry right-justified in the FROM and TO fields.
2. Leading zeros may be omitted.
3. A numeric field cannot be longer than 15 numbers. The IBM 1130 system, however, limits numeric fields to 14 characters.
4. Alphanumeric fields cannot be longer than 256 characters. Remember that an alphanumeric field may still be considered this type even though it contains all numbers, as long as calculations, editing, or zero suppression does not have to be done.

Information for the field location entries are obtained from a card layout form or from a typical data card in the file. Figure 2-12 shows the relationship of the Card Layout Form to the coding entered in the Field Location area of the Input Specifications form for the introductory program.

Decimal Positions (Column 52).   If a data item is alphabetic or alphanumeric no entry is needed in this column. However, if the data is numeric and calculations, editing, or zero suppression is required, then a numeric entry must be made in this field. Decimal position value may be any number from 0 to 9, and the use of one of these numbers will indicate to the computer that the field defined as input is numeric. The effect of entries in this field is as follows:

1. If the input data field is a whole number a 0 will assign a decimal after the last number or the low order number. For example, if the number read from a data card was 24515 and the decimal position on the Input Specifications form contained a zero, the decimal assignment in storage would be after the low order 5, as 24515. However, if a two was entered in the decimal position column, the number would be handled in storage as 245.15.
2. A value of 1 through 9 denotes the number of decimal positions in the input data field. This value must not exceed the field length described in columns 44–51 or Field Location. Obviously, no more than nine decimal positions may be assigned to any number.
3. If the input data field is to be treated as alphabetic or alphanumeric, then no entry is needed in this field. This means that no calculation, editing, or zero suppression may be done on this field.

Refer to Figure 2-12 again and notice the decimal position field (column 52) is blank. According to rule 3 given above, a blank indicates the contents of the field are either alphabetic or alphanumeric. Account Number (ACTNO)

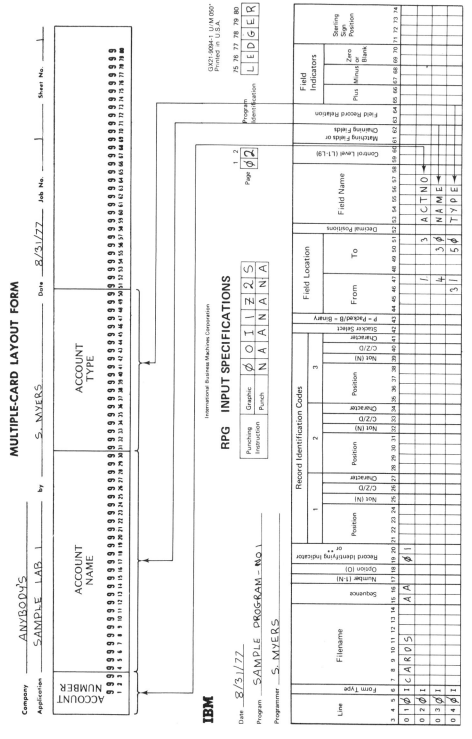

Fig. 2-12. Relationship of Card Layout Form to Input Specifications form.

44

could have been made numeric by entering a zero in column 52. However, it is not going to be used in calculations or edited so the entry is not necessary. Obviously, Account Name (NAME) and Account Type (TYPE) are alphabetic and no number should be entered in this field. If a number was mistakenly entered in the Account Name (NAME) decimal position field the computer would indicate an error because the field is longer than 15 characters. On the other hand, if an alphanumeric or alphabetic field was 15 characters or smaller the computer would not indicate an error but the output would be numbers and not alphabetic characters.

Field Name (Columns 53–58).   The input fields defined on the card layout form must be given a mnemonic name that is entered left-justified in the respective field. The name should be as easy to read and interpret as possible to aid debugging and documentation. All the rules for forming and using field names are as follows:

1. Field names must begin with an alphabetic character, but the others in the name may be numeric.
2. A field name may be no longer than six characters.
3. A field name may contain no imbedded blanks or special characters.
4. The name must be left-justified in the field on the Input Specifications form which means it must begin in column 53.

A field name, in addition to being read in an input, may be created in the Calculation Specifications form as the result of some mathematical operation. This will be introduced in Chapter 4. Refer to Figure 2-12 again and notice that all of the field names follow the rules stated above. An important point to remember is that the spelling of a field name defined anywhere in the program must be exactly the same when it is referred to again or a warning error will result that could cause incorrect final results.

OUTPUT-FORMAT SPECIFICATIONS FORM

All RPG II output coding is specified on the Output-Format Specifications form that is illustrated in Figure 2-13. An examination of the figure will reveal that two major sections are defined on the form; the File Identification and the Field Description sections with an overlapping area called Control. These terms are not printed on the form, but are used in Figure 2-13 to identify the logic areas for purpose of explanation.

The File Identification section of the Output-Format Specifications form specifies the following:

1. Output files
2. Timing of output

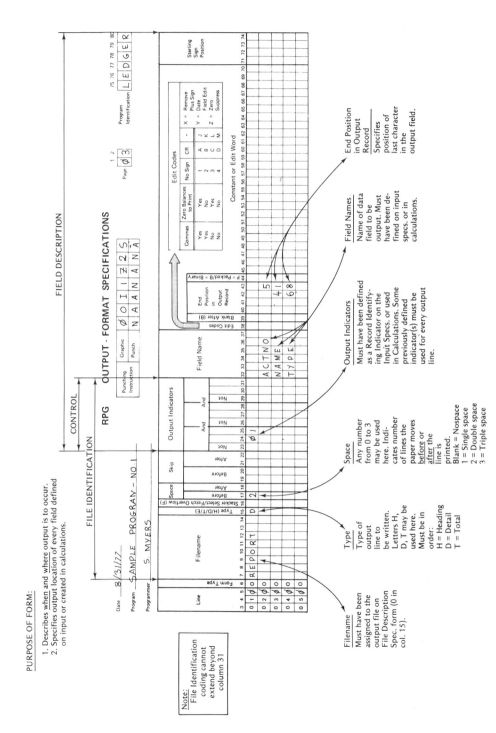

Fig. 2-13. Output-Format Specifications form.

46

3. The stacker to which the read or punched cards will be returned on the reader device

4. Line spacing

5. Skipping control by carriage control tape (or buffer) channels

6. Under what conditions output will happen

In addition, the section labeled Control in Figure 2-13 may control output by indicators that were assigned to a particular file, record, or field within a record.

On the other hand, the Field Description section describes:

1. What fields are to be included on output

2. Where the individual fields are to be placed on the output media

3. Any special conditions related to fields to be printed or punched

The coding entries specified on the Output-Format Specifications form for the introductory program in this chapter will be explained in the following paragraphs. Reference will be made to Figure 2-13 as each field area is discussed.

Filename (Columns 7–14).   Any output file name used here must have been previously defined on the File Description form. Remember output files on the File Description form were so indicated by the letter O in column 15. The file name must be entered left-justified in this field and follow the rules for forming file names listed on page 34. Figure 2-13 shows the correct entry for the output file REPORT. Notice that the file name is only mentioned once and not repeated on every line of the form. If the file name was repeated, an error would result, preventing compilation.

Type (Column 15).   The H, D, T, and E letters that appear in this field heading inform the computer about the time output is to occur. Output must be coded on the Output-Format Specifications form to execute in the following sequence:

1. Heading lines (H)	discussed in Chapter 3
2. Detail lines (D)	
3. Total lines (T)	discussed in Chapter 4
4. Exception lines (E)	discussed in Chapter 8

The following definitions of the line types may help in a further understanding of their use in RPG II programs.

Heading Lines: Usually contain unchanging information such as headings. However, variable field information also may be output at heading time.

Detail Lines: Have a direct relationship to the input data records. Most of the data in a detail record comes from the input record or from calculations performed on data from the input record.

Total Lines: Usually contain data that is the end result of specific calculations on many detail records.

As indicated above, the discussion of Heading Lines, Total Lines, and Exception Lines will be reserved for later chapters. Detail Line output, however, will be discussed in this section.

Refer to Figure 2-13 and notice the letter D is entered in column 15. This indicates the output line is a Detail Line. The introductory lab for this chapter does not have headings, totals, or exception output; consequently, these line types are not needed for the program. A Heading Line (H) could have been used here without error, however, according to the explanation of Detail Lines given above, it is more logical to use a D.

Space (Columns 17 and 18). This field includes two separate columns—the Before (column 17) and After (column 18)—that are used to control line spacing in the body of a report. Three is the largest number that may be used in either column. If a three was entered in both the Before and After columns, six spaces would be advanced on the printer and the next line of printing would begin on the sixth line giving five blank spaces between the lines. If no spacing is required after a line is printed, a zero must be entered in the After column to prevent any line spacing.

Refer to Figure 2-13 and notice that a 2 is entered in the Before field (column 17). The result of this spacing is shown at the bottom of the figure. Notice that one blank space is inserted between the printed lines. If a 1 had been entered in column 17, no blank space would result and each line would be printed directly below the preceding one. On the other hand, if a 3 was entered in column 17 (Before), two blank spaces would appear. The effects of entries in column 17 (Before) and column 18 (After) are illustrated in Figure 2-14. Any combination of Before and After entries may be made; however, maximum line spacing is six unless dummy output lines are placed in between. Usually when many spaces have to be advanced at one time a feature called *skipping* is used which will be discussed in Chapter 3.

Output Indicators (Columns 23–31). Figure 2-15 shows the relationship of the Record Identifying Indicator (01) assigned to the record type in the Input Specifications to the indicator used in the Output-Format Specifications form. Notice that the same indicator (01) is entered on both forms. When a data record is read, the Record Identifying Indicator for that record type automatically turns on and stays on until the last output instruction of the RPG II

The effect of entries specified in column 17 (Before) and/or column 18 (After) are shown in the following examples:

Example 1: A 1 entered in column 17 (Before)
PREVIOUS LINE HERE
NEXT LINE PRINTED HERE

Example 2: A 2 entered in column 17 (Before)
PREVIOUS LINE HERE
      space
NEXT LINE PRINTED HERE

Example 3: A 3 entered in column 17 (Before)
PREVIOUS LINE HERE
      space
      space
NEXT LINE PRINTED HERE

Example 4: A 1 entered in column 18 (After)
LINE PRINTED HERE
NEXT LINE WOULD BE PRINTED HERE

Example 5: A 2 entered in column 18 (After)
LINE PRINTED HERE

NEXT LINE WOULD BE PRINTED HERE

Example 6: A 3 entered in column 18 (After)
LINE PRINTED HERE
      space
      space
NEXT LINE WOULD BE PRINTED HERE

Example 7: It is possible to get a maximum of five spaces between two lines of print by specifying a 3 in the after field for a print line and a 3 in the before field of the next line type to be printed.
LINE PRINTED HERE
      space
      space
      space
      space
      space
NEXT LINE WOULD BE PRINTED HERE

Fig. 2-14. Effects of Before and After Space coding.

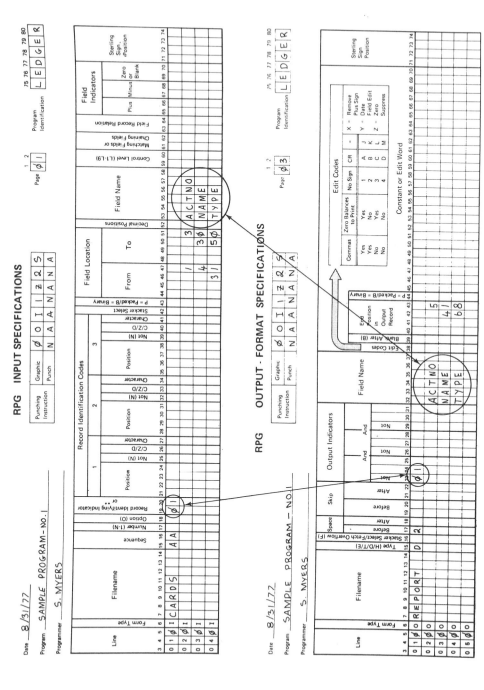

Fig. 2-15. Relationship of Record Identifying Indicator Assigned on the Input Specifications to its use on the Output-Format Specifications.

program is executed or tested; then it turns off. The on and off status of Record Identifying Indicators occurs for every record processed in a data file.

The use of the Record Identifying Indicator (01) on output *conditions* the line of output so it only occurs when the indicator is on. If a different indicator (02 for example) had been entered in columns 24 and 25 by mistake, nothing would have been printed and the error would be identified by the error listing printed after the source listing during compilation. Every line type of output must be conditioned by an indicator or incorrect output may result. Other indicators used in the RPG II language will be presented in subsequent chapters.

The reader should remember that any indicator from 01 to 99 could have been assigned on the Input Specifications as long as the same indicator was used to condition output.

Field Name (Columns 32–37).   Coding for this field and subsequent ones on this form *cannot* begin on the same line with entries in columns 7–31 but must begin on a new line when field coding is started in column 32.

The field names entered in this field must have been defined (i.e., given a field name, size, and type) on the Input or Calculation Specifications form. Look at Figure 2-15 and observe that the input fields ACTNO, NAME, and TYPE are defined on the Input Specifications form and repeated exactly on the Output-Format Specifications. Any misspelling of field names will result in an undefined field causing errors in your program.

Furthermore, the fields do not have to be listed in the same order on output as they appeared on input even though in Figure 2-15 they are in the same order. Later it will be seen how output fields may be created as a result of a calculation operation.

End Position in Output Record (Columns 40–43).   Entries made in this field are right-justified. End position refers to the right-most (low-order) digit of the field or constant that was formatted on the Printer Spacing Chart.

Refer to Figure 2-16 and notice how the end position entry for ACTNO, NAME, and TYPE fields in the Output-Format Specifications are related to the last character of the field in the Printer Spacing Chart. For example, five is the print position of the last character for the ACTNO field: 41 the NAME field, and 68 the TYPE field.

This is why the Printer Spacing Chart is so important to RPG II source program coding for printed reports. Many frustrating hours of unnecessary debugging may be saved by an accurate chart.

All of the RPG II source program coding entries for the introductory program have been discussed in this chapter. Other coding entries will be presented as they are needed for programs introduced in later chapters.

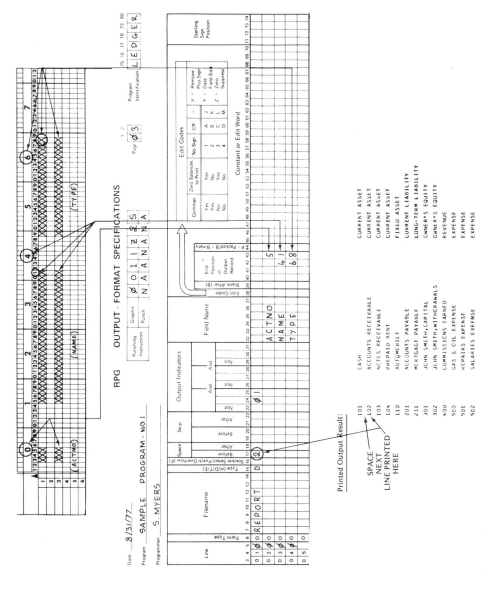

Fig. 2-16. Relationship of Printer Spacing Chart to Output-Format Specifications form and printed report.

52

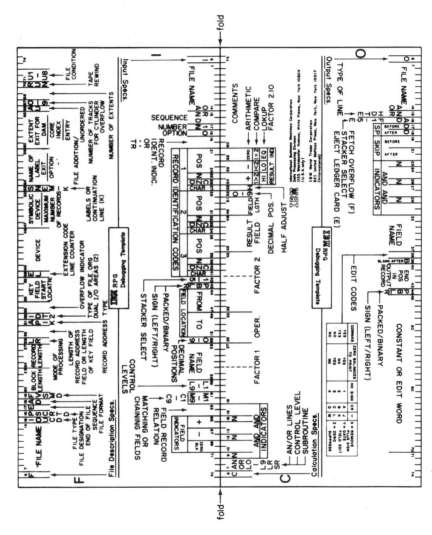

Fig. 2-17. Debugging template.

53

DEBUGGING AID

After the specification forms are completed, the source cards keypunched, the job stream set up and the program loaded into the card reader, terminal errors may be in the source program that prevent compilation and ultimate execution. Because RPG II source program coding is strictly column oriented, every entry must be in its specified location or errors result. An examination of a source listing (Figure 2-19) indicates that the field and column headings are not detailed on the computer listing. Consequently, it may be difficult if not impossible to determine whether an entry is in the correct column without checking the actual source program cards against the coding forms. This would be both tedious and difficult.

A convenient tool, called a Debugging Template as shown in Figure 2-17, is available to facilitate the location of errors in a source program listing.

Notice that a separate template section is included for File Description (F), Input Specifications (I), Calculations (C), and Output-Format Specifications (0). The back of the card, which is not shown, has template sections for Control Card, Extension Specifications, Line Counter Specifications, and Telecommunications Specifications.

An example of the use of the template is depicted in Figure 2-18. Column 6 on the template is aligned with the F, I, C, or O on the program listing and placed horizontally along the line that is being checked. A comparison between the columns on the Debugging Template and the RPG II source program listing will indicate exactly in which columns the characters are entered. A misplaced or incorrect entry may easily be identified by the Debugging Template.

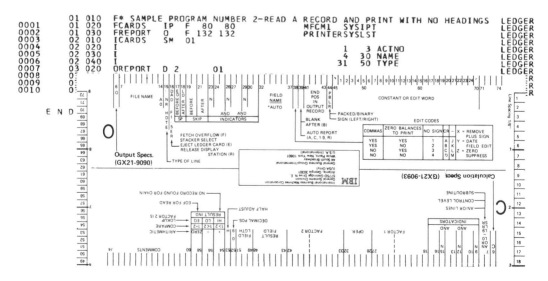

Fig. 2-18. Example of how Debugging Template is used.

Data File:

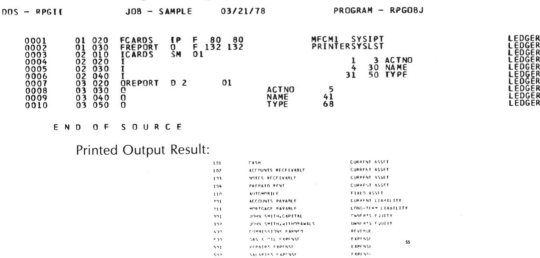

```
502SALARIES EXPENSE          EXPENSE

501REPAIRS EXPENSE           EXPENSE

500GAS & OIL EXPENSE         EXPENSE

400COMMISSIONS EARNED        REVENUE

302JOHN SMITH,WITHDRAWALS    OWNER'S EQUITY

301JOHN SMITH,CAPITAL        OWNER'S EQUITY

211MORTGAGE PAYABLE          LONG-TERM LIABILITY

201ACCOUNTS PAYABLE          CURRENT LIABILITY

110AUTOMOBILE                FIXED ASSET

104PREPAID RENT              CURRENT ASSET

103NOTES RECEIVABLE          CURRENT ASSET

102ACCOUNTS RECEIVABLE       CURRENT ASSET

101CASH                      CURRENT ASSET
```

Source Program Listing by the Computer:

DOS – RPGII   JOB – SAMPLE   03/21/78   PROGRAM – RPGOBJ

```
0001     01 020  FCARDS    IP  F  80   80      MFCM1  SYSIPT        LEDGER
0002     01 030  FREPORT   O   F  132  132     PRINTERSYSLST        LEDGER
0003     02 010  ICARDS    SM  01                                  LEDGER
0004     02 020  I                                 1    3  ACTNO   LEDGER
0005     02 030  I                                 4   30  NAME    LEDGER
0006     02 040  I                                31   50  TYPE    LEDGER
0007     03 020  OREPORT   D  2        01                          LEDGER
0008     03 030  O                           ACTNO     5           LEDGER
0009     03 040  O                           NAME     41           LEDGER
0010     03 050  O                           TYPE     68           LEDGER
```

END OF SOURCE

Printed Output Result:

```
101    CASH                      CURRENT ASSET
102    ACCOUNTS RECEIVABLE       CURRENT ASSET
103    NOTES RECEIVABLE          CURRENT ASSET
104    PREPAID RENT              CURRENT ASSET
110    AUTOMOBILE                FIXED ASSET
201    ACCOUNTS PAYABLE          CURRENT LIABILITY
211    MORTGAGE PAYABLE          LONG-TERM LIABILITY
301    JOHN SMITH,CAPITAL        OWNER'S EQUITY
302    JOHN SMITH,WITHDRAWALS    OWNER'S EQUITY
400    COMMISSIONS EARNED        REVENUE
500    GAS & OIL EXPENSE         EXPENSE           55
501    REPAIRS EXPENSE           EXPENSE
502    SALARIES EXPENSE          EXPENSE
```

Fig. 2-19.   Illustrated data file, source program listing, and printed output.

Figure 2-19 shows the source program listing, printed output, and arrangement of the data file. The job control language needed to compile a source program and execute it differs for every system. Consequently, the respective manufacturer's programmer's manual should be used as a reference to identify the arrangement of the job stream.

This chapter completes the basic coding rules needed to code card input and printed output (without headings). A thorough examination of the coding sheets and source listing of the sample program should provide the reader with an understanding of the steps involved in writing an RPG II source program to generate a printed report. Before any additional concepts are introduced at least one RPG II source program should be written and if possible keypunched, compiled, and executed.

QUESTIONS

1. Name the five RPG II coding forms.
2. What are the minimum form types that must be used for any RPG II source program? Explain the function of each.
3. What seven areas are common to all the RPG II coding forms? Which ones are actually keypunched in the source program cards? Which one(s) *must* be keypunched in the source cards to prevent compilation from cancelling?
4. If the number 02130 appeared in the first five columns of a source program card what would it indicate? What would the number 02131 indicate?
5. What is a control card? When must it be used?
6. What is meant by the compilation order of an RPG II source program?
7. What are the minimum entries that must be included in the File Description Specifications coding form for an input file? An output file? (Try to use the Device assignments, etc. for the computer system available to you when answering this question.)
8. Included in the Filename section of a File Description Specifications form shown below are six file names. Indicate if any of the entries are incorrect and why?

Line			Form type	Filename							
3	4	5	6	7	8	9	10	11	12	13	14
,0	2		F	A	I	2	3	4			
0	3	∅	F	7	S	A	L	E			
0	4	∅	F	C	A	R	D			N	
0	5	∅	F					C	A	S	H
0	6	∅	F	T	I	M	E	/			
0	7		F	B	A	N	K				

9. What is the minimum number of files that must be used in any RPG II source program?
10. What are the two logical sections of the Input Specifications form? What is the function of each section?
11. A line of Record Identification coding cannot extend beyond what column on the Input Specifications form?

12. Explain the entries in this section of an Input Specifications form.

Line			Form type	Filename								Sequence		Number (1-N)	Option (O)	Record identifying indicator or **	
3	4	5	6	7	8	9	10	11	12	13	14	15	16	17	18	19	20
0	1	Ø	I	S	A	M	P	L	E			A	Z			2	I

13. What are Record-Identifying indicators? For what purpose are they used?
14. From what preliminary planning tool do field sizes and locations come from?
15. Indicate if anything is wrong with the following entries, and, if so, explain why it is wrong.

Field location								Decimal positions	Field name					
From				To										
44	45	46	47	48	49	50	51	52	53	54	55	56	57	58
			I	I	7			2	S	A	L	E		
		I	8	4	8					N	A	M	E	
Ø	Ø	4	9	4	9	8			G	R	O	U	P	
		5	Ø	5	8				D	I	S		N	T
		5	9						S	T	A	T	E	

16. What is the source of the file name that is entered in the output coding form? How often is it mentioned on the form type? If output coding extended to another page(s) would the file name be entered on the first line of each page?

17. What entries may be made in column 15 of the Output-Format Specifications form? Explain the meaning of each. In what sequence must they be used?

18. If a 3 was specified in the Before field, column 17, how many blank spaces would be provided between two lines of printing?

19. What are the logical sections of the Output-Format Specifications form? Explain the function of each.

20. When a line of coding begins in column 7 on the output form how far may it extend?
21. From where do the Record Identifying Indicators come that are specified on the Output-Format form in the indicator field? What are their functions in the source program?
22. Where in an RPG II source program are the field names defined that are used in the Field Name columns of the output form?
23. What does the entry in the End Position in Output Record field indicate? Where does this number originate?
24. Examine the Output-Format Specifications form given below and explain the meaning of each entry.

Line	Form Type	Filename	Type (H/D/T/E)	Stacker Select/Fetch Overflow (F)	Space Before	Space After	Skip Before	Skip After	Output Indicators Not	And Not	And Not	Field Name	Edit Codes	Blank After (B)	End Position in Output Record
3 4 5	6	7 8 9 10 11 12 13 14	15	16	17	18	19 20	21 22	23 24	25 26	27 28	29 30 31	32 33 34 35 36 37	38	39	40 41 42 43
0 1 0	O	LIST .		D	3	3			9 9						
0 2 0	O											EMPNO			1 0
0 3 0 0												NAME			4 5

EXERCISES

2-1. Format a Card Layout Form (or Punch Card) for the following data record information:

PART NUMBER   4 alphanumeric characters long
PART NAME   25 alphanumeric characters long
QUANTITY ON HAND   6 numbers long

2-2. From the following Card Layout Form information, format a Printer Spacing Chart. Place your fields anywhere on the chart. However, indicate *double spacing* for the report.

EMPLOYEE NUMBER	EMPLOYEE NAME	PHONE NUMBER	
9 9 9 9 9	9 9 9 9 9 9 9 9 9 9 9 9 9 9 9 9 9 9 9 9 9 9 9 9 9	9 9 9 9 9 9 9	9 9 9 9 9 9 9 9 9 9 9 9 9 9 9 9 9 9 9 9 9 9 9 9 9 9 9 9 9 9 9 9 9 9 9 9 9 9 9 9 9 9 9
1 2 3 4 5	6 7 8 9 10 11 12 13 14 15 16 17 18 19 20 21 22 23 24 25 26 27 28 29 30	31 32 33 34 35 36 37 38	39 40 41 42 43 44 45 46 47 48 49 50 51 52 53 54 55 56 57 58 59 60 61 62 63 64 65 66 67 68 69 70 71 72 73 74 75 76 77 78 79 80

2-3. On a blank File Description Specifications form enter the coding for the following information:

An input file, STATES, that consists of Hollerith data cards will be read on an IBM 2560 Card Reader/Punch unit. The output file, CAPITALS, will be printed on paper 132 positions wide by an IBM 3203 line printer. Program will be compiled and executed on an IBM 370 DOS/VS system.

2-4. From the following Card Layout Form, code the Input Specifications for the input file defined in Exercise 3 (above).

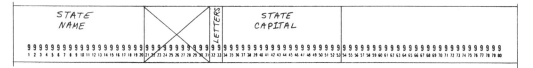

2-5. From the following Printer Spacing Chart code the Output-Format Specifications form. Use the Input Specifications form from Exercise 4 for the field size information, etc.

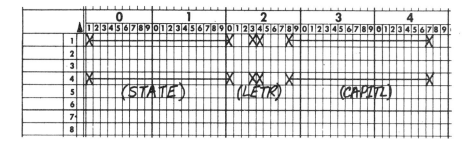

2-6. DEBUGGING AN RPG II SOURCE PROGRAM

Given below is an RPG II source program listing with diagnostic errors. The program did not compile because of *terminal errors* that prevented compilation of a source program. Some errors are noted only as *warnings*. However, these also should be corrected as incorrect final results could be included in the finished report.

CORRECT THE CODING LINES THAT ARE INCORRECT BY REWRITING THEM ON THE REQUIRED SPECIFICATIONS FORM. ALSO, LOCATE AND UNDERSTAND THE MEANING OF THE *NOTES* GIVEN IN THE DIAGNOSTICS.

Source Program Listing:

```
DOS - RPGII          JOB - SAMPLE     03/21/78              PROGRAM - RPGOBJ

0001    01 020    FCARDS    IP  F  80  80    MFCM1 SYSIPT            LEDGER
0002    01 030    FREPORT   O   F 132 132    PRINTER SYSLST         LEDGER     NOTE 083
0003    02 010    ICARDS        $    01                             LEDGER
0004    02 020    I                              1    3 ACTNO       LEDGER     NOTE 076
0005    02 030    I                              4   30 NAME        LEDGER     NOTE 321
0006    02 040    I                             31   81 TYPE        LEDGER     NOTE 202
0007    03 010    ORFPORT   D   2            02
0008    03 020    O         D   1            $                      LEDGER
0009    03 030    O                          01    ACCTNO           LEDGER
0010    03 040    O                                NAME      41     LEDGER
0011    03 050    O                                TYPE      68     LEDGER
```

              E N D   O F   S O U R C E

Diagnostics:

```
DOS - RPGII          JOB - SAMPLE     03/21/78              PROGRAM - RPGOBJ

                                       T A B L E S   A N D   M A P S

RESULTING INDICATOR TABLE
ADDRESS  RI     ADDRESS  RI     ADDRESS  RI     ADDRESS  RI     ADDRESS  RI     ADDRESS  RI
029D  0A       028F  LR       02C0  H0       02CA  1P       02CD  01

FIELD NAMES
ADDRESS  FIELD    ADDRESS  FIELD    ADDRESS  FIELD    ADDRESS  FIELD    ADDRESS  FIELD    ADDRESS  FIELD
01DD  *ERROR     0345             0348  TYPE      ACTNO
                 ACTNO  0004                        ACCTNO                                       NOTE 399
                        0009                        NAME                                         NOTE 398
                        0010                                                                     NOTE 398
```

```
DOS - RPGII          JOB - SAMPLE     03/21/78              PROGRAM - RPGOBJ

                              M E S S A G E   T E X T

NOTE 076    SPEC TYPE NOT I, C, OR O IN POSITION 6. SPEC IS DROPPED.
NOTE 083    SEQUENCE ENTRY IN POSITIONS 15-16 IS BLANK OR INVALID. AA IS ASSUMED.
NOTE 202    INDICATOR IS INVALID OR UNDEFINED. DROP ENTRY.
NOTE 321    TO ENTRY (POSITIONS 48-51) IS BEYOND RECORD LENGTH. SPEC IS DROPPED.
NOTE 398    FIELD NAME UNDEFINED. SPEC IS DROPPED.
NOTE 399    FIELD NAME UNREFERENCED. WARNING.
```

61

LABORATORY ASSIGNMENTS

LABORATORY ASSIGNMENT 2-1:
EMPLOYEE SOCIAL SECURITY NUMBER LIST

From the Card Layout Form and Printer Spacing Chart information given below write an RPG II source program to obtain the required printed report. Your device and symbolic assignments (if needed) must be according to those required for the computer system used for compilation and execution.

Input Format of Data Records:

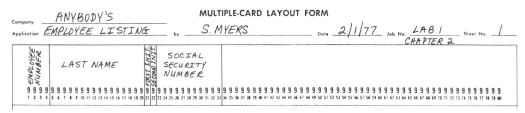

Design of Printed Report:

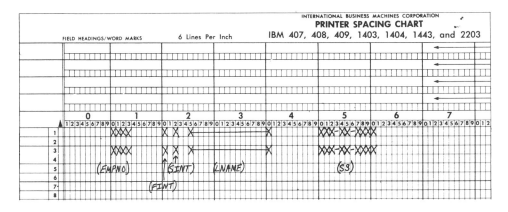

Data To Be Used in Program:

Employee Number	Last Name	Initials 1st	2nd	Social Security
0001	WASHINGTON	G	G	017-32-1799
0016	LINCOLN	A	T	018-09-1864
0018	GRANT	U	S	018-22-1885
0032	ROOSEVELT	F	D	018-82-1945
0033	TRUMAN	H	S	018-84-1973
0034	EISENHOWER	D	D	018-90-1971
0039	CARTER	J		019-77-19??

The completed lab assignment must include the following:

1. Filled in Specification Forms
2. Source Program Deck
3. Source Program Listing
4. Printed Report

LABORATORY ASSIGNMENT 2-2:
CUSTOMER MAILING LIST

From the Card Layout Form and Printer Spacing Chart information given below write an RPG II source program to obtain the required printed report. Your device and symbolic assignments must be those used with the computer system you will use for compilation.

Input Format of Data Records:

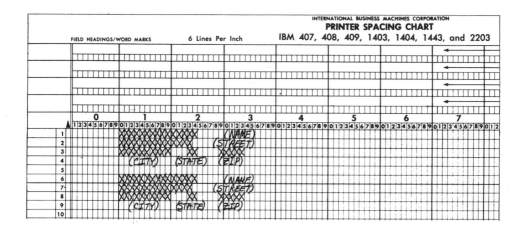

Output Format of Printed Report:

Data To be Used in Program:

Name	Street	City	State	Zip
ANDREW GUMP	1 SUN AVENUE	MIAMI	FL	08881
DICK TRACY	CELL 8	ALCATRAZ	CA	07770
BEETLE BAILEY	"A" COMPANY	FORT DIX	NJ	06666
CHARLIE BROWN	8 DOGHOUSE ST.	ANYWHERE	??	?????
MOON MULLINS	16 TIDE ROAD	LAKEVILLE	CT	06633
LI'L ABNER	80 PATCH LANE	DOG PATCH	SC	09999
YOUR NAME	YOUR STREET	YOUR CITY	"	"

The completed lab assignment must contain the following:

1. Filled-in Specification Forms
2. Source Program Deck
3. Source Program Listing
4. Printed Report

3
REPORT HEADINGS
AND EDITING

Chapter 2 presented the basic coding concepts required to print a simple report without headings or numeric data field editing. Typically, reports do have headings and the input data contain numeric fields that require editing for readability. This chapter introduces the RPG II source program coding procedures used to produce report headings and edit numeric fields.

The report illustrated in Figure 3-1 shows that headings are included at the beginning of the printed output and the numeric fields contain dollar signs, decimals, and commas.

An examination of Figure 3-1 shows that three heading lines are printed in the report. The first line contains the date, heading constants, and page number; the second and third lines contain heading constants. Also notice the variable input data record field information is printed below the headings.

In addition, the report shows the result of numeric field editing. Editing refers to the suppression of leading zeros and the insertion of decimals and commas in a numeric field. Refer to Figure 3-1 again and notice the numeric fields do have leading zeros suppressed (eliminated when contents of field are smaller than maximum size assigned), and commas and decimals inserted.

The RPG II coding procedures for headings and numeric field editing will be presented in the following paragraphs.

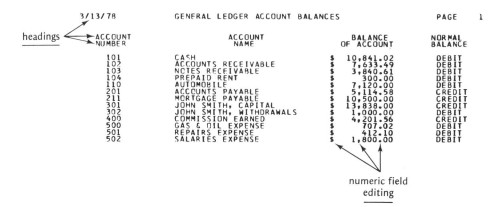

Fig. 3-1. Printed report with Headings and numeric field editing.

PRINTER SPACING CHART FORMAT FOR HEADINGS

Figure 3-2 shows the Printer Spacing Chart format for the sample program discussed in this chapter ·which contains headings and numeric editing. Notice the actual heading words (constants) are entered in their appropriate print positions on the form. The first heading line contains the variable field, (UDATE); the constant, GENERAL LEDGER ACCOUNT BALANCES; the constant, PAGE; and the variable field for the page number which is shown as XXØX.

The variable field (UDATE), positions 1–8, represents the current date which is automatically printed by the computer when this field name is used on output coding. If any date other than the current date was required it would have to be included in an input data record like any other variable information.

The XXØX after the constant PAGE is another internal feature of the computer that numbers the pages of a printed report automatically when the variable field name PAGE is used on output coding. Page numbering starts with 0001 and may go to 9999.

The constants on the heading lines will be printed as shown every time the RPG II program is executed. Remember the names in parenthesis are variable field names that contain changing information as each input data record is processed.

The Hs and Ds alongside the line numbers indicate the type of line formatted on the report. The definition of Heading Lines (Chapter 2) stated that they usually contain only unchanging constants whereas Detail Lines are directly related to the input data and do contain changing field information. The use of Hs and/or Ds, however, is the programmer's choice as long as all the Hs are used in the source program before any Ds.

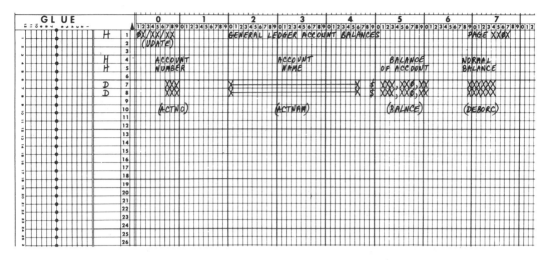

Fig. 3-2. Printer Spacing Chart with Headings.

FORMS CONTROL

Forms Control refers to the vertical spacing of lines in a printed report. One type of forms control was introduced in Chapter 2 when *line spacing* was discussed. The entering of a 1, 2, or 3 in the Before field (column 17) or the After field (column 18) controlled the spacing of lines in a report. Additional control of line spacing, however, is usually required and can only be performed by *skipping*.

The printed result from the introductory source program in Chapter 2 did not start the report on a page separate from the source program listing pages but was a continuation of it. Furthermore, if the report had continued on to another page, lines would have been printed (or close to it) on the perforated line on the continuous forms paper. Hence, additional coding must be entered in the RPG II program to provide for forms to advance to the top of a new page and overflow to another page if the report extends beyond one page.

The ability of the printer to skip is called carriage control and may be performed by a *carriage control tape* or a *buffer software* program which is part of the system software. IBM printers like the 1403 use carriage control tapes; but recent designs such as the 3203 printer use a buffer software program to control forms skipping.

Look at Figure 3-2 again and notice the area labelled GLUE on the extreme left of the chart. This represents the carriage control tape that controls the skipping of paper during printing. The tape printed on the spacing chart is only a representation of an actual control tape. A complete tape has 140 horizontal lines. Hence, the tape must be cut according to the length of the paper or form used. The length of a form may be determined by the total number of lines it contains or its length in inches.

For example, if a form was 50 lines long the tape would have to be cut at line 50 and glued into a loop by alignment with the end marked GLUE. On the other hand, if six lines per inch (eight may also be used) printing was required and the form was 15 inches long, the tape would be cut on line 90 (six inches by 15 inches). A standard control tape is normally used for continuous blank paper; however, when special preprinted continuous forms are used (checks, invoices, etc.) custom-made tapes have to be punched and installed in the printer for the job.

Figure 3-3 shows the relationship of the carriage control tape to the line printer. The round holes prepunched in the center of the tape are used by the drive sprocket on the line printer to move the tape and control skipping. When the tape is mounted on the printer these holes are placed over the drive sprocket; the switch for six or eight lines per inch placed in the desired setting; the carriage restore button pressed; and the paper aligned accordingly.

Refer back to Figure 3-2 and notice there are numbers printed horizontally across the top of the tape that range from 1 to 12. These represent *channels* that control the skipping of lines at the beginning, in the body, or at the last line of each page of a report. Normally a punch in channel 1 on any line will indicate first line of printing and a punch in channel 12, the last line of printing for the page (called the overflow line). Punches in other channels (02-11) in the carriage control tape are used when *skipping* is required in the body of a report.

Figure 3-4 illustrates an example of top of page, body, and overflow skipping controlled by channels punched in a control tape. The form formatted

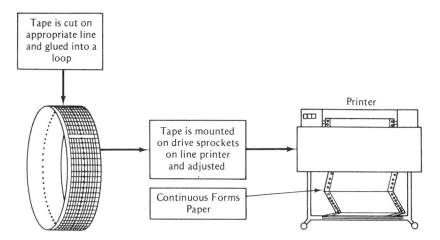

Fig. 3-3. Relationship of Carriage Control Tape to printer.

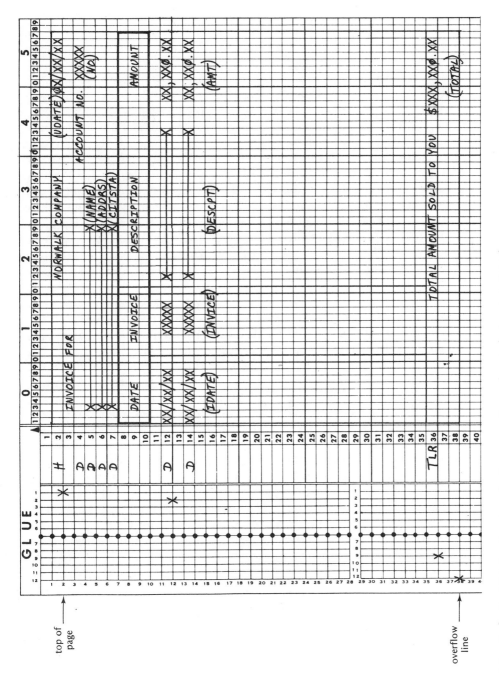

Fig. 3-4. Formatted Printer Spacing chart representing a forms design preprinted on continuous forms paper.

69

on the Printer Spacing Chart represents a preprinted form printed on continuous paper. The constants included in the form (NORWALK COMPANY, INVOICE FOR, ACCOUNT NO., etc.) are preprinted on the paper by a printing company, not by the computer. The heavy lines outlining the form and in the body are also preprinted.

Vertical line advance for the report illustrated in Figure 3-4 is controlled by the skipping and spacing coded in the RPG II source program. For example, when the program executes, the continuous forms is advanced to the top of the page (channel 01 in the tape) and the UDATE field contents are printed. Line *spacing* then advances the carriage to the ACCOUNT NO. line and the variable (NO) is printed. The variable fields NAME, ADDRS, and CITSTA line spacing is controlled by space coding in the RPG II source program. The RPG II coding entries for spacing were explained in Chapter 2.

The forms advance to line 12 (Figure 3-4) is controlled by an 02 channel punch. This channel punched in the tape allows the printer to skip over the DATE, INVOICE, DESCRIPTION, and AMOUNT constants preprinted on the form. After the last data card for the customers is processed, the printer carriage advances to channel 09 (line 36) and the total amount field (TOTAL) is printed.

Next the computer senses the overflow channel (12) and advances the forms paper to the top of the next form (channel 01). This sequence of *skipping* and *spacing* will be executed for the next customer invoice form and continue until the data file is completely processed or the paper exhausted.

Recent designs of line printers have eliminated the need for a carriage control tape and instead use a software program supplied by the computer manufacturer. For example, the IBM 3203 line printer has this feature and forms control is executed by a punch card formatted for the channel required in the program. Figure 3-5 illustrates the format of a punch card needed for the report shown in Figure 3-4.

Every column on the punch card represents a line of print. If the report was longer than 80 lines (columns available on the Hollerith card) another punch card would have to be used to obtain the total required number of lines. An examination of Figure 3-5 shows that a punch is contained in columns 2, 12, 36, 38, and 40. These represent the channels used for this report (Figure 3-4). The one punch in column 2 indicates that channel 01 (top of the page) is on line 2 of the report. The paper will advance to this line before the report is printed. In addition, the two punch in column 12 indicates the 02 channel is on line 12; and the nine punch in column 36 represents channel 09 assigned to line 36 of the report. The letter C (standard punch for overflow line) in column 38 represents the overflow line that will print and then automatically advance the paper to another page. Finally, the X (standard punch for forms length) in column 40 indicates the length of the form (distance between perforated lines). This card must be included in a special job stream and processed by the computer before the report forms are run.

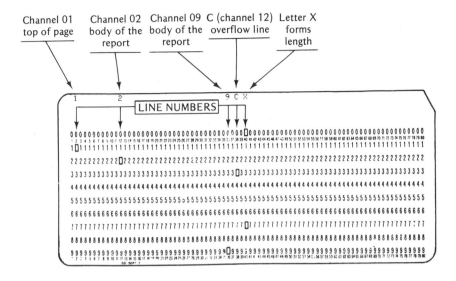

Fig. 3-5.   Formatted punch card for channels required in printed report Illustrated in Fig. 3-4.

The RPG II source program coding for skip control, page overflow, and headings will be discussed in the following text.

RPG II SOURCE PROGRAM CODING FOR SKIPPING, OVERFLOW, AND HEADINGS

Figure 3-6 shows the sample RPG II source program for a printed report with headings, numeric input, and editing. An examination of the figure will reveal that the only changes in the program for skipping, page overflow, and headings are included in the File Description and Output-Format Specification forms.

Figure 3-7 shows the coding entries needed on the Output-Format Specifications form to control skipping and page overflow. The 01 entered in columns 19 and 20 represents the channel number punched in the carriage control tape or entered in the computer by a software program. This number entered in the Skip Before field will cause the printer to advance to the top of a new page *before* printing the heading line.

The First Page Indicator (1P) in columns 24 and 25 informs the computer when to print this line. The 1P indicator turns on automatically when the program begins to execute *before* any variable input data records are read. Any constants included in columns 45-70 may be printed at "1P time" and reserve words such as UDATE, UDAY, UMONTH, and PAGE. These fields are not input data fields but are contained in the computer. If the Record Identifying Indicator 20 (assigned in columns 19 and 20 of the Input Specifications) had been entered in columns 24 and 25 for this heading line, it would be printed each time a record was processed. Usually headings are printed only once per page and not repeated before every detail line.

The letters OR entered in columns 14 and 15, line 020, and OF, in columns 24 and 25, line 020, indicate an OR relationship with the preceding line, In other words, it means to execute this line of output if the 1P indicator is *on* or when the computer senses the overflow line (channel 12) to repeat the headings on the top of the next page. If line 020 was not included in the source program, the headings conditioned by the OF indicator would not be printed on any additional pages of the report. Sometimes this feature may be desirable.

When overflow is required and the coding is entered on the Output-Format Specifications form, the letters OF must also be entered in columns 33 and 34 of the File Description Specifications form for the printer output file. If the entry is not made in the File Description form a terminal error will be generated during compilation. In addition to the letters OF, other entries, including OA to OG and OV, may also be used to indicate overflow forms control.

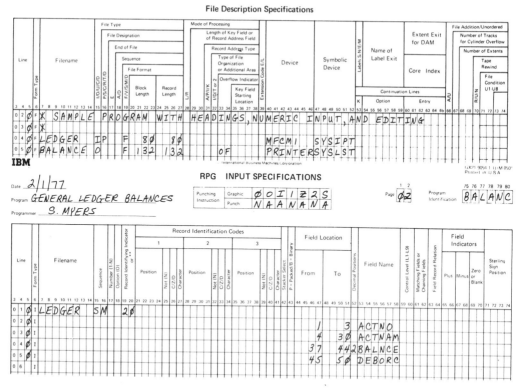

Fig. 3-6. RPG II sample source program written on specification forms that shows Coding for numeric input fields, headings, and editing. (continued on next page)

IBM

International Business Machines Corporation

GX21-3090-1 U/M (50)
Printed in U.S.A.

RPG   OUTPUT - FORMAT SPECIFICATIONS

Date 2/1/77
Program GENERAL LEDGER BALANCES
Programmer S. MYERS

Punching Instruction — Graphic: Ø O I Z 2 S   Punch: N A A N A N A

1 2
Page Ø3
Program Identification BALANC

Edit Codes

	Commas	Zero Balances to Print	No Sign	CR	-	X = Remove Plus Sign
	Yes	Yes	1	A	J	Y = Date Field Edit
	Yes	No	2	B	K	
	No	Yes	3	C	L	Z = Zero Suppress
	No	No	4	D	M	

Constant or Edit Word

Line	Form Type	Filename	Type (H/D/T/E)	Stacker Select/Fetch Overflow (F)	Space Before	Space After	Skip Before	Skip After	Output Indicators And / And / Not / Not / Not	Field Name	Edit Codes	Blank After (B)	End Position in Output Record	P = Packed/B = Binary	Constant or Edit Word
01	O	BALANCE	H			3	Ø1		1P						
02	O	OR							OF						
03	O									UDATE	Y		8		
04	O												41		'GENERAL LEDGER ACCOUNT'
05	O												50		'BALANCES'
06	O												72		'PAGE'
07	O									PAGE	Z		77		
08	O		H			1			1P						
09	O	OR							OF						
10	O												11		'ACCOUNT'
11	O												36		'ACCOUNT'
12	O												59		'BALANCE'
13	O												73		'NORMAL'
14	O		H			2			1P						
15	O	OR							OF						

IBM

International Business Machines Corporation

GX21-3090-1 U/M 050
Printed in U.S.A.

RPG   OUTPUT - FORMAT SPECIFICATIONS

Date 2/1/77
Program GENERAL LEDGER BALANCES
Programmer S. MYERS

Punching Instruction — Graphic: Ø O I Z 2 S   Punch: N A A N A N A

1 2
Page Ø4
Program Identification BALANC

Edit Codes

	Commas	Zero Balances to Print	No Sign	CR	-	X = Remove Plus Sign
	Yes	Yes	1	A	J	Y = Date Field Edit
	Yes	No	2	B	K	
	No	Yes	3	C	L	Z = Zero Suppress
	No	No	4	D	M	

Constant or Edit Word

Line	Form Type	Filename	Type (H/D/T/E)	Stacker Select/Fetch Overflow (F)	Space Before	Space After	Skip Before	Skip After	Output Indicators	Field Name	Edit Codes	Blank After (B)	End Position in Output Record	P = Packed/B = Binary	Constant or Edit Word
01	O												10		'NUMBER'
02	O												34		'NAME'
03	O												60		'OF ACCOUNT'
04	O												74		'BALANCE'
05	O		D		1				20						
06	O									ACTNO			9		
07	O									ACTNAM			46		
08	O									BALNCEI			60		
09	O									DEBORC			74		
10	O												49		'$'
11	O														

Fig. 3-6.   (concluded)

73

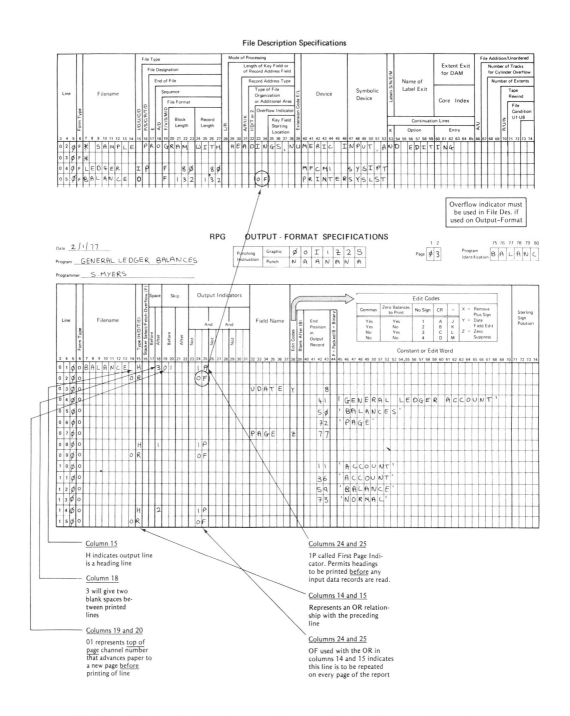

Fig. 3-7. File description and output-format coding for form overflow, skipping, and headings.

Look at Figure 3-6 again and notice that all of the heading lines contain coding for overflow. This is not a necessary requirement for all reports and heading overflow may be assigned to output print lines as needed. Notice, however, that overflow is not assigned to the detail line containing variable field information (line 050, page 4 of the source program, Figure 3-6). If the overflow indicator was assigned to the detail line and channel 12 (overflow channel) sensed the line, the line would be repeated on the following page. This feature is not usually desirable in a printed report.

Figure 3-8 illustrates the result of page overflow coding for headings. Notice the overflow line is on print line 23 of the report. When this line is sensed by the channel 12 punch in the carriage control tape or buffer program, the last output record for the page will be printed and the overflow will occur and cause the printer to skip over the perforated line. The carriage will stop on the next page when it senses a channel 01 punch in the tape or buffer program.

Because forms overflow was defined for the sample program in both the File Description (columns 33 and 34) and Output-Format Specifications (columns 24 and 25) the headings will be repeated on every page of the report. The variable data field lines will be printed as each input data record is processed and heading overflow will continue on every page. It is not necessary that every heading be repeated on overflow but only those required should be repeated. For example, the first heading line 1/20/77, etc., could have been eliminated on page overflow by omitting the OR OF line from the source program for this output line.

Report Headings

Figure 3-9 shows the relationship of the Printer Spacing Chart format to the Output-Format Specifications coding for headings. Locate the heading GENERAL LEDGER ACCOUNT BALANCES on the first line of the chart. Notice the letter T of the word ACCOUNT is entered in column 41. Now look at the Output-Format Specifications form and you can see that 41 is entered in columns 42 and 43 of the End Postion in Output Record field (columns 40–43).

Further examination of the Output-Format coding form indicates that the constant GENERAL LEDGER ACCOUNT is enclosed in apostrophes (numeric H on the IBM 029 keypunch) and entered in the Constant or Edit Word field (columns 45–70). Any constant or edit word (discussed later) must be enclosed in apostrophes or an error will be indicated for the line of coding in the source listing during compilation of the program.

Also notice the entire heading could not be entered on one line of coding but had to extend to another line. Consequently, the word BALANCES is entered on the next line of coding and given its respective end position. Note that even though the UDATE field, constants GENERAL LEDGER ACCOUNT, etc., appear on separate Output-Format coding lines they will be

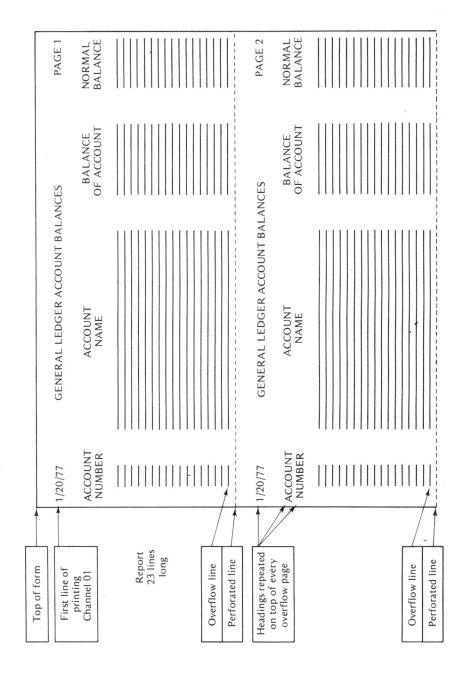

76

Fig. 3-8. Printed result of Forms Overflow Control.

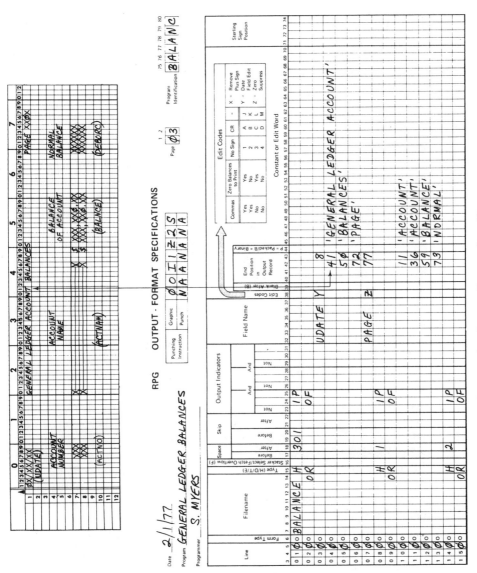

Fig. 3-9. Relationship of Printer Spacing Chart to the Output-Format Specifications form coding for headings.

printed on one horizontal line on output because they are conditioned by the entries made in columns 7–31. Any constant entries in the source program will appear on printed output exactly as they are coded (and keypunched); there-fore, correct spelling and end position locations are important for satisfactory output.

The example shown in Figure 3-9 is not to be construed as the only approach for the coding of headings for this report. RPG II source program coding for headings in the Constant Field columns is flexible and the words may be arranged in any format the programmer wants providing the Printer Spacing Chart format is followed.

Numeric Input Fields

Input data fields are made numeric by entering a number from zero to nine in column 52 of the Input Specifications form. The number entered in this column will depend upon the number of decimal positions contained in the numeric field. For example, a numeric number that contains no decimal position would require a zero in column 52. On the other hand, if two decimal positions (usually a dollar and cents amount) were included in the field, then a two would be entered in the decimal position field. The field must remain blank for any alphabetic or alphanumeric fields. If a number was incorrectly specified in column 52 for an alphabetic field, only numbers would be printed because the computer would only read the digit portion of the punch and not the zone area. In any case, if calculations, editing, and/or zero suppression are to be performed on data contained in an input field, the appropriate number must be entered in column 52.

Figure 3-10 illustrates the relationship of a data record for the sample program discussed in this chapter to the Input Specifications coding for the one numeric field in the record and the field contents in computer storage after the record is processed. Notice that the decimal point is not keypunched into the data card. *Decimal points, commas, etc. are never keypunched into numeric data fields for the RPG II programming language.* The decimal point is assigned automatically (implied) in storage and does not require a storage position as do the numbers in the variable field. The implied decimal point is important to the computer because it aligns numeric amounts, regardless of field lengths, by the decimal point before performing any mathematical operation.

Refer to Figure 3-10 again and notice the BALNCE field is included in columns 37–44 of the data card. This makes the field eight digits long; and the two in column 52 indicates that two decimal positions are included in the field size of eight.

In addition, numeric fields may *not be longer than 15 digits* and no more than nine decimal positions may be assigned to a numeric field. Furthermore,

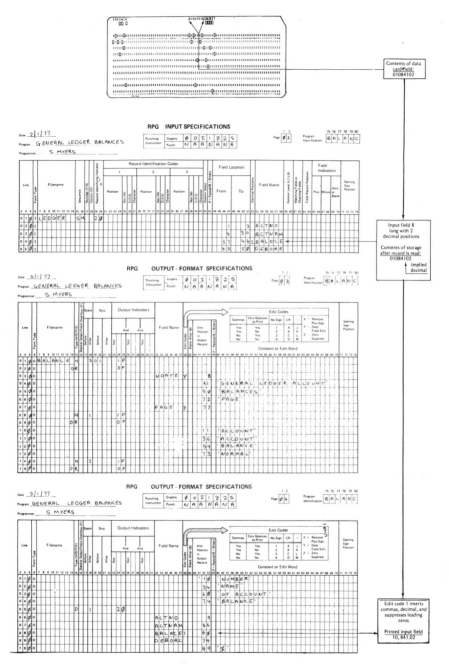

Fig. 3-10. Relationship of a numeric field in a data record to the Input Specifications and edited result on the Output-Format Specifications.

the decimal position entered in column 52 *must not be larger than the length* of the field defined in the FROM field (columns 44–47) and the TO field (columns 48–51) of the Input Specifications form.

As will be seen in Chapter 4, numeric fields may be created in calculations as the result of a mathematical operation.

EDITING OF NUMERIC FIELDS

Only fields that have been defined as numeric may be edited. Editing refers to the zero suppression, insertion of decimal points, comma insertion, blanking of zero fields, and sign removal, and the addition or insertion of special characters in a numeric field on printed output. The editing of numeric fields may be performed by the use of Edit Codes which are entered in column 38 of the Output-Format Specifications form alongside the field to be edited. Editing may also be performed by the use of Edit Words that are entered left-justified in the Constant or Edit Word field (columns 45–70). The coding logic and results of both methods will be discussed in the following paragraphs.

Edit Codes

The edit codes may be divided into two types; simple and combination. Simple edit codes, which include X, Y, and Z, do not cause a numeric field to be punctuated but only perform unique functions. The editing effect of these simple codes is as follows:

X   not used

Y   causes a date field to be edited as follows:

3 digits	(n)n/n
4 digits	(n)n/nn
5 digits	(n)n/nn/n
6 digits	(n)n/nn/nn

The parenthesis in the first position of the examples given above indicates that any leading zero in the date field will automatically be suppressed. For example, if a date field contained the quantity 081178, it would appear as 8/11/78 on printed output if the Y edit code was used. Because of the convenience of this edit code, date fields should be coded as six–digit numeric fields whenever possible.

The Z edit code causes all leading zeros to be suppressed and any signs to be removed without any decimal insertion. Hence, if a field contained 001234, the use of the Z edit code in column 38 would result in 1234 as the printed output.

The combination edit codes 1, 2, 3, 4, A, B, C, D, J, K, L, and M will do one of four basic editing functions to a numeric field:

1. Add commas and decimal point
2. Add commas, decimal point, and suppress leading zeros (high-order digits)
3. Add commas, decimal point, and add a minus sign or the letters CR at the end of a field if it is negative
4. Insert decimal point, zero suppress leading zeros, and add a minus sign or the letters CR at the end of a field if it is negative.

Figure 3-11 illustrates the effect of individual edit codes on data fields.

Edit codes	Positive number- two decimal positions	Positive number- no decimal positions	Negative number- three decimal positions**	Negative number- no decimal positions**	Zero balance- two decimal positions	Zero balance- no decimal positions	Negative number -two decimal positions- end position specified as 10								
							Output print positions								
							3	4	5	6	7	8	9	10	11
Unedited	1234567	1234567	0012b	0012b	000000	000000				0	0	4	1	2	
1	12,345.67	1,234.567	.120	120	.00	0				4	.	1	2		
2	12,345.67	1,234.567	.120	120						4	.	1	2		
3	12345.67	1234.567	.120	120	.00	0				4	.	1	2		
4	12345.67	1234.567	.120	120						4	.	1	2		
A	12,345.67	1,234.567	.120CR	120CR	.00	0			4	.	1	2	C	R	
B	12,345.67	1,234.567	.120CR	120CR					4	.	1	2	C	R	
C	12345.67	1234.567	.120CR	120CR	.00	0			4	.	1	2	C	R	
D	12345.67	1234.567	.120CR	120CR					4	.	1	2	C	R	
J	12,345.67	1,234.567	.120 −	120 −	.00	0				4	.	1	2	−	
K	12,345.67	1,234.567	.120 −	120 −						4	.	1	2	−	
L	12345.67	1234.567	.120 −	120 −	.00	0				4	.	1	2	−	
M	12345.67	1234.567	.120 −	120 −						4	.	1	2	−	
X	1234567	1234567	00012b	00012b	000000	000000				0	0	4	1	2	
Y*			0/00/12	0/01/20	0/00/00	0/00/00		0	/	4	1	/	2		
Z	1234567	1234567	120	120							4	1	2		

*The Y code suppresses the leftmost zero only. It edits a three through six digit field according to the following pattern:

  n/nn
nn/nn
n/nn/nn
nn/nn/nn

**The b represents a blank. This is caused by a negative zero not corresponding to a printable character.

Source: International Business Machines Corporation,
Data Processing Division *IBM 1130 RPG Coding,* Number C21-5002-1 (Rochester, Minnesota: IBM, 1969), p. 121.

Fig. 3-11.   Edit Code Examples.

The column headings indicate how the field was specified as related to decimal position, sign, and zero balance. The use of a particular edit code will frequently depend on the programmer's personal preference.

Examine Figure 3-10 again and determine what edit codes were used in the sample program output. Locate line 030 on the first page of the Output-Format form and notice the edit code Y is entered in column 38 alongside the UDATE field. This edit code will print the field on output as 1/20/77 instead of 012077. The edit code Y has suppressed the leading zero and inserted slashes within the printed field. Remember, however, the input field storage size is six long whereas the output printed result is eight long because of editing. UDATE, UDAY, UMONTH, UYEAR are reserved words stored in the computer that will cause the current date to print when any of these words are used. Note that UDATE gives the month, day, and year whereas UDAY would only print the day part of the UDATE field. Furthermore, these fields are not defined on the Input Specifications form.

Refer back to Figure 3-10 and locate line 070 of the first page of the Output-Format form. Notice the field name PAGE is edited by the edit code Z. Because the PAGE field is a standard four digits long it would begin printing as 0001 if zero suppression was not provided. The use of the edit code Z suppresses (eliminates) the leading zeros and prints the first page as 1, and so on. Also, because there are no decimal points or commas in the PAGE field the use of any other edit code would be illogical.

The field name PAGE has a special use in RPG II in that it provides for automatic page numbering on the pages of a printed report. The use of PAGE in the Field Name field (columns 32–37) will begin report page numbering with 0001 and continue to 9999. If it was necessary to begin a report with a larger page number than 0001, the PAGE field must be defined on either Input or the Calculation Specifications form.

Locate line 080 of the second page of the Output-Format form (Figure 3-10) and notice an edit code 1 is entered in column 38 alongside the BALNCE field name. The result of this edit code on the printed output field is shown in Figure 3-10. Notice that zero suppression and comma and decimal insertion are provided in the printed field.

A convenient reference to the function of the individual edit codes is provided in the Output-Format Specifications form. Locate the large arrow beginning at the top of column 38 and follow it to the right to the Edit Code chart printed on the form. Find the column labeled No Sign and refer to the edit code 1 on the first line. Reference to the two columns to the left of the edit code number indicates the function of the code. The edit code 1 will provide commas in the field and print .00 if the numeric field contains two decimal points and is blank or contains all zeros. The edit code A would give the same result as edit code 1, but add the letter CR to the right of the number if the field was negative. An examination of Figure 3-11 will show the edit results of the available edit codes in the RPG II language.

Dollar Signs

Dollar signs may be coded as floating or fixed on the Output-Format Specification form. Reference to Figure 3-10, line 100 on the second page of the form shows that a dollar sign ($) is entered in the Constant Field and enclosed in apostrophes with an end position of 49. This is referred to as a *fixed dollar sign* in that it has its own end position and will be printed there everytime the line is executed. The print position location for the dollar sign is obtained from the Printer Spacing Chart. If the variable output data field (BALNCE) overlapped the dollar sign because of incorrect end position coding, the contents of the field would suppress the sign and it would not appear in printed output.

A floating dollar sign is also entered in the Constant Field and enclosed in apostrophes, only it is entered on the same line as the field name to which it refers. Figure 3-12 shows the coding for a fixed and floating dollar sign and the printed result.

Refer to Figure 3-12 and notice the dollar sign is entered in the Constant Field on the same line as the field name to which it applies on the printed report. When a floating dollar sign is used, an edit code must be entered in column 38 or an error will result.

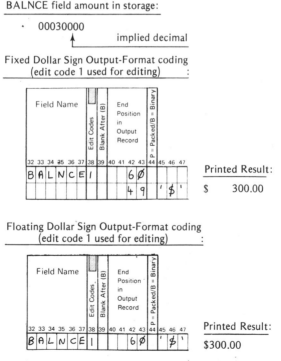

Fig. 3-12. Examples of Fixed and Floating Dollar Sign coding.

Edit Words

The use of Edit Codes should be sufficient for the editing requirements of numeric fields on printed output; however, when special editing is required it may be necessary to use Edit Words to accomplish the needed result.

An examination of the top part of Figure 3-13 indicates an Edit Word consists of three parts: the body, status, and expansion. The body of an Edit Word begins at the left-hand side and must include the *same number or more positions as the data field to be edited*. If less positions are provided, an error will result during compilation of the source program.

The status section of the Edit Word is the area to the right of the body. If an Edit Word does not provide for a CR or minus sign (−), this part of the word would not exist.

The expansion area continues to the right of the status, or of the body if the status section does not exist, and ends with the low-order or extreme right-hand character in the edit word.

Figure 3-13 also lists the rules for forming edit words along with an explanation of the examples depicted at the bottom of the figure.

The changes in the editing of the numeric fields included in the sample program in this chapter using Edit Words instead of Edit Codes are illustrated in Figure 3-14.

COMPUTER OUTPUT

RPG II source programs illustrated in this text are compiled and executed on an IBM 370/115 DOS/VS computer system. During compilation of programs, the computer prints several pages of diagnostics in addition to the source listing. Every computer system, even from the same manufacturer, does not have exactly the same supportive information; hence, the listings shown in Figure 3-15 (other than the source part), are not to be construed as the standard format for all RPG II compilers.

Refer to the top section of Figure 3-15 and notice the area entitled RPG CONTROL CARD OPTIONS. Listed below the title are the Control Card Options that were and could be used in the Control Card which precedes the RPG II source program card deck. Several options are automatically assigned by the computer system and not by the programmer. The Control Card used for the sample program contains only the page, line number, and H in column 6.

Page 002 of the listing is the source program generated from the source deck. The numbers to the extreme left are sequence numbers automatically printed by the computer. If the page and line numbers (columns 1–5 on the source cards) were omitted from the program, the computer still sequences the coding lines on the listing. The RPG II compiler references line errors by the sequence numbers and not the programmer-supplied page and line numbers. The words END OF SOURCE are not part of the program but are printed by the computer after the last source program card is processed.

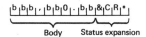

Body   Status expansion

Rules for forming an edit word

1. An edit word must be enclosed in apostrophes.
2. A blank in the body of the edit word is replaced with the character from the corresponding position of the data field specified in *Field Name*.
3. An ampersand in the body or status portion causes a blank in the edited field. It remains unchanged in the expansion portion.
4. A zero is used for zero-suppression. It is placed in the rightmost position where zero suppression is to stop. It is replaced with the character from the corresponding position of the data field, unless that character is zero. Column 38 (edit codes) must be left blank.
5. If leading zeros are desired, the edit word must contain one more position than the field to be edited. A zero must be placed in the high-order position of the edit word.
6. An asterisk in the body of the edit word is used for asterisk protection and zero suppression. It is placed in the rightmost position where zero suppression is to stop. It is replaced with the non-zero character from the corresponding position of the data field. Each suppressed zero is replaced by an asterisk. An asterisk preceding a zero is interpreted as representing asterisk protection.
7. A dollar sign in the body of the edit word written immediately to the left of the zero-suppression code causes the insertion of a dollar sign in the position to the left of the first significant digit. This is the *floating dollar* sign. A dollar sign that is entered immediately after the initial single-quote mark is fixed (printed in the same location each time). This is the *fixed dollar* sign.
8. The decimal and commas are printed in the same relative positions they were written in the edit word.

If they are to the left of significant digits, they are blanked out or replaced by an asterisk.
9. All other characters used in the body of the edit word are printed if they are to the right of significant digits in the data field. If they are to the left of high-order significant digits in the data word, they are blanked out. If asterisk protection is used they are replaced with an asterisk.
10. The letters CR or the minus symbol in the status portion of the edit word are undistributed if the sign in the data field is minus. If the sign is plus, CR and — are blanked out.
11. Characters to the right of the status portion of the edit word are undistrubed.
12. The edit word may be larger than the field to be edited.

Figure 5-6 illustrates the use of constants and edit words. The numbers to the left refer to the item numbers in the follow text.

1. The constant 26.75 is in the output record ending in position 96. The fieldname specification must be blank.
2. The constant DEPARTMENT TOTAL is contained in the output record ending in position 96. The field name must be blank.
3. This example illustrates zero suppression to the left of significant digits. The letters CR are written because the amount field can contain a negative value.
4. The floating dollar-sign protection enters the $ to the left of the first significant digit.
5. Asterisk protection enters as many asterisks to the left of the first significant digit as required to fill out the number of positions specified in the edit word.

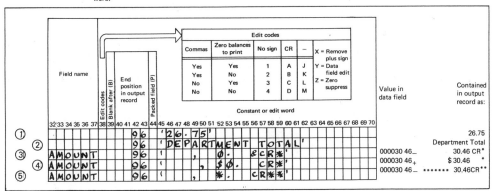

Source: International Business Machines Corporation,
Programming Publications, *IBM 1130 RPG Language,* Number C21-5002-1 (Rochester, Minnesota: IBM, 1969), p. 123.

Fig. 3-13.   Edit Word rules and examples.

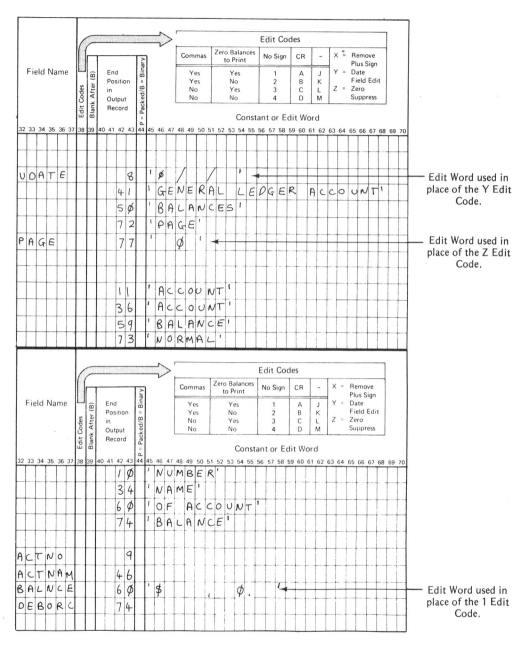

Fig. 3-14. Editing of numeric fields in sample program with Edit Words instead of Edit Codes.

DDS - RPGII   JOB - MYERS   03/21/78

H

RPG CONTROL CARD OPTIONS

POSITION	FUNCTION	OPTION	ENTRY
15	DEBUG	NO	
21	INVERTED PRINT	STD	
26	ALTERNATE COLLATING.SEQ	NONE	
40	FORCE SIGN	BOTH	
41	1P FORM ALIGNMENT	NO	
42	INDICATOR SETTING	NO	
43	FILE TRANSLATION	NO	
50	FORMAT DUMP	YES	
51	CONVERSION NOTES	NO	
75 - 80	PROGRAM NAME	RPGOBJ	

COMPILER OPTIONS ARE - LIST, NODECK AND LINK.   PARTITION SIZE IS - 00072K   DISK

DDS - RPGII   JOB - MYERS   03/21/78   PROGRAM - RPGOBJ

```
0001 01 020 F* SAMPLE PROGRAM WITH HEADINGS,NUMERIC INPUT,AND EDITING.                 BALANC
0002 01 030 F*                                                                          BALANC
0003 01 050 FFLEDGER IP F  80  80           MFCM1 SYSIPT                                 BALANC
0004 02 010 FBALANCE O  F 132 132    OF      PRINTERSYSLST                               BALANC
0005 02 030 ILEDGER SM 20                                                               BALANC
0006 02 040 I                                          1   3 ACTNO                       BALANC
0007 02 050 I                                          4  30 ACTNAM                      BALANC
0008 03 010 I                                         37  42BALANCE                      BALANC
0009 03 020 I                                         45  50 DEBORC                      BALANC
0010 03 030 I                                                                            BALANC
0011 03 040 IBALANCE H 301            UDATE Y     8  'GENERAL LEDGER ACCOUNT'            BALANC
0012 03 050 I           OR                        40  'BALANCES'                         BALANC
0013 03 060 I                                     52  'PAGE'                             BALANC
0014 03 070 I                                     77                                     BALANC
0015 03 090 O           H 1             PAGE Z                                           BALANC
0016 03 100 O           OR                        11  'ACCOUNT'                          BALANC
0017 03 110 O                                     36  'ACCOUNT'                          BALANC
0018 03 120 O                                     59  'BALANCE'                          BALANC
0019 03 130 O                                     73  'NORMAL'                           BALANC
0020 03 140 O           H 2                        10  'NUMBER'                          BALANC
0021 03 150 O           OR                         34  'NAME'                            BALANC
0022 04 010 O                                      60  'OF ACCOUNT'                      BALANC
0023 04 020 O                                      74  'BALANCE'                         BALANC
0024 04 030 O                                                                            BALANC
0025 04 040 O           D 1    20       ACTNO      9                                     BALANC
0026 04 050 O                           ACTNAM    46                                     BALANC
0027 04 060 O                           BALNCE1   60                                     BALANC
0028 04 070 O                           DEBORC    74                                     BALANC
0029 04 080 O                                      49  '$'                               BALANC
0030 04 090 O                                                                            BALANC
0031 04 100 O                                                                            BALANC
```

Fig. 3-15.   Source program listing with diagnostics listings.

T A B L E S   A N D   M A P S

RESULTING INDICATOR TABLE

ADDRESS	RI	ADDRESS	RI	ADDRESS	RI	ADDRESS	RI	ADDRESS	RI	ADDRESS	RI
02A2	OF	028F	LR	02C0	H9	02CA	1P	02CD	20	02CD	1P

FIELD NAMES

ADDRESS	FIELD	ADDRESS	FIELD	ADDRESS	FIELD	ADDRESS	FIELD	ADDRESS	FIELD
01DD	*ERROP	0345	ACTNO	0348	ACTNAM	0363	BALNCE	0368	DEBQRC
01F7	UDATE	036E	PAGE						

ADDRESS LIST

BEGINNING OF LITERALS/EDITS	000371
DETERMINE RECORD TYPE	0003F4
INPUT FIELD EXTRACTION	00041C
BUILD OUTPUT FIELDS	00043E
DETAIL LINES	00040C
TOTAL LINES	000556
TOTAL LINE EPILOG	000558
OVERFLOW LINES	00059A
POINTER TO FIB LIST	0005F8
INITIALIZATION	00070C
DETAIL CALCS	000964
TOTAL CALCS	00096A
DETERMINE FILE TO PROCESS	00099C
GET INPUT RECORD	000AF8
TERMINATION	000AF8

NO ERROR(S) IN PROGRAM

END OF COMPILATION - PROGRAM LENGTH HEX - 000BCC   DEC - 003020

Fig. 3-15. (continued)

The TABLES AND MAPS SECTION is divided into two areas: the RESULTING INDICATOR TABLE section and the FIELD NAMES. The Resulting Indicator Table section lists the indicators used in the program (OF, 1P, and 20). The LR indicator (Last Record) turns on automatically when the end of the data file is sensed by the /* card included at the end of any data file. It was not used in the sample program but could be used if source program instructions were to be performed after the last data record was read. Chapter 4 will introduce the use of the LR indicator in RPG II programs.

The H0 indicator listed in this section was not defined by the programmer but is assigned internally by the RPG II compiler to test for errors that will halt compilation and cancel the program. Halt Indicators (H0-H9) may, however, be assigned by the programmer to test for errors on input, calculations, and output, and follow a coded error routine to prevent cancellation of the compilation or execution phase.

The FIELD NAMES section lists the field names used in the source program and the stored location (ADDRESS) of the field. Examine the section and notice the field *ERROR. This *does not* indicate an error in the program, but represents a reserved word that the programmer may use in calculations to cancel select errors that could terminate a program during the processing of a data file.

Page 004 of the listing identifies the address of functional areas in the RPG II compilation stage. This area is useful when a core dump of the program is used when a difficult error has to be found. The words NO ERROR(S) IN PROGRAM indicate the program compilation contained no *terminal* or *warning* errors. Errors may, however, exist in a source program or data file (divide by zero, input/output, unidentified record, etc.) that will not be listed during compilation but occur when the records in the data file are processed. A core dump is sometimes necessary to locate these errors.

The printed report for the sample RPG II source program is illustrated in Figure 3-16. Any output results should be carefully checked by the programmer to insure the coding results are in accordance with the job specifications and data base.

```
3/13/78              GENERAL LEDGER ACCOUNT BALANCES                      PAGE    1

    ACCOUNT                  ACCOUNT                   BALANCE           NORMAL
    NUMBER                    NAME                    OF ACCOUNT         BALANCE
     101          CASH                            $    10,841.02          DEBIT
     102          ACCOUNTS RECEIVABLE             $     7,633.49          DEBIT
     103          NOTES RECEIVABLE                $     3,840.61          DEBIT
     104          PREPAID RENT                    $       300.00          DEBIT
     110          AUTOMOBILE                      $     7,120.00          DEBIT
     201          ACCOUNTS PAYABLE                $     5,114.58          CREDIT
     211          MORTGAGE PAYABLE                $    10,500.00          CREDIT
     301          JOHN SMITH, CAPITAL             $    13,838.00          CREDIT
     302          JOHN SMITH, WITHDRAWALS         $     1,000.00          DEBIT
     400          COMMISSION EARNED               $     4,201.56          CREDIT
     500          GAS & OIL EXPENSE               $       707.02          DEBIT
     501          REPAIRS EXPENSE                 $       412.10          DEBIT
     502          SALARIES EXPENSE                $     1,800.00          DEBIT
```

Fig. 3-16. Printed report created from sample RPG II program.

QUESTIONS

1. How is skipping controlled? When should it be used in a source program?
2. If a heading is to appear only once on a page of a report, what indicator should be used in the Output Indicator field in the output form?
3. If headings are to be printed on every page of a printed report, what indicator is used to cause this to happen, and on what coding forms and columns is it entered?
4. What, if anything, is wrong with the following RPG II source program coding for a heading line? Note 10 is a Record-Identifying Indicator.

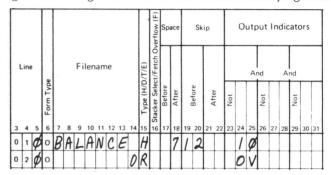

5. How and on what coding form are input data fields made numeric?
6. What is the maximum length of a numeric field? What is the maximum number of decimal positions that may be assigned to a numeric field?
7. May the number of decimal positions assigned to a numeric field exceed the field length for the field?
8. If an alphabetic field is incorrectly made numeric what will be the printed result for the field on output?
9. What, if anything, is wrong with the following partial Output-Format form coding for a heading?

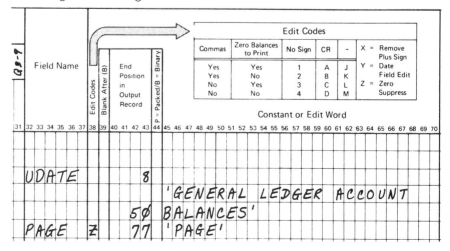

10. In the following examples of the contents of fields in storage, what is the edited result when the edit code indicated is specified? The decimal position assigned is two.

Contents of Field	Edit Code
ØØØØØØØØ	1
ØØØØØØØØ	2
Ø7125839	3
Ø125Ø765	B
ØØ36Ø818	M
ØØØØ9999	Z

11. What will be the result on the following amounts in storage if the Y edit code is specified in column 38 of the Output-Format Specifications form?

120178	ØØØ879
Ø81178	ØØ1977

12. UDATE is the reserved word that may be used in an RPG II source program to print the current date. Does this variable field have to be defined on the Input Specifications form?

13. What words would have to be entered in the Output-Format Specifications form to print the current day, month, or year individually?

14. On a blank Output-Format Specifications form enter the coding needed to edit the variable numeric field AMOUNT which is seven digits long with two decimal positions. *Use Edit Codes*.

Contents of Field	Desired Edited Result
ØØØØ721	$7.21
ØØØØØØØ	$.ØØ
ØØØ1842	$18.42
ØØ2ØØØØ	$200.00CR
103452̄1	$10345.21 −

15. On a blank Output-Format Specifications form enter the coding needed to edit the variable numeric field BALNCE which is eight digits long with two decimal positions. Use Edit Words to accomplish the edited result.

ØØØØØØ7̄7	$.77 CR*
Ø2222855	$2,228.55 *
ØØØØØ199	$*****1.99
ØØØØ4488	$44.88 DEBIT

16. In addition to the source program listing, what are some of the other items included in the pages of the compilation listing? Explain briefly the function of each section.

EXERCISES

3-1. From the following report, format a Printer Spacing Chart. Assume the maximum field sizes are:

Salesman Number	4 numeric digits
Salesman Name	25 alphabetic characters
Sale Amount	8 digits with two decimal positions

Printed Report:

ØX/XX/XX	WEEKLY SALES REPORT	PAGE XXØX
SALESMAN NUMBER	**SALESMAN NAME**	**AMOUNT OF SALE**
1234	ALEXANDER DUMAS	$77,000.01
678	WILLIAM SHAKESPEARE	.90
18	GEORGE BERNARD SHAW	603.15

Determine your own vertical and horizontal spacing on the Printer Spacing Chart.

3-2. From the Printer Spacing Chart you formatted in Exercise 1, and the input field sizes given, complete the File Description, Input, and Output-Format Specification forms for an RPG II program to print the required report.

3-3. On a blank Output-Format Specifications form complete the output coding to print a report based upon the following Printer Spacing Chart:

LABORATORY ASSIGNMENTS

LABORATORY ASSIGNMENT 3-1:
DATA PROCESSING PERSONNEL SALARY LIST

From the Card Layout Form and Printer Spacing Chart information given below write an RPG II source program to obtain the required printed report. The device and symbolic assignments (if needed) must be according to those required for the computer system used for compilation and execution.

Input Format of Data Records:

MULTIPLE-CARD LAYOUT FORM

Company _NORWALK_

Application _SALARY LISTING_ by _S. MYERS_ Date _2/14/77_ Job No. _Lab 3-1_ Sheet No. _1_

SALARY	NO. OF EMP.

```
9999999999999999999999999|9 9|9 9|9 9 9 9 9 9 9 9 9 9 9 9 9 9 9 9 9 9 9 9 9 9 9 9 9 9 9 9 9 9 9 9 9 9 9 9 9 9 9 9 9 9 9 9 9 9 9 9
1 2 3 4 5 6 7 8 9 10 11 12 13 14 15 16 17 18 19 20 21 22 23 24 25|26 27 28|29 30|31 32 33|34 35 36 37 38 39 40 41 42 43 44 45 46 47 48 49 50 51 52 53 54 55 56 57 58 59 60 61 62 63 64 65 66 67 68 69 70 71 72 73 74 75 76 77 78 79 80
```

Design of Printed Report:

```
        0         1         2         3         4         5         6         7
        1234567890123456789012345678901234567890123456789012345678901234567890123456789012
H  1  XØ/XX/XX                                          PAGE XXØX
   2
H  3  AVERAGE WEEKLY SALARY OF DATA PROCESSING PERSONNEL
   4
   5
H  6  NUMBER OF        JOB TITLE              AVERAGE
H  7  EMPLOYEES                              WEEKLY SALARY
   8
D  9    XØX      X------------------X      $ XXØ,XX
  10
D 11    XØX      X------------------X      $ XXØ,XX
  12
  13   (EMP)       (TITLE)                (SALARY)
  14
  15
  16
  17    (1.) Headings on top of every page.
  18
  19
  20    (2.) $ signs are fixed.
  21
```

Data To Be Used in Program:

Job Title	Salary	Number of Employees
APPLICATION PROGRAMMERS	24000	010
SYSTEMS PROGRAMMERS	32000	002
COMPUTER OPERATORS	18500	004
SYSTEMS ANALYST	40700	002
KEYPUNCH OPERATORS	15200	011
PROGRAMMER TRAINEES	19100	003
RECORDS CLERK	14600	001
DATA PROCESSING MANAGER	50200	001

The completed labratory assignment must include the following:

1. Filled in Specification Forms
2. Source Program Deck
3. Source Program Listing
4. Printed Report

LABORATORY ASSIGNMENT 3-2:
FEDERAL INCOME TAX AVERAGE ITEMIZED DEDUCTION SCHEDULE

From the Card Layout Form and Printer Spacing Chart information given below write an RPG II source program to obtain the required printed report. Your device and symbolic assignments (if needed) must be in accordance to those required for the computer system used for compilation and execution.

This schedule lists the average itemized deductions entered on Schedule A of the 1040 Individual Taxpayer's Federal Tax Return for Adjusted Gross Income brackets. Proof of the deduction still rests on the individual taxpayer if he or she elects to itemize instead of using the standard deduction.

Input Format of Data Records:

Company _NORWALK_

Application _Federal Income Tax_   by _S. MYERS_   Date _1/1/78_   Job No. _Lab. 3-2_   Sheet No. _1_

MULTIPLE-CARD LAYOUT FORM

LOW AGI	HIGH AGI	CONTRIBUTION	INTEREST	TAXES	MEDICAL	

Data To Be Used in Program:

Low AGI	High AGI	Contributions	Interest	Taxes	Medical
5000	6000	312	768	631	751
6001	7000	323	838	616	695
7001	8000	307	911	767	698
8001	9000	317	878	780	615
9001	10000	326	950	791	533
10001	15000	364	1153	1024	506

Design of Printed Report:

		0	1	2	3	4	5
		1234567890	1234567890	1234567890	1234567890	1234567890	12345678901
H	1			*1977*			
H	2			*FEDERAL INCOME TAX*			
H	3		*AVERAGE ITEMIZED DEDUCTION*				
	4						
H	5	*ADJUSTED*		*CONTRIBUTIONS*	*INTEREST*	*TAXES*	*MEDICAL*
H	6	*GROSS INCOME*					
	7						
D	8	*$0X,XXX TO $0X,XXX*		*$ XXX*	*$0XXX*	*$0XXX*	*$ XXX*
	9						
D	10	*$0X,XXX TO $0X,XXX*		*$ XXX*	*$0XXX*	*$0XXX*	*$ XXX*
	11						
	12						
	13			*Dollar signs are fixed.*			
	14						
	15						

The completed laboratory assignment must include the following:

1. Filled in Specification Forms
2. Source Program Deck
3. Source Program Listing
4. Printed Report

4
CALCULATION SPECIFICATIONS, RESULTING INDICATORS, AND FIELD INDICATORS

The previous chapters presented the RPG II coding rules for the File Description, Input, and Output-Format Specifications forms for example programs not requiring calculations. Most business and accounting applications do require calculations, and a thorough understanding of RPG II calculation coding procedures is important to effective programming. This chapter will introduce the Calculation Specifications coding rules for arithmetic functions. In addition, Resulting and Field Indicators, which give control over calculations and/or output, will be presented.

THE CALCULATION SPECIFICATIONS FORM

Any calculation coding needed in a program is entered in the standard Calculation coding form. Figure 4-1 illustrates the form with the major logic areas identified. These terms are not printed on the form, but serve to explain the major functional sections.

Columns 7–17 are labeled with the word WHEN, because indicators entered in these fields tell the computer when this line of calculation is to be executed. Any Record Identifying Indicator (01–99), discussed in Chapter 2, may be used in columns 9–17 along with Resulting and Field Indicators which

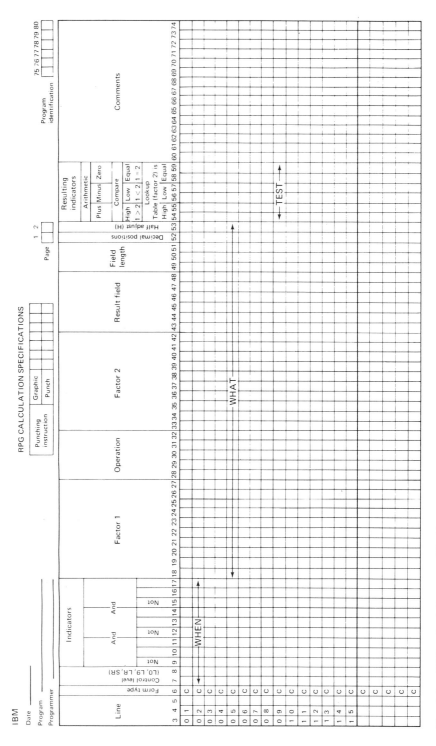

Fig. 4-1. RPG calculation specifications.

98

will be discussed later in this chapter. Control Level Indicators (L0–L9) are used in columns 7 and 8, and they will be discussed in Chapter 6.

The area labeled WHAT, which includes Factor 1, Operation, Factor 2, Result Field, Field Length, Decimal Positions, and Half-adjust, informs the computer about the arithmetic operation to be performed and on what fields it will be performed. Comments about the section labeled TEST will be made later in this chapter when Resulting Indicators are discussed.

The Comments field (columns 60–74) is used to identify or explain a line of calculation and does not have to be used, as it does not become part of the object program. Comments entered in this area do not have to be enclosed in apostrophes and do not require an asterisk in column 7.

The Calculation Specifications form, in addition to containing the features common to all forms, has the letter C preprinted in column 6 for every line of coding. The RPG II coding rules for this form are presented in the text that follows and reference should be made to Figure 4-1 to understand and identify the field location discussed.

Control Fields (Columns 7–8).   Will be discussed in Chapter 6.

Indicators (Columns 9–17).   Any indicator type available in the RPG II language may be used to condition a line of calculations. Record Identifying Indicators, discussed in Chapter 2, and Resulting and Field Indicators, introduced later in this chapter, may be used to condition a line of calculations along with other indicator types presented later in the text.

If the Indicator fields are blank, the line of calculations will be executed every time a record is processed. Some lines of calculations may be unconditioned and others may be conditioned by one or more indicators. The logic of the program will dictate *when* the line is to be executed.

Examine Figure 4-1 and notice only three indicators may be entered on any one line (columns 9–17). If additional indicators are required to condition a line of calculations, the letters AN may be entered in columns 7 and 8 to further condition the line. Figure 4-2 illustrates the Indicator field coding for an AN relationship (lines 010 and 020).

Lines 030 and 040 (Figure 4-2) illustrate an example of the OR relationship of indicators used to condition a line of calculations. In the example shown, line 040 will execute if either indicator 02 or 12 is on.

The N20 indicator entered in columns 9–11 illustrates the use of the NOT (off) condition of an indicator. This calculation will only execute if indicator 20 is *not on.*

The examples of AND, AN, OR, and NOT relationship of indicators are not to be considered required coding procedures; they only add flexibility to source program coding. Indicators should not be used indiscriminately, but assigned to a line of calculations and/or output according to program logic. The more indicators used in a program the more difficult it will be to debug the program.

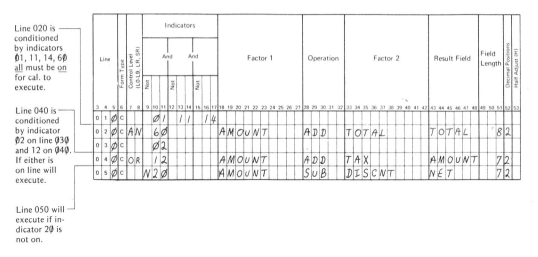

Line 020 is conditioned by indicators Ø1, 11, 14, 6Ø all must be on for cal. to execute.

Line 040 is conditioned by indicator Ø2 on line Ø3Ø and 12 on Ø4Ø. If either is on line will execute.

Line 050 will execute if indicator 2Ø is not on.

Fig. 4-2. AN, OR, and NOT conditioning of calculations.

A very important point to remember now that may possibly save many hours of debugging is that only *one Record Identifying Indicator* may condition a line of calculations and/or output. Record Identifying Indicators are those assigned to a record type in columns 19 and 20 of the Input Specifications form. As a record is processed, the respective Record Identifying Indicator is turned on and remains on for the program cycle and then turns off after the last instruction in the program is executed. The book has only illustrated *one record type* file at this point; however, when *multirecord* files are discussed, this rule must be followed. Record Identifying Indicators may be used, however, with one or more Resulting Indicators, Field Indicators, etc.

Factor 1 (Columns 18–27) and Factor 2 (Columns 33–42). These fields represent the two quantities used on a line of calculations. The field names must be entered left-justified in the designated columns (Factor 1 and Factor 2) and must have been defined in Input Specifications or created in the Result Field of the Calculations Specifications form. Any field names used in Factors 1 or 2 must follow the rules for forming field names described in Chapter 2.

In addition to field names, Factors 1 or 2 may contain a numeric or alphanumeric literal. Numeric literals are entered left-justified in either Factor 1 or 2 depending on the program logic. Figure 4-3, example 4, illustrates an example of a numeric literal. Alphanumeric literals will be discussed in Chapter 7.

When addition or multiplication operations are performed, it does not matter which quantity is assigned to either factor. However, with subtraction or division, it is important which field name or literal is specified in Factors 1 and 2.

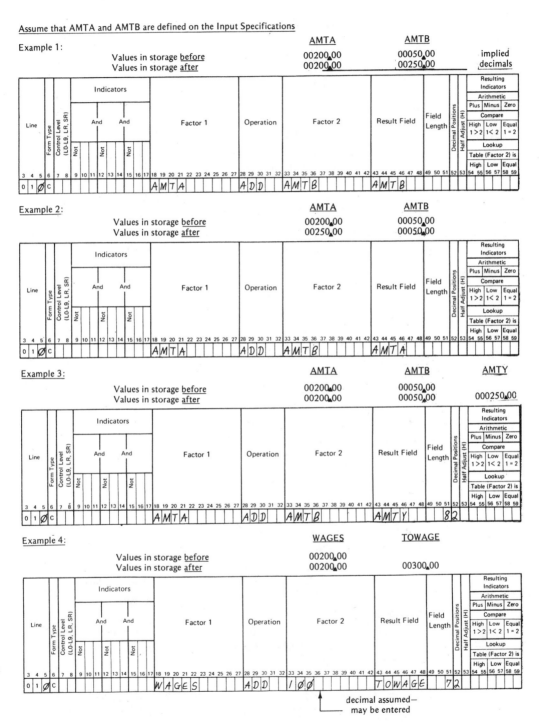

Fig. 4-3. RPG II addition operation examples showing the values in field storage before and after the operation is executed.

Operation (Columns 28–32). The arithmetic functions are expressed in RPG as follows:

Function	RPG Operation
Addition	ADD
Subtraction	SUB
Division	DIV
Multiplication	MULT

The spelling of these RPG operation names must be exact and they must always be left-justified in the Operation field starting in column 28.

Result Field (Columns 43–48). The name entered in this field may be created as the result of a mathematical operation, or it may be one of the field names that appears in Factors 1 or 2. If one of the names in Factors 1 or 2 is used for the result field, the original quantity of this field will be lost after the first record is processed. Therefore, if the original quantities in either field should be saved, a result field with a different name must be created. Any name used in this field, of course, must follow the same rules as other field names.

Field Length (Columns 49–51). The length of the Result Field is entered right-justified in this field. When creating the field length, be careful to make certain it is large enough, or the high order digits may be truncated or lost. A good rule to follow for addition is to make the result field one position longer than the longest factor field length. For the results of subtraction or division, the result field would normally be a satisfactory length if the size of the largest factor variable field name was used. However, we must be careful when a result field is specified in multiplication. A helpful rule to follow for multiplication results is to add the maximum number of digits that could be contained in Factor 1 to the maximum number that could be contained in Factor 2. For example, if a three-digit number was multiplied by a four-digit number, the maximum number of digits would be seven.

Decimal Positions (Column 52). This field specifies the number of decimal positions that will be assigned to the Result Field. A decimal entry must be made for the result of all mathematical operations unless the field was defined somewhere else in the program. Note that any number from $\emptyset$ to 9 may be used in this column and nothing greater than nine. It may help in determining decimal location if we remember that the number of decimal positions for the result of a multiplication will be the sum of the number of decimal positions in Factor 1 and the number in Factor 2.

Half-adjust (Column 53). This field is used only if the Result Field should have less decimal points than any of the factors. In mathematical terminology it is called rounding and Figure 4-4 shows how the computer does it in its

Addition:

Rule 1	Rule 2	Rule 3	Rule 3	Rule 3
+2	−3	+5	+3	+8
+2	−3	−5	−9	−6
+4	−6	Ø	−6	+2

Subtraction:

	Example 1	Example 2	Example 3
Minuend:	+3 = +3	+3 = +3	−5 = −5
Subtrahend:	+3 −3	−3 +3	+7 −7
Difference:	Ø	+6	−12

Multiplication:

Rule 1	Rule 1	Rule 2	Rule 2
+3	−3	+3	−3
+8	−8	−8	+8
+24	+24	−24	−24

Division:

Rule 1	Rule 1	Rule 2	Rule 2
$\begin{array}{r} +3 \\ -3\overline{)-9} \end{array}$	$\begin{array}{r} +3 \\ +3\overline{)+9} \end{array}$	$\begin{array}{r} -3 \\ -3\overline{)+9} \end{array}$	$\begin{array}{r} -3 \\ +3\overline{)-9} \end{array}$

Half-adjusting (rounding):

SALE = 1871.09
TAXPCT = 7%
The result of muliplication would be as follows:

$$\begin{array}{r} 1871.09 \\ \underline{0.07} \\ 130.9763 \\ \underline{+5} \\ 130.9813 \end{array}$$

If result field only specified *two* decimal positions, with *half-rounding* 5 would be added to the third digit to the right of the decimal.

Therefore the result field would contain 130.98 and the 1 and 3 digits would automatically be truncated (dropped).

Fig. 4-4. Examples of the algebraic rules for addition, subtraction, multiplication, division, and half-rounding.

unique way. If rounding or half-adjusting is desired, an H must be entered in column 53. If it is not wanted, the field must be left blank. Half-adjusting is not commonly used with the results of addition or subtraction but is frequently used with the results of multiplication or division.

Resulting Indicators (Columns 54–59). The use of Resulting Indicators to test the result of an arithmetic operation will be discussed later in this chapter. Other uses of Resulting Indicators will be discussed when the Compare (COMP) operation and Tables are introduced in subsequent chapters.

Comments (Columns 60–74). These columns are used to explain or document each line of calculations to help in debugging or general classification. Entries made in this field do not have to be used and in no way affect the compilation or execution of the program. As was discussed before, comments within the source program are made by entering an asterisk in column 7 of any source program card. Comments in this field area are only a supplement to others that may be used.

RPG II ADDITION

Examples of the addition operation calculation form coding are depicted in Figure 4-3 along with the values in the fields before and after the operation. In example 1 AMTA is added to AMTB placing the result of the operation in the AMTB field. Consequently, the original contents of the AMTB field will be replaced with the sum of the two fields. If any of the Factor 1 or Factor 2 field contents should be saved for further reference, a new Result Field should be created. Also notice that this line of calculation is not conditioned by an indicator; therefore, it would be performed every time a record was read. The field length is seven digits long with two decimal positions as indicated by the 2 specified in the decimal position field. A $\emptyset$ to 9 entry must be made in the decimal position column or the field would not be defined as numeric. If any field was defined on input or somewhere else in calculations, either before or after a line, it would not have to be defined again. This is a good rule to keep in mind, because if the same field is defined twice, a *multidefined* field error will result during compilation. The IBM 370 or System/3 computer systems will give a warning error and assume the first field size assigned. However, on the IBM 1130 a multidefined field error will cause a terminal error and cancel the program compilation.

Example 2 follows the same logic as example 1 except that the Result Field is the same as Factor 1 which will cause the original content of field AMTA to be replaced by the result of the addition. This line is also not conditioned by any indicator and will be performed every time a record is read.

The calculations for example 3, AMTA added to AMTB, places the sum in a newly-created field AMTY. If the AMTY field is created for the first time it must be given a field length and decimal positions or it would be considered unreferenced and prevent processing. The contents of Factors 1 and 2 will remain the same as the sum of their addition and will be stored in the new field AMTY. Notice that this line is not conditioned by any indicator.

Example 4 illustrates the use of a *numeric literal* in a calculation operation. There are four rules for using numeric literals:

1. They must be left-justified either in Factor 1 or 2.

2. If a whole number, numeric literals do not have to contain a decimal point as it will be assumed by the computer. If decimal positions are required, the decimal point must be included in the literal.

3. Other than the decimal point, no other punctuation may be included in the literal.

4. Numeric literals may be used with any arithmetic operation.

In the examples illustrated in Figure 4-3 none of the calculation lines were conditioned by an indicator. Many times the logic of the program will require that individual lines of calculation must be conditioned by an indicator or indicators. Any of the available RPG II indicators may be used to condition a line of calculations.

Because RPG causes the contents of Factor 2 to be added to the contents of Factor 1 algebraically, we should be at least familiar with the rules of algebraic addition:

Rule 1: Adding two plus fields results in the sum of the two fields having a plus sign.

Rule 2: Adding two minus fields results in the sum of the two fields having a minus sign.

Rule 3: Adding two fields with different signs $(+, -)$ results in the difference between the two fields and carries the sign of the larger number.

Examples of the algebraic addition rules are shown in Figure 4-4. Furthermore, remember that any number that does not have a sign is always considered positive.

RPG II SUBTRACTION

Figure 4-5 illustrates examples of coding for the RPG subtraction operation. It is very important to distinguish between the top and bottom numbers of a subtraction operation. Factor 1 always contains the minuend, or top number, and Factor 2 always contains the subtrahend, or bottom number, and the result of the subtraction is called the difference. Refer back to Figure 4-4 and notice

Assume QUANA and QUANB are defined on the Input Specifications

Example 1:

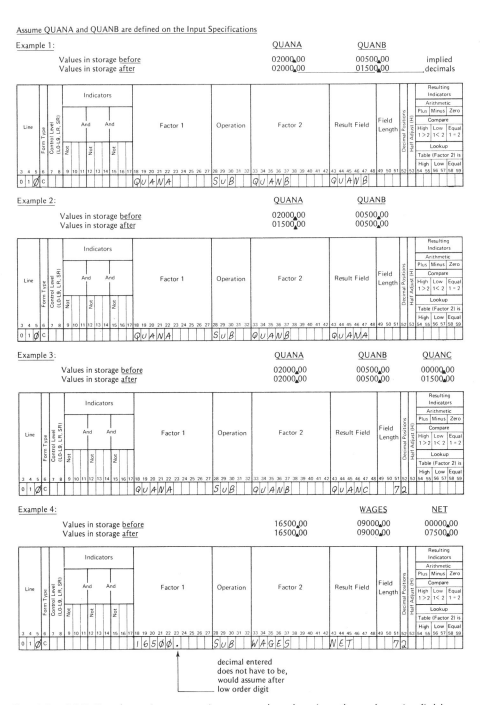

Fig. 4-5. RPG II subtraction operation examples showing the values in field storage before and after the operation is executed.

which numbers of the examples are labeled the minuend, subtrahend, and difference.

The coding entered in example 1 of Figure 4-5 indicates that QUANB, the subtrahend, is to be subtracted from QUANA, the minuend, and the difference stored in QUANB. The original value of QUANB will, of course, be replaced by the difference. Again it cannot be overemphasized that the minuend must be entered in Factor 1 and the subtrahend in Factor 2 or improper answers will result.

The coding specified in example 2 follows the same logic as example 1 only the answer will be stored in QUANA replacing the original value in that field. Because QUANA and QUANB are input fields (or if they had been previously defined in calculations) the field length entry is not needed. However, when a field is created for the first time as a result of calculations, it must be defined.

Notice that the coding in example 3 stores the difference in a new Result Field, QUANC, which must be given a field length and decimal position entry to prevent a terminal error during compilation. The values contained in QUANA and QUANB will not be lost because the difference is stored in QUANC.

Example 4 illustrates the use of a numeric literal in a subtraction operation. Notice the literal does contain a decimal point; however, it does not have to as this will not result in an error because it will be assumed by the computer and implied after the low-order digit. The logic of the arithmetic operation will determine whether the literal is entered in Factor 1 or 2.

RPG II MULTIPLICATION

Multiplication in RPG causes the contents of the variable field name in Factor 1 to be multiplied by the contents of the variable field name in Factor 2 with the product stored in a variable field name in the Result Field. With the multiplication operation it doesn't matter which field name is specified in the factors.

A little processing time is saved, however, if the field with the smallest size is entered in Factor 1. Figure 4-6 illustrates examples of multiplication with the half-rounding feature used where needed.

Examples 1 and 2 of Figure 4-6 illustrate calculation coding for multiplication where one of the field values is replaced by the product of the MULT operation. In example 1, the original value of FIELDB, and in example 2, the value in FIELDA, will be replaced by the product of the multiplication.

Example 3 illustrates a multiplication operation where a new Result Field is created. Notice that the answer is rounded to the nearest cent. The values in HOURS and RATE will remain the same after the operation is executed.

Example 4 shows the use of a numeric literal for calculations. The literal could be entered left-justified in either Factor 1 or 2. However, because it is

Assume FIELDA and FIELDB are defined on the Input Specifications
as six digits long with two decimal positions and four long with
four decimal positions respectively.

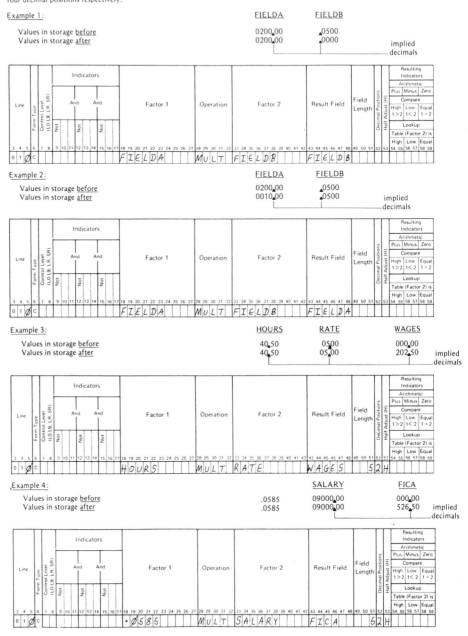

Example 1:

	FIELDA	FIELDB
Values in storage before	0200.00	.0500
Values in storage after	0200.00	.0000

implied decimals

Example 2:

	FIELDA	FIELDB
Values in storage before	0200.00	.0500
Values in storage after	0010.00	.0500

implied decimals

Example 3:

	HOURS	RATE	WAGES
Values in storage before	40.50	0500	000.00
Values in storage after	40.50	05.00	202.50

implied decimals

Example 4:

		SALARY	FICA
Values in storage before	.0585	09000.00	000.00
Values in storage after	.0585	09000.00	526.50

implied decimals

Fig. 4-6. RPG II multiplication operation examples showing the values in field storage before and after operation is executed.

more efficient to place the smaller quantity in Factor 1, the example follows this rule.

The rules for determining the size of a Result Field for a multiplication operation and the number of decimal points are restated in Figure 4-7. Notice in the first example of Figure 4-7 that Factor 1 contains a three-digit number with three decimal positions, and Factor 2, a two-digit number with two decimal positions which, when added together according to the rule, will give five digits with five decimal positions. Half-rounding may be used to reduce the number of decimal positions down to the required size.

Rule for Field Length:

The field length for the product of a multiplication should be the sum of the maximum number of digits that could be contained in Factor 1 and the maximum number that could be contained in Factor 2.

Rule for decimal position:

The number of decimal positions for the result of multiplication should be the sum of the number of decimal positions in Factor 1 and the number in Factor 2.

Examples:

	FACTOR 1	×	**FACTOR 2**	=	**RESULT**
Contents of field	0.999	×	0.99	=	0.99999
Contents of field	99.99	×	0.999	=	099.99999
Contents of field	999.	×	99.	=	99999

Fig. 4-7. Rules for determining field length and decimal positions for products of multiplication.

The raising of a number to a power may be accomplished in RPG II by multiplication with a feature called *looping* which will be presented in Chapter 8.

RPG II DIVISION

The terms used in division are explained in Figure 4-8. It is very important that Factor 2 is always the divisor and Factor 1 the dividend with the Result Field the answer or quotient. The variable field names specified in Factor 1, Factor

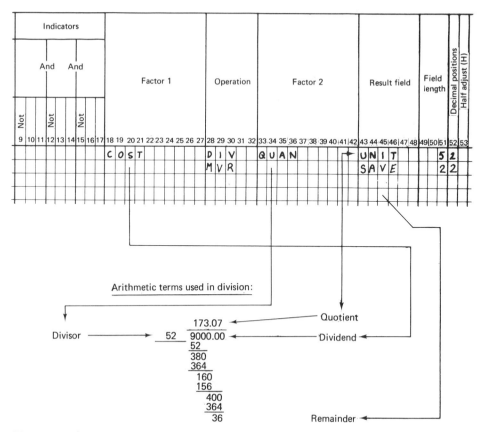

Fig. 4-8. Terms used in division and RPG calculation specifications coding for division.

2, and the Result Field may all be the same names, all may be different, or any two alike. However, the contents of Factor 2, the divisor, may never be zero because the computer *will never allow division by zero*. On the other hand, Factor 1 may be zero, which would result in a zero answer for the quotient; but the program will still execute. Refer to Figure 4-8, line Ø1Ø, and notice that the variable field COST, the dividend, is to be divided by the variable field QUAN that will result in a quotient or answer called UNIT. Any of these field names may have been created in the Calculation Specifications form either before or after this line or defined previously on input. If it is remembered that Factor 2 is the divisor and Factor 1 the dividend, the most difficult aspect of division will be understood.

The algebraic rules for division are the same as the rules for multiplication, and are repeated below.

1. Division of numbers with like signs results in a sign of plus.

2. Division of numbers with unlike signs results in a sign of minus.

If any remainder (the amount that does not appear in the quotient) results from the division it will be lost unless the Move Remainder (MVR) operation is used. Figure 4-8 also shows the coding on line Ø3Ø that is needed to correctly use this rather infrequently used function. The RPG rules for using this operation include:

1. Factor 1 and Factor 2 must always be blank on the Calculation Specifications form.

2. The operation code MVR is placed left-justified in the Operation Field columns 28–32.

3. A variable field name is placed in the Result Field.

4. The remainder will have the same sign as the dividend.

5. Half-adjustment is allowed with the MVR operation; however, it is not allowed in the Divide Operation that created the remainder.

6. Any control levels or indicators entered in columns 7–17 of this form must be the same for both the division and Move Remainder operations.

7. The MVR operation must immediately follow the divide operation.

The length of the Result Field in the MVR operation must be *equal to the number of decimal positions included in the dividend (Factor 1)* or *the sum of the decimal position in the divisor (Factor 2) and quotient (Result Field)*, whichever is greater.

RPG II arithmetic may seem awkward at first, but as more programs are written the student should develop the proficiency to solve any application problem for the business environment. The following paragraphs will illustrate the use of RPG II arithmetic operations in an application program.

EXAMPLE APPLICATION PROGRAM: A SALES JOURNAL

Because of the volume of accounting transactions that take place in a business daily, weekly, or monthly, more than one book of original entry (journal) may be needed to record information from source documents. The most commonly used books include the sales journal, purchase journal, cash receipts journal, cash disbursements journal, and the general journal. In addition, if a company has many transactions that result in sales and/or purchase returns and allowances it may be practical to use a sales returns and allowances journal, or a purchase returns and allowances journal, or perhaps both.

The suggested use of each of the common journals is as follows:

1. The sales journal records all sales of merchandise on account. (Cash sales are recorded in the cash receipts journal.)

2. The purchase journal records all purchases of merchandise on account. (Cash purchases of merchandise are recorded in the cash disbursements journal.)

3. The cash receipts journal records all cash received by an organization regardless of its source.

4. The cash disbursement journal records all cash paid out by an organization.

5. The general journal, commonly referred to simply as the journal, is used to record transactions of a general nature, as its name implies. It contains all transaction data which cannot be recorded in any of the other books of original entry employed in an accounting system.

Figure 4-9 shows the typical design for sales, purchase, cash receipts, cash disbursements, and general journals. However, the design of these journals will depend on the needs of the user with more or less columns as required. In other words, the journals may often be custom designed and still be acceptable in the accounting profession.

Figure 4-10 illustrates a "one amount column" sales journal with entries recorded for the month of October. Transactions are recorded daily by entering the date in the date columns, name of charge customer in the account debited column, and the amount of the sales in the single amount column. The F or folio column is used in manual data processing systems for posting reference to the accounts receivable subsidiary ledger, but is not needed in a computerized accounting system. An accounts receivable ledger is usually an alphabetical or account number listing of a company's customers, and daily posting is required to maintain daily updated balances. The posting procedure in a manual system would need some identification providing the information that a customer's account had been posted. In the sales journal illustrated this is indicated by a check mark. Also, the total of all the customers' current balances in the subsidiary ledger must equal the balance in the general ledger account referred to as accounts receivable.

At the end of the month the total of charge sales is computed and posted as a debit to the general ledger account accounts receivable and a credit to the

SALES JOURNAL — PAGE 8

Date		Account debited	Invoice number	Folio	Amount
19 Nov.	3	J.T. Burgess	761	✓	5 0 0 00

PURCHASES JOURNAL — PAGE 8

Date		Account credited	Date of invoice	Terms	Folio	Amount
19 Nov.	8	Monroe Mfg. Co.	11/6	2/10. n/60	✓	1 0 0 0 00

CASH RECEIPTS JOURNAL — PAGE 9

Date		Account credited	Explanation	Folio	Sundry accounts credit	Accounts receivable credit	Sales credit	Sales discount debit	Cash debit
19 Nov.	1	Rent earned	Tenant's November rent	711	1 5 0 00				1 5 0 00

CASH DISBURSEMENTS JOURNAL — PAGE 7

Date		Account debited	Explanation	Folio	Sundry accounts debit	Accounts payable debit	Purchases discount credit	Cash credit
19 Nov.	15	Sales salaries expense	Salaries for first half	611	2 2 5 00			2 2 5 00

GENERAL JOURNAL — PAGE 17

Date	Account titles and explanation	Folio	Debit	Credit

Source: Pyle, William W., and John Arch White, *Fundamental Accounting Principles* (5th ed.), Homewood, Illinois; Richard D. Irwin, Inc., 1969, p. 171.

Fig. 4-9.   Basic design of the journals.

general ledger account, sales. An entire accounting system or subsystem should only be computerized when the volume of transactions warrants it. Obviously once programs are written and perfected they should be able to handle accounting transactions with great speed and accuracy. However, the degree of accuracy depends on the recording and keypunching of source document information.

Now that we have refreshed our memories in reference to some basic accounting tools—the books of original entry—we should be ready to begin planning the steps needed for writing an RPG source program for a simple sales journal.

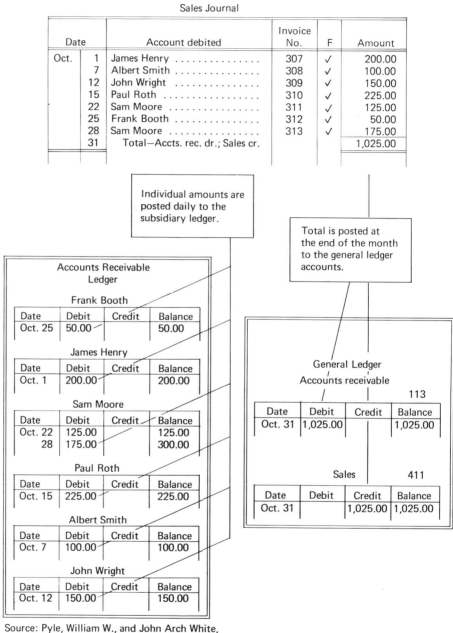

Sales Journal

Date		Account debited	Invoice No.	F	Amount
Oct.	1	James Henry	307	✓	200.00
	7	Albert Smith	308	✓	100.00
	12	John Wright	309	✓	150.00
	15	Paul Roth	310	✓	225.00
	22	Sam Moore	311	✓	125.00
	25	Frank Booth	312	✓	50.00
	28	Sam Moore	313	✓	175.00
	31	Total—Accts. rec. dr.; Sales cr.			1,025.00

Individual amounts are posted daily to the subsidiary ledger.

Total is posted at the end of the month to the general ledger accounts.

Accounts Receivable Ledger

Frank Booth

Date	Debit	Credit	Balance
Oct. 25	50.00		50.00

James Henry

Date	Debit	Credit	Balance
Oct. 1	200.00		200.00

Sam Moore

Date	Debit	Credit	Balance
Oct. 22	125.00		125.00
28	175.00		300.00

Paul Roth

Date	Debit	Credit	Balance
Oct. 15	225.00		225.00

Albert Smith

Date	Debit	Credit	Balance
Oct. 7	100.00		100.00

John Wright

Date	Debit	Credit	Balance
Oct. 12	150.00		150.00

General Ledger

Accounts receivable   113

Date	Debit	Credit	Balance
Oct. 31	1,025.00		1,025.00

Sales   411

Date	Debit	Credit	Balance
Oct. 31		1,025.00	1,025.00

Source: Pyle, William W., and John Arch White,
Fundamental Accounting Principles (5th ed.).
Homewood, Illinois; Richard D. Irwin, Inc.,
1969, p. 171.

Fig. 4-10.   Single column sales journal.

Design of Input for the Sales Journal

One of the preliminary tasks in the design of punch cards is to determine the size of the fields required to handle input data. Field sizes should be determined practically and not made too large, as more information may have to be added to the card in the future. Re-examination of Figure 4-10 will show the information that must be read to develop a sales journal which includes date, customer name, invoice number, and invoice amount. Provision must be made for all of this information on our input data cards and the appropriate size of each field must be planned accordingly. We know that a date consists of month, day, and year, and a standard six–digit field for date will be used in all programs presented in this text. The use of a six–digit numeric field is in lieu of printing the name of the month, day, and year.

In order to provide for relatively long customer names, this field size should be 29 columns in width. The invoice number field size may be determined by referring to a source document—the sales invoice—for the present and possible future size of this item. Consequently, six card columns will be allowed for this field.

The largest foreseeable dollar sale must also be considered when planning the size of the invoice amount field. Consultation with the sales department would guide our decision. A field size of seven, including two decimal positions, should be allocated to this item since this would allow a maximum sale of $99,999.99, probably more than needed for most sales transactions. A card layout form for a Hollerith card is shown with the fields designated in Figure 4-11. Again, remember that we could have placed these fields anywhere on the card, not only in the first available columns.

Repeating several concepts concerning the punching of data cards may be timely at this point. It must be remembered that alphanumeric or alphabetic data is punched left-justified in the assigned field and numeric data is right-justified. In addition, commas and decimals are never punched into a numeric input field. A punched Hollerith data card for this program is illustrated in Figure 4-12.

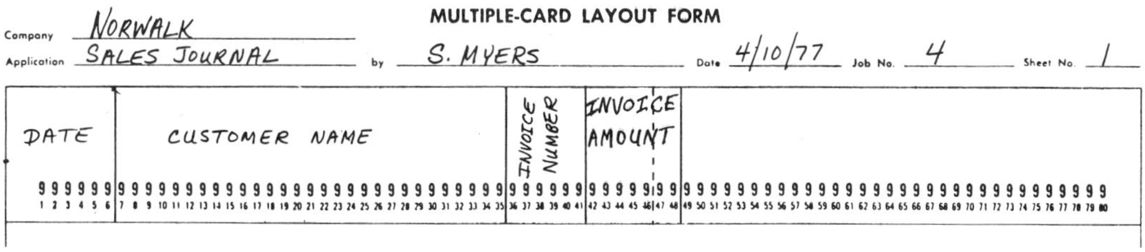

Fig. 4-11. Card Layout Form formatted for Sales Journal Input.

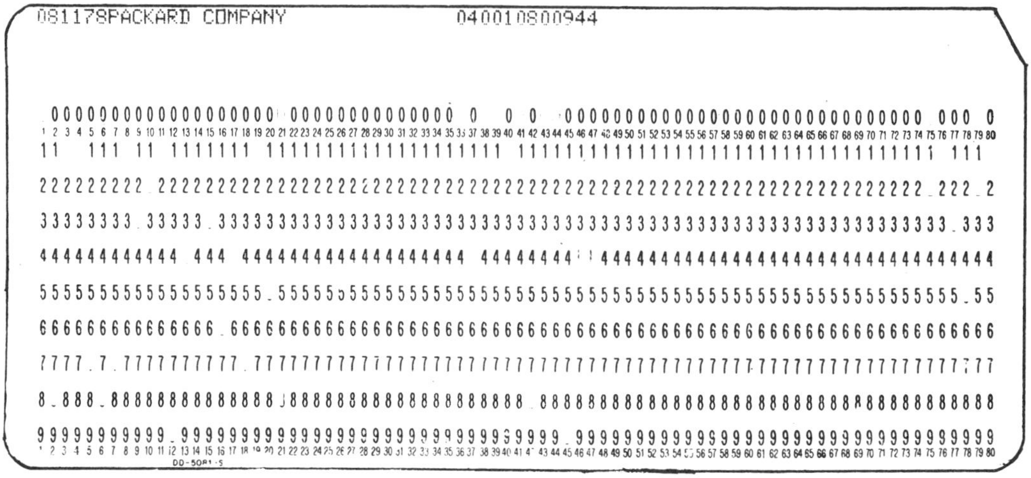

Fig. 4-12. Punched data card for Sales Journal Program

Design of Output for the Sales Journal

Figure 4-13 illustrates the Printer Spacing Chart for the sales journal program. In addition to the Heading (H) and Detail line (D) notice another line type is formatted on the chart. The TLR lines indicate that the column-total line, total amount of sales (TOTSAL), and the double final total line are printed only at *Total Time after the last record* is processed. The letter T is used for Total Time output and the LR indicator is an internal indicator that turns on automatically after the last record of the data file is processed.

End of file on most computer systems is sensed by a record containing a slash asterisk (/*) in columns 1 and 2. Hence, every data file must include a /* card after the last data record. When this card is sensed, the LR indicator turns on and executes any calculation and/or output coding conditioned by the Last Record Indicator. Until the /* record is sensed, any coding conditioned by the LR indicator will be ignored. Furthermore, Total Time (T) for any output file must follow Heading (H) and Detail (D) time. In order to execute at the correct time during execution of the program, the LR indicator must be used with Total Time (T in column 15 of the output form) and *not with* Heading or Detail time.

Look at Figure 4-13 again and notice the column total line (— — — — — — — — — — —) is entered immediately after the second detail line. This does not infer that the total is printed after the second detail line, but indicates the vertical spacing requirements of the report. The TLR lines will be printed only after all the detail records are processed regardless of the number of input data records.

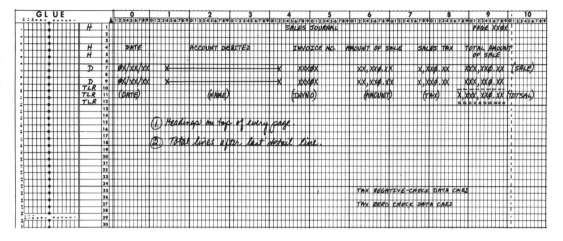

Fig. 4-13. Printer Spacing Chart for Sales Journal application program.

RPG II Source Program Coding for Sales Journal

An examination of the source program coding for the sales journal program in Figure 4-14 will reveal that the File Description and Input Specifications entries follow RPG II rules previously discussed. A Calculation Specifications form is used in this application program that illustrates many of the calculation procedures introduced in this chapter.

Calculation Specifications

Figure 4-15 shows the calculation entries for the sales journal program in greater detail. Line 020 of the form shows an example of multiplication with a numeric literal. The AMOUNT, defined on input, is multiplied by the numeric literal .07 (seven percent) to give the state's sales tax (TAX) levied on every sale. Notice the literal is left-justified in Factor 2 and includes the required decimal point. If the decimal point had been omitted, the literal would be interpreted by the computer as a 7. or 700 percent. Because this is a multiplication operation, the literal could have been entered in Factor 1 instead of Factor 2 without causing an error.

Also notice the Result Field TAX, the product of the operation, is given a field length and decimal position. This field was not defined on input and instead is created in calculations. Consequently, it must be given a field length and decimal position to define it or an error would result during compilation. The letter H in column 53 indicates the Result Field TAX is rounded to the nearest cent. According to the rules of multiplication, the maximum size of

File Description Specifications

Line	Filename	File Type	File Designation	End of File	Sequence	File Format	Block Length	Record Length	Mode of Processing	Device	Symbolic Device	Name of Label Exit	Extent Exit for DAM	Core Index	File Addition/Unordered
0 2 Ø	F	X THIS PROGRAM PRINTS A SALES JOURNAL FOR CHARGE CUSTOMERS......													
0 3 Ø	F	CHARGSALIP	F	8Ø	8Ø						MFCMI	SYSIPT			
0 4 Ø	F	SALEJRL O	F	132	132		OF				PRINTERSYSLST				
0 5	F														

RPG INPUT SPECIFICATIONS

Date _____
Program _____
Programmer _____

Punching Instruction — Graphic / Punch

Page Ø2 Program Identification SALESJ

Line	Filename	Sequence	Number (1 N)	Record Identifying Indicator or	Record Identification Codes Position 1	C/Z/D	Character	Position 2	C/Z/D	Character	Position 3	C/Z/D	Character	Field Location From	To	Decimal Positions	Field Name	Control Level (L1-L9)	Field Indicators Plus	Minus	Zero or Blank
0 1 Ø	I CHARGSALSM		5Ø																		
0 2 Ø	I													1	6Ø	DATE					
0 3 Ø	I													7	35	NAME					
0 4 Ø	I													36	41Ø	INVNO					
0 5 Ø	I													42	482	AMOUNT					
0 6	I																				

RPG CALCULATION SPECIFICATIONS

Date _____
Program _____
Programmer _____

Punching Instruction — Graphic / Punch

Page Ø3 Program Identification SALESJ

Line	Form Type	Control Level (L0-L9, LR, SR)	Indicators And / And	Factor 1	Operation	Factor 2	Result Field	Field Length	Decimal Positions	Resulting Indicators Plus Minus Zero / Compare High Low Equal	Comments
0 1 Ø	C			X CALCULATE SALES TAX BASED ON STATE'S 7% RATE...........							
0 2 Ø	C			AMOUNT	MULT	.Ø7	TAX	72H			
0 3 Ø	C			ADD TAX TO AMOUNT TO GIVE TOTAL AMOUNT OF SALE....							
0 4 Ø	C			TAX	ADD	AMOUNT	SALE	82			
0 5 Ø	C			X ADD TOTAL AMOUNT OF EACH SALE TO A TOTAL OF ALL SALES FIELD							
0 6 Ø	C			SALE	ADD	TOTSAL	TOTSAL	92			
0 7	C										

Fig. 4-14. Source program coding for the Sales Journal program. (continued on next page)

RPG OUTPUT - FORMAT SPECIFICATIONS

Date _____ Program _____ Programmer _____

Punching Instruction: Graphic / Punch

Edit Codes:

	Commas	Zero Balances to Print	No Sign	CR	-
	Yes	Yes	1	A	J
	Yes	No	2	B	K
	No	Yes	3	C	L
	No	No	4	D	M

X = Remove Plus Sign Y = Date Field Edit Z = Zero Suppress

Line	Form Type	Filename	Type (H/D/T/E)	Space Before	Space After	Skip Before	Skip After	Output Indicators	Field Name	Edit Codes	Blank After (B)	End Position in Output Record	P	Constant or Edit Word
01	O	SALEJRL	H	3	0	1		IP						
02	O		OR					OF						
03	O											56		'SALES JOURNAL'
04	O											94		'PAGE'
05	O								PAGE	Z		99		
06	O		H	1				IP						
07	O		OR					OF						
08	O											7		'DATE'
09	O											34		'ACCOUNT DEBITED'
10	O											56		'INVOICE NO.'
11	O											73		'AMOUNT OF SALE'
12	O											85		'SALES TAX'
13	O											100		'TOTAL AMOUNT'
14	O		H	2				IP						
15	O		OR					OF						

RPG OUTPUT - FORMAT SPECIFICATIONS

Date _____ Program _____ Programmer _____

Punching Instruction: Graphic / Punch

Edit Codes:

	Commas	Zero Balances to Print	No Sign	CR	-
	Yes	Yes	1	A	J
	Yes	No	2	B	K
	No	Yes	3	C	L
	No	No	4	D	M

X = Remove Plus Sign Y = Date Field Edit Z = Zero Suppress

Line	Form Type	Filename	Type (H/D/T/E)	Space Before	Space After	Skip Before	Skip After	Output Indicators	Field Name	Edit Codes	Blank After (B)	End Position in Output Record	P	Constant or Edit Word
01	O											97		'OF SALE'
02	O		D	2		50								
03	O								DATE	Y		9		
04	O								NAME			42		
05	O								INVNO	Z		52		
06	O								AMOUNT	1		70		
07	O								TAX	1		84		
08	O								SALE	1		98		
09	O		T	1				LR						
10	O											98		'- - - - - - - - -'
11	O		T	1				LR						
12	O								TOTSAL	1		98		
13	O		T	0				LR						
14	O											98		'= = = = = = = = = ='
15	O													

Fig. 14-14. (concluded)

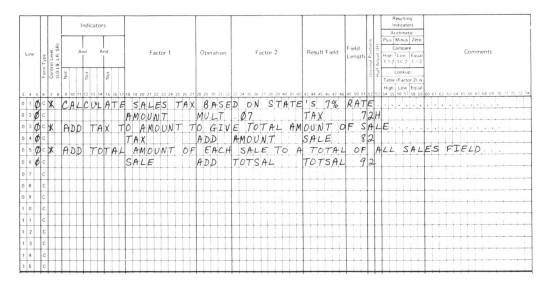

Fig. 4-15. Sales Journal application program calculation coding. Addition, multiplication, numeric literal, and half-rounding are used in the calculation coding.

TAX could be nine with four decimal positions; however, rounding to the cent would give a size of seven with two decimal positions. The rule for determining Result Field sizes for a multiplication operation must be followed or high-order digits could be truncated (lost).

Line 040 adds the TAX field (created on line 020) to the input field AMOUNT giving a new field SALE. The SALE field must be defined and should be given a larger field size than AMOUNT to allow for any additional high-order digits that could result from addition. Notice, however, the SALE field is not half-rounded because both the fields in Factors 1 and 2 contain only two decimal positions. If an H was entered in column 53 for this line of calculations, a warning error would result during compilation, but the program would compile successfully.

The coding entered on line 060 causes the SALE field, created on line 040, to be added to the accumulator field TOTSAL. This field (TOTSAL) accumulates the total amount of SALE which is computed for each record processed and will be printed after all the data records in the file are read. Notice that TOTSAL is entered in Factor 2 and the Result Field. In order to be used as an accumulator field TOTSAL must be entered as a Factor and Result Field. As each record is processed and SALE computed, the SALE amount will be added to the previous amount contained in TOTSAL and continue until the last record is processed. The TOTSAL field was not defined anywhere else in the program and is initialized and defined (given a storage position) after successful compilation of the source program.

Output-Format Specifications

Figure 4-16 illustrates the second page of the Output-Format Specifications coding which contains the only new coding entries required for the sales journal program. Other coding entries for output include previously discussed concepts.

An examination of Figure 4-16 will reveal that lines 090, 110, and 130 are coded as T (total lines) conditioned by the LR (last record indicator). The LR lines will be ignored during processing of the data records until the end of file (/*) marker is sensed, when LR will turn on and execute the total lines. TOTSAL will contain the sum of all the SALE fields which is computed for every data record processed. Hence, the total line (– – – – – – – – – – – – –), TOTSAL, and the final total line (= = = = = = = = = = = = =) will only print when end of file is sensed and LR turns on.

Figure 4-17 shows the source program listing and printed sales journal. If the report had extended to more than one page, the total lines would only be printed on the last page, not on every page.

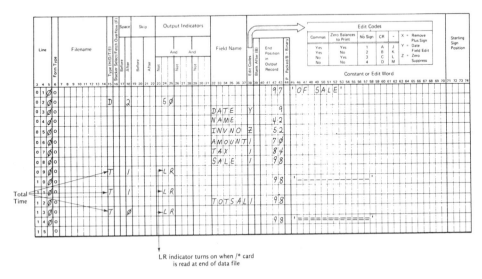

Fig. 4-16. Output-Format Specifications coding for Sales Journal application program showing coding for Last Record Time (LR).

Source Program Listing:

```
       01 020  F* THIS PROGRAM PRINTS A SALES JOURNAL FOR CHARGE CUSTOMERS......    SALESJ
0001   01 030  FCHARGSALIP  F  80  80              MFCM1 SYSIPT                      SALESJ
0002   01 040  FSALEJRL  O   F 132 132      OF     PRINTERSYSLST                     SALESJ
0003   02 010  ICHARGSALSM  50                                                      SALESJ
0004   02 020  I                                        1    60DATE                 SALESJ
0005   02 030  I                                        7    35 NAME                SALESJ
0006   02 040  I                                       36    41 INVNO               SALESJ
0007   02 050  I                                       42   482AMOUNT               SALESJ
       03 010  C* CALCULATE SALES TAX BASED ON STATE'S 7% RATE..................    SALESJ
0008   03 020  C          AMOUNT    MULT .07        TAX       72H                    SALESJ
       03 030  C* ADD TAX TO AMOUNT TO GIVE TOTAL AMOUNT OF SALE.................    SALESJ
0009   03 040  C          TAX       ADD  AMOUNT     SALE      82                     SALESJ
       03 050  C* ADD TOTAL AMOUNT OF EACH SALE TO A TOTAL OF ALL SALES FIELD...    SALESJ
0010   03 060  C          SALE      ADD  TOTSAL     TOTSAL    92                     SALESJ
0011   04 010  OSALEJRL  H  301       1P                                            SALESJ
0012   04 020  O          OR          OF                                            SALESJ
0013   04 030  O                                       56  'SALES JOURNAL'          SALESJ
0014   04 040  O                                       94  'PAGE'                    SALESJ
0015   04 050  O                             PAGE  Z   99                           SALESJ
0016   04 060  O         H   1        1P                                            SALESJ
0017   04 070  O          OR          OF                                            SALESJ
0018   04 080  O                                        7  'DATE'                    SALESJ
0019   04 090  O                                       34  'ACCOUNT DEBITED'         SALESJ
0020   04 100  O                                       56  'INVOICE NO.'             SALESJ
0021   04 110  O                                       73  'AMOUNT OF SALE'          SALESJ
0022   04 120  O                                       85  'SALES TAX'               SALESJ
0023   04 130  O                                      100  'TOTAL AMOUNT'            SALESJ
0024   04 140  O         H   2        1P                                            SALESJ
0025   04 150  O          OR          OF                                            SALESJ
0026   04 160  O                                       97  'OF SALE'                 SALESJ
0027   04 170  O         D   2        50                                            SALESJ
0028   04 180  O                             DATE  Y    9                           SALESJ
0029   04 190  O                             NAME      42                           SALESJ
0030   04 200  O                             INVNO Z   52                           SALESJ
0031   05 010  O                             AMOUNT1   70                           SALESJ
0032   05 020  O                             TAX   1   84                           SALESJ
0033   05 030  O                             SALE  1   98                           SALESJ
0034   05 040  O         T   1        LR                                            SALESJ
0035   05 050  O                                       98  '------------'           SALESJ
0036   05 060  O         T   1        LR                                            SALESJ
0037   05 070  O                             TOTSAL1   98                           SALESJ
0038   05 080  O         T   0        LR                                            SALESJ
0039   05 090  O                                       98  '============'           SALESJ
```

     E N D   O F   S O U R C E

Printed Report:

SALES JOURNAL

DATE	ACCOUNT DEBITED	INVOICE NO.	AMOUNT OF SALE	SALES TAX	TOTAL AMOUNT OF SALE
8/01/78	HUDSON MOTOR CAR COMPANY	40000	4,121.00	288.47	4,409.47
8/11/78	PACKARD COMPANY	40010	80,094.40	5,606.61	85,701.01
8/14/78	THE HUPMOBILE CORPORATION	40021	6,738.20	471.67	7,209.87
8/19/78	THE TUCKER CAR COMPANY	40030	19.90	1.39	21.29
8/21/78	AUBURN INCORPORATED	40040	356.70	24.97	381.67
8/27/78	BRICKLIN LIMITED	40050	9,990.10	699.31	10,689.41
8/31/78	THE LOCOMOBILE CAR COMPANY	40062	20,000.00	1,400.00	21,400.00

PAGE   1

```
                                                             -------------
                                                              129,812.72
                                                             =============
```

Fig. 4-17. Source program listing and printed report for the Sales Journal program.

RESULTING INDICATORS

Locate columns 54–59 on the Calculation Specifications form in Figure 4-18. Notice the field area is entitled *Resulting Indicators* with subdivisions of these indicators given below the title. This chapter is concerned with only the *Arithmetic* Resulting Indicators (Plus, Minus, Zero) reserving the Compare and Lookup types for subsequent chapters.

The value in any field entered as a Result Field (columns 43–48) may be tested for a positive, minus, or zero condition by entering any RPG II indicator in the respective field. For example, Figure 4-18 shows that indicator 1∅ is entered in the Plus field, 2∅ in the Minus, and 3∅ in the Zero. Any of the

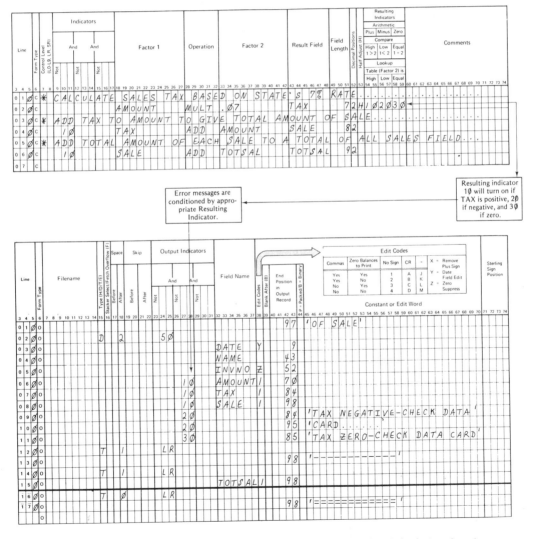

Fig. 4-18.   Relationship of Resulting Indicators assigned on the Calculation Specifications form to Output-Format Specifications.

Source Program Listing:

```
DOS - RPGII          JOB - SALES      03/13/78           PROGRAM - SALESJ

       01 020  F* THIS PROGRAM PRINTS A SALES JOURNAL FOR CHARGE CUSTOMERS......   SALESJ
0001   01 030  FCHARGSALIP  F   80   80        MFCM1 SYSIPT                         SALESJ
0002   01 040  FSALEJRL  O  F 132 132       OF  PRINTERSYSLST                       SALESJ
0003   02 010  ICHARGSALSM  50                                                     SALESJ
0004   02 020  I                                        1    60DATE                 SALESJ
0005   02 030  I                                        7    35 NAME                SALESJ
0006   02 040  I                                       36    410INVNO               SALESJ
0007   02 050  I                                       42    482AMOUNT              SALESJ
       03 010  C* CALCULATE SALES TAX BASED ON STATE'S 7% RATE................     SALESJ
0008   03 020  C            AMOUNT    MULT .07      TAX     72H102030               SALESJ
       03 030  C* ADD TAX TO AMOUNT TO GIVE TOTAL AMOUNT OF SALE..............     SALESJ
0009   03 040  C     10     TAX       ADD  AMOUNT   SALE    82                      SALESJ
       03 050  C* ADD TOTAL AMOUNT OF EACH SALE TO A TOTAL OF ALL SALES FIELD...   SALESJ
0010   03 060  C     10     SALE      ADD  TOTSAL   TOTSAL  92                      SALESJ
0011   04 010  CSALEJRL H  301        1P                                           SALESJ
0012   04 020  O           OR         OF                                           SALESJ
0013   04 030  O                                       56 'SALES JOURNAL'          SALESJ
0014   04 040  O                                       94 'PAGE'                    SALESJ
0015   04 050  O                                PAGE Z, 99                          SALESJ
0016   04 060  O           H  1       1P                                           SALESJ
0017   04 070  O           OR         OF                                           SALESJ
0018   04 080  O                                        7 'DATE'                    SALESJ
0019   04 090  O                                       34 'ACCOUNT DEBITED'         SALESJ
0020   04 100  O                                       56 'INVOICE NO.'             SALESJ
0021   04 110  O                                       73 'AMOUNT OF SALE'          SALESJ
0022   04 120  O                                       85 'SALES TAX'               SALESJ
0023   04 130  O                                      100 'TOTAL AMOUNT'            SALESJ
0024   04 140  O           H  2       1P                                           SALESJ
0025   04 150  O           OR         OF                                           SALESJ
0026   05 010  O                                       97 'OF SALE'                 SALESJ
0027   05 020  O           D  2       50                                           SALESJ
0028   05 030  O                                DATE Y  9                           SALESJ
0029   05 040  O                                NAME    42                          SALESJ
0030   05 050  O                                INVNO Z 52                          SALESJ
0031   05 060  O                            10  AMOUNT1 70                          SALESJ
0032   05 070  O                            10  TAX   1 84                          SALESJ
0033   05 080  O                            10  SALE  1 98                          SALESJ
0034   05 090  O                            20          84 'TAX NEGATIVE-CHECK DATA' SALESJ
0035   05 100  O                            20          95 'CARD......'             SALESJ
0036   05 110  O                            30          85 'TAX ZERO-CHECK DATA CARD' SALESJ
0037   05 120  O           T  1       LR                                           SALESJ
0038   05 130  O                                        98 '------------'           SALESJ
0039   05 140  O           T  1       LR                                           SALESJ
0040   05 150  O                                TOTSAL1 98                          SALESJ
0041   05 160  O           T  0       LR                                           SALESJ
0042   05 170  O                                        98 '============'           SALESJ

              E N D   O F   S O U R C E
```

Printed Report:

DATE	ACCOUNT DEBITED	INVOICE NO.	AMOUNT OF SALE	SALES TAX	TOTAL AMOUNT OF SALE
		SALES JOURNAL			PAGE 1
8/01/78	HUDSON MOTOR CAR COMPANY	40000	TAX ZERO-CHECK DATA CARD		
8/11/78	PACKARD COMPANY	40010	80,094.40	5,606.61	85,701.01
8/14/78	THE HUPMOBILE CORPORATION	40021	6,738.20	471.67	7,209.87
8/19/78	THE TUCKER CAR COMPANY	40030	19.90	1.39	21.29
8/21/78	AUBURN INCORPORATED	40040	TAX NEGATIVE-CHECK DATA CARD......		
8/27/78	BRICKLIN LIMITED	40050	9,990.10	699.31	10,689.41
8/31/78	THE LOCOMOBILE CAR COMPANY	40062	20,000.00	1,400.00	21,400.00

					125,021.58
					============

Fig. 4-19. Source program listing and printed report for Sales Journal program
modified with Resulting Indicators used to condition calculations and output.

available RPG II indicators could have been used in the fields; however, *no Record Identifying Indicator should be assigned as a Resulting Indicator*, since unpredictable calculations and/or output could result.

Refer back to Figure 4-18 and notice lines 040 and 060 are conditioned by the 1Ø (Plus) indicator which means that these lines will execute only if the value in TAX is positive. If 2Ø or 3Ø turned on because the value in TAX was either minus or zero the calculations on lines 040 and 060 would not be executed.

The Resulting Indicators, 1Ø, 2Ø, and 3Ø, are also used on the Output-Format Specifications to condition the required output line information. Locate lines 060, 070, and 080 in Figure 4-18 and notice that they are conditioned by the 1Ø (Plus) indicator turned on if the TAX field is positive. On the other hand, lines 090 and 100 are conditioned by the 2Ø indicator and will be printed only when the value in TAX is negative.

Finally, the 110 line is conditioned by 3Ø which will execute only if the value in TAX is zero. Because the print line (020) is conditioned by the Record Identifying Indicator 50, assigned on input to the data records, the DATE, NAME, and INVNO field values will be printed for every record processed regardless of the test status of the Result Field TAX.

Resulting Indicators add another control aspect to RPG II source program coding that may help to eliminate errors that could result in the termination of program execution or incorrect output. For example, because an amount cannot be divided by zero, the testing of a field value for zero, which may be used as the divisor in a division operation, could prevent unnecessary cancellation of the program during processing of the data file. When the programmer elects to use Resulting Indicators in a source program depends upon the logic and requirements of the application.

Figure 4-19 illustrates the source program listing for the modified sales journal program and the resultant printed report showing the error messages for a negative and zero value in the TAX field. Error messages serve as a communication device that may help in identifying errors or exceptions during the processing of data. Again their use often depends only upon the programmer's individual preferences.

SQUARE ROOT

The square root of a number may be computed in RPG II by the use of the SQRT operation. The following must be considered when this operation is used:

1. The Operation column, Factor 2, and the Result field are used with the SQRT operation. (Factor 1 is never used.)

2. If the value contained in the variable field (or numeric literal) named in Factor 2 is negative the job will halt.

3. The number of positions in the Result Field may be equal, greater, or less than the number of decimal positions in the value in Factor 2.

4. Any indicator may condition the SQRT operation.

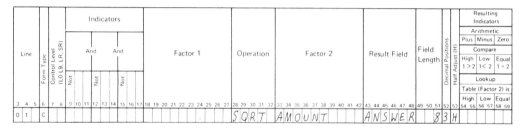

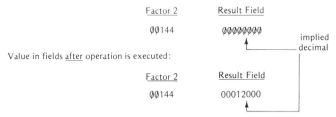

Fig. 4-20. Calculation Specifications coding for the Square Root Operation (SQRT).

5. An entire array may be used with the SQRT operation providing Factor 2 and the Result Field are both arrays (Chapter 14).

Figure 4-20 illustrates the Calculation Specification form entries used with the SQRT operation.

FIELD INDICATORS

Additional control of calculations and/or output is available to the programmer by the use of *Field Indicators*. Field Indicators are defined in columns 65–70 on the Input Specifications form. Look at Figure 4-21 and notice the Field Indicator columns are divided into three separate fields: Plus (columns 65–66), Minus (columns 67–68), and Zero or Blank (columns 69–70). The status of a numeric input field may be tested for all these conditions whereas an alphanumeric or alphabetic field may only be tested for a blank condition.

The coding entries made in Figure 4-21 are supplemental entries that could be made to test the status of input data fields used in the example sales journal program illustrated previously. Any indicator, 01–99, or Halt Indicators (H0 to H9) may be used in these fields to test the status of the value in an input field. Subsequent calculations and/or output may be controlled by the indicator turned on in one of the Field Indicator columns.

For example, the computer does not allow for a divide by zero division and will cancel the job (or halt) if detected during execution of a data file. The programmer may test the status of the input field used as the divisor in the division operation (Factor 2) to insure it is positive or negative and not zero or blank. Again, remember if a data field is defined as numeric on input (number entered in column 52) and the value in the field is blank, the computer will assume zeros in the RPG II language.

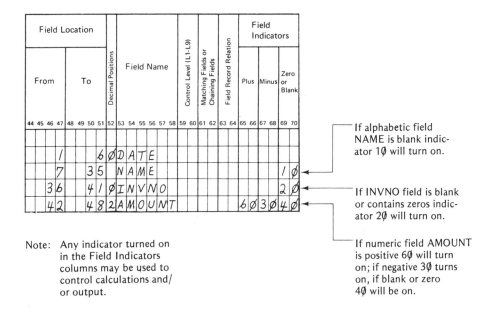

Fig. 4-21.   Examples of Field Indicator coding in the Input Specifications coding form.

EXAMPLE PROGRAM USING SQUARE ROOT AND FIELD INDICATORS

The source program in Figure 4-22 illustrates the use of the Square Root operation (SQRT) and Field Indicators. Examination of the Input Specifications form will show the input field NUMBER is tested by the Field Indicators entered in columns 65–70. If the value in the variable field (NUMBER) is positive, 60 will be turned on if negative, 70 will go on; and 80 will be turned on if blank or zero. Any one of the other 01–99 indicators could have been used here; however, the indicator assigned as the Record-Identifying indicator (columns 19 and 20) in the Input Specifications should *never* be used as a Field Indicator. Incorrect calculations or output could result if a Record-Identifying Indicator was entered in the Field Indicators columns.

The Square Root operation (SQRT) on line 010 of the Calculation Specifications is conditioned by the Record-Identifying Indicator 9∅ and the Field Indicator 6∅. Consequently, the operation will execute only if the input field value is positive.

The headings for the report on the Output-Format Specifications form follow previously discussed coding rules; however, additional logic is shown in the output coding.

Locate line 070 of the output form and notice the detail line is conditioned by the Record Identifying Indicator 90. Everytime a data card is read, this line will be executed and the value in the NUMBER field will be printed regardless of its input status. However, the Result Field (ROOT) will be

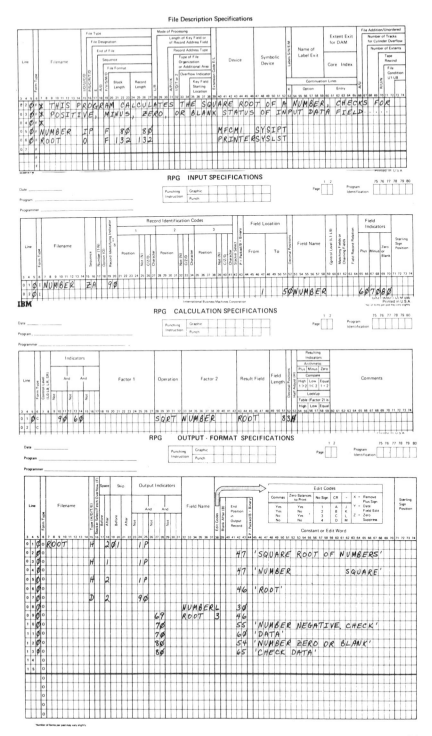

Fig. 4-22. Source program coding forms for Square Root program using Field Indicators and error messages.

printed only if the input field value is positive because it is conditioned by the 60 indicator entered in columns 27 and 28 of line 090.

In addition, *error messages* are used in the program to inform the user of the status of the input field. If the value in the NUMBER field is negative, 70 will turn on; the value in NUMBER will be printed and the message NUMBER NEGATIVE CHECK DATA printed. On the other hand, if the value in the input field is blank or zero, the field indicator 80 will turn on and the error message NUMBER ZERO OR BLANK CHECK DATA printed. Any programmer-designed error messages may be used in source programs as a communication link with the computer.

Refer to Figure 4-22 again and notice the print line 070 is conditioned by the Record-Identifying Indicator 90 and not the individual field indicators. If, for example, indicator 60 had been entered in columns 27 and 28 on the same line as the 90 indicator, the line would only print when the value in the NUMBER field was positive. The error messages conditioned by Field Indicators 70 and 80 would never be printed regardless of the input field status.

Field Indicators do not have to be used in every program but are an additional RPG II language coding feature that may help identify and control errors in programs and reports. The source program listing and printed report are shown in Figure 4-23.

Source Program Listing:

```
DOS - RPGII                JOB - SQROOT      03/13/78              PROGRAM - RPGOBJ

0001    01 050   FNUMBER   IP  F  80  80            MFCM1 SYSIPT                      SQROOT
0002    01 060   FROOT     O   F 132 132            PRINTERSYSLST                    SQROOT
0003    02 010   INUMBER   ZA  90                                                    SQROOT
0004    02 020   I                                    1    50NUMBER        607080    SQROOT
0005    03 010   C    90 60           SQRT NUMBER   ROOT     83H                     SQROOT
0006    04 010   OROOT     H   201   1P                                              SQROOT
0007    04 020   O             H   1  1P             47 'SQUARE ROOT OF NUMBERS'     SQROOT
0008    04 030   O             H   1  1P                                            SQROOT
0009    04 040   O             H   2  1P             47 'NUMBER          SQUARE'     SQROOT
0010    04 050   O             H   2  1P             46 'ROOT'                       SQROOT
0011    04 060   O                                                                   SQROOT
0012    04 070   O             D   2     90                                          SQRCOT
0013    04 080   O                          NUMBERL  30                              SQROOT
0014    04 090   O                          ROOT  3  46                              SQROOT
0015    04 100   O                     60            55 'NUMBER NEGATIVE CHECK'      SQROOT
0016    04 110   C                     70            60 'DATA'                       SQROOT
0017    04 120   O                     80            54 'NUMBER ZERO OR BLANK'       SQROOT
0018    04 130   O                     80            65 'CHECK DATA'                 SQROOT

        END OF SOURCE
```

Printed Report:

```
SQUARE ROOT OF NUMBERS
    NUMBER              SQUARE
                         ROOT

    746-      NUMBER NEGATIVE CHECK DATA
       0      NUMBER ZERO OR BLANK CHECK DATA
   87411          295.654
     144           12.000
   60000          244.949
   92000          303.315
```

Fig. 4-23.   Source program listing and printed report.

QUESTIONS

1. What are the correct RPG operation names for the following arithmetic functions?

Addition   Division
Subtraction   Multiplication
Move Remainder

2. Below is a list of arithmetic terms. Identify where they should be specified on the Calculation Specifications form.

Quotient	Sum	Difference
Subtrahend	Divisor	Dividend
Product	Addend	Multiplier
Multiplicand	Remainder	

3. If a five-digit number with two decimals is multiplied by a three-digit number with three decimals, how large should the Result Field be and with how many decimal positions?

4. On a blank Calculation Specifications coding form enter the coding needed to multiply SALES by RATE with the answer stored in TAX. The SALES field is seven digits long with two decimal positions and RATE is three long with three decimals.

5. What would be the result of the following multiplication?

	Factor 1	**Factor 2**
(a)	+23.8	+4.0
(b)	−19	−5.0
(c)	+8.7	−2.1

6. What sign will the quotient carry after the following division?

	Factor 1	**Factor 2**
(a)	+21.04	2.00
(b)	−82.26	−6.1
(c)	−15.55	4.5

7. Half-adjust the following numbers to two decimal points.

(a)	45.2891	(d)	73.44444
(b)	18.134	(e)	.4567
(c)	99.9959	(f)	26.7896

8. On a blank Calculation Specifications coding form enter the coding needed to divide QUANT by DOZ and store in the field NUM. QUANT is six positions long with no decimal points and DOZ is two positions long with no decimals.

9. On a blank Calculations Specifications coding form enter the coding needed to multiply PURCHA by DISRAT and store the' answer in DISAMT. PURCHA is eight digits with two decimal positions and DISRAT is three positions long with three decimals. Then subtract DISAMT from PURCHA and store the answer in NETPUR.

10. What type of indicators may be specified in the indicator field columns 9–17?

11. If a line of calculations is conditioned by an indicator how does this affect that line? What if no indicator is entered in this field?

12. Specifiy whether the entry in the respective field is left- or right-justified.

Factor 1	Factor 2
Operation	Result field
Field length	Indicators

13. How many Record Identifying Indicators may condition a line of calculations?

14. On a blank Calculation Specifications form divide COST by UNIT and store the answer in NET. COST is eight long with two decimal positions and UNIT is five long with no decimal positions. Move any remainder to a field called HOLD. You must also determine the correct size of the HOLD field to complete your coding.

15. How is an input numeric field included in a data card punched to make it minus? Positive?

16. On a blank Calculation Specifications form subtract COST from SPRICE and store result in GPROFT. Then divide GPROFT by SPRICE and store result in PERCNT. Use the appropriate Resulting indicator(s) to test the calculation coding operations to prevent the program from terminating.

17. What are the rules for using the Square Root operation (SQRT)?

18. Where and when are Field Indicators used?

EXERCISES

4-1. Banks use two methods for making loans to borrowers—the *Loan Method* and the *Discount Method*. With the Loan Method the borrower receives the full principal of the loan and at maturity pays the principal and total interest. Under the Discount Method banks take out the interest before the principal is received and the borrower receives the net amount. At maturity the borrower pays only the principal.

   Consequently, the Discount Method results in a higher effective interest rate than the Loan Method. The effective interest on a bank loan under the Discount Method may be computed by the following formula:

$$\frac{D}{P} \times \frac{12}{T} = I$$

where: D = The amount of interest taken (discount) out of loan before
it is received

P = The net proceeds of the loan

12 = The months in the calendar year (days may be used here)

T = The term of the note in months (if days are used for the
factor above, they must be used here)

Required:

Write the necessary RPG source program calculations to solve the formula. Consider the following field sizes and round the answer (I) to the
nearest tenth of a percent (example: 6.06% expressed as a percentage or
.0606 expressed as the decimal value).

Field Name	Field Size	Decimal Positions
D	6	2
P	8	2
T	3	Ø

4-2. Write the RPG II Calculation coding for the following flowchart logic.
Use the Arithmetic Resulting Indicators for coding.

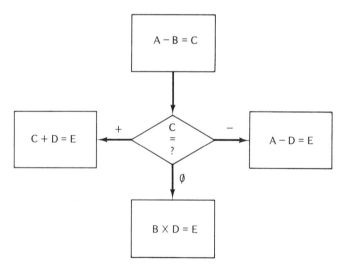

4-3. From the following flowchart logic, code the RPG II calculations using
Input Specifications Field Indicators. FIELDA is a numeric input field
which is to be tested for Plus, Minus, Blank, or Zero status. The appropriate Field Indicator must be used to condition the corresponding
calculation operation.

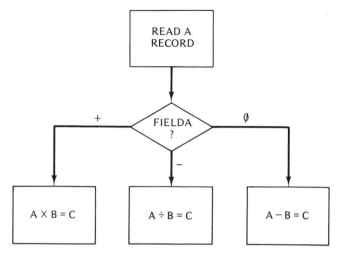

4-4. Write the RPG II calculation coding needed to solve the following formula. Include the necessary tests in your coding to prevent the program from terminating because of the incorrect status (minus number) of the number for which the square root is to be determined.

$$\sqrt{\frac{X - Y}{Z}}$$

4-5. DEBUGGING AN RPG II SOURCE PROGRAM

Given below is an RPG II source program listing that contains executable errors that resulted in an incorrect printed report.

Source Listing:

```
        01 020  F* THIS PROGRAM CONTAINS ERRORS THAT DID NOT PREVENT COMPILATION      SALESJ
        01 021  F* BUT DID GIVE INCORRECT PRINTED OUTPUT................................SALESJ
0001    01 030  FCHARGSALIP   F   80  80           MFCM1  SYS1PT                       SALESJ
0002    01 040  FSALEJRL O    F  132 132      OF    PRINTERSYSLST                      SALESJ
0003    02 010  ICHARGSALSM   50                                                       SALESJ
0004    02 020  I                                        1    6 DATE                   SALESJ
0005    02 030  I                                        7   35 NAME                   SALESJ
0006    02 040  I                                       36   410INVNO                  SALESJ
0007    02 050  I                                       42   482AMOUNT                 SALESJ
        03 010  * CALCULATE SALES TAX BASED ON STATE'S 7% RATE..................       SALESJ
0008    03 020  C          AMOUNT    MULT .07        TAX      56H                      SALESJ
                                                              $
        03 030  C* ADD TAX TO AMOUNT TO GIVE TOTAL AMOUNT OF SALE................      SALESJ            NOTE 150
0009    03 040  C          TAX       ADD  AMOUNT     SALE     82                       SALESJ
        03 050  C* ADD TOTAL AMOUNT OF EACH SALE TO A TOTAL OF ALL SALES FIELD...      SALESJ
0010    03 060  C          SALE      ADD  TOTSAL     TOTSAL   92                       SALESJ
0011    04 010  CSALEJRL H    301      1P                                              SALESJ
0012    04 020  O             OR       OF                                              SALESJ
0013    04 030  O                                    56  'SALES JOURNAL'               SALESJ
0014    04 040  O                                    94  'PAGE'                        SALESJ
0015    04 050  O                            PAGE Z  99                                SALESJ
0016    04 060  O          H   1      1P                                               SALESJ
0017    04 070  O             OR       OF                                              SALESJ
0018    04 080  O                                    7   'DATE'                        SALESJ
0019    04 090  O                                    34  'ACCOUNT DEBITED'             SALESJ
0020    04 100  O                                    56  'INVOICE NO.'                 SALESJ
0021    04 110  O                                    73  'AMOUNT OF SALE'              SALESJ
0022    04 120  O                                    85  'SALES TAX'                   SALESJ
0023    04 130  O                                    100 'TOTAL AMOUNT'                SALESJ
0024    04 140  O          H   2      1P                                               SALESJ
0025    04 150  O             OR       OF                                              SALESJ
0026    04 160  O                                    97  'OF SALE'                     SALESJ
0027    04 170  O          D   2      50                                               SALESJ
0028    04 180  O                            DATE Y  9                                 SALESJ
0029    04 190  O                            NAME 1  42                                SALESJ
0030    04 200  O                            INVNO Z 52                                SALESJ
0031    05 010  O                            AMOUNTI 70                                SALESJ
0032    05 020  O                            TAX  1  84                                SALESJ
0033    05 030  O                            SALE 1  98                                SALESJ
0034    05 040  O          T   1      LR                                               SALESJ
0035    05 050  O                                    98  '----------'                  SALESJ
0036    05 060  O          T   1      LR                                               SALESJ
0037    05 070  O                            TOTSL 1  98                               SALESJ
0038    05 080  O          D   0      LR                                               SALESJ
0039    05 090  O                                    98  '=========='                  SALESJ
```

E N D   O F   S O U R C E

Diagnostics:

T A B L E S   A N D   M A P S

RESULTING INDICATOR TABLE

ADDRESS RI	ADDRESS RI	ADDRESS RI	ADDRESS RI	ADDRESS RI	ADDRESS RI	ADDRESS RI
02A2 OF	02BF LR	02C0 HO	02CA 1P	02CD 50		

FIELD NAMES

ADDRESS FIELD	ADDRESS FIELD	ADDRESS FIELD	ADDRESS FIELD	ADDRESS FIELD

01DD   *ERROR
0370   TAX
	0345 DATE
	0373 SALE
	        0037
	        0028
	        0029
		034B NAME
		0378 TOTSAL TOTSL
			0368 INVNO
			037D PAGE
				036C AMOUNT

NOTE 398
NOTE 413
NOTE 413

M E S S A G E   T E X T

NOTE 150   DECIMAL POSITIONS EXCEED FIELD LENGTH. ASSUME FIELD LENGTH.

NOTE 398   FIELD NAME UNDEFINED. SPEC IS DROPPED.

NOTE 413   EDIT SPECIFIED WITH ALPHAMERIC FIELD. DROP EDITING.

Printed Report (Incorrect):

SALES JOURNAL   PAGE   1

DATE	ACCOUNT DEBITED	INVOICE NO.	AMOUNT OF SALE	SALES TAX	TOTAL AMOUNT OF SALE
080178	HUDSON MOTOR CAR COMPANY	40000	4,121.00	.47000	4,121.47
081178	PACKARD COMPANY	40010	80,094.40	.60800	80,095.00
081478	THE HUPMOBILE CORPORATION	40021	6,738.20	.67400	6,738.87
081978	THE TUCKER CAR COMPANY	40030	19.90	.39300	20.29
082178	AUBURN INCORPORATED	40040	356.70	.96900	357.66
082778	BRICKLIN LIMITED	40050	9,990.10	.30700	9,990.40
083178	THE LOCOMOBILE CAR COMPANY	40062	20,000.00	.00000	20,000.00

CORRECT THE CODING LINES THAT ARE INCORRECT BY REWRITING THEM ON THE REQUIRED SPECIFICATION FORMS. ALSO, LOCATE AND INTERPRET THE MEANING OF THE NOTES GIVEN IN THE DIAGNOSTICS.

LABORATORY ASSIGNMENTS

LABORATORY ASSIGNMENT 4-1:
PURCHASE JOURNAL

The purchase journal used as part of the accounting system of a company may be designed according to the needs of the user. It may be a multicolumn design to provide for the purchase of anything on credit including inventory items for resale or supplies used within the company. The purchase journal design for this assignment is a *single-amount* column journal used only to record the purchase of merchandise for resale to customers.

Input Format of Data Records:

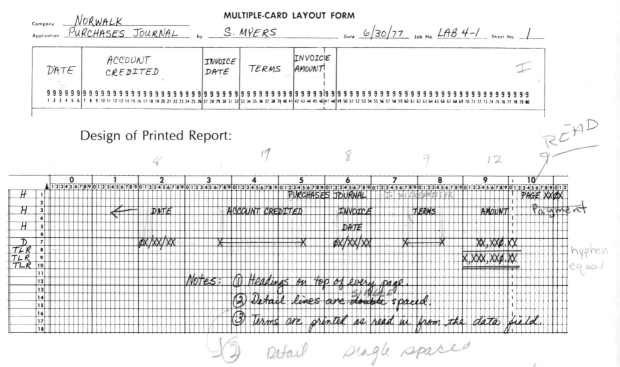

MULTIPLE-CARD LAYOUT FORM

Company _NORWALK_
Application _PURCHASES JOURNAL_ by _S. MYERS_   Date _6/30/77_ Job No. _LAB 4-1_ Sheet No. _1_

DATE	ACCOUNT CREDITED	INVOICE DATE	TERMS	INVOICE AMOUNT		I

Design of Printed Report:

READ

PURCHASES JOURNAL   J. WICKENMEYER   PAGE XXØX   Payment

| DATE | ACCOUNT CREDITED | INVOICE DATE | TERMS | AMOUNT | hyphen equal |

ØX/XX/XX   X————X   ØX/XX/XX   X————X   XX,XXØ.XX
X,XXX,XXØ.XX

Notes: ① Headings on top of every page.
② Detail lines are ~~double~~ spaced.
③ Terms are printed as read in from the data field.

① Detail single spaced

Data to be Used in Program: Note: (Keypunch terms as shown)

Transaction Date 1-6	Account Credited 7-26	Invoice Date 27-32	Terms 33-41	Amount 42-48
062978	QUALITY USED CARS	062878	2/10,N/30	0260000
071078	LINDQUIST HARDWARE	060878	1/10,N/30	0007244
073078	KEATING FORD	072978	2/15,N/60	1450012
081178	MEYER SUPPLY CO.	080978	2/10,N/30	0087539
092578	SEARS	092378	1/30,N/90	0100088
101578	MONTGOMERY WARD	101578	1/10,N/60	0099900
110178	R. A. LALLI COMPANY	110178	3/15,N/90	0246785
121278	PEERLESS FOUNDRY	121078	2/10,N/60	3378194

No decimals

The completed laboratory assignment must include the following:

1. Completed Specifications Forms layout chart
2. Source Program Deck   date 1
3. Source Program Listing ✓
4. Printed Report ✓

LABORATORY ASSIGNMENT 4-2:
PROFIT ANALYSIS REPORT OF SOUP BRANDS

From the information given below write an RPG II source program to print a soup brand profit analysis report by dollar and percent profit. The percent of profit is determined by dividing the dollar profit by cost. Also required in the report is an overall average for all soup brands determined by adding the percent of profit for each soup brand to a total field and dividing that field by the number of soup brands at last record time.

Input Format of Data Records:

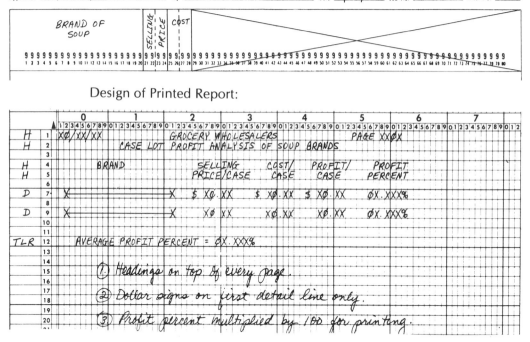

Design of Printed Report:

Data To Be Used in Program:

Brand	SP	Cost
CAMPBELL'S	0648	0504
LIPTON INSTANT	1440	1188
HEINZ'S	0792	0576
MOM'S HOME STYLE	1728	1224
NESTLE'S INSTANT	1404	1116
PANTRY PRIDE	1476	1044
A & P	0720	0792

The completed laboratory assignment must include the following:

1. Filled in Specification Forms
2. Source Program Deck
3. Source Program Listing
4. Printed Report

LABORATORY ASSIGNMENT 4-3:
COMPUTATION OF SIMPLE INTEREST

From the information given below write an RPG II source program to compute the simple interest on loans. Simple interest is the rent paid to a lender for the privilege of borrowing money. Simple interest is charged on personal loans, car loans, installment loans, and home mortgages.

The formula for computing simple interest is:

$$I = P \times R \times T$$

where   I = Dollar amount of simple interest

P = Principal (amount borrowed) on which interest is computed

R = Annual interest rate expressed as a decimal

T = Number of days, months, or years for which the money will be loaned (time is always converted to years or percentage of a year to make formula compatible)

Input Format of Data Records:

MULTIPLE-CARD LAYOUT FORM

Company   *NORWALK*

Application   *SIMPLE INTEREST*   by   *S. MYERS*   Date   *3/31/77*   Job No.   *LAB 4-3*   Sheet No.   *1*

PRINCIPAL	INTEREST RATE	TIME	

9 9 9 9 9 9 9 9 9 9 9 9 9 9 9 9 9 9 9 9 9 9 9 9 9 9 9 9 9 9 9 9 9 9 9 9 9 9 9 9 9 9 9 9 9 9 9 9 9 9 9 9 9 9 9 9 9 9 9 9 9 9 9 9 9 9 9 9 9 9 9 9 9 9 9 9 9 9 9 9
1 2 3 4 5 6 7 8 9 10 11 12 13 14 15 16 17 18 19 20 21 22 23 24 25 26 27 28 29 30 31 32 33 34 35 36 37 38 39 40 41 42 43 44 45 46 47 48 49 50 51 52 53 54 55 56 57 58 59 60 61 62 63 64 65 66 67 68 69 70 71 72 73 74 75 76 77 78 79 80

Design of Printed Report:

		0	1	2	3	4	5	6	7
H	1			SIMPLE INTEREST LOAN SCHEDULE AS OF ØX/XX/XX (UDATE)					
	2								
	3								
H	4	PRINCIPAL	ANNUAL INTEREST	TIME IN	INTEREST	TOTAL			
H	5	AMOUNT	RATE	DAYS	ON LOAN	AMOUNT DUE			
	6								
D	7	$XXX,XXØ.XX	XØ.XXX%	XXØX	$XX,XXØ.XX $X,XXX,XXØ.XX				
	8								
D	9	$XXX,XXØ.XX	XØ.XXX%	XXØX	$XX,XXØ.XX $X,XXX,XXØ.XX				

(1) Dollar signs are floating.

(2) Headings on top of every page.

(3) Interest rate must be multiplied by 100 to get required output field.

Data To Be Used in Program:

P	R	T (days)
12000000	.08500	0120
00300000	07000	0185
01025000	09100	0730
00047500	10250	0092
00100000	12125	0060
2 dec. pos.	5 dec. pos.	0 dec. pos.

LABORATORY ASSIGNMENT 4-4:
DETERMINATION OF ECONOMIC ORDER QUANTITY

The costs of carrying an item in inventory include deterioration, obsolescence, handling, clerical labor, taxes, insurance, storage, and a predetermined return on investment. These costs are weighed against the costs of inadequate inventory which may lead to loss of sales, loss of customer goodwill, production stoppage, extra purchasing costs, and a higher small-quantity purchase cost.

Because of these inventory considerations companies have relied upon mathematical models as guidelines for their decision-making process as to "how much to order and when." One helpful decision-making tool is a determination of the ECONOMIC ORDER QUANTITY OF AN ITEM which indicates the optimum quantity to order of any one item.

In order to determine the Economic Order Quantity of any one item of inventory, the number of units needed annually, cost per order, unit cost of the item, and its carrying cost must be known. Once these factors are determined for the purchased item the following formula may be used to determine the ideal Economic Order Quantity:

$$\text{Economic Order Quantity} = \sqrt{\frac{2 \times \text{units needed annually} \times \text{ordering cost}}{\text{item unit cost} \times \text{inventory carrying cost \%}}}$$

$$\text{or} \qquad \text{EOQ} = \sqrt{\frac{2 \times U \times OC}{UC \times ICC}}$$

Input Format of Data Records:

Company **NORWALK**
Application **ECONOMIC ORDER QUANTITY** by **S. MYERS** Date **4/1/77** Job No. **LAB 4-4** Sheet No. **1**

MULTIPLE-CARD LAYOUT FORM

Design of Printed Report:

Format your own Printer Spacing Chart to your own design preference. However, the following information must be included in the report:

NAME OF ITEM	ANNUAL REQUIREMENTS	ECONOMIC ORDER QUANTITY	ORDERS PER YEAR
X_____X	XX,XØX	* XX,XØX	XØX

Note: Orders per year are determined by dividing Annual Requirements by the Economic Order Quantity.

Data To Be Used in Program:

Item Name	Annual Quantity	Order Cost 0 decimal positions	Unit Cost 2 decimal positions	Carrying Cost %
LEFT-HAND MONKEY WRENCH	10000	025	00550	0250
DOGGIE BOOTS	04000	010	01000	0400
MEN'S SHAVER (DIESEL)	20000	018	14500	1000
ATOMIC TOOTH BRUSH	40000	020	20750	1400

5
MULTIPLE RECORD
FILE CONCEPTS
AND MOVE OPERATIONS

Previous chapters presented example programs in which the input files included only one *record type* (design). Many applications, however, require that more than one record type be included in the input data file(s). Figure 5-1 illustrates the Multiple Card Layout Form used for the record formats in the example cash receipts journal application program.

An examination of Figure 5-1 reveals that three record types are included in the data file. Each record format contains its own logical information and is formatted accordingly. The first record formatted on the form is used to record miscellaneous (sundry) transactions: the second, the payment of accounts receivable; and the third, cash sales. Hence, each record type is a physical record used to record a specific accounting transaction. The numbers 08, 16, and 20 to the left of column 1 (Figure 5-1) are the Record Identifying Indicators used in the source program for the corresponding record format. In actual practice they probably would not be entered on the form and are used here only for reference purposes.

Because there is more than one record type in this data file, each one must be coded so that the computer can distinguish between them and execute the related instructions. Consequently, Record Identification Codes have to be entered in the records to identify the type being processed. The code used for record type 08 is SUN which is entered in columns 78, 79, and 80 of every data record of this format. The second record type (16) is coded by the letters CASH

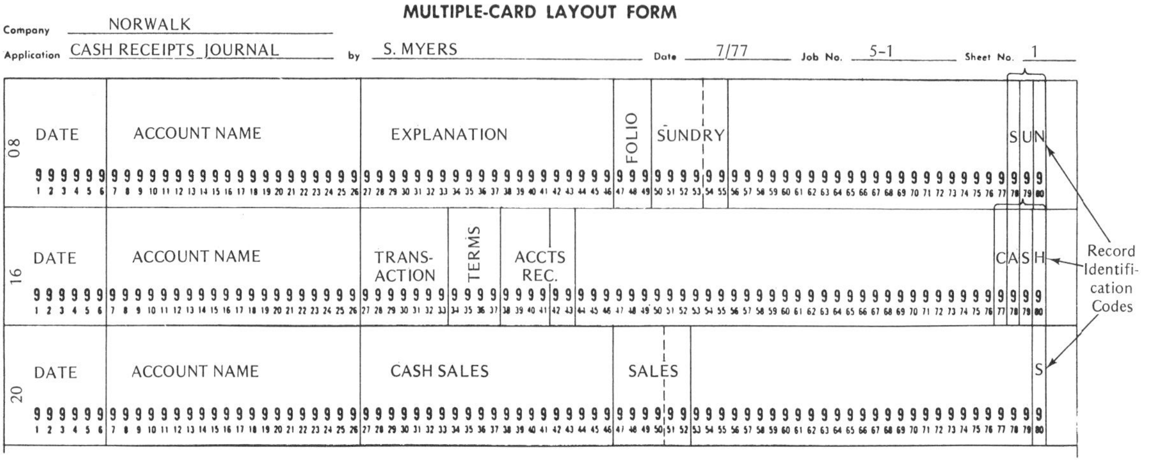

Fig. 5-1. Card Layout Form for the Cash Receipts Journal program using three record types in the data file.

in columns 77, 78, 79, and 80, whereas record 20 is coded by the character S in column 80.

Record Identification Codes may be entered in any available columns in a record, not only the last positions. The location of these codes often depends upon existing record formats or, for new applications, on the programmer's option. Furthermore, as many characters as desired may be used to code a data record; however, columns should not be assigned that are not necessary, as storage is usually a valuable commodity within any input media. Also, any number, letter, or special character ($, *, #, etc.) may be used to code a record type as long as it is part of the character set of the printer or display unit on the computer.

ARRANGEMENT OF DATA FILE

Accounting transactions are usually recorded in ascending order by date; therefore, any input data file for a journal must be *sorted* in ascending date order before it is processed. Figure 5-2 shows the arrangement of the data cards in the file used in the example Cash Receipts Journal program.

Notice two important things about the data file: first, the records are sorted in ascending order by date (columns 1–6) and second, each record is coded with its required Record Identification Code. If the respective code was omitted in a data card during keypunching, an error that prevented further execution of the file would result. An error routine may, however, be coded in the program to prevent program cancellation during execution of the data file. Care should be exercised, however, to insure that the data cards are correctly recorded to prevent any additional processing procedures.

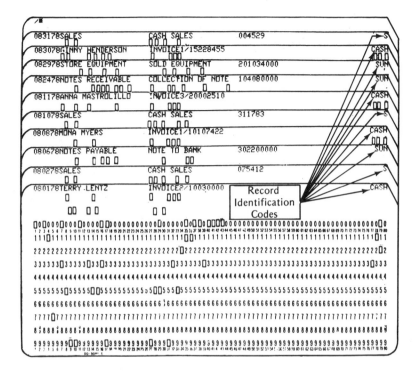

Fig. 5-2.   Data file arrangement for Cash Receipts program.

ACCOUNTING APPLICATION—THE CASH RECEIPTS JOURNAL

The Cash Receipts Journal is used to record the receipt of cash regardless of the source. In a merchandising concern cash receipts would typically result from cash sales recorded on cash registers and totaled for the day and from checks received in the mail from customers. Other receipts of cash may, of course, come from borrowing money by signing a promissory note, loan, or by the sale of an asset.

Instead of using the General Journal to record all transactions, cash receipts may be recorded in one journal so they are easily determined. Figure 5-3 depicts one form of a Cash Receipts Journal. The design will usually depend on the needs of the individual company and no one design should be considered as absolute. An examination of the column titles in the example will indicate the information normally needed for an entry in this book of original entry.

For example, the *account credited* column refers to the ledger account affected by the transaction. The first transaction, dated October 1, is for a cash

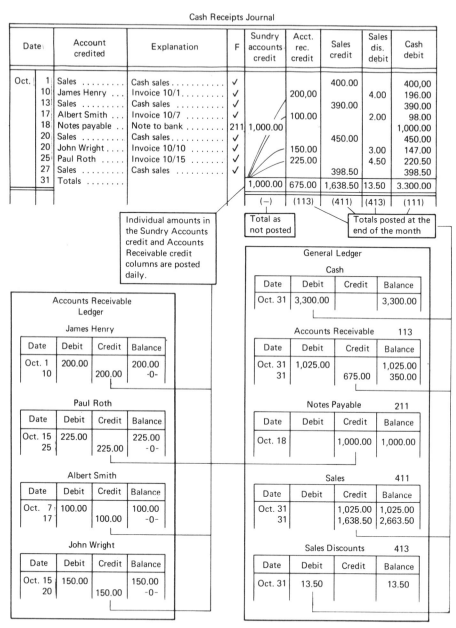

Source: William W. Pyle and John Arch White,
Fundamental Accounting Principles
(Homewood, Illinois: Richard D. Irwin,
Inc., 1969), p. 174.

Fig. 5-3. Example of Cash Receipts Journal.

sale. Notice that a column is provided for sales and cash. The sales column indicates that this amount is credited, which is in accordance with the basic accounting rules of increasing revenue accounts by crediting. On the other hand, cash is an asset and all asset accounts are increased by debiting. The totals of these two account columns are posted to the General Ledger only at the end of the month, not daily. Obviously this procedure saves a great deal of labor by eliminating much of the posting.

When a customer makes a payment on an open account, the entry should be made as shown for October 10. The customer's name is entered in the *account credited* column and the dollar amount placed in the *account receivable* column and the *cash* column. This entry, however, is posted daily to the Accounts Receivable Ledger so that a customer's account is updated daily to reflect the current balance. Furthermore, at the end of the month the total of the account receivable column is posted to the respective general ledger account along with the other column totals.

A *sales discount* column is provided for cash discounts allowed to customers who pay their invoices within the discount period specified by the company. For example, terms stated as 2/10, n/30 indicate that the amount must be paid 30 days after the invoice date to maintain a good credit rating. However, a two percent discount will be granted if the invoice is paid within 10 days after the invoice date; hence, the discount period.

In addition, a *sundry* or miscellaneous account column is included for transactions that affect accounts that do not have a separate column in the Cash Receipts Journal. Notice that the number of the account must be used as shown by the entry for October 18 in Figure 5-3 that affects a Notes Payable account. If a great deal of notes payable transactions were normally involved in a month's transactions, then a separate column could easily be provided in the journal.

After the column totals are totaled, the sum of the debits must equal the credits before any posting is done in the general ledger. Notice, however, that the sum for the sundry column is not posted but is used only as a check figure to prove the equality of debits and credits. Figure 5-3 explains the posting requirements of this journal to the Subsidiary and General Ledgers. The application program that will be shown in this chapter for the Cash Receipts Journal, however, will not be part of a system and therefore will not require posting, but will be a stand-alone program illustrating this particular journal.

SOURCE PROGRAM CODING FOR THE CASH RECEIPTS JOURNAL PROGRAM

An examination of Figure 5-4 will reveal that additional entries are introduced in the RPG II source program for the Cash Receipts Journal example program using multirecord file concepts. Input, Calculations, and Output-Format Specification forms contain new coding procedures explained in this chapter.

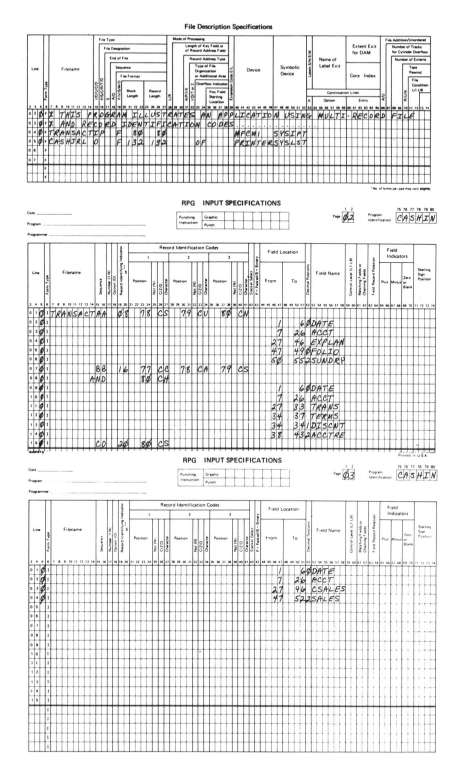

Fig. 5-4. Cash Receipts Journal source program coding.

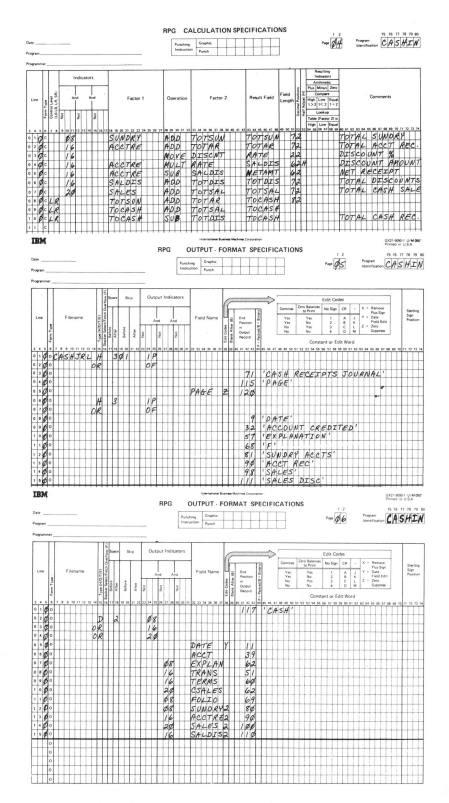

Fig. 5-4. Cash Receipts Journal source program coding (continued).

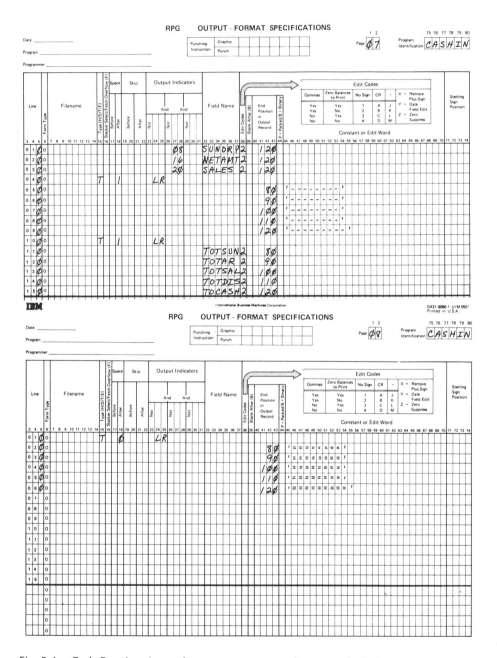

Fig. 5-4. Cash Receipts Journal source program coding (concluded).

The Input Specifications form detailed in Figure 5-5 shows the additional coding entries needed for defining the three record types (08, 16, and 20) that were formatted on the layout form in Figure 5-1. Locate line 010 and notice, in addition to the file name, sequence letters, and the Record Identifying Indicators, entries are made in the Record Identification Code Fields. This area (columns 21–41) of the Input form consists of three identical sections. Each section includes four fields: Position, Not (N), C/Z/D, and Character, which are used to describe the location, presence (or absence), and type of record

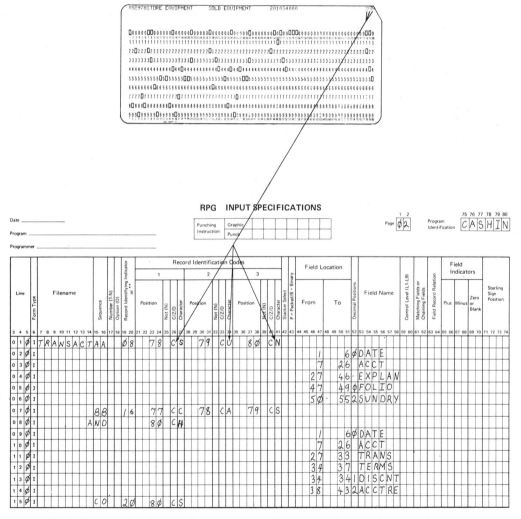

Fig. 5-5. Relationship of data card identification code to source program Input Specifications coding.

code. For example, the 08 record type is coded by the character S in column 78, U in column 79, and N in column 80. This indicates that these characters must be punched in every data card for this logical record type. The three sections of the Record Identification Codes area of the form are in an AND relationship indicating the record must contain the letter S *and* the letter U *and* the letter N in order to be processed. Refer back to Figure 5-5 and observe the relationship of the data card entry for the code to the source program coding. If only one letter was entered incorrectly the related record would not be processed.

Line 070 shows record type 16 is coded by the characters C *and* A *and* S *and* H. Notice the fourth letter (H) is entered on line 080 which allows the *and* relationship to continue by entering the letters AND in columns 14, 15, and 16. Any number of characters may be included as codes in a data card in this manner. Also notice the input file name (TRANSACT) was *not* entered again for record type 16 or 20. The input file name is only entered once regardless of the number of record types in the data file.

Line 150 shows that record type 20 is only coded by the character S in column 80.

The Position field of each section indicates where the respective code is located within the record. Remember these codes may be entered in any unused columns in the data record and not necessarily the last positions.

The Not (N) columns of the sections may be used to indicate that this character is not to be included as a code for the record type. Use of this column offers additional flexibility in assigning codes to data records.

The C/Z/D fields indicate what portion of the character will be read. Any card column includes a Zone area (12, 11, and 0) and a Digit area (rows 1–9). Hence, if the character C is entered in this field both the Zone and Digit areas of the character will be examined. However, if the letter Z is entered, only the Zone area will be read; and if a D is used, only the digit area will be studied. Some processing time will be saved, however, if a C is used for identifying the type of Record Identification Code instead of a Z or D. Figure 5-6 illustrates the meaning of the C, Z, and D entry in this field.

Any character may be entered in the Character field including letters, numbers, and special characters; their use depends on the code(s) entered in the respective data record(s).

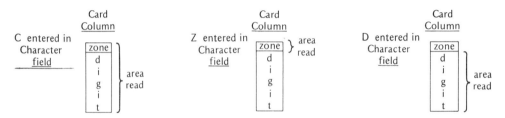

Fig. 5-6.   Processing affect of entering a C, Z, or D in the Character Field for a Record Identification Code entry.

CALCULATION SPECIFICATIONS CODING FOR THE CASH RECEIPTS JOURNAL PROGRAM

Because the three record types (08, 16, 20) included in the data file for the Cash Receipts Journal program refer to different transactions, the calculation coding line must be conditioned accordingly as shown in Figure 5-7. For example, record type 08 contains information about miscellaneous (sundry) transactions and the only required arithmetic for that record type is to accumulate the SUNDRY variable field information into a total field, TOTSUN. Along with the other column totals in the journal, TOTSUN will be printed at last record time (LR).

Line 04010 (Figure 5-7) shows the coding to accumulate SUNDRY to TOTSUN. Notice the coding line is conditioned by the appropriate Record Identifying Indicator.

Lines 04020 to 04060 are conditioned by indicator 16 and include the necessary coding for recording the receipt of an accounts receivable payment. Line 04020 adds the accounts receivable amount (ACCTRE) to a newly-created field, TOTAR, which is also printed at LR time.

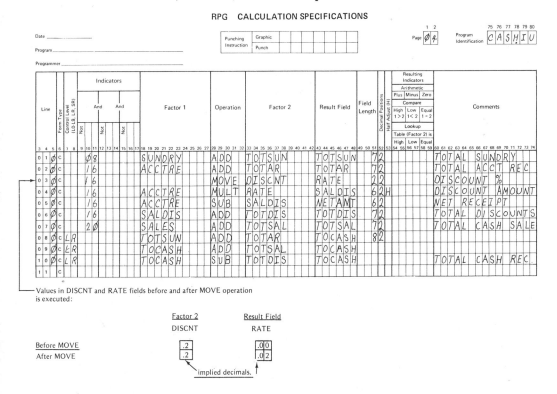

Fig. 5-7. Affect of MOVE operation on the values of the fields entered in Factor 2 and the Result Field.

Line 04030 uses a new operation, MOVE, to move the DISCNT field, which is defined on the Input Specifications form (Figure 5-5, line 130), to a new field, RATE. Note that the DISCNT field is defined as one character long and is located in column 34 (Figure 5-5), the first position of the TERMS field. The procedure of renaming part or all of another field is referred to as *redefining* a field. It does not destroy or affect the field redefined.

Refer back to Figure 5-7 and examine the affect of the MOVE operation on the two fields before and after the move. Notice the DISCNT field, which is one character long with one decimal position, is moved into RATE—defined as two characters with two decimals. The field (or literal) in Factor 2 is referred to as the *sending field* and the field named in the Result Field is called the *receiving field* in any MOVE (or MOVEL) operation.

The correct decimal equivalent for the cash discount percent is obtained by use of the MOVE operation. Before the move, the amount in DISCNT was .2, which arithmetically indicates 20 percent, the incorrect discount percent for this example. By moving this figure into the RATE field, the low-order positions of the *receiving field* (RATE) are filled first, resulting in .02, the correct decimal value for a two-percent discount. A comprehensive discussion of the MOVE operations is included at the end of this chapter. The reader may refer to it now or continue with the logic of the Cash Receipts Journal program in the following text.

The coding on line 04050 subtracts the monetary discount, SALDIS, from the accounts receivable amount (ACCTRE) to give a net amount paid (NETAMT). On line 04060 the sales discount amount (SALDIS) is added to a total discount field (TOTDIS) that will be printed at LR time.

Cash sale transactions (record type 20) are accumulated on line 04070 by adding cash sales (SALES) to a total sales field (TOTSAL).

Lines 04080 to 04100 are executed at LR time and include the arithmetic operations to calculate the final amount for the total net cash amount received in the accounting period. Line 04080 adds the total sundry amount (TOTSUN) to total accounts receivable (TOTAR) giving a newly-created field for total net cash receipts (TOCASH). The operation on line 04090 adds total cash sales (TOTSAL) to the TOCASH field—a gross total of all receipts. Finally, the calculations on line 04100 subtract total sales discounts (TOTDIS) from total net cash receipts (TOCASH) to give the final net amount for TOCASH. Along with the other column totals in the Cash Receipts Journal, TOCASH will be printed at LR time. Refer to Figure 5-10 for the printed result of the journal.

OUTPUT-FORMAT CODING FOR CASH RECEIPTS JOURNAL PROGRAM

Refer to Figure 5-8, which details page 6 of the source program, and locate lines 06020, 06030, and 06040. The coding entered indicates the fields included in this line are to be printed when either Record Identifying Indicator 08, 16,

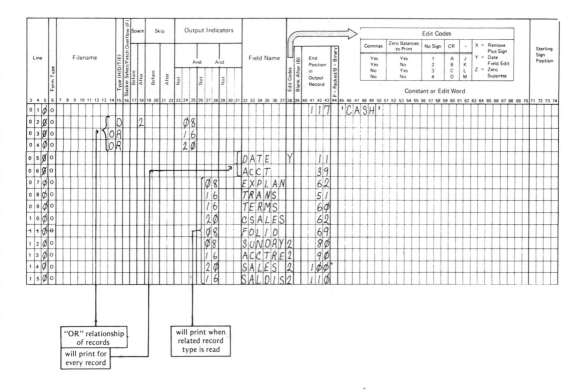

Fig. 5-8. Output-Format Coding Form illustrating use of the OR relationship of the records in a multirecord data file.

or 20 is on. The letters OR entered in columns 14 and 15 (lines 06030 and 06040) indicate an *or* relationship. In other words, if any of the three record types included in the data file for the Cash Receipts Journal program is processed, the line will be printed with the respective record information.

Further examination of Figure 5-8 will reveal, however, that *all* the fields included in this line are not to be printed for every record type. Lines 06050 and 06060 contain the variable fields DATE and ACCT and the contents of these fields will be printed regardless of the record type processed (08, 16, or 20) because they are not conditioned by an indicator. Reference to Figure 5-1 will indicate these fields are formatted in the same location for the three record types. Notice that other fields in the records refer to different information.

Refer back to Figure 5-8 and notice that other fields on the print line are conditioned by the related Record Identifying Indicator. For example, EX-PLAN on line 06070 is a field in the 08 type record (Figure 5-1) and should only be printed when the 08 data record is processed. In order to control the printing of this field the Record Identifying Indicator 08 is entered in columns 27 and 28 alongside the respective field name. Hence, the contents of the field will be printed only when indicator 08 is on. Note, however, any of the available Output Indicator columns (24 and 25 or 30 and 31) could have been used to condition the printing of the EXPLAN field. Reference to the other variable fields in this print line will indicate that every one is conditioned by its related Record Identifying Indicator. Refer to Figure 5-1 to determine what fields are included in each record type. When multirecord data are processed and the output of the fields is in an *or* relationship, this coding procedure is usually necessary to prevent incorrect results.

Figure 5-9 illustrates the processing logic for the multirecord file for the Cash Receipts Journal program.

Figure 5-10 details the complete source program listing and the printed Cash Receipts Journal.

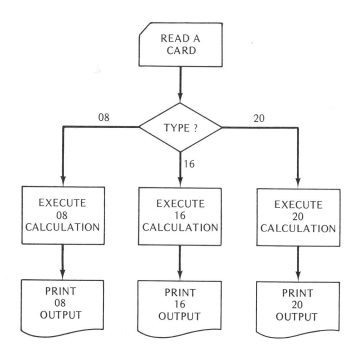

Note: Only one Record Identifying Indicator may be on at any time in the processing cycle. If 08 is on 16 and 20 will be off and so forth.

Any calculations and/or output conditioned by the corresponding indicator will be executed only when the respective indicator is on. Any instructions not conditioned by an indicator will be executed for every record type read.

Fig. 5-9. Multiple record processing logic.

```
          01 020  F* THIS PROGRAM ILLUSTRATES AN APPLICATION USING MULTI RECORD FILE   CASHIN
          01 030  F* AND RECORD IDENTIFICATION CODES................               CASHIN
0001      01 040  FTRANSACTIP F  80  80              MFCM1 SYSIPT              CASHIN
0002      01 050  FCASHJRL O  F 132 132          OF  PRINTERSYSLST            CASHIN
0003      02 010  ITRANSACTAA  08  78 CS   79 CU   80 CN                      CASHIN
0004      02 020  I                                    1   60DATE             CASHIN
0005      02 030  I                                    7   26 ACCT            CASHIN
0006      02 040  I                                   27   46 EXPLAN          CASHIN
0007      02 050  I                                   47   490FOLIO           CASHIN
0008      02 060  I                                   50   552SUNDRY          CASHIN
0009      02 070  I            BB  16  77 CC   78 CA   79 CS                   CASHIN
0010      02 080  I            AND     80 CH                                   CASHIN
0011      02 090  I                                    1   60DATE             CASHIN
0012      02 100  I                                    7   26 ACCT            CASHIN
0013      02 110  I                                   27   33 TRANS           CASHIN
0014      02 120  I                                   34   37 TERMS           CASHIN
0015      02 130  I                                   38   432ACCTRE          CASHIN
0016      02 140  I                                   34   341DISCNT          CASHIN
0017      02 150  I            CC  20  80 CS                                   CASHIN
0018      03 010  I                                    1   60DATE             CASHIN
0019      03 020  I                                    7   26 ACCT            CASHIN
0020      03 030  I                                   27   46 CSALES          CASHIN
0021      03 040  I                                   47   522SALES           CASHIN
0022      04 010  C     08       SUNDRY    ADD  TOTSUN    TOTSUN  72     TOTAL SUNDRY  CASHIN
0023      04 020  C     16       ACCTRE    ADD  TOTAR     TOTAR   72     TOTAL ACCT REC.CASHIN
0024      04 030  C     16                 MOVE DISCNT    RATE    22     DISCOUNT %    CASHIN
0025      04 040  C     16       ACCTRE    MULT RATE      SALDIS  62H    DISCOUNT AMOUNTCASHIN
0026      04 050  C     16       ACCTRE    SUB  SALDIS    NETAMT  62     NET RECEIPT   CASHIN
0027      04 060  C     16       SALDIS    ADD  TOTDIS    TOTDIS  72     TOTAL DISCOUNTSCASHIN
0028      04 070  C     20       SALES     ADD  TOTSAL    TOTSAL  72     TOTAL CASH SALECASHIN
0029      04 080  CLR          TOTSUN    ADD  TOTAR     TOCASH  82                 CASHIN
0030      04 090  CLR          TOCASH    ADD  TOTSAL    TOCASH                    CASHIN
0031      04 100  CLR          TOCASH    SUB  TOTDIS    TOCASH         TOTAL CASH REC.CASHIN
0032      05 010  OCASHJRL H    301       1P                                        CASHIN
0033      05 020  O       OR              OF                                        CASHIN
0034      05 030  O                                     71 'CASH RECEIPTS JOURNAL'  CASHIN
0035      05 040  O                                    115 'PAGE'                    CASHIN
0036      05 050  O                         PAGE   Z   120                           CASHIN
0037      05 060  O       H    3            1P                                       CASHIN
0038      05 070  O       OR              OF                                        CASHIN
0039      05 080  O                                      9 'DATE'                    CASHIN
0040      05 090  O                                     32 'ACCOUNT CREDITED'        CASHIN
0041      05 100  O                                     57 'EXPLANATION'             CASHIN
0042      05 110  O                                     68 'F'                       CASHIN
0043      05 120  O                                     81 'SUNDRY ACCTS'            CASHIN
0044      05 130  O                                     90 'ACCT REC'                CASHIN
0045      05 140  O                                     98 'SALES'                   CASHIN
0046      05 150  O                                    111 'SALES DISC'              CASHIN
0047      06 010  O       D    2            08                                       CASHIN
0048      06 020  O       OR                16                                       CASHIN
0049      06 030  O       OR                20                                       CASHIN
0050      06 040  O                         DATE  Y    11                            CASHIN
0051      06 050  O                         ACCT        39                           CASHIN
0052      06 060  O                08       EXPLAN      62                           CASHIN
0053      06 070  O                16       TRANS       51                           CASHIN
0054      06 080  O                16       TERMS       60                           CASHIN
0055      06 090  O                20       CSALES      62                           CASHIN
0056      06 100  O                08       FOLIO       69                           CASHIN
0057      06 110  O                08       SUNDRY2     80                           CASHIN
0058      06 120  O                16       ACCTRE2     90                           CASHIN
0059      06 130  O                20       SALES 2    100                           CASHIN
0060      06 140  O                16       SALDIS2    110                           CASHIN
0061      06 150  O                08       SUNDRY2    120                           CASHIN
0062      07 010  O                16       NETAMT2    120                           CASHIN
0063      07 020  O                20       SALES 2    120                           CASHIN
0064      07 030  O       T    1       LR                                           CASHIN
0065      07 040  O                                    80 '--------'                 CASHIN
0066      07 050  O                                    90 '--------'                 CASHIN
0067      07 060  O                                   100 '--------'                 CASHIN
0068      07 070  O                                   110 '--------'                 CASHIN
0069      07 080  O                                   120 '--------'                 CASHIN
0070      07 090  O       T    1       LR                                           CASHIN
0071      07 100  O                         TOTSUN2    80                            CASHIN
0072      07 110  O                         TOTAR 2    90                            CASHIN
0073      07 120  O                         TOTSAL2   100                            CASHIN
0074      07 130  O                         TOTDIS2   110                            CASHIN
0075      07 140  O                         TOCASH2   120                            CASHIN
0076      07 150  O       T    0       LR                                           CASHIN
0077      08 010  O                                    80 '========'                 CASHIN
0078      08 020  O                                    90 '========'                 CASHIN
0079      08 030  O                                   100 '========'                 CASHIN
0080      08 040  O                                   110 '========'                 CASHIN
0081      08 050  O                                   120 '========'                 CASHIN
0082      08 060  O                                   120 '========'                 CASHIN
```

     E N D   O F   S O U R C E

DATE	ACCOUNT CREDITED	EXPLANATION		F	SUNDRY ACCTS	ACCT REC	SALES	SALES DISC	CASH
		CASH RECEIPTS JOURNAL						PAGE	1
8/01/78	TERRY LENTZ	INVOICE	2/10			300.00		6.00	294.00
8/02/78	SALES	CASH SALES					754.12		754.12
8/06/78	NOTES PAYABLE	NOTE TO BANK		302	2,000.00				2,000.00
8/08/78	MONA MYERS	INVOICE	1/10			1,074.22		10.74	1,063.48
8/10/78	SALES	CASH SALES					3,117.83		3,117.83
8/11/78	ANNA MASTROLILLO	INVOICE	3/20			25.10		.75	24.35
8/24/78	NOTES RECEIVABLE	COLLECTION OF NOTE		104	800.00				800.00
8/29/78	STORE EQUIPMENT	SOLD EQUIPMENT		201	340.00				340.00
8/30/78	GINNY HENDERSON	INVOICE	1/15			2,284.55		22.85	2,261.70
8/31/78	SALES	CASH SALES					45.29		45.29
					3,140.00	3,683.87	3,917.24	40.34	10,700.77

Fig. 5-10. Source program listing for Cash Receipts Journal and printed report.

ALTERNATIVE CODING FOR CASH RECEIPTS JOURNAL PROGRAM USING FIELD RELATION INDICATORS

Figure 5-11 illustrates an alternative method for coding the Input Specifications form for the Cash Receipts Journal program. Notice the three record types (08, 16, 20) are now in an *or* relationship as indicated by lines 02010 to 02040.

Supplemental to the use of the *or* coding method is the use of *Field Relation Indicators* (columns 63 and 64 of the Input Specifications form). Examine Figure 5-11 and notice that except for the DATE and ACCT fields, which are common to all three record types, every input field is conditioned by its relative indicator. A Record Identifying Indicator, entered in columns 63 and 64 on the same line as the field to which it relates, indicates that a storage position will be provided in the computer's core storage only when the respective indicator is on.

For example, if record 08 is read, a storage area will be provided for DATE, ACCT, EXPLAN, FOLIO, and SUNDRY fields. The other fields (TRANS through SALES) will be ignored because they are conditioned by indicators 16 and 20 in the Field Relation Indicator columns. The use of Field Relation Indicators for this application is important to prevent incorrect data information from being processed because the fields of the three record types overlap each other and relate to different logical information.

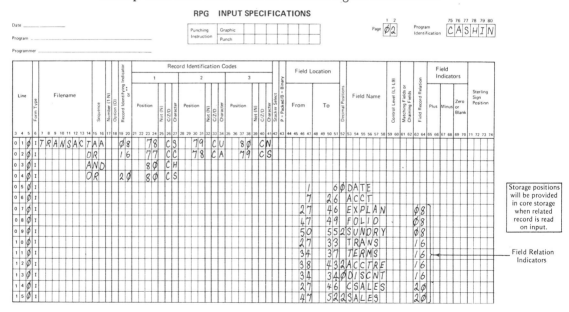

Fig. 5-11. Alternative coding method for Input Specifications Form using an OR relationship and Field Relation Indicators.

```
          01 020  F* ALTERNATIVE CODING FOR CASH RECEIPTS PROGRAM USING 'OR'        CASHIN
          01 030  F* RELATIONSHIP ON INPUT AND FIELD RECORD RELATION INDICATORS...... CASHIN
          01 040  F*                                                                 CASHIN
0001      01 050  FTRANSACTIP  F  80  80              MFCM1  SYSIPT                   CASHIN
0002      01 060  FCASHJRL  O  F 132 132      OF      PRINTERSYSLST                   CASHIN
0C03      02 010  ITRANSACTAA    08  78 CS  79 CU  80 CN                             CASHIN
0004      02 020  I         OR    16  77 CC  78 CA  79 CS                            CASHIN
0005      02 030  I         AND       80 CH                                          CASHIN
0006      02 040  I         OR    20  80 CS                                          CASHIN
0007      02 050  I                                 1    60DATE                      CASHIN
0008      02 060  I                                 7    26 ACCT                     CASHIN
0009      02 070  I                                27    46 EXPLAN      08            CASHIN
0010      02 080  I                                47    49 FOLIO       08            CASHIN
0011      02 090  I                                50   552SUNDRY       08            CASHIN
0012      02 100  I                                27    33 TRANS       16            CASHIN
0013      02 110  I                                34    37 TERMS       16            CASHIN
0014      02 120  I                                38   432ACCTRE       16            CASHIN
0C15      02 130  I                                34   341DISCNT       16            CASHIN
0016      02 140  I                                27    46 CSALES      20            CASHIN
0017      02 150  I                                47   522SALES        20            CASHIN
0018      04 010  C      08       SUNDRY   ADD  TOTSUN    TOTSUN  72    TOTAL SUNDRY   CASHIN
0019      04 020  C      16       ACCTRE   ADD  TOTAR     TOTAR   72    TOTAL ACCT REC.CASHIN
0020      04 030  C      16                MOVE DISCNT    RATE    22    DISCOUNT %     CASHIN
0021      04 040  C      16       ACCTRE   MULT RATF      SALDIS  62H   DISCOUNT AMOUNTCASHIN
0022      04 050  C      16       ACCTRE   SUB  SALDIS    NETAMT  62    NET RECEIPT    CASHIN
0023      04 060  C      16       SALDIS   ADD  TOTDIS    TOTDIS  72    TOTAL DISCOUNTSCASHIN
0024      04 070  C      20       SALES    ADD  TOTSAL    TOTSAL  72    TOTAL CASH SALECASHIN
0025      04 080  CLR             TOTSUN   ADD  TCTAR     TOCASH  82                   CASHIN
0026      04 090  CLR             TOCASH   ADD  TOTSAL    TOCASH                       CASHIN
0027      04 100  CLR             TOCASH   SUB  TOTDIS    TOCASH        TOTAL CASH REC.CASHIN
0028      05 010  OCASHJRL H  301      1P                                             CASHIN
0029      05 020  O         OR          CF                                            CASHIN
0030      05 030  O                                71  'CASH RECEIPTS JOURNAL'        CASHIN
0031      05 040  O                               115  'PAGE'                         CASHIN
0032      05 050  O                          PAGE Z  120                              CASHIN
0033      05 060  O         H  3        1P                                            CASHIN
0034      05 070  O         OR          OF                                           CASHIN
0035      05 080  O                                 9  'DATE'                         CASHIN
0036      05 090  O                                32  'ACCOUNT CREDITED'             CASHIN
0037      05 100  O                                57  'EXPLANATION'                  CASHIN
0038      05 110  O                                68  'F'                            CASHIN
0039      05 120  C                                81  'SUNDRY ACCTS'                 CASHIN
0040      05 130  O                                90  'ACCT REC'                     CASHIN
0041      05 140  C                                98  'SALES'                        CASHIN
0042      05 150  C                               111  'SALES DISC'                   CASHIN
0043      06 010  O                               117  'CASH'                         CASHIN
0044      06 020  O         D  2        08                                            CASHIN
0045      06 030  O         OR          16                                            CASHIN
0046      06 040  O         OR          20                                            CASHIN
0047      06 050  O                          DATE  Y  11                              CASHIN
0048      06 060  O                          ACCT     39                              CASHIN
0049      06 070  O                     08   EXPLAN   62                              CASHIN
0050      06 080  O                     16   TRANS    51                              CASHIN
0051      06 090  O                     16   TERMS    60                              CASHIN
0052      06 100  O                     20   CSALES   62                              CASHIN
0053      06 110  O                     08   FOLIO    69                              CASHIN
0054      06 120  O                     08   SUNDRY2  80                              CASHIN
0055      06 130  O                     16   ACCTRE2  90                              CASHIN
0056      06 140  O                     20   SALES 2  100                             CASHIN
0057      06 150  O                     16   SALDIS2  110                             CASHIN
0058      07 010  O                     08   SUNDRY2  120                             CASHIN
0059      07 020  C                     16   NETAMT2  120                             CASHIN
0060      07 030  O                     20   SALES 2  120                             CASHIN
0061      07 040  O         T  1        LR                                            CASHIN
0062      07 050  O                                80  '---------'                    CASHIN
0063      07 060  O                                90  '---------'                    CASHIN
0064      07 070  O                               100  '---------'                    CASHIN
0065      07 080  C                               110  '---------'                    CASHIN
0066      07 090  O                               120  '--------'                     CASHIN
0067      07 100  O         T  1        LR                                            CASHIN
0068      07 110  O                          TOTSUN2  80                              CASHIN
0069      07 120  O                          TOTAR 2  90                              CASHIN
0070      07 130  O                          TOTSAL2  100                             CASHIN
0071      07 140  O                          TOTDIS2  110                             CASHIN
0072      07 150  O                          TOCASH2  120                             CASHIN
0073      08 010  O         T  0        LR                                            CASHIN
0074      08 020  O                                80  '========='                    CASHIN
0075      08 030  O                                90  '========='                    CASHIN
0076      08 040  O                               100  '========='                    CASHIN
0077      08 050  O                               110  '========='                    CASHIN
0078      08 060  O                               120  '========='                    CASHIN

     E N D   O F   S O U R C E
```

Fig. 5-12. Source program listing for alternative input coding for Cash Receipts Journal program.

An examination of the complete source program listing in Figure 5-12 will reveal that calculation and output-format coding are not affected by this alternative coding procedure. The use of Field Relation Indicators has the advantage of reducing the coding steps in a source program. For example, the DATE and ACCT fields were coded three times in the first program example for the Cash Receipts Journal (Figure 5-5); however, in the alternative approach the fields only had to be coded once (Figure 5-11).

The reader should be aware that the coding methods presented in this example and elsewhere in the text are not to be construed as the only approach for an application program. The example programs are specifically designed to illustrate an RPG II coding procedure.

SEQUENCE CHECKING OF RECORD TYPES ON INPUT

It is often necessary to check the input sequence of record types in a multirecord data file. The Cash Receipts Journal program presented before included more than one record type, but did not *sequence check* the arrangement of the records on input. Because the data records for that program were sorted in ascending date order, the logic of the application does not require the sequence check of records. However, some applications may require this feature to insure the correct calculation and output results. An income statement program will be used to explain the Input Specifications coding procedures for sequence checking the record types in a multirecord data file.

The card layout form in Figure 5-13 shows the format of the record types used in the example program. Notice each record type is coded by its respective Record Identification Code. The codes are all located in column 80, but could have been assigned to any unused column within the records.

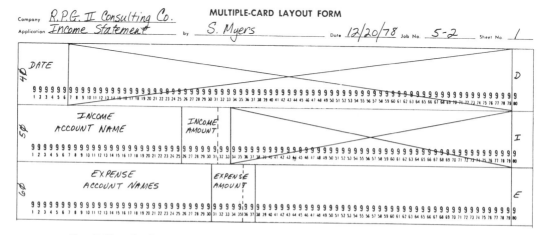

Fig. 5-13. Card Layout Form for the Income Statement program using three record types in the data file.

Figure 5-14 illustrates the arrangement of the data cards in the file. Notice the date card is first and the income card, second, followed by the expense cards. In order for the income statement to print correctly (Figure 5-15) the data records must be arranged in this order. If, for example, the expense cards (record type 60) were incorrectly placed in the data deck first instead of last, the expense record information would be printed before the data and income values. This is because all input records follow the fixed RPG II logic cycle. Consequently, when a record type is read and the related Record Identifying Indicator turned on, all calculations and output coding lines

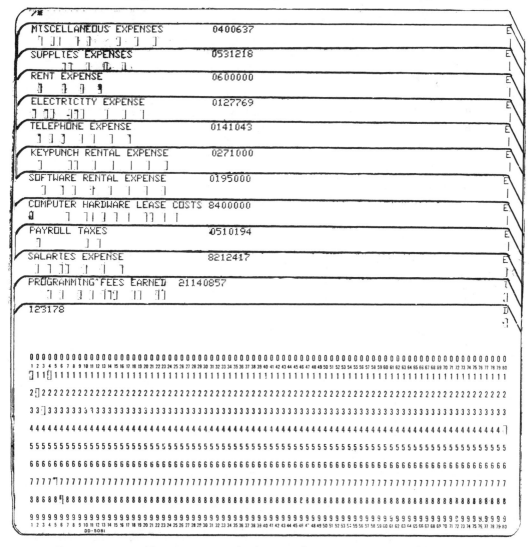

Fig. 5-14.   Data file arrangement for Income Statement program using sequence checking of records on input.

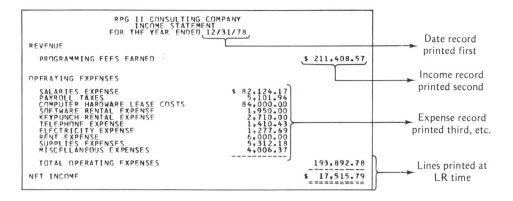

Fig. 5-15. Identification of record types on Income Statement printout.

conditioned by the respective indicators in the source program will be executed. Comments on the Income Statement printout in Figure 5-15 indicate the printing sequence of the input record information.

INPUT SPECIFICATIONS CODING FOR THE SEQUENCE CHECKING OF INPUT DATA RECORDS

An examination of the Input Specifications form in Figure 5-16 will indicate that new RPG II coding entries are used on lines 02010, 02030, and 02060 in columns 15, 16, and 17. The following paragraphs explain the meaning and use of the additional input coding.

Sequence (Columns 15–16). A two-character entry must be placed in these columns for every record type in a file. Depending on the requirements of the program, the entry may be either two alphabetic or numeric characters. Any combination of two letters of the alphabet should be used when:

1. The file only has one record type, or

2. The input records are not in a predetermined sequence, or

3. Processing is not to terminate when any input records are out of sequence, or

4. The specific record type is not part of a predetermined sequence

Program examples previously presented in the text have used two alphabetic letters in this field because there either has been only one record type in the data file or sequence checking was not critical to the logic of the source program instructions.

On the other hand, a two-number entry should be made when;

1. A file contains more than one record type within a group, and

IBM

International Business Machines Corporation

RPG   INPUT SPECIFICATIONS

GX21-9094-1 U/M 050'
Printed in U.S.A.

Date _____

Program _____

Programmer _____

Punching Instruction — Graphic / Punch

Page $\emptyset 2$

Program Identification: $INCOME$ (75 76 77 78 79 80)

Line	Form Type	Filename	Sequence	Number (1 N) Option (O)	Record Identifying Indicator	Record Identification Codes 1 — Position / Not (N) / C/Z/D / Character	2 — Position / Not (N) / C/Z/D / Character	3 — Position / Not (N) / C/Z/D / Character	Stacker Select P=Packed/B=Binary	Field Location From	To	Decimal Positions	Field Name	Control Level (L1,L9)	Matching Fields or Chaining Fields	Field Record Relation	Field Indicators Plus / Minus / Zero or Blank	Sterling Sign Position
0 1	I	LEDGER	Ø11	4Ø		8Ø	CD											
0 2	I									1	6Ø		DATE					
0 3	I		Ø21	5Ø		8Ø	CI											
0 4	I									1	25		INAME				*	
0 5	I									26	332		INCOME					
0 6	I		Ø3N	6Ø		8Ø	CE											
0 7	I									1	3Ø		EXNAME					
0 8	I									31	372		EXPNSE					
0 9	I																	
1 0	I																	
1 1	I																	
1 2	I																	
1 3	I																	
1 4	I																	
1 5	I																	

Fig. 5-16. Input Specifications form for Income Statement program using sequence checking of data records.

2. The RPG II program is to check for all record types and/or whether their sequence in the file or group is correct.

A combination of these entries may be made for the records in a file. For example, some record types may be sequence checked and others may not.

Figure 5-17 details the logic related to the sequence checking of the three record types in the data file for the Income Statement program. Notice the date card is read first, followed by the income card, and then the expense cards. When sequence checking is provided in the program instructions, any records sorted out of the required sequence would cause the program execution to terminate.

Number (Column 17).   An entry is made in this column only when numbers are entered in columns 15 and 16. Examine Figure 5-18 and notice the number 1 is entered in this field for lines 02010 and 02030. This informs the computer that only one card of this type should be present in the data file (or record group). Reference to the data file listing in Figure 5-15 indicates only one date card and income card are included; however, notice that more than one expense record is present in the file. Refer back to Figure 5-18 and observe the letter N is entered in column 17 for the expense records. Use of the letter N in this field indicates any number of this record type may be present in the data file. In all cases, when sequence checking is provided in the program instructions, the number 1 is used when only one record of that type is required in the

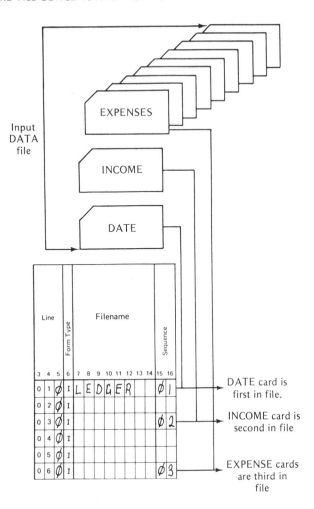

Fig. 5-17. Entries for Sequence Field.

file or record group. On the other hand, the N is used when more than one record of that type is included.

Option (Column 18). If a particular record type must be in a file, or if sequence checking is not to be performed, this column must be blank. However, if the sequence of the record types is to be checked, but the presence of this record type is optional, then the letter O must be placed in this field. In the Income Statement example program all the record types are required. Consequently, this field is blank for the three record types. Figure 5-19 details the Input Specifications coding entries for the Option field.

The reader must understand that sequence checking is not a standard coding procedure for all programs. It should be included in the RPG II

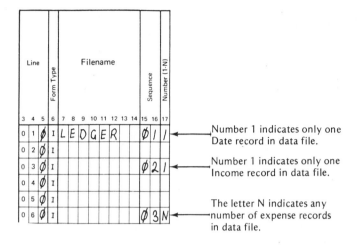

Number 1 indicates only one Date record in data file.

Number 1 indicates only one Income record in data file.

The letter N indicates any number of expense records in data file.

Fig. 5-18.   Entries for Number Field, column 17.

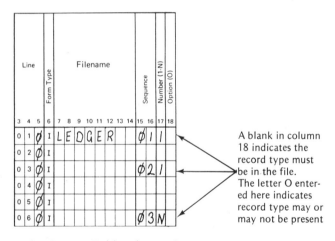

A blank in column 18 indicates the record type must be in the file. The letter O entered here indicates record type may or may not be present

Fig. 5-19.   Entries for Option Field, column 18.

instructions only when the logic of the program requires that record types be sequence checked, or to insure the accuracy of the data in the file. Remember any records out of sequence will cause the program execution to cancel and if the user is processing a huge card file it may be an inconvenience which is not worth the trouble.

The complete source program for the Income Statement application is detailed in Figure 5-20 along with the printed report. Notice that previously discussed coding procedures are used in calculation and output coding. Especially examine the coding entries on line 03070. Resulting Indicators (70 and 80) are used in the appropriate fields to test the Result Field NET for a

Positive, Zero, and Minus result. The related constant is conditioned on output to reflect the status of the field. Reference to lines 06010 and 06020 will show that the constants INCOME and (LOSS) are conditioned by the corresponding Resulting Indicator that was turned on from the result on line 03070.

THE MOVE OPERATIONS

Move operations (MOVE and MOVEL) are often needed in RPG II source programs when data has to be moved from one data field to another without performing an arithmetic operation. The rules for using the MOVE and MOVEL operations are listed below.

Source Program Listing:

```
        01 020  F*THIS PROGRAM ILLUSTRATES THE USE OF SEQUENCE CHECKING OF THREE    INCOME
        01 030  F*RECORD TYPES IN A FILE FOR AN INCOME STATEMENT APPLICATION....     INCOME
        01 040  F*                                                                   INCOME
0001    01 050  FLEDGER    IP  F   80   80              MFCM1  SYSIPT                 INCOME
0002    01 060  FINCOME    O   F  132  132              PRINTERSYSLST                INCOME
0003    02 010  ILEDGER    011 40   80 CD                                            INCOME
0004    02 020  I                                            1     60DATE            INCOME
0005    02 030  I           021 50   80 CI                                           INCOME
0006    02 040  I                                            1    25 INAME           INCOME
0007    02 050  I                                           26    332INCOME          INCOME
0008    02 060  I           03N 60   80 CE                                           INCOME
0009    02 070  I                                            1    30 EXNAME          INCOME
0010    02 080  I                                           31    372EXPNSE          INCOME
        03 010  C* ACCUMULATE EACH EXPENSE AMOUNT INTO A TOTAL EXPENSE FIELD.........INCOME
        03 020  C*                                                                   INCOME
0011    03 030  C      60        EXPNSE    ADD  TOTEXP    TOTEXP  82                  INCOME
        03 040  C*                                                                   INCOME
        03 050  C* AT LAST RECORD TIME SUBTRACT TOTAL EXPENSE FROM INCOME............INCOME
        03 060  C*                                                                   INCOME
0012    03 070  CLR          INCOME    SUB  TOTEXP    NET      82 807080             INCOME
        03 080  C*                                                                   INCOME
        03 090  C* IF NET IS MINUS WILL INDICATE A NET LOSS FOR YEAR.................INCOME
0013    04 010  OINCOME  H  101       1P                                            INCOME
0014    04 020  O                                           50  'RPG II CONSULTING COMPAN'  INCOME
0015    04 030  O                                           51  'Y'                 INCOME
0016    04 040  O         H   1       1P                                            INCOME
0017    04 050  O                                           46  'INCOME STATEMENT'  INCOME
0018    04 060  O         D   2       40                                            INCOME
0019    04 070  O                                           43  'FOR THE YEAR ENDED'  INCOME
0020    04 080  O                             DATE   Y      52                      INCOME
0021    04 090  O         D   2       50                                            INCOME
0022    04 100  O                                           16  'REVENUE'           INCOME
0023    04 110  O         D   3       50                                            INCOME
0024    04 120  O                             INAME         36                      INCOME
0025    04 130  O                             INCOME1       75                      INCOME
0026    04 140  O                                           64  '$'                 INCOME
0027    04 150  O         D   2       50                                            INCOME
0028    05 010  O                                           27  'OPERATING EXPENSES'  INCOME
0029    05 020  O         D   0       50                                            INCOME
0030    05 030  O                                           50  '$'                 INCOME
0031    05 040  O         D   1       60                                            INCOME
0032    05 050  O                             EXNAME        41                      INCOME
0033    05 060  O                             EXPNSE1       60                      INCOME
0034    05 070  O         T   1       LR                                            INCOME
0035    05 080  O                                           60  '----------'        INCOME
0036    05 090  O         T   1       LR                                            INCOME
0037    05 100  O                                           35  'TOTAL OPERATING EXPENSES'  INCOME
0038    05 110  O                             TOTEXP1       75                      INCOME
0039    05 120  O         T   1       LR                                            INCOME
0040    05 130  O                                           75  '----------'        INCOME
0041    05 140  O         T   1       LR                                            INCOME
0042    05 150  O                                           12  'NET'               INCOME
0043    06 010  O                                80         19  'INCOME'            INCOME
0044    06 020  O                                70         19  '(LOSS)'            INCOME
0045    06 030  O                             NET    1      75                      INCOME
0046    06 040  O                                           64  '$'                 INCOME
0047    06 050  C         T   0       LR                                            INCOME
0048    06 060  O                                           75  '============'      INCOME

        END OF SOURCE
```

Fig. 5-20. Source program listing and printed report for the Income Statement application program. (continued on next page)

Printed Income Statement:

```
              RPG II CONSULTING COMPANY
                 INCOME STATEMENT
             FOR THE YEAR ENDED 12/31/79

REVENUE

   PROGRAMMING FEES EARNED                          $ 211,408.57


OPERATING EXPENSES

   SALARIES EXPENSE                    $ 82,124.17
   PAYROLL TAXES                          5,101.94
   COMPUTER HARDWARE LEASE COSTS         84,000.00
   SOFTWARE RENTAL EXPENSE                1,950.00
   KEYPUNCH RENTAL EXPENSE                2,710.00
   TELEPHONE EXPENSE                      1,410.43
   ELECTRICITY EXPENSE                    1,277.69
   RENT EXPENSE                           6,000.00
   SUPPLIES EXPENSES                      5,312.18
   MISCELLANEOUS EXPENSES                 4,006.37
                                        ----------
   TOTAL OPERATING EXPENSES                            193,892.78

NET INCOME                                          $  17,515.79
                                                    ============
```

Fig. 5-20.   (concluded)

1. The operation (MOVE or MOVEL) must be left-justified in the operation field of the Calculation Specifications form.

2. Factor 1 is never used with the MOVE or MOVEL operations.

3. Decimal alignment is not performed in the MOVE or MOVEL operations.

4. A numeric literal or the contents of a variable numeric field may be moved into an alphanumeric field or vice versa.

5. Any acceptable RPG II indicator may be used to condition the calculation line for a MOVE or MOVEL operation.

6. The MOVE operation causes the literal or contents of the variable field in Factor 2 to be moved to the low-order positions of the Result Field. If the Result Field is smaller than the literal or field in Factor 2 any high-order characters will be truncated.

7. The MOVEL operation causes the literal or contents of the variable field in Factor 2 to be moved to the high-order positions in the Result Field. If the field defined in the Result Field is smaller than the literal or field in Factor 2 any low-order characters will be truncated.

8. If the Result Field is larger than the literal or field in Factor 2 any high-order characters in the Result field before the MOVE will remain after the operation is executed. Under the same circumstances when the MOVEL operation is used, any low-order characters will not be replaced by the literal or field contents in Factor 2.

9. The contents of storage values in Factor 2 will not be disturbed by the MOVE or MOVEL operations.

Figure 5-21 illustrates the Calculation Specifications for five unrelated MOVE and MOVEL operations. Line 010 causes the storage contents of FIELDA to be moved into the storage area named FIELDX. The MOVE

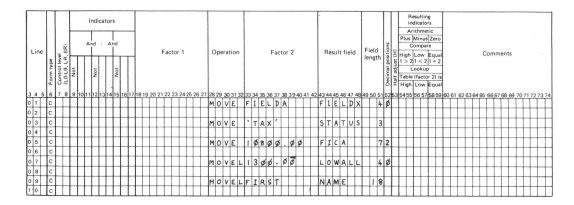

Fig. 5-21. Calculation specifications coding examples of the MOVE and MOVEL operations.

statement specified on line 030 moves the alphanumeric literal TAX into a storage area called STATUS. Notice that apostrophes encompass the literal TAX. All alphanumeric literals must be enclosed in apostrophes whereas numeric literals are not. Line 050 illustrates an example of moving a numeric literal into a variable field. Remember that decimal alignment is not performed for the MOVE operations.

The MOVEL operation specified on line 070 causes a negative literal to be moved into a smaller result field. This would cause the low-order digits to be truncated. All numbers are assumed to be positive unless specified as negative. When a number is identified as negative the negative sign must be keypunched *over the last digit* of the number. The last operation, line 090, causes the storage contents of the FIRST field to move left into the storage area NAME.

Examples of the technique in which data is handled internally in the computer when the MOVE operation is used are illustrated in Figure 5-22. Notice in Example 1 that the contents of the SALARY field, which is specified in Factor 2, is moved into the receiving field HOLD, defined as five character long with two decimal positions. The SALARY field must have been previously defined on input or created in calculations. In this example, the sending field SALARY is the same length as the receiving field HOLD. When the data is moved into the HOLD field it fills the low-order positions first, commencing with the right-most position and filling in the next available position to the left. Consequently, if the receiving field is smaller than the contents of the variable field or literal specified in Factor 2, the high-order positions of the sending field will be lost. On the other hand, if the receiving field is larger, any of the characters that were in the receiving field before the move will remain there because RPG II MOVE operations do not initialize the Result field to zero before the move is executed.

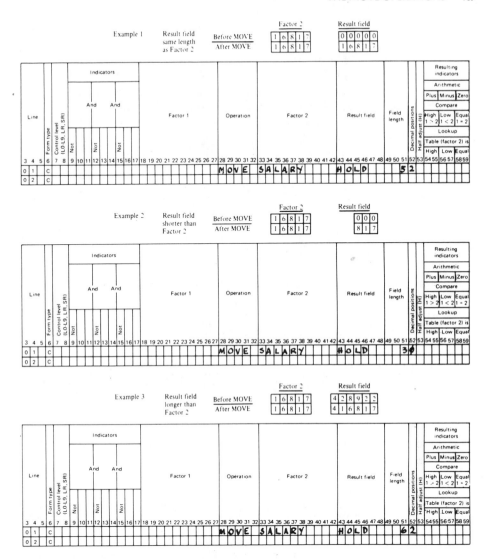

Fig. 5-22. Results of the MOVE operation.

Also, notice the contents of the SALARY field are not affected by the MOVE operation and the amount is now included in two fields, the SALARY and HOLD fields.

Example 2, Figure 5-22, illustrates the result of moving data into a smaller field. Observe that the high-order digits of the sending field are lost because the receiving field, HOLD, is smaller and the MOVE operation causes the low-order positions to be filled in first. Often the MOVE and MOVEL operation features are useful and the characteristics mentioned in these paragraphs are not to be construed as undesirable; they make the operations an invaluable programming tool.

Example 3, Figure 5-22, shows the movement of a data item into a Result field which is larger than the size specified for Factor 2. Therefore, any high-order characters previously stored in the Result field will remain there after the move is completed unless, of course, replaced by data of equivalent size. Examine the contents of the fields after the move is completed and notice that the high-order number 4 of the original contents of the Result field is not

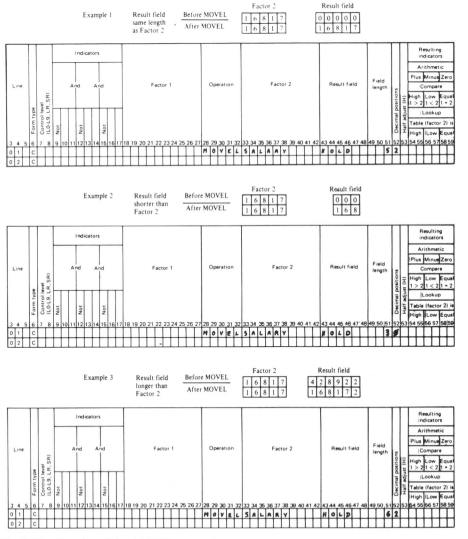

Fig. 5-23.   Results of the MOVEL operation.

replaced by the data that was moved into the HOLD field. Hence, when a Result field is larger than the contents of Factor 2, the Result field should be set to zero before the move operation is executed, unless, of course, the high-order positions of the Result field are to be saved.

The MOVEL operation performs basically the same function as the MOVE operation except the left-most positions in the receiving field are occupied first, followed by filling the next available position to the right.

Figure 5-23 shows the results of the MOVEL operation when the receiving field (HOLD) is the same size, smaller, and larger than the sending field (SALARY). An examination of example 1 will reveal that when the sending and receiving fields are the same size, the contents of the Result field after the MOVEL is completed will be the same as the contents of Factor 2.

On the other hand, example 2 indicates that when the Result field is smaller than Factor 2, the low-order positions of the sending field will be lost because the MOVEL operation causes the data to be moved into the high-order positions first.

Furthermore, when the receiving field is larger than Factor 2, as shown in example 3, the contents of the low-order position in the Result field before the MOVEL is executed will remain after the MOVEL is completed because Result fields are not set to zero before the data is moved.

Both the MOVE and MOVEL operations give additional flexibility to the RPG language and provide a convenient way to manipulate data internally within the computer.

QUESTIONS

1. What is meant by a Multirecord file?
2. How does the computer distinguish between records in a Multirecord file when the file is processed?
3. How many Record Identifying Indicators may be on at the same time?
4. If an output instruction is not conditioned by any indicator, when will it be executed?
5. In what columns are the letters OR entered on the Input Specifications form? On the Output-Format Specifications form?
6. What does use of the OR coding accomplish on input and output coding?
7. What are Field Relation Indicators? Where and when are they used?
8. In what positions in a record may Record Identification Codes be entered? How many characters may be used to identify the record type?
9. When is the AND relationship used on Input Specifications coding? When is it used on Output Format Specifications coding?
10. When should the sequence checking of records in a multirecord file be used?
11. What Input Specification columns are used for the sequence checking of record types?
12. If the records in a multirecord file are to be sequence–checked, what must be done to the file before it is processed?
13. If only one record in a multirecord file is out of the required sequence, what will happen during processing?
14. Explain the meaning of each field entry on the partial Input Specification form shown below:

Sequence	Number (1-N) Option (O)	Record Identifying Indicator or **	Record Identification Codes													Stacker Select
			1				2				3					
			Position	Not (N)	C/Z/D	Character	Position	Not (N)	C/Z/D	Character	Position	Not (N)	C/Z/D	Character		
14	15 16	17 18	19 20	21 22 23 24	25	26	27	28 29 30 31	32	33	34	35 36 37 38	39	40	41	42
Ø11		Ø1		4Ø	C	X										
Ø2N		11		8Ø	D	2										
Ø3N09Ø			1		C	S	2NC	T								

15. Explain the meaning of the following coding entries on the partial Output-Format Specifications form shown below:

ip	Output Indicators			Field Name		Edit Codes
		And	And			
After	Not	Not	Not			
21 22	23 24	25 26 27	28 29 30 31	32 33 34 35 36 37	38	
				FIELDA		
			14	FIELDB		
		20		FIELDC		
		98		FIELDD		

16. Explain the function of the coding entries on the partial Input Specifications form presented below:

Decimal Positions	Field Name	Control Level (L1-L9)	Matching Fields or Chaining Fields	Field Record Relation	Pli'
52	53 54 55 56 57 58	59 60	61 62	63 64	65
	ABC				
	BCD			Ø1	
	CDE			Ø2	
	DEF			Ø3	

17. What happens in a MOVE operation if the receiving field is two positions smaller than the sending field? If it is longer?
18. What happens in a MOVEL operation if the receiving field is one position smaller than the sending field? If it is longer?
19. Is decimal alignment performed in MOVE or MOVEL operation?
20. In a MOVE or MOVEL operation what happens to a negative sign in a Factor 2 field?
21. Shown below are the original contents of the three Factor 2 and Result fields. Determine the contents of the Result field after the MOVE operation is executed.

Before MOVE   After MOVE

Factor 2   Result   Result

J O N E S   J O H N

1 1 1 Ø 2 4   1 8

9 7 3   1 9 7 2

22. Shown below are the original contents of the three Factor 2 and Result fields. Determine the contents of the Result field after the MOVEL operation is executed.

Before MOVEL

Factor 2	Result
J O H N	J O N E S
1 1 1 Ø 2 4	Ø Ø 7 4
1 9 7	1 8 7 4

After MOVEL

Result

EXERCISES

5-1. From the following card layout form complete the Input Specifications sheet. Describe each record type on a separate line, *do not* use the OR relationship for this exercise. Use input file name INVENTY.

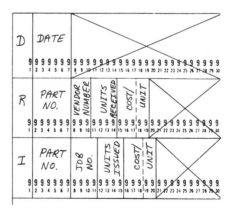

5-2. Rewrite the Input Specifications form from the information in Exercise 1 and use the OR relationship method for input of the record types along with Field Relation Indicators.

5-3. Rewrite the Input Specifications from the information in Exercise 1 using *sequence checking* to check the input of R and I record types in the file. Assume records are in a D, R, I order. Only *one* date card is included in the file, but any number of R and I records in each part number group.

5-4. Write the Calculation Specifications coding for the record information included in Exercise 1. The calculations for record type R require that Units Received be multiplied by Cost/Unit to give the total cost for the part. Total cost for each part must be added to a grand total field for all part receipts.

Type I records also require that Units Issued be multiplied by Cost/Unit to give the cost of the issue. The cost of issue amount must also be accumulated to a grand total field for all issues.

5-5. Write the Output-Format Specifications coding from the report design information included in the Printer Spacing Chart given below. Use information from Exercise 1 for field sizes and names.

		0	1	2	3	4	5
		1234567890	1234567890	1234567890	1234567890	1234567890	123456789
H	1	PART RECEIPT AND ISSUE REPORT					
D	2		AS OF ØX/XX/XX				
	3						
D	4	PART NO.	RECEIVED	ISSUED			
	5						
D	6	XXXXXX	X,XXX,XXØ.XX				
D	7	XXXXXX		X,XXX,XXØ.XX			
	8						
	9						
TLR	10	TOTALS XX,XXX,XXØ.XX	XX,XXX,XXØ.XX				
	11						
	12						
	13	NOTES:					
	14						
	15	(1) Headings on top of every page.					
	16						
	17	(2) Detail lines are single spaced.					
	18						
	19						

5-6. On a blank Calculation Specifications form write the necessary coding (using the MOVE and MOVEL operations to separate the six–digit date field, 081179, into its Month, Day, and Year elements.

5-7. DEBUGGING AN RPG II SOURCE PROGRAM
Given on the following pages is an RPG II source program listing with diagnostic messages. The program compiled but did not print the correct report because of compilation errors.

CORRECT THE CODING LINES THAT ARE INCORRECT BY REWRITING THEM ON THE REQUIRED SPECIFICATIONS FORM. ALSO, LOCATE AND INTERPRET THE NOTES GIVEN IN THE DIAGNOSTICS.

Source Program Listing:

```
        01 020  F*THIS PROGRAM ILLUSTRATES THE USE OF SEQUENCE CHECKING OF THREE    INCOME
        01 030  F*RECORD TYPES IN A FILE FOR AN INCOME STATEMENT APPLICATION....     INCOME
        01 040  F*                                                                   INCOME
0001    01 050  FLEDGER  IP  F  80  80        MFCM1 SYSIPT                           INCOME
0002    01 060  FINCOME  O   F 132 132        PRINTERSYSLST                          INCOME
0003    02 010  ILEDGER  011 40  80  D                                              INCOME

0004    02 020  I                                                                   INCOME        NOTE 095
0005    02 030  I         SM1 50  80 CI              1    60DATE                     INCOME
                          $
0006    02 040  I                                   1    25 INAME                   INCOME        NOTE 084
0007    02 050  I                                  26   332INCOME                   INCOME
0008    02 060  I         03  30  80 CE                                             INCOME
                          $
0009    02 070  I                                   1    30 EXNAME                  INCOME        NOTE 086
0010    02 080  I                                  31   378EXPNSE                   INCOME
                                                       $
        03 010  C* ACCUMULATE EACH EXPENSE AMOUNT INTO A TOTAL EXPENSE FIELD........INCOME        NOTE 112
        03 020  C*                                                                  INCOME
0011    03 030  C    60       EXPNSE     ADD  TOTEXP    TOTEXP 82                    INCOME
        03 040  C*                                                                  INCOME
        03 050  C* AT LAST RECORD TIME SUBTRACT TOTAL EXPENSE FROM INCOME...........INCOME
        03 060  C*                                                                  INCOME
0012    03 070  CLR          INCOME     SUB  TOTEXP    NET     82 807080            INCOME
        03 080  C*                                                                  INCOME
        03 090  C* IF NET IS MINUS WILL INDICATE A NET LOSS FOR YEAR................INCOME
0013    04 010  CINCOME  H  101    1P                                              INCOME
0014    04 020  O                                   50  'RPG II CONSULTING COMPAN'  INCOME
0015    04 030  O                                   51  'Y'                         INCOME
0016    04 040  O         H  1    1P                                               INCOME
0017    04 050  O                                   46  'INCOME STATEMENT'          INCOME
0018    04 060  O         D  2    40                                               INCOME
0019    04 070  O                                   43  'FOR THE YEAR ENDED'        INCOME
0020    04 080  O                           DATE Y  52                              INCOME
0021    04 090  O         D  2    50                                               INCOME
0022    04 100  O                                   16  'REVENUE                    INCOME
0023    04 110  O         D  3    50                                               INCOME
0024    04 120  O                           INAME   36                              INCOME
0025    04 130  O                           INCOME1 75                              INCOME
0026    04 140  O                                   64  '$'                         INCOME
0027    04 150  O         D  2    50                                               INCOME
0028    05 010  O                                   27  'OPERATING EXPENSES'        INCOME
0029    05 020  O         D  0    50                                               INCOME
0030    05 030  O                                   50  '$'                         INCOME
0031    05 040  O         D  1    60                                               INCOME
                                                       $
0032    05 050  O                           EXNAME  41                              INCOME        NOTE 202
0033    05 060  O                           EXPNSE1 60                              INCOME
0034    05 070  O         T  1    LR                                               INCOME
0035    05 080  O                                   60  '----------'               INCOME
0036    05 090  O                                   35  'TOTAL OPERATING EXPENSES'  INCOME
0037    05 100  O                           TOTEXP1 75                              INCOME
0038    05 110  O         T  1    LR                                               INCOME
0039    05 120  O                                   75  '----------'               INCOME
0040    05 130  O         T  1    LR                                               INCOME
0041    05 140  O                                   12  'NET'                       INCOME
0042    05 150  O                                   19  'INCOME'                     INCOME
0043    06 010  O                      81                                          INCOME
                                       $
0044    06 020  O                      70           19  '(LOSS)'                    INCOME        NOTE 202
0045    06 030  O                           NET   1 75                              INCOME
0046    06 040  O                                   64  '$'                         INCOME
0047    06 050  O         T  0    LR                                               INCOME
0048    06 060  O                                   73  '=========='               INCOME
```

            END OF SOURCE

Diagnostic Messages:

                    T A B L E S   A N D   M A P S

RESULTING INDICATOR TABLE

ADDRESS	RI	ADDRESS	RI	ADDRESS	RI	ADDRESS	RI	ADDRESS	RI	ADDRESS	RI	ADDRESS	RI	
029D	0A	02BF	LR	02C0	H0	02CA	1P	02CD	30	02CE	40	02CF	50	
02D0	70	02D1	80											
				0008			30							NOTE 388
				0011			60							NOTE 387
				0012			80							NOTE 388
				0012			80							NOTE 388

FIELD NAMES

ADDRESS	FIELD	ADDRESS	FIELD	ADDRESS	FIELD	ADDRESS	FIELD	ADDRESS	FIELD
01DD	*ERRCR	0349	DATE	034D	INAME	0366	INCOME	036B	EXNAME
0389	EXPNSE	038D	TOTEXP	0392	NET				

Printed Report with Errors:

MESSAGE TEXT

NOTE 084   SEQUENCE ENTRY IN POSITIONS 15-16 IS INVALID. ASCENDING NUMERIC SEQUENCE IS
            ASSUMED.
NOTE 086   NUMBER ENTRY (POSITION 17) IS INVALID. ASSUME N.
NOTE 095   C/Z/D ENTRY IN POSITIONS 26, 33, OR 40 IS NOT C, Z, OR D. ASSUME C.
NOTE 112   DECIMAL ENTRY IN POSITION 52 IS GREATER THAN UNPACKED FIELD LENGTH. ASSUME FIELD
            LENGTH.
NOTE 202   INDICATOR IS INVALID OR UNDEFINED. DROP ENTRY.
NOTE 387   INDICATOR REFERENCED BUT NOT DEFINED. DROP INDICATOR.
NOTE 388   INDICATOR DEFINED BUT NOT REFERENCED. WARNING.

```
                    RPG II CONSULTING COMPANY
                         INCOME STATEMENT
                                              .0000000
                  FOR THE YEAR ENDED 12/31/78

                                              .0000000
         REVENUE

            PROGRAMMING FEES EARNED                        $ 211,408.57

         OPERATING EXPENSES
                                               $    .0000000
               SALARIES EXPENSE                    .8212417
               PAYROLL TAXES                       .0510194
               COMPUTER HARDWARE LEASE COSTS       .8400000
               SOFTWARE RENTAL EXPENSE             .0195000
               KEYPUNCH RENTAL EXPENSE             .0271000
               TELEPHONE EXPENSE                   .0141043
               ELECTRICITY EXPENSE                 .0127769
               RENT EXPENSE                        .0600000
               SUPPLIES EXPENSES                   .0531218
               MISCELLANEOUS EXPENSES              .0400637
                                               ------------
               TOTAL OPERATING EXPENSES                           1.91
                                                           ------------
         NET INCOME                                        $ 211,406.66
                                                           ============
```

LABORATORY ASSIGNMENTS

LABORATORY ASSIGNMENT 5-1:
SCHEDULE OF ACCOUNTS RECEIVABLE

A schedule of Accounts Receivable is a listing of the account balances of the customers accounts in the Accounts Receivable Ledger.

From the following information write an RPG II source program to obtain a Schedule of Accounts Receivable report.

Input Design:

Input Design:

Record ID code

DATE				D

9 9 9 9 9 9 9 9 9 9 9 9 9 9 9 9 9 9 9 9 9 9 9 9 9 9 9 9 9 9 9 9 9 9 9 9 9 9 9 9 9 9 9 9 9 9 9 9 9 9 9 9 9 9

1 2 3 4 5 6 7 8 9 10 11 12 13 14 15 16 17 18 19 20 21 22 23 24 25 26 27 28 29 30 31 32 33 34 35 36 37 38 39 40 41 42 43 44 45 46 47 48 49 50 51 52 53 54 55

CUST. NO.	CUSTOMER NAME	ACCOUNT BALANCE	AC

9 9 9 9 9 9 9 9 9 9 9 9 9 9 9 9 9 9 9 9 9 9 9 9 9 9 9 9 9 9 9 9 9 9 9 9 9 9 9 9 9 9 9 9 9 9 9 9 9 9 9 9 9

1 2 3 4 5 6 7 8 9 10 11 12 13 14 15 16 17 18 19 20 21 22 23 24 25 26 27 28 29 30 31 32 33 34 35 36 37 38 39 40 41 42 43 44 45 46 47 48 49 50 51 52 53 54 55

Record ID codes

Calculations. Accumulate the balance of all the customers and print the total at LR time. Also, create a count field so the number of records processed may be determined.

Output Design:

		0	1	2	3	4	5	6	7
H	1	PAGE XXØX		EVERYBODY COMPANY					
H	2			SCHEDULE OF ACCOUNTS RECEIVABLE					
H	3			ØX/XX/XX					
	4								
H	5	CUSTOMER NUMBER		CUSTOMER NAME			ACCOUNT BALANCE		
	6								
D	7	XXXXX	X————		——X	$ XXX,XXØ.XX		
D	8	XXXXX	X————		——X	XXX,XXØ.XX		
TLR	9								
TLR	10						$X,XXX,XXØ.XX		
TLR	11								
	12								
TLR	13		RECORDS PROCESSED = XXXØX						
	14								
	15								
	16	NOTES							
	17								
	18	① HEADINGS ON TOP OF EVERY PAGE.							
	19								
	20	② DOLLAR SIGN ON FIRST DETAIL LINE ONLY.							
	21								
	22	③ DOLLAR SIGNS ARE FIXED.							
	23								
	24								

detail — total
Print out balance

Data for this assignment is as follows:

Customer Number	Customer Name	Account Balances
11111	ALWAYS ABLE	00219215
11121	MARY BEST	00051322
11444	I. M. CURRENT	00020010
12345	LARS DEFICIT	00797788
12356	HUGH DENT	00011154
13344	NEVER EARLY	00485673
14455	T. O. FATSO	00061487
15376	I. C. GUNN	01065936
16443	Y. HOLD	00004128
17777	I. ITCH	00613366
18123	H. I. JUMP	00032446
19996	E. Z. KIDD	00444444
20019	I. M. A. LUMOX	00056784

L 1 customer total
LR - Total

Note: Use any six character date for report date

LABORATORY ASSIGNMENT 5-2:
CASH DISBURSEMENTS JOURNAL (CHECK REGISTER)

The Cash Disbursements Journal (also called check register) is used in an accounting system to record all cash disbursements. Individual columns in the journal are included when the activity of that transaction category is great. Write an RPG II source program from the information given below:

Input Design.   From the following Card Layout, code the Input Specifications form using the OR relationship method and Field Relation Indicators.

Calculations.   Accumulate the column totals as indicated in the Printer Spacing Chart shown below. Any purchase discount percent must be multiplied by the account payable amount to give the cash discount. All cash discounts are subtracted from the gross accounts payable to give the net amount of cash to be paid.

Output Design.   The Printer Spacing Chart for the Cash Disbursements Journal is detailed below:

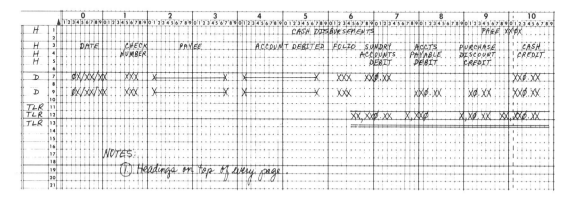

Data for this assignment is as follows:

Check Date	Check Number	Payee of Check	Folio	Account Debited	Sundry Amount	Accts. Payable Amount	Purchase Discount Percent
012578	098	EAST SALES CO.		PURCHASES		10000	020
13078	099	ACME MFG. COMPANY		ACME MFG. COMPANY		20000	020
022778	100	SMITH AND SON INC		SMITH AND SON INC		30000	025
031578	101	APEX REALTY	043	RENT EXPENSE	25000		
032778	102	ARIZONA SUPPLY CO		ARIZONA SUPPLY CO		95000	015
040178	103	WESTERN SUPPLY CO		WESTERN SUPPLY CO		80000	010
043078	104	MATCHLESS TOOL CO		MATCHLESS TOOL CO		60000	030
050178	105	JERRY HALE	080	SALARIES EXPENSE	08600		
060178	106	ELSIE TRUCKING CO	590	DELIVERY EXPENSE	01500		
072578	107	SAVO AND SONS	110	OFFICE EQUIPMENT	05000		

LABORATORY ASSIGNMENT 5-3:
DISCOUNTING NOTES RECEIVABLE

Companies that maintain large accounts receivable may ask that their long-term or slower paying customers give them a promissory note in lieu of the open account. This is particularly important when a company needs cash for their own obligations as the customer's notes (notes receivable) may be easily discounted at a bank. The mathematics of discounting a customer's note is as follows:

Determining the Cash Proceeds

As far as the bank is concerned, it is making a loan to the borrower based on the maturity value of the note, including any interest, because that is the amount the bank will collect from the maker at the maturity date. The discount that the bank deducts is based on a stipulated rate of the maturity value for the period of time the note has to run.

The sequence for computing the proceeds of a discounted note is:

1. The maturity value, or the principal plus the total interest to maturity, is determined.

2. The discount period, or the number of days the note still has to run after the date of the discount, is found.

3. The discount is computed at the stipulated bank rate for the discount period.

4. The discount is deducted from the maturity value to find the cash proceeds.

This sequence may be stated as:

$$MV - (MV \times D \times RL) = P$$

where

MV = the maturity value
D = the rate of discount
RL = the remaining life of the note
P = the cash proceeds

Assume that on April 19, 1969, the Faison Company receives a 6-percent, 60-day note for $2,000 from Edward Goodson in settlement of a past-due open account. This transaction is recorded as follows:

1969
Apr. 19   Notes Receivable   2000
      Accounts Receivable-Edward Goodson   2000
        To record receipt of a 6%, 60-day note from
        Goodson in settlement of a past-due open account.

On May 1, 1969, the Faison Company, needing short-term funds, decides to discount Goodson's note at the bank's rate of 5-percent. Calculation of the proceeds follows:

1. Maturity value of note (principal of $2,000 plus total interest of $20) $2,020.00
2. Due date   June 18
3. Period of discount:

May 1–May 31 (not counting May 1)	30 days
June 1–June 18 (including June 1)	18 days
	48 days

4. Discount at 5% for 48 days on the maturity value:

Interest on $2,020 at 6% for 60 days	$20.20
Less interest on $2,020 at 6% for 12 days	
$\left(\frac{1}{3} \times \$20.20\right)$	4.04
Interest on $2,020 at 6% for 48 days	$16.16
Less interest on $2,020 at 1% for 48 days	
$\left(\frac{1}{6} \times \$16.16\right)$	2.69
Discount (or interest) on $2,020 at 5% for 48 days	13.47
Total cash proceeds	$2,006.53

Source: Albert Slavin, Isaac N. Reynolds, and Lawrence H. Malchman, Basic Accounting for Managerial and Financial Control (New York: Holt, Rinehart, and Winston, Inc., 1968), p. 263.

Input Design.   The input data record format of the two record types in the file is formatted below. Use sequence checking to check the sequence of the records. Each record group must include the 01 record type first, followed by the related 02 record. Only one of each record type should be included in the file for every note.

Field Description	Field Name	Card Columns	Dec. Pos.	Type
Record Type 01				
Customer name	CUST	1–25		A
Maker of note	MAKER	26–51		A
Date of note	DATE	52–57	0	N
Time of note	TIME	58–61	0	N
Interest rate of note	RATE	62–65	4	N
Maturity date of note	MDATE	66–71		A
Principal of note	PRINPL	72–79	2	N
Record Identification Code (digit 1 in column 80)				
Record Type 02				
Discount period*	DISTIM	1–4	0	N
Discount rate	DRATE	9–12	4	N
Record Identification Code (digit 2 in column 80)				

*Note: Discount period (DISTIM) is the period of time that the bank will hold the note.

Calculations. Calculate the simple interest on the note and add this amount to the principal to give the maturity value. The formula for simple interest is:

$$\text{Principal} \times \text{Rate} \times \text{Time} = \text{Simple Interest}$$

Then: $\text{Principal} + \text{Simple Interest} = \text{Maturity Value (MV)}$

After the maturity value is computed solve the formula to determine the cash proceeds from discounting the note:

$$MV - (MV \times D \times RL) = P$$

(see "Determining the Cash Proceeds" given earlier for the complete solution)

Note: Use Resulting Indicators in calculations to determine whether the result of discounting a note is income or expense. Condition the related output lines accordingly.

Output Design. From the sample report given below *format your own Printer Spacing Chart*. Your heading and field locations may be your own design. However, your report must include all the information in the following printout. Provide for INCOME EARNED or INTEREST EXPENSE depending on whether there are more or less net proceeds than the principal amount.

```
                         NOTES DISCOUNTED, LAST NATIONAL BANK
---------------------------------------------------------------------------
I.B.M. SALES AND SERVICE
        WILLIAM MARTIN
        DATE OF NOTE            MATURITY DATE          TIME        INTEREST
          12/15/71                 3/14/72           90 DAYS        .0650

        PRINCIPAL              INTEREST             MATURITY VALUE
        $3,500.00               $56.10                $3,556.10
                               DISCOUNT  INFORMATION
        ---------------------------------------------------------------------
        DISCOUNT PERIOD        DISCOUNT RATE
          45 DAYS                .0550

        DISCOUNT AMOUNT        NET PROCEEDS
          $24.11                $3,531.99

        INTEREST EARNED
          $31.99
```

Data for the Laboratory Assignment: Record Type 01

Customer Name	Maker of Note	Date of Note	Time of Note	Interest Rate	Maturity Date	Principal
JAMES A. FILBERT	1ST NATIONAL BANK	061078	0090	0800	090878	00240000
JAMES P. BROWN	CLEAN WORK COMPANY	013178	0120	0750	053178	00880000
BECKER AND BECKER COMPANY	MAGNOLIA REFUSE REMOVAL	081178	0036	0900	091678	00092400
YEVGENY YEVTUSHENKO	SOPWITH CAMEL	0141478	0090	0850	071378	02175000
HUBERT HYMPHREY DRUGS	RICHARD M. NIXON LAW, INC	110278	0045	0700	121778	00030000

Data for the Laboratory Assignment: Record Type 02

Discount Period	Discount Rate
80	0700
82	0600
32	0700
74	0825
16	0650

Note: The first record from Record Type 01 must be grouped with the first record from Record Type 02, the second record from Record Type 01 with 02, and so on.

6
CONTROL LEVEL INDICATORS

The efficient and effective use of RPG II depends upon a complete understanding of the various indicator types included in the language. Record Identifying (01–99), Resulting, First Page, Overflow, Field Relation, and Last Record (LR) Indicators have been introduced and discussed in previous chapters.

Another class of indicators called Control Level (L1–L9) are part of the repertoire of indicators often needed in RPG II programs. A typical use of the Control Level Indicators is for applications requiring subtotals within the body of a report. We have learned the Last Record Indicator (LR) will cause totals, etc., to be printed when the end-of-file record (/*) is read, but LR does not provide for subtotal printing or control. Control Level Indicator coding provides for this additional feature in program instructions.

First, a sample program will be illustrated and discussed depicting the use of one Control Level Indicator (L1) for the control of calculations and output for a savings account application. Next, an application will be presented using four Control Level Indicators (L1–L4) to obtain the calculations and output for a printed report.

Before the use of Control Level Indicator coding is discussed, however, an understanding of three new terms must be acquired: Control Level Fields, Control Groups, and Control Breaks.

SAVINGS ACCOUNT APPLICATION PROGRAM USING ONE CONTROL LEVEL INDICATOR (L1)

The data file illustrated in Figure 6-1 shows the arrangement of the records and Control Level terminology. Notice the records are sorted by account number (columns 1–4) first in a B, then in a W or D order (column 80). As with most applications, the arrangement of the data file is important for correct processing and end results.

Refer back to Figure 6-1 and identify how the new Control Level terminology relates to the data file. Each term will be defined in the following paragraphs.

Control Level Fields

Control Level Fields are variable data fields defined on input which are used to identify a different record or group of records within a data file. Examination of Figure 6-1 will show the Control Level Field for this example is entered in

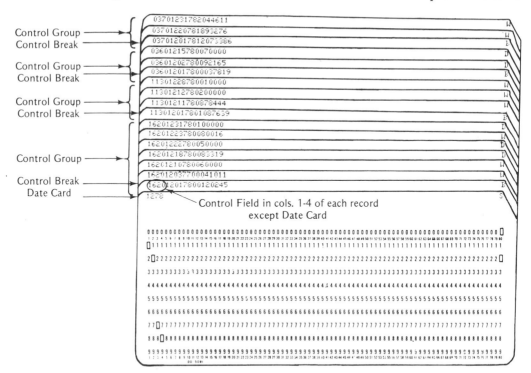

Fig. 6-1. Data File for savings account example program showing Control Fields, Control Breaks, and Control Groups.

columns 1–4 which is the account number for this application. Notice the records for the account number 1620 are all grouped together as are the records for account numbers 1130, 0360, and 0370. If the records were not arranged by group for this application the instructions in the program would not process the file correctly.

Control Level Fields may be any variable field and may be located in any position within the record. This sample program only requires the use of one Control Level Field; however, up to nine (L1–L9) may be assigned in one program.

Three important RPG II coding considerations for Control Fields are:

1. Related Control Fields must be in the same location of every record in the group or file, and

2. The related Control Fields must be the same type (numeric or alphanumeric), and

3. They must be the same length

For example, an examination of Figure 6-1 will show that the Control Fields are all located in the same columns (1–4), have the same length (4 characters), and are numeric.

Control Level Groups

A Control Level Group refers to data records that have the same information in the Control Field(s). The Control Level Groups in Figure 6-1 are the seven records for account number 1620, four records for 1130, three for 0360, and three for 0370.

How the records are arranged within the group depends on the processing logic. In this example, the Balance record (B in column 80) must be the first record of the group followed by either deposit or withdrawal records (D and W in column 80). Remember the arrangement of the records in the data file is critical to successful program execution and end results.

Control Level Breaks

A Control Level Break occurs when a change is sensed in the Control Field. For example, when the value in the account number field changes from 1620 to 1130, a Control Break occurs and the corresponding Control Level Indicator (L1 in this example) turns on. Subsequent calculations and/or output instructions may be conditioned accordingly. Because the sample program has only one Control Field, only the L1 indicator will turn on.

If the data file was sorted incorrectly and an account number 1130 record was placed as the second card in the 1620 group, a Control Break would occur after the first 1620 record was read. The 1130 record would be processed and a

Control Break would occur when the next 1620 record was read. This would, of course, result in an invalid calculation and/or output results.

The RPG II source program coding entries will be discussed in the following paragraphs for Control Level Indicator usage.

RPG II SOURCE PROGRAM CODING
FOR SAVINGS ACCOUNT APPLICATION

Figure 6-2 shows the RPG II source program for the Savings Account Application program using one Control Level Indicator (L1). Examination of the coding forms will reveal that File Description Specifications coding is not affected by Control Level coding and uses the standard entries previously discussed. However, Input, Calculations, and Output-Format coding forms do show that the L1 indicator is entered.

Input Specifications Coding

Examine the Input Specifications form in Figure 6-3 and notice the L1 Control Level Indicator is entered in the Control Level Field (columns 59 and 60). Depending on the logic of the application, any appropriate field may be assigned as the Control Level Field(s) in a program. For this application the account number field (ACTNO) is the logical field to assign as the· Control Field.

All Control Level Indicator assignments must begin with L1 and increase numerically as more Control Fields are needed in a program. For example, in the next sample program presented in this chapter, four Control Fields are used and are assigned L1, L2, L3, and L4 accordingly.

Further examination of the input form in Figure 6-3 indicates the OR relationship method, with related Field Relation Indicators, is used to define the input records and fields. This coding approach has nothing to do with Control Level Indicator coding or usage, but only represents the programmer's choice for input coding.

Notice the Control Field is defined as being located in columns 1–4 and is numeric. The respective values in the data cards must agree with this location and field type. Sequence checking was not possible for this application because the deposit and withdrawal cards appear in the file according to transaction date sequence. However, in all account groups the balance card must be first (Figure 6-1).

The L1 indicator entered in columns 59 and 60 will only turn on when the value in that field changes. When the L1 indicator turns on, any subsequent calculations and/or output may be conditioned by it.

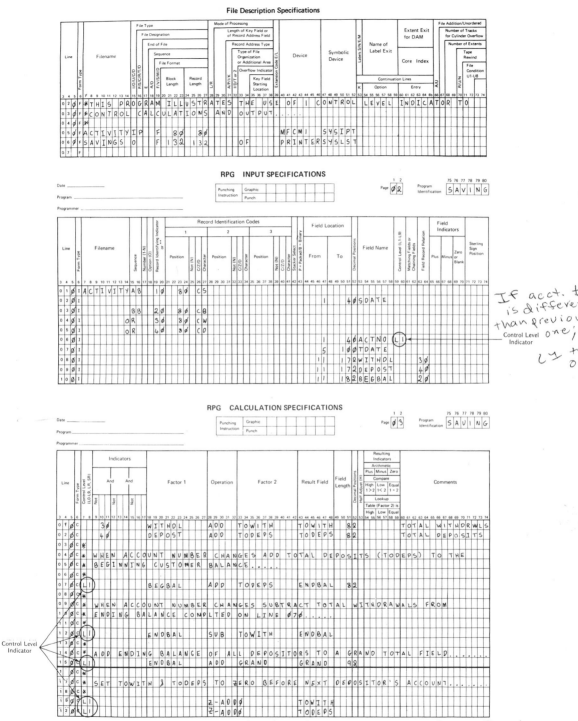

Fig. 6-2. Source program coding for savings account program using one Control Level Indicator (L1).

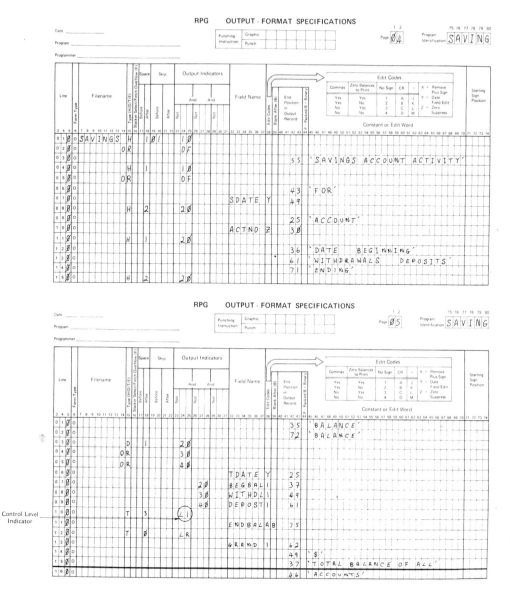

Fig. 6-2. Source program coding for savings account program using one Control Level Indicator (L1). (Concluded).

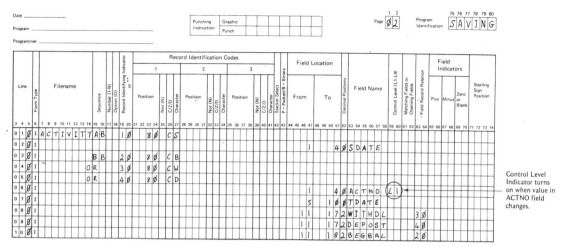

Fig. 6-3. Input Specifications form for savings account program using one Control Level Indicator (L1).

Calculation Specifications Coding

The Calculation Specifications form in Figure 6-4 shows new RPG II coding concepts. On line 03010 the amount in the withdrawal field (WITHDAL) is added to a total withdrawal field (TOWITH) to accumulate the total withdrawals for each depositor. Notice the coding line is conditioned by the appropriate Record Identifying Indicator (30) assigned to the record type on input. Line 03020 accumulates each deposit (DEPOST) into a total deposit field (TODEPS). This operation is also conditioned by the related indicator (40) and executes only when that record type is processed.

The coding on line 03070 is conditioned by the L1 Control Level Indicator which turns on when a change is sensed in the contents of the Control Field (ACTNO). Notice the L1 indicator is entered in the Control Field, columns 7 and 8, and not in any field included in columns 9–17. Any calculation line conditioned by an indicator in columns 7 and 8 informs the computer the operation is only to be executed at *Total Time.* If L1 had been entered in any field included in columns 9–17 the line would be executed at *Detail Time* which would be incorrect for this application. The calculation operation entered on this line adds the total accumulated deposits for the depositor (TODEPS) to the beginning balance (BEGBAL) to give a new field called ENDBAL.

The coding on line 03120 subtracts the total withdrawals (TOWITH) from ENDBAL to give a new amount for ENDBAL. The ending balance field (ENDBAL) represents the depositor's balance after the depositor's last record is

L1 lines are executed when value changes in ACTNO Control Field.

L1 must be entered in cols. 7 and 8 for Total Time.

Line	Indicators	Factor 1	Operation	Factor 2	Result Field	Field Length	Comments
010	30	WITHOL	ADD	TOWITH	TOWITH	8 2	TOTAL WITHDRWLS
020	40	DEPOST	ADD	TODEPS	TODEPS	8 2	TOTAL DEPOSITS
030	*	WHEN ACCOUNT NUMBER CHANGES ADD TOTAL DEPOSITS (TODEPS) TO THE					
040	*	BEGINNING CUSTOMER BALANCE					
060	L1	BEGBAL	ADD	TODEPS	ENDBAL	8 2	
080	*	WHEN ACCOUNT NUMBER CHANGES SUBTRACT TOTAL WITHDRAWALS FROM					
100	*	ENDING BALANCE COMPUTED ON LINE 070					
120	L1	ENDBAL	SUB	TOWITH	ENDBAL		
140	*	ADD ENDING BALANCE OF ALL DEPOSITORS TO A GRAND TOTAL FIELD					
150	L1	ENDBAL	ADD	GRAND	GRAND	9 2	
170	*	SET TOWITH & TODEPS TO ZERO BEFORE NEXT DEPOSITOR'S ACCOUNT					
190	L1		Z-ADD0		TOWITH		
200	L1		Z-ADD0		TODEPS		

Fig. 6-4. Calculation Specifications for savings account program using one Control Level Indicator (L1).

processed. If a depositor does not have any deposits and/or withdrawals for the period, these lines will still execute but contain zero values in TOWITH and TODEPS.

The coding on line 03150 adds each depositor's ending balance (ENDBAL) to a grand total amount for all depositors (GRAND). At Last Record time (LR) GRAND will contain the total balance amount of all depositors.

Lines 03190 and 03200 introduce a new coding operation used in this program application to initialize a field to zero before the next depositor's record group is processed. An explanation of the functions and characteristics of the Z-ADD (and Z-SUB) operations are presented below.

THE Z-ADD AND Z-SUB OPERATIONS

The Z-ADD operation is used in the sample program (lines 03190 and 03200) to initialize a field to zero before the next record group is processed. If initializing was not performed the amount from the previous depositor would be added to the new depositor's deposits and withdrawals.

There are many ways of initializing a field to zero (i.e., multiply by zero or subtract the field from itself); however, RPG II has convenient operations for initializing fields to any numeric value, not only zero. The functions and characteristics of the Z-ADD and Z-SUB operations are as follows:

1. The field name in the Result Field is set to zero, then
2. The contents of the field name or numeric literal are moved into the low-order position of the Result Field
3. Field names and literals must be numeric
4. Automatic decimal alignment is performed (MOVE operations do not do this)
5. Factor 1 is never used with this operation
6. The contents of Factor 2 are not lost

Figure 6-5 illustrates the coding for three Z-ADD operations and the values in Factor 2 and the Result Field before and after the operation is executed.

In Example 1 the ENDBAL field is set to zero. Because the field length is not entered it indicates the field was defined previously in the program. Variable fields, however, may be created by using the Z-ADD (or Z-SUB) operation like any other arithmetic operation.

The coding in example 2 first sets the RATE field to zero and then moves the numeric literal .0585 into the field's storage area. Remember decimal alignment is performed in this operation. If RATE, for example, had been defined as three long with three decimal positions instead of four and four, the low-order (five in this example) number would be truncated.

Example 3 illustrates the operation where the contents of the variable field entered in Factor 2 (PCT) are moved into the variable field in the Result Field after HOLD is set to zero. Notice the value contained in PCT before the Z-ADD is executed is included in both PCT and HOLD after the operation is performed.

Even though the Z-SUB operation is not used in this program, an explanation of its function is timely. The Z-SUB operation performs exactly the same functions as the Z-ADD except the sign of the variable field value or literal is reversed. For example, if the contents of Factor 2 were negative, the Result Field would be positive after the operation is executed. On the other hand, if the Factor 2 value was positive, the Result Field value would be negative. Consequently, the variable field value in the Result Field will always have a sign opposite the value contained in the variable field or numeric literal specified in Factor 2.

At first glance the reader may think the Z-ADD and Z-SUB operations are the same as the MOVE operations discussed in Chapter 5. They are, however, completely different in function and use. The MOVE operations *do*

Example 1:

Initializing a variable field to zero

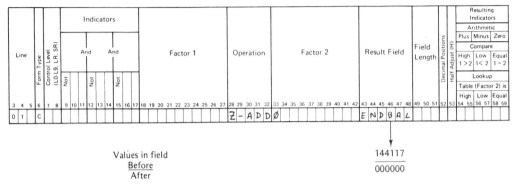

Values in field

Before	144117
After	000000

Example 2:

Initializing a variable field to zero and entering a numeric
literal into it.

RPG   CALCULATION SPECIFICATIONS

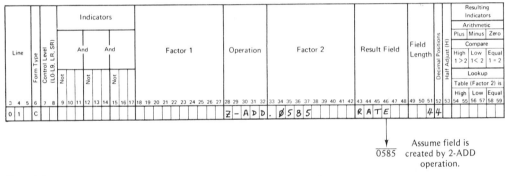

0585   Assume field is
created by 2-ADD
operation.

Example 3:

Initializing a variable field to zero and entering the values
contained in the variable field from Factor 2 into it.

RPG   CALCULATION SPECIFICATIONS

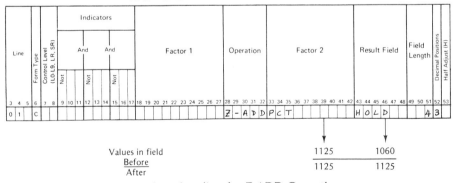

Values in field

Before	1125	1060
After	1125	1125

Fig. 6-5.   Examples of coding for Z-ADD Operation.

not initialize the Result Field to zero before the move and *do not* perform decimal alignment. On the other hand, the Z-ADD and Z-SUB operations *do not* allow for the movement of alphanumeric data.

OUTPUT-FORMAT SPECIFICATIONS CODING

Continuing with an explanation of the Savings Account Application program, the Output-Format Specifications form in Figure 6-6 shows that the L1 Control Level Indicator is used to condition a line of output. Examination of the figure will reveal that lines 04010 to 05090 follow coding procedures discussed previously. Line 05100, however, illustrates the use of a Control Level Indicator for conditioning a line of output.

Notice the line is a total line (T in column 15) which will be printed only when a change in the account number (ACTNO) field value is sensed. If the line was defined as a detail line (D in column 15) the line would print when the first record of every group was read and not the last. This would, at least for this example, give incorrect results.

Another new coding entry is introduced on line 05110. Notice the letter B is entered in column 39 on the Output-Format form. The B in this column sets a numeric output field to zero or an alphanumeric field to blanks after the contents of the field have been moved to an output storage area. Use of this entry provides a convenient method of clearing output fields before another record is processed which is especially useful for subtotal fields.

In the sample program, if the letter B was not entered in column 39 for the ENDBAL field on output, the balance of the previous depositor would remain in storage. In the extreme case where a depositor had no balance or withdrawal or deposit activity for the period, the ending balance (ENDBAL) of the previous depositor would be carried through calculations and printed on output. We will see in the next sample program where this entry is needed to prevent the incorrect accumulation of total fields.

A complete source program listing is illustrated in Figure 6-7 for the Savings Account Program using one Control Level Indicator (L1). The reader should examine the listing and identify the relationship of the Control Level Indicator (L1) usage from one coding form to the next. Notice the L1 lines in the Calculation and Output-Format forms are entered last. *Total Time* coding must follow any *Heading* and *Detail Time* coding as dictated by the RPG II compiler logic cycle. The heirarchy of H, D, T coding must be followed in RPG II source program coding to prevent terminal errors and cancellation of the program.

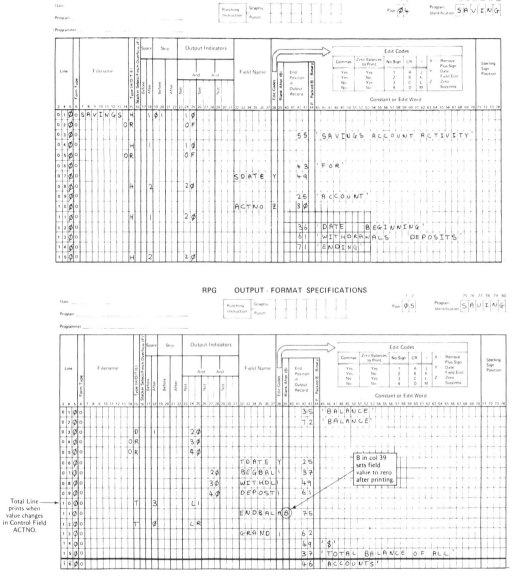

Fig. 6-6. Output-Format coding for savings account program using one Control Level Indicator (L1).

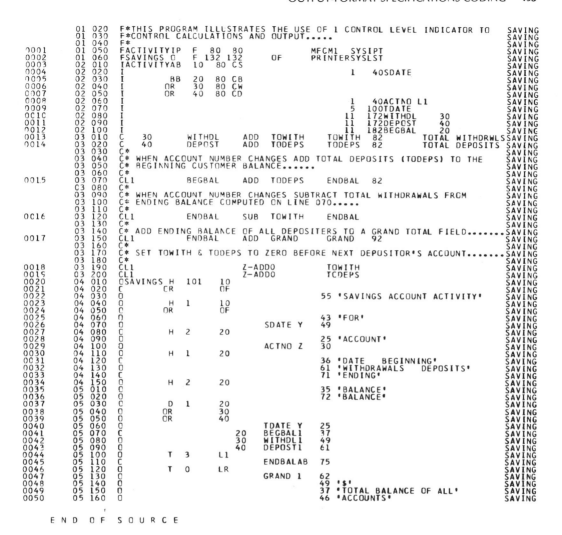

```
          01 020  F*THIS PROGRAM ILLUSTRATES THE USE OF 1 CONTROL LEVEL INDICATOR TO     SAVING
          01 030  F*CONTROL CALCULATIONS AND OUTPUT.....                                  SAVING
          01 040  F*                                                                      SAVING
  0001    01 050  FACTIVITYIP   F   80   80              MFCM1  SYSIPT                     SAVING
  0002    01 060  FSAVINGS O    F  132  132        OF    PRINTERSYSLST                     SAVING
  0003    02 010  IACTIVITYAB   10   80 CS                                                 SAVING
  0004    02 020  I                                      1    40SDATE                      SAVING
  0005    02 030  I           BB   20   80 CB                                              SAVING
  0006    02 040  I           OR   30   80 CW                                              SAVING
  0007    02 050  I           OR   40   80 CD                                              SAVING
  0008    02 060  I                                      1    40ACTNO L1                   SAVING
  0009    02 070  I                                      5   100TDATE                      SAVING
  0010    02 080  I                                     11   172WITHDL       30            SAVING
  0011    02 090  I                                     11   172DEPOST       40            SAVING
  0012    02 100  I                                     11   182BEGBAL       20            SAVING
  0013    03 010  C    30        WITHDL     ADD  TOWITH   TOWITH   82        TOTAL WITHDRWLSSAVING
  0014    03 020  C    40        DEPOST     ADD  TODEPS   TODEPS   82        TOTAL DEPOSITS SAVING
          03 030  C*                                                                      SAVING
          03 040  C* WHEN ACCOUNT NUMBER CHANGES ADD TOTAL DEPOSITS (TODEPS) TO THE       SAVING
          03 050  C* BEGINNING CUSTOMER BALANCE......                                     SAVING
          03 060  C*                                                                      SAVING
  0015    03 070  CL1           BEGBAL     ADD  TODEPS   ENDBAL   82                       SAVING
          03 080  C*                                                                      SAVING
          03 090  C* WHEN ACCOUNT NUMBER CHANGES SUBTRACT TOTAL WITHDRAWALS FROM          SAVING
          03 100  C* ENDING BALANCE COMPUTED ON LINE 070.....                             SAVING
          03 110  C*                                                                      SAVING
  0016    03 120  CL1           ENDBAL     SUB  TOWITH   ENDBAL                            SAVING
          03 130  C*                                                                      SAVING
          03 140  C* ADD ENDING BALANCE OF ALL DEPOSITERS TO A GRAND TOTAL FIELD.......SAVING
  0017    03 150  CL1           ENDBAL     ADD  GRAND    GRAND    92                       SAVING
          03 160  C*                                                                      SAVING
          03 170  C* SET TOWITH & TODEPS TO ZERO BEFORE NEXT DEPOSITOR'S ACCOUNT.......SAVING
          03 180  C*                                                                      SAVING
  0018    03 190  CL1                      Z-ADDO        TOWITH                            SAVING
  0019    03 200  CL1                      Z-ADDO        TODEPS                            SAVING
  0020    04 010  OSAVINGS H   101   10                                                   SAVING
  0021    04 020  O         CR         OF                                                 SAVING
  0022    04 030  O                                      55 'SAVINGS ACCOUNT ACTIVITY'    SAVING
  0023    04 040  O         H  1        10                                                SAVING
  0024    04 050  O         OR         OF                                                 SAVING
  0025    04 060  O                                      43 'FOR'                          SAVING
  0026    04 070  O                             SDATE Y  49                                SAVING
  0027    04 080  O         H  2        20                                                SAVING
  0028    04 090  O                                      25 'ACCOUNT'                      SAVING
  0029    04 100  O                             ACTNO Z  30                                SAVING
  0030    04 110  O         H  1        20                                                SAVING
  0031    04 120  O                                      36 'DATE     BEGINNING'           SAVING
  0032    04 130  O                                      61 'WITHDRAWALS    DEPOSITS'      SAVING
  0033    04 140  O                                      71 'ENDING'                       SAVING
  0034    04 150  O         H  2        20                                                SAVING
  0035    05 010  O                                      35 'BALANCE'                      SAVING
  0036    05 020  O                                      72 'BALANCE'                      SAVING
  0037    05 030  O         D  1        20                                                SAVING
  0038    05 040  O         OR         30                                                 SAVING
  0039    05 050  O         OR         40                                                 SAVING
  0040    05 060  O                             TDATE Y  25                                SAVING
  0041    05 070  O                        20   BEGBAL1  37                                SAVING
  0042    05 080  O                        30   WITHDL1  49                                SAVING
  0043    05 090  O                        40   DEPOST1  61                                SAVING
  0044    05 100  O         T  3       L1   ENDBALAB  75                                   SAVING
  0045    05 110  O                             ENDBALAB  75                               SAVING
  0046    05 120  O         T  0       LR                                                 SAVING
  0047    05 130  O                             GRAND 1  62                                SAVING
  0048    05 140  O                                      49 '$'                            SAVING
  0049    05 150  O                                      37 'TOTAL BALANCE OF ALL'         SAVING
  0050    05 160  O                                      46 'ACCOUNTS'                     SAVING

    END  OF  SOURCE
```

Fig. 6-7. Source program listing for savings account program using one Control Level Indicator (L1).

The Printer Spacing Chart and printed report for the sample program are shown in Figure 6-8. Notice that comments are made on the report indicating when the respective line is printed.

This sample program has illustrated the use of one Control Level Indicator (L1) to condition calculations and output. The program presented in the following paragraphs uses four Control Level Indicators to obtain the required printed report.

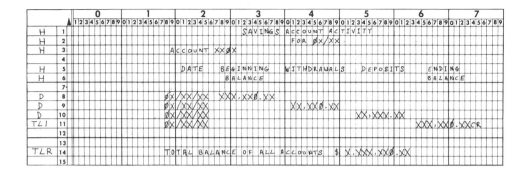

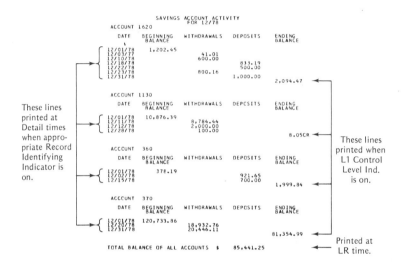

Fig. 6-8.   Printer Spacing Chart and printed report for savings account program using one Control Level Indicator (L1).

MULTIPLE CONTROL LEVEL INDICATOR (L1–L4) APPLICATION PROGRAM

Figure 6-9 illustrates the printed detail report for the sample program presented in the following paragraphs which uses four Control Level Indicators. Each subtotal is identified with the appropriate Control Level Indicator used in the source program to condition the print line. Notice that Salesman Sales is an L1 total; Department Sales, an L2 total; Store Sales, an L3 total; and State Sales, an L4 total.

Control Level Indicators (L1–L9) are assigned to variable input Control Fields in ascending order. The lowest subtotal of a group is always assigned L1

```
DATE   SALESMAN DEPT STORE STATE  WEEKLY SALES     TOTALS AS OF  3/21/78
1/02/79  0111    03   145    7      $256.12
1/09/79  0111    03   145    7      $441.70
1/16/79  0111    03   145    7      $384.20
1/23/79  0111    03   145    7      $302.44

                                          $1,384.46        SALESMAN SALES ◄——— L1 total
1/02/79  0112    03   145    7      $189.76
1/09/79  0112    03   145    7      $500.38
1/16/79  0112    03   145    7      $198.37
1/23/79  C112    03   145    7      $246.18

                                          $1,134.69        SALESMAN SALES ◄——— L1 total
                                          $2,519.15        DEPARTMENT SALES ◄—— L2 total
1/02/79  0113    05   145    7      $612.55
1/09/79  0113    05   145    7      $800.00
1/16/79  0113    05   145    7      $999.19
1/23/79  0113    05   145    7      $737.47

                                          $3,149.21        SALESMAN SALES ◄——— L1 total
                                          $3,149.21        DEPARTMENT SALES ◄—— L2 total
                                          $5,668.36        STORE SALES ◄——————— L3 total
1/02/79  2114    12   200    7      $645.33
1/09/79  2114    12   200    7      $301.76
1/16/79  2114    12   200    7      $888.88
1/23/79  2114    12   200    7      $532.86

                                          $2,368.83        SALESMAN SALES ◄——— L1 total
                                          $2,368.83        DEPARTMENT SALES ◄—— L2 total
                                          $2,368.83        STORE SALES ◄——————— L3 total
                                          $8,037.19        STATE SALES ◄———————— L4 total
1/02/79  2218    14   211    8      $184.79
1/09/79  2218    14   211    8      $733.74
1/16/79  2218    14   211    8      $472.52
1/23/79  2218    14   211    8      $900.09

                                          $2,291.14        SALESMAN SALES ◄——— L1 total
                                          $2,291.14        DEPARTMENT SALES ◄—— L2 total
                                          $2,291.14        STORE SALES ◄——————— L3 total
                                          $2,291.14        STATE SALES ◄———————— L4 total
                                         $10,328.33        UNITED STATES SALES ◄ LR total
```

Fig. 6-9. Printed detail sales report showing Control Level totals by salesman, department, store, state and United States.

and the others L2, L3, etc., as needed. In the example shown here the Salesman Total is lowest, with Department next, and so forth. Control Level Indicator assignments to Control Fields must begin with L1 and cannot be randomly selected like Record Identifying Indicators.

When a higher Control Level Indicator turns on because of a change in the value of a Control Field, all the lower Control Level Indicators turn on at the same time. For example, when L4 turns on because of a change in the value of the State Number input Control Field, L3, L2, and L1 will also turn on and execute any calculations and/or output conditioned by those indicators. The United States Total amount (Figure 6-9) is printed at LR time.

Figure 6-10 shows the data file arrangement for the four Control Level sample program. The Control Fields are identified in the first record group as 111 for Salesman Number; 3, Department Number; 145, Store Number; and 7, the State Number. A Control Group includes only those records which have the same values in the Control Fields. Even though Department, Store, and State remained the same when the Salesman Number changed from 111 to 112, a Control Break was sensed because a different Control Group was identified by the change in the value in the Control Field.

Refer to Figure 6-10 and notice when Salesman Number and Department changed, the L1 and L2 Control Breaks took place. When Salesman, Department, and Store Numbers changed, L1, L2, and L3 Control Level Breaks occurred. Finally, when a change is sensed in all the values stored in

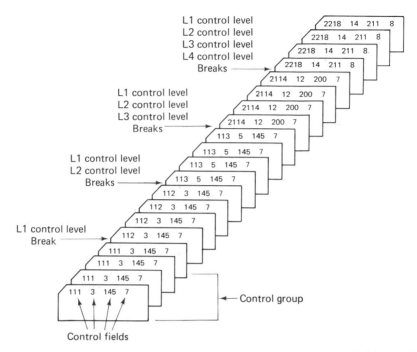

Fig. 6-10. Sample program data file showing control levels, fields, breaks, and groups for four Control Breaks.

Salesman, Department, Store, and State, all four Control Level Breaks are executed. The reader should be able to appreciate that the *data file must be sorted* in the required order before processing by the program. If records are placed out of order, incorrect Control Breaks would occur resulting in invalid output.

RPG II SOURCE CODING FOR SAMPLE PROGRAM USING FOUR CONTROL LEVEL INDICATORS

Because the File Description Specifications coding form is not affected by Control Level Indicator usage, it is not shown for this sample program. Input, Calculations, and Output-Format Specifications are used for Control Level Indicators and will be discussed in the following paragraphs.

Input Specifications Coding

Figure 6-11 shows the Control Level Indicators entered in columns 59 and 60 of the input form. Notice the L1 indicator is assigned to the SALMAN field, L2 to DEPTS, L3 to STOR, and L4 to STAT. Obviously, SALMAN is the lowest

REPORT PROGRAM GENERATOR   INPUT SPECIFICATIONS

IBM System 360

Date: 1/12/73
Program: LEVEL NUMBERS
Programmer: ANYBODY

Page: 0 2
Program identification: [blank]

Punching instruction — Graphic: 0 / I N N S   Punch: N A N A N A

Line	Form type	Filename	Sequence	Number (1-N)	Option (O)	Resulting indicator	Record identification codes 1 — Position	Not (N)	C/Z/D	Character	2 — Position	Not (N)	C/Z/D	Character	3 — Position	Not (N)	C/Z/D	Character	Stacker select	Packed (P)	Field location From	To	Field name	Control level (L1-L9)	Matching fields or chaining fields	Field record relation	Plus	Minus	Zero or blank	Sterling sign position
01	I	SALEREPTAR				06																								
02	I																				1	6	08DATES							
03	I																				11	14	48SALMAN	L1						
04	I																				21	22	228DEPTS	L2						
05	I																				31	33	338STOR	L3						
06	I																				41	41	418STAT	L4						
07	I																				51	56	562WEKSAL	L						

Fig. 6-11. Input-Specifications coding for four Control Levels.

199

Control Field and STAT, the highest. The Control Fields are all numeric ($\emptyset$ in column 52), but could have been alphanumeric without error. However, if one Control Field of a group is defined as numeric the others must be defined the same. Some cannot be numeric and others alphanumeric; they all must be the same type. When a change in the value of the Control Field is sensed the appropriate Control Level Indicator(s) will turn on.

Calculation Specifications Coding

Figure 6-12 illustrates the Control Level Indicator coding in the Calculation Specifications form for the four Control Break program. The coding on line 03010 adds the value in the input field WEKSAL to a total field SALSUM for every data record processed. Notice the line is not conditioned by any indicator. It could have been conditioned by the 06 Record Identifying Indicator; however, because there is only one record type in the file it is not necessary.

When a change in the contents of the Salesman Number field (SAL-MAN) is sensed on input, the L1 Control Level Indicator turns on. The coding on line 03020 (Figure 6-12) is executed and the value in SALSUM is added to a Department Total field (DEPSUM). It is important that the Control Level Indicator (L1) be entered in columns 7 and 8 of the Control Field of the Calculation Specifications form. This field instructs the computer to execute the instruction at *Total Time*. If the L1 indicator was entered in one of the fields in columns 9–17, the instruction would be executed at *Detail Time* which would be incorrect for this application.

The L2 Control Break occurs when a change is sensed in the Department Number input field DEPTS. A re-examination of Figure 6-12 shows that line 03030 is conditioned by L2 and adds DEPSUM to a Store Total field STOSUM. Remember, when L2 turns on because of a change in Department Number, L1 will be on at the same time. Consequently, line 03020 will be executed along with the instructions on line 03030.

An L3 Control Break occurs when a change is sensed in the STOR (Store Number) field. Reference to columns 6–12 will indicate that Store Sum (STOSUM) is added to STASUM (State Sum) when this Control Break takes place. When L3 turns on, L2 and L1 will be on also which will cause lines 03020 and 03030 to execute for the same cycle.

The same identical sequence of instructions is followed when an L4 Control Break is sensed. STASUM (State Sum) is added to TOTSUM (United States Total), a total field for all states. Reference to the Printed Report in Figure 6-9 will show the printed effect of each Control Level Break and corresponding total amount. The $10,328.33 (United States Total) represents the total amount of sales for all salesmen and is printed only at LR time.

REPORT PROGRAM GENERATOR   CALCULATION SPECIFICATIONS
IBM System 360

Date: 1/12/73
Program: LEVEL NUMBERS
Programmer: ANYBODY

Punching instruction — Graphic: ∅ O / I Z 2 S — Punch: N A N A N A

Page: 1 2 ∅ 3

Program identification: 75 76 77 78 79 80

Line	Form type	Control level (L0-L9, LR)	Indicators	Factor 1	Operation	Factor 2	Result field	Field length	Decimal positions	Comments
0 1	C			WEKSAL	ADD	SALSUM	SALSUM	6	2	
0 2	C	L1		SALSUM	ADD	DEPSUM	DEPSUM	7	2	
0 3	C	L2		DEPSUM	ADD	STOSUM	STOSUM	8	2	
0 4	C	L3		STOSUM	ADD	STASUM	STASUM	9	2	
0 5	C	L4		STASUM	ADD	TOTSUM	TOTSUM	11	2	

Fig. 6-12. Calculation Specifications coding for sample program using four Control Level Indicators.

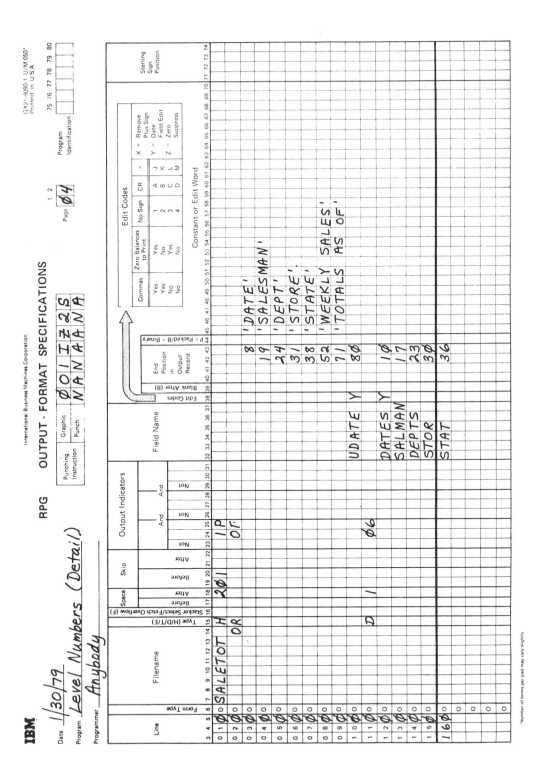

Fig. 6-13. Output-Format coding for program using four Control Level Indicators (L1–L4). (continued on next page)

202

Date: 1/30/79
Program: Level Numbers (Detail)
Programmer: Anybody

Page: 05

Program Identification: 0 1 1 2 2 8 / N A N A N A

Edit Codes

		Zero Balances to Print	No Sign	CR	-
Commas	Yes	Yes	1	A	J
	Yes	No	2	B	K
	No	Yes	3	C	L
	No	No	4	D	M

X = Remove Plus Sign
Y = Date Field Edit
Z = Zero Suppress

P = Packed/B = Binary

Line	Form Type	Type (H/D/T/E)	Space After	Output Indicators	Field Name	Edit Codes	Blank After (B)	End Position in Output Record	Constant or Edit Word
01	O	T	22	L1	WEKSAL2	2		50	'$'
02	O				SALSUM2B			72	
03	O							102	'SALESMAN SALES'
04	O	T	2	L2				72	'$'
05	O				DEPSUM2B			104	
06	O								'DEPARTMENT SALES'
07	O	T	2	L3				72	'$'
08	O				STOSUM2B			99	
09	O								'STORE SALES'
10	O	T	2	L4				72	'$'
11	O				STASUM2B			99	
12	O								'STATE SALES'
13	O	T	8	LR				72	'$'
14	O				TOTSUM2			107	
15	O								'UNITED STATES SALES'
16	O								

*Number of forms per pad may vary slightly

Fig. 6-13. (concluded)

203

Output-Format Specifications Coding

Examination of the Output-Format forms in Figure 6-13 shows that lines 04010 to 04090 are printed at *Heading Time* when the First Page Indicator is on (1P or page overflow [OF]. The Detail Line, conditioned by the 06 Record Identifying Indicator assigned to the records on input, will be printed when the information included in fields for every data record is processed (Figure 6-15). Also, notice lines 05010 to 05150 are Total Lines conditioned by the related Control Level Indicator.

When a change is sensed in the Salesman Number (SALMAN) input field, L1 will turn on and lines 05010 to 05030 will execute. If a change is sensed in the Department Number field (DEPTS), both L2 and L1 will turn on causing those output lines conditioned by the indicators to print. In addition,

```
0001    01 010   FSALEREPTIPF F   80   80              MFCM1  SYSIPT
0002    01 020   FSALETOTSO    F  132  132      OF      PRINTERSYSLST
0003    02 010   ISALEREPTAP   06
0004    02 020   I                                            1    60DATES
0005    02 030   I                                           L1   140SALMANL1
0006    02 040   I                                           21   220DEPTS L2
0007    02 050   I                                           31   330STOR  L3
0008    02 060   I                                           41   410STAT  L4
0009    02 070   I                                           51   562WEKSAL
0010    03 010   C           WEKSAL      ADD   SALSUM    SALSUM   62
0011    03 020   CL1         SALSUM      ADD   DEPSUM    DEPSUM   72
0012    03 030   CL2         DEPSUM      ADD   STOSUM    STOSUM   82
0013    03 040   CL3         STOSUM      ADD   STASUM    STASUM   92
0014    03 050   CL4         STASUM      ADD   TOTSUM    TOTSUM  112
0015    04 010   OSALFTOTSH  201     1P
0016    04 020   O       OR          OF
0017    04 030   O                                          8  'DATE'
0018    04 040   O                                         19  'SALESMAN'
0019    04 050   O                                         24  'DEPT'
0020    04 060   O                                         31  'STORE'
0021    04 070   O                                         38  'STATE'
0022    04 080   O                                         52  'WEEKLY  SALES'
0023    04 090   O                                         71  'TOTALS  AS  OF'
0024    04 100   O                              UDATE Y    80
0025    04 110   O       D   1       06
0026    04 120   O                              DATES Y    10
0027    04 130   O                              SALMAN     17
0028    04 140   O                              DEPTS      23
0029    04 150   O                              STOR       30
0030    04 160   O                              STAT       36
0031    05 010   O                              WEKSAL2    50  '$'
0032    05 020   O       T   22      L1
0033    05 030   O                              SALSUM2B   72  '$'
0034    05 040   O                                        102  'SALESMAN SALES'
0035    05 050   O       T   2       L2
0036    05 060   O                              DEPSUM2B   72  '$'
0037    05 070   O                                        104  'DEPARTMENT SALES'
0038    05 080   O       T   2       L3
0039    05 090   O                              STOSUM2B   72  '$'
0040    05 100   O                                         99  'STORE SALES'
0041    05 110   O       T   2       L4
0042    05 120   O                              STASUM2B   72  '$'
0043    05 130   O                                         99  'STATE SALES'
0044    05 140   O       T   2       LR
0045    05 150   O                              TOTSUM2    72  '$'
0046    05 160   O                                        107  'UNITED STATES SALES'
```

E N D   O F   S O U R C E

Fig. 6-14. RPG II source program listing for the sales detail report using four Control Level Indicators.

when L3 turns on, L2 and L1 will also be on which will execute output lines conditioned by L3, L2, and L1 Control Level Indicators. Finally, when L4 turns on because of a change in the value contained in the STAT field, L3, L2, and L1 will be on and all four total lines will be printed. Furthermore, when end of file is sensed and LR turns on, all the lower Control Level Indicators will be on and the respective total printed (see last group of total in Figure 6-15).

Notice the total fields (SALSUM, DEPSUM, STOSUM, and STASUM) are set to zero after printing by the letter B in column 39. If the letter was not entered in the Blank After field (column 39) each group total would include the totals for the previous group. The only total amounts that would be correct would be for the first Control Group.

The source program listing for the sample program using four Control Level Indicators is detailed in Figure 6-14. Examine the listing and study the interrelationship of the L1–L4 indicators to each coding form.

Figure 6-15 shows the Printer Spacing Chart and Printed Report for the program. The report is called *Detail Report* because it includes all the information for each Control Field on every line. Another report classification will be discussed in the following paragraphs.

DETAIL AND GROUP REPORTS

Even though there are many different formats of printed reports, they may be classified into two major categories: Detail Printed Reports and Group Printed Reports.

The report that was illustrated in Figure 6-15 is called a Detail Report because it prints the information for every record processed. However, because of individual preferences, report requirements, or readability, a report may need less detailed information. Figure 6-16 depicts a Group Report containing the same information as Figure 6-15 but with less detail.

The RPG II coding to affect this change is slightly different than that required for a Detail Report. All the coding for the File Description, Input, and Calculation Specifications is identical for both Detail and Group Reports. However, minor changes are needed on the Output-Format form to change a Detail Report to Group.

Examine Figure 6-17 and notice on lines 04120 to 04150 the respective Control Level Indicator is entered in columns 24 and 25 on the same line as the Control Field. Any of the other Output Indicator columns could have been used without error.

When a record is processed, the DATES and WEKSAL field values will be printed for every record, but SALMAN, DEPTS, STOR, and STAT will print only when the designated Control Level Indicator(s) is on. Refer back to

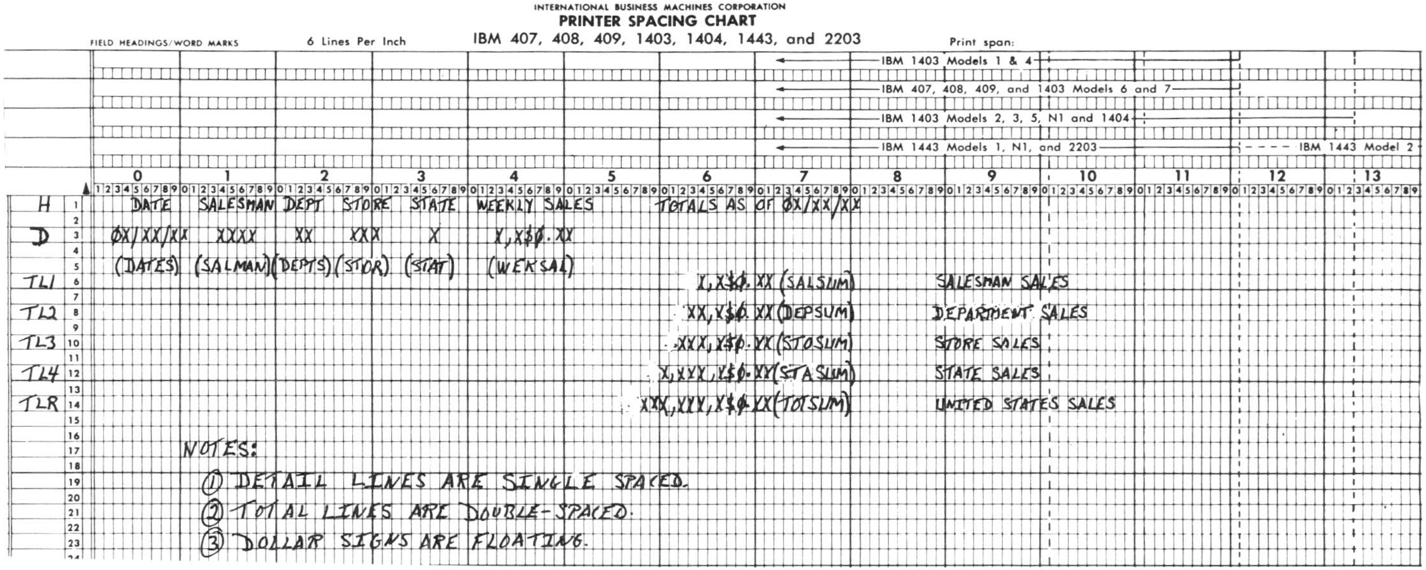

Fig. 6-15. Printed Spacing Chart for sample program using four Control Level Indicators (L1–L4). (continued on next page)

Printed Report:

DATE	SALESMAN	DEPT	STORE	STATE	WEEKLY SALES	TOTALS AS OF 3/21/78	
1/02/79	0111	03	145	7	$256.12		
1/09/79	0111	03	145	7	$441.70		
1/16/79	0111	03	145	7	$384.20		
1/23/79	0111	03	145	7	$302.44		
						$1,384.46	SALESMAN SALES
1/02/79	0112	03	145	7	$189.76		
1/09/79	0112	03	145	7	$500.38		
1/16/79	0112	03	145	7	$198.37		
1/23/79	0112	03	145	7	$246.18		
						$1,134.69	SALESMAN SALES
						$2,519.15	DEPARTMENT SALES
1/02/79	0113	05	145	7	$612.55		
1/09/79	0113	05	145	7	$800.00		
1/16/79	0113	05	145	7	$999.19		
1/23/79	0113	05	145	7	$737.47		
						$3,149.21	SALESMAN SALES
						$3,149.21	DEPARTMENT SALES
						$5,668.36	STORE SALES
1/02/79	2114	12	200	7	$645.33		
1/09/79	2114	12	2000	7	$303.76		
1/16/79	2114	12	2000	7	$888.88		
1/23/79	2114	12	200	7	$532.86		
						$2,368.83	SALESMAN SALES
						$2,368.83	DEPARTMENT SALES
						$2,363.83	STORE SALES
						$8,037.19	STATE SALES
1/02/79	2218	14	211	8	$184.79		
1/09/79	2218	14	211	8	$733.74		
1/16/79	2218	14	211	8	$472.52		
1/23/79	2218	14	211	8	$900.09		
						$2,291.14	SALESMAN SALES
						$2,291.14	DEPARTMENT SALES
						$2,291.14	STORE SALES
						$2,291.14	STATE SALES
						$10,328.33	UNITED STATES SALES

Fig. 6-15. (Concluded)

207

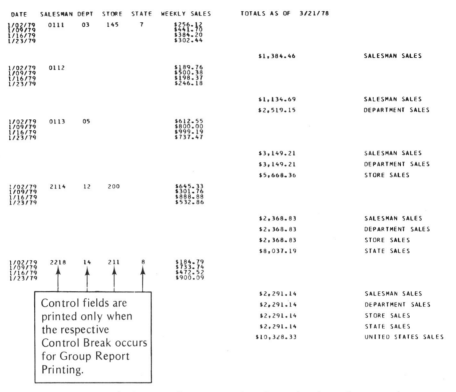

Control fields are printed only when the respective Control Break occurs for Group Report Printing.

Fig. 6-16. Printed *Group* sales report showing sales by salesman, department, store, state, and United States.

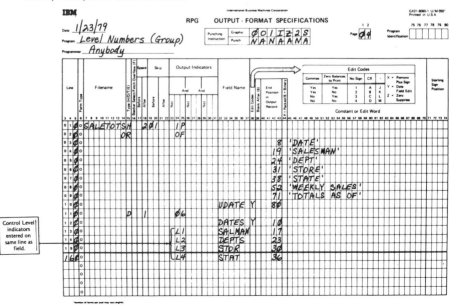

Fig. 6-17. Output-Format Specifications coding for Group Report.

the printed group report in Figure 6-15 and notice the Control Field numbers are only printed when the Control Break(s) occurs, and not for every record.

The source program listing for the Group Report is shown in Figure 6-18. Again notice the only additional entries appear in the output coding lines 04130 to 04160.

Reports may be condensed further by printing only the Control Group Totals when the Control Break occurs and there are no Detail Lines. The type of report frequently depends on the user's requirements.

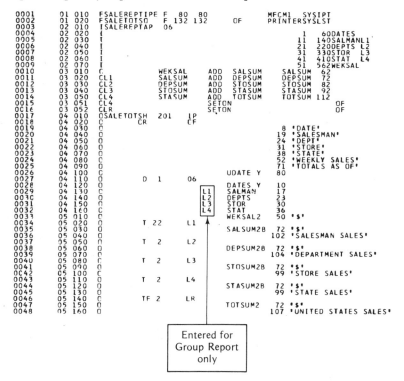

Fig. 6-18. RPG II source program listing for group sales report using control level indicators.

Additional Control for Overflow Printing

Refer back to Figure 6-18 and examine the source program for page overflow coding. Notice the entries follow normal RPG II coding for overflow which provides for the printing of headings on the top of every page in a report. Regardless of the print line in the report, page overflow will automatically occur when channel 12 is sensed. The report generated by the program in Figure 6-18 is repeated again in the following figure (Figure 6-19) for convenience.

DATE	SALESMAN	DEPT	STORE	STATE	WEEKLY SALES		TOTALS AS OF 3/21/78
1/02/79	0111	03	145	7	$256.12		
1/09/79					$441.70		
1/16/79					$384.20		
1/23/79					$302.44		
						$1,384.46	SALESMAN SALES
1/02/79	0112				$189.76		
1/09/79					$500.38		
1/16/79					$198.37		
1/23/79					$246.18		
						$1,134.69	SALESMAN SALES
						$2,519.15	DEPARTMENT SALES
1/02/79	0113	05			$612.55		
1/09/79					$800.00		
1/16/79					$999.19		
1/23/79					$737.47		
						$3,149.21	SALESMAN SALES
						$3,149.21	DEPARTMENT SALES
						$5,668.36	STORE SALES
1/02/79	2114	12	200		$645.33		
1/09/79					$301.76		
1/16/79					$888.88		
1/23/79					$532.86		
						$2,368.83	SALESMAN SALES
						$2,368.83	DEPARTMENT SALES
						$2,368.83	STORE SALES
						$8,037.19	STATE SALES
1/02/79	2218	14	211	8	$184.79		
1/09/79					$733.74		
1/16/79					$472.52		
1/23/79					$900.09		
						$2,291.14	SALESMAN SALES
						$2,291.14	DEPARTMENT SALES
						$2,291.14	STORE SALES
						$2,291.14	STATE SALES
						$10,328.33	UNITED STATES SALES

Fig. 6-19. Group Report in which all data is printed on one page.

Examination of the report in Figure 6-19 shows that all the information is printed on one page. Assume, however, the user wants to have each state's sales information on a separate page(s) and the UNITED STATES SALES total on a separate page with headings. Figure 6-20 illustrates the required output. The way the program is written in Figure 6-18, each state's sales information would be printed on a separate page only if channel 12 (overflow channel) was sensed at the same time as a change in the State field took place and the L4 control level indicator turned on. The probability of these two things taking place at the same time would be unlikely.

Two additional features of RPG II provide the needed control of page overflow to obtain the required results. First, the SETON and SETOF operations will be introduced and then used to modify the application program in Figure 6-18 to allow for the printing of each state's information on a separate page. Second, the Fetch Overflow feature will be discussed which provides for the printing of headings and the UNITED STATES TOTAL on a separate page.

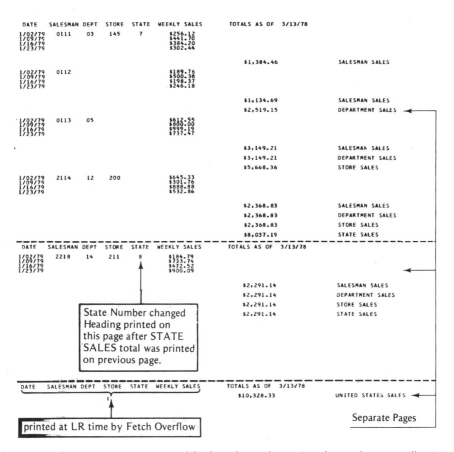

Fig. 6-20. Group Report modified so that information for each state will print on a separate page and Last Record Totals with required headings will print on a separate page.

SETON AND SETOF OPERATIONS

Record Identifying Indicators that are turned on by an input record, Resulting Indicators that may be turned on by the result of an arithmetic operation or Compare statement, and Level Indicators that may be turned on by a change in a control field have all been discussed in previous chapters. The previously discussed indicator types are the ones most commonly used in RPG source programs. However, program logic may require that an indicator or indicators be systematically turned on or off to provide a needed result in a program. For example, a special indicator may have to be turned on or off to condition a calculation and/or output instruction(s).

Figure 6-21 illustrates unrelated lines of coding showing the method of entering the SETON and SETOF operations in the Calculation Specifications. Notice that the operations are left-justified in the Operation field and that Factor 1, Factor 2, and the Result fields are not used. A maximum of three indicators may be turned on or off for each individual operation and more than one SETON or SETOF may be used in a program.

The following features must be considered when using the SETON and SETOF operations:

1. If the LR indicator is turned on during total calculations by a SETON operation, processing is terminated after the output of the total lines.

2. If the OV or OF indicator is changed by a SETON or SETOF operation during total or detail calculations, the RPG object program resets the indicator at the end of the associated total, detail, or exception output. Therefore, overflow printing will not be affected.

3. The indicators H1–H9, L1–L9, and all Record Identifying Indicators defined in columns 19 and 20 of the Input Specifications form can be turned on by the SETON operation. However, they will all be turned off by the RPG object program following detail output.

4. Setting indicators L1–L9 or LR on or off will not automatically set the lower-level indicators on or off.

When using the SETON or SETOF operations it must be remembered that all of the RPG indicators except LØ, 1P, and MR may be turned on or off in a program.

Because the SETON and SETOF operations are introduced in this chapter does not infer that they are only used with Control Level Indicators. The operations may be used at any time in calculations when the logic of the program requires their usage. For example, the SETOF operation (not used in this application) should be used to turn off any Resulting Indicators assigned in a program. Resulting Indicators that test the result of a calculation or COMP operation (Chapter 7) may remain on when the next record is processed, which could result in incorrect or unwanted output.

Examine the source program listing in Figure 6-22 and locate line 03051 in the calculation form. The line is conditioned by the L4 Control Level Indicator which turns on when a change in the value of the STAT field is detected. Because the modified report requires (Figure 6-20) that each state's information be printed on separate pages, the overflow indicator (OF) is turned on at L4 time by the SETON operation. All of the total information (Salesman, Department, Store, and State) related to the previous state will be printed; then page overflow will occur and the overflow headings will be printed followed by Detail and Total lines for the next state group. Note the Headings are printed on the next page *after* the totals are printed, *not before*.

Fig. 6-21. Examples of SETOF and SETON operations coding.

Line	Form type	Control level (L0-L9, LR)	Indicators Not	And	Not	And	Not	Factor 1	Operation	Factor 2	Result field	Field length	Decimal positions	Half adjust (H)	Resulting indicators — Compare High 1>2 / Plus	Low 1<2 / Minus	Equal 1=2 / Zero or blank	Comments
01	C			Ø1					SETON						40			
02	C								SETON						9Ø	67	Ø	
03	C								SETOF							21		
04	C			11					SETOF						84	12	99	
05	C																	

213

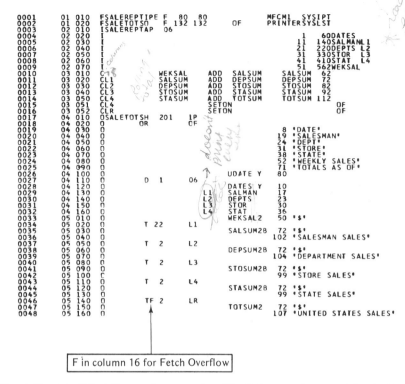

```
0001   01 010  FSALEREPTIPE F  80  80             MFCM1 SYSIPT
0002   01 020  FSALETOTSO   F 132 132      OF     PRINTERSYSLST
0003   02 010  ISALEREPTAP     06
0004   02 020  I                                       1   60DATES
0005   02 030  I                                      11  140SALMANL1
0006   02 040  I                                      21  220DEPTS L2
0007   02 050  I                                      31  330STOR  L3
0008   02 060  I                                      41  410STAT  L4
0009   02 070  I                                      51  562WEKSAL
0010   03 010  C       WEKSAL      ADD  SALSUM    SALSUM    62
0011   03 020  CL1     SALSUM      ADD  DEPSUM    DEPSUM    72
0012   03 030  CL2     DEPSUM      ADD  STOSUM    STOSUM    82
0013   03 040  CL3     STOSUM      ADD  STASUM    STASUM    92
0014   03 050  CL4     STASUM      ADD  TOTSUM    TOTSUM   112
0015   03 051  CL4                      SETON               OF
0016   03 052  CLR                      SETON               OF
0017   04 010  OSALETOTSH     201    1P
0018   04 020  O        OR           OF
0019   04 030  O                                       8  'DATE'
0020   04 040  O                                      19  'SALESMAN'
0021   04 050  O                                      24  'DEPT'
0022   04 060  O                                      31  'STORE'
0023   04 070  O                                      38  'STATE'
0024   04 080  O                                      52  'WEEKLY SALES'
0025   04 090  O                                      71  'TOTALS AS OF'
0026   04 100  O      D  1     06       UDATE Y      80
0027   04 110  O                        DATES Y      10
0028   04 120  O                     L1 SALMAN       17
0029   04 130  O                     L2 DEPTS        23
0030   04 140  O                     L3 STOR         30
0031   04 150  O                     L4 STAT         36
0032   04 160  O                        WEKSAL2      50
0033   05 010  O                        SALSUM2B     72  '$'
0034   05 020  O      T 22    L1                    102  'SALESMAN SALES'
0035   05 030  O
0036   05 040  O                        DEPSUM2B     72  '$'
0037   05 050  O      T  2    L2                    104  'DEPARTMENT SALES'
0038   05 060  O
0039   05 070  O                        STOSUM2B     72  '$'
0040   05 080  O      T  2    L3                     99  'STORE SALES'
0041   05 090  O
0042   05 100  O                        STASUM2B     72  '$'
0043   05 110  O      T  2    L4                     99  'STATE SALES'
0044   05 120  O
0045   05 130  O                        TOTSUM2      72  '$'
0046   05 140  O      TF 2    LR                    107  'UNITED STATES SALES'
0047   05 150  O
0048   05 160  O
```

F in column 16 for Fetch Overflow

Fig. 6-22. Modified Group Report using SET ON operations and Fetch Overflow to control page overflow printing.

The printing of the UNITED STATES SALES total at LR time requires that the headings be printed on the following page *before* the Last Record total is printed. In order to accomplish this sequence of output, the *Fetch Overflow* feature must be used.

Fetch Overflow

RPG II compiler logic instructs program control to execute any total time instructions before page overflow occurs. Consequently, for the report in Figure 6-20 it would not be possible to print the overflow headings before totals on a separate page. The UNITED STATES SALES total could be printed alone on a separate page by entering the top of page channel (01) in the Before field, columns 19 and 20. However, this would not provide for the required headings that precede the printing of the final total (Figure 6-20).

The *Fetch Overflow* feature instructs program control to "fetch" any heading, detail, or total lines conditioned by an overflow indicator and print them on the next page *before* the total. The coding to accomplish the desired result is entered on line 03052 of calculations and line 05140 of the output sections of the source program in Figure 6-22.

Refer to line 03052 of calculations and notice the OF indicator is turned on by the SETON operation at LR time when the end-of-file record (/*) is processed at the end of the data file. RPG II program control automatically turns on the overflow indicator when channel 12 is sensed. However, if Last Record Time (LR) occurs before the line assigned to channel 12 is reached, the overflow indicator would not turn on and overflow printing would not execute at the proper time. Consequently, the coding on line 03052 of calculations is necessary to turn on the overflow indicator when LR is on regardless of the line of output.

Supplemental to the Fetch Overflow coding for this application is the letter F entered in column 16 on line 05140 of output. The F entry fetches the overflow indicator turned on in calculations and executes any output lines conditioned by overflow (line 04020) to print on the following page *before* the Last Record total UNITED STATES SALES is printed.

The Fetch Overflow feature will be discussed again in Chapter 8 when Exception Time output is presented.

RPG II LOGIC

RPG II has a built-in logic cycle that controls the sequence of processing for all programs written in this language. Every data record processed follows the same sequential flow of steps with some alternative branches based on the result of a decision. Figure 6-23 depicts the logical steps followed in every RPG II program. Notice the steps in the flowchart are referenced with numbers 1 to 25 for the purpose of explanation. The sequence of RPG II processing logic will be followed step by step through the flowchart.

Step 1:   Before a data record is read and any detail output is performed, all heading output will occur.

Steps 2 and 3: The computer will test for carriage overflow which controls the advancing to the top of a new page by sensing a punch in the 12 channel of the carriage control tape (see Chapter 2). If channel 12 is sensed, page overflow will occur; however, provision for the proper coding must have been made in the File Description and Output-Format Specifications coding sheets.

Step 4:   If carriage overflow is not sensed by the computer, the OF indicator will automatically be turned off.

Step 5:   Testing for a halt condition is made at this point in the cycle. The programmer may write provisions into the program for error conditions that will cause processing to halt if an error

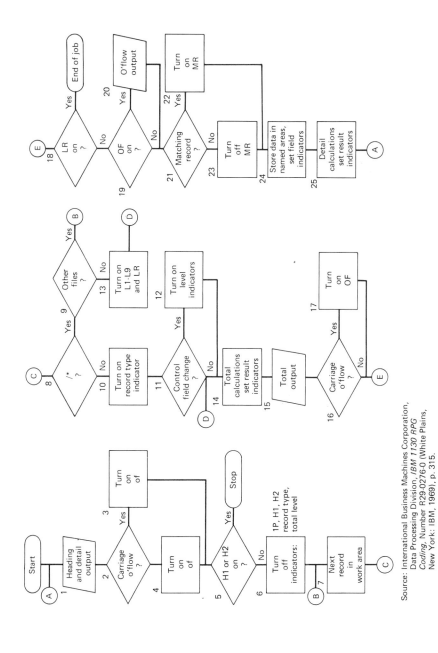

Source: International Business Machines Corporation,
Data Processing Division, *IBM 1130 RPG
Coding,* Number R29-0276-0 (White Plains,
New York: IBM, 1969), p. 315.

Fig. 6-23. RPG fixed logic flowchart.

results on input. If an error condition is sensed, an H1 or H2 indicator will be turned on that will cause processing to stop and control to pass to an external decision that would have to be made by the computer operator or programmer.

Step 6: If a halt indicator is not turned on, all other indicators will be automatically turned off including first page (1P), record identifying (Ø1-99), control level (L1–L9), and the last record (LR) indicators.

Step 7: A data record is now placed in the input work area, but is not stored in a field area at this stage of the cycle. Therefore, it is not available for processing until later.

Step 8: A test is made for the last record card at this step. Consequently, a last record card must be included at the end of a data file so that the computer will sense when the end of a file has been reached and any last record calculations and/or output may be performed. A commonly used end of file card is the slash asterisk card (/*). However, some computer systems may require a different card to indicate the end of a file condition.

Step 9: If the last record indicator card is sensed, the program will be tested to determine if other input files are included in the program. If the test indicates that there are other input files, control will loop back to step 7 and the previous steps will be executed again. The NO result of the decision test that causes step 13 to be executed will be discussed later when control level indicators are introduced.

Step 10: If the end-of-file card is not sensed, a Record Identifying Indicator (Ø1-99) will be turned on. An indicator of this type was assigned to a record in the Input Specifications form.

Step 11: A test for control break will be made at this step. If the test results in a YES, appropriate control level indicators will be turned on, as shown in step 12. A NO result will cause step 14 to be executed.

Step 12: If step 11 resulted in a YES decision the Control Level Indicators (L1 to L9) used for that Control Field will turn on. If a higher Control Level Indicator turns on, any lower Level Indicators will also be on.

Step 13: This step follows the same logic as step 12, except that the L1 to L9 indicators are automatically switched on at the end of the last file processed (these may be multiple input files). This enables all subtotals and last record totals to be printed when end of file is sensed.

Step 14: If a control level indicator (L1–L9) or last record indicator (LR) had been turned on in step 13, total calculations would be performed at this step. However, if this condition did not occur for this record, any resulting indicator (01–99) that may have been used to condition the result of a calculation is turned on.

Step 15: Any Total Time output conditioned by a control level indicator (L1–L9) or last record indicator is performed at this step in the cycle.

Steps 16 and 17: The test for overflow is made again at this stage of the cycle. If a punch in channel 12 of the carriage control tape is sensed (or buffer program) is sensed, the OF indicator will be turned on. However, if the channel is not sensed, the indicator will not be switched on and overflow will not occur.

Step 18: If the end-of-file record (/*) had been sensed in step 8, the last record indicator (LR) would have been turned on and the job would end at this step. If LR was not on, control would advance to step 19.

Steps 19 and 20: A test is made for page overflow indicator (OF) which might have been turned on in step 17. If the OF indicator is on, any heading, detail, or total lines will be printed, after which control will branch back to the main job stream. However, if the OF indicator was not on, control would pass to step 21.

Steps 21, 22 and 23: These steps will be discussed later in the text when sequential file processing is introduced.

Step 24: The data record that was placed in an input work area (step 7) is now stored in a storage area and is available for processing. Calculations may now be performed on the record data.

Step 25: This is the last step of the RPG logic cycle for a detail record. Detail calculations that were conditioned by a record identifying indicator (01–99), are executed at this time. All resulting indicators, columns 54–59 of the Calculations Specifications, that may have been used to condition the result of a calculation, are turned on. After completion of this step, control returns to step 1 where any detail or heading output will be executed.

In order to be an effective RPG II programmer a knowledge of the RPG II Fixed Logic Cycle should be acquired. The most important concept to understand from examination of the logic cycle is when the available RPG II indicators are turned on and off during the processing of a data file. Hence, a review of the RPG II indicator types is important before additional coding concepts are introduced.

SUMMARY OF RPG II INDICATORS

A summary of the RPG II indicators discussed in the text at this point is presented in the following paragraphs:

First Page Indicator (1P)

The First Page Indicator is turned on (step 3 of the logic cycle) *before* any data records are placed in the work area. All output lines (records) conditioned by 1P will be executed. In addition, any output *not* conditioned by *any* indicator will also execute. Consequently, all output must be conditioned (columns 23–31 of output form) by an indicator to prevent unwanted or incorrect output. The 1P indicator is automatically turned off (step 6) before a data record is placed in the work area and remains off for the duration of the program.

Overflow Indicator (OA–OG, and OV)

Overflow Indicators are turned on when channel 12 in the carriage control tape or a 12 punch in the buffer program card (see Chapter 3) is sensed. The last line of the page (overflow line) will be printed, paper will advance to the top of next page, headings will be printed that are conditioned for overflow printing, and the overflow indicator will automatically turn off.

Record Identifying Indicators (01–99)

Record Identifying Indicators are assigned to the record types on input (columns 19 and 20), and are turned on and off automatically as the record type is read. They *do not* have to be assigned in any required order. If a file contains more than one record type, Record Identification Codes must be used to distinguish each record type from the other. Notice in the Logic Flowchart (Figure 6-18) the Record Identifying Indicators are turned on in step 10 if end of file was not sensed. These indicators remain on at both detail and total times.

Field Record Relation Indicators (01–99)

Field Record Relation Indicators are entered in columns 63 and 64 of the input form on the same line as the variable field to which they relate. These indicators must be the same as those assigned as Record Identifying and turn on when any of those indicators are on. They are usually only used in a multirecord file application when the OR relationship method is used for the input of data record types in the program.

Field Indicators (may be any indicator in RPG II except 1P or overflow)

Field Indicators are entered in columns 65 –70 of the input form on the same line as the field they are testing for Plus, Minus, or Zero (Blank) value. They should not be the same as any Record Identifying Indicator assigned because unpredictable results could occur. Any indicator turned on is used to condition subsequent calculations and/or output.

Resulting Indicators (may be any indicator in RPG II except 1P or overflow)

Resulting Indicators are entered in columns 54 –59 of the Calculation form. Their function, which was discussed in Chapter 4, is to test the value of a Result Field for Plus, Minus, or Zero. Again, in order to prevent unpredictable results, any indicators used as Resulting should not be Record Identifying Indicators. The Compare and Lookup function of Resulting Indicators will be discussed in later chapters. The logic of some programs may require that these indicators be set off (SETOF) before the next record is processed.

Control Level Indicators (L1–L9)

Control Level Indicators are used to condition calculations and/or output and are turned on when a change in the value of an input Control Field is sensed. When a new record is read and the respective Record Identifying Indicator is turned on, the Control Level Indicator will be off until a Control Break is sensed. If assigned at Detail Time, they will turn on when the first record of a group is processed. When assigned at Total Time, they will turn on when the last record of a group is processed. Any higher Control Level Indicators will turn on lower ones automatically. For example, if L3 is on, L2 and L1 will also be on.

Reference to step 12 in Figure 6-18 shows that a Control Break is sensed when the input record is still in the work area before it is transferred to the field storage area (step 24). Hence, the old record is still in storage when a Control Break is sensed.

Last Record Indicator (LR)

The Last Record Indicator turns on when the end-of-file record is sensed. Any Control Level Indicators (L1–L9) used in the program will automatically turn on and output conditioned by those indicators will be executed before LR output.

QUESTIONS

1. What are the Control Level Indicators? What do they do?
2. What are Control Fields? Control Groups? Control Breaks?
3. In what coding forms and respective columns are Control Level Indicators specified?
4. If the L5 Control Level Indicator was turned on what other Control Level Indicators will be on at the same time?
5. What entry should be made in column 39 of the Output-Format Specifications when control level indicators are used to print an accumulated total after an accumulated total is sensed? What effect does this coding have?
6. What are the two broad classifications of reports? Explain their differences.
7. What does the /* card do at the end of a card file?
8. Examine the RPG flowchart, Figure 8-1, and explain what happens at steps 11 and 12.
9. How would an RPG source program for a detailed report be modified to obtain a group report? How many coding forms are affected in making this change?
10. What, if anything, is wrong with the following *related* lines of coding for a record defined in the Input Specifications?

Field name	Control level (L1-L9)	Matching fields or chaining fields	Field record relation	Field indicators Plus	Minus	Zero or blank
53 54 55 56 57 58	59 60	61 62	63 64	65 66	67 68	69 70
E M P N O	L 5					
S E C T O N	L 4					
D E P T	L 2					
D I V I S N	L 3					

11. What, if anything, is wrong with the lines of *related* coding in the Calculation Specifications form?

Indicators And Not	And Not	Not	Factor 1	Operation	Factor 2	Result field
9 10 11	12 13 14	15 16 17	18 19 20 21 22 23 24 25 26 27	28 29 30 31 32	33 34 35 36 37 38 39 40 41 42	43 44 45 46 47 48
L 1			V O T E R S	A D D	V O T O T L	V O T O T L
L 3			V O T O T L	A D D	C O U N T Y	C O U N T Y
L 4			C O U N T Y	A D D	D I S T C T	D I S T C T
L 2			D I S T C T	A D D	S T A T E	S T A T E

12. When is the Z-ADD operation used? Name the rules for using this operation.
13. How does the Z-SUB operation differ from the Z-ADD?
14. What if anything is wrong with the four lines of coding given below?

RPG CALCULATION SPECIFICATIONS

Line	Form Type	Control Level (L0-L9, LR, SR)	And Not	And Not	Not	Factor 1	Operation	Factor 2	Result Field	Field Length	Decimal Positions	Half Adjust (H)	Plus / High 1>2	Minus / Low 1<2	Zero / Equal 1=2
0 1	C					A	Z-ADD	B	C	7 0					
0 2	C					D	Z-ADD		E	6 2					
0 3	C						Z-ADD	'ABC'	HOLD	3					
0 4	C						Z-ADD	.07	PCT	3 3					
0 5	C						Z-SUB	X	Z	3 2			1 2		

15. When is the First Page Indicator on during the RPG II Logic Cycle?
16. When do Record Identifying Indicators turn on during the logic cycle?
17. When a Control Level Indicator turns on, what other indicators may be on at the same time?
18. What indicators turn on when the end-of-file record is sensed?
19. When does the Overflow Indicator (OF, etc.) turn on?
20. If an output line is not conditioned by any indicator when will the line be printed?
21. In a single input file processing run how many Record Identifying Indicators will be on at the same time?
22. When do Field Relation Indicators turn on in an RPG II program?
23. When do Resulting Indicators turn on in an RPG II program?
24. At what step in the RPG II Logic Flowchart is a detail record actually placed in storage and available for processing?
25. What are the SETON and SETOF operations used for in source program coding?
26. In what coding form and columns are the entries made for the SETON and SETOF operations? How many indicators may be turned on or off by these operations?
27. Explain the logic of the Fetch Overflow feature.
28. What coding forms and columns are used to facilitate overflow printing of headings at Last Record Time?

EXERCISES

6-1. An input file (PARTS) consists of data records with the following format:

P	PART NO.	JOB NO.	DEPT. NO.	DESCRIPTION	QUANTITY USED	COST/ ITEM	

```
99999 999 999 9999999999999999999 9999 99999 9999999999999999999999999999999999999999999
1  2 3 4  5  6 7 8  9 10 11 12 13 14 15 16 17 18 19 20 21 22 23 24 25 26 27 28 29 30 31 32 33 34 35 36 37 38 39 40 41 42 43 44 45 46 47 48 49 50 51 52 53 54 55 56 57 58 59 60 61 62 63 64 65 66 67 68 69 70 71 72 73 74 75 76 77 78 79 80
```

Write the Input Specifications using Control Level Indicators where Part Number is the lowest Control Field and Department Number the highest.

6-2. From the information included in Exercise 1 write the Calculation Specifications coding. Cost must be multiplied by Quantity to obtain the total cost amount for the part. The total part cost must be added to a total job field and the amount in this field added to a total department field. Refer to Printer Spacing Chart in Exercise 3 for total field sizes.

6-3. From the Printer Spacing Chart given below write the Output Format Specifications coding.

		0	1	2	3	4	5	6
		1234567890	1234567890	1234567890	1234567890	1234567890	1234567890	1234567890
H	1			PART USAGE REPORT				
H	2	ØX/XX/XX		BY JOB AND DEPT		PAGE XXØX		
	3							
H	4	PART NO	DESCRIPTION		TOTAL COST			
	5							
D	6	XXXX	X_____	X	$ X,XXX,XXØ.XX			
	7							
D	8	XXXX	X_____	X	X,XXX,XXØ.XX			
	9							
	10							
TL1	11		JOB NO XØX TOTAL		$ XX,XXX,XXØ.XX X			
	12							
TL2	13		DEPT NO ØX TOTAL		$ XXX,XXX,XXØ.XX XX			
	14							
TLR	15		PLANT TOTAL		$ X,XXX,XXX,XXØ.XX XXX			
	16							
	17							
	18							
	19		Notes - Headings on top of every page.					
	20							

6-4. Modify your coding in Exercises 2 and 3 so that each Department's data is printed on a separate page and the Plant Total with Heading lines 1 and 2 printed on a page by themselves.

6-5. DEBUGGING AN RPG II SOURCE PROGRAM

Given below is an RPG II source program listing which includes errors. Examine the listing, interpret the errors, and *correct the coding lines that include errors by rewriting them on the required specifications form.*

Source Program Listing:

```
              01 020  F*THIS PROGRAM ILLUSTRATES THE USE OF 1 CONTROL LEVEL INDICATOR TO      SAVING
              01 030  F*CONTROL CALCULATIONS AND OUTPUT.....                                  SAVING
              01 040  F*                                                                      SAVING
      0001    01 050  FACTIVITYIP  F   80  80                     MFCM1 SYSIPT               SAVING
      0002    01 060  FSAVINGS  O  F  132 132         OF          PRINTERSYSLST             SAVING
      0003    02 010  IACTIVITYAB  10  80 CS                                                  SAVING
      0004    02 020  I                                            1    40SDATE              SAVING
      0005    02 030  I            BB  20  80 CB                                              SAVING
      0006    02 040  I         OR      30  80 CW                                            SAVING
      0007    02 050  I         OR      40  80 CD                                            SAVING
      0008    02 060  I                                            1    40ACTNO    L1        SAVING
      0009    02 070  I                                            5   100IDATE             SAVING
      0010    02 080  I                                           11   172WITHDL      30    SAVING
      0011    02 090  I                                           11   172DEPOST      40    SAVING
      0012    02 100  I                                           11   182BEGBAL      20    SAVING
      0013    03 010  C    30       WITHDL   ADD  TOWITH   TOWITH  82       TOTAL WITHDRWLSSAVING
      0014    03 020  C    40       DEPOST   ADD  TODEPS   TODEPS  82       TOTAL DEPOSITS SAVING
              03 030  C*                                                                      SAVING
              03 040  C* WHEN ACCOUNT NUMBER CHANGES ADD TOTAL DEPOSITS (TODEPS) TO THE      SAVING
              03 050  C* BEGINNING CUSTOMER BALANCE......                                     SAVING
              03 060  C*                                                                      SAVING
      0015    03 070  CL1          BEGBAL   ADD  TODEPS   ENDBAL  82                         SAVING
              03 080  C*                                                                      SAVING
              03 090  C* WHEN ACCOUNT NUMBER CHANGES SUBTRACT TOTAL WITHDRAWALS FROM         SAVING
              03 100  C* ENDING BALANCE COMPUTED ON LINE 070.....                            SAVING
              03 110  C*                                                                      SAVING
      0016    03 120  C            ENDBAL   SUB  TOWITH   ENDBAL                             SAVING
              03 130  C*  $                                                                   SAVING          NOTE 137
              03 140  C* ADD ENDING BALANCE CF ALL DEPOSITERS TO A GRAND TOTAL FIELD.......SAVING
      0017    03 150  CL2          ENDBAL   ADD  GRAND    GRAND   92                         SAVING
              03 160  C*                                                                      SAVING
              03 170  C* SET TOWITH & TODEPS TO ZERO BEFORE NEXT DEPOSITOR'S ACCOUNT.......SAVING
              03 180  C*                                                                      SAVING
      0018    03 190  CL1          ZADD 0   TOWITH                                           SAVING
              03 200  CL1      Z-ADDO   TODEPS                  $                            SAVING          NOTE 141
      0019                                                                                   SAVING
      0020    04 010  OSAVINGS H  101    10                                                  SAVING
      0021    04 020  O          OR       OF                                                 SAVING
      0022    04 030  O                                        55 'SAVINGS ACCOUNT ACTIVITY'SAVING
      0023    04 040  O          H    1   10                                                 SAVING
      0024    04 050  O          CR       OF                                                 SAVING
      0025    04 060  O                                        43 'FOR'                      SAVING
      0026    04 070  O                          SDATE Y       49                            SAVING
      0027    04 080  O          H    2   20                                                 SAVING
      0028    04 090  O                                        25 'ACCOUNT'                  SAVING
      0029    04 100  O                          ACTNO Z       30                            SAVING
      0030    04 110  O          H    1   20                                                 SAVING
      0031    04 120  O                                        36 'DATE     BEGINNING'       SAVING
      0032    04 130  O                                        61 'WITHDRAWALS   DEPOSITS'   SAVING
      0033    04 140  O                                        71 'ENDING'                   SAVING
      0034    04 150  O          H    2   20                                                 SAVING
      0035    05 010  O                                        35 'BALANCE'                  SAVING
      0036    05 020  O                                        72 'BALANCE'                  SAVING
      0037    05 030  O          D    1   20                                                 SAVING
      0038    05 040  O         OR       30                                                  SAVING
      0039    05 050  O         OR       40                                                  SAVING
      0040    05 060  O                          TDATE Y       25                            SAVING
      0041    05 070  O                    20    BEGBAL1       37                            SAVING
      0042    05 080  O                    30    WITHDL1       49                            SAVING
      0043    05 090  O                    40    DEPOST1       61                            SAVING
      0044    05 100  O          T    3        L3  $                                         SAVING          NOTE 202
      0045    05 110  C                          ENDBALAB      75                            SAVING
      0046    05 120  O          T    0        LR                                            SAVING
      0047    05 130  O                          GRAND 1       62                            SAVING
      0048    05 140  O                                        49 '$'                        SAVING
      0049    05 150  O                                        37 'TOTAL BALANCE CF ALL'     SAVING
      0050    05 160  O                                        46 'ACCOUNTS'                 SAVING

        E N D   O F   S O U R C E
```

Diagnostics:

T A B L E S   A N D   M A P S

RESULTING INDICATOR TABLE

ADDRESS	RI	ADDRESS	RI	ADDRESS	RI	ADDRESS	RI	ADDRESS	RI	ADDRESS	RI	ADDRESS	RI
02A2	OF	02B6	L1	02BF	LR	02C0	HO	02CA	1P	02CD	10	02CE	20
02CF	30	02D0	40		0017			L2						

NOTE 387

FIELD NAMES

ADDRESS	FIELD	ADDRESS	FIELD	ADDRESS	FIELD	ADDRESS	FIELD	ADDRESS	FIELD
01DD	*ERROR	0361	SDATE	0364	ACTNO	0367	TDATE	036B	WITHDL
036F	DEPOST	0373	BEGBAL	0378	TOWITH	037D	TODEPS	0382	ENDBAL
0387	GRAND								

M E S S A G E   T E X T

NOTE 137   NON-LEVEL SPEC FCLLOWS A LEVEL SPEC. ASSUME LO IN POSITIONS 7-8.

NOTE 141   INVALID OPERATION. SPEC IS DROPPED.

NOTE 202   INDICATOR IS INVALID OR UNDEFINED. DROP ENTRY.

NOTE 387   INDICATOR REFERENCED BUT NOT DEFINED. DROP INDICATOR.

LABORATORY ASSIGNMENTS

LABORATORY ASSIGNMENT 6-1:
MONTHLY CUSTOMER INVOICES

From the Card Layout Form and Printer Spacing Chart information given below write an RPG II source program to obtain the required printed report. You will have to use the L1 Control Level Indicator in your program.

Input Format of Data Records:

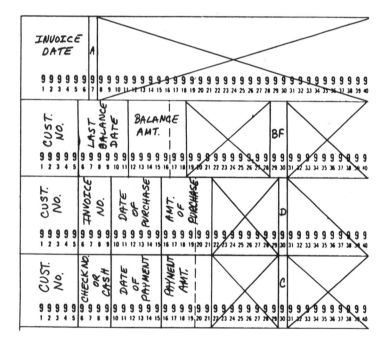

Calculations. Any purchases are to be added to the beginning of the month's balance and payments are to be subtracted. The total of purchases and payments must be accumulated for *each* customer as well as the total purchases, payments, and ending balances of *all* customers. (See Printer Spacing Chart for total requirements.)

Design of the Printed Report:

		0	1	2	3	4	5	6	7
H	1				MONTHLY INVOICE				
D	2				AS OF ØX/XX/XX				
	3								
D	4	ACCOUNT NO. XXXXX							
D	5				PURCHASES PAYMENTS				
D	6	BALANCE AS OF ØX/XX/XX						XX,XXØ.XXCR	
	7								
D	8	ØX/XX/XX INVOICE XXXX		X,XXØ.XX				XX,XXØ.XXCR	
	9								
D	10	ØX/XX/XX(CHECK NO XXXX)				X,XXØ.XX		XX,XXØ.XXCR	
	11	(CASH							
TLI	12	TOTAL ACTIVITY		XX,XXØ.XX XX,XXØ.XX				XX,XXØ.XXCR	END OF MONTH
	13								BALANCE
	14								
TLR	15	TOTAL PURCHASES FOR ALL CUSTOMERS XXX,XXØ.XX							
TLR	16	TOTAL PAYMENTS BY ALL CUSTOMERS XXX,XXØ.XX							
	17								
TLR	18	TOTAL BALANCE OF CUSTOMERS X,XXX,XXØ.XX							
	19								
	20								
	21								
	22								
	23								
	24								

USE ANY SIX-CHARACTER DATE FOR DATE CARD.

Data for Laboratory Assignment 6-1

Balance cards Cols. 1–5   6–11   12–18   29–30

11111	013179	0012010	BF
22222	013179	0287178	BF
33333	013179	0001045	BF
4444	013179	0000000	BF
55555	013179	0000400 −	BF (acct has credit balance)

Purchase cards Cols. 1–5   6–9   10–15   16–21   30

11111	0100	020179	030009	D
22222	0101	020379	025160	D
11111	0102	020479	005637	D
33333	0103	020579	010000	D
44444	0104	021079	061231	D
33333	0105	021879	070000	D
55555	0106	022879	041283	D

Payment cards Cols. 1–5   6–9   10–15   16–21   30

11111	0711	021079	042019	C
22222	0012	021279	287178	C
33333		022479	081500	C (blank in cols 6–9
44444	0410	022679	021079	C indicate cash sale)

Note: Records *must be* sorted by customer group in ascending date order within each group. Balance card for each customer first in group.

2 record
types in file

LABORATORY ASSIGNMENT 6-2:
DETAIL AND GROUP REPORTS FOR THREE CONTROL TOTALS

From the Card Layout Form and Printer Spacing Chart information given below write an RPG II source program to obtain the required printed report. Notice the report includes three Control Breaks and related subtotals.

Input Format of Data Records:

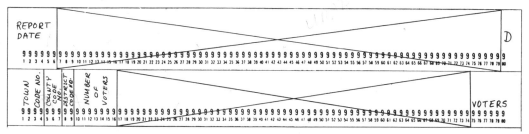

Calculations. Accumulate totals for each town, county, district, and state. (See Printer Spacing Chart for Control Group total sizes.) Because each district's data is to be printed on separate pages with headings and the state total at LR time is to be printed with headings on a separate page, enter the needed calculations to provide for this output.

fetch overflow

district change = change page change

Design of Printed Report. If the VOTERS field is blank, print an error message in the VOTERS output position. Use your own wording for this message. The state total and report headings are to be printed on a separate page. Enter the required coding on output to execute this requirement.

```
        0         1         2         3         4         5         6         7         8
       1234567890123456789012345678901234567890123456789012345678901234567890123456789
 H  1                                       STATE OF CONFUSION
 H  2                          VOTERS REPORT BY TOWN COUNTY AND DISTRICT
 H  3                                     FOR YEAR ENDING 0X/XX/XX
 H  4
    5
 H  6                          TOWN    COUNTY       DISTRICT              VOTERS
    7
 D  8                          XXXX    XXX          XX                   XXX XXX
 D  9                          XXXX    XXX          XX                   XXX XXX
   10
TL1 11  TOWN                        TOTAL VOTERS FOR TOWN    XXXX.......X,XXX,XOX X
   12
TL2 13  COUNTY                       TOTAL VOTERS FOR COUNTY  XXX.......XX,XXX,XOX XX
   14
TL3 15  DISTRICT                     TOTAL VOTERS FOR DISTRICT XX.......XXX,XXX,XOX XXX
   16
TLR 17  last page           TOTAL VOTERS IN STATE.........X,XXX,XXX,XOX
   18
   19
   20       Notes:
   21
   22          ① Headings on top of every page.
   23
   24
   25          ② If voters input field is blank
   26             print error message in voters positions
   27
   28
   29
   30
```

75-80 VOTERS

Data for Laboratory Assignment:

TOWN	COUNTY	DISTRICT	VOTERS
1-4	5-7	8-9	10-16
1000	100	10	215,625
1000	100	10	82,784
1000	100	10	104,716
1000	100	10	12,899
1000	100	10	267,004	683,028
1100	100	10	57,800
1100	100	10	14,111
1100	100	10	118,923
1100	100	10	73,807
1100	100	10	200,749	465,390
2000	200	20	111,111
2000	200	20	67,242
2000	200	20	104,338
2000	200	20	99,917
2000	200	20	178,615	561,223
3100	378	31	222,234
3100	378	31	33,845
3100	378	31	117,871
3100	378	31	64,899
3100	378	31	45,348	484,197
4890	999	55	88,888	88,888

2,282,726

LABORATORY ASSIGNMENT 6-3:
MONTHLY SALES REPORT USING TWO LEVEL INDICATORS

Write an RPG II source program from the input and output information given in the Card Layout Form and Printer Spacing Chart. Notice in the Printer Spacing Chart that the individual weekly sales are not printed but the total sales amount for the week is printed instead.

Format of Input Records:

Calculations. Each salesman's daily sales are to be added to a total field and when a Control Break occurs (L1) the total weekly sales for the salesman will be added to the Monthly-Sales-To-Date amount. Totals must also be provided for Branch and Company Sales. (See Printer Spacing Chart for field size requirements of totals.)

Design of Printed Report. Each Branch sales information must be printed on a *separate page*. Total Company Sales must be printed after the last Branch total.

Printer Spacing Chart:

```
                    MONTHLY SALES REPORT BY                    PAGE XXØX
H                   BRANCH AND SALESMAN
H                        ØX/XX/XX   (UDATE)
D   BRANCH ØX

D   SALESMAN     SALESMAN NAME       WEEKLY          MONTHLY
D   NUMBER                            SALES            SALES
TL1    XØX     X                X   $ XXX,XXØ.XX   $X,XXX,XXØ.XX
TL1    XØX     X                X     XXX,XXØ.XX   X,XXX,XXØ.XX
TL2           TOTAL BRANCH SALES      XXXX,XXØ.XX  XX,XXX,XXØ.XX X
TLR           TOTAL COMPANY SALES  XXXXXX,XXØ.XX  XXX,XXX,XXØ.XX XX

              Notes:
              ① Repeat headings on every page.
              ② Print branch sales on separate pages.
              ③ $ signs are fixed.
```

Data For Lab:

Note the data records must be sorted by Branch Number and each Salesman Number in the related group. For example, Salesman Number 123 month-to-date record must be the first record of the group followed by the three daily sales records for the Salesman. The month-to-date and daily sales records for Salesman Number 234 would follow and so on for the complete file.

Month-to-date records

cols	1	2–4	5–6	7–26	27–35
	M	123	10	RICHARD MACY	001242415
	M	234	10	JOHN GIMBEL	000863579
	M	345	10	JOHN WANAMAKER	001000000
	M	456	20	BERT ALTMAN	000080000
	M	567	20	ROGER PEET	003200000

Daily Sales records

cols	1	2–4	5–6	7–11	12–14	15–20
	S	123	10	10000	020	031079
	S	123	10	00500	200	031279
	S	123	10	60000	002	031579
	S	234	10	09000	100	031079
	S	345	10	01200	500	031179
	S	345	10	50000	010	031579
	S	456	20	02800	050	031079
	S	456	20	12000	010	031179
	S	567	20	35000	002	031879
	S	567	20	01850	200	031979

Note: One field in the Daily Sales records is not needed for the required report. Fields are often included in records that are not used for every report. The student should be aware of this and plan the program accordingly.

7
THE COMPARE (COMP) OPERATION, BRANCHING, AND LOOPING CONCEPTS

THE COMPARE (COMP) OPERATION

In addition to the normal arithmetic functions including addition, subtraction, multiplication, and division, there are many other RPG II operations that may be used in the Calculation Specifications form. One of these is the Compare (COMP) operation which instructs the computer to compare the value in a variable field or literal (numeric or alphanumeric) entered in the Factor 1 field (columns 18–27) of the calculation form, with the value in the variable field or literal entered in Factor 2 (columns 33–42). The result of the comparison will turn on an indicator(s) specified in the Resulting Indicator fields columns 54 to 59.

The COMP operation is used in conjunction with the *collating sequence* of the computer. The collating sequence, which is predetermined by the manufacturer determines which character is higher or lower than another. The normal collating sequence of the IBM series of computers is given in Figure 7-1.

Examination of the collating sequence in Figure 7-1 indicates that a blank is the lowest character and nine the highest. In other words, if a variable field containing a zero was compared to a field containing a nine the field with the nine value would be higher according to the *collating sequence* illustrated in Figure 7-1. An understanding of the collating sequence is important for the COMP operation, sorting, and general programming logic. The collating

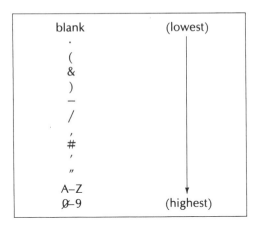

Fig. 7-1. Collating Sequence of IBM computers.

sequence of computers has been standardized by most manufacturers, however, the programmer should examine the programmer's manual related to the computer used to identify any minor differences.

Figures 7-2, 7-3, 7-4, and 7-5 illustrate the coding for the COMP operation and comparison examples for numeric and alphanumeric fields and literals. Examine Figure 7-2 and notice the COMP operation is left-justified in the Operation field of the calculation form. Notice also only Factor 1 and 2 are used and *not* the Result, Field Length, Decimal Positions, or Half Adjust fields. Any number of indicators (columns 7–17) may be used to condition a COMP operation, their use depends on the logic of the program.

Subsequent calculations and/or output may be conditioned by the indicator(s) turned on by the result of a comparison of the fields or literals entered

RPG CALCULATION SPECIFICATIONS

Line	Form Type	Control Level (L0-L9, LR, SR)	Indicators			Factor 1	Operation	Factor 2	Result Field	Field Length	Decimal Positions	Half Adjust (H)	Resulting Indicators

Value in fields:

	AMT1	AMT2	INDICATOR "ON"
Example 1	1234	1235	45
Example 2	1234	0033	44
Example 3	1234	1234	90

In the calculation line: `01 C   AMT1   COMP   AMT2         44 45 90`

Fig. 7-2. Comparison of two positive numeric field values.

in Factor 1 and 2. One or more indicators may be used in the Resulting Indicator columns 54–59 to test for the result of the comparison. The field values or literals may be tested in the following ways:

1. If the value in the variable field or literal in Factor 1 is *higher than* that in Factor 2, the indicator entered in columns 54 and 55 (High) will turn on.

2. If the value in the variable field or literal in Factor 1 is *less than* that in Factor 2, the indicator entered in columns 56 and 57 (Low) will turn on.

3. If the value in the variable field or literal in Factor 1 is *equal to* that in Factor 2, the indicator entered in columns 58 and 59 (Equal) will turn on.

Refer back to Figure 7-2 and notice the value in AMT1 is compared to the value in AMT2. In Example 1, indicator 45 will turn on because the value 1234 contained in AMT1 is less than (according to the collating sequence in Figure 7-1) the 1235 value in the AMT2 field. Indicator 44 will turn on in Example 2 because the value in AMT1 is higher than the value in AMT2. Because the values in the AMT1 and AMT2 fields for Example 3 are equal, indicator 90 will turn on. When a comparison is made between the variable fields or literals in Factors 1 and 2, all the High, Low, and Equal Resulting Indicators do not have to be used. Program logic may require that only one of the compare results be tested for the conditioning of subsequent calculations and/or output.

Figure 7-3 illustrates a comparison of two numeric variable fields when the value in field A is negative and B is positive. Notice only one indicator is specified in the Low Resulting Indicator field. Indicators could be entered in the High and Equal fields and these conditions tested too. Program logic will dictate which conditions should be tested. Indicator 09 turns on, in this

RPG   CALCULATION SPECIFICATIONS

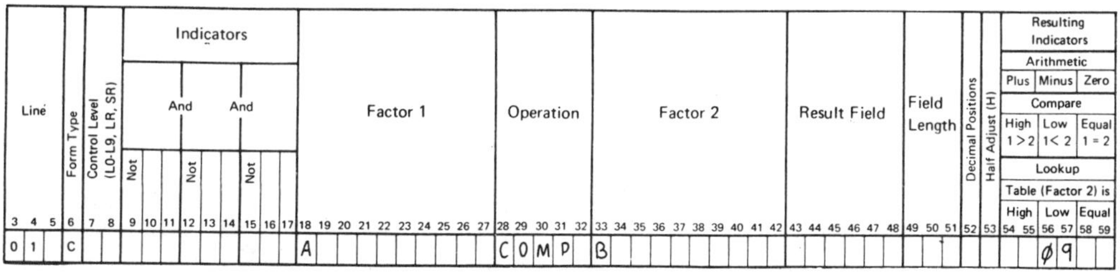

Value in fields: A   B   INDICATOR "ON"

Example   −51   51   09

Fig. 7-3. Comparison of a negative value with a positive value.

example, because -51 is less than $+51$. Remember an unsigned number is assumed to be positive and a negative number is less than a positive number.

Another important point to remember is that a *blank* in the value of a numeric field is interpreted as a *zero*. Consequently, ƀ51 would be equal to 051 in any comparison or sort operation. Note the letter ƀ with a line through it (ƀ) is the standard sign for a blank.

Figure 7-4 shows the comparison of an alphanumeric field with an alphanumeric literal. In example 1, the value in the variable field CITY is equal to the alphanumeric literal 'CHICAGO' which turns on indicator 80. Examination of example 2 indicates that indicator 79 (Low) is turned on because the value in the variable field is ALBANY which is less than the literal

RPG   CALCULATION SPECIFICATIONS

Value in fields	CITY	LITERAL	INDICATOR "ON"
Example 1	CHICAGO	CHICAGO	80
Example 2	ALBANY	CHICAGO	79
Example 3	NEW YORK	CHICAGO	78

Fig. 7-4.   Comparison of alphanumeric field with an alphanumeric literal.

CHICAGO according to the collating sequence (Figure 7-1). Reference to example 3 reveals that indicator 78 turned on because the value NEW YORK in the variable field CITY is higher than the literal CHICAGO. As a reminder notice the alphanumeric literal CHICAGO is enclosed in *apostrophes* which follows the RPG II coding rule for using alphanumeric literals.

Figure 7-5 illustrates the comparison of a numeric field with a numeric literal. Note that numeric literals *are not* enclosed in apostrophes. The decimal point may be omitted in a numeric literal as it will be assumed after the low-order number. However, if a decimal amount is required in the literal it must be entered in its required location.

Indicator 10 turned on in example 1 because the values are equal. The value 16200.00 is equal to 16200 even though decimal positions are not indicated in the numeric literal. In example 2, indicator 02 turns on because the value in the variable field WAGES is less than the numeric literal. The COMP operation in example 3 causes indicator 01 to turn on because the value in WAGES is higher than the literal.

When a comparison is made between two variable fields or a variable field and a literal, the values must be the *same type*. In other words, a numeric

RPG CALCULATION SPECIFICATIONS

Line	Form Type	Control Level (L0-L9, LR, SR)	Indicators			Factor 1	Operation	Factor 2	Result Field	Field Length	Decimal Positions	Half Adjust (H)	Resulting Indicators
			And	And									Arithmetic
			Not	Not	Not								Plus / Minus / Zero
													Compare
													High 1>2 / Low 1<2 / Equal 1=2
													Lookup (Factor 2) is
													High 54 55 / Low 56 57 / Equal 58 59
0 1	C	L				WAGES	COMP	16200					01 02 10

Value in fields	WAGES	LITERAL	INDICATOR "ON"
Example 1	16200.00	16200	10
Example 2	10174.18	16200	02
Example 3	21700.12	16200	01

Fig. 7-5. Comparison of a variable field value with a numeric literal.

field may only be compared to another numeric field or literal and an alphanumeric field may only be compared to another alphanumeric field or literal. The computer will not allow the comparison of an alphanumeric field or literal with a numeric field or literal. Any variable field used in a COMP operation must be previously defined in either input or calculations.

In addition, the programmer should be careful in the assignment of Resulting Indicators. If a Record Identifying Indicator is used as a Resulting Indicator an incorrect compare operation could result. Any indicators used as Resulting Indicators do not have to be assigned in any required sequence; use of a particular indicator is at the programmer's discretion.

An example of the use of the COMP operation will be discussed by application to a trial balance program, which is presented in the following text. Other examples of the COMP are used in conjunction with Branching and Looping discussed later in this chapter.

ACCOUNTING APPLICATION—THE TRIAL BALANCE

The underlying principle of double-entry bookkeeping is that debits must equal credits. According to established practice, a debit is the left side of an account and a credit the right side. Therefore, to debit an account is to enter an amount on the left side and to credit an account is to enter an amount on the right side. For simplicity of illustration an account is commonly represented by a simple T; however, an actual account is normally kept on standard ledger paper, as illustrated in Figure 7-6. Notice that the T comes from the center line and the top horizontal line of the ledger paper.

The "T" Account:

The common account form:

	Date	Explanation	F	Debit	Date	Explanation	F	Credit
	1969 July 1		1	5 0 0 0 00	1969 July 1		1	3 0 0 00
					3		1	3 0 0 0 00
					3		1	1 0 0 0 00

Cash Account no: *1*

The balance column account:

	Date	Explanation	Folio	Debit	Credit	Balance
	1969 July 3		1	1 0 0 0 00		1 0 0 0 00
	5		1	3 5 0 00		1 3 5 0 00
	9		1		1 5 0 00	1 2 0 0 00

Office Equipment Account no: *7*

Normal balance of account classifications:

Type of account	Increases are recorded as—	And the normal balance is—
Asset	Debits	Debit
Contra asset	Credits	Credit
Liability	Credits	Credit
Owner equity:		
Capital	Credits	Credit
Withdrawals	Debits	Debit
Revenue	Credits	Credit
Expense	Debits	Debit

Fig. 7-6. Account forms and normal balances.

Another form of ledger accounts that is used extensively in computerized systems is the balance column account that is illustrated in Figure 7-6. This account design has three columns in which to enter amounts: a debit column, credit column, and balance column. When the balance column account form is used, the balance of an account is available at a glance, whereas when the standard T account is used, the debit and credit sides have to be footed (added) and the balance of the account computed by subtracting one side from the other.

Accounts used in any accounting system may be placed into five broad categories including: assets, liabilities, owner's equity, revenue, and expenses. Each account classification has strict rules for increasing or decreasing the account balances. Figure 7-6 also depicts the rules for increasing and decreasing the accounts used in any accounting system. In order to maintain equality between debits and credits, when an account is debited some other account must be credited keeping debits equal to credits after every business transaction.

For example, when a check is written to pay an employee's salary, the asset cash would be decreased by crediting for the amount and a wage expense account would be debited to increase it for the corresponding amount. Because it is not within the scope of this book to present the principles of bookkeeping and accounting, any of the popular bookkeeping or accounting textbooks should be referenced for a complete presentation or overview.

At the end of a month a trial balance is usually prepared to check for the equality of debits and credits of the ledger accounts. If the debit balance of the ledger accounts equals the credit balance, we may be reasonably certain that:

1. Equal debits and credits have been recorded for all transactions.
2. The debit or credit balance of each account has been correctly computed.
3. The addition of the account balances in the trial balance has been correctly performed.[1]

However, if the totals of debits and credits of the account do not equal, one or more of the following errors may have been made:

1. The entering of a debit as a credit, or vice versa
2. Arithmetic mistakes in balancing accounts
3. Clerical errors in copying account balances into the trial balance
4. Listing a debit balance in the credit column of the trial balance, or vice versa
5. Errors in addition of the trial balance[2]

[1]Walter B. Meigs, *Accounting: The Basis For Business Decisions* (New York: McGraw-Hill Book Company, 1967), p. 50.

[2]*Ibid.*, p. 50.

Cash (Account No. 1)

19—	1		I	20,000	19—	3		I	7,000
Sept.	20	7,500	I	500	Sept.	5		I	5,000
						30		I	1,000

Accounts receivable (Account No. 2)

| 19— | | | | | 19— | | | | |
| Sept. | IO | 1,500 | I | 2,000 | Sept. | 20 | | I | 500 |

Land (Account No. 20)

| 19— | | | | | 19— | | | | |
| Sept. | 3 | $ 5,000 | I | 7,000 | Sept. | 10 | | 1 | 2,000 |

Building

| 19— | | | | | | | | | |
| Sept. | 5 | | I | 12,000 | | | | | |

Office equipment (Account No. 25)

| 19— | | | | | | | | | |
| Sept. | 14 | | 1 | 1,500 | | | | | |

Accounts payable (Account No. 30)

19—					19—				
Sept.	30		1	1,000	Sept.	5	7,500	I	7,000
						14		I	1,500

James Roberts, Capital (Account No. 50)

| | | | | | 19— | | | | |
| | | | | | Sept. | 1 | | 1 | 20,000 |

Trial
balance at
month-end
Process
ledger is
in balance

Roberts Real Estate Company
Trial balance
September 30, 19—

Cash	$ 7,500	
Accounts receivable	1,500	
Land	5,000	
Building	12,000	
Office equipment	1,500	
Accounts payable		$ 7,500
James Roberts, capital		20,000
	$27,500	$27,500

Fig. 7-7. Example of ledger and trial balance.

238

That the total of the debit balances of the accounts equals the total of credit balances does not indicate conclusively that errors have not been made. A transaction could have been completely eliminated by not posting to the ledger from the journals, the wrong account may have been debited or credited, or a number transposed as 123 instead of 132 to the account debited and credited. Even though hidden errors may not be revealed by the trial balances, it is still a useful accounting tool that must be prepared as a key step in the accounting cycle.

Figure 7-7 shows a ledger of accounts with the debit and credit sides footed and the balance determined for each account. The trial balance for this ledger is shown below the last ledger account. Notice that the heading of the trial balance contains the name of the company, name of the statement, and the date of the statement. Statement headings are a necessity in all accounting reports, whether formal or informal. The trial balance has only two amount columns, one for debit balances and the other for the credit balances of the ledger accounts. Furthermore, the accounts must be listed as they appear in the ledger, with assets normally first, then liabilities, owner's equity, revenue, and expenses.

Refer to Figure 7-6 and examine the illustration showing the normal balance of each account classification. If an account balance has an abnormal balance, it must be placed in the debit or credit column and circled or written in red ink to indicate that it is not the normal balance of that account. For example, if the cash account had a credit because of overdrawing, the checking account balance should be placed in the credit column of the trial balance and circled to indicate it is not normal.

RPG II CODING FOR THE TRIAL BALANCE

One of the first steps in the preparation of any RPG program is to prepare the card layout form for the data cards. If a card, tape, or disk file already exists for a ledger, the same field sizes would have to be used in order to provide continuity with a system already developed. Assume that this trial balance application program is not part of a system and will be written as a separate program.

Figure 7-8 illustrates the card layout form for the program which contains two record types: one for the date card and another for the data cards containing account names, amounts, and code for debit or credit balance. Any columns of the cards could have been assigned to the fields without any resulting errors.

Another preliminary step in RPG programming is the printer spacing chart that is shown in Figure 7-9. This is, of course, only a suggested format as the trial balance could have been properly spaced in many different ways. Examine the form for horizontal and vertical spacing, punctuation, and field name requirements.

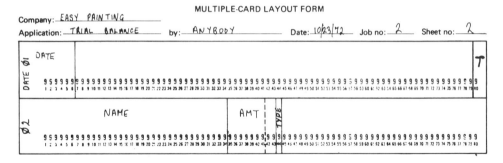

Fig. 7-8. Card layout form for data cards of trial balance program.

After the preliminary steps of preparing the card layout form and the printer spacing chart are completed, the actual coding of the RPG source program can be accomplished as all the information needed is available.

Line Ø2Ø of the File Description form, Figure 7-10, depicts the coding for the card input file LEDGER which contains records with a maximum record length of 80 card columns to be read on an IBM 2560 card read/punch unit. In addition, line Ø3Ø shows the output file TRIBAL and indicates that it will be printed on an IBM 3203 line printer with a maximum of 132 print positions specified. The OF in columns 33 and 34 of this line of coding is used in conjunction with the OF which is specified in the output indicator columns of the Output-Format Specifications form in order to provide for the printing of headings on the top of every page in the event the report continues over to more than one page.

Examination of the Input Specifications form in Figure 7-11 indicates that two record types are included in the data file. The record type assigned Record Identifying Indicator 08 contains the Trial Balance report date. A separate date record is needed because accounting reports are typically prepared after the related statement date which would make UDATE inappropriate. In order to distinguish between the two record types in the data file the data record is identified by the Record Identification Code T punched in column 80.

Record type 11 includes the account name (NAME), account balance (AMT), and the normal balance (debit or credit) of the account (TYPE). This information is contained in the General Ledger of the company and the amounts represent the end-of-accounting period account balances.

A line by line explanation of the calculation instruction in Figure 7-12 is presented in the following paragraphs.

Line 03010. When record type 11 is processed the value in the TYPE field, which is either D for debit or C for credit, is compared to the alphanumeric literal 'D'. If the value in TYPE is equal to 'D', Resulting Indicator 30, entered

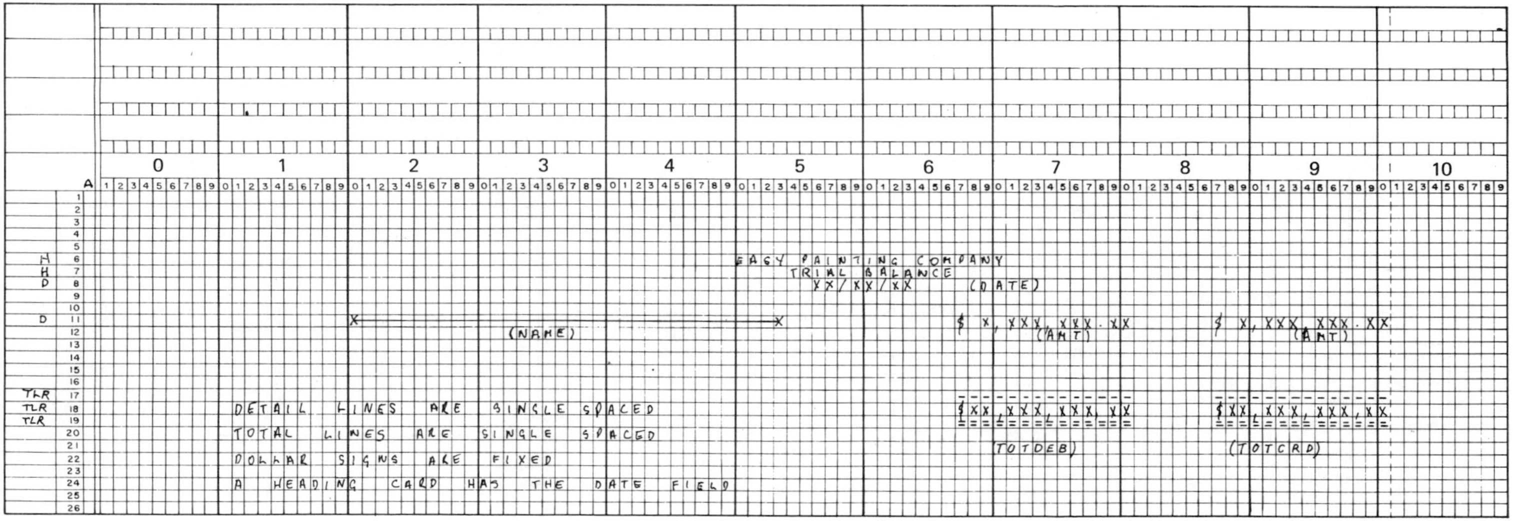

Fig. 7-9. Printer spacing chart for trial balance program.

File description specifications

Line	Form type	Filename	File type (I/O/U/C/D)	File designation (P/S/C/R/T/D)	End of file (E)	Sequence (A/D)	File format (F/V/S/M/D)	Block length	Record length	L/R	Mode of processing (A/P/I/K)	Record address type (I/D/T or 2)	Type of file organization or additional area	Key field starting location	Extension codes E/L	Device	Symbolic device	Labels S/N/E/M	Name of label exit	Option K	Continuation lines: Option / Entry	Core index	Extent exit for DAM (A/U)	File condition U1-U8 / (R/U/N)	Number of extents / Tape rewind	Number of tracks for cylinder overflow	File addition/unordered
02	F	LEDGER	I	P			F	80	80							MFCM1											
03	F	TRIBAL	O				F	132	132				OF			PRINTER											
04																											

Fig. 7-10. File Description Specifications coding for the trial balance.

242

Programmer ______________

RPG INPUT SPECIFICATIONS

Line (3–5)	Form Type (6)	Filename (7–14)	Sequence (15–16)	Number (1-N) (17)	Option (O) (18)	Record Identifying Indicator or ** (19–20)	Record Identification Codes 1: Position (21–24)	1: Not (N) (25)	1: C/Z/D (26)	1: Character (27)	2: Position (28–31)	2: Not (N) (32)	2: C/Z/D (33)	2: Character (34)	3: Position (35–38)	3: Not (N) (39)	3: C/Z/D (40)	3: Character (41)	Stacker Select (42)	P = Packed/B = Binary (43)	Field Location From (44–47)	Field Location To (48–51)	Decimal Positions (52)	Field Name (53–58)	Control Level (L1-L9) (59–60)	Matching Fields or Chaining Fields (61–62)	Field Record Relation (63–64)	Field Indicators Plus (65–66)	Minus (67–68)	Zero or Blank (69–70)	Sterling Sign Position (71–74)
01Ø	I	LEDGER	LF			Ø8	8Ø		C	T																					
02Ø	I																				1	6	Ø	DATE							
03Ø	I		FS			11																									
04Ø	I																				1	34		NAME							
05Ø	I																				35	43	2	AMT							
06Ø	I																				44	44		TYPE							

Fig. 7-11. Input Specifications coding for the trial balance.

Programmer ______________________

RPG CALCULATION SPECIFICATIONS

Line (3–5)	Form Type (6)	Control Level (L0-L9, LR, SR) (7–8)	Indicators (9–11)	Indicators And (12–14)	Indicators And (15–17)	Factor 1 (18–27)	Operation (28–32)	Factor 2 (33–42)	Result Field (43–48)	Field Length (49–51)	Decimal Positions (52)	Half Adjust (H) (53)	Resulting Indicators: Plus / High 1>2 (54–55)	Resulting Indicators: Minus / Low 1<2 (56–57)	Resulting Indicators: Zero / Equal 1=2 (58–59)	Comments (60–74)
010	C		11			TYPE	COMP	'D'						20	30	
020	C		20			CREDIT	ADD	1	CREDIT	1	0					
030	C		20			CREDIT	COMP	1							40	
040	C		30			AMT	ADD	TOTDEB	TOTDEB	10	2					
050	C		20			AMT	ADD	TOTCRD	TOTCRD	10	2					

Fig. 7-12. Calculation Specifications coding for trial balance.

in columns 58 and 59, will turn on. When an equal condition exists a debit balance is indicated. Assets and expense accounts have normal debit balances. On the other hand, if the value in TYPE is less than the letter D, an account with a normal credit balance is sensed and indicator 20 turns on.

Line 03020.   If the account has a credit balance (letter C in the TYPE field), Resulting Indicator 20 will turn on and the numeric literal 1 is added to a newly created field CREDIT. This instruction is needed to identify when the first credit account is read and to control printing of the dollar sign for the credit column of the trial balance. Examine Figure 7-13 for the printing requirements of dollar signs in the report.

Line 03030.   The instruction on this line compares the value in CREDIT with the numeric literal 1 and if equal Resulting Indicator 40 will turn on. Look at Figure 7-13, line 04130, and notice the dollar sign is conditioned by indicators 40 and 20. Consequently, the fixed dollar sign for the credit column of the trial balance will print only when an account with a credit balance (indicator 20) and when the value in CREDIT is 1 (indicator 40). Examination of the report in Figure 7-16 shows that the dollar sign is printed only once alongside the first

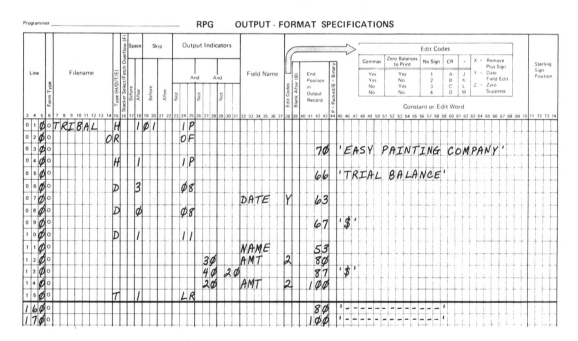

Fig. 7-13. Output-Format Specifications coding for the trial balance.

credit amount. This special coding is not needed for the debit column because Cash is always the first account in the trial balance and has a normal debit balance.

Line 03040. The value in the AMT field for accounts with debit balances are accumulated in the TOTDEB field. The value in TOTDEB will be printed at Last Record Time (LR) after all the data cards are processed (see Figure 7-14).

Line 03050. The instruction here performs the same function as that on line 03040 except the value in the AMT field for accounts that have credit balances is accumulated in the TOTCRD field.

The output coding is illustrated in Figures 7-13 and 7-14. Examination of Figure 7-13 indicates that previously discussed coding procedures are followed. Note, however, how the dollar sign for the debit column of the trial balance is conditioned for printing. Locate line 04080 and notice how it is conditioned by the Record Identifying Indicator 08 assigned to the date record. Because there is only one date record in the file the dollar sign will only print once. If Record Identifying Indicator 11 had been used to condition this output instruction the dollar sign would be repeated for every record processed. A zero is entered in the *space after* field to prevent any spacing until the first debit amount is printed alongside the dollar sign for the debit column. See the report in Figure 7-16 for the printed result of this coding.

Refer back to Figure 7-13 and locate line 04120. The AMT field is conditioned by Resulting Indicator 30 which turned on if the TYPE field value was D, indicating a debit balance. Consequently, the AMT value will be printed in this location only when the account has a debit balance.

The dollar sign on line 04130 is printed only when Resulting Indicators 40 and 20 are on. Remember indicator 20 was turned on by the COMP operation on calculation line 03010 (Figure 7-12) if the TYPE field value was C indicating a credit balance for the account. Indicator 40 turned on as the result of the COMP operation on line 03030 of calculations when the value in the CREDIT field was 1. This coding controls the printing of the dollar sign for the credit column of the trial balance so it will be printed only once alongside the first credit amount. Again, see Figure 7-16 for the printed result of this coding.

Finally, the AMT value for credit accounts will be printed when Resulting Indicator 20 is on as shown in Figure 7-13, line 04140.

After the last data record of the file has been processed and the end-of-file record read, the Last Record Indicator (LR) will automatically be switched on permitting all final printing to execute. Lines 04160 and 04170 of Figure 7-13 indicate that two lines of dashes representing total lines will be printed after the last data record of the file is processed.

The Output-Format Specifications coding is continued in Figure 7-14, line Ø1Ø. Again this line of coding will only be performed after the last record is

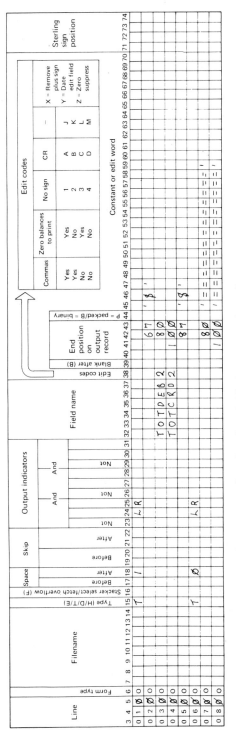

Fig. 7-14. Output-Format specifications coding for the trial balance (continued).

processed and the last record card is read. The total debits (TOTDEB) and total credits (TOTCRD) with fixed dollar signs will be printed in their respective positions. Finally, the double lines customary after final total figures in accounting reports and statements will be printed by the coding entered on lines Ø6Ø, Ø7Ø, and Ø8Ø at LR time.

The actual computer-executed source program with listing and resultant printed output is presented in Figure 7-15 and Figure 7-16.

```
0001    01 010    FLEDGER    IP   F   80  80              MFCM1  SYSIPT       TRIBAL
0002    01 020    FTRIBAL    O    F  132 132       OF      PRINTERSYSLST       TRIBAL
0003    02 010    ILEDGER    LF   08   80 CT                                   TRIBAL
0004    02 020    I                                           1    60DATE      TRIBAL
0005    02 030    I               FS  11                                       TRIBAL
0006    02 050    I                                          1    34 NAME      TRIBAL
0007    02 060    I                                         35   432AMT        TRIBAL
0008    02 070    I                                         44   44 TYPE       TRIBAL
0009    03 010    C          11            TYPE      COMP 'D'                2030 TRIBAL
0010    03 020    C          20            CREDIT    ADD  1       CREDIT 10    TRIBAL
0011    03 030    C          20            CREDIT    COMP 1                  40 TRIBAL
0012    03 040    C          30            AMT       ADD  TOTDEB  TOTDEB 102   TRIBAL
0013    03 050    C          20            AMT       ADD  TOTCRD  TOTCRD 102   TRIBAL
0014    04 010    OTRIBAL    H     101     1P                                  TRIBAL
0015    04 020    O                OR      OF                                  TRIBAL
0016    04 030    O                                          70 'EASY PAINTING COMPANY' TRIBAL
0017    04 040    O          H     1       1P                                  TRIBAL
0018    04 050    O                                          66 'TRIAL BALANCE' TRIBAL
0019    04 060    O          D     3       08                                  TRIBAL
0020    04 070    O          D     C       08          DATE  Y   63            TRIBAL
0021    04 080    O          D     C       08                                  TRIBAL
0022    04 090    O                                          67 '$'            TRIBAL
0023    04 100    O          D     1       11                                  TRIBAL
0024    04 110    O                                    NAME      53            TRIBAL
0025    04 120    O                                30  AMT   2   80            TRIBAL
0026    04 130    O                                40 20         87 '$'        TRIBAL
0027    04 140    O                                20  AMT   2  100            TRIBAL
0028    04 150    O          T     1       LR                80 '------------' TRIBAL
0029    04 160    O                                         100 '------------' TRIBAL
0030    04 170    O                                                            TRIBAL
0031    05 010    O          T     1       LR                                  TRIBAL
0032    05 020    O                                          67 '$'            TRIBAL
0033    05 030    O                                TOTDEB2    80               TRIBAL
0034    05 040    O                                TOTCRD2   100               TRIBAL
0035    05 050    O                                          87 '$'            TRIBAL
0036    05 060    O          T     O       LR                                  TRIBAL
0037    05 070    O                                          80 '==========='  TRIBAL
0038    05 080    O                                         100 '==========='  TRIBAL
```

END OF SOURCE

Fig. 7-15. Source listing of trial balance program using the Compare (COMP) operation.

```
                        EASY PAINTING COMPANY
                             TRIAL BALANCE
                               10/05/77

CASH                                            $      1,525.00
ACCOUNTS RECEIVABLE                                    1,115.00
MERCHANDISE INVENTORY                                 14,540.00
STORE SUPPLIES                                           675.00
PREPAID INSURANCE                                        220.00
STORE EQUIPMENT                                        9,890.00
ACCUMULATED DEPRECIATION STORE EQ                                  $      3,210.00
ACCOUNTS PAYABLE                                                          2,225.00
EARL DALE, CAPITAL                                                       17,045.00
EARL DALE, WITHDRAWALS                                7,800.00
SALES                                                                    74,455.00
SALES RETURNS AND ALLOWANCES                            310.00
SALES DISCOUNTS                                        1,145.00
PURCHASES                                            41,320.00
PURCHASE RETURNS AND ALLOWANCES                                             750.00
PURCHASES DISCOUNTS                                                         435.00
FREIGHT IN                                              565.00
SALES SALARIES                                       11,435.00
RENT EXPENSE                                          6,000.00
ADVERTISING EXPENSE                                     815.00
HEATING AND LIGHT EXPENSE                               765.00
                                                 --------------    --------------
                                            $        98,120.00    $       98,120.00
                                                 ==============    ==============
```

Fig. 7-16. Printed trial balance generated from program in Figure 7-15.

BRANCHING

Two of the most important features of a computer are the abilities to branch and loop within a program. The branching feature permits the skipping or hopping forward during the execution of program instructions. In other words, instead of following stored instruction in the normal sequential order, or one after the other, branching will cause control to break away from a line of instruction and execute some instruction not immediately following the one being executed.

Branching may be conditional or unconditional and may include more than one branch for each decision. Conditional branching means that more than one alternative path may be followed depending on a condition that resulted or was tested. For example, examine the conditional branching flowchart in Figure 7-17 and notice that a test is made for which indicator is on. If indicator Ø1 is on, program control will cause instructions to skip around the calculations and go to the end of the calculation instructions. On the other hand, if indicator Ø2 is on, the normal sequence of instructions would be followed, or one after the other.

The RPG coding for branching is illustrated in the same figure. Notice the use of two new RPG operations: the GOTO and TAG commands. These two operation names must always be used together or branching will not be possible. Both operations are entered left-justified in the operation field of the Calculation Specifications coding form. Notice that the GOTO command is entered in the field beginning in column 28, and that a field name is specified in Factor 2 on the same coding line. Any field name not used elsewhere in the program may be entered in Factor 2, but it must fulfill the requirements for the forming of field names that were discussed in Chapter 2. Also notice that the TAG command specified on line Ø9Ø is preceded by a field name in Factor 1 of the coding line. The field name entered in Factor 1 must be exactly the same as the field name that was specified in Factor 2 of the GOTO command. TAG commands are the entry point for a particular GOTO statement and must be identified with the same field name.

GOTO statements may be conditioned by indicators as depicted on line 010. In fact for this application, if the indicator had been omitted from line 010, the GOTO operation would be executed every time, regardless of the record type processed, and the calculations on lines 020 to 080 *would never* be executed. The TAG statement, however, must *never* be conditioned by any indicator. Notice the Result Field is not used with either the GOTO or TAG statements, Factor 1 is not used with the GOTO operation, and Factor 2 is not used with the TAG statement. There is no limit to the number of GOTO statements that may be used in a program; their use depends on the requirements of the program or programmer preference. In addition, more than one GOTO statement may refer to the same TAG statement in the program.

Refer back to Figure 7-17 and notice lines 020 to 080 are conditioned by the 02 Record Identifying Indicator. The 02 indicator could have been omitted

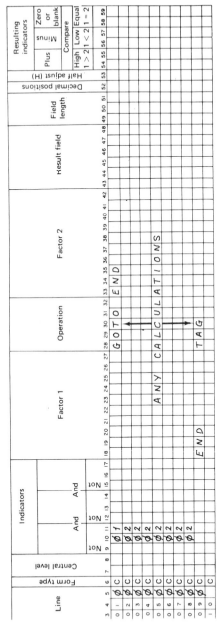

Fig. 7-17. Conditional branching flowchart with RPG coding control.

250

from these lines because the GOTO operation on line 010 would prevent any calculations from executing at 01 time. In order to save storage and reduce processing time, indicators should be omitted where possible. They are entered in Figure 7-17 only for reference purposes.

Figure 7-18 shows a conditional branch involving three decisions. If the result of the calculation specified on line Ø1Ø is a minus, indicator 9Ø will be turned on and the next sequential instruction is conditioned with the 9Ø indicator, which will execute the GOTO statement and transfer control to the entry point ROUTIN TAG on line Ø8Ø. All the instructions on lines Ø3Ø through Ø7Ø will be skipped and never be processed when indicator 9Ø is turned on. After skipping to line Ø8Ø, the instructions specified on lines Ø9Ø to 11Ø will be executed because they are conditioned by the 9Ø indicator.

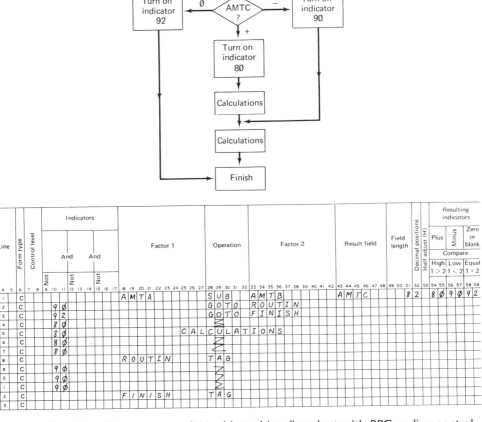

Fig. 7-18. Three-way conditional branching flowchart with RPG coding control.

On the other hand, if AMTC, the result field, is zero, indicator 92 will be turned on and line Ø2Ø will not be executed because it is not conditioned by this indicator. However, the GOTO statement on line Ø3Ø will be executed, transferring control to line 12Ø, the entry point for the respective GOTO statement. Notice that lines Ø4Ø through 11Ø will never be executed if resulting indicator 92 is on. Furthermore, if the result field AMTC is positive, indicator 8Ø will be switched on and lines Ø2Ø and Ø3Ø will not be executed because they are not conditioned by the 8Ø result indicator. However, lines Ø4Ø through Ø7Ø will be executed.

The only difference between conditional and unconditional branching is that unconditional is not dependent on a test condition. For example, Figure 7-17 illustrated a conditional branch and in order to make an unconditional branch the decision symbol would be left out and branching would be performed every time a card was read. Unconditional branching should be used with discretion as incorrect calculations and/or output could result by unintentionally "skipping over" needed calculations.

Many combinations of branching may be used in RPG programs. It must be remembered, however, that the branching discussed so far has only been concerned with the *forward* skipping instructions, not going *back* to a previously executed instruction. The ability of a computer to go back to a previous instruction is called *looping* and will be discussed in the following paragraphs.

LOOPING

Looping is an even more powerful use of the GOTO and TAG operations as it enables control to be transferred to a preceding instruction and to repeat an operation as many times as needed. This powerful feature of a computer is necessary for iterative methods of calculation when an answer is obtained after repeating the same instructions a predetermined number of times.

A typical example of an iterative operation using the looping principle is the raising of a number to a power, as in squaring or cubing calculations. A flowchart is illustrated in Figure 7-19 with the Calculation Specification lines references alongside the symbols so the flowchart logic may be coordinated with the Calculation Specifications coding sheet presented in Figure 7-20.

Notice that a Z-ADD operation, which was discussed in Chapter 6, is entered on line 010 of Figure 7-20. It is used in this program to create the RAISE field for the first record processed and initialize the field to zero for subsequent records. A Z-ADD operation is also entered on line 020. Here the contents of the variable field NUMBER are moved to a newly created result field SAVE because the original contents of the NUMBER field will be lost after one pass through the loop. Because the original value for NUMBER will be printed on output, it must be saved, and the use of the Z-ADD operation will accomplish the desired result. The SAVE field, specified as the result field on line 020, must be given a field size because it was not defined in input or

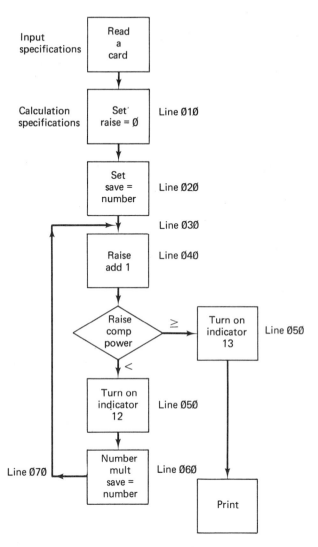

Fig. 7-19. Flowchart for the raising of a number to a power logic.

other calculations. In addition, the SAVE field has to be given a field size that is the same or larger than NUMBER or high-order digits will be lost (truncated).

Continuing with the explanation of the program, line Ø3Ø is the entry point for the GOTO operation specified on line Ø7Ø. Notice that when line Ø7Ø is executed, the program control will go *back* to a previously executed instruction; that is the logic of looping.

The coding specified on line Ø4Ø provides for an accumulator where the number of times the loop is executed is calculated. Line Ø5Ø compares the accumulator field, RAISE, with the input field, POWER, which contains the

REPORT PROGRAM GENERATOR CALCULATION SPECIFICATIONS

IBM System/360

Date: 12/27/72

Program: RAISING NUMBER TO POWER

Programmer: ANYBODY

Punching instructions							
Graphic	Ø	O	Z	2	S	5	I
Punch	N	A	A	N	A	N	A

Page (1 2): Ø3

Program identification (75–80): POWERS

Line (3–5)	Form type (6)	Control level (L0-L9, LR) (7–8)	Indicators (9–17)	Factor 1 (18–27)	Operation (28–32)	Factor 2 (33–42)	Result field (43–48)	Field length (49–51)	Decimal positions (52)	Half adjust (H) (53)	Resulting indicators: Plus / Compare High 1 > 2 (54–55)	Minus / Low 1 < 2 (56–57)	Zero or blank / Equal 1 = 2 (58–59)	Comments (60–74)
01Ø	C				Z-ADD	Ø	RAISE	3	Ø					
02Ø	C				Z-ADD	NUMBER	SAVE	4	Ø					
03Ø	C			START	TAG									
04Ø	C			RAISE	ADD	1	RAISE							
05Ø	C			RAISE	COMP	POWER					13	12	13	
06Ø	C		12 N13	NUMBER	MULT	SAVE	NUMBER							
07Ø	C		12 N13		GOTO	START								
08Ø	C													

Fig. 7-20. Calculation specifications coding for the raising of a number to a power program.

number indicating the amount of times the loop is to be performed. If the number in the field RAISE is lower than POWER, Resulting Indicator 12 will be switched on, permitting the calculations on line Ø6Ø to execute where NUMBER is multiplied by SAVE, giving NUMBER as the result. Line Ø7Ø will also be executed when indicator 12 is on, which sends program control back to line Ø3Ø to repeat the sequence of instructions over again.

Some means must be provided for the exiting from a loop or it will go on to infinity. This is often a common programming error that must be considered when writing any computer programs involving loops regardless of the language used. In this program, exit from the loop is accomplished by the Resulting Indicator 13 specified in columns 54, 55, 58, and 59 of line Ø5Ø. When the contents of the field RAISE is greater than or equal to the contents of the input field, POWER, indicator 13 will be turned on, permitting exit from the loop and the printing of the answer.

The source program listing showing the coding for the File Description Input and Output Specification is illustrated in Figure 7-21. There are no new RPG coding concepts introduced in these coding sections, but follow RPG language rules already discussed in the previous chapters. The printed output for three numbers raised to a desired power is also shown in Figure 7-21.

This simple program example applies the mechanics of the looping process in RPG. Many detailed and complicated programs may require several loops within the same program, but the logic and coding requirements are basically the same. Another more detailed application program requiring the use of looping will be presented in the remainder of this chapter. The program involves the computing of compound interest for a principal amount based on a stated interest rate and time period.

Source listing:

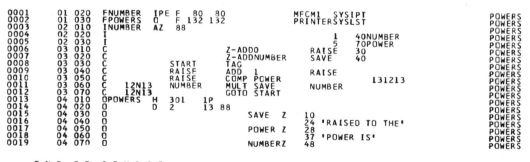

Printed output:

```
12 RAISED TO THE    2 POWER IS        144
16 RAISED TO THE    3 POWER IS        4096
 9 RAISED TO THE    4 POWER IS        6561
```

Fig. 7-21. Source listing and printed report for program to raise a number to a power.

COMPOUND INTEREST

Before an RPG source program can be written for any application, some understanding of the concepts of the problem must be already known or learned. Therefore, the principle of compound interest will be presented before the coding procedures for this process are discussed.

When interest is computed on the combined total of principal and prior interest, it is called compound interest.[1]

Figure 7-22 illustrates the mechanics of computing compound interest. Notice that the interest is computed on the sum of the principal and interest at the end of each year which results in a higher earned interest amount. The procedure of computing compound interest may be conveniently expressed by the formula in Figure 7-22.

The solution for the computation enclosed in parentheses will result in the compound amount of one dollar. To obtain only the compound interest on a dollar for n, the number of interest periods, 1 must be subtracted from this result.

In the event the interest periods are computed semiannually, quarterly, monthly, weekly, or even daily, the interest rate must be divided by the number of interest periods per annum. Also, the number of payments per annum must

$$a = (1 + i)^n$$
$$a = \text{Compound interest}$$
$$i = \text{Annual interest rate}$$
$$n = \text{Number of periods}[2]$$

Problem:
    Calculate the amount of interest produced by $100 with interest at 6% compounded annually for four years.

Solution:

```
$100 X 6% = $    6.00  First year's interest
            + 100 .00  Principal
            $106. 00   Balance-end of first year
$106 X 6% = +  6. 36   Second year's interest
            $112. 36   Balance-end of second year
$112.36 X 6% = + 6. 74 Third year's interest
            $119. 10   Balance-end of third year
$119.10 X 6% = + 7. 15 Fourth year's interest
            $126. 25   Balance-end of fourth year
            −100. 00   Balance at beginning
            $ 26. 25   Amount of compound interest
```

Fig. 7-22. Example of compound interest procedure.

[1]Diamond and Pintel, *Mathematics of Business*, p. 86.

be multiplied by the number of years for which the interest is being computed to obtain the correct quantity for n, the total number of interest periods.

For example, if the interest were to be compounded quarterly, or four times a year, and the compound interest on a principal amount of five years is required, five years would be multiplied by four giving 20 as the amount for n. The interest rate per annum would also have to be divided by four giving the interest rate of 1.25 percent per quarter. This simple arithmetic procedure is important to remember about compound interest because the greater the number of interest periods during a year, the higher the compound interest received. In other words, it is more advantageous to a savings account depositor to have interest compounded daily than weekly.

Before examining the RPG compound interest application program presented in this chapter, the reader should solve question 6 in the Questions and Exercises section to gain a complete understanding of the mechanics of compound interest so the RPG coding may be more easily understood.

RPG II CODING FOR COMPOUND INTEREST

The card layout form for the input records for this program is illustrated in Figure 7-23. Two card types, Ø1 and Ø2, are used for input. The Ø1 card is assigned to the date or header card, and the Ø2 card type for the data cards which include fields for principal, interest rate, time period, and alphanumeric literal for year, month, or days. Both card types are coded with a Record Identification Code in column 80 that is necessary in order for the computer to distinguish between the two input cards.

All of the output format information for the printed report is shown on the printer spacing chart, Figure 7-24. Notice that the dollar signs are floating

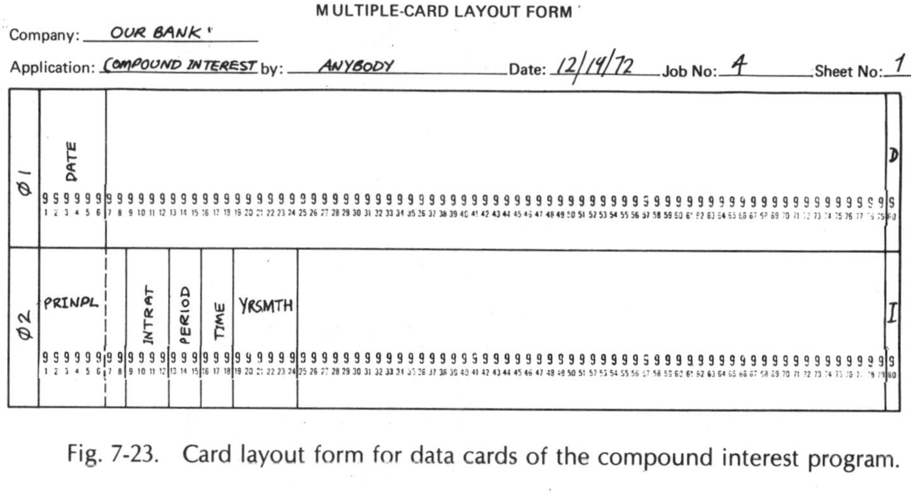

MULTIPLE-CARD LAYOUT FORM

Company: _OUR BANK '_

Application: _COMPOUND INTEREST_ by: _ANYBODY_ _____ Date: _12/19/72_ Job No: _4_ _____ Sheet No: _1_

Fig. 7-23.   Card layout form for data cards of the compound interest program.

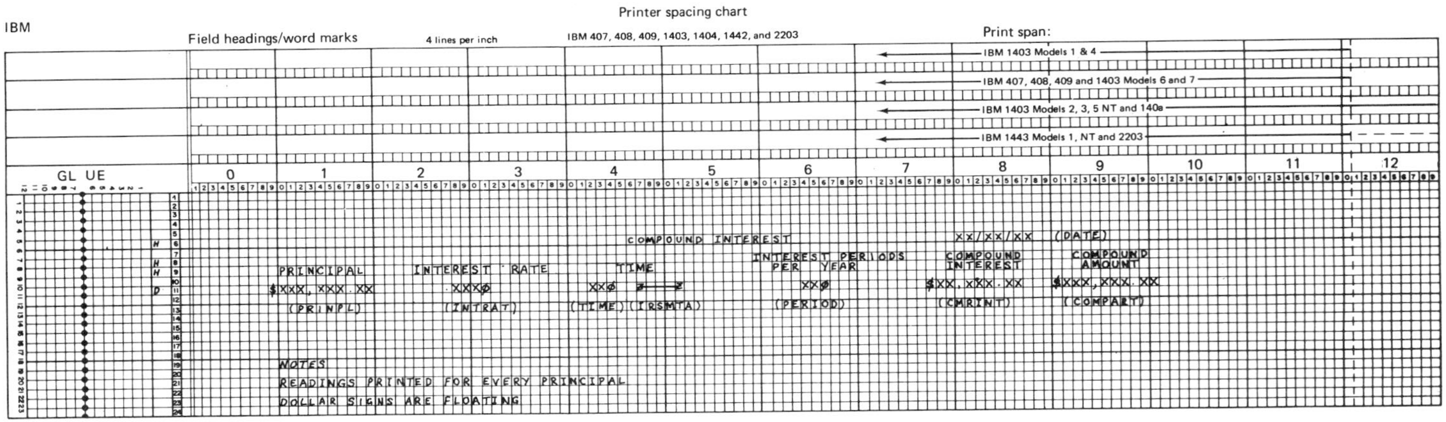

258

Printer spacing chart

IBM

Field headings/word marks — 4 lines per inch — IBM 407, 408, 409, 1403, 1404, 1442, and 2203 — Print span:

IBM 1403 Models 1 & 4
IBM 407, 408, 409 and 1403 Models 6 and 7
IBM 1403 Models 2, 3, 5 NT and 140a
IBM 1443 Models 1, NT and 2203

GL UE

```
                                    COMPOUND  INTEREST          XX/XX/XX   (DATE)
                                              INTEREST PERIODS  COMPOUND   COMPOUND
                                                   PER  YEAR    INTEREST   AMOUNT
      PRINCIPAL      INTEREST  RATE      TIME
      $XXX,XXX.XX          XXXØ        XXØ  #--#       XXØ       $XX,XXX.XX  $XXXX,XXX.XX
      (PRINPL)        (INTRAT)    (TIME)(IRSMTA)      (PERIOD)   (CMRINT)   (COMPAMT)


      NOTES
      READINGS PRINTED FOR EVERY PRINCIPAL
      DOLLAR SIGNS ARE FLOATING
```

Fig. 7-24.   Printer Spacing Chart for the compound interest program.

File description specifications:

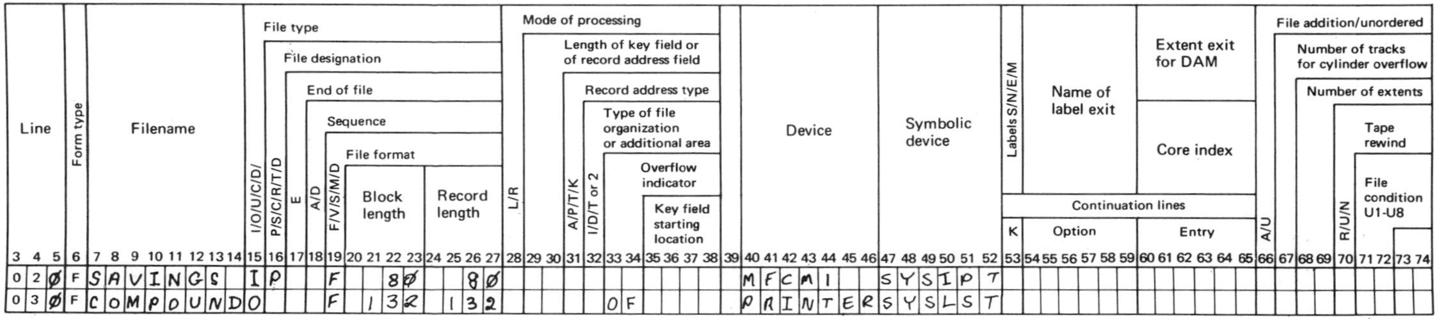

Fig. 7-25. File Description Specifications coding for the compound interest program.

Line	Form type	Filename	File type (I/O/U/C/D)	(P/S/C/R/T/D)	Block length	Record length	Mode of processing	Device	Symbolic device
0 2	0	SAVINGS	I	P	F 80	80		MFCM1	SYSIPT
0 3	0	COMPOUND	O		F 132	132	OF	PRINTER	SYSLST

and zero suppression is required for interest rate, time, and interest periods per year. Compound interest and compound amount are created in calculations whereas the other output information is obtained from the Input Specifications form.

There is nothing different about the File Description coding, Figure 7-25, for this program. Previously studied RPG coding rules are applied for the coding of the input file, SAVINGS, and the output file, COMPOUND.

The two input card types with their respective fields are described on the Input Specifications form, Figure 7-26. Notice that the DATE field, the only field in card type Ø1, is specified as numeric so that editing may be performed on printed output. All of the fields in card type Ø2, except for YRSMTH, are specified as numeric by the entry in the decimal position field, column 52. Four decimal positions are assigned to the interest rate field, INTRAT, so that enough positions are provided for fractional interest rates. For example, an interest rate of 6.25 percent must be expressed as the decimal equivalent or .0625, thereby resulting in four decimal positions. Two decimal positions are specified for the principal (PRINPL) field to allow for amounts less than a whole dollar.

A flowchart for the compound interest calculation logic that is illustrated in Figure 7-27 is coordinated with the RPG calculation coding presented in the Calculation Specifications form, Figure 7-28. Notice that the line number of each calculation is referenced with the respective flowchart symbol. The preparation of a flowchart should be a preliminary step to the writing of any detailed or complicated calculations as it serves as a convenient reference to the necessary coding logic.

Follow the flowchart and reference every step to a line on the Calculation Specifications form. First, a card is read and tested for type. If the card type is Ø1 the date will be printed and when a Ø2 card type is read, calculations will be performed. The first line of calculations, line Ø1Ø, creates the COUNT field and initializes it to zero. A field size must be assigned to the COUNT field in calculations because it is newly formed and was not defined as an input field. If the field is used in the result field more than once, any one of the result references may be given the size, not necessarily the first use of the name. Obviously, the field must be numeric and large enough, or high-order digits may be lost.

Lines Ø2Ø through Ø4Ø calculate the compound interest on $1 as expressed by the following formula:

$$a = (1 + i)^n$$

When the number of interest periods per year is greater than one, the interest rate per annum must be reduced accordingly. For example, if the interest rate per annum is 6 percent and interest is compounded quarterly, 6 would have to be divided by 4 giving 1.50 percent, the interest rate per quarter. This calculation is performed on line Ø2Ø when INTRAT is divided by

Input specifications

Date: 12/19/72
Program: COMPOUND INTEREST
Programmer: ANYBODY

Punching instructions	
Graphic	0 0 I I 4 2 S
Punch	N A A N A N A

Page 1 2: 0 2

Program identification (75 76 77 78 79 80): C O M I N T

Line	Form type (6)	Filename (7-14)	Sequence (15-16)	Number (1-N) (17)	Option (O) (18)	Record identifying indicator or ** or -- (19-20)	Record ID code 1 — Position (21-24)	Not(N) (25)	C/Z/D (26)	Character (27)	Field location From (45-48)	To (49-51)	Decimal positions (52)	Field name (53-58)
01	I	SAVINGS	AA			01	80		C	D				
02	I										1	6	0	DATE
03	I		AB			02	80		C	I	1	8	2	APRINPL
04	I										9	12	4	INTRAT
05	I										13	15	0	PERIOD
06	I										16	18	0	TIME
07	I										19	24		YRSMTH
08	I													

Fig. 7-26. Input Specifications coding for the compound interest program.

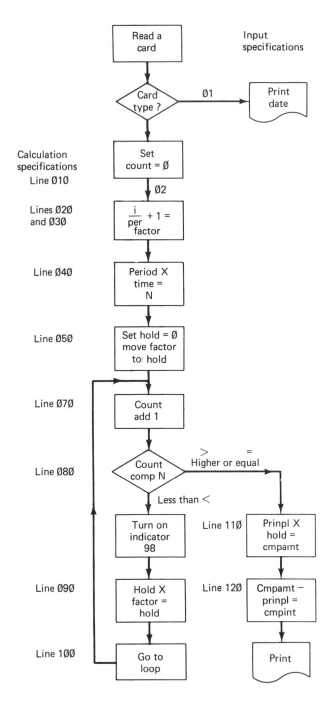

Fig. 7-27. Flowchart for compound interest calculation logic.

REPORT PROGRAM GENERATOR   CALCULATION SPECIFICATIONS
IBM System/360

Date: 12/19/73
Program: Compound Interest
Programmer: Anybody

Punching instructions — Graphic: 0 1 I Z Z S   Punch: N A N A N A
Page: 01

Program identification (75-80): COMINT

Line	Form type	Indicators (And/Not)	Factor 1	Operation	Factor 2	Result field	Field length	Dec positions	Half adjust	Resulting indicators (Compare: Low/Equal)
01	C	02	INTRAT	Z-ADD	0	COUNT	40	0		
02	C	02	BETWN	DIV	PERIOD	BETWN	55	5	H	
03	C	02	BETWN	ADD	1	FACTOR	65			
04	C	02	PERIOD	MULT	TIME	FACTOR	50			
05	C	02		Z-ADDFACTOR		N	65			
06	C		LOOP	TAG						
07	C	02	COUNT	ADD	1	COUNT				
08	C	02	COUNT	COMP	N					98
09	C	02 98	HOLD	MULT	FACTOR	HOLD				
10	C			GOTO	LOOP					
11	C		PRINPL	MULT	HOLD	CMPAMT	82	2	H	
12	C		CMPAMT	SUB	PRINPL	CMPINT	82	2	H	
13	C									
14	C									

Fig. 7-28. Calculation Specifications coding for the compound interest program.

263

PERIOD placing the result in an intermediate field BETWN. The calculation operation on line Ø3Ø adds 1 to the result field BETWN, completing the quantity within the parentheses of the formula for one year.

N, or the total number of interest periods for the problem, is computed by multiplying the number of interest periods per year by the time in years as indicated on line Ø4Ø.

The Z-ADD operation on line Ø5Ø creates the field HOLD, sets it to zero, and then moves the contents of FACTOR into this field. Hence, the contents of FACTOR are then stored in two places, HOLD and FACTOR areas, which is necessary so that the original contents of the FACTOR field may be saved and used again as required for the calculation specified on line Ø9Ø. However, the contents of HOLD will be changed after every pass is made through the loop, but the field FACTOR, which is the multiplier, will remain the same.

LOOP TAG, specified on line Ø6Ø, is the entry point for the GOTO statement on line 1ØØ. Notice that the TAG operation is not conditioned by an indicator and contains no field names or literals in the result field and Factor 2. Any incorrect coding of the TAG statement will prevent execution of the GOTO operation.

The number of times that the loop has been performed is determined by the COUNT field specified on line Ø7Ø. This field was initialized on line Ø1Ø and the constant 1 is added every time that the loop is executed. The coding on line Ø8Ø compares the amount in COUNT with n, the total number of interest periods. If COUNT is lower, indicator 98 will be turned on, permitting the calculations on line Ø9Ø and the following GOTO statement to be executed, which will return control back to line Ø6Ø, the entry point for the loop.

Exit from the loop is provided on line Ø8Ø. When the contents of COUNT are higher or equal to n, the operations on lines Ø9Ø and 1ØØ will not be executed, thereby allowing control to drop down to line 11Ø and finally line 12Ø where compound amount, CMPAMT, and compound interest, CMPINT, will be calculated.

After calculations are completed on a principal amount, the required information will be available for output. An examination of Figures 7-29 and 7-30 will indicate, with the exception of DATE, that all detail output will be performed when Record Identifying Indicator Ø2 is turned on by the respective input record. If indicator Ø1 had been specified for all of the output the answer would not be available at that time for output. Indicator usage is the most sensitive concept of the RPG language and good programming practice suggests that detail output should be conditioned with the last Record Identifying Indicator that was turned on by the last record read in from the Input Specifications. This procedure insures that all input information is in core storage and available for subsequent output.

The RPG source program listing by the computer is shown in Figure 7-31, and the printer output is illustrated in Figure 7-32 which includes the information and results of calculations on four principal amounts. By a careful

IBM

RPG OUTPUT-FORMAT SPECIFICATIONS:

Date: 12/7/72
Program: COMPOUND INTEREST
Programmer: ANYBODY

Page: 0 4 (1 2)

Punching instruction — Graphic: 0 0 1 N 2 S   Punch: N A N A A N A

Program identification (75–80): C O M I N T

Edit codes

Commas	Zero balances to print	No sign	CR	−
Yes	Yes	1	A	J
Yes	No	2	B	K
No	Yes	3	C	L
No	No	4	D	M

X = Remove plus sign
T = Date edit field
Z = Zero suppress

Constant or edit word

Line	Form type	Filename	Type (H/D/T/E)	Before	After	Output indicators	Field name	Edit codes	End position	Constant or edit word
01	O	COMPOUNDH	H	01	3 01					
02	O	OR				01 OF				
03	O						DATE	Y	63	'COMPOUND INTEREST'
04	O		H	1		02			87	
05	O						INTEREST		74	'INTEREST COMPOUND'
06	O						COMPOUND		86	'PERIODS'
07	O						COMPOUND		99	'COMPOUND'
08	O									
09	O		H	2		02			18	'PRINCIPAL'
10	O						PRINCIPAL		37	'INTEREST RATE'
11	O						INTEREST		43	'TIME'
12	O						TIME		69	'PER YEAR'
13	O						PER		86	'INTEREST'
14	O						INTEREST		98	'AMOUNT'
15	O						AMOUNT			

Fig. 7-29. Output-format Specifications coding for the compound interest program.

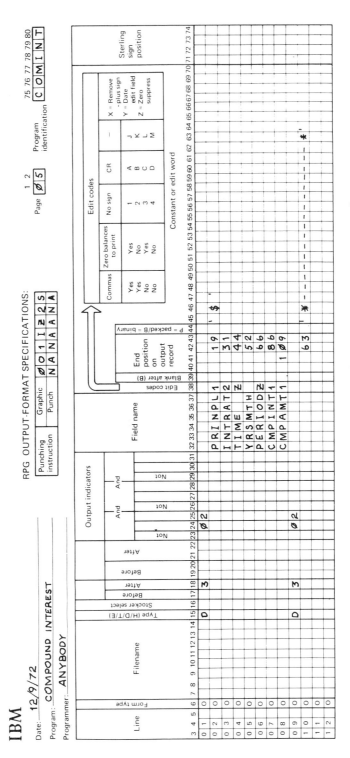

Fig. 7-30. Output-format Specifications coding for the compound interest program (continued).

```
0001    01 020  FSAVINGS IP  F      80              MFCM1 SYSIPT        COMINT
0002    01 030  FCOMPOUNDO   F 120 120    OF        PRINTERSYSLST       COMINT
0003    02 010  ISAVINGS AA   01  80 CD                                 COMINT
0004    02 020  I                                        1   60DATE     COMINT
0005    02 030  I        AB  02  80 CI                                  COMINT
0006    02 040  I                                        1   82PRINPL   COMINT
0007    02 050  I                                        9  124INTRAT   COMINT
0008    02 060  I                                       13  150PERIOD   COMINT
0009    02 070  I                                       16  180TIME     COMINT
0010    02 080  I                                       19   24 YRSMTH  COMINT
        03 000  I* INITIALIZE COUNT FIELD TO ZERO.........................COMINT
0011    03 010  C              Z-ADDO         COUNT    40                COMINT
        03 010  C* CALCULATE PERIOD INTEREST RATE......                  COMINT
0012    03 020  C     02  INTRAT    DIV  PERIOD    BETWN    55H          COMINT
0013    03 030  C     02  BETWN     ADD  1         FACTOR   65           COMINT
        03 031  C* CALCULATE TOTAL INTEREST PERIODS                      COMINT
0014    03 040  C     02  PERIOD    MULT TIME      N        50           COMINT
        03 041  C* STORE MULTIPLIER IN ANOTHER STORAGE POSITION.....     COMINT
0015    03 050  C     02            Z-ADDFACTOR    HOLD     65           COMINT
0016    03 060  C         LOOP      TAG                                  COMINT
        03 061  C* ACCUMULATE NUMBER OF TIMES THROUGH LOOP...            COMINT
0017    03 070  C     02  COUNT     ADD  1         COUNT                 COMINT
        03 071  C* IF COUNT IS LESS THAN N TURN ON 98 AND EXECUTE NEXT TWO LINES COMINT
0018    03 080  C     02  COUNT     COMP N                    98         COMINT
0019    03 090  C     02 98 HOLD    MULT FACTOR    HOLD                  COMINT
0020    03 100  C     98            GOTO LOOP                            COMINT
        03 101  C* COMPUTE COMPOUND AMOUNT OF PRINCIPAL                  COMINT
0021    03 110  C         PRINPL    MULT HOLD      CMPAMT   82H          COMINT
0022    03 120  C         CMPAMT    SUB  PRINPL    CMPINT   82H          COMINT
0023    04 010  OCOMPOUNDH  301    01                                   COMINT
0024    04 020  O        OR          OF                                 COMINT
0025    04 030  O                                    63 'COMPOUND INTEREST' COMINT
0026    04 040  O                               DATE Y 87                COMINT
0027    04 050  O        H   1      02                                  COMINT
0028    04 060  O                                    74 'INTEREST PERIODS' COMINT
0029    04 070  O                                    86 'COMPOUND'       COMINT
0030    04 080  O                                    99 'COMPOUND'       COMINT
0031    04 090  O        H   2      02                                  COMINT
0032    04 100  O                                    19 'PRINCIPAL'      COMINT
0033    04 110  O                                    37 'INTEREST RATE'  COMINT
0034    04 120  O                                    43 'TIME'           COMINT
0035    04 130  O                                    69 'PER YEAR'       COMINT
0036    04 140  O                                    86 'INTEREST'       COMINT
0037    04 150  O                                    98 'AMOUNT'         COMINT
0038    05 010  O        D   3      02                                  COMINT
0039    05 020  O                        PRINPL1     19 '$'             COMINT
0040    05 030  O                        INTRAT2     31                 COMINT
0041    05 040  O                        TIME  Z     44                 COMINT
0042    05 050  O                        YRSMTH      52                 COMINT
0043    05 060  O                        PERIODZ     66                 COMINT
0044    05 070  O                        CMPINT1     86                 COMINT
0045    05 080  O                        CMPAMT1    109                 COMINT
0046    05 090  O        D   3      02                                  COMINT
0047    05 100  O                                    63 '*------------------*' COMINT
```

E N D   O F   S O U R C E

Fig. 7-31. Source listing of compound interest program.

```
                          COMPOUND INTEREST              8/11/79

                                          INTEREST PERIODS  COMPOUND   COMPOUND
PRINCIPAL    INTEREST RATE  TIME              PER YEAR      INTEREST   AMOUNT
 $100.00       .0600          4   YEARS           1          26.25              126.25


                                    *---------------*


                                          INTEREST PERIODS  COMPOUND   COMPOUND
PRINCIPAL    INTEREST RATE  TIME              PER YEAR      INTEREST   AMOUNT
 $950.00       .0500         25   YEARS           2        2,314.83            3,264.83


                                    *---------------*


                                          INTEREST PERIODS  COMPOUND   COMPOUND
PRINCIPAL    INTEREST RATE  TIME              PER YEAR      INTEREST   AMOUNT
$1,200.00      .0400         13   YEARS           4         812.89            2,012.89


                                    *---------------*


                                          INTEREST PERIODS  COMPOUND   COMPOUND
PRINCIPAL    INTEREST RATE  TIME              PER YEAR      INTEREST   AMOUNT
 $100.00       .0400          4   YEARS           4          17.25              117.25


                                    *---------------*
```

Fig. 7-32. Printer output for the compound interest program.

study of this program and the previous one that determined the power of a number, the student should understand the mechanics and use of the looping process in RPG.

Another powerful tool of RPG has been introduced. However, the mere reading of RPG rules and principles is not enough for the learning of a programming language. Programs must be written in order to gain the knowledge necessary for a complete understanding. Consequently, at least one of the lab assignments at the end of this chapter should be written, keypunched, compiled, and debugged so that a finished RPG source program and correct, printed report are obtained.

QUESTIONS

1. What is the Compare Operation name? In what coding forms is it used? Is it right- or left-justified in its respective field? What is entered in the Result Field in any compare statement?
2. When comparing the variable field or literal in Factor 1 with the variable field or literal in Factor 2, what conditions are possible?
3. What indicators may be used in the Resulting Indicator fields High, Low, and Equal? Do they have to be assigned in any order?
4. What if anything is wrong with the following unrelated lines of COMP Operation coding:

RPG CALCULATION SPECIFICATIONS

Line	Form Type	Control Level (L0-L9, LR, SR)	Not	Indicators And Not	And Not	Factor 1	Operation	Factor 2	Result Field	Field Length	Decimal Positions	Half Adjust (H)	Resulting Indicators — Arithmetic: Plus 1>2 / Minus 1<2 / Zero 1=2; Compare High 1>2 / Low 1<2 / Equal 1=2; Lookup Table (Factor 2) is High / Low / Equal
0 1	0	C		0 1		'NEWARK'	COMP	16200.00	CITY	1 2			4 0
0 2		C											
0 3	0	C				.0585	COMP	PCT					
0 4		C											
0 5	0	C	L1			A	COMP	B	C				0 1 0 2 0 3
0 6		C											
0 7	0	C				0 0 3 2	COMP	3 2					1 0

5. Determine the result of the following compares:

	FIELDA	FIELDB	$A > B, A < B, A = B$?
A.	0585	.0585	
B.	−90	90	
C.	00200	200.00	
D.	RPGbII	RPGII	
E.	MYERS,S	MYERSbS	
F.	DONbbbb	DONALDS	
G.	bbbBYTE	BYTEbbb	
H.	NEWbYORK	NEWJERSEY	

Note: small letter b denotes blank spaces.

6. Compute the compound interest on the following:

Principal	Rate	Compounded	Years
$600.00	6%	Annually	4
$400.00	3%	Annually	5
$500.00	4%	Quarterly	3
$200.00	5%	Semi-Annually	2

7. What is conditional branching? unconditional branching?
8. What are the two RPG II operation names used in branching?
9. State the rules for forming and using these operation names.
10. What, if anything, is wrong with the following lines of coding (consider each line as unrelated to any other)?

Line	Form Type	Control Level (L0-L9, LR, SR)	Indicators And Not	Indicators And Not	Indicators And Not	Factor 1	Operation	Factor 2	Result Field	Field Length	Decimal Positions
0 1	C						GOTO	START	BEGIN	80	
0 2	C					FIRST	GO TO				
0 3	C						TAG	LOOP			
0 4	C						TAG	GOTO			
0 5	C						GOTO	ENTER			

11. What, if anything, is wrong with the following *related* lines of coding? There are two record types in the file and the first record type is the report date card. The second record type contains the fields used for calculations.

RPG   CALCULATION SPECIFICATIONS

Line	Form Type	Control Level (L0-L9, LR, SR)	Indicators And Not	Indicators And Not	Indicators And Not	Factor 1	Operation	Factor 2	Result Field	Field Length	Decimal Positions	Half Adjust (H)
0 1	C						GOTO	END				
0 2	C					A	MULT	B	C	62		H
0 3	C					C	DIV	D	E	52		
0 4	C					END	TAG					

12. What is meant by Looping? How does it differ from Branching?

EXERCISES

7-1. Write the Calculation Specifications for the flowchart given below using the GOTO and TAG operations. Assign your own Resulting Indicators for the result of the COMP operation.

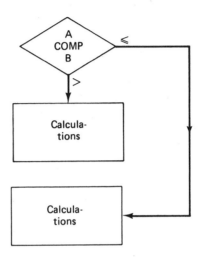

7-2. Prepare a flowchart and complete the Calculation Specifications for the following formula. Ignore Result Field sizes and use the letter in the formula for field names. Assign your own field names for Result Fields.

$$X = \left(\frac{Y^2}{Z^2} \right)^n$$

7-3. From the flowchart given on the next page write the Calculation Specifications coding for the logic. Use field names given in the flowchart symbols and assign your own Record Identifying and Resulting Indicators. Ignore any Result Field sizes.

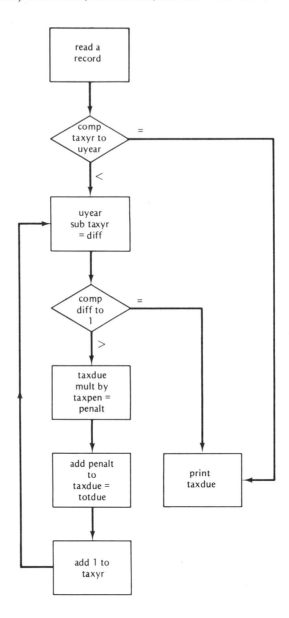

LABORATORY ASSIGNMENTS

LABORATORY ASSIGNMENT 7-1:
PAYROLL REGISTER

A payroll register is used to record the year-to-date and weekly payroll information for each employee. Information as Federal Income Tax withheld to date, Social Security Tax withheld to date, current week's pay, current week's Federal Income Tax withheld, current week's Social Security Tax withheld, and Net Pay are some of the data items recorded in a payroll register. From the information given below write an RPG II source program for the payroll register formatted in the Printer Spacing Chart.

Input Record Format:

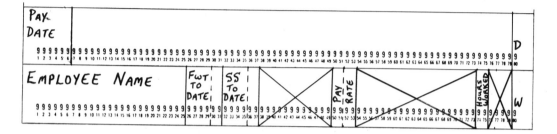

Calculations. From the flowchart given below write the calculation coding for the payroll register. Even though Federal Income Tax withheld amounts are based on number of exemptions, payroll period (weekly, biweekly, etc.), marital status, and amount of wages, use a constant of 15 percent to simplify the program coding.

The Social Security (SS) is based on a maximum wage of $17,700 at a tax rate of 6.05 percent for 1978. The maximum $17,700 amount and 6.05 percent are subject to change. Consequently, the reader should be aware of these changes in subsequent years. The 1070.85 constant given in the flowchart is computed by multiplying $17,700 by .0605 which represents the maximum social security tax dollars that may be withheld from any employee's wages for 1978. Any earnings greater than $17,700 would not be subject to the Social Security Tax. On the other hand, there is no maximum amount for Federal Income Taxes withheld. All wages earned for the payroll year are subject to Federal Income Tax withheld.

Data for Laboratory Assignment:

Employee Name	Federal Income Tax Withheld -to-Date	Social Security Tax Withheld -to-Date	Hourly Pay Rate	Hours Work
JOSEPH BLACKBURN	168000	067760	0650	40
THOMAS WHITEHOUSE	265500	107085	0710	35
JAMES SMITTY	300000	107085	0450	40
SEAN MASSEY	255000	102850	1000	45
BETTY BURPO	000000	000000	0875	30

FLOWCHART:

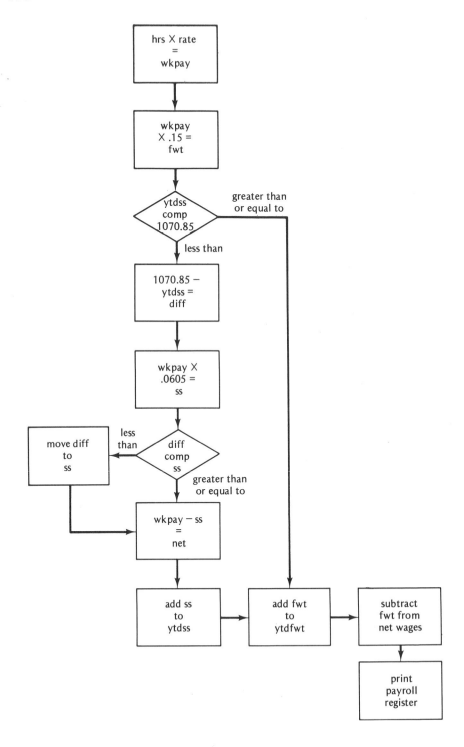

Printed Report Format:

```
                0         1         2         3         4         5         6         7
       1234567890123456789012345678901234567890123456789012345678901234567890123456789012
H  1                                      PAYROLL REGISTER                            PAGE XXXX
D  2                                  FOR WEEK ENDING ØX/XX/XX
   3
D  4              EMPLOYEE NAME            FUT TO    SS TO     WEEK WAGES   WEEK    WEEK    NET
D  5                                       DATE      DATE                  FUT     SS     PAY
   6
D  7  X                               X  X,XXØ.XX  X,XXØ.XX    XXØ.XX     XXØ.XX  XØ.XX   XXØ.XX
   8
D  9  X                               X  X,XXØ.XX  X,XXØ.XX    XXØ.XX     XXØ.XX  XØ.XX   XXØ.XX
  10
  11
  12
  13      HEADINGS ON TOP OF EVERY PAGE
  14
```

LABORATORY ASSIGNMENT 7-2:
PRESENT VALUE OF A FUTURE AMOUNT

Sometimes it is desired to determine what principal amount must be invested today to have a definite future sum at a later date considering the interest the money will earn and the time period in which it will be earned.

This procedure is called compound present worth and involves the following steps:

Step 1: Compute the present worth of $1 by dividing 1 by the compound amount of a dollar, expressed by formula as:

$$v^n = \frac{1}{(1 + i)^n}$$

where:

i = interest rate per annum

n = number of interest periods

v^n = present value of $1

Step 2: Then, multiply the present value of $1 (determined by the procedure illustrated above) by the number of dollars to be produced. This may be expressed by the following formula:

$$P = S \times v^n$$

Where:

S = desired future sum

v^n = present worth of $1

P = amount that must be invested today to have S in a predetermined number of years

Example. How much has to be invested today to have $1,000 in five years if the principal can earn 6 percent compounded yearly?

Step 1:

$$v^n = \frac{1}{(1 + i)^n}$$

$$v^n = \frac{1}{(1 + .06)^5}$$

$$v^n = .74726 \quad \text{(This is the present value of a dollar, or the amount that has to be invested now to have a dollar five years from now if money can earn 6 percent.)}$$

Step 2:

$$P = S \times v^n$$

or: $$P = 1,000 \times .74726$$

$$P = 747.26 \quad \text{(This is the amount that must be invested today to have \$1,000 five years from now if the investment can earn 6 percent.)}$$

Based upon the preceding arithmetic logic, write an RPG II source program from the following input and output formats:

Design of Input Records:

Calculations. Write the calculations from the logic in the formulas explained in steps 1 and 2 of the Present Value logic explained previously. Notice the formula in step 1 is based upon the Compound Interest logic illustrated in the chapter. The Present Value Factor of \$1 (v^n) should be carried to five decimal positions for accuracy

Design of the Printed Report:

H	1	PAGE XXØX LAB I CHAPTER 7 ØX/XX/XX	
H	2	PRESENT WORTH APPLICATION	
H	3	TO DETERMINE THE AMOUNT THAT	
H	4	MUST BE INVESTED TODAY TO HAVE	
H	5	A PREDETERMINED AMOUNT AT	
H	6	A FUTURE TIME	
D	9	INVESTOR.................X————————————X	
D	11	INTEREST RATE PER ANNUM...ØX.XXX PERCENT	
D	13	TIME..................ØX YEARS	
D	15	INTEREST PERIODS PER YEAR.ØX	
D	17	FUTURE AMOUNT \$ XX,XXØ.XX	
D	19	PRESENT WORTH OF \$1.......X.XXXXX	
D	21	AMOUNT THAT MUST BE	
D	22	INVESTED TODAY TO HAVE	
D	23	FUTURE AMOUNT.........\$XX,XXØ.XX	

Data for Laboratory Assignment.

Investor's Name	Int. Rate Per Annum	Time	Int. Per. Per Annum	Future Amt.
ANDREW GUMP	06000	04	01	0010000
DICK TRACY	05000	05	04	0237550
GEORGE HARRISON	05500	05	12	0200000

LABORATORY ASSIGNMENT 7-3:
AGING OF ACCOUNTS RECEIVABLE

Companies that sell a large amount of their goods on account usually experience some customers who do not pay. These bad debts may be recognized and written off as they actually occur, or, when a company maintains a large balance of total accounts receivable, the bad debt expense may be estimated for each operating period. Bad debts are important for tax purposes because they are allowed as legitimate deductions and should be recorded for each period by an adjusting entry.

Typically, bad debt expense may be estimated by using a percent of charge sales, a percent of the accounts receivable balance, or by an analysis of the accounts receivable accounts. The analysis of accounts receivable is commonly called Aging of Accounts Receivable.

The Aging of Accounts Receivable will be the procedure used for this laboratory assignment. Included below are the field information, calculation procedure, output design, and data for the lab.

Input. A card file, ACCSTREC, contains the following record type and fields:

Description	Field Name	Location	Decimal Position	Type
Customer number	CUSTNO	1-5	0	N
Customer name	CUSTNM	6-26		A
Invoice month	INVMON	27-28	0	N
Invoice day	INVDAY	29-30	0	N
Invoice year	INVYR	31-32	0	N
Invoice number	INVOIC	34-37	0	N
Amount of invoice	AMT	39-47	2	N

1. Record Identification Codes (column 79, character 3, and column 80, character 0)

Note: Assign control level indicator L1 to INVOIC and L2 to CUSTNO.

Calculations. Compare each invoice date to determine whether it is current, zero to three months overdue, three to six months overdue, or more than six months overdue. Accumulate the total amounts overdue for each customer based on the invoice date and the months overdue or current. When a customer number changes, print out the totals for that customer and also obtain a grand total for all the amount due or current in each time category (see output format).

Output. The suggested design of your output follows:

ANALYSIS OF ACCOUNTS RECEIVABLE
5/02/73

CUSTOMER NUMBER	CUSTOMER NAME	INVOICE NUMBER	INVOICE DATE	INVOICED AMOUNT	CURRENT	INVOICE AGED BY INVOICE DATE		
						0-3 MONTHS	3-6 MONTHS	OVER 6 MONTHS
05006	MR. K. ANDERSSON	1002	02/25/73	500.00	.00	500.00	.00	.00
	CUSTOMER TOTAL			500.00	.00	500.00	.00	.00
06005	MRS. L. BACKY	3501	03/04/73	1,100.25		1,100.25		
		3509	03/27/73	50.37		50.37		
		6074	04/01/73	30.00		30.00		
		7006	04/06/73	25.75	25.75			
	CUSTOMER TOTAL			1,206.37	25.75	1,180.62	.00	.00
08010	MRS. M. CARSON	0089	06/25/72	30.45				30.45
		1003	12/20/72	40.25			40.25	
		1257	12/23/72	30.99			30.99	
		3047	01/24/73	95.03		95.03		
		5089	02/16/73	73.00		73.00		
	CUSTOMER TOTAL			269.72	.00	168.03	71.24	30.45
12367	MR. F. DONNELLY	0230	07/30/72	14.25				14.25
		0500	10/30/72	3.75			3.75	
		1050	09/10/72	62.10				62.10
		6025	04/25/73	42.30	42.30			
	CUSTOMER TOTAL			122.40	42.30	.00	3.75	76.35
	GRAND TOTAL			2,098.49	68.05	1,848.65	74.99	106.80

279

The data for the assignment is as follows:

CUSTNO	CUSTNM	INVMON	INVDAY	INVYR	INVOIC	AMT
05006	MR. K. ANDERSSON	02	25	73	1002	500.00
06005	MRS. L. BACKY	03	04	73	3501	1100.25
06005	MRS. L. BACKY	03	27	73	3509	50.37
06005	MRS. L. BACKY	04	01	73	6074	30.00
06005	MRS. L. BACKY	04	06	73	7006	25.75
08010	MRS. M. CARSON	06	25	72	0089	30.45
08010	MRS. M. CARSON	12	20	72	1003	40.25
08010	MRS. M. CARSON	12	23	72	1257	30.99
08010	MRS. M. CARSON	01	24	73	3047	95.03
08010	MRS. M. CARSON	02	16	73	5089	73.00
12367	MR. F. DONNELLY	07	30	72	0230	14.25
12367	MR. F. DONNELLY	10	30	72	0500	3.75
12367	MR. F. DONNELLY	09	10	72	1050	62.10
12367	MR. F. DONNELLY	04	25	73	6025	42.30

Your finished lab should include the following items:

1. RPG coding sheets
2. Source program listing
3. Printed report
4. Printer Spacing Chart

8
THE EXCEPTION (EXCPT) OPERATION

The powerful EXCPT operation which adds flexibility to RPG II coding will be introduced in this chapter. Use of this operation will be shown by its inclusion in two application programs presented in the following paragraphs. First, the logic of the EXCPT operation and its application will be illustrated by a simple program that prints the information included in a record group a predetermined number of times. Second, another example of the Exception (EXCPT) coding is illustrated by an accounting application program for a depreciation method.

THE EXCEPTION (EXCPT) OPERATION CODE

The EXCPT operation permits the output of information contained in a record, or the result of calculations immediately from calculations instead of at output time. In other words, the result of every pass through a loop, for example, will be immediately available for output not only when all calculations are completed and control has passed to output instructions.

A simple example of EXCPT usage is the printing of shipping labels when more than one label is required for each customer. If Exception (EXCPT) operation coding was not used, the instructions in the program would follow the normal RPG II logic cycle, and only one label would be printed for a customer.

File description specifications:

Line	Form type	Filename	I/O/U/C	P/S/C/R/T	End of file	A/D	F/V	Block length	Record length	L/R	Length of record address field	Record address type	Type of file organization	K/I	I/O	Overflow indicator	Key field starting location	Extension code I/L	Device	Symbolic device	Labels (S/N, or E)	Name of label exit	Extent exit for DAM	Comments
0 2 Ø	F	NAMES	I	P			F	8Ø	8Ø										MFCMI	SYSIPT				
0 3 Ø	F	LABELS	O				F	132	132										PRINTER	SYSLST				

Input specifications:

Line	Form type	Filename	Sequence	Number (1N)	Option (O)	Resulting indicator	1 Position	1 Not (N)	1 C/Z/D	1 Character	2 Position	2 Not (N)	2 C/Z/D	2 Character	3 Position	3 Not (N)	3 C/Z/D	3 Character	Stacker select	Packed (P)	From	To	Decimal positions	Field name	Control level (L1-L9)	Matching fields on chaining fields	Final received solutions	Field indicators Plus	Field indicators Minus	Field indicators Zero or blank	Sterling sign position
0 Ø	I	NAMES	Ø1	1		11	8Ø		C	N																					
0 2 Ø	I																				1	79		NAME							
0 Ø	I		Ø2	1		12	8Ø		C	A																					
0 4 Ø	I																				1	35		STREET							
0 5 Ø	I																				36	79		CITSTA							
0 6 Ø	I		Ø3	1		13	8Ø		C	M																					
0 7 Ø	I																				1	4	Ø	NUM							

Fig. 8-1. RPG II source program coding for label program using Exception (EXCPT) operation coding.

Calculation specifications:

Line	Form type	Control level (L0-L9, LR)	Indicators	Factor 1	Operation	Factor 2	Result field	Field length	Decimal positions	Half adjust (H)	Resulting indicators: Plus (High 1 > 2)	Minus (Low 1 < 2)	Zero or blank (Equal 1 = 2)	Comments
0 1 Ø	C			RETURN	TAG									
0 2 Ø	C		13		EXCPT									
0 3 Ø	C		13	NUM	SUB	1	NUM						88	
0 4 Ø	C		N88 13		GOTO	RETURN								

Output-Format specifications:

Line	Form type	Filename	Type (M/D/T/E)	Space Before	Space After	Skip Before	Skip After	Output indicators	Field name	Edit codes	Blank after (B)	End position on output record	P = packed/B = binary	Constant or edit word	Sterling sign position
1 Ø	O	LABELS	E	3	2			13							
0 2 Ø	O								NAME			98			
0 3 Ø	O		E		2			13							
0 4 Ø	O								STREET			54			
0 5 Ø	O		E		3			13							
0 6 Ø	O								CITSTA			63			

Edit codes

Commas	Zero balances to print	No sign	CR	–	X = Remove plus sign; Y = Date field edit; Z = Zero suppress
Yes	Yes	1	A	J	
Yes	No	2	B	K	
No	Yes	3	C	L	
No	No	4	D	M	

Coding entries required for EXCPT operation coding.

Fig. 8-1. (concluded)

284

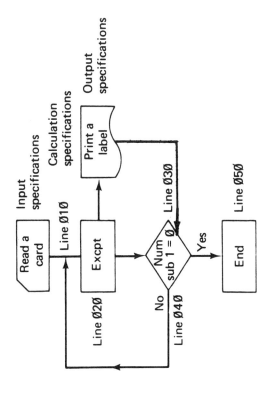

Fig. 8-2. Sample label program logic for EXCPT Operation coding. (continued on next page)

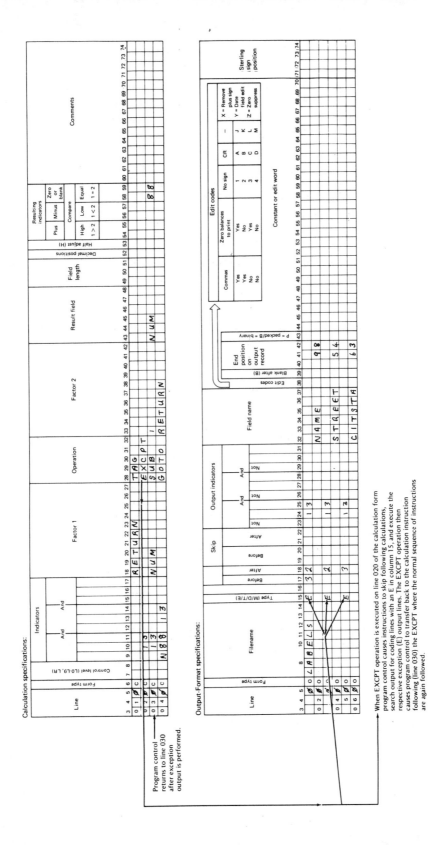

Fig. 8-2. (concluded)

285

Figure 8-1 illustrates the source program coding for the label program. An examination of the File Description and Input Specifications indicates no coding entries are used in these forms for EXCPT coding. Notice on input that sequence checking (discussed in Chapter 5) of the three record types in each customer group is provided to insure the records are in the required order.

New coding entries are required in the Calculation and Output-Format Specifications, however, to provide for EXCPT operation coding. Examine the calculation form (Figure 8-1) and locate line 020. Notice the EXCPT operation is entered left-justified in the Operation field (columns 28-32) and that Factor 1, Factor 2, Result Field, Field Length, Decimal Positions, Half-Adjust, and the Resulting Indicator fields are not used with the operation. In addition to any conditioning indicators (columns 7-17) the EXCPT operation characters are the only entries entered for an exception instruction.

Refer to the output form in Figure 8-1 and locate lines 010, 030, and 050. Notice the letter E is entered in the line type field, column 15. The letter E indicates the line is an exception line and must be used in conjunction with the EXCPT operation, coded in calculations. Hence, the letters H (Heading), D (Detail), and T (Total) may not be used to execute exception time output. This does not infer that Heading, Detail, and Total lines cannot be used in the same program with Exception lines, but only that an E must be used to indicate when and where the particular exception line is to be output. Supplemental to previously discussed coding procedures, the letter E in column 15 is the only new entry needed on the output form to facilitate exception time output.

Exception time output records (E in column 15) may be entered anywhere in the output file(s), no order has to be followed for H, D, T, and E output type lines. However, performance is improved if the H, D, T, and E order is followed for the output records within a file.

Examine Figure 8-1 and notice the Exception Lines on the output form are conditioned by Record Identifying Indicator 13. Reference to the input form (Figure 8-1) shows three record types (11, 12, and 13) defined on input. If indicator 11 or 12 had been used to condition the exception lines, all the information for the record group would not be stored and available for processing. The data for output lines 010 and 020 would be available when the 11 record type was read, and the information for lines 030 and 040 would be available when the 12 record type was read. Each time a record type was processed the EXCPT operation could be executed and the respective line output. However, it is more efficient to output after the three record types are read and the data stored because the EXCPT operation only has to be executed once for each record group instead of three times.

Exception Operation Logic

The flowchart in Figure 8-2 shows the flow of logic for the sample label program using the EXCPT operation. Notice the calculation coding form line numbers are referenced alongside the respective flowchart symbol. The line numbers are coordinated and included in the flowchart to enable the reader to follow the logic and entries used for EXCPT coding.

When record types 11 and 12 are read, lines 020, 030, and 040 are examined but ignored because they are conditioned by the 13 indicator. After the 13 record type is read and all the information for the group is in storage, the EXCPT operation on line 020 is executed and control skips over all following calculations, branches to output, and executes any exception lines conditioned by the 13 Record Identifying Indicator. After every exception line is output, control automatically branches back to line 030, the instruction immediately following the EXCPT operation. This is the *built-in* design feature of the EXCPT and requires no additional coding to execute exception time output.

After control branches back to line 030 the constant 1 is subtracted for the input field NUM which contains the number of times that output is to be printed for each record group. When the value in NUM is zero, the Resulting Indicator 88, which is specified in the Zero Field (columns 58 and 59), will turn on, preventing line 040 from executing. However, if the result in NUM is greater than zero, line 040 will execute and control will loop back to line 010 and follow the same sequence of operations. Everytime a loop is made, and the EXCPT executed, another label will be printed.

Notice the absence of coding to indicate an end-of-job condition. It is not needed in RPG II because control will automatically read another record after all instructions in the program have been examined and executed. The next record group will be processed following the same program logic until the end-of-file is sensed and the last card processed.

The example program has presented a simple yet powerful use of the EXCPT operation. Without this operation, the program would have to be executed the same number of times as there are labels for each customer which would be inefficient and impractical. The source program listing and printed output are shown in Figure 8-3. The printed labels would be individual and attached in a continuous roll to facilitate printing.

Another, more complicated use of the EXCPT operation will be illustrated in an accounting application for a depreciation method called Double Rate Declining Balance.

THE CONCEPT OF DEPRECIATION

Before the RPG application program for the double-rate declining balance method of depreciation is discussed, a review of the concepts and methods of depreciation will be presented.

Service, retail, and manufacturing businesses typically have assets that are used in the production of income. The broad class of assets is commonly referred to as tangible fixed assets or plant and equipment items, the cost of which represents a bundle of services to be received over the life of the asset.

```
0001    01 020   FNAMES    IP  F   80    80          MFCM1  SYSIPT                    LABELS
0002    01 030   FLABELS   O   F  132   132          PRINTERSYSLST                    LABELS
0003    02 010   INAMES        011  11   80 CN                                        LABELS
0004    02 020   I                                             1   79 NAME            LABELS
0005    02 030   I             021  12   80 CA                                        LABELS
0006    02 040   I                                             1   35 STREET          LABELS
0007    02 050   I                                            36   79 CITSTA          LABELS
0008    02 060   I             031  13   80 CM                                        LABELS
0009    02 070   I                                             1   40NUM              LABELS
0010    03 010   C                     RETURN    TAG                                  LABELS
0011    03 020   C      13                        EXCPT                               LABELS
0012    03 030   C      13    NUM                  SUB  1         NUM           88     LABELS
0013    03 040   C      N88 13                     GOTO RETURN                        LABELS
0014    04 010   OLABELS   E  32        13         NAME     93                        LABELS
0015    04 020   O                                                                    LABELS
0016    04 030   O         E   2        13         STREET   54                        LABELS
0017    04 040   O                                                                    LABELS
0018    04 050   O         E   3        13         CITSTA   63                        LABELS
0019    04 060   C                                                                    LABELS
```

E N D   O F   S O U R C E

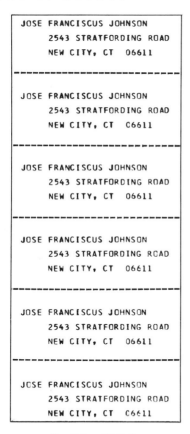

Fig. 8-3. RPG II source program listing and printed output for the label program using the EXCPT operation.

Because of the elements of time and use, assets are subject to deterioration and obsolescence, which means that their cost should, therefore, be written off against revenue over the estimated useful life of the respective asset.

The method of writing off the cost of a tangible fixed asset is called depreciation and may be defined as "a system of accounting, which aims to distribute the cost or other basic value of tangible capital assets, less salvage (if any), over the estimated useful life of the unit . . . in a systematic and rational manner. It is a process of allocation, not of valuation."

Notice that the definition of depreciation clearly states that it is not a method of valuation. Market values are ignored in accounting for assets regardless of how much the market has changed as compared with original cost. Assets are always recorded at cost and the base is never changed to reflect market fluctuations.

Three basic things must be considered when determining the amount of depreciation to be taken each year: the cost, salvage value, and estimated useful life of the tangible fixed asset.

The cost of the tangible fixed asset includes all of the normal expenditures needed to place the asset in use. Invoice amount, less discount, plus freight, insurance, storage, assembly, setup, and installation may be a few of the expenditures included in the cost of an asset. Instead of writing off these expenditures in the year incurred, they are allocated over the useful life of the asset.

Salvage or trade-in value represents that portion of an asset's cost that will be recovered at the end of its useful life. For example, the suggested life of a taxi cab is three years and at the end of that time, it will normally have a trade-in value. Consequently, any trade-in value must be estimated or too much depreciation would be taken each year during the life of the asset. Many reference sources are available to help in determining the salvage or trade-in value of an asset. For some assets, however, the salvage value may be nothing more than a guess and others may be worthless at the end of their productive life.

Estimated useful life is the period of time that an asset is productive in the producing of goods and services for a company. The estimated useful life of an asset often depends on the type of asset, its use, and obsolescence. It may often be difficult to determine in many cases, so the Internal Revenue Service has published information regarding the suggested useful life of many tangible fixed assets.

METHODS OF DEPRECIATION

Now that the three elements needed for determining the depreciation of a tangible fixed asset have been discussed, the methods of depreciation will be introduced.

Many acceptable methods of depreciation are available for determining the amount of annual depreciation expense for a tangible fixed asset. Four of the most commonly used methods include Straight-line, Units-of-production, Sum-of-the-years' digits, and the Double-rate Declining Balance methods. Each of the above methods is allowable for tax deductible purposes and offers the businessman certain advantages. The mathematics needed for each method, along with the advantages, will be discussed in the following paragraphs.

The Straight-Line Method

The simplest and easiest-to-use method of depreciation is the straight-line method. When this method of allocating the cost of an asset is used an equal amount is taken each year as depreciation expense. The mathematics used for straight-line depreciation may be expressed by the following formula:

$$\text{Annual Depreciation} = \frac{\text{Cost} - \text{Salvage}}{\text{EUL}}$$

An examination of the above formula will indicate that salvage value (if any) is subtracted from the cost of the asset, and the net amount is divided by the estimated useful life (EUL). The result is the annual depreciation expense for every year in the life of the asset. For example, if an asset had a cost of $5,000 with a salvage value of $500 and an estimated life of five years, the annual depreciation expense deduction would be determined by subtracting $500 from $5,000 giving a net amount of $4,500. The net amount would then be divided by the estimated useful life of five years giving $900 as the annual depreciation deduction for each year of the asset's useful life.

The advantages of the straight-line method are that it is simple and acceptable for tax purposes for all types of tangible fixed assets. In addition, the method also provides for a constant amount of depreciation expense deduction which has the tendency to smooth out fluctuations in income because of larger or smaller expense deductions.

The Units-of-Production Method

The Units-of-Production method of depreciation allocates the cost of an asset not on the basis of life, but on how much it is used. The more an asset is used, the greater the amount of depreciation that will be taken by this method. Consequently, the Units-of-Production method is particularly suited to assets when useful life is determined by use or obsolescence. The formula used in the computation of this method is as follows:

$$\frac{\text{Depreciation per}}{\text{Unit of Product}} = \frac{\text{Cost-Salvage}}{\text{Estimated Total}} \frac{}{\text{Units of Production}}$$

Notice in the above formula that depreciation is determined per unit of product by subtracting salvage from cost and dividing the net amount by the estimated total units that the asset will produce in its life. For example, using the same cost of $5,000 and salvage value of $500 that was used in the straight-line example, assume that an estimated total of 90,000 units will be produced by a machine. Salvage would be subtracted from cost and the net amount of $4,500 would be divided by 90,000 units giving a depreciation per unit of $.05. If the machine produced 20,000 units for a particular year, $1,000 of depreciation expense would be allowed for that year. On the other hand, if no units were produced no depreciation expense could be taken.

This method is simple, but more importantly its advantage is that it charges depreciation expense against income for an operating period in direct proportion to use. Also, from a logical point of view, the more an asset is used the faster it will usually wear out.

The Sum-of-the-Years' Digits Method

The Sum-of-the-Years' Digits method is one of the so-called accelerated methods of depreciation which allocates a larger depreciation expense deduction in the early years of the life of an asset. Its use is permissible for tax purposes and provides an obvious tax advantage if an asset is not kept for its entire useful life.

Two arguments are often cited for using accelerated methods of depreciation. First, because of the rapid development of technology, the faster obsolescence may occur, and, if an asset can be depreciated faster, the financial implications of replacing obsolete equipment may be relieved to some extent by the taking of a greater depreciation expense in the early years of an asset's life.

Another argument in favor of the Sum-of-the-Years' Digits method depreciation and other accelerated methods is that repair expenses normally increase as an asset becomes older. Therefore, the reduced depreciation expense in the later years of the asset's life, coupled with the increased repair costs, has a tendency to balance out the expenses associated with a particular asset.

The formula for the Sum-of-the-Years' Digits method is as follows:

$$\frac{\text{Digit Year}}{\text{Sum-of-the-Years' Digits}} \times (\text{Cost} - \text{Salvage}) = \text{Annual Depreciation}$$

The numerator of the fraction in the above example is the number of the digit year and the denominator is the sum of all the digit years. For example, consider the same information for the previously discussed depreciation methods. The digit years include 1, 2, 3, 4, and 5, resulting in a sum of 15, the denominator of the fraction. The numerator for the first year depreciation would be 5; the second year, 4; the third, 3; the fourth, 2; and the fifth, 1.

Sum-of-the-years' digits method:

Year	Calculation	Annual Depreciation	Accumulated Depreciation	Book Value
1	5/15 X 4,500	$ 1,500	$ 1,500	$ 3,500
2	4/15 X 4,500	1,200	2,700	2,200
3	3/15 X 4,500	900	3,600	1,400
4	2/15 X 4,500	600	4,200	800
5	1/15 X 4,500	300	4,500	500*

*The book value at the end of the fifth year is equal to the salvage value.

Double-rate declining balance method:

Year	Calculation	Annual Depreciation	Accumulated Depreciation	Book Value
1	40% X 5,000	$ 2,000	$ 2,000	$ 3,000
2	40% X 3,000	1,200	3,200	1,800
3	40% X 1,800	720	3,920	1,080
4	40% X 1,080	432	4,352	648
5	40% X 648	148**	4,500	500

**The depreciation for the fifth year according to the calculation is $259.20. However, if all of this amount was taken it would bring the book value below the estimated salvage of $500, which, of course, is not allowed. Hence, the depreciation expense for the fifth year is limited to the lesser amount of $148.

Fig. 8-4. Schedule of sum-of-the-years' digits and double-rate declining balance methods of depreciation.

Consequently the fractions would be 5/15, 4/15, 3/15, 2/15, and 1/15 accordingly.

Finally the depreciation for each year of the asset's life would be determined by multiplying cost minus salvage, or $4,500 by the appropriate fraction for the respective year's depreciation expense. Figure 8-4 shows a schedule of the depreciation expense computed for every year of an asset's life using the Sum-of-the-Years' Digits method of depreciation. Notice that less depreciation is taken for each year of an asset's life.

The Double-Rate Declining Balance Method:

Another accelerated depreciation method, and the one used as the basis for the RPG II application program, is the Double-Rate Declining Balance method. Under this method, up to twice the straight-line rate may be taken as the annual depreciation percent. For example, consider the sample data used for the other three methods presented previously. The asset has a five-year life, and with the Straight-Line method 20 percent of the depreciable amount (cost-salvage) would be the allowable depreciation expense for every year of the asset's life. Consequently, the *double-rate* would be twice the straight-line rate, or 40 percent.

On the other hand, if an asset had a four-year life, the double-rate would be 50 percent; a 10-year life, 20 percent, and so forth. Figure 8-4 illustrates the mechanics of the Double-Rate Declining Balance method of depreciation. Notice this is the only method in which salvage (trade-in) is not subtracted from cost before the annual depreciation amount is determined.

Now that the methods and mathematics of depreciation has been introduced, the RPG II coding for the Double-Rate Declining Balance method of depreciation will be presented.

RPG II CODING FOR THE DOUBLE-RATE DECLINING BALANCE PROGRAM

An examination of the source listing (Figure 8-5) for the Double-Rate Declining Balance method of depreciation will reveal that previously discussed coding procedures are used in the File Description and Input Specifications. However, the EXCPT operation coding introduced in this chapter is used in calculations along with the corresponding E entry in column 15 of the Output-Format form.

Closer examination of the calculation form shows that two EXCPT operations are used in the instructions. One controls the exception output of headings and the other the year's depreciation, accumulated depreciation, and book value which are determined from every pass through the loop. Any number of EXCPT operations may be used in calculations. The logic of the program and/or programmer preference are the only parameters which determine when this operation is used. A line-by-line discussion of the calculation instructions will be explained in the following section.

Calculation Logic

Line 03010.   The input field Purchase Date (PYEAR) is moved into a year field (PYR) to separate the year of purchase from the other date elements.

Line 03020.   The purchase year (PYR) is added to the constant 1900 to create a date suitable for printing (WKYR). See Figure 8-6 for printed output.

Line 03040.   The EXCPT operation entered on this line causes program control to skip all the following calculations, and to search output for an exception line conditioned by the 02 Record Identifying Indicator. After all the exception lines conditioned by the 02 indicator are executed, control will automatically branch back to the SETOF operation on line 03060.

Line 03060.   The SETOF operation turns off the 02 Record Identifying Indicator. If this was not done 02 would still be on when the next EXCPT (line 04140) was executed which would cause the headings to repeat for every pass through the loop. This does not affect the access of input data because the data is already stored in its field locations.

```
0001   01 020   FCRDF    IPE F  80  80              MFCM1 SYSIPT
0002   01 030   FPRNT    O   F 132 132              PRINTERSYSLST
0003   02 010   ICRDF    BB  02  80 CB
0004   02 020   I                                          1  20 ASSET
0005   02 030   I                                         21 260PYEAR
0006   02 040   I                                         27 320SDATE
0007   02 050   I                                         33  56 VENDOR
0008   02 060   I                                         57 642CCST
0009   02 070   I                                         65 712SVALUE
0010   02 080   I                                         72 730EUL
0011   03 010   C                      MOVE PYEAR     PYR    20
0012   03 020   C          PYR         ADD  1900      WKYR   40
       03 030   C*SKIP TO OUTPUT AND PRINT EXCEPTION LINES CONDITIONED BY 02 INDICATOR
0013   03 040   C                      EXCPT
       03 050   C*SETOF 02 INDICATOR SO HEADINGS WILL NOT BE REPEATED ON NEXT EXCPT
0014   03 060   C                      SETOF               02
       03 070   C* MOVES COST OF ASSET TO BOOK VALUE FIELD
0015   03 080   C          Z-ADDCOST   BOOK    60
       03 090   C*COMPUTE STRAIGHT LINE RATE
0016   03 100   C          1.00        DIV  EUL       WKUL   32
       03 110   C*COMPUTE TWICE THE STRAIGHT LINE RATE
0017   03 120   C          2           MULT WKUL      WKUL
0018   03 130   C          LOOP        TAG
       03 140   C*COMPUTE THE ANNUAL DEPRECIATION AMOUNT ROUNDED TO NEAREST DOLLAR
0019   03 150   C          BOOK        MULT WKUL      ANDEP  60
0020   04 010   C          BOOK        SUB  ANDEP     BOOK
0021   04 020   C          BOOK        COMP SVALUE                  1111
       04 030   C* IF BOOK VALUE IS LESS THAN OR EQUAL TO SALVAGE EXECUTE FOLLOWING 3 LINES
0022   04 040   C    11    ACDEP       ADD  SVALUE    TOTAL  60
0023   04 050   C    11    COST        SUB  TOTAL     ANDEP
0024   04 060   C    11                Z-ADDSVALUE    BOOK
0025   04 070   C          ANDEP       ADD  ACDEP     ACDEP  60
0026   04 080   C          EUL         SUB  1         EUL
0027   04 090   C          EUL         COMP 0                       12
       04 100   C*IF USEFUL LIFE (EUL) IS LESS THAN ZERO GO TO END OF CALCULATIONS
0028   04 110   C    12                GOTO OUTA
       04 120   C*SETON INDICATOR 60 TO CONDITION EXCPT OUTPUT FOR EACH YEAR DEPRECIATION
0029   04 130   C                      SETON               60
0030   04 140   C                      EXCPT
       04 150   C*INCREMENT THE DEPRECIATION YEAR USED IN PRINTING BY 1
0031   05 010   C          1           ADD  WKYR      WKYR
       05 020   C*IF ASSET NOT FULLY DEPRECIATED RETURN AND REPEAT INSTRUCTIONS
0032   05 030   C                      GOTO LOOP
0033   05 040   C          OUTA        TAG
       05 050   C*TURN OFF ALL RESULTING INDICATORS USED IN CALCULATIONS
0034   05 060   C                      SETOF               1160
       05 070   C*INITIALIZE ACC. DEP FIELD TO ZERO BEFORE NEXT ASSET INFO IS COMPUTED
0035   05 080   C                      Z-ADD0         ACDEP
0036   05 090   OPRNT    E 2 01        02
0037   05 100   O                                      5 'ASSET'
0038   05 110   O                      ASSET         40
0039   05 120   O        F 1           02
0040   05 130   O                                     13 'PURCHASE DATE'
0041   05 140   O                      PYEAR Y       28
0042   05 150   O        F 1           02
0043   06 010   O                                      9 'DATE SOLD'
0044   06 020   O                      SDATE Y       28
0045   06 030   O        E 1           02
0046   06 040   O                                      8 'SUPPLIER'
0047   06 050   O                      VENDOR        44
0048   06 060   O        E 1           02
0049   06 070   O                                      4 'COST'
0050   06 080   O                      COST  1       30
0051   06 090   O        E 1           02
0052   06 100   O                                     13 'SALVAGE VALUE'
0053   06 110   O                      SVALUE1       30
0054   06 120   O        E 1           02
0055   06 130   O                                      4 'LIFE'
0056   06 140   O                      EUL           22
0057   06 150   O        E 2           02
0058   07 010   O                                      4 'YEAR'
0059   07 020   O                                     22 'ANNUAL'
0060   07 030   O                                     46 'ACCUMULATED'
0061   07 040   O                                     66 'BOOK VALUE'
0062   07 050   O        E 11          02
0063   07 060   O                                     26 'DEPRECIATION'
0064   07 070   O                                     47 'DEPRECIATION'
0065   07 080   O        F 1           60
0066   07 090   O                      WKYR  Z        4
0067   07 100   O                      ANDEP 1       26
0068   07 110   O                      ACDEP 1       46
0069   07 120   O                      BOOK  1       66

END OF SOURCE
```

Fig. 8-5. Source program listing of double-rate depreciation program.

```
ASSET                 SCREW MACHINE
PURCHASE DATE         12/01/72
DATE SOLD              0/00/00
SUPPLIER              XYZ CORP
COST                      500.00
SALVAGE VALUE             100.00
LIFE                  05

YEAR            ANNUAL              ACCUMULATED          BOOK VALUE
             DEPRECIATION          DEPRECIATION

1972              200                   200                  300
1973              120                   320                  180
1974               72                   392                  108
1975                8                   400                  100
1976                0                   400                  100
```

Fig. 8-6. Printed report for Double-Rate Depreciation program showing an asset fully depreciated the fourth year.

Line 03080.   The contents in the input field COST are moved into the newly created field BOOK (Book Value) so the original value of COST is saved as BOOK will change after each pass through calculation. The mathematics of the Double-Rate Declining Balance depreciation method requires that annual depreciation be computed on the last year's book value. Also remember any field created in calculations must be given a field size or it will be undefined and result in an error during compilation.

Line 03100.   A straight-line percent is computed in this instruction by dividing the constant, 1.00, by the Estimated Useful Life of the asset (EUL).

Line 03120.   The double-rate used in the depreciation method is computed by multiplying the straight-line rate by the constant, 2.

Line 03130.   The LOOP TAG operation specified on this line is the entry point for the GOTO LOOP instruction entered on line 05030.

Line 03150.   The book value (BOOK), which is the original cost of the asset for the first computation, is multiplied by the depreciation rate (WKUL) giving the annual depreciation for the year (ANDEP).

Line 04010.   This instruction subtracts the annual depreciation (ANDEP) from the previous book value (BOOK) to give a new value for BOOK which is used in the computation of the next year's depreciation.

Line 04020.   The book value (BOOK) is compared to the salvage value (SVALUE) for every pass through the loop. When BOOK is equal to or less than SVALUE, Resulting Indicator 11 will turn on and the next three coding lines will be executed. If, however, BOOK is greater than SVALUE the following three instructions will be examined but ignored because they are conditioned by the 11 indicator which did not turn on.

Lines 04040, 04050, and 04060.   If BOOK is less than or equal to SVALUE, line 04040 will be executed where accumulated depreciation (ACDEP) is added to SVALUE giving an intermediate field TOTAL. The instruction on line 04050 subtracts TOTAL from COST which results in the annual depreciation (ANDEP) for the respective year. Finally, the SVALUE is moved into BOOK on line 04060 because BOOK may never be below the salvage value of a depreciable asset.

The logic of the instructions on lines 04040, 04050, and 04060 may be explained by examining the printed report (Figure 8-6) for the program. Locate the 1974 depreciation line and notice the book value is 108. When 40 percent of BOOK is computed it results in $43 rounded, and subtracted from BOOK gives a book value of $65 which is below the allowable salvage value limit. Consequently, the amount that may be taken as annual depreciation for the year is the amount by which book value exceeded salvage for the previous year. The amount by which book value exceeded salvage was $8, the allowable amount of annual depreciation for 1975.

Line 04070.   The annual depreciation (ANDEP) computed on either line 03150 or 04050 is added to accumulated depreciation (ACDEP). Remember, the accumulated depreciation amount indicates the amount of depreciation taken on an asset to date.

Line 04080.   Because depreciation expense is determined on every year for the life of an asset and no more, the EUL must be reduced by one after a pass through the loop so a limit may be placed on the number of times the loop is executed.

Lines 04090 and 04110.   The instruction on line 04090 compares the estimated useful life (EUL) to zero, and if less than zero, Resulting Indicator 12 will turn on. Because line 04110 is conditioned by the 12 indicator, control will branch to line 05040 and skip over the instructions on lines 04120 to 05030. However, if EUL is not less than zero, the GOTO will be ignored and the instruction on line 04130 will be executed. This is how to provide for the exit from the loop in this program. Any looping instructions must have instructions for an exit or the calculations will go on to infinity.

Line 04130.   The SETON operation on this line turns on an indicator used to control the printing of the year's depreciation lines in the report. Any indicator not previously assigned in the program could be used here. Remember the 02 Record Identifying Indicator assigned to the records on input controlled the printing of exception time heading information and was later turned off to prevent the duplication of headings on subsequent output. Consequently, another indicator has to be used to control the printing of annual depreciation lines.

Line 04140. The EXCPT operation caused program control to branch to output and executed the exception lines conditioned by the 60 indicator. After the exception lines are output, control automatically branches back to the following line (line 04150) and the sequence of instructions are again followed.

Line 05010. The depreciation year (WKYR) is incremented by the constant, 1, on this line. The report includes the depreciation history for the life of an asset; therefore, each year's depreciation is computed accordingly.

Line 05030. The GOTO operation here causes program control to branch back to line 03130 where the sequence of instructions to compute the annual depreciation for the year are repeated. This sequence would be skipped over if EUL had been less than zero, thereby preventing the possibility of going into a perpetual loop.

Line 05040. The OUTA TAG instruction on this line is the entry point for the GOTO OUTA on line 04110.

Line 05060. All Resulting Indicators are set off to prevent any unwanted output when the next asset's record is processed.

Line 05080. The accumulated depreciation field (ACDEP) is initialized to zero before the next record is processed to prevent the carry-over of accumulated depreciation from one asset to the next.

The calculation logic and corresponding coding has been presented in a line-by-line discussion. Notice that comment lines in the source program caused the line numbers to appear as if instructions were skipped. Any line number not following the previous one indicates that a comment line interceded.

Output Logic Coding

Refer back to Figure 8-5 and notice lines 05090 to 07070 are exception lines (E in column 15) conditioned by the 02 indicator. The general information for the report is printed on these lines when the first EXCPT (line 03040) is executed. After the information is printed once for the asset the 02 indicator is turned off in calculations to prevent any duplication of print lines. Look at the printed report in Figure 8-6 and identify which print lines are output at exception time when the 02 indicator is on.

Lines 07080 to 07120 are exception lines conditioned by the 60 indicator turned on by the SETON operation on line 04130 in the calculation form. The output line conditioned by the 60 indicator is executed after every pass through the loop. The number of print lines conditioned by the 60 indicator depends on the estimated useful life (EUL) of the asset. Examine Figure 8-6 again and locate the lines output by the second EXCPT when 60 is on.

The logic presented for this application is not the only approach to this application. Each program is a creative process and the programmer writing the instructions will use his or her own logic and coding preferences. Hence, it is not to be construed that this program or any program in the text incorporates the only or even best coding procedures.

Overflow Control at Exception Time

The program presented in the preceeding section did not use any Heading (H), Detail (D), or Total (T) lines in output. In addition, the printing of heading information was not provided for on output in the event of page overflow. It may be desirable to have some heading information repeated on every page of a report if the pages become separated. This is provided for in RPG II by entering an overflow indicator (OA-OG, and OV) in one of the Output Indicator fields (columns 23-31). Overflow printing may be used with any H, D, or T line in an OR relationship with an output line, or alone. Normal RPG II coding, however, does not allow the printing of overflow lines at exception

RPG OUTPUT SPECIFICATIONS

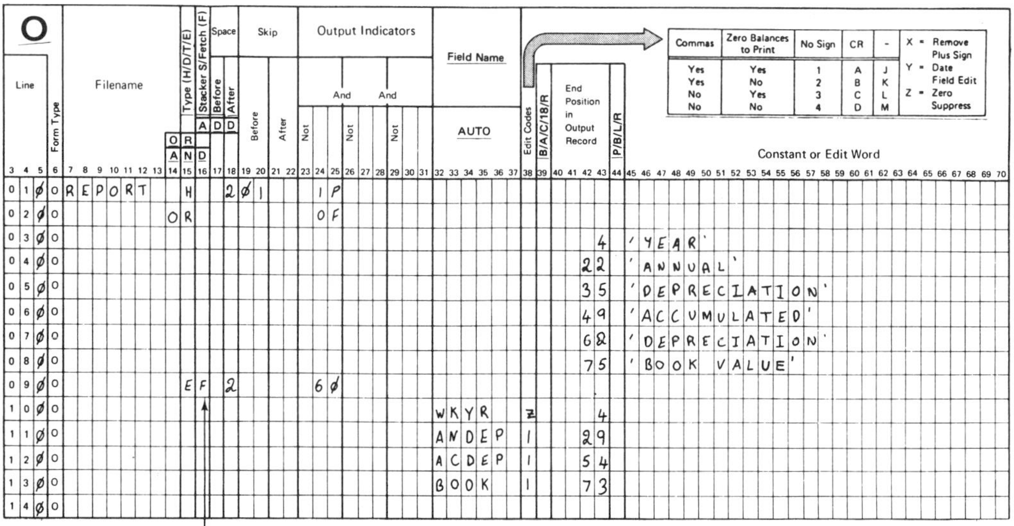

Line	Form Type	Filename	Type (H/D/T/E)	Stacker S/Fetch (F)	Space Before	Space After	Skip Before	Skip After	Output Indicators	Field Name	Edit Codes	B/A/C/18/R	End Position in Output Record	P/B/L/R	Constant or Edit Word
01ø	O	REPORT	H		2		ø1		1P						
02ø	O	OR							OF						
03ø	O												4		'YEAR'
04ø	O												22		'ANNUAL'
05ø	O												35		'DEPRECIATION'
06ø	O												49		'ACCUMULATED'
07ø	O												62		'DEPRECIATION'
08ø	O												75		'BOOK VALUE'
09ø	O		E	F	2				6ø						
10ø	O									WKYR	Z		4		
11ø	O									ANDEP	1		29		
12ø	O									ACDEP	1		54		
13ø	O									BOOK	1		73		
14ø	O														

If the Overflow line (channel 12) is sensed when printing the exception lines, the letter F in column 16 of the output form will "fetch" the Heading line to be printed on page overflow. The line (s) will be printed on the next page before the exception line output is continued. Overflow lines must be coded on output (line 020) to execute the required Fetch Overflow feature.

Fig. 8-7. Fetch Overflow Feature used with Exception Time Output to facilitate Page Overflow printing.

time. The *Fetch Overflow* feature discussed in Chapter 6 does provide for the printing of headings at exception time output when the overflow line is sensed.

Figure 8-7 illustrates an example of output coding to print the heading lines conditioned by an overflow indicator (line 020) when overflow is sensed (channel 12) during the printing of an exception line. Notice the only entry needed to execute the Fetch Overflow feature is the letter F in column 16 of the exception line. When overflow is sensed, the Fetch Overflow will "fetch" the overflow lines, print them on the next page, and then continue with exception time printing. Note any overflow line is printed *before* the next exception line. In order for this feature to execute, overflow lines must be provided for on output. If there are not any overflow lines the Fetch Overflow has nothing to "fetch."

QUESTIONS

1. Explain the logic of the EXCPT operation.
2. What coding forms are used with the EXCPT operation? What columns or fields of the respective forms are used?
3. How many EXCPT operations are permitted in one RPG II program?
4. When is the EXCPT operation used in a program? Name some applications where the EXCPT may be used.
5. When is the Fetch Overflow feature used with exception time output?

EXERCISES

8-1. Complete the Calculation coding for the following logic. You must use the SETOF operation to control printing of headings. Use names in the symbols for variable field names.

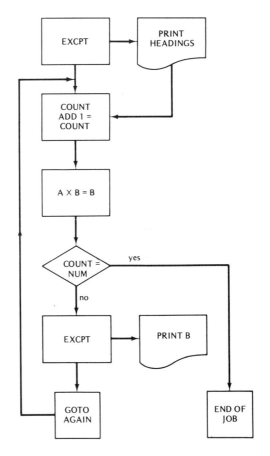

8-2. Refer to your coding in Exercise 1 and complete the output coding for the following report format. Use the Fetch Overflow feature to provide for headings on top of every page if the overflow line is sensed during exception time output.

		0	1	2	3
		1234567890	1234567890	1234567890	1234567890
H	1	ØX/XX/XX	EXERCISE 8-1	PAGE XXØX	
	2				
E	3	CHANGING VALUES FOR B			
	4				
E	5	XXX.XXØX			
E	6	XXX.XXØX			
	7				
	8				
	9	NOTE:			
	10				
	11	PRINT HEADING LINE			
	12	ON TOP OF EVERY			
	13	OVERFLOW PAGE			
	14				
	15				
	16				
	17				
	18				
	19				
	20				
	21				
	22				
	23				
	24				

8-3. Refer to Chapter 7 and the source program listing for the "raising a number to a power" program in Figure 7-21. Notice the answer is printed when the required power is determined. Modify the program so that the power from each pass through the loop is printed. For example, if a number is raised to the fourth power print the result for the second and third power of the number as well as the fourth.

8-4. DEBUGGING AN RPG II SOURCE PROGRAM

Given below is an RPG II source program that contains errors. Correct the coding lines that are incorrect by rewriting them on the required Specifications form.

```
0001   01 020  FNAMES    IP  F  80   80      MFCM1  SYSIPT         LABELS
0002   01 030  FLABELS   O   F  132  132     PRINTERSYSLST         LABELS
0003   02 010  INAMES    011 11   80 CN                            LABELS
0004   02 020  I                                  1  79 NAME       LABELS
0005   02 030  I         021 12   80 CA                            LABELS
0006   02 040  I                                  1  35 STREET     LABELS
0007   02 050  I                                 36  79 CITSTA     LABELS
0008   02 060  I         031 13   80 CM                            LABELS
0009   02 070  I                                  1  40NUM         LABELS
0010   03 010  C     88      RETURN    TAG                         LABELS
                                                                            NOTE 332
0011   03 020  C     13              EXCPTLOOP                     LABELS
                                                                            NOTE 336
0012   03 030  C     13      NUM     SUB  1      NUM            88 LABELS
0013   03 040  C                     GOTO RETURN                   LABELS
0014   04 010  OLABELS   H  32      13                             LABELS
0015   04 020  O                        NAME      93                LABELS
0016   04 030  O         E   2      13                             LABELS
0017   04 040  O                        STREET    54                LABELS
0018   04 050  O         E   3      13                             LABELS
0019   04 060  O                        CITSTA    63                LABELS
```

        E N D   O F   S O U R C E

                      T A B L E S   A N D   M A P S

RESULTING INDICATOR TABLE

ADDRESS RI	ADDRESS RI	ADDRESS RI	ADDRESS RI	ADDRESS RI	ADDRESS RI	ADDRESS RI
029D OA	02BF LR	02C0 H0	02CA 1P	02CD 11	02CE 12	02CF 13
02D0 88						
		0003	11			
		0005	12			

FIELD NAMES

ADDRESS FIELD	ADDRESS FIELD	ADDRESS FIELD	ADDRESS FIELD	ADDRESS FIELD
01DD *ERROR	0349 NAME	0398 STREET	03BB CITSTA	03E7 NUM
03EC RETURN				

                              M E S S A G E   T E X T

        NOTE 332   CONDITIONING INDICATORS INVALID. ASSUME BLANK.
        NOTE 336   FACTOR 2 CANNOT BE SPECIFIED. BLANK ASSUMED.
        NOTE 388   INDICATOR DEFINED BUT NOT REFERENCED. WARNING.

LABORATORY ASSIGNMENTS

LABORATORY ASSIGNMENT 8-1:
STRAIGHT-LINE DEPRECIATION SCHEDULE

Write an RPG II source program for the depreciation schedules for fixed assets using the straight-line method of depreciation. The mathematics and procedure of this method is fully explained in this chapter: however, the formula is repeated below for convenience:

$$\text{Annual Depreciation} = \frac{\text{Cost} - \text{Salvage(Trade-in)}}{\text{Estimated Useful Life}}$$

Format of Data Records.   Note the last two digits of the Purchase Date field must be redefined on input to isolate the Purchase Year which is needed in calculations. If the reader prefers, the MOVE or Z-ADD operation could be used in calculations to accomplish the same thing.

ASSET NAME	PURCHASE DATE	COST	SALVAGE VALUE	EUL		SL

```
999999999999999999999999 9999999 999999 9 999999999 9 9 9999999999999999999999999999 99
1 2 3 4 5 6 7 8 9 10 11 12 13 14 15 16 17 18 19 20 21 22 23 24 25 26 27 28 29 30 31 32 33 34 35 36 37 38 39 40 41 42 43 44 45 46 47 48 49 50 51 52 53 54 55 56 57 58 59 60 61 62 63 64 65 66 67 68 69 70 71 72 73 74 75 76 77 78 79 80
```

Calculations.   Reference to the straight-line method of depreciation section in this chapter indicates the annual depreciation amount is the same for every year of an asset's life. However, the depreciation year, accumulated depreciation, and book value amounts change for every year. Depreciation is only an estimate; consequently, all result fields used as output may be rounded to the nearest dollar. Refer to the Printer Spacing Chart for Result Field sizes.

The calculation logic is given in the Flowchart which appears on the next page.

Format of Printed Report:

NOTES:
① HEADINGS ON TOP OF EVERY PAGE
② ROUND ANNUAL DEP., ACCUMULATED DEP., AND BOOK VALUE TO NEAREST DOLLAR....

[handwritten notes:] each year has a print line   half adjust   Book value = salvage val at end of year

FLOWCHART FOR STRAIGHT LINE DEPRECIATION LOGIC

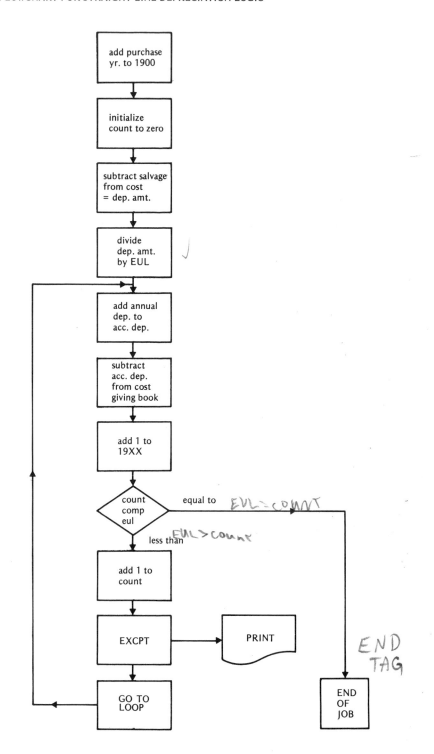

Data for Laboratory Assignment:

Asset Name	Purchase Date	Cost of Asset	Salvage Value	Estimated Useful Life(yrs)
TWO-FAMILY, ROSE AVE.	010578	09000000	0000000	40
IBM SELECTOMATIC	021078	00150000	0030000	05
HEWITT-PACKARD CAL.	031578	00480000	0050000	10
CHEVROLET EL CAMINO	041578	00711897	0150000	06

Note: Company takes full-year depreciation regardless of month asset is purchased.

LABORATORY ASSIGNMENT 8-2:
SUM-OF-THE-YEARS' DIGITS DEPRECIATION

Write an RPG source program to compute depreciation expense by the sum-of-the-years' digits method of depreciation.

The formula is as follows:

$$\frac{\text{Digit Year}}{\text{Sum-of-the-Years' Digits}} \times (\text{Cost} - \text{Salvage}) = \begin{array}{l}\text{Annual} \\ \text{depreciation} \\ \text{amount}.\end{array}$$

Use the following formula in your program to determine the denominator of the above formula. This formula must also be part of your source program.

$$\text{Sum-of-the-Years' Digits} = \text{EUL} \times \left(\frac{1 + \text{EUL}}{2}\right)$$

Input fields must include:

Record Type Ø1

Description	Location	Type
Vendor	1-3Ø	Alphanumeric
Asset name	31-6Ø	Alphanumeric
Purchase date	61-66	Numeric
Sale date	67-72	Numeric

Record identification code (character A, column 8Ø)

Record Type Ø2

Description	Location	Decimal Position	Type
EUL*	1-2		Numeric
Cost	3-11	2 dec. pos.	Numeric
Salvage	12-18	2 dec. pos.	Numeric

Record identification code (character B, column 8Ø)

*Note: EUL is the abbreviation for Estimated Useful Life of the asset.

Output may be of your own design, but must include the following information:

Asset name	X_____X
Purchase date	XX/XX/XX
Date sold	XX/XX/XX
Vendor	X_____X
Cost	$X,XXX,XXX.XX
Salvage value	$XX,XXX.XX
Useful life	XX

YEAR	ANNUAL DEPRECIATION	ACCUMULATED DEPRECIATION	BOOK VALUE
19XX	$ XX,XXX	$ X,XXX,XXX	$ X,XXX,XXX

Your finished lab should contain the following items:

1. Flowchart for calculation logic
2. Printer Spacing Chart
3. Card Layout Form
4. RPG coding sheets
5. Source program listing
6. Printed output

Use the following data for your lab:

	ASSET 1	**ASSET 2**	**ASSET 3**	**ASSET 4**
ASSET	Printer for IBM 1130	Kitchen Unit	Telephone Display Store	International Trailer
PURCHASE DATE	01/14/72	01/30/68	01/02/71	01/03/69
DATE SOLD	00/00/00	09/12/73	00/00/00	00/00/00
VENDOR	Conn. Machine Supply Co.	Stamford Vending Corp.	Southern New England Tel.	Hertz Rental Service of Wilton
COST	$6,500.00	$18,000.00	$120,000.00	$7,000.00
SALVAGE VALUE	$ 500.00	$ 3,000.00	$ 15,000.00	$1,000.00
USEFUL LIFE	5 years	4 years	20 years	5 years

LABORATORY ASSIGNMENT 8-3:
MORTGAGE (LOAN) AMORTIZATION SCHEDULE

Banks and other lending institutions must provide the mortgagor with an amortizations schedule of the monthly or yearly payments. Included in the schedule is information concerning the balance of the original principal after each payment; applicable dollar amount of interest for the period; amount of the monthly or yearly mortgage payment; the amount of the payment that applies against the principal; and the end-of-year principal balance.

Format of Data Records:

Calculations. The calculations for determining the amortization payment per month (or year), simple interest due on each payment, applicable principal portion of payment, and end-of-period principal balance are calculated by solving the following formulas:

Formula for Computation of Mortgage (Amortization) Payments:

$$\text{PAYMENT} = \frac{P \times}{\dfrac{1 - \dfrac{1}{(1 + i)^n}}{i}}$$

Note: $(1 + i)^n$ is the compound interest formula.

where:

$i =$ the annual interest rate charged on the mortgage (has to be divided by the number of interest payments in a year to obtain interest rate per period).

I = interest per period

N = Number of periods

$n =$ the total number of payment periods for the life of the mortgage. If, for example, a 20-year mortgage required monthly payments, the total number of payments (n) would be 20 years × 12 months per year which equals 240.

$P =$ Original amount of mortgage (principal).

Steps in Solution of Formula:

1. Compute the compound interest formula $(1 + i)^n$.

2. Divide the compound amount determined in step 1 into 1 to obtain the present value of a dollar.

3. Subtract the present value of a dollar (determined in step 2) from 1. This represents the compound discount on 1 for the interest rate and payment periods of loan.

4. Divide the result obtained in step 3 by i, then raise to n which gives the present value of an annuity.

5. Divide the original amount of the mortgage (principal) by the result found in step 4. This represents the payment required to amortize the mortgage over its life. This payment figure includes an interest part and principal payment part.

Formula for Computation of Interest Due for Each Period. The payment computed in step 5 includes interest and principal payment. In order to determine the interest portion of the payment the following simple interest formula must be used:

$$I = P \times \frac{R}{\text{\# of interest periods}}$$

where:

I = the simple interest in dollars.   where

P = principal amount in dollars and cents. (The original principal amount will decline after a payment.) Hence, P will represent the end-of-period principal for interest determination.

R = annual rate of interest: must be divided by number of interest periods per year.

T = the time in years, months, or days.

Computation of Principal Payment. The amount of mortgage payment applicable to the principal is computed by subtracting the interest computed above from the payment amount. The following formula may be used to compute principal portion of payment:

$$\frac{\text{Principal}}{\text{payment}} = \text{Payment} - \text{Interest}$$

Computation of End-of-Period Principal Balance. The end-of-period principal balance is determined by subtracting the applicable principal payment from the previous end-of-period balance.

$$Princ - Pay =$$

Format of Printed Report:

```
                    MORTGAGE AMORTIZATION SCHEDULE
LOAN NUMBER-XXXPX    MORTGAGOR-X_____X    INTEREST RATE/YR- PV. XXX

MONTH    BEGINNING     INTEREST    MORTGAGE    PRINCIPAL        END-OF-PERIOD
         PRINCIPAL     DUE         PAYMENT     PAYMENT          PRINCIPAL

XPX      XXX,XXP.XX    XX,XXP.XX   XX,XXP.XX   XX,XXP.XX        XXX,XXP.XX
XPX      XXX,XXP.XX    XX,XXP.XX   XX,XXP.XX   XX,XXP.XX        XXX,XXP.XX

NOTES:
  ① HEADINGS ON TOP OF EVERY PAGE
  ② CONVERT DECIMAL PERCENT TO PERCENT FOR PRINTING
```

Data for Laboratory Assignment:

Loan No	Mortgagor	Time of Loan (yrs)	Percent of Loan	Principal of Loan	Interest Per./Yr.
00221	RELIABLE SOFTWARE CO.	05	12500	02000000	04
05670	SIMPLIFIED TAX SERVICE	10	10000	06000000	12
08888	ABC MANUFACTURING CO.	30	09500	20000000	02

9
DISK FILE CONCEPTS AND SEQUENTIAL DISK FILES

DISK CONFIGURATION

Previous chapters have discussed the techniques associated with the processing of card input and printer output files. Figure 1-2 of Chapter 1 showed that many devices may be used in addition to card readers and line printers to process input and output. One of the most powerful devices, which has gained popularity because of drastically reduced initial purchase costs and inherent benefits is the magnetic disk with drive unit. Disk storage has proven to be a valuable feature that has made the computer a more powerful and versatile machine because of the following reasons:

1. Less physical room is occupied by data files stored on disk as compared to cards.

2. Disk data files may be processed with greater speed than card files.

3. Files stored on disk may be *random accessed* faster than tape or card files.

4. Records may be added to a data file stored on disk, a feature not possible with tape files and awkward for card files. The need to recreate the file if records have to be added or updated is eliminated.

5. The object code output (and source code) from source programs may be stored on disk permitting faster processing and making object decks unnecessary.

6. User programs can be stored on disk and nested so that one automatically executes another.

The general concept of magnetic disk files and programs follows the same logic as those maintained in card form except that records are physically written on disk as magnetic impulses instead of holes in a punch card. Perhaps it may be useful to compare a long-playing record to a magnetic disk used with a computer system. However, instead of scratches on the surface of the disk, the disk used with a computer stores the information as invisible magnetic impulses similar to the tape used on a tape recorder. In other words, the data may be erased and new information stored in the same location as often as needed without damage to the disk. Common terminology related to disks includes the following:

Disk Drive: The hardware unit which holds the disk pack and controls the operation of the disk. Figure 9-1 shows the outside design of a disk drive on an IBM 370 system.

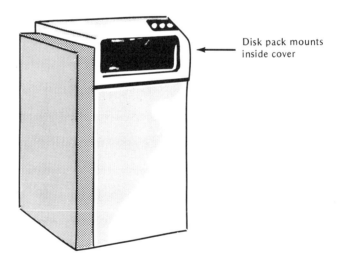

Disk pack mounts inside cover

Fig. 9-1. IBM 3340 disk drive unit.

Disk Pack: A self-contained portable unit which encases the magnetic disks (platters). Disks are used as a storage media for data files, system and user software.

Volume: Refers to a disk pack, data cell, data drum, diskette, or reel of magnetic tape.

Data Set: (Another name for a data file.) Might only be a small area on a disk pack or large enough to include more than one physical disk pack.

Figure 9-2 shows the internal features of the 3348 disk pack which are important to the programmer. The mechanical design is not shown but only the logical areas used for data files, programs, and other software storage.

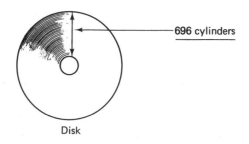

Disk

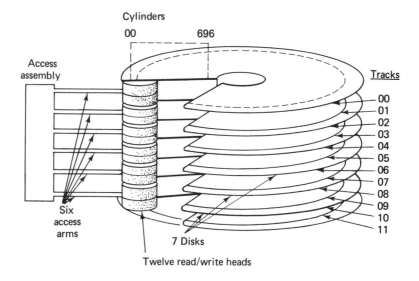

Fig. 9-2. Internal construction of 3348 disk pack.

The inside structure of the 3348 pack contains seven magnetic disks (platters) and six arms, each with two read/write heads. Reexamine Figure 9-2 and notice the logically-defined storage areas are identified by *Cylinders* and *Tracks*.

A description of the two areas follows:

Cylinders. A disk pack (volume) is divided into areas called cylinders. The 3348 disk illustrated in Figure 9-2 has 696 cylinders with an additional three for overflow in the event one of the normally-used 696 cylinders becomes defective. The horizontal and vertical movements are accentuated by instructions from the computer and used to locate a specific cylinder, track, and record.

Each cylinder on the 3348 disk pack has 100,000 bytes (characters) of storage capacity. The maximum storage of the pack is 100,000 × 696 cylinders, or 69.6 million bytes. Depending on the disk pack design, some have more or less storage.

Tracks. Disk packs are further subdivided into tracks (heads). Examine Figure 9-2 and notice each cylinder is divided into 12 writing surfaces called tracks or heads. The tracks are numbered from 00 to 11, or 12 tracks per cylinder. Storage capacity of a track is 100,000 ÷ 12, or approximately 8,333 bytes (characters).

The disk pack discussed is not the only design available. Some have only one disk (platter) and, of course, have less cylinders and tracks for storage. On the other hand, other designs have more cylinders and tracks and have larger storage capacities. The type of disk pack used will depend on the computer system and/or disk drives.

DISK FILE ORGANIZATION METHODS

Disks are used to store data files, user programs, and the system's software (compilers, supervisor, etc.). Maintenance and application programmers are concerned primarily with two uses of disks. First, for the storage of data files, and second, for the storage of the object code from the compilation of a source program. The RPG II coding methods for the creation and processing of data files stored on disk will be presented in the following sections.

Data files stored on disk may be organized as *sequential, indexed-sequential,* and *direct.* Figure 9-3 shows the methods of organization and related processing methods. The method of organization will usually depend on the data file used in applications. For example, a file that is normally processed completely could be efficiently organized as sequential. A payroll file would be an example of a file that might be sequentially organized because it is usually processed in its entirety when the week's payroll is run. On the other hand, a file that has limited access, as an accounts receivable file, would be more efficiently organized as indexed-sequential or direct.

Figure 9-3 also indicates the processing techniques available for each file organization type. Regardless of the file type, it may be processed sequentially (one record after the other, as in a card file) or *randomly.*

Random processing refers to the process method when a data file is accessed for a limited number of select records and not the complete file. A sequential file processed randomly requires that the first record, then the second, third, and so forth, be read and examined until the appropriate record is located. Consequently, if one record were to be accessed and it was located at the end of the sequentially-organized file, every record in the file would have to be examined before the required record was found. This method of processing is both time consuming and inefficient when a file is frequently processed randomly. Indexed-sequential disk files, however, provide for more efficient random processing. This file organization method will be discussed in Chapter 11.

Even though sequential files are slower to random process, they have advantages. First, sequentially-organized files require less storage than

		METHOD OF ORGANIZATION		
		Sequential	Indexed-sequential	Direct
METHOD OF PROCESSING	Sequential	a) Sequential processing of a sequential file	b) Sequential processing of an indexed-sequential file	Sequential processing of a direct file
	Random	c) Random processing of a sequential file	d) Random processing of an indexed-sequential file	Random processing of a direct file

Fig. 9-3. Methods of file organization and processing.

indexed-sequential files; second, they are easy to create and maintain; and third, they are faster to process when the file has a high percentage of activity.

The logic of sequential disk-file creation from card input is shown in Figure 9-4. Note the characters (bytes) from each card record are written as magnetic impulses on a track(s). The number of tracks reserved for a data file depends on its present or future size. Hence, the programmer must determine how many tracks and cylinders have to be used for the file before it is created.

In addition, every computer system has its own unique Job Control Language (JCL) for the creation and subsequent processing of data files stored on disk. The JCL needed for disk files may range from the very simple, such as a Burroughs B1700 system, to the complex IBM 370 DOS/VS system. Appendix II shows some of the job control cards needed in the job stream to create and process disk stored data files for may computer systems.

Now that an introduction to basic disk concepts has been presented, the creation, sequential processing, random processing, updating, and addition of sequentially organized files will be discussed in this and the next chapter.

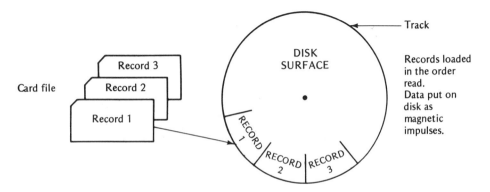

Fig. 9-4. Logic of sequential disk file creation.

CREATION (LOADING) OF A
SEQUENTIALLY-ORGANIZED DISK FILE

An employee payroll rate file in cards will be used as the data base for the application programs to create the sequential disk file and later process it for the required reports and maintenance functions. The fields in the one-record type included in the file are illustrated in the Card Layout Form shown in Figure 9-5. Notice the records are coded with an R in column 79 and a T in column 80.

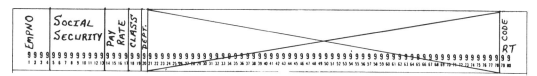

Fig. 9-5. Card layout form showing field format in the record type for the employee rate sequential file in cards.

The data file in card form is illustrated in Figure 9-6. Notice the records are arranged in ascending order by employee number. A sequential file could, however, be created (loaded) in descending order, or in no order at all. Future use of the file and speed of sorting are factors which may determine whether the file is sorted before or after loading.

Examine the file in Figure 9-6 and notice two of the records are missing the Record Identification Code (R in column 79 and T in column 80). If the creation program tests for ID codes and they are missing in a record(s), execution of the program will be cancelled or halted. Provision must be made

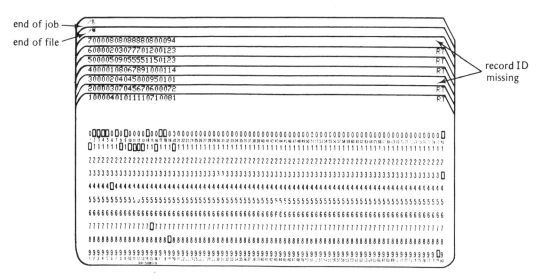

Fig. 9-6. Data file in cards arranged in ascending sequence by employee number. Used as data base for application program for employee rate files.

in the program to isolate any records not coded so the user can be aware of their existence in addition to not cancelling the program run. The disk file creation program explained later provides for any uncoded records.

Also notice in Figure 9-6 the end-of-file record (/*) and the end-of-job records which follow the last record in the data deck. Every file must have an end-of-file record regardless of the media used for storage. The end-of-job record (1 &) informs the computer that the job has ended and another job is to be accepted when programs are batched.

The RPG II coding procedures to create a sequential disk file from the card file in Figure 9-6 will now be discussed.

RPG II CODING FOR THE CREATION OF A SEQUENTIAL DISK FILE FROM CARD INPUT

Figure 9-7 shows the RPG II coding needed in the Employee Payroll Rate program to create a sequential disk file from card input. Examination of the coding forms will indicate that few new coding entries are needed in the

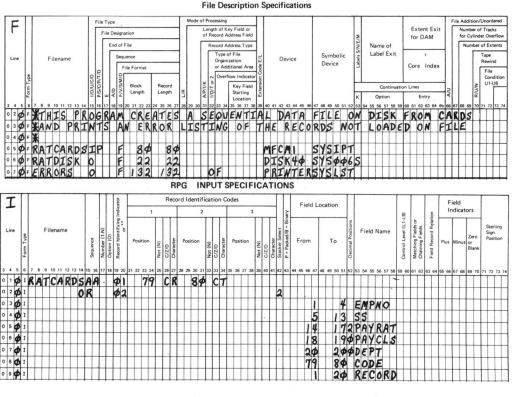

Fig. 9-7. RPG II program that creates a sequential disk file from card input for the Employee Pay Rate Application. (Continued on next page.)

RPG   CALCULATION SPECIFICATIONS

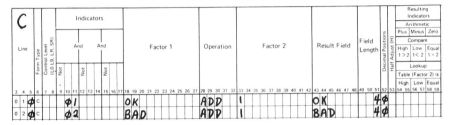

RPG   OUTPUT - FORMAT SPECIFICATIONS

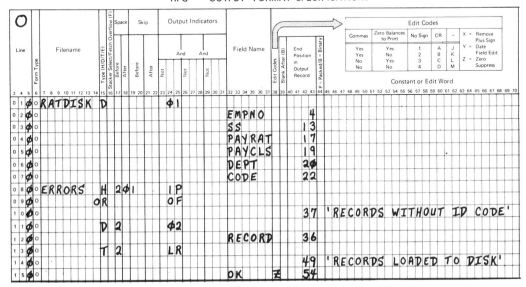

RPG   OUTPUT - FORMAT SPECIFICATIONS

Fig. 9-7.   (Concluded)

program to create a file. The forms that include the new coding entries will be discussed individually.

Look at the File Description form in Figure 9-8 and locate the following new entries:

Columns 7–14 (Filename). The program has one input card file (RATCARDS) and two output files (RATDISK and ERRORS). One output

File Description Specifications

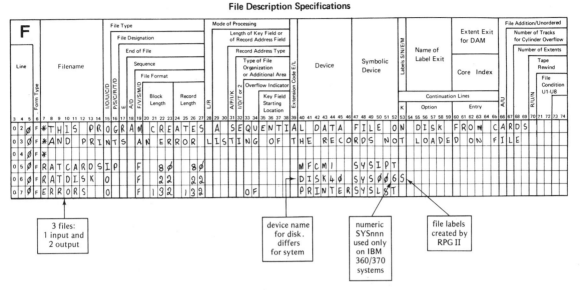

Fig. 9-8. File description coding for employee payroll rate application program showing new entries.

file (RATDISK) is the sequential file created in this program and the other (ERRORS) is a printer file for identifying records without Record Identification Codes.

This is called a multifile program because of the two output files. More than one input and output file may be used in a program. In fact, a maximum of 50 files may be used in an RPG II program with an IBM 370 system.

Columns 40–46 (Device). A new device name (DISK40) is used for the sequential disk file defined as an output file (RATDISK). The file is created (loaded) from card input. Device names are unique to the respective computer system and the RPG II programmer's manual should be referenced to determine device names. Appendix I lists some of the device names found on computer systems.

Columns 47–52 (Symbolic Device). Symbolic Device assignments are unique to IBM 360 and 370 systems and are not used on System/3, Burroughs B1700, Digital, or Data General computers. The entry used here is determined by the system used and the available SYSnnn numbers established when the system is generated. SYS006 is randomly used here; however, any assignment from SYS001 to SYS255 could be used if all the SYSNOs are available on the system.

Column 53 (Labels S/N/E/M). The letter S informs the computer of the standard label routine provided by the RPG II language to be used to write the file identifying label which contains information relating to the data file. The information usually includes the file name, date created, expiration date, blocking factor, record length, and cylinder and tracks location. This entry is not needed for all systems. The E and N options for this field are used for user-written labels and the M is for unlabeled tape files. These entries require complicated user-written subroutines and are beyond the scope of this book.

Examine the Input Specifications form in Figure 9-9 and locate lines 010 and 020. Only one record type was indicated for the file (Figure 9-5) coded by the letter R in Column 79 and a T in column 80. If a record is missing this code when the data file is processed, it will cause program execution to cancel or, depending on the computer system, to at least halt. In order to overcome this, another record type (02) is entered in an OR relationship. Notice the 02 record type does not contain any Identification Codes which will allow any incorrect records to be processed, thereby preventing cancellation or a halt in execution. This will allow the complete file to be processed.

Any unidentified records are isolated in a separate stacker by the entry in the Stacker Select field (column 42). Most card readers have more than one stacker for the return of processed cards. If a stacker number is not entered in column 42, cards will return to stacker 1. However, if a different stacker is required for certain card types the appropriate stacker number must be entered as shown in Figure 9-9.

Refer back to the data file in Figure 9-6 and notice two records are without Record Identification Codes. When the file is processed, the two

RPG INPUT SPECIFICATIONS

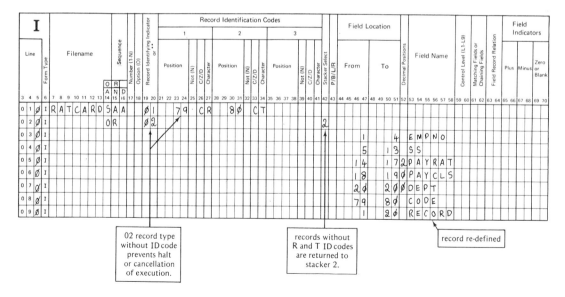

Fig. 9-9. Input specifications coding for employee payroll rate program.

unidentified records, 3000 and 7000, will be returned to stacker 2 because they are the 02 type record. Records 1000, 2000, 4000, 5000, and 6000 are properly identified and are the 01 type which return to stacker 1. Mistakes are made in recording information on cards, etc; consequently, the programmer should provide for errors in programs.

Another previously introduced concept is the redefining of a record on input. Locate line 090 and notice card columns 1–20 are redefined as a RECORD field. This field is used to print out the unidentified records in card format. The individual fields could have been used to print any incorrect cards; however, defining the record as one field saves programming time.

The Calculation Specifications form is not required for disk file creation; however, if a record count or other calculations are needed it must be used. Figure 9-10 shows the Calculation form for the Employee Payroll Rate program. Requirements of the application indicate that the number of records loaded on the disk file and the number of records without ID codes be printed at LR time (Figure 9-11). Messages serve as a communication link between the programmer and computer and inform the programmer of errors in data.

Line 010 of the calculation form accumulates the number of records with the correct ID codes and line 020 accumulates the number of records without the ID. At Last Record time (LR) the fields OK and BAD will contain their respective number of records and be available for output.

Figure 9-11 illustrates the Output-Format Specifications forms for the example program. Examination of the forms shows that two files are formatted on output. The sequential disk file, RATDISK, is loaded with the 01 type records at detail time. Any 02 records without the correct Identification Code are not loaded on the file, but will be printed.

Notice two important features about the output fields in the disk file RATDISK. First, there is *no editing* of the numeric fields. When a disk file is

RPG CALCULATION SPECIFICATIONS

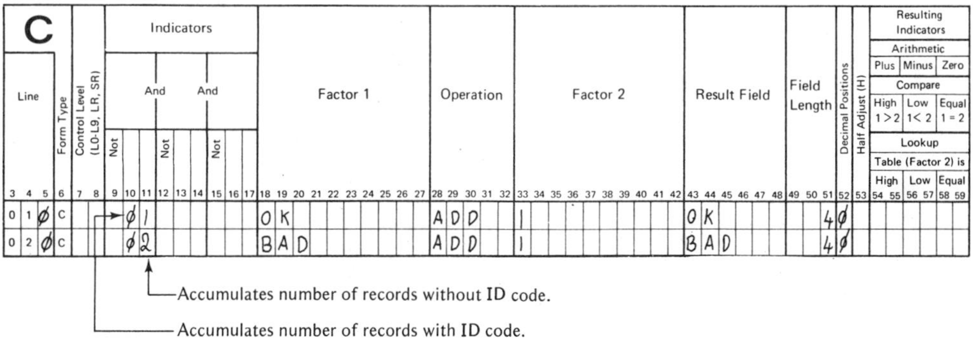

Fig. 9-10. Calculation specifications for employee rate program.

created, editing is never used in the output of numeric fields to disk as incorrect results would occur. Second, the fields are loaded next to each other. Disk space should not be wasted and unless a field(s) is to be added later there should not be any unused positions between fields. Note that the Identification Code is loaded in the two positions (21 and 22) after the DEPT field instead of in positions 79 and 80 as in the card records. The CODE field was defined on input and entered on output because it will be used to identify the disk records when RATDISK is processed.

Look at Figure 9-11 again and notice that spacing and skipping are not entered for the disk file. These functions are not performed on disk files, only for printer output.

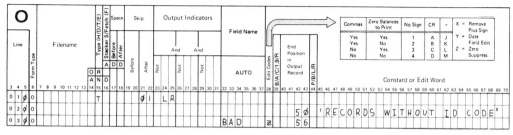

Fig. 9-11. Output-Format Specifications coding for employee payroll rate program.

```
        01 020  F*THIS PROGRAM CREATES A SEQUENTIAL DATA FILE ON DISK FROM CARDS   CREATE
        01 030  F*AND PRINTS AN ERROR LISTING OF THE RECORDS NOT LOADED ON FILE     CREATE
        01 040  F*                                                                  CREATE
0001    01 050  FRATCARDSIP   F  80  80           MFCM1 SYSIPT                       CREATE
0002    01 060  FRATDISK  O   F  22  22           DISK40 SYS006S                     CREATE
0003    01 070  FERRORS   O   F 132 132      OF   PRINTERSYSLST                      CREATE
0004    02 010  IRATCARDSAA   01   79 CR   80 CT                  2                  CREATE
0005    02 020  I          OR  02                                                   CREATE
0006    02 030  I                                          1    4 EMPNO             CREATE
0007    02 040  I                                          5   130SS                CREATE
0008    02 050  I                                         14   172PAYRAT            CREATE
0009    02 060  I                                         18   190PAYCLS            CREATE
0010    02 070  I                                         20   200DEPT              CREATE
0011    02 080  I                                         79   80 CODE              CREATE
0012    02 090  I                                          1   20 RECORD            CREATE
0013    03 010  C     01      OK        ADD 1       OK         40                    CREATE
0014    03 020  C     02      BAD       ADD 1       BAD        40                    CREATE
0015    04 010  ORATDISK  D            01                                           CREATE
0016    04 020  O                           EMPNO    4                              CREATE
0017    04 030  O                           SS      13                              CREATE
0018    04 040  O                           PAYRAT  17                              CREATE
0019    04 050  O                           PAYCLS  19                              CREATE
0020    04 060  O                           DEPT    20                              CREATE
0021    04 070  O                           CODE    22                              CREATE
0022    04 080  OERRORS   H   201    1P                                             CREATE
0023    04 090  O          OR         OF                                            CREATE
0024    04 100  O                                  37 'RECORDS WITHOUT ID CODE'     CREATE
0025    04 110  O         D  2        02                                            CREATE
0026    04 120  O                           RECORD  36                              CREATE
0027    04 130  O         T  2        LR                                            CREATE
0028    04 140  O                                  49 'RECORDS LOADED TO DISK'      CREATE
0029    04 150  O                           OK   Z  54                              CREATE
0030    05 010  O         T     01 LR                                               CREATE
0031    05 020  O                                  50 'RECORDS WITHOUT ID CODE'     CREATE
0032    05 030  O                           BAD  Z  56                              CREATE
```

E N D   O F   S O U R C E

Fig. 9-12. Source program listing of employee payroll rate program.

The output file ERRORS prints the 02-type records which are those without the correct ID code. In addition, two messages are printed with the related count field indicating the number of records loaded to disk and the number not loaded because they are missing the ID code. The printer output file is not a requirement for creating disk files, but does serve as a useful communication link between the computer and the user.

Furthermore, it does not matter which file is entered first on the output forms. The ERRORS file could have been coded first, followed by the disk file RATFILE. However, files are usually entered on the output (and input) form in the order they appear in the File Description Specifications.

Figure 9-12 shows the source program listing for the Employee Payroll Rate program discussed in this section.

The printed output for the records without the correct Identification Codes is illustrated in Figure 9-13. Notice that five records were loaded on the disk file and two were not loaded because of incorrect or missing ID codes.

```
RECORDS WITHOUT ID CODE

    30000204045000950101

    70000808088880800094

                RECORDS LOADED TO DISK     5

                RECORDS WITHOUT ID CODE      2
```

Fig. 9-13. Printed report for identifying records without the correct ID Code and count of records loaded to disk.

Depending on the computer system used, the records not loaded may be corrected and added to the sequential file by an RPG II program for file adds.

Even though program execution did not cancel or halt, and the data file was processed successfully, there is no guarantee that the records and related fields were correctly loaded on disk. An incorrect end position on output or wrong input format are errors that may not be easily identified unless other checks are made. *Utility programs*, written by the software suppliers, are available for purchase or rent and perform many useful operational functions. COPY and DITTO are a few of the utility packages which relieve the user of the responsibility for writing programs to perform many daily maintenance functions.

One of the functions found in these software packages enables a disk file to be accessed and to print out the individual records for examination. Figure 9-14 shows the output of the disk file created by the source program in Figure 9-12. This is only one print format of the many available in the COPY or DITTO utilities.

Examine Figure 9-14 and locate the left-hand side. Notice the cylinder number, 010; the track number, 00 (the first track on the cylinder); and the

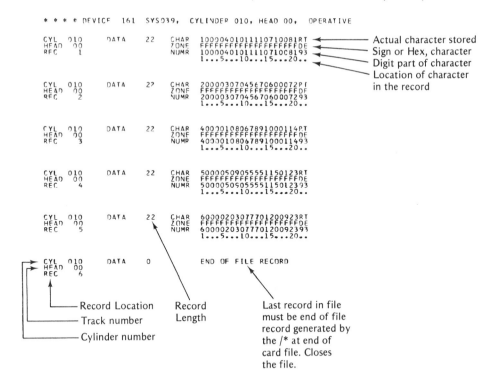

Fig. 9-14. Sequential disk file printed by a utility program. Shows cylinder, track, record, and character locations.

location where the individual records on the tracks are listed. The DATA 22 indicates this is a data record with a record length of 22 bytes (characters). The last record (number 6) is the end-of-file record which contains no data; hence, the reason for the zero.

The data area is shown in the right-hand side of Figure 9-14. The four lines starting from the bottom of each record have the following meanings:

Bottom row: Indicates the storage position of each byte in the record. This record is 22 bytes long as indicated in the File Description form for the source program.

NUMR: Represents the digit part of a character. Every number, character, and most special characters have a digit section (0–9). The entry on this line indicates the digit used in the respective character.

ZONE: The letter F represents a positive sign for output and a D would indicate the number was negative. The letters D and E in positions 21 and 22, along with the related numbers 9 and 3 in the NUMR row, are the hexadecimal representation of the letter R and T in the CHAR row.

CHAR: This row represents the character (byte) stored in each indicated position. It shows the actual number, character, or special character.

The END-OF-FILE RECORD must be part of every data file or the file would never close, preventing a normal end-of-job termination. This record is generated when the end-of-file record (/*) is processed at the end of the card data file.

One record, a section of records, or an entire data file may be accessed by this type of utility program. This is not part of the RPG II compiler, but a separate software package offered by many software suppliers.

ALTERNATIVE DISK FILE CREATION CODING TO SAVE STORAGE AND SPEED PROCESSING

A technique called *blocking* may be used in RPG II programs to save storage and decrease process time. Blocking may be defined as *the placing together of logical records in a group (physical record) instead of individually for storage on a direct access device or tape*.

Two new terms, logical and physical records, are introduced in the blocking definition which are defined as follows:

Logical Record: The characters and fields related to a transaction. A card containing information for an accounting transaction is a logical record.

Physical Record: Is the same size as a logical record in an unblocked file. In a blocked file it is two or more logical records in length. Maximum block size depends on the storage device used and/or the computer system.

When records are written on a disk or tape, a space exists between them where nothing is entered. This takes up room that could be used for additional records. In addition, as the data file is processed, each record is individually read into the input area. If there are 100 records in the file, 100 read and "write commands" would have to be executed by the computer if the complete file was read. Figure 9-15 illustrates a data file with unblocked records. Notice only one record at a time is read into the input area which means the computer must execute four read/write commands. Because the records are unblocked, the logical and physical records are the same size.

Figure 9-16 shows the format of blocked records where the *Blocking Factor* is 4. The Blocking Factor is the number of logical records grouped to make one physical record. In this example, the number of logical records is four, which determines the size of the physical record. If the logical records were 80 bytes long, the physical record would be 80 times 4, or 320 bytes. The physical record must be the exact multiple of the logical record length.

Notice the absence of any gaps in Figure 9-16 between records in the block. A gap will still exist, however, between the physical records, so the larger the block of logical records the less space wasted for gaps.

Block size is limited, however, by the computer system and/or the device used. For example, the IBM System/3 computer reads and writes from disk in 256 character blocks. If a record was 80 bytes long, space would automatically be allocated for 256 bytes. For efficiency, any block size for this system should be 256 bytes, or multiples thereof.

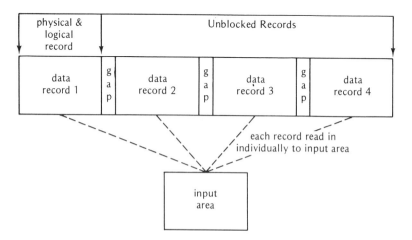

Fig. 9-15. Format of unblocked data records on disk.

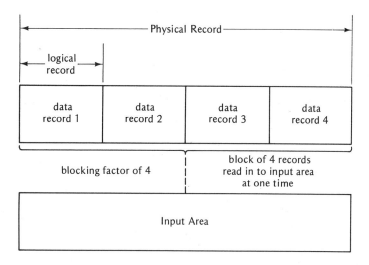

Fig. 9-16.   Format of blocked records on disk.

The maximum block sizes for direct access devices may be determined from the language manual for the system used. For convenience a few devices are presented below:

Device	Maximum Block Length in Bytes	
IBM 2311 Drive	3625	(without keys)
	3605	(with keys)*
IBM 3300 Storage	9999	(without keys)
Facility	9999	(with keys)*
IBM 3340 Disk	8368	(without keys)
Facility	8293	(with keys)*
IBM 2314 Storage	7294	(without keys)
Facility	7249	(with keys)*

*Keys are used with ISAM (Indexed-Sequential) files which are presented in Chapter 11.

RPG II Coding for Blocking

The only coding entries needed in an RPG II source program to provide for blocking are entered in columns 20–23 (Block length field) of the File Description Specifications form. Figure 9-17 illustrates the entry which indicates a blocking factor of five. The logical record size is 17 (columns 24–27) and when multiplied by five gives the physical record size of 85 bytes (columns 20–23). Any multiple of 17 could have been used for the block size, limited only by the device or system. The blocking factor of five was picked randomly by the programmer. However, if a previously-created file is processed, the correct block size must be known or the file could not be accessed.

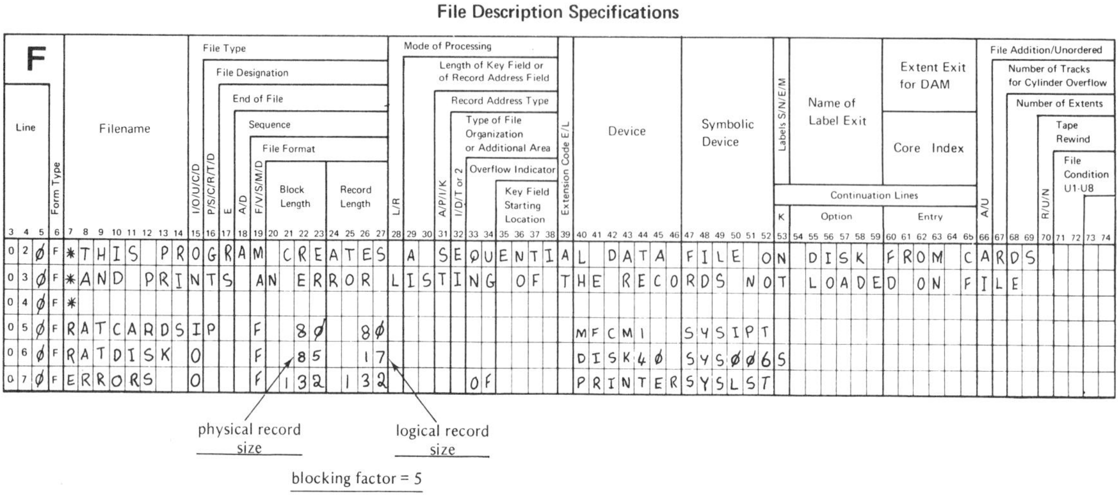

File Description Specifications

F		Line		Form Type	Filename						I/O/U/C/D	P/S/C/R/T/D	E	A/D	F/V/S/M/D	File Type / File Designation / End of File / Sequence / File Format	Block Length	Record Length	L/R	Mode of Processing / Length of Key Field or of Record Address Field / Record Address Type / Type of File Organization or Additional Area / A/P/I/K / I/D/T or 2 / Overflow Indicator / Key Field Starting Location		Extension Code E/L	Device	Symbolic Device	Labels S/N/E/M	Name of Label Exit / K / Continuation Lines / Option	Entry	Core Index	Extent Exit for DAM	File Addition/Unordered / Number of Tracks for Cylinder Overflow / Number of Extents / Tape Rewind / File Condition U1-U8 / R/U/N

0 2	Ø	F	*	T H I S		P R O G R A M		C R E A T E S		A		S E Q U E N T I A L		D A T A		F I L E		O N		D I S K		F R O M		C A R D S					
0 3	Ø	F	*	A N D	P R I N T S		A N	E R R O R	L I S T I N G		O F		T H E		R E C O R D S		N O T		L O A D E D		O N		F I L E						
0 4	Ø	F	*																											
0 5	Ø	F	R A T C A R D S	I P			F		8 Ø		8 Ø						M F C M 1		S Y S I P T											
0 6	Ø	F	R A T D I S K	O			F		8 5	1 7							D I S K 4 Ø		S Y S Ø Ø 6 5											
0 7	Ø	F	E R R O R S	O			F	1 3 2	1 3 2				O f				P R I N T E R		S Y S L S T											

physical record size — logical record size

blocking factor = 5

Fig. 9-17. File Description Specifications form for employee payroll rate program modified for blocking and packing.

Only data records stored on a direct access device (disk, cell, drum, or diskette) and tape may be blocked. If the Block Length field is blank, a blocking factor of one is assumed.

Observe in Figure 9-17 the logical record size in columns 24–27 has been changed for the example program from an original 22 bytes to 17. The shorter record size is caused by the packing of numeric fields, discussed in the following paragraphs.

PACKED DECIMAL FORMAT

All *numeric fields* may be *packed* on a storage media (tape, disk, diskette, cell, or drum) to save room. If numeric data is not packed on input, RPG II automatically converts it to packed decimal format for internal processing. This saves the real storage of the computer. If an input numeric field is already in packed format, the conversion routine is ignored and some processing time is saved.

Packing does nothing more than utilize the zone area of the numeric character bytes. Numbers do not use the zone part of the byte, only the digit area. Therefore, the zone will remain unused unless packing is indicated on output. Figure 9-18 shows the comparison between a three-digit numeric field in unpacked and packed formats. Notice that one byte of storage is saved because of packing.

Two formulas are available when using packed decimal fields. One is used to determine the *packed output size* of an *unpacked numeric input field* and the other for determining the *unpacked output size* of a *packed numeric input field*. Figure 9-19 illustrates the formulas and example calculations.

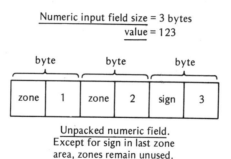

Numeric input field size = 3 bytes
value = 1 2 3

Unpacked numeric field.
Except for sign in last zone
area, zones remain unused.

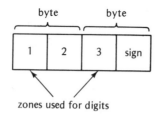

Output field size after packing = 2 bytes

zones used for digits

Packed numeric field

Fig. 9-18. Comparison of unpacked and packed numeric fields.

RPG II Coding For Packed Decimal Output

Only two coding forms are used for packed decimal numeric fields. The Input Specifications is used when the input field is in packed numeric format and the Output-Format Specifications if any fields are to be packed on output. The coding for packing an output field will be discussed here and input coding later in the chapter.

Look at Figure 9-20 and notice the only new entry on the output form is the letter P in column 44 on lines 030 and 040. This is the only entry needed to pack an output field.

PAYCLS and DEPT were also defined as numeric on input (Figure 9-20) but are too small to pack. A field must be at least three bytes long to pack and reduce the number of storage positions. For example, the PAYCLS field is two bytes long and if packed (using the formula in Figure 9-19) would still be two bytes. Therefore, nothing would be gained by packing.

The Social Security field (SS) was nine bytes long on input (see Figure 9-7) and when packed is reduced to five bytes which results in a savings of four bytes. In addition, the Pay Rate field (PAYRAT) was defined at four bytes on input and when packed is condensed to three, or a reduction in storage of one

Formula for determining the size of a packed output field:

$$\text{Packed field size} = \frac{N+1}{2}$$

$$N = \text{Unpacked field size}$$

Example:

$$\text{Unpacked field size} = 4 \text{ bytes (digits)}$$

$$\text{Substituting:} \frac{4+1}{2} = 2.5 \quad \text{or 3 as the size of the packed output field}$$

Note: Any remainder increases whole number by 1

Formula for determining the output size of a packed input field:

$$\text{Unpacked field size} = (2 \times N) - 1$$

$$N = \text{Packed field size}$$

Example:

$$\text{Packed field size} = 3 \text{ bytes (digits)}$$

$$\text{Substituting:} (2 \times 3) - 1 = 5 \quad \text{the unpacked output field size}$$

Note: The original field size was 4 before packing and unpacking the packed field increases the unpacked size by 1 byte. This feature must be considered when editing and in calculations.

A *rule of thumb* is to make any unpacked numeric fields an *odd number length*. This will utilize all of the available positions in the packed field, and is more efficient.

Fig. 9-19. Formulas used for determining input and output field sizes when packing is used.

byte. The total storage savings for one data record because of packing is five bytes. This may not seem significant for a few records, but for a large data file it results in a considerable storage savings which otherwise would be wasted.

Figure 9-21 shows the source program listing for the Employee Payroll Rate program modified with blocking and packing. The result of these coding techniques is twofold: processing time is reduced by blocking, and disk storage is saved by packing of numeric fields.

Figure 9-22 shows the contents of the sequential disk file (RATDISK) after it is created with blocking and packing specified. If this utility program printout is compared with the listing in Figure 9-14, significant differences will be obvious between the two. The differences are caused by blocking and packing.

Examine Figure 9-22 and notice the cylinder and head numbers are the same as in Figure 9-14, but the REC number is one and not six. Because of

RPG OUTPUT - FORMAT SPECIFICATIONS

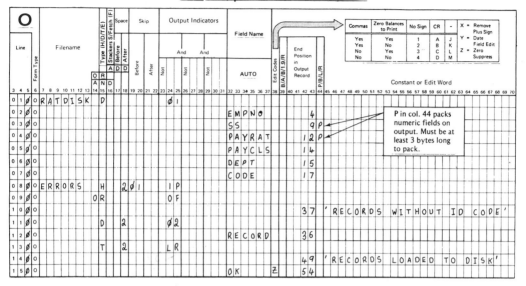

RPG OUTPUT - FORMAT SPECIFICATIONS

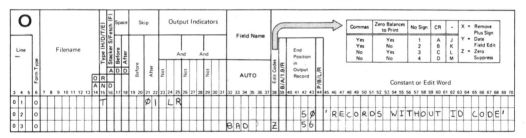

Fig. 9-20. Output-format specifications coding for employee payroll rate program using packed numeric fields on output to disk.

blocking, the logical records are grouped into one physical record. The REC always refers to the physical records.

Except for different positions, the Employee Number field (EMPNO), Pay Class (PAYCLS), Department (DEPT), and Identification Code (CODE), appear in the same format in both listings. However, the Social Security (SS) and Pay Rate (PAYRAT) are packed fields and have a different format. SS originally occupied nine positions in Figure 9-14, but because of packing is reduced to five (see Figure 9-22). Notice the letter C is printed in the NUMR row in the last position of the field. This indicates the field is positive. Also, observe that nothing is printed in the CHAR row when a field is packed, where the actual character is printed in this row if the field is not packed. Sometimes an extraneous character may print in the CHAR row of a packed field. This may be confusing to the user, but is not part of the field and should be ignored.

```
            01 020  F*THIS PROGRAM CREATES A SEQUENTIAL DATA FILE ON DISK FROM CARDS    CREATE
            01 030  F*AND PRINTS AN ERROR LISTING OF THE RECORDS NOT LOADED ON FILE      CREATE
            01 040  F*                                                                   CREATE
0001        01 050  FRATCARDSIP  F  80   80              MFCM1  SYSIPT                    CREATE
0002        01 060  FRATDISK  O  F  85   17              DISK40 SYS006S                   CREATE
0003        01 070  FERRORS   O  F 132  132       OF     PRINTERSYSLST                    CREATE
0004        02 010  IRATCARDSAA  01   79 CR   80 CT                                       CREATE
0005        02 020  I            OR   02                              2                   CREATE
0006        02 030  I                                             1     4 EMPNO           CREATE
0007        02 040  I                                             5    13OSS             CREATE
0008        02 050  I                                            14   172PAYRAT           CREATE
0009        02 060  I                                            18   190PAYCLS           CREATE
0010        02 070  I                                            20   200DEPT             CREATE
0011        02 080  I                                            79    80 CODE            CREATE
0012        02 090  I                                             1    20 RECORD          CREATE
0013        03 010  C       01       OK        ADD 1      OK        40                    CREATE
0014        03 020  C       02       BAD       ADD 1      BAD       40                    CREATE
0015        04 010  ORATDISK D          01                                               CREATE
0016        04 020  O                       EMPNO     4                                   CREATE
0017        04 030  O                       SS        9P                                  CREATE
0018        04 040  O                       PAYRAT   12P                                  CREATE
0019        04 050  O                       PAYCLS   14                                   CREATE
0020        04 060  O                       DEPT     15                                   CREATE
0021        04 070  O                       CODE     17                                   CREATE
0022        04 080  OERRORS   H  201       1P                                             CREATE
0023        04 090  O            OR         OF                                            CREATE
0024        04 100  O                                   37 'RECORDS WITHOUT ID CODE'      CREATE
0025        04 110  O         D  2         02                                             CREATE
0026        04 120  O                       RECORD   36                                   CREATE
0027        04 130  O         T  2         LR                                             CREATE
0028        04 140  O                                   49 'RECORDS LOADED TO DISK'       CREATE
0029        04 150  O                       OK       Z 54                                 CREATE
0030        05 010  O         T      01 LR                                                CREATE
0031        05 020  O                                   50 'RECORDS WITHOUT ID CODE'      CREATE
0032        05 030  O                       BAD      Z 56                                 CREATE
```

E N D   O F   S O U R C E

Fig. 9-21. Source program listing of employee payroll program modified by blocking and packing.

A packed field is read by starting in the ZONE row of the first position of the field and then reading the number in the NUMR row directly under this position. The next number is read in the second position of the ZONE row and then the number under that and so forth. The method of reading a packed field appears in Figure 9-23.

The Pay Rate (PAYRAT) field appears in positions 10–12 in Figure 9-22. This is an example where a field adds another digit because of packing.

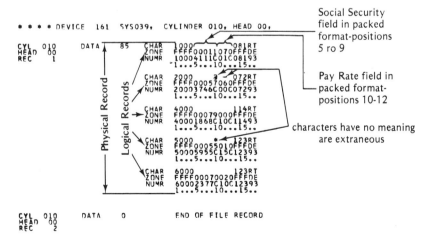

Fig. 9-22. Sequential disk file printed by a utility program showing cylinder, track, record, and character locations when blocking and packing is specified in source program.

	Packed field (from Fig. 9-22)		Method of Reading
ZONE	00011	start →	00011
			WWW
NUMR	4111C		4111C ← end

When unpacked gives:

040101111+

Fig. 9-23. Method of reading a packed field.

The PAYRAT field was four bytes long on input and now is five bytes in packed format (zero in ZONE 'row of position 10 adds digit). This must be considered in any calculations and editing if the value is used for one of these functions. Again, if any field is to be used for packing, an odd numbered size will prevent unwanted zeros in the high-order positions.

Once a disk file is created (loaded), it may be processed sequentially (complete file), added to, random processed, and up dated. The RPG II coding needed to process a sequential disk file and the addition of records will be presented in the remainder of this chapter. Random processing and updating of sequential disk files will be reserved for Chapter 10.

SEQUENTIAL PROCESSING OF A SEQUENTIAL DISK FILE

Figure 9-24 shows the source program to process the sequential disk file (RATDISK) created in Figure 9-21. Examine the source listing and notice the sequential disk file (RATDISK) is now an input file. The records in this file are to be processed one after the other and are printed in the report format shown

```
        01 020  F*THIS PROGRAM SEQUENTIALLY PROCESSES AN ENTIRE DISK FILE          ECHO
0001    01 030  FRATDISK IP  F   85   17             DISK40 SYS006S                 ECHO
0002    01 040  FLISTING  O   F 132 132       OF     PRINTERSYSLST                  ECHO
0003    02 010  IRATDISK AA   01   16 CR   17 CT                                    ECHO
0004    02 030  I                                           1    4 EMPNO            ECHO
0005    02 040  I                                       P   5   90SS                ECHO
0006    02 050  I                                       P  10  122PAYRAT            ECHO
0007    02 060  I                                          13' 140PAYCLS            ECHO
0008    02 070  I                                          15  150DEPT              ECHO
0009    04 080  CLISTING H   201      1P                                            ECHO
0010    04 090  O              OR            OF                                     ECHO
0011    04 100  O                                UDATE Y    9                       ECHO
0012    04 110  O                                          46 'LISTING OF RATE FILE REC' ECHO
0013    04 120  O                                          50 'ORDS'                ECHO
0014    04 130  O                                          60 'PAGE'                ECHO
0015    04 140  O                                PAGE  Z   65                       ECHO
0016    04 150  O              H   2      1P                                        ECHO
0C17    05 010  O                                          30 'EMPLOYEE    SS NO.'  ECHO
0018    05 020  O                                          52 'PAY RATE   PAY CLASS' ECHO
0019    05 030  O                                          57 'DEPT'                ECHC
0020    05 040  O              D   2      01                                        ECHO
0021    05 050  O                                EMPNO     18                       ECHO
0022    05 060  O                                SS        32 'O   -   -        '    ECHO
0023    05 070  O                                PAYRAT1   40                       ECHO
0024    05 080  O                                PAYCLS    48                       ECHO
0025    05 090  O                                DEPT      56                       ECHO
0026    05 100  O                                          34 '$'                   ECHO

      END  OF  SOURCE
```

Fig. 9-24. Source listing of program to process a sequential file sequentially

RPG INPUT SPECIFICATIONS

						Record Identification Codes													Field Location						
I						1			2			3													

Hand-entered rows:

Line	Form Type	Filename	Sequence	Number (1-N)	Option (O)	Record Identifying Indicator or **	Position	Not (N)	C/Z/D	Character	Position	Not (N)	C/Z/D	Character	Position	Not (N)	C/Z/D	Character	Stacker Select	P/B/L/R	From	To	Decimal Positions	Field Name	Control Level (L1-L9)	Matching Fields or Chaining Fields	Field Record Relation
01	0	I	RATDISK	AA		01	1 6		C	R	1 7		C	T													
02	0	I																		1	4		EMPNO			
03	0	I																P	5	9 0	S	SS			
04	0	I																P	1 0	1 2 2		PAYRAT			
05	0	I																	1 3	1 4 0		PAYCLS			
06	0	I																	1 5	1 5 0		DEPT			

ID codes
in disk
<u>records</u>

indicates
packed
input
field

location of
field in
<u>disk records</u>

packed
fields
must be
<u>numeric</u>

Fig. 9-25. Input Specifications for program to process a sequential disk file sequentially.

in Figure 9-26. It is very important that the same Record and Block size established when the file was created is used in any program to access the file. Notice the record size is 17 and the block size is 85 bytes which is the same as in the creation program (Figure 9-21). All the other entries in the File Description Specifications are the same as when the file was created, including the device name, symbolic device, and S (standard labels).

Because of a new coding entry, the Input Specifications form is shown separately in Figure 9-25. When the disk file was created, the SS and PAYRAT fields were packed on output and in order to access these fields the computer must be informed they are already in packed format.

Examine Figure 9-25 and notice the letter P is entered in column 43 on the same line as the SS and PAYRAT fields. The P in this column informs the computer the field is already in packed decimal format and not to use the automatic conversion routine to convert it to packed decimal for internal processing. If a P is not entered for a field that is packed, a *data check* will occur which, depending on the system, will cancel or at least halt the job.

The positions in the input fields were determined by the program to create the file (see Figure 9-21). A disk layout form could be formatted and used as part of the documentation for the program indicating field position within the disk records. Notice in Figure 9-25 the packed size is entered for SS and PAYRAT, not the unpacked size.

The report generated from the sequential processing program is shown in Figure 9-26. Because the file was processed sequentially (not randomly) every record in the disk file was printed.

```
4/11/78                    LISTING OF RATE FILE RECORDS          PAGE    1
             EMPLOYEE      SS NO.     PAY RATE   PAY CLASS DEPT
                 1000    040-10-1111  $  7.10        08        1
                 2000    030-70-4567  $  6.00        07        2
                 4000    010-80-6789  $ 10.00        11        4
                 5000    050-90-5555  $ 11.50        12        3
                 6000    020-30-7770  $ 12.00        12        3
```

Fig. 9-26. Printed report generated from program to process a sequential file sequentially

RPG II Coding for Adding Records to a Sequential Disk File

RPG II allows data records to be added to a sequential disk file after it is initially created. Data records are added at the end of the file in the order they are read. The add records do not have to be in any sorted order; however, if the file has either an ascending or descending order by some control field, adds may destroy this sequence and require another sort. If it is anticipated that records may be added to a file after it is created, extra space (cylinders and tracks) must be assigned to accomodate the additional records.

Source program coding to add records to a sequential disk file is identical in logic and entries as programs to create (load) the file, except for two additional entries. Figure 9-27 identifies the entries needed in an RPG II source program to facilitate file addition.

One of the entries appears in the File Description Specifications. Notice on line 050 (Figure 9-27) the letter A has been entered in column 66. The A must be entered on the coding line defining the disk file to which the records are to be added. Other than previously discussed entries, this is the only entry required on this form to add records to a sequential disk file.

The other entry appears on line 010 of the Output-Format Specifications form. Locate this line (Figure 9-27) and notice the letters ADD are entered in columns 16, 17, and 18 on the same line as the file name RATDISK. The File and Output Specification entries automatically generate RPG II compiler routines to do the housekeeping chores needed to add data records to an existing file.

Figure 9-28 shows the source program listing for the program to add records to the Employee Payroll Rate file. Examination of the listing will show that input, calculations, and the printer output file are not affected by the coding for file addition. Figure 9-29 illustrates the utility program listing (DITTO, COPY, etc.) of the file after the two records have been added. Remember the add records must have exactly the same format as the records in the disk file.

The ability to add to a sequential disk file is not available on all systems. For example, the IBM 360 and 370 series of computers do not provide for

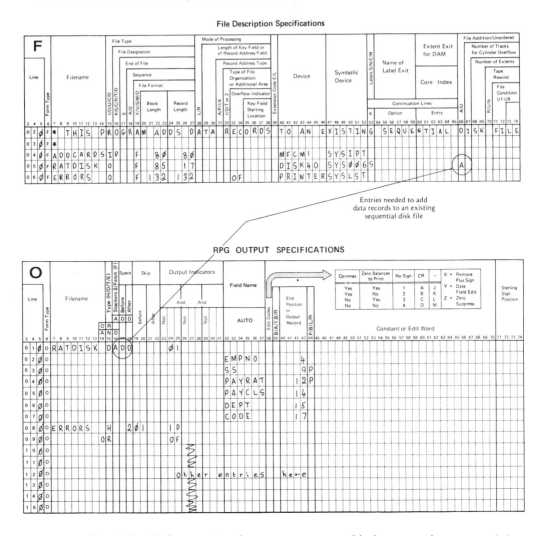

Fig. 9-27. Coding entries for a program to add data records to an existing sequential disk file.

addition to sequential disk files in the RPG II language (however, they do for indexed-sequential files). Consequently, if records have to be added, two alternatives are available. One, the records may be physically placed in the card file and the disk file recreated. Second, a new disk file could be created from the add card records and the SORT/MERGE utility program could be used to merge the original file and the adds file into a new disk file. Both of these methods are obviously less convenient than adding directly to an existing disk file.

```
              01 020   F* THIS PROGRAM ADDS RECORDS TO A SEQUENTIAL DISK FILE.........         ADDS
              01 030   F*                                                                      ADDS
              01 040   F*                                                                      ADDS
0001          01 050   FRATCARDSIP  F  80  80            MFCM1   SYSIPT                         ADDS
0002          01 060   FRATDISK O   F  85  17            DISK40 SYS006S                         ADDS
0003          01 070   FERRORS   O  F 132 132       OF   PRINTERSYSLST                          ADDS
0004          02 010   IRATCARDSAA  01  7S CR   80 CT                                           ACDS
0005          02 020   I       OR   02                   2                                      ADDS
0006          02 030   I                                        1    4 EMPNO                    ADDS
0007          02 040   I                                        5   130SS                       ADDS
0008          02 050   I                                       14  172PAYRAT                    ADDS
0009          02 060   I                                       18  190PAYGLS                    ADDS
0010          02 070   I                                       20  200DEPT                      ADDS
0011          02 080   I                                       79   80 CODE                     ADDS
0012          02 090   I                                        1   20 RECORD                   ADDS
0013          03 010   C    01        OK        ADD  1         OK        40                     ADDS
0014          03 020   C    02        BAD       ADD  1         BAD       40                     ADDS
0015          04 010   ORATDISK D            01                                                 ADDS
0016          04 020   O                               EMPNO      4                             ADDS
0017          04 030   O                               SS         9P                            ADDS
0018          04 040   O                               PAYRAT    12P                             ADDS
0019          04 050   O                               PAYGLS    14                             ADDS
0020          04 060   O                               DEPT      15                             ADDS
0021          04 070   C                               CODE      17                             ADDS
0022          C4 080   OERRORS   H   201      1P                                                ADDS
0023          04 090   O       OR           OF                                                  ADDS
0024          04 100   O                                        37 'RECORDS WITHOUT ID CODE'    ADDS
0025          04 110   O         D   2       02                                                 ADDS
0026          04 120   O                               RECORD    36                             ADDS
0027          04 130   O         T   2       LR                                                 ADDS
0028          04 140   C                                        49 'RECORDS LOADED TO DISK'     ADDS
0029          04 150   O                               OK    Z   54                             ADDS
0030          05 010   C         T       01 LR                                                  ADDS
0031          05 020   C                                        50 'RECORDS WITHOUT ID CODE'    ADDS
0032          05 030   O                               BAD   Z   56                             ADDS


        E N D   O F   S O U R C E
```

Fig. 9-28.   Source program listing for program to add records to a sequential disk file after it has been created.

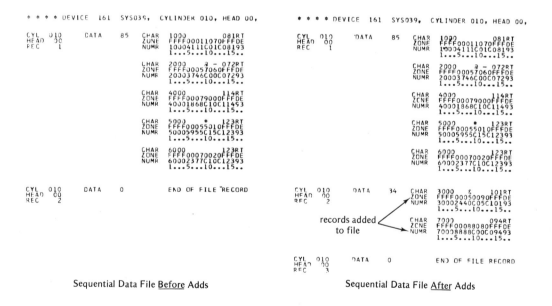

Sequential Data File Before Adds   Sequential Data File After Adds

Fig. 9-29.   Listing of sequential disk file *before* and *after* data records are added.

QUESTIONS

1. What types of data may be stored on disk?
2. Name some advantages of using disk for storage as compared to cards and magnetic tape.
3. Information is stored in what logical areas on a disk pack?
4. Explain how information is located on a disk.
5. How many cylinders on a 3348 disk pack? How many tracks on each cylinder? How are the tracks numbered?
6. Name the methods of organizing disk files.
7. How may the files named in question 6 be processed? Which organization method provides for faster random processing?
8. What coding forms are used to create a sequential disk file? On which forms do the new entries appear? What fields are used for these entries?
9. As compared to a printer output file, what are some of the output coding restrictions when creating a disk file?
10. Sequential disk files have to be loaded with data records in what order? What determines the order in which records are loaded?
11. What is blocking? Name two advantages of blocking. May card and printer files be blocked?
12. Define *blocking factor*. How large may the blocking factor be?
13. What coding form and field are used to block records?
14. Define the term *packed numeric format*. May all field types be packed?
15. What coding form and related field are used to pack a field on output?
16. Name the coding form and field used to indicate that a field is in packed format on input.
17. Determine the packed output size of the following unpacked input fields: six bytes, two bytes, seven bytes, three bytes, and four bytes.
18. Determine the unpacked output size of the following packed input fields: four bytes, two bytes, three bytes, and five bytes.
19. What coding forms are used for the entries to add records to a sequential disk file? What are the entries and where are they located on the forms?
20. Where on a sequential disk file are the records added? What provision must be made when the file is created if it is anticipated that records may be added in the future?

EXERCISES

9-1. Write the File Description Specifications to create a sequential disk file from the following information:

Input card file:	CARDIN
Output disk file:	SEQDISK
Output printer file:	LISTING

The data records in the CARDIN file are 80 bytes long. Use a record of 80 and a blocking factor of 10 to create a sequential disk file (SEQDISK). Printer width is 132 characters.

9-2. From the card layout form given below write the Input Specifications for the CARDIN file defined in Exercise 1. Have unidentified data records return to stacker 2.

CUST. NO.	CUSTOMER NAME	STREET ADDRESS	CITY	STATE	ZIP	CREDIT MAX. (0 dec.)	CODE CI
9999	99999999999999999999999999	999999999999999999999	999999999999999	99	99999	999999	99
1 2 3 4	5 6 7 8 9 10 11 12 13 14 15 16 17 18 19 20 21 22 23 24 25 26 27 28 29 30	31 32 33 34 35 36 37 38 39 40 41 42 43 44 45 46 47 48 49 50	51 52 53 54 55 56 57 58 59 60 61 62 63 64 65	66 67	68 69 70 71 72	73 74 75 76 77 78 79 80	79 80

9-3. From the information included in Exercises 9-1 and 9-2 write the Calculation Specifications to accumulate the number of records loaded on disk and the number of unidentified records not loaded. Also, provide for a total count field for total records read.

9-4. Write the Output-Format Specifications to create the sequential disk file, SEQDISK. Pack the customer number, zip code, and credit limit fields. Load the fields in each record next to each other without unused spaces. The record identification code included in the card records is to be loaded in the disk records.

The format of the printer report is shown in the printer spacing chart below.

		0	1	2	3	4	5
H	1			CUSTOMER RECORDS NOT LOADED		PAGE XX0X	
H	2			TO FILE ON 0X/XX/XX			
	3						
D	4			XXXX			
	5						
D	6			XXXX			
	7			(CUST NO)			
	8						
TLR	9		NUMBER OF RECORDS LOADED.........X,XX0				
	10						
TLR	11		NUMBER OF RECORDS NOT LOADED....X,XX0				
	12						
TLR	13		TOTAL RECORDS READ.............XX,XX0				
	14						
	15						
	16		HEADINGS ON TOP OF EVERY PAGE				
	17						
	18						
	19						

LABORATORY ASSIGNMENTS

LABORATORY ASSIGNMENT 9-1:
CREATION OF A SAVINGS ACCOUNT MASTER SEQUENTIAL DISK' FILE.

A national bank has branches in all 50 states. Write an RPG II source program to create a sequential disk file on disk from card input. The information on the data cards includes the following fields:

Format of input records:

ACCT. No.	DEPOSITOR'S NAME	BRANCH NAME	STATE	ACCT. BALANCE	CODE BAL.

Check the Account Balance field for a zero or blank value. If it is zero or blank, the record information is not to be loaded to disk. Also code input so that any unidentified records will not cancel execution of program. Use a blocking factor of five for records.

Calculations. Provide for an accumulator field for the number of records with zero balances, the number without ID codes, and the total number of records in the card file.

Output Coding. Load the records without any blank spaces between the fields to the disk records. Pack the Account Balance field and store the Record Identification Code (BAL) in the disk records in the *first three positions*. Provide for error messages as indicated in the Printer Spacing Chart given below:

		0	1	2	3	4	5
H	1		DEPOSITORS RECORDS WITH ZERO BALANCES				PAGE XXØX
H	2		AND/OR WITHOUT ID CODE				
H	3		AS OF ØX/XX/XX				
	4						
H	5		RECORDS WITHOUT ID				RECORDS WITH
	6						ZERO BALANCES
	7						
D	8		XXXXX				XXXXX
	9						
D	10		XXXXX				XXXXX
	11						
	12						
TLR	13		TOTAL NUMBER OF RECORDS IN FILE....XXØX				
TLR	14		NUMBER WITHOUT ID CODE.......XXØX				
TLR	15		NUMBER WITH ZERO BALANCE.....XXØX				
	16						
	17		NOTES:				
	18						
	19		HEADINGS ON TOP OF EVERY PAGE				

Data for Laboratory Assignment 9-1:

Account Number	Depositor's Name	Branch Name	State	Account Balance	ID Code
64321	HENRY FORD	DETROIT	MI	21584519	BAL
55114	LOUIS CHEVROLET	TARRYTOWN	NY		
88397	WALTER P. CHRYSLER	SAN DIEGO	CA	01000000	BAL
74891	BENJAMIN DODGE	CHICAGO	IL	04100000	
91784	WILLIAM BRICKLIN	TORONTO	ND	09000000	BAL
49814	JOHN STUDEBAKER	KANSAS CITY	KA		BAL
34444	STANLEY STEAMER	BUFFALO	NY	37100000	BAL

LABORATORY ASSIGNMENT 9-2:
SEQUENTIAL PROCESSING OF SEQUENTIAL DISK FILE CREATED IN LABORATORY ASSIGNMENT 9-1

Sequentially process the sequential disk file you created in Laboratory Assignment 9-1. Refer to the output of Laboratory Assignment 9-1 for field locations within the disk record. Remember the blocking factor and packed field.

Calculations. Accumulate the Account Balance field to a total field for all depositors. See Printer Spacing Chart below for the size of this total field.

Design of the printed report:

LABORATORY ASSIGNMENT 9-3:
ADDING RECORDS TO A SEQUENTIAL DISK FILE

Modify the program you wrote in Laboratory Assignment 9-1 to add records to the sequential disk file created in that assignment. Correct the records that were not loaded on the file because of zero balances and/or no record identification code, and add them to the file.

Check the results of the execution of the add program by executing the program from Laboratory Assignment 9-2 or, if available, the utility program on your system to access a disk file. The format, blocking factor, and packing requirements must be the same for all add records as the existing format of the disk records.

LABORATORY ASSIGNMENT 9-4:
CREATION OF A CUSTOMER MASTER RECORD SEQUENTIAL DISK FILE

Create a sequential disk file called CUSTMER from the following two card record types:

Input record formats:

Note: *One disk record* is to be created from the *two-card record* types for each customer. Sequence check every customer group on input. Pack the Zip Code, Account Balance, Store Number, and Telephone Number fields in the disk records. Load the fields in the disk records next to each other without unused spaces.

Load the Record Identification Code from each record type (letters T and B) in the last two positions of the disk records. Use a blocking factor of four.

Calculations. Provide for a count field of the total number of records processed.

Output Requirements. Load one disk record from the two-input card records to the disk file CUSTMER. Provide for a printed report of a listing of the Customer Number, Account Balance, and Last Balance Date (date in cards).

The current date (UDATE) is to be output to the disk records replacing the last balance date in cards.

		0	1	2	3	4	5
		1234567890	1234567890	1234567890	1234567890	1234567890	1234567890
H	1	ØX/XX/XX	ACCOUNT BALANCE AND ACTIVITY			PAGE XXØX	
H	2		REPORT OF CUSTOMERS				
	3						
H	4		CUSTOMER	ACCOUNT	LAST BALANCE		
H	5		NUMBER	BALANCE	DATE		
	6						
D	7		XXXX	XXX,XXØ.XX	ØX/XX/XX		
	8						
D	9		XXXX	XXX,XXØ.XX	ØX/XX/XX		
	10						
	11						
	12		TOTAL RECORDS PROCESSED XXØX				

Data For Laboratory Assignment 9-4:

Record Type Coded with Character T in Column 80:

Customer Number	Customer Name	Street Address	City	State	Zip
1234	JOHN FIRESTONE	20 TYRE LANE	AKRON	OH	05456
2345	WILLIAM GOODYEAR	19 TUBE ROAD	DETROIT	MI	06606
3456	JAMES GOODRICH	81 VALVE TERRACE	CHICAGO	IL	04404
4567	CLAUDE MICHELIN	1 PARIS PLACE	FRANCE	PA	06611
5678	ANTHONY PIRELLI	33 FIAT BOULEVARD	ROME	NY	06608
6789	TOYO KOGO	12 HIROSHIMA ROAD	TOKYO	CA	06666

Record Type Coded with Character B in Column 80:

Customer Number	Account Balance	Balance Date	Store No.	Customer Tel. No.
1234	00018112	083179	0001	2032889999
2345	01041879	063079	0005	2127445555
3456	12000000	043079	0002	2063334441
4567	00091822	073179	0003	2136666666
5678	01800000	053179	0004	2015558888
6789	00045600	083179	0002	2142221111

The data records must be grouped together according to customer number. Sequence checking is required. Therefore a record coded with the character T must be placed before the corresponding customer's record for the type coded with the character B.

10
PROCESSING AND UPDATING FILES BY THE MATCHING RECORDS METHOD AND BY THE READ OPERATION

ONE MATCHING FIELD

The matching feature of the RPG II language provides for a convenient method of sequentially and randomly processing multiple input files stored on disk, tape, and cards. In addition, matching records may be used to update field information in records stored on disk and tape. Examples of using matching records to process more than one file simultaneously may include:

1. Two or more card files
2. A card file and a sequentially organized disk file (or tape)
3. Two or more magnetic tape files
4. Two or more sequential disk files
5. A card file and an indexed-sequential disk file
6. A sequential disk file and an indexed-sequential disk file.

The examples listed above should not be considered as the only alternatives for which the matching record concept may be used. Many other multiple file combinations are available, but the maximum number of files that may be processed in one program is limited by the particular configuration used.

When two or more files are to be processed at one time, the computer must determine which record is to be processed next. Because RPG only

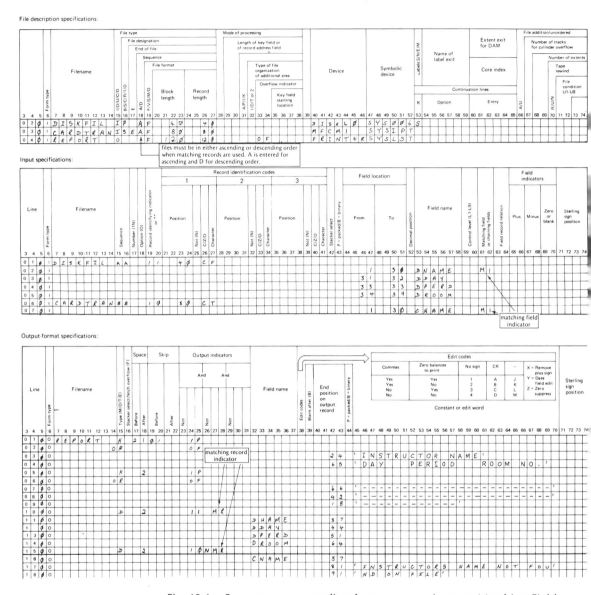

Fig. 10-1.   Source program coding for program using one Matching Field.

processes one record at a time, the matching record technique will provide the facility to determine which file will supply the next record.

An example program will be used to explain the matching record concept when only one field from two separate files is to be matched. Figure 10-1 shows the File Description Specifications coding for the sample program. Two input files are specified, a sequentially organized master disk file (DISKFIL) and a transaction card file (CARDTRAN). Furthermore, notice that the master disk file (DISKFIL) is designated as the primary file by the letter P entered in column 16 and the transaction file (CARDTRAN) is specified as secondary by the letter S in the same column. When more than one input file is used in a program only one file may be designated as primary and any other input files must be considered secondary. Usually the master file, or the one that contains the permanent record information, is specified as primary and, therefore controls the processing of the program. Furthermore, remember that output files are not specified either as primary or secondary, and no entry is required in column 16 of the File Description Specifications coding form.

Look at Figure 10-1 again and notice the letter A is entered in the Sequence Field (column 18). This entry indicates the two data files, DISKFIL and CARDTRAN, are sorted in ascending order. When matching record coding is used to process files the files *must be* sorted in the *same* sequence (ascending or descending by control field). If the data files are sorted in descending sequence, a D would be entered in column 18.

Figure 10-2 shows the arrangement of the two data files used in the sample program. DISKFIL is arranged in ascending sequence (from JORGAN to MYERS) by the DNAME matching field. CARDTRAN is also sorted in ascending sequence (from HOOPLE to MYERS) by the CNAME field. If the files were sorted from MYERS to JORGAN and MYERS to HOOPLE respectively, they would be in descending order and the letter D instead of an

DISKFILE				**CARDTRAN**
DNAME	DDAY	DPERD	DROOM	CNAME
JORGAN, JAMES	M	2	B-25	HOOPLE, HARVEY
JORGAN, JAMES	T	3	B-14	JORGAN, JAMES
JORGAN, JAMES	TH	4	A-28A	MORGAN, ROBERT
JORGAN, JAMES	T	3	B-14	MYERS, STANLEY
MORGAN, ROBERT	M	1	B-17A	
MORGAN, ROBERT	M	2	B-18	
MORGAN, ROBERT	M	5	A-29	
MORGAN, ROBERT	T	2	A-29	
MORGAN, ROBERT	TH	5	B-25	
MYERS, STANLEY	M	1	B-16	
MYERS, STANLEY	T	2	B-25	
MYERS, STANLEY	W	3	B-21	
MYERS, STANLEY	TH	4	B-23	
MYERS, STANLEY	F	2	B-17A	
MYERS, STANLEY	F	7	B-25	

Fig. 10-2. Data record values in master sequential disk file and card transaction file for program using one Matching Field.

A would be entered in column 18 of the File Description form.

An examination of the Input Specifications form in Figure 10-1 will show that an M1 (Matching Field Indicator) is entered in columns 61 and 62 alongside the DNAME field in the DISKFIL and CNAME in the record for the CARDTRAN card file. The M1 indicator is called a Matching Field Indicator ·which indicates in this program that only one field value is to be matched to facilitate processing. As many as nine matching field indicators (M1-M9) may be used in a program.

Two rules must be followed when assigning matching field indicators to the fields in two or more files. *First, the fields must be exactly the same length, and second, they must be the same type (numeric, alphabetic, or alphanumeric). The fields, however, do not have to be in the same location in the matching records.* The assignment of matching field indicators must begin with M1 and if additional fields within the records are to be matched the indicators are assigned in ascending sequence (M2, M3, etc.). The next sample program presented in this chapter will illustrate the use of three matching fields.

The use of matching field indicators in the Input Specifications will determine which file will supply the record to be processed next. After program control reads a record from each file, the matching fields (DNAME and CNAME) are compared in the input buffer area before being stored in core. The processing logic for two data files using matching fields is illustrated in Figure 10-3.

The records in the primary and secondary files (Figure 10-3) are lettered for the purpose of illustration only and are not an integral part of the records. Because the order in which records are processed is important in the matching record technique, the letters are also used in Figure 10-3 to identify which record is selected for processing for the entire job.

The sequence of processing the two data files in the sample program is controlled by the two rules stated in Figure 10-3 when the matching record method is used. During program execution one record from each file is read into an *input buffer area* and a comparison is made of the matching field values. Because the files are sorted in ascending order (Figure 10-2), and the matching field value HOOPLE is lower in the collating sequence than JORGAN, and the field values *do not match*, record P from the secondary file is selected for processing first. This follows the logic stated in rule 1 of Figure 10-3.

Another record from the secondary file is immediately read into the input area vacated by record P. A comparison is again made and because the matching field values in records A and Q are equal, record A from the primary file is selected for processing in accordance with rule 2 of Figure 10-3. Record B will then be read into the input buffer area and a comparison made in the matching field values. There is a match in the field values so record B will be processed next. The processing logic stated in rules 1 and 2 (Figure 10-3) will be followed for the remaining records in the files. For convenience the processing sequence of the other records in the files is given at the bottom of Figure 10-3.

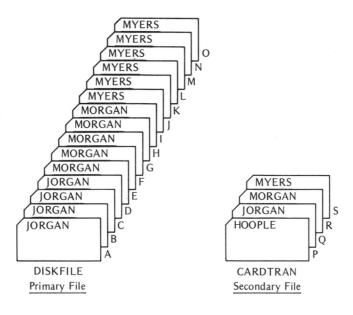

DISKFILE
Primary File

CARDTRAN
Secondary File

INPUT AREAS:

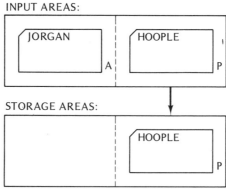

STORAGE AREAS:

Rule 1:

    If the records in the input areas do not match (value in matching field) and the files are in ascending order, select the record with the lowest matching field value. Hence, HOOPLE is lower than JORGAN and is selected for processing first.

    If files were in descending order the record with the highest value in the matching fields would have been processed first. Remember both files must be sorted in same sequence for matching record logic to execute.

    After record P is read into storage another record from the secondary file is read into the input area (record Q). The value in the matching field in the primary file is compared to the value in the matching field in the secondary. Because the values are equal (match) the information in rule 2 is followed:

Rule 2:

    If the records in the input areas match (value in matching fields are equal), select the primary record(s) first.

Fig. 10-3. Matching record logic for processing a primary file and one secondary file. (Continued on next page.)

Input Areas:

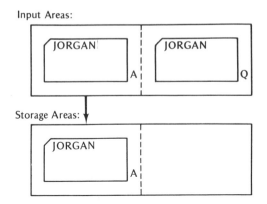

The remaining records in the two files are processed according to the two rules or a B, C, D, Q, E, F, G, H, I, R, J, K, L, M, N, O, S order.

Fig. 10-3. (Concluded)

During the process run the value in the matching field (DNAME) from the primary disk file (DISKFIL) will be compared to the matching field, CNAME, in the secondary card file (CARDTRAN) and, if equal, a special *Matching Record Indicator* (MR) will automatically turn on. The MR indicator may then be used to control any required calculations and/or output. In the program example presented, no calculations are needed; therefore, MR will only condition the printing of output.

Figure 10-4 illustrates the relationship of the Matching Fields (DNAME and CNAME) in the Input Specifications form and the Matching Record Indicator (MR) in the output form. Notice Record Identifying Indicator 11, assigned to the records in the primary file (DISKFIL), is used with MR to condition the first detail line.

Confusion often results concerning which Record Identifying Indicator to assign with the MR indicator (or NMR) in calculations or output. The rule stated below will aid in the determination of what indicator to use with MR.

Rule for assigning MR and a Record Identifying Indicator in calculations and/or output:

If all data required for calculations or output is available from one record, assign MR and the Record Identifying Indicator for that record

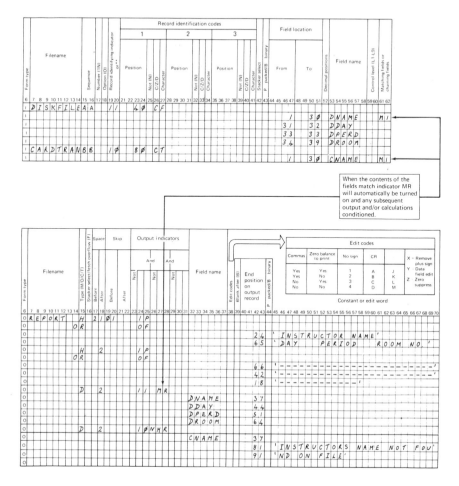

Fig. 10-4. Coding relationship between Input Specifications form and Output-Format Specifications for program using one Matching Field.

type. If, however, data is required from both a primary and secondary record (or result field) assign MR and the Record Identifying Indicator for the secondary record.

The preceding rule is controlled by the processing logic of the matching record method. When a match occurs, all the records in the primary file that match the secondary file are processed first, followed by any records in the secondary file for that match. Refer back to Figure 10-3 and read rules 1 and 2.

Examine the output form in Figure 10-4 and notice all the fields in the first detail line are from the 11 record type; therefore, the 11 indicator is used to condition this detail line along with the MR indicator. Reference to Figure

10-3 shows that records A, B, C, and D are processed first because the values match in the primary and secondary records and according to rule 2 (Figure 10-3) the primary records are processed first. Q, from the secondary file, is processed after the primary records because it has a lower matching field value than record E. The field value in the secondary input area is still JORGAN but the value in the primary input is now MORGAN. JORGAN is less than MORGAN (according to the collating sequence); consequently, it is processed first.

Further examination of the output form in Figure 10-4 shows the last detail line is conditioned by Record Identifying Indicator 10 and NMR. Indicator NMR indicates that the MR indicator is not on. When a disk record is not found that matches the secondary record, MR or 11 will not be on. Consequently, the indicator from the secondary file (CARDTRAN) has to be used to condition the error message INSTRUCTOR NAME NOT FOUND ON FILE. This additional coding is not required but does serve to indicate possible errors that may exist in the data files.

Figure 10-5 shows the source program listing and printed output for the sample program using one matching field. Notice the error message for HOOPLE, HARVEY. This was printed because no matching record was found in the primary file for that record.

Source Listing:

```
F************************************************************************************
F*    PROGRAM TO ACCESS THE INSTRUCTORS' DATA FILE.                                *
F************************************************************************************
F*    NAMES OF INSTRUCTORS ARE READ IN ON CARDS AND THEIR NAMES ARE MATCHED        *
F*    TO THE DATA FILE RECORDS. ALL OF THE PARTICULAR INSTRUCTOR'S RECORDS         *
F*    FROM THE FILE ARE PRINTED. IF THERE IS NO MATCHING NAME ON THE FILE          *
F*    AN ERROR MESSAGE IS PRINTED.                                                 *
F************************************************************************************
0001   01 020   FDISKFILEIP AF   40   40           DISK40 SYS008S              MATCHR
0002   01 030   FCARDTRANISEAF   80   80           MFCM1  SYSIPT               MATCHR
0003   01 040   FREPORT   O    F 132 132    OF      PRINTERSYSLST              MATCHR
0004   02 010   IDISKFILEAA   11   40 CF                                       MATCHR
0005   02 020   I                                    1   30 DNAME   M1         MATCHR
0006   02 030   I                                   31   32 DDAY               MATCHR
0007   02 040   I                                   32   33 DPERD              MATCHR
0008   02 050   I                                   34   39 DROOM              MATCHR
0009   02 060   ICARDTRANBB   10                                              MATCHR
0010   02 070   I                                    1   30 CNAME   M1         MATCHR
0011   03 010   OREPORT   H 2101     1P                                        MATCHR
0012   03 020   O         OR         OF                                        MATCHR
0013   03 030   O                                   24 'INSTRUCTOR NAME        MATCHR
0014   03 040   O                                   65 'DAY    PERIOD    ROOM NO. MATCHR
0015   03 050   O         H   2     1P                                         MATCHR
0016   03 070   O                                   66 '------------------------' MATCHR
0017   03 080   O                                   42 '------------------------' MATCHR
0018   03 090   O                                   18 '-------------'          MATCHR
0019   03 100   O         D   2     11 MR                                      MATCHR
0020   03 110   O                            DNAME  37                         MATCHR
0021   03 120   O                            DDAY   44                         MATCHR
0022   03 130   O                            DPERD  51                         MATCHR
0023   03 140   O                            DROOM  64                         MATCHR
0024   03 150   O         D   2     10NMR                                      MATCHR
0025   04 010   O                            CNAME  37                         MATCHR
0026   04 020   O                                   81 'INSTRUCTORS NAME NOT FOU' MATCHR
0027   04 030   O                                   91 'ND ON FILE'            MATCHR
```

Fig. 10-5. Source listing of program using one Matching Field (M1). (Continued on next page.)

Printed Report:

INSTRUCTOR NAME	DAY	PERIOD	ROOM NO.
HOOPLE,HARVEY			INSTRUCTORS NAME NCT FOUND ON FILE
JORGAN,JAMES	M	2	B-25
JORGAN,JAMES	T	3	B-14
JORGAN,JAMES	TH	4	A-28A
JORGAN,JAMES	T	3	B-14
MORGAN,ROBERT	M	1	B-17A
MORGAN,ROBERT	M	2	B-18
MORGAN,ROBERT	M	5	A-29
MORGAN,ROBERT	T	2	A-29
MORGAN,ROBERT	TH	5	B-25
MYERS,STANLEY	M	1	B-16
MYERS,STANLEY	T	2	B-25
MYERS,STANLEY	W	3	B-21
MYERS,STANLEY	TH	4	B-23
MYERS,STANLEY	F	2	B-17A
MYERS,STANLEY	F	7	B-25

Fig. 10-5.   (Concluded)

SPLIT MATCHING FIELDS (M1-M9)

The previous program illustrated the use of one matching field requiring only the matching field indicator, M1. However, it may sometimes be necessary to have more than one matching field in order to process two or more input files. Depending on the system used, up to nine matching fields may be specified to obtain the required match.

When more than one matching field indicator is specified in two or more fields, the M1 or lowest matching field indicator should be assigned to the lowest data classification, and the higher matching field indicator to the highest data classification. For example, if a field for city and one for state are specified on input and they are to be matched as split fields, M1 should be assigned to the city field and M2 to the state field.

The example program that will illustrate the use of split matching fields will use the same data as in the previous program for the master disk file except the data will be rearranged in sequential order by class day and class period as well as instructor. Figure 10-6 illustrates the arrangement of the data in the master disk file and the transaction file records. Notice that the transaction file (CARDTRAN) now contains additional fields for class day and period. The objective of the program is to find the classroom that is occupied by an individual instructor, on a select school day, for a particular period.

Examine the Input Specifications form, Figure 10-7 and notice that the

	DISKFILE			
	DNAME	DDAY	DPERD	DROOM
A.	JORGAN, JAMES	M	2	B-25
B.	JORGAN, JAMES	T	3	B-14
C.	JORGAN, JAMES	TH	4	A-28A
D.	JORGAN, JAMES	TH	8	B-15
E.	MORGAN, ROBERT	M	1	B-17A
F.	MORGAN, ROBERT	M	2	B-18
G.	MORGAN, ROBERT	M	5	A-29
H.	MORGAN, ROBERT	T	2	A-29
I.	MORGAN, ROBERT	TH	5	B-25
J.	MYERS, STANLEY	F	2	B-17A
K.	MYERS, STANLEY	F	7	B-15
L.	MYERS, STANLEY	M	1	B-16
M.	MYERS, STANLEY	T	2	B-25
N.	MYERS, STANLEY	TH	4	B-23
O.	MYERS, STANLEY	W	3	B-21

	CARDTRAN		
	CNAME	DDAY	DPERD
P.	HOOPLE, HARVEY	F	6
Q.	JORGAN, JAMES	TH	4
R.	MORGAN, ROBERT	M	1
S.	MORGAN, ROBERT	T	2
T.	MORGAN, ROBERT	TH	7
U.	MYERS, STANLEY	F	2
V.	MYERS, STANLEY	W	3

Fig. 10-6. Data contents of master sequential disk file and card transaction file for program using three Matching Fields.

matching field indicator M1 is assigned to the matching field DPERD in the master disk file and CPERD in the transaction card file, M2 is assigned to the fields DDAY and CDAY, and M3 to DNAME in the disk file and CNAME to the matching field in the card records. Hence, the lowest matching field indicator, M1, is assigned to the lowest level, or class period (DPERD and CPERD), M2 is assigned to the next higher level, the class day (DDAY and CDAY), and M3 is assigned to the highest level, or instructor name (DNAME and CNAME).

Examine Figure 10-7 and observe how the matching field values are arranged for matching. DPERD is the low-order field in the disk record matching group, DDAY the next highest, and DNAME the high-order field. The letter b (for blank position in a field) is entered as needed to indicate the actual size of the field. Notice the fields are arranged for matching the same way in the card file CARDTRAN, with CPERD the low-order field and CNAME the high-order. Because of this automatic matching field arrangement it is important that the correct matching field indicator is assigned to the related fields.

The same matching field rules must be followed for split matching fields; that is, the fields must all be the same type (numeric, alphanumeric, or alphabetic). In other words, DNAME and CNAME could not be alphabetic when DDAY, CDAY, DPERD, and CPERD are defined as numeric. All the fields would have to be alphabetic.

In addition, the related fields assigned with the same matching field indicator must be the same size. CPERD must be the same size as DPERD; DDAY the same as CDAY; and DNAME the same size as CNAME.

RPG   INPUT SPECIFICATIONS

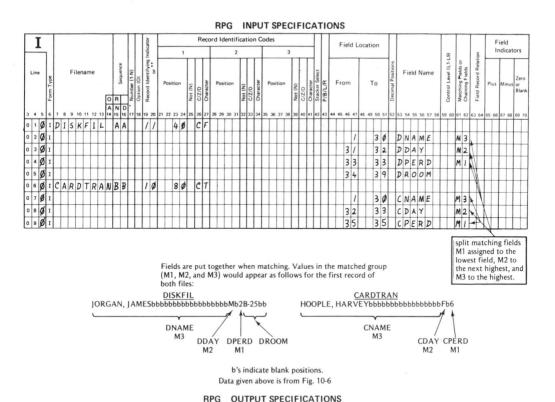

Fields are put together when matching. Values in the matched group (M1, M2, and M3) would appear as follows for the first record of both files:

DISKFIL
JORGAN, JAMESbbbbbbbbbbbbbbbbbbMb2B-25bb

DNAME M3   DDAY M2   DPERD M1   DROOM

CARDTRAN
HOOPLE, HARVEYbbbbbbbbbbbbbbbbbbFb6

CNAME M3   CDAY M2   CPERD M1

split matching fields M1 assigned to the lowest field, M2 to the next highest, and M3 to the highest.

b's indicate blank positions.
Data given above is from Fig. 10-6

RPG   OUTPUT SPECIFICATIONS

```
O   01 O REPORT    H  21Ø1   1P
    02 O        OR           ØF
    03 O                               24  'INSTRUCTOR NAME'
    04 O                               65  'DAY     PERIOD     ROOM NO-'
    05 O           H  2      1P
    06 O        OR           ØF
    07 O                               66  '_ _ _ _ _ _ _ _ _ _ _ _ _'
    08 O                               42  '_ _ _ _ _ _ _ _ _ _ _'
    09 O                               18  '_ _ _ _ _ _'
    10 O           D  2      1Ø
    11 O                    CNAME      37
    12 O                    CDAY       44
    13 O                    CPERD      51
    14 O              MR    DROOM      64
    15 O              NMR              81  '*-NOTE   NO MATCHING RECO'
    16 O              NMR              89  'RD FOUND'
```

Fig. 10-7. Input and Output-Format Specifications coding for program using three Matching Fields.

Figure 10-7 also illustrates the Output-Format Specifications coding for the sample split matching-field program. Notice that Record Identifying Indicator 10 is used to condition the detail line (line 100). The 10 indicator was assigned to the records in the secondary file and because the data for this output record is from both the primary and secondary file, the Record Identifying Indicator for the secondary records must be used. This rule was stated on pages 350–51.

Re-examine Figure 10-7 and notice the MR indicator is entered on line 140 in columns 27 and 28. This is still an AND relationship with the 10 indicator, but allows CNAME, CDAY, and CPERD to print whether there is a match or not. The error message, *NOTE NO MATCHING RECORD FOUND, will print when a match is not found.

The source program listing is illustrated in Figure 10-8 along with the resulting printed output. Look at the printed output and notice that a matching record cannot be found on the DISKFIL for two records. A record for HOOPLE, HARVEY does not exist on the disk file. In addition, a seventh period class is not included in the disk file for MORGAN, ROBERT, hence, no match. In order for MR to turn on, all the matching fields in the group (M1, M2, and M3) must match.

Source program listing:

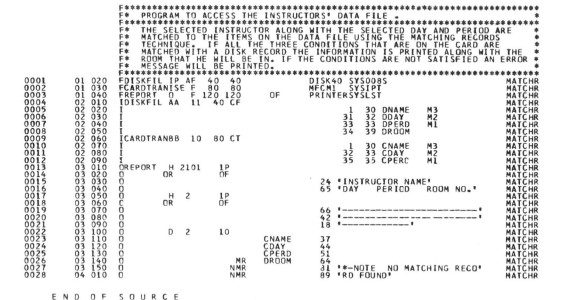

Fig. 10-8.   RPG source program listing and printer output for program using three Matching Fields.

Printed output:

```
  INSTRUCTOR NAME                   DAY   PERIOD   ROOM NO.
------------------------------------------------------------------

  HOOPLE,HARVEY                      F       6     *-NOTE   NO MATCHING RECORD FOUND

  JORGAN,JAMES                      TH       4     A-28A

  MORGAN,ROBERT                      M       1     B-17A

  MORGAN,ROBERT                      T       2     A-29

  MORGAN,ROBERT                     TH       7     *-NOTE   NO MATCHING RECORD FOUND

  MYERS,STANLEY                      F       2     B-17A

  MYERS,STANLEY                      W       3     B-21
```

Fig. 10-8.   (Concluded)

UPDATING A SEQUENTIAL DISK FILE BY THE MATCHING RECORD METHOD

RPG II coding for the creation, sequential processing, and addition to sequential disk files was presented in Chapter 9, and random processing, using matching records, was detailed in the preceding paragraphs of this chapter. Another commonly used processing function is the update of field(s) in records stored on a direct access device (disk, diskette, data cell, drum) or magnetic tape. The ability to update information within a data record eliminates the need to recreate a file every time changes are needed in a record or records. Regardless of the file organization type (sequential, indexed-sequential, or direct), RPG II allows for the update of any record(s) residing in a data file on a direct access device or magnetic tape unit.

A sample program using the same data base as in the previous, random, processing program that used three matching fields will be used to illustrate the required coding to update records stored in a sequential disk file. The disk file (DISKFIL) data is repeated again in Figure 10-9 along with the data for the card file (UPDATES) which contain the update field information.

Examine Figure 10-9 and notice the only field to be updated (changed) is the room field (DROOM) in the disk records. Any number of data record fields may be updated; however, because the required, matched record is found by matching on three fields, *no field assigned as a Matching Field* may be changed when updating.

Included in the UPDATES file are six records, three of which either have no matching disk file (DISKFIL) record and/or have a blank room (UROOM) value. Output provides for error messages for records that do not meet the requirements of the program. This is not a requirement in Matching Record coding but does serve as a useful communication link between the user and the computer.

DISKFIL				UPDATES			
DNAME	DDAY	DPERD	DROOM	UNAMES	UDAYS	UPERDS	UROOM
JORGAN, JAMES	M	2	B-25	ANDREWS, JOE			
JORGAN, JAMES	T	3	B-14	BROWN, JOHN			
JORGAN, JAMES	TH	4	A-28A	JORGAN, JAMES	TH	4	D-005
JORGAN, JAMES	TH	8	B-15	MORGAN, ROBERT	M	2	D-006
MORGAN, ROBERT	M	1	B-17A	MYERS, STANLEY	T	2	
MORGAN, ROBERT	M	2	B-18	MYERS, STANLEY	W	3	D-008
MORGAN, ROBERT	M	5	A-29				
MORGAN, ROBERT	T	2	A-29				
MORGAN, ROBERT	TH	5	B-25	new value to			
MYERS, STANLEY	F	2	B-17A	be entered			
MYERS, STANLEY	F	7	B-15	in DROOM			
MYERS, STANLEY	M	1	B-16	in DISKFIL			
MYERS, STANLEY	T	2	B-25				
MYERS, STANLEY	TH	4	B-23				
MYERS, STANLEY	W	3	B-21				

Sequential disk file to be updated	Card file containing update records

Fig. 10-9. Records in the sequential disk file (DISKFIL) and records in the card file (UPDATES) containing the update field information.

The complete source program coding for the update program is illustrated in Figure 10-10. Examination of the figure will reveal that few changes are required in previously discussed RPG II coding to update a disk file. The required update coding and program logic is discussed in the following paragraphs supported by individual figures for every coding form used in the program.

Look at the File Description coding form in Figure 10-11 and notice the only new entry to update a disk file is the letter U in column 15 for the file to be updated (DISKFIL). The letter U indicates the file is an update file which informs the computer it is *both an input and output file*. Consequently, the records in the file must be defined on the *input and output forms*. See Figure 10-10 and locate the input form line 060 and the first output form line 010. The file name, DISKFIL, is entered on both of the forms because it is an update file and, therefore, must be defined on input and output.

When the matching record method is used to update a disk file it must be specified as a secondary file (S in column 16 of File Description form). Because of the processing sequence of the RPG II logic cycle, if the update file was specified as primary it would not update correctly. It must be remembered when the records of two or more files match, the primary record is always processed first (see Figure 10-3, Rule 2); therefore, the primary record(s) would be processed before it was updated and would not be available for updating.

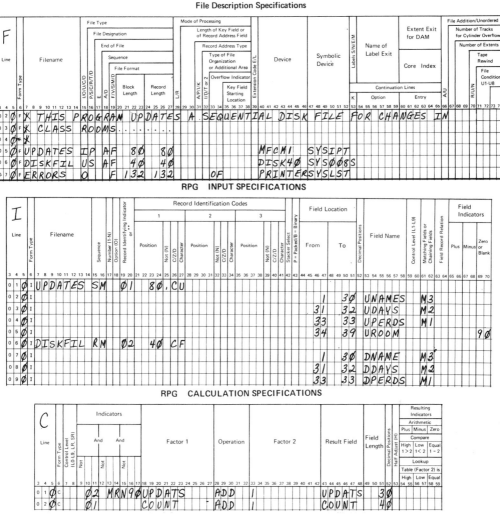

Fig. 10-10. Source program for updating a sequential disk file using the Matching Records Method. (Continued on next page.)

As with all files using matching records, an A or D must be entered in column 18 of File Description to indicate the sorted sequence. All files used in a program that include records with matching fields must be sorted in the same sequence (A or D). Any sort error will cause file processing to halt, or on some systems, cancel program execution.

Further examination of Figure 10-11 reveals that no additional or new coding entries are required in the File Description form to update a disk file. The UPDATES input card file contains the update record information and the

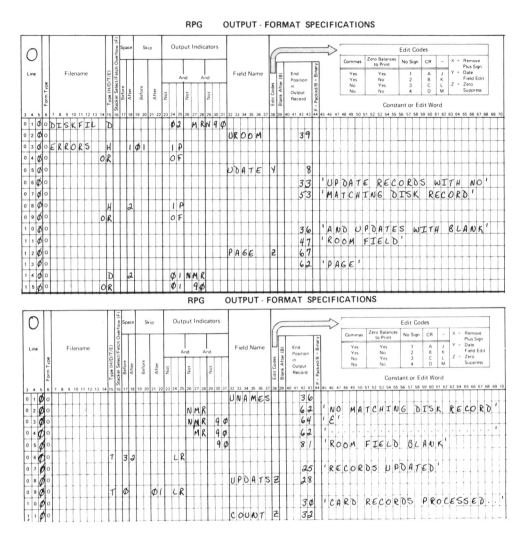

Fig. 10-10. Source program for updating a sequential disk file using the Matching Records Method (Concluded).

ERRORS printer file (not required) provides for printed error messages useful in identifying data errors.

Examine the Input Specifications form in Figure 10-12 and notice the fields in the records from the card input file (UPDATES) and the sequential disk file (DISKFIL) are defined. In addition to the Matching Field Indicators, the UROOMS field is tested for a blank value. If the field is blank, the 90 indicator will turn on and is used to condition subsequent calculations and output (see Figures 10-13 & 10-14). Notice the files are entered in the input form in the same order they appear in the File Description Specifications.

File Description Specifications

File Description Specifications

Line	Form Type	Filename	I/O/U/C/D	P/S/C/R/T/D	E	A/D	F/V/S/M/D	Block Length	Record Length	L/R	A/P/I/K	I/D/T or 2			Extension Code E/L	Device	Symbolic Device	Labels S/N/E/M	Name of Label Exit	K	Option	Entry	A/D	R/U/N	File Condition U1-U8

Line	
0 2	F * THIS PROGRAM UPDATES A SEQUENTIAL DISK FILE FOR CHANGES IN
0 3	F * CLASS ROOMS . . . .
0 4	F *
0 5	F UPDATES IP AF 80 80 MFCM1 SYSIPT
0 6	F DISKFIL US AF 40 40 DISK40 SYS0008 S
0 7	F ERRORS O F 132 132 OF PRINTER SYSLST

- U must be entered in col. 15 for file to be updated
- When matching records is used update file must be secondary
- When matching records is used both file must be sorted in same sequence. Either ascending or descending

Fig. 10-11. File Description Specifications coding for sample program for updating a sequential disk file.

RPG INPUT SPECIFICATIONS

Line	Form Type	Filename	Sequence	Number (1-N)	Option (O)	Record Identifying Indicator or **	Position (1)	Not (N)	C/Z/D	Character	Position (2)	Not (N)	C/Z/D	Character	Position (3)	Not (N)	C/Z/D	Character	P/B/L/R	From	To	Decimal Positions	Field Name	Control Level (L1-L9)	Matching Fields or Chaining Fields	Field Record Relation	Plus	Minus	Zero or Blank

Line	
0 1	I UPDATES SM 01 80 C U
0 2	I 1 30 UNAMES M3
0 3	I 31 32 UDAYS M2
0 4	I 33 33 UPERDS M1
0 5	I 34 39 UROOMS 90
0 6	I DISKFIL RM 02 40 C F
0 7	I 1 30 DNAME M3
0 8	I 31 32 DDAYS M2
0 9	I 33 33 DPERDS M1

- When the values in the 3 fields in an UPDATES file record matches the values in the 3 fields in a DISKFIL record MR (Matching Record Indicator) will turn on.
- 90 turns on if UROOMS is blank. Used to check status of this field.

Fig. 10-12. Input Specifications coding for sample program for updating a sequential disk file.

361

Other than defining the records and fields (only those used in the program have to be defined even though others may exist in the records) of the update and transaction files, no additional or new coding entries are needed for an update program using the matching record method.

The sample program does not have any required calculations for the update of disk records, but does have two optional accumulator fields included. The coding on line 010 of the calculation form provides for a count of the disk records successfully updated. The line is conditioned by the Record Identifying Indicator assigned to the DISKFIL records (secondary file), the matching record indicator (MR), and *not* 90. Hence, a one will be added to the accumulator field UPDATS only if the fields from the primary and secondary file match and the UROOM field is not blank.

The coding on line 020 of the calculation form accumulates the number of card file (UPDATES) records read. This will include the records with the correct update information as well as the records that do not match the disk file and/or have a blank room field.

As shown on the first page of the output forms (Figure 10-14, line 010) disk file (DISKFIL) is updated when a matching record is found, if the room field is not blank, and when the secondary file (DISKFIL) record identifying indicator (02) is on. The value in the card file record field UROOM is entered in the disk file position for DROOM which changes (or updates) the original value in that disk record field.

The program also provides for a printer file for error messages. Figure 10-14 shows the coding used in the sample program to print errors for which

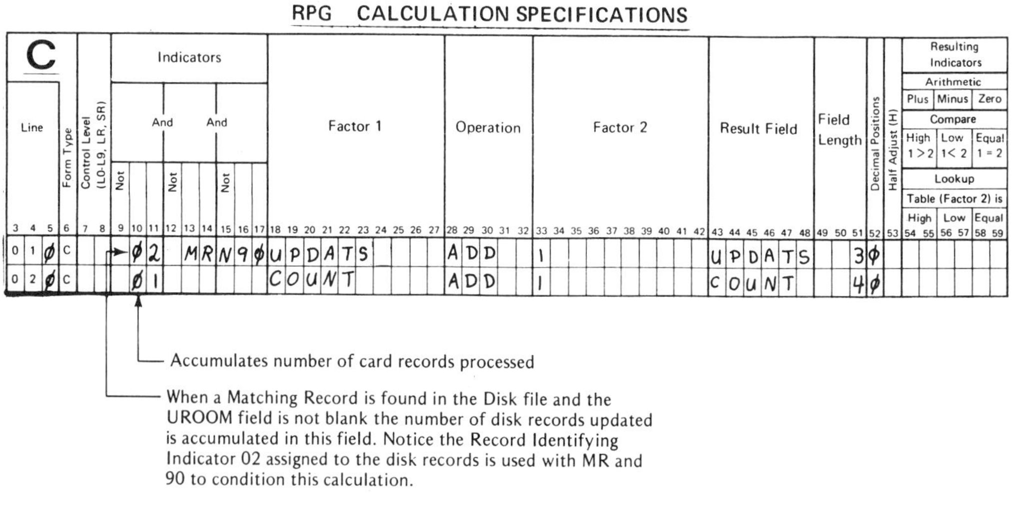

RPG CALCULATION SPECIFICATIONS

Accumulates number of card records processed

When a Matching Record is found in the Disk file and the UROOM field is not blank the number of disk records updated is accumulated in this field. Notice the Record Identifying Indicator 02 assigned to the disk records is used with MR and 90 to condition this calculation.

Fig. 10-13. Calculation Specifications coding for sample program for updating a sequential disk file.

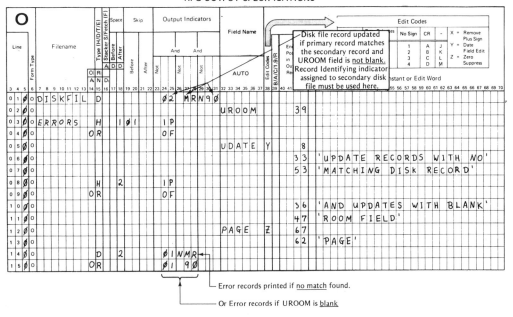

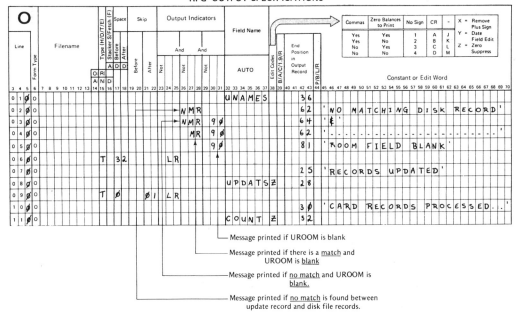

Fig. 10-14. Output-Format Specifications coding for sample program for updating a sequential disk file.

testing takes place in the input card records. Locate line 140 of the first output form and notice it is conditioned by the 01 Record Identifying Indicator assigned to the card file records. If a match cannot be found between the records of the primary and secondary files, the 02 indicator would not be on for a *not match* (NMR) condition. Therefore, in order for the appropriate card record to be identified, the 01 indicator is used with the NMR indicator to provide for an error message for this condition. In addition, the OR relationship on line 150 of the first output form provides for any records which do match but have a blank room (UROOM) field.

Lines 020 to 050 in the second output form (Figure 10-14) condition the respective error messages. The indicator logic and related messages are detailed at the bottom of Figure 10-14. Furthermore, the two accumulator fields (UPDATS and COUNT) are printed at Last Record Time (LR) when end-of-file is sensed in the UPDATES card file.

The source program listing is illustrated in Figure 10-15 with the error messages generated by card record not having a matching disk file record, not having a blank room field, or both conditions.

Anytime disk or tape records are changed by a program, a listing of the updated records and the records immediately before and after should be examined to insure the program executed any update functions correctly.

Source listing:

```
        01 020  F*THIS PROGRAM UPDATES A SEQUENTIAL DISK FILE FOR CHANGES IN        UPDATE
        01 030  F* CLASS ROOMS........                                              UPDATE
        01 040  F*                                                                  UPDATE
0001    01 050  FUPDATES IP AF  80   80             MFCM1  SYSIPT                    UPDATE
0002    01 060  FDISKFIL US AF  40   40             DISK40 SYS008S                   UPDATE
0003    01 070  FERRORS   O  F 132  132      OF     PRINTERSYSLST                    UPDATE
0004    02 010  IUPDATES SM  01  80 CU                                              UPDATE
0005    02 020  I                                          1   30 UNAMES  M3        UPDATE
0006    02 030  I                                         31   32 UDAYS   M2        UPDATE
0007    02 040  I                                         33   33 UPERDS  M1        UPDATE
0008    02 050  I                                         34   39 UROOM          90 UPDATE
0009    02 060  IDISKFIL RM  02  40 CT                                             UPDATE
0010    02 070  I                                          1   30 DNAME   M3        UPDATE
0011    02 080  I                                         31   32 DDAYS   M2        UPDATE
0012    02 090  I                                         33   33 DPERDS  M1        UPDATE
0013    03 010  C     02 MRN90UPDATS     ADD  1      UPDATS  30                     UPDATE
0014    03 020  C        01         COUNT ADD  1      COUNT   40                     UPDATE
0015    04 010  ODISKFIL D         02 MRN90                                         UPDATE
0016    04 020  O                           UROOM  39                               UPDATE
0017    04 030  OERRORS  H  101    1P                                               UPDATE
0018    04 040  O        OR        OF                                               UPDATE
0019    04 050  O                  UDATE Y   8                                      UPDATE
0020    04 060  O                          33  *UPDATE RECORDS WITH NO*             UPDATE
0021    04 070  O                          53  *MATCHING DISK RECORD*               UPDATE
0022    04 080  O        H    2    1P                                               UPDATE
0023    04 090  O        OR        OF                                               UPDATE
0024    04 100  O                          36  *AND UPDATES WITH BLANK*             UPDATE
0025    04 110  C                          47  *ROOM FIELD*                         UPDATE
0026    04 120  O                  PAGE  Z  67                                      UPDATE
0027    04 130  O                          62  *PAGE*                               UPDATE
0028    04 140  O        D    2    01NMR                                            UPDATE
0029    04 150  O        OR        01 90                                            UPDATE
0030    04 160  O                  UNAMES   36                                      UPDATE
0031    05 010  O                  NMR      62  *NO MATCHING DISK RECORD*           UPDATE
0032    05 020  O                  NMR 90   64  *&*                                 UPDATE
0033    05 030  O                  MR  90   62  *...................*              UPDATE
0034    05 040  O                      90   81  *ROOM FIELD BLANK*                  UPDATE
0035    05 050  C        T  32    LR                                               UPDATE
0036    05 060  O                          25  *RECORDS UPDATED....*               UPDATE
0037    05 070  O                  UPDATSZ  28                                      UPDATE
0038    05 080  O        T  0     01 LR                                            UPDATE
0039    05 090  O                          30  *CARD RECORDS PROCESSED..*          UPDATE
0040    05 100  O                  COUNT Z  34                                      UPDATE
```

Fig. 10-15. Source listing for updates program using three Matching Fields and error messages.

Error listing:

```
3/13/78    UPDATE RECORDS WITH NO MATCHING DISK RECORD
              AND UPDATES WITH BLANK ROOM FIELD            PAGE    1

        ANDREWS,JOE                      NO MATCHING DISK RECORD & ROOM FIELD BLANK
        BROWN,JOHN                       NO MATCHING DISK RECORD
        MYERS,STANLEY                    ....................... ROOM FIELD BLANK


        RECORDS UPDATED....  3
        CARD RECORDS PROCESSED..   6
```

Fig. 10-15. (Concluded)

Figure 10-16 shows a utility program listing of the data file (DISKFIL) *before* the sample program processed the update card records and Figure 10-17 illustrates the three records *after* the updated disk file records were changed. The only field updated in the program is the room field which is located in positions 34–39 of the disk records. Even though the sample program only provided for the update of one field, any number of fields in a record may be changed. However, no value in a field may be changed which is used as a Matching Field in the program.

Even though there were six records in the update card file (UPDATES) (see Figure 10-9) only three were used to update the disk file because the other three either had no matching disk record, a blank room field (tested on input), or both. The printed error listing in Figure 10-15 identifies the update records not used to update the master disk file.

PROCESSING A DISK FILE USING THE READ OPERATION CODE

Instead of using the Matching Records Method of processing a sequential disk file, the file may be defined as a *Demand File* and processed by the *READ operation code*. When this technique is used, data records are retrieved from the Demand File during calculations rather than waiting for the next normal logic cycle. Every record processed follows the same fixed RPG II logic cycle; the READ operation code, however, temporarily alters it so records may be accessed from the Demand File in the calculation phase of the cycle (see Chapter 6, Figure 6-3, for logic flowchart). Hence, a Demand File is one that provides records on demand rather than according to the logic cycle of the RPG II compiler.

A Demand File may be an input (I), update (U), or combined (C) file as defined by entering the appropriate letter in column 15 of the File Description form. Regardless of the file organization type (sequential, indexed-sequential, or direct) the file is processed sequentially. Individual records are retrieved from the Demand File only by the READ operation code. A sample program using the same data base and input fields as the previously presented program

```
* * * * DEVICE  161  SYS039,  CYLINDER 009, HEAD 00,  OPERATIVE 3340 PRIMARY

CYL  009    DATA   40    CHAR   JORGAN,JAMES                     M 2B-25   T
HEAD  00                 ZONE   DCDCCD6DCDCE444444444444444444444D4FC6FF44E
REC    1                 NUMR   169715811452000000000000000004022025003
                                1...5...10...15...20...25...30...35...40

CYL  009    DATA   40    CHAR   JORGAN,JAMES                     T 3B-14   T
HEAD  00                 ZONE   DCDCCD6DCDCE444444444444444444444E4FC6FF44E
REC    2                 NUMR   169715811452000000000000000003032014003
                                1...5...10...15...20...25...30...35...40

CYL  009    DATA   40    CHAR   JORGAN,JAMES                     TH4A-28A  T
HEAD  00                 ZONE   DDDCCD6DCDCE444444444444444444444ECFC6FFC4E
REC    3                 NUMR   169715811452000000000000000003841028103
                                1...5...10...15...20...25...30...35...40

CYL  009    DATA   40    CHAR   JORGAN,JAMES                     TH8B-15   T
HEAD  00                 ZONE   DDDCCD6DCDCE444444444444444444444ECFC6FF44E
REC    4                 NUMR   169715811452000000000000000003882015003
                                1...5...10...15...20...25...30...35...40

CYL  009    DATA   40    CHAR   MORGAN,ROBERT                    M 1B-17A  T
HEAD  00                 ZONE   DDDCCD6DDCCDE444444444444444444444D4FC6FFC4E
REC    5                 NUMR   469715896259300000000000000004012017103
                                1...5...10...15...20...25...30...35...40

CYL  009    DATA   40    CHAR   MORGAN,ROBERT                    M 2B-18   T
HEAD  00                 ZONE   DDDCCD6DDCCDE444444444444444444444D4FC6FF44E
REC    6                 NUMR   469715896259300000000000000004022018003
                                1...5...10...15...20...25...30...35...40

CYL  009    DATA   40    CHAR   MORGAN,ROBERT                    M 5A-29   T
HEAD  00                 ZONE   DDDCCD6DDCCDE444444444444444444444D4FC6FF44E
REC    7                 NUMR   469715896259300000000000000004051029003
                                1...5...10...15...20...25...30...35...40

CYL  009    DATA   40    CHAR   MORGAN,ROBERT                    T 2A-29   T
HEAD  00                 ZONE   DDDCCD6DDCCDE444444444444444444444E4FC6FFC4E
REC    8                 NUMR   469715896259300000000000000003021029003
                                1...5...10...15...20...25...30...35...40

CYL  009    DATA   40    CHAR   MORGAN,ROBERT                    TH5B-25   T
HEAD  00                 ZONE   DDDCCD6DCDCCDE44444444444444444444ECFC6FF44E
REC    9                 NUMR   469715896259300000000000000003852025003
                                1...5...10...15...20...25...30...35...40

CYL  009    DATA   40    CHAR   MYERS,STANLEY                    F 2B-17A  T
HEAD  00                 ZONE   DECDE6EECDDCE444444444444444444444C4FC6FFC4E
REC   10                 NUMR   485928231535800000000000000006022017103
                                1...5...10...15...20...25...30...35...40

CYL  009    DATA   40    CHAR   MYERS,STANLEY                    F 7B-15   T
HEAD  00                 ZONE   DECDE6EECDDCE444444444444444444444C4FC6FF44E
REC   11                 NUMR   485928231535800000000000000006072015003
                                1...5...10...15...20...25...30...35...40

CYL  009    DATA   40    CHAR   MYERS,STANLEY                    M 1B-16   T
HEAD  00                 ZONE   DECDE6EECDDCE444444444444444444444D4FC6FF44E
REC   12                 NUMR  - 485928231535800000000000000004012016003
                                1...5...10...15...20...25...30...35...40

CYL  009    DATA   40    CHAR   MYERS,STANLEY                    T 2B-25   T
HEAD  00                 ZONE   DECDE6EECDDCE444444444444444444444E4FC6FF44E
REC   13                 NUMR   485928231535800000000000000003022025003
                                1...5...10...15...20...25...30...35...40

CYL  009    DATA   40    CHAR   MYERS,STANLEY                    TH4B-23   T
HEAD  00                 ZONE   DECDE6EECDDCE444444444444444444444ECFC6FF44E
REC   14                 NUMR   485928231535800000000000000003842023003
                                1...5...10...15...20...25...30...35...40

CYL  009    DATA   40    CHAR   MYERS,STANLEY                    M 3B-21   T
HEAD  00                 ZONE   DECDE6EECDDCE444444444444444444444E4FC6FF44E
REC   15                 NUMR   485928231535800000000000000006032021003
                                1...5...10...15...20...25...30...35...40

CYL  009    DATA    0            END OF FILE RECORD
HEAD  00
REC   16
```

Values in fields
<u>before</u> updated

Fig. 10-16. Utility program listing of sequential disk file *before* updating by sample program using three Matching Fields.

```
* * * * DEVICE  161  SYS039,  CYLINDER 009, HEAD 00,  OPERATIVE 3340 PRIMARY 1

CYL  009   DATA   40   CHAR   JCRGAN,JAMES                     M 2B-25  T
HEAD  00                ZONE   DDDCCD6DCDCE4444444444444444444D4FC6FF44E
REC    1                NUMR   1697158114520000000000000000004C22025C03
                               1...5...10...15...20...25...30...35...40

CYL  009   DATA   40   CHAR   JORGAN,JAMES                     I 3B-14  T
HEAD  00                ZONE   DDDCCD6DCDCE4444444444444444444E4FC6FF44E
REC    2                NUMR   1697158114520000000000000000003032014003
                               1...5...10...15...20...25...30...35...40

CYL  009   DATA   40   CHAR   JCRGAN,JAMES                  TH40-005 T
HEAD  00                ZONE   DDDCCD6DCDCE44444444444444444ECFC6FF44E
REC    3                NUMR   1697158114520000000000000000003844000503
                               1...5...10...15...20...25...30...35...40

CYL  009   DATA   40   CHAR   JCRGAN,JAMES                  TH8B-15  T
HEAD  00                ZONE   DDDCCD6DCDCE44444444444444444ECFC6FF44E
REC    4                NUMR   1697158114520000000000000000003882015003
                               1...5...10...15...20...25...30...35...40

CYL  009   DATA   40   CHAR   MCRGAN,ROBERT                    M 1B-17A T
HEAD  00                ZONE   DDDCCD6DDCCDE44444444444444444D4FC6FFC4E
REC    5                NUMR   4697158962593000000000000000004012017103
                               1...5...10...15...20...25...30...35...40

CYL  009   DATA   40   CHAR   MCRGAN,ROBERT                    M 2D-006 T
HEAD  00                ZONE   DDDCCD6DDCCDE44444444444444444D4FC6FF44E
REC    6                NUMR   4697158962593000000000000000004024000603
                               1...5...10...15...20...25...30...35...40

CYL  009   DATA   40   CHAR   MCRGAN,ROBERT                    M 5A-29  T
HEAD  00                ZONE   DDDCCD6DDCCDE44444444444444444D4FC6FF44E
REC    7                NUMR   4697158962593000000000000000004051029003
                               1...5...10...15...20...25...30...35...40

CYL  009   DATA   40   CHAR   MCRGAN,ROBERT                    I 2A-29  T
HEAD  00                ZONE   DDDCCD6DDCCDE44444444444444444E4FC6FF44E
REC    8                NUMR   4697158962593000000000000000003021029003
                               1...5...10...15...20...25...30...35...40

CYL  009   DATA   40   CHAR   MCRGAN,ROBERT                  TH5B-25  T
HEAD  00                ZONE   DDDCCD6DDCCDE44444444444444444ECFC6FF44E
REC    9                NUMR   4697158962593000000000000000003852025003
                               1...5...10...15...20...25...30...35...40

CYL  009   DATA   40   CHAR   MYERS,STANLEY                    F 2B-17A T
HEAD  00                ZONE   DECDE6EECDDCE44444444444444444C4FC6FFC4E
REC   10                NUMR   4859282315358000000000000000006022017103
                               1...5...10...15...20...25...30...35...40

CYL  009   DATA   40   CHAR   MYERS,STANLEY                    F 7B-15  T
HEAD  00                ZONE   DECDE6EECDDCE44444444444444444C4FC6FF44E
REC   11                NUMR   4859282315358000000000000000006072015003
                               1...5...10...15...20...25...30...35...40

CYL  009   DATA   40   CHAR   MYERS,STANLEY                    M 1B-16  T
HEAD  00                ZONE   DECDE6EECDDCE44444444444444444D4FC6FF44E
REC   12                NUMR   4859282315358000000000000000004012016003
                               1...5...10...15...20...25...30...35...40

CYL  009   DATA   40   CHAR   MYERS,STANLEY                    I 2B-25  T
HEAD  00                ZONE   DECDE6EECDDCE44444444444444444E4FC6FF44E
REC   13                NUMR   485928231535800C0000000000C0C003022025003
                               1...5...10...15...20...25...30...35...40

CYL  009   DATA   40   CHAR   MYERS,STANLEY                  TH4B-23  T
HEAD  00                ZONE   DECDE6EECDDCE44444444444444444ECFC6FF44E
REC   14                NUMR   4859282315358000000000000000003842023003
                               1...5...10...15...20...25...30...35...40

CYL  009   DATA   40   CHAR   MYERS,STANLEY                    W 3D-008 T
HEAD  00                ZONE   DECDE6EECDDCE44444444444444444E4FC6FF44E
REC   15                NUMR   485928231535800000000000000006034000803
                               1...5...10...15...20...25...30...35...40

CYL  009   DATA   C    END OF FILE RECCRD
HEAD  00
REC   16
```

Value in field
After Update

Fig. 10-17. Utility program listing of Sequential Disk File *after* updating by sample program using three Matching Fields.

367

for updating a sequential file using three matching fields (Figure 10-15) will be modified to illustrate the RPG II coding entries for Demand Files and the READ operation.

The source program coding for the sample update using a Demand File and the READ operation is given in the individual figures that follow. Examination of the forms indicates the only new entries used for Demand Files and the READ operation are entered in the File Description and Calculation Specification forms. Input and Output-Format Specification forms are not affected and use previously discussed standard coding procedures.

The File Description coding for a Demand File is illustrated in Figure 10-18. Notice the only change needed to specify a disk file as a Demand File is the letter D in column 16. All other coding entries for the file remain the same. However, in order to process the Demand File all records within the files must be sorted in either ascending or descending sequence. The U in column 15 (discussed previously) indicates the file is an update file that has to be defined on input and output. Also notice that columns 17 18, 33, 34 and 39 must always be blank.

No additional coding entries are required in the Input Specifications for a Demand File. Input coding is shown in Figure 10-19 only to explain how the fields in the card and disk records are redefined. In the matching records program (Figure 10-15) three fields were used to extract a disk record when the related, matching, field values from the card record match. The same fields are used in this program but are now redefined as one field in the disk record (DFIELD) and one in the card record (UFIELD). By redefining the fields as one field eliminates the need to use the MOVE and MOVEL operations in calculations to create the fields used in the compare operations required in this program.

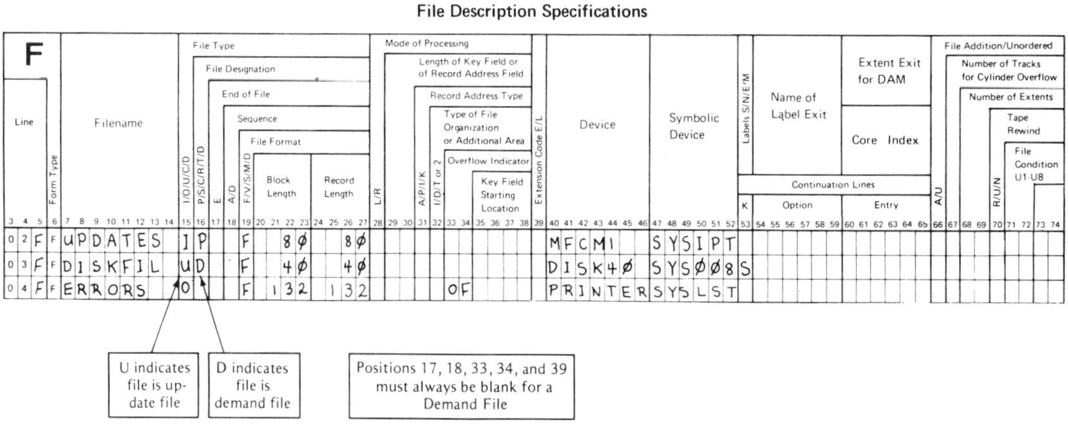

File Description Specifications

Fig. 10-18. File Description coding entries needed to define a Disk File as a Demand File.

RPG   INPUT SPECIFICATIONS

Line	Form Type	Filename	Sequence	Number (1 N)	Option (O)	Record Identifying Indicator or **	Position	Not (N)	C/Z/D	Character	Position	Not (N)	C/Z/D	Character	Position	Not (N)	C/Z/D	Character	Stacker Select P/B/L/R	From	To	Decimal Positions	Field Name	Control Level (L1-L9)	Matching Fields or Chaining Fields	Field Record Relation	Plus	Minus	Zero or Blank
0 1 0	I	UPDATES	SM			0 1	8 0		C	U																				
0 2 0	I																		1	3 0		UNAMES						
0 3 0	I																		1	3 3		UFIELD						
0 4 0	I																		3 4	3 9		UROOM						9 0
0 5 0	I	DISKFIL	RM			0 2	4 0		C	T																				
0 6 0	I																		1	3 3		DFIELD						

Name, Day, and Period Fields
are redefined in UFIELD and DFIELD

Fig. 10-19. Input Specifications coding for the sample program using a Demand File and the READ operation code. No special coding is needed on input for Demand File processing.

Before calculation coding is discussed, the logic of processing a Demand File by the READ operation code must be understood. This logic is detailed in Figure 10-20. Two important points are noted in the Demand File/READ operation logic. First, the search of a Demand File *does not* begin at the first record for each search record processed. The logic explanation in Figure 10-20 indicates the search begins at the disk record following the last one successfully found. Second, if a related record cannot be found in the Demand File for a search record the Demand File would be scanned until the end-of-file record is sensed and the file would automatically be closed and no longer available for processing. To avoid this, a routine must be provided for in calculations.

A line-by-line explanation of the calculation coding in Figure 10-21 will be presented in the following paragraphs.

Line 010. Indicators 98 and 99 that could have been turned on by the compare (COMP) on line 160 are set off to prevent any unwanted subsequent instructions from executing.

Lines 020 to 050. Comments.

Line 060. The value in the redefined input field (UFIELD) is compared with the value in DFIELD; if equal indicator 98 is turned on. This compare is performed only if 97 was turned on in the compare operation on line 160 when the disk value is higher than the card value. If the next card record is equal to the disk record, the disk record would not be updated if this compare was not used.

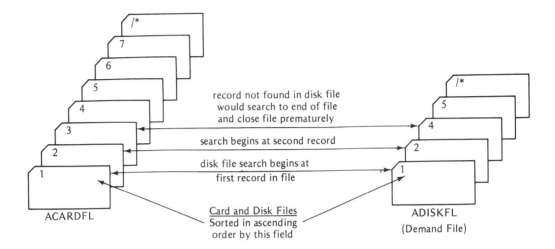

Processing logic:

A data record is read from the card file and the READ operation code searches the disk file until an equal record is found. If a related card record is found in the disk file, the disk record information is extracted for processing. Another card record is then read and the disk file search <u>begins at the record following the</u> one previously extracted. Remember the search <u>does not</u> start at the beginning of the disk file for each card record processed, but at the record following the one just processed. In the example given above when card record 2 is read the disk file search will begin at disk record 2 and <u>not</u> 1.

If a related card record cannot be found in the disk file the disk file will be searched until the end-of-file record is read and the file will be closed. This will prevent any card records following the card record without a related disk record from being used to search the disk file. Therefore, a routine must be provided for in calculations to prevent end-of-file from being read until all the records in the search file are processed. In the example given above, a related disk record does not exist for card record 3, consequently, the disk file would be searched until end of file is sensed and card records 5, 6, and 7 would not be able to process the disk file because it would be closed. The calculation logic for this program explains how this may be avoided.

Fig. 10-20. Processing logic for a Demand File processed by the READ operation code.

Line 070. If the compare on line 060 resulted in an equal condition, indicator 97 is turned off to prevent any erroneous error messages from printing when the disk record is found and updated.

Line 080. When 98 is on (turned on as a result of an equal compare on line 060) the GOTO operation is executed and calculations are skipped over (except for the two card-count calculation lines: lines 190 and 200). Because 98 is on, the disk record is updated with the room change (the indicators used to condition the update file DISKFIL are found in Figure 10-22).

Line 090. The AGAIN TAG is the entry point for the loop so DISKFIL may be searched until an equal to or higher than relationship exists between UFIELD and DFIELD.

Line	Form Type	Control Level	Indicators (And/And)	Factor 1	Operation	Factor 2	Result Field	Field Length	Dec Pos	Resulting Indicators	Comments
010	C		01		SETOF					99 98	
020	C		*	IF THE VALUE IN THE PREVIOUS CARD RECORD IS HIGHER THAN THE DISK							
030	C		*	RECORD VALUE COMPARE UFIELD WITH DFIELD. IF = SETON 98 (LINE 060)							
040	C		*	THEN SETOF 97 (LINE 070), THEN GO TO END OF CALCULATIONS AND UPDATE							
050	C		*								
060	C		97	UFIELD	COMP	DFIELD				98	
070	C		98		SETOF					97	
080	C		98		GOTO	END					
090	C				AGAIN	TAG					
100	C				READ	DISKFIL				20	
110	C		20		GOTO	END					
120	C		*	COMPARE CARD RECORD WITH DISK RECORD. IF = TURN ON 98 & UPDATE							
130	C		*	DISKFIL RECORD, IF LESS THAN, READ ANOTHER DISK RECORD, IF HIGHER							
140	C		*	THAN TURN ON 97 & PRINT ERROR MESSAGE.							
150	C		*								
160	C			DFIELD	COMP	UFIELD				97 99 98	
170	C		99		GOTO	AGAIN					
180	C			END	TAG						
190	C		98 N90	UPDATS	ADD	1	UPDATS	30			
200	C		01	COUNT	ADD	1	COUNT	40			

Fig. 10-21. Calculation coding for sample program using a Demand File processed by the READ operation code.

Line 100. The READ operation code extracts a record from DISKFIL on demand instead of only at the normal RPG II cycle of processing records. The disk record following the one previously processed is read. Remember the READ operation does not begin a search of the Demand File at the first record for every card record processed.

Line 110. If the end-of-file record in the disk file (DISKFIL) is sensed, indicator 20 is turned on by the READ operation on line 100, the GOTO END operation executed, and all looping calculations skipped. Once end of file is sensed, the file is closed and may no longer be accessed.

Lines 120 to 150. Comments.

Line 160. The values in DFIELD and UFIELD are compared. If they are equal, 98 is turned on and the disk record updated (see Figure 10-22) with the new room field value. If less than, indicator 99 turns on, line 170 is executed, and program control loops back to line 090 and reads another disk record on demand (line 100). If higher than, indicator 97 is turned on and program control follows the normal RPG II logic cycle and related error messages are printed (see Figure 10-22). Note when the next card record is processed, 97 is still on, and the compare on line 060 is made to check for an equal condition of the two fields before a new record is read from the disk file (line 100).

Line 170. If the value in DFIELD (the disk record) is less than the value in the card record field (UFIELD), 99 was turned on and program control loops back to read another disk record.

Line 180. Entry point for the GOTO operations on lines 080 and 110.

Line 190. Accumulates the number of disk records found and updated.

Line 200. Accumulates a count of all the card records processed.

The output coding illustrated in Figure 10-22 is identical to the coding in Figure 10-15 except the error messages are now conditioned by a 97 indicator turned on in calculation line 160 when the value in FIELD is higher than the value in UFIELD.

The source program listing for the sample program illustrating the use of the READ operation code to process a Demand File is shown in Figure 10-23 along with the resulting error messages. Results of the update are the same as that illustrated in Figures 10-16 and 10-17.

This program has illustrated the use of the READ operation code with a Demand File (the only file it may be used with). The READ operation is often used with display files (cathode ray tube input and/or output) and with matching record programs when more than two files are used for input.

Some of the rules and limitations of Demand Files and the READ operation code are as follows:

1. All files defined as Demand Files and processed by the READ operation code must be sorted in the same order (ascending or descending sequence).

2. Matching field indicators, control level indicators, and look-ahead fields cannot be used with the Demand File. Other files in the program may use these, however.

3. A Demand File may be an input, update, or combined file.

4. Sequential and indexed-sequential (ISAM) files may be defined as a Demand File and processed by the READ operation code.

5. Demand Files may be processed only by the READ operation code.

6. Any indicator, except H0 (Halt Indicator), may be used in columns 58 and 59 in the calculation form with the READ operation code.

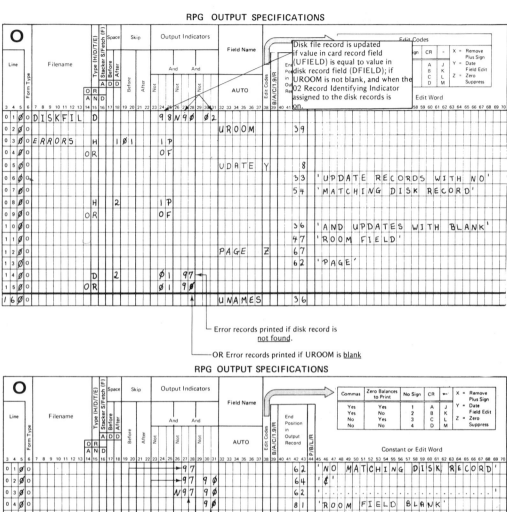

Fig. 10-22. Output-Format Specifications coding for sample program for updating a Demand File using the READ operation code.

Source program listing:

```
           01 020  F*THIS PROGRAM UPDATES A SEQUENTIAL DISK FILE (DEFINED AS A DEMAND      DEMAND
           01 030  F* FILE) FOR CHANGES IN CLASSROOMS USING THE READ OPERATION CODE.....•DEMAND
           01 040  F*                                                                      DEMAND
0001       01 050  FUPDATES IP   F  80   80            MFCM1  SYSIPT                        DEMAND
0002       01 060  FDISKFIL UD   F  40   40            DISK40 SYSO08S                       DEMAND
0003       01 070  FERRORS   O   F 132  132       OF   PRINTERSYSLST                        DEMAND
0004       02 010  IUPDATES SM   01   80 CU                                                 DEMAND
0005       02 020  I                                        1   30 UNAMES                   DEMAND
0006       02 030  I                                        1   33 UFIELD                   DEMAND
0007       02 040  I                                       34   39 UROOM            90       DEMAND
0008       02 050  IDISKFIL RM   02   40 CT                                                 DEMAND
0009       02 060  I                                        1   33 DFIELD                   DEMAND
0010       03 010  C     01                    SETOF                       9998             DEMAND
           03 020  C*IF THE VALUE IN THE PREVIOUS CARD RECORD IS HIGHER THAN THE DISK       DEMAND
           03 030  C*RECORD VALUE COMPARE UFIELD WITH DFIELD. IF = SETON 98 (LINE 050)      DEMAND
           03 040  C*THEN SETOF 97 (LINE 070), THEN GO TO END OF CALCULATIONS AND UPDATEDEMAND
           03 050  C*                                                                       DEMAND
0011       03 060  C     97       UFIELD    COMP DFIELD                       98             DEMAND
0012       03 070  C     98                 SETOF                       97                  DEMAND
0013       03 080  C     98                 GOTO END                                        DEMAND
0014       03 090  C              AGAIN     TAG                                             DEMAND
0015       03 100  C                        READ DISKFIL                     20             DEMAND
0016       03 110  C     20                 GOTO END                                        DEMAND
           03 120  C*COMPARE CARD RECORD WITH DISK RECORD. IF = TURN ON 98 & UPDATE         DEMAND
           03 130  C*DISKFIL RECORD, IF LESS THAN, READ ANOTHER DISK RECORD, IF HIGHER      DEMAND
           03 140  C*THAN TURN ON 97 & PRINT ERROR MESSAGE.                                 DEMAND
           03 150  C*                                                                       DEMAND
0017       03 160  C              DFIELD    COMP UFIELD                   979998             DEMAND
0018       03 170  C     99                 GOTO AGAIN                                       DEMAND
0019       03 180  C              END       TAG                                             DEMAND
0020       03 190  C     98N90    UPDATS    ADD  1          UPDATS  30                       DEMAND
0021       03 200  C     01       COUNT     ADD  1          CCUNT   40                       DEMAND
0022       04 010  ODISKFIL D            98N90 02                                            DEMAND
0023       04 020  O                                UROOM      39                            DEMAND
0024       04 030  OERRORS   H   101      1P                                                 DEMAND
0025       04 040  O            OR         CF                                                DEMAND
0026       04 050  O                                UDATE Y    8                             DEMAND
0027       04 060  O                                          33 'UPDATE RECORDS WITH NO'    DEMAND
0028       04 070  O                                          54 'MATCHING DISK RECORD'      DEMAND
0029       04 080  O            H   2      1P                                                DEMAND
0030       04 090  O            OR         OF                                                DEMAND
0031       04 1C0  O                                          36 'AND UPDATES WITH BLANK'    DEMAND
0032       04 110  O                                          47 'ROOM FIELD'                DEMAND
0033       04 120  O                                PAGE  Z   67 'PAGE'                      DEMANC
0034       04 130  O                                          62 'PAGE'                      DEMAND
0035       04 140  O            D   2      01 97                                             DEMAND
0036       04 150  O            OR         01 90                                             DEMAND
0037       04 160  O                                UNAMES    36                             DEMAND
0038       05 010  O                                97        62 'NO MATCHING DISK RECORD'   DEMAND
0039       05 020  O                                97 90     64 '&'                         DEMAND
0040       05 030  O                                N97 90    62 '....................'      DEMAND
0041       05 040  O                                90        81 'ROOM FIELD BLANK'          DEMAND
0042       05 050  O            T 32      LR                                                 DEMAND
0043       05 060  O                                          25 'RECORDS UPDATED....'       DEMANC
0044       05 070  O                                UPDATSZ   28                             DEMAND
0045       05 080  O            T 0      01 LR                                               DEMAND
0046       05 090  O                                          30 'CARD RECORDS PROCESSED..'  DEMAND
0047       05 100  O                                COUNT Z   34                             DEMAND
```

Error message report:

```
9/26/77    UPDATE RECORDS WITH NOMATCHING DISK RECORD
           AND UPDATES WITH BLANK ROOM FIELD              PAGE    1

    ANDREWS,JOE                        NO MATCHING DISK RECORD & ROOM FIELD BLANK

    BROWN,JOHN                         NO MATCHING DISK RECORD

    MYERS,STANLEY                      ....................  ROOM FIELD BLANK


    RECORDS UPDATED....  3
    CARD RECORDS PROCESSED..   6
```

Fig. 10-23. Source program listing and error message report for sample program for processing a Demand File by the READ operation code.

QUESTIONS

1. How many matching field indicators are available in the RPG II language? On what forms and in what columns are they entered?
2. When matching field indicators are assigned to fields in two different input files what are some of the specific rules that must be observed?
3. When two fields match, what internal indicator is automatically turned on? What may the indicator be used for?
4. When two matching fields match, which file will supply the next record to be processed? If the fields do not match, which file will supply the next record to be processed?
5. In what order will the following records be processed when matching fields are used? Assume EMPNO1 is included in the primary file and EMPNO2 in the secondary file.

EMPNO1		EMPNO2	
(a)	01234	(e)	01234
(b)	22222	(f)	01235
(c)	33312	(g)	41111
(d)	41111		

6. If three matching fileds are specified for a match, how will the contents of the fields be arranged for the match if M1 contains 18; M2, 44; and M3, 72?
7. Given below are the contents of two matching input fields. When will the MR indicator be turned on?

			Field Name	Contents
(a)	Primary file:	EMPREC	EMP1	17804
	Secondary file:	EMPTRAN	EMP2	45102
(b)	Primary file:	EMPREC	EMP1	-34512
	Secondary file:	EMPTRAN	EMP2	34512

8. What order must two or more input (or update) files be sorted before matching records are used to process them? What must be entered in column 18 of the File Description Specifications form? Is this entry used for an output file(s)?
9. When updating a disk sequential file what entries must be made in the File Description Specifications to provide for the update operation? Should the disk (or tape) file to be updated be primary or secondary? Why?
10. On what coding forms are the fields entered for the file to be updated? If only one field is to be updated in a disk record do all the fields have to be defined on input?

11. What if anything is wrong with the following coding?

RPG   INPUT SPECIFICATIONS

Line	Form Type	Filename	Sequence	Number (1,N)	Option (O)	Record Identifying Indicator	Position 1	Not (N)	C/Z/D	Character	Position 2	Not (N)	C/Z/D	Character	Position 3	Not (N)	C/Z/D	Character	Stacker Select P=Packed/B=Binary	From	To	Decimal Positions	Field Name	Control Level (L1-L9)	Matching Fields or Chaining Fields	Field Record Relation	Plus	Minus	Zero or Blank
01	0 I	CARDS		AA		01																							
02	0 I																			2	60		CUSTNO		M1				
03	0 I																			7	10		BRANCH		M3				
04	0 I																			11	12		STATE		M2				
05	0 I																			13	20	2	ACTBAL		M4				
06	0 I				AB		02																						
07	0 I																			2	5		CUSTNO		M1				
08	0 I																			6	80		BRANCH		M2				
09	0 I																			9	10		STATE		M3				
10	0 I																			11	18	25	SALE		M4				

12. Explain the processing logic of the READ operation code. In what type files may it be used?

13. What are the coding forms and columns used for the READ operation?

14. Assume a disk file includes 1000 data records sorted in ascending sequence by employee number. If the READ operation is used to process this file and disk record 400 was processed, would the first record in the disk file be processed next? Explain your answer.

15. What are some of the restrictions when using the READ operation?

16. What are a few of the available methods of sorting a large data file?

17. In a multifile program, on which file should letter E (end-of-file) be assigned?

EXERCISES

10-1. A sequentially organized master inventory file called ITMFIL resides on disk with the following record format:

Field Description	Positions	Char.	Bytes	Dec. Pos.	Type
Item number	1–5	5	5		A
Department number	6–8	3	3		A
Amount on hand	9–11	5	3	0	N

Note: The disk records were loaded with a blocking factor of 10.

Required:

Write the File Description and Input Specifications coding to update ITMFIL for sales and purchases of department items. Assign M1 to Item number and M2 to Department number. The format of the records in the update file, SALORPU, are as follows:

10-2. Write the Calculation Specifications for updating the file defined in Exercise 10-1. When a successful match is found, update the amount on hand for sales and purchases of items. Provide for two count fields; one for the disk records updated and one for the number of card records that have no matching disk record.

10-3. Write the Output-Format Specifications to update the ITMFIL when a match is found. The balance of the new amount on hand will be entered in the respective disk record.

10-4. Refer to Exercises 10-1 and 10-2 and write the output coding for an error report listing in the following format:

		0	1	2	3	4
		1234567890	1234567890	1234567890	1234567890	1234567890
H	1	ØX/XX/XX	UPDATE RECORDS	WITH NO	PAGE	XXØX
H	2		MATCHING DISK	RECORD		
	3					
H	4	ITEM NO	DEPT NO	AMOUNT	ID CODE	
	5					
D	6	XXXXX	XXX	XXXØ	X	
D	7	XXXXX	XXX	XXXØ	X	
	8					
TLR	9	DISK RECORDS UPDATED........XXXØ				
	10					
TLR	11	NO MATCHING DISK RECORD....XXXØ				
	12					
	13	NOTE: HEADINGS ON TOP OF EVERY PAGE				
	14					

10-5. Modify Exercises 10-1, 10-2, 10-3, and 10-4 so the ITMFIL is updated by the READ operation code instead of Matching Records. Remember all of the coding forms are not affected by the READ operation.

10-6. How would you change your coding in Exercises 10-2, 10-3, and 10-4 so that calculations and output are conditioned by a Control Level Indicator (L1 and L2)? Assume there are several records for each item and the files are sorted in ascending sequence.

LABORATORY ASSIGNMENTS

LABORATORY ASSIGNMENT 10-1:
UPDATING A SEQUENTIAL DISK FILE USING ONE MATCHING FIELD

A file resides on disk for savings account information for depositors. The disk record information and format is given in the layout form below along with the data for the disk file. Note you may have created this disk file if you completed Laboratory Assignment 9-1 in Chapter 9. If the assignment was not required, you will have to create the disk file before you can complete this assignment.

Existing Disk File Record Format. (If not already on disk you will have to create this file.)

RECORD NAME _____Ø1_____

PAGE _1_ OF _1_
DATE _9/30/77_

DISK/TAPE FILE DOCUMENTATION

FILE NAME - In Program	FILE NAME - For File Management	PACK OR TAPE ID
SEQDISK	LAB 9-1, S. MYERS	222222

ALL FILES:	DISK FILES:	TAPE FILES:
RECORD LENGTH **64**	MULTIPLE PACKS Y (N)	MULTIPLE REELS Y N
BLOCK FACTOR **5**	KEY FIELD LOC'N ___ to ___	REEL SIZE _____
BLOCK LENGTH **320**	ORGANIZATION:	RETEN. CYCLE _____
SPACE AVAIL. FOR	☒ SEQ. ☐ INDEXED	(days)
EXPANSION **8YTES**	☐ DIRECT ☐ OTHER _____	

FIELD NAME OR DESCRIPTION	POSITIONS FROM	POSITIONS TO	NO. OF CHARS.	NO. OF BYTES	DEC. POS'N	TYPE A/N/P*	REMARKS
'ID' CODE	1	3	3	3		A	letters BAL
ACCOUNT NUMBER	4	8	5	5		A	
DEPOSITOR'S NAME	9	38	3Ø	3Ø		A	
BRANCH NAME	39	57	19	19		A	
STATE	58	59	2	2		A	
ACCOUNT BALANCE	60	64	8	5	2	P	

* A = alpha; N = numeric; P = packed

Data for the Sequential Disk File. (If you completed Laboratory Assignment 9-1 this is the same data.)

Account Number	Depositor's Name	Branch Name	State	Account Balance	ID Code
64321	HENRY FORD	DETROIT	MI	21584519	BAL
55114	LOUIS CHEVROLET	TARRYTOWN	NY		
88397	WALTER P. CHRYSLER	SAN DIEGO	CA	01000000	BAL
74891	BENJAMIN DODGE	CHICAGO	IL	04100000	
91784	WILLIAM BRICKLIN	TORONTO	ND	09000000	BAL
49814	JOHN STUDEBAKER	KANSAS CITY	KA		BAL
34444	STANLEY STEAMER	BUFFALO	NY	37100000	BAL

Required for Laboratory Assignment 10-1:

Write a source program to update the disk file using the Matching Record Method. Only one Matching Field Indicator has to be used which is to be assigned to the Account Number Field. The format of the update records is as follows:

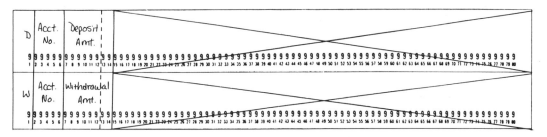

Calculations. Deposit amounts in the records coded with the character D in column 1 are to be added to the disk record field for account balance when a record from the primary and secondary fields match. Records coded with the character W in column 1 are withdrawal amounts which are subtracted from the disk file account balance for the related depositor. Provide for two accumulator fields; one for the number of disk records updated and one for the total number of card records read.

Output Coding. For every card record successfully matched with a disk record, update the depositor's disk record account balance. Provide for a listing of card records that have no matching disk record. The printer format of the error report is given below:

Format of Printed Report:

		0	1	2	3	4
		1 2 3 4 5 6 7 8 9 0	1 2 3 4 5 6 7 8 9 0	1 2 3 4 5 6 7 8 9 0	1 2 3 4 5 6 7 8 9 0	1 2 3 4 5 6 7 8
H	1	ØX/XX/XX	CARD RECORDS WITHOUT A		PAGE XXØX	
H	2		MATCHING DISK RECORD			
	3					
	4					
D	5			XXXXX (ACTNO)		
	6					
D	7			XXXXX		
	8					
	9					
TLR	10		NUMBER OF DISK RECORDS UPDATED...XXØ			
	11					
TLR	12		NUMBER OF CARD RECORDS READ.......XXØ			
	13					
	14					
	15		NOTE:			
	16					
	17		HEADINGS ON TOP OF EVERY PAGE.			
	18					

Additional Requirement. Check the contents of the disk file to determine if your program updated the records correctly. Use the *utility program* (if available) on your system to do this or *write your own* RPG II program to echo check the disk file.

Data To Be Used in Update Records:

Column 1	Columns 2–6	Columns 7–14
D	34444	01000000
W	34444	03000000
W	34444	05000000
D	74891	00500000
W	91784	08000000
D	41111	00750000

Note: The records in the disk file and card file must be sorted in the same sequence when the Matching Records Method is used.

LABORATORY ASSIGNMENT 10-2:
UPDATING A SEQUENTIAL DISK FILE USING THE READ OPERATION

Refer to the disk record format, card record layout, calculation requirements, and printed report format in Laboratory Assignment 10-1 and write an update program using the READ operation code instead of Matching Records. Remember both files must be sorted in the same sequence for the READ operation to process the disk file. Refer to the coding logic detailed in this chapter for the READ operation.

LABORATORY ASSIGNMENT 10-3:
UPDATING A SEQUENTIAL DISK FILE USING TWO MATCHING FIELDS

A master customer sequential file resides on disk. The disk record information and format is given in the layout form below. You may have created this disk file if you completed Laboratory Assignment 9-4 in Chapter 9. If the assignment was not required you will have to create the disk file before you can complete this assignment. Matching fields ($M1$ and $M2$) for this program are customer number and name.

Existing Disk File Record Format. (If not already on disk you will have to create this file.)

RECORD NAME _CUSTOMER RECORDS_

PAGE _1_ OF _1_
DATE _10/1/77_

DISK/TAPE FILE DOCUMENTATION

FILE NAME - In Program	FILE NAME - For File Management	PACK OR TAPE ID
CUST FIL	_LAB 9-4 – S. MYERS_	_222222_

ALL FILES:
RECORD LENGTH _99_
BLOCK FACTOR _4_
BLOCK LENGTH _396_
SPACE AVAIL. FOR
EXPANSION _5900_ BYTES

DISK FILES:
MULTIPLE PACKS   Y Ⓝ
KEY FIELD LOC'N ___ to ___
ORGANIZATION:
☒ SEQ.   ☐ INDEXED
☐ DIRECT ☐ OTHER ___

TAPE FILES:
MULTIPLE REELS Y N
REEL SIZE ___
RETEN. CYCLE ___
(days)

FIELD NAME OR DESCRIPTION	POSITIONS FROM	TO	NO. OF CHARS.	NO. OF BYTES	DEC. POS'N	TYPE A/N/P*	REMARKS
CUSTOMER NUMBER	1	4	4	4		A	
CUSTOMER NAME	5	33	29	29		A	
STREET ADDRESS	34	57	24	24		A	
CITY	58	72	15	15		A	
STATE	73	74	2	2		A	
ZIP	75	77	5	3	Ø	P	
ACCOUNT BALANCE	78	82	8	5	2	P	
BALANCE DATE	83	88	6	6	Ø	N	
STORE NUMBER	89	91	4	3	Ø	P	
CUST. TELEPHONE No.	92	97	10	6	Ø	P	
'ID' CODE	98	99	2	2			letters T+B

* A = alpha; N = numeric; P = packed

Data for the Sequential Disk File. (If you completed Laboratory Assignment 9-4 this is the same data.) Note that *two* card records are used to create *one* disk record

Record Type Coded With Character T in Column 80:

Customer Number	Customer Name	Street Address	City	State	Zip
1234	JOHN FIRESTONE	20 TYRE LANE	AKRON	OH	05456
2345	WILLIAM GOODYEAR	19 TUBE ROAD	DETROIT	MI	06606
3456	JAMES GOODRICH	81 VALVE TERRACE	CHICAGO	IL	04404
4567	CLAUDE MICHELIN	1 PARIS PLACE	FRANCE	PA	06611
5678	ANTHONY PIRELLI	33 FIAT BOULEVARD	ROME	NY	06608
6789	TOYO DOGO	12 HIROSHIMA ROAD	TOKYO	CA	06666

Record Type Coded With Character B in Column 80:

Customer Number	Account Balance	Balance Date	Store No.	Customer Tel. No.
1234	00018112	083179	0001	2032889999
2345	01041879	063079	0005	2127445555
3456	12000000	043079	0002	2063334441
4567	00091822	073179	0003	2136666666
5678	01800000	053179	0004	2015558888
6789	00045600	083179	0002	2142221111

The data records must be grouped together according to customer number. Sequence checking is required; therefore, a record with the character T must be placed *before* the corresponding customer's record for the type coded with the character B.

Format of Update Records:

The update records perform the following functions:

Column 80 ID

A	This record type updates the master disk file for a change in the customer's address.
S	Updates the account balance for an additional sale.
P	Updates the account balance for payments on account.
T	Updates the master disk file for a change in telephone number.

(handwritten margin notes: 74, 12, 14, 14, 29, 18, + , 132)

Calculations.   Add any additional sale amounts to the account balance and deduct payments on account from the customer's account balance. Provide for two accumulator fields: one for the number of master disk records updated and another for the total number of card records read.

Output Coding.   For every card record matched with a disk record, update the customer's record with the related update information. Provide for a listing of all card records that have no matching disk record. The printer format of the error report is given below:

Format of Printed Report:

```
          0         1         2         3         4         5         6
          1234567890123456789012345678901234567890123456789012345678901234567890
H   1            ØX/XX/XX  RECORDS WITHOUT MATCHING DISK RECORD      PAGE XXØX
H   3            CUST   CUSTOMER NAME                           RECORD
H   4            NO.                                            CODE
D   6            XXXX   X                                 X         X
D   8            XXXX   X                                 X         X
TLR 11       DISK RECORDS UPDATED.....XXØ
TLR 13       CARDS PROCESSED..........XXØ
```

Additional Requirements.   Check the contents of the disk file to determine if your program correctly updated the disk records. Use the utility program on your system to do this (if available) or *write* your own RPG II source program to echo-check the file.

Data To Be Used for the Assignment:

Record Type for Address Changes:

Columns 1–4	Columns 5–33	Columns 34–57	Columns 58–72	Columns 73–74	Columns 75–79	Column 80
1234	JOHN FIRESTONE	9 PARK PLACE	BRIDGEPORT	CT	06611	A
6789	TOYO KOGO	2 MAZDA ROAD	SAN DIEGO	CA	92100	A
2345	WILLIAM GOODRICH	17 WHEEL LANE	HONOLULU	HI	96800	A

Record Types for Account Balance Change (Sales and Payments):

Columns 1–4	Columns 5–33	Columns 34–41	Columns 42–79 not used	Column 80
1234	JOHN FIRESTONE	00018112	(not used)	P
3456	JAMES GOODRICH	01000000	"	S
4576	CLAUDE MICHELIN	00010000	"	P

Record Type for Telephone Number Change:

Columns 1–4	Columns 5–33	Columns 34–43	Columns 44–79 not used	Column 80
5678	ANTHONY PIRELLI	2049990000	(not used)	T

Depending on sequence in the disk file (A or D), the card records must be sorted in the same ascending or descending sequence. If this is not done the execution of the compiled program will either halt or, on some systems, cancel.

LABORATORY ASSIGNMENT 10-4:
UPDATING A SEQUENTIAL DISK FILE USING THE READ OPERATION

Refer to the disk record format, card record layout, calculation requirements, and printed report format in Laboratory Assignment 10-3 and write an update program using the READ operation code instead of Matching Records. Remember both files must be sorted in the same sequence for the READ operation to process the disk files. Refer to the coding logic detailed in this chapter for the READ operation.

11
INDEXED-SEQUENTIAL (ISAM) DISK FILE CONCEPTS

INDEXED-SEQUENTIAL (ISAM) FILE ORGANIZATION METHOD

Chapter 9 introduced basic disk file concepts and the RPG II coding for the creation of and addition to sequential disk files. The random processing and update by the Matching Records Method and the READ operation code were presented in Chapter 10. This chapter introduces the RPG II coding for the creation and processing of indexed-sequential (ISAM) disk files.

Whether a file is sequential, indexed-sequential, or direct, each organization method has unique advantages and disadvantages. For example, it was mentioned in Chapter 9 that sequential disk files have the advantage of using less disk space, are simple to load, and faster to process when the file has a high record activity. On the other hand, disadvantages include slow random access when the file has a low percentage of record activity, the inability to add records to an existing file on some systems, and, if records may be added, the sorted integrity of the file is destroyed. Because of these disadvantages a data file may be more efficiently processed and maintained if it is organized as an ISAM file.

Indexed-sequential disk files (referred to as ISAM for the remainder of this text) overcome some of the disadvantages of the sequential organization method. First, ISAM disk files are faster to random access when relatively few records are processed; second, all systems provide for the addition of records to ISAM files; and third, when records are added, the sorted integrity of the file is not destroyed. Disadvantages are that they use more storage than sequential files, are slower to process if the file has a large percentage of random access, and become slower to process if a large percentage of records have been added.

Figure 11-1 illustrates the logical and physical differences between a sequential and indexed-sequential disk file. Notice the sequential file consists only of a Prime Data Area. All data records loaded to the file are stored in the order they are read. If the file is to be processed later by Matching Records or the READ operation code, the records must be sorted in ascending or descending order by some field or fields.

Further examination of Figure 11-1 indicates the ISAM file has four separate areas including the Index, Prime Data Area, Cylinder Overflow, and Independent Overflow Area. The purpose and features of each area will be discussed in the following paragraphs.

Index. The index, which is unique to an ISAM file, provides for faster random processing of a file. When a sequential disk file is processed randomly, the file is searched sequentially until the required record is found. If the record was located at the end of the file the entire file would be scanned. The index overcomes this disadvantage because the location of individual records is indexed and enables the record to be directly accessed without searching the file sequentially.

When an ISAM file is created, two indexes are automatically created which include the *Cylinder Index* and *Track Index*. The programmer is not directly concerned with the separate indexes; however, the purpose of each is presented here to facilitate a greater understanding of how a record is located directly from an ISAM file.

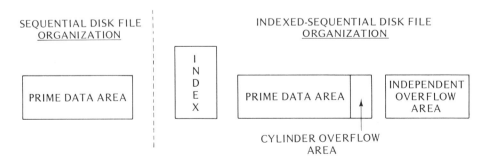

Fig. 11-1. Logical comparison of Sequential Disk File Organization Method to Indexed-Sequential Access Method (ISAM).

Data records are loaded and later referenced in an ISAM file by a key field within each record. Key fields may be an employee number, customer number, part number, social security number, names, etc. They must be unique for each record and duplicate keys are not allowed. Key fields may be numeric, alphanumeric, or alphabetic, and from 1 to 29 characters in length (up to 99 on IBM 370).

When the ISAM file is loaded, the records may be sorted in ascending order by key field or, on some systems (System/3 for example), may be in any order (unordered). If the records are loaded in an unordered sequence, the index, however, is automatically sorted in ascending order even though the data records remain in the original, loaded order. Figure 11-2 illustrates the logic of loading (creating) an ISAM disk file in unordered sequence. Remember on some systems the records must be sorted in ascending order before loading or program execution will be cancelled.

As the file is loaded with data records, the Cylinder Index and Track Index (one for each cylinder used for prime data) are automatically created. The highest numbered data record key field value is stored in the Cylinder Index for every cylinder used for the prime data area of the file. Look at Figure 11-3 and notice the highest number on cylinder 10 is key field value 100; cylinder 11, 200, and cylinder 12, 300.

At the same time the Cylinder Index is loaded, a Track Index is created for each prime data area cylinder. The highest record key value for each track on the respective cylinder is stored in each cylinder's Track Index. Notice in Figure 11-3 the highest key in track 01 is 15; track 02, 30; track 03, 45, and so forth. Each data record stored on the tracks has the record's key field stored with it.

The procedure of locating an individual data record, which is done for random processing or updating, involves a search of the Cylinder Index, Track Index, and individual data records. When a file is opened and a record read, the key field value in the record is used to first search the Cylinder Index. Refer to Figure 11-3 and assume a data record with a key field of 25 is used to random process the ISAM file. The key field entries in the Cylinder Index are searched until a key field value higher than 25 is found. In the example shown, the first key field higher than 25 is stored on cylinder 10. Hence, the record is stored somewhere on cylinder 10.

The address of the cylinder's Track Index is used to locate that index and it is then searched until a key is found higher than 25. Examine Figure 11-3 and notice the first key higher than 25 is stored on track 02. Finally, track 02 will be searched until the required key is found and the individual record information extracted for processing. All of the operations are executing in millionths of a second and the programmer is not aware of the individual indexes or search procedures. These concepts are mentioned here to make the user gain a fuller understanding of overall disk concepts and logic.

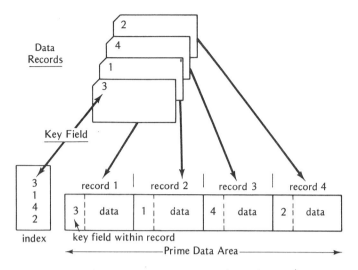

After ISAM disk file is created (loaded) the index is automatically sorted in ascending sequence. The records in the prime data area, however, remain in the same sequence as when the file was created.

The index and prime area after the automatic sort will be in the following key-field order:

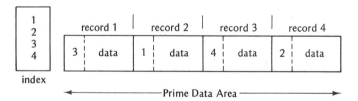

Notice after the automatic sort of the index the index is now in ascending order by key field, but the prime data area records remain in the original order.

NOTE: ISAM files loaded on an IBM 360 or 370 system must have data records sorted in ascending order before creating the file.

Fig. 11-2. Logic of creating an ISAM disk file when the key fields are in an unordered sequence.

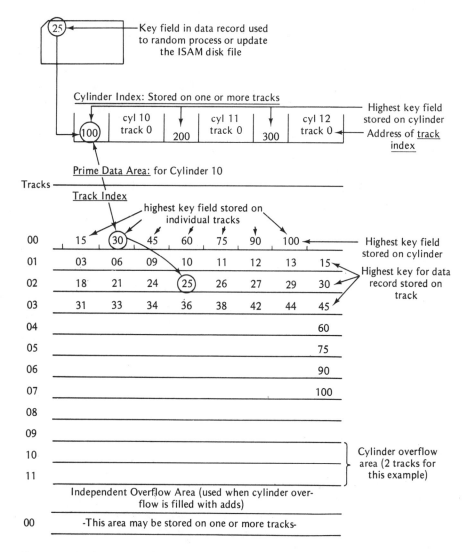

Fig. 11-3.   Cylinder index, track index, cylinder overflow and independent over-flow logic for ISAM disk files.

The Prime Data Area

The prime data area for any disk file organization type is where the data records are stored. The logical records in a disk file may be stored on disk in the following formats.

Fixed-unblocked.   Each logical record is the same length. Because the records are unblocked, the physical and logical records are same length (see Chapter 9 for explanation of logical and physical records). The letter F is entered in column 19 of the File Description Specifications form to specify that records are in fixed format. In an unblocked file the record length and block length fields would have the same entry. The format of the records is illustrated below.

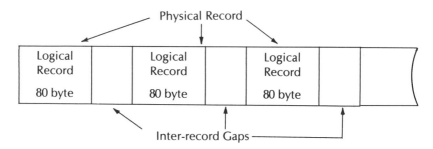

Fixed-blocked.   All logical records in file are the same length but are stored in blocks (physical record). Blocking eliminates the interrecord gap between individual logical records thereby decreasing storage used by the file and increasing processing speed. A gap, however, still exists between the blocks of records.

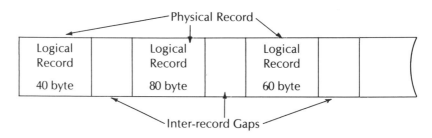

Variable-unblocked.   Logical records vary in length, and are used when more than one record type is stored in the file and each has a different length. This format saves disk storage for files that include records with variable lengths. The letter V is entered in column 19 of the File Description form instead of an F. The largest record length for the record types must be entered in the Record Length and Block Length fields. The format for this prime data organization method follows:

Variable-blocked.   Logical records vary in byte length. They are used when more than one record type is stored in the file and each has a different length. This format saves even more room than the variable-unblocked format because the interrecord gap is eliminated between individual, logical records. The letter V must be entered in column 19 of the File Description form for the disk file. The block size must be the sum of the individual records plus four bytes for the block length and an additional four bytes for each data record stored in the block. In the example shown the block size would be:

$$40 + 80 + 60 + 12 \text{ (four bytes for each record)}$$
$$+4 \text{ (for block length area)} = 196 \text{ bytes.}$$

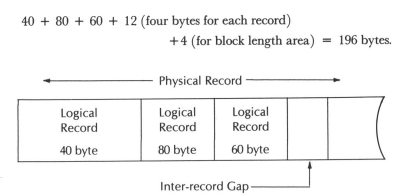

The most widely used formats are either fixed-unblocked or fixed-blocked. Variable formats are used primarily when disk or tape storage is limited.

Again the programmer does not have to be particularly concerned with the actual physical format of the record formats, but should be concerned with the advantages, disadvantages, and use of each.

Overflow Areas

Two overflow areas are optional with ISAM file organization and include the Cylinder Overflow and Independent Overflow areas. An overflow area is provided only if additional data records are to be added to the ISAM disk file that may exceed the existing prime data area. Overflow areas are not available for sequential or direct files and any records added are loaded at the end of the file. When the prime data area is full (sequential and direct) no more records may be added and the file would have to be reorganized.

The Cylinder Overflow area resides on some tracks of every cylinder used for the prime data area. On some systems it is created automatically and usually occupies from one to three tracks. Figure 11-4 illustrates the logic of adding a data record to an ISAM file.

Examine Figure 11-4 and notice four records with key field values 5, 17, 22, and 24 are added to the existing ISAM disk file. When a record is added it is placed in between other records to maintain the required ascending order. Notice the record with key field 5 is inserted between records 4 and 6. Because the track was full, record 12, which was the last record on track 1 before the adds, is moved to the Overflow area. In addition, record 17 is placed between records 16 and 19, and record 22 is stored as the last record on track 2. Observe that record 24 is also added, however, because track 2 is now full. Record 24 is added in the cylinder overflow area.

When the Cylinder Overflow area is full, additional adds will automatically be stored in the Independent Overflow area if provided for in the Job Control for the program. Furthermore, if many records are added to an ISAM

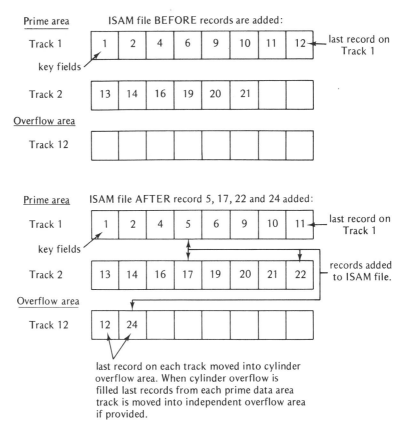

Fig. 11-4. Arrangement of an ISAM file *before* and *after* additional data records are added.

file, the access speed to the file is greatly reduced and should be reorganized by copying it to a different location. The reorganization will store all the add records in the prime data area and thereby increase access speed efficiency.

The Cylinder Overflow area may be used without an Independent Overflow area and vice versa. Remember overflow areas are optional and should only be included for the ISAM file if records are to be added after the file is created.

Now that basic ISAM disk file concepts have been introduced, the RPG II coding entries will be presented for the creation, sequential access, addition, limits processing, random processing, and updating of ISAM files.

RPG II CODING FOR THE CREATION
OF AN ISAM DISK FILE

An examination of the coding sheets for the source program in Figure 11-5 to create an ISAM disk file will indicate the only entries affected by the creation of an ISAM disk file are those in the File Description Specifications form. Input, Calculations, and Output-Format Specifications coding remain identical to that required for the creation of a sequential disk file.

Figure 11-6 illustrates the new entries in the File Description form to create an ISAM disk file along with the relationship of the length of the key field entry to the data records. The records used as the data base for all the programs in this chapter are also shown in Figure 11-6.

It is evident after an examination of Figure 11-6 that only a few new entries are required for the creation of an ISAM disk file. A summary of the new entries include the following:

1. The length of the key field must be specified in columns 29 and 30.
2. The letter A (or P or K) must be entered in column 31.
3. The letter I must be entered in column 32.
4. The key field starting location in the disk file record must be entered in columns 35 to 38.

These new entries will be explained in the following paragraphs.

Length of Key Field or of Record Address Field (Columns 29–30).   Typical key fields may be an employee number, customer number, part number, or some other suitable field used to identify a data record. In the File Description coding example in Figure 11-6, the key field is four positions (bytes) long. Notice the entry is right-justified in the field. The maximum length of key fields will again depend on the computer system used. When an ISAM file is created,

File Description Specifications

Line	Form Type	Filename	I/O/U/C/D P/S/C/R/T/D	E	A/D F/V/S/M/D	File Format	Block Length	Record Length	L/R	A/P/I/K I/D/T or Overflow Indicator	Extension Code E/L	Device	Symbolic Device	Labels S/N/E/M	Name of Label Exit	Core Index	Continuation Lines Option / Entry	A/U	R/U/N	File Condition U1-U8
0 2 0	F	INPUT	IP	E	F		80	80				MFCM1	SYSIPT							
0 3 0	F	INVEN	O		F		550	55		4AI	I	DISK40	SYS006	S				I		

RPG INPUT SPECIFICATIONS

Line	Form Type	Filename	Sequence	Number (1 N)	Option (O)	Record Identifying Indicator or **	Position (1) Not(N)	C/Z/D	Character	Position (2) Not(N)	C/Z/D	Character	Position (3) Not(N)	C/Z/D	Character	Stacker Select P=Packed/B=Binary	From	To	Decimal Positions	Field Name	Control Level (L1-L9)	Matching Fields or Chaining Fields	Field Record Relation	Plus	Minus	Zero or Blank
0 1 0	I	INPUT	AA			01											1	4		PARTNO						
0 2 0	I																5	45		NAME						
0 3 0	I																46	49	0	UCOST						
0 4 0	I																50	53	0	QUANT						

RPG CALCULATION SPECIFICATIONS

Line	Form Type	Control Level (L0-L9, LR, SR)	And (Not)	And (Not)	(Not)	Factor 1	Operation	Factor 2	Result Field	Field Length	Decimal Positions	Half Adjust (H)	Plus	Minus	Zero	High 1>2	Low 1<2	Equal 1=2	High	Low	Equal
0 1 0	C	01				QUANT	MULT	UCOST	TOTAL	70											

RPG OUTPUT - FORMAT SPECIFICATIONS

Line	Form Type	Filename	Type (H/D/T/E)	Stacker Select/Fetch Overflow (F)	Space Before	Space After	Skip Before	Skip After	Output Indicators And (Not)	And (Not)	(Not)	Field Name	Edit Codes	End Position in Output Record	B=Packed/B=Binary	Constant or Edit Word
0 1 0	O	INVEN	D						01							
0 2 0	O											PARTNO		4		
0 3 0	O											NAME		45		
0 4 0	O											UCOST		48 P		
0 5 0	O											QUANT		51 P		
0 6 0	O											TOTAL		55 P		

Fig. 11-5. Source program coding to create an ISAM disk file.

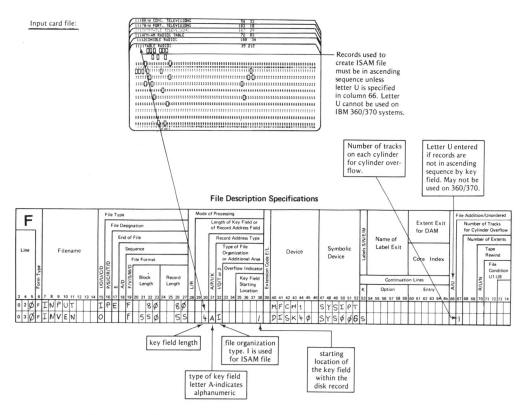

Fig. 11-6. File description coding for sample program to create an ISAM file. Special entries for ISAM files are identified.

the key fields are stored in the indexes as shown in Figure 11-3 and with each data record.

Record Address (Column 31).   The letter A entered in this field (Figure 11-6) indicates the key field is alphanumeric. The letter P may also be entered for an ISAM file which informs the computer the key field is packed numeric. The letter K was used on some systems and if used on a system that will not accept it, this letter will automatically "default" to a P-type key field. This field is blank for a sequential disk file. Other letters may be used here but relate to direct and addrout files which will be discussed later.

Type of File Organization or Additional Area (Column 32).   When an indexed-sequential file is created or processed, the letter I must be specified in this field which informs the computer that the file to be created is the indexed-sequential type. The entry initializes manufacturer-supplied software systems that perform any required housekeeping chores so the file may be loaded on disk.

Key Field Starting Location (Columns 35–38). Notice in Figure 11-6 that the number one is entered right-justified in this field. The entry specifies the location of the key field within the data record stored in the ISAM disk file. For example, the record size assigned to the records in the disk file is 55 bytes and the key field is specified as starting in the first position in the disk records. The fact that the key field is located in the first four positions of the card file's data records (Figure 11-6) does not indicate the key field location has to be in the same position in the disk records.

Look at Figure 11-6 again and notice the letter U may be entered in column 66 for the ISAM file if the data records used to load the disk file are not in ascending sequence. IBM 360/370 systems do not support this entry and the data records must be in sorted, ascending order by key field. Other systems do, however, support unordered sequence and sort the index in ascending order after the file is loaded. The records in the prime data area remain in the order in which they were loaded.

All other entries in the File Description form have been discussed in previous chapters including blocking, device, symbolic device, and standard labels. The reader may want to refer to Chapter 9 for the discussion of these general disk file entries.

An examination of the Input, Calculations, and Output-Format forms in Figure 11-5 indicates no special entries are used to create an ISAM disk file. However, three important points should again be noted regarding the output coding for any disk file creation: first, editing is not used with numeric output fields when stored on disk; second, spacing and skipping is never specified for disk files; third, only numeric fields may be packed on output (see Chapter 9) and when the file is later processed (defined as input) any packed fields must be identified as packed on input.

When a disk file is created or processed, the computer's unique control cards must be included in the job stream. Job control cards execute systems programs (supplied by the manufacturer) that facilitate the loading and/or processing operations needed to create or process a disk file. Also, job control cards are different for every manufacturer and model of computer and their format must be determined from the programmer's manuals supplied by the various computer manufacturers. Appendix Two illustrates and describes some of the job streams and control cards used in RPG II disk-file creation and processing programs.

The source program listing for the sample program that creates an ISAM disk file is illustrated in Figure 11-7. A utility program listing of the file after it is created is shown in Figure 11-8 to verify that the data records are loaded in the format specified.

Once the ISAM disk file is created, several methods of processing are available. First, the sequential processing of the entire file will be discussed followed by addition, limits-processing, random processing, and updating operations.

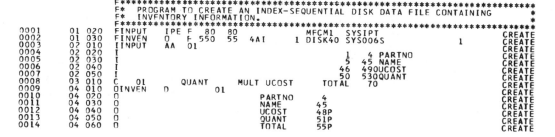

```
F************************************************************************************
F*    PROGRAM TO CREATE AN INDEX-SEQUENTIAL DISK DATA FILE CONTAINING          *
F*    INVENTORY INFORMATION.                                                   *
F************************************************************************************
0001  01 020  FINPUT   IPE F  80   80            MFCM1  SYSIPT                    CREATE
0002  01 030  FINVEN   O  F 550   55  4AI      1 DISK40 SYS006S              1    CREATE
0003  02 010  IINPUT   AA  01                                                     CREATE
0004  02 020  I                                           1   4 PARTNO            CREATE
0005  02 030  I                                           5  45 NAME             CREATE
0006  02 040  I                                          46 490UCOST            CREATE
0007  02 050  I                                          50 530QUANT            CREATE
0008  03 010  C    01      QUANT      MULT UCOST      TOTAL  70                   CREATE
0009  04 010  OINVEN   D        01                                                CREATE
0010  04 020  O                          PARTNO     4                             CREATE
0011  04 030  O                          NAME      45                             CREATE
0012  04 040  O                          UCOST     48P                            CREATE
0013  04 050  O                          QUANT     51P                            CREATE
0014  04 060  O                          TOTAL     55P                            CREATE
```

Fig. 11-7. RPG II source program listing for sample program to create an indexed-sequential disk file.

```
DATA   550  CHAR  1111TABLE RADIOS                                      *
            ZCNE  FFFFECCDC4DCCCDE4444444444444444444444444444444440050220040
            NUMR  1111312350914962000000000000000000000000000003C01C072C
                  1...5...10...15...20...25...30...35...40...45...50...55

            CHAR  1112CONSOLE RADIOS                                     <
            ZCNE  FFFFCDDEDCC4DCCCDE4444444444444444444444444444444(18CC4CC32
            NUMR  1112365263509149620000000000000000000000000000008C03C069C
                  1...5...10...15...20...25...30...35...40...45...50...55

            CHAR  1114FM-AM RADIOS TABLE                                 z
            ZCNE  FFFFCD6CD4DCCCDE4ECCDC4444444444444444444444444440020030096
            NUMR  1114640140914962031235000000000000000000000007C08C057C
                  1...5...10...15...20...25...30...35...40...45...50...55

            CHAR  1115PORTABLE TELEVISIONS                               a
            ZCNE  FFFFDDDECCDC4ECDCECECDDE4444444444444444444444440170090083
            NUMR  1115769312350353559296520000000000000000000006C02C044C
                  1...5...10...15...20...25...30...35...40...45...50...55

            CHAR  1117B/W PORT. TELEVISIONS                              <
            ZCNE  FFFC6E4DDDE44ECDCECECDDE444444444444444444444440130080024
            NUMR  1117216076538035355929652000000000000000000008C01C039C
                  1...5...10...15...20...25...30...35...40...45...50...55

            CHAR  1118B/W CONS. TELEVISIONS                              <
            ZCNE  FFFFC6E4CDDE44ECDCECECDDE444444444444444444444440080030094
            NUMR  1118216036528035355929652000000000000000000005C03C011C
                  1...5...10...15...20...25...30...35...40...45...50...55
```

Fig. 11-8. Utility program listing of data records in Indexed-Sequential disk file created by source program illustrated in Fig. 11-7.

SEQUENTIAL PROCESSING OF INDEXED-SEQUENTIAL FILES

Figure 11-9 illustrates the RPG II source program listing for the program to process an ISAM file sequentially (sometimes called an echo check). Notice in the File Description form the file is defined exactly as when created (Figure 11-6), except the file is now an *input file*. Therefore, the only change needed in the File Description form is the letter I in column 15 instead of the letter O.

All of the fields entered in the Input Specifications form must be defined according to their disk record field sizes and types. Because unit cost (UCOST), quantity (QUANT), and total (TOTAL) fields were packed on output when the file was created, they must be identified as packed on the input form. The letter P is entered in column 43 alongside the numeric field that is packed in the disk records. As was mentioned in Chapter 9, the computer automatically packs all numeric fields in storage before processing. Informing the computer that a field is already packed (P in column 43 on the input field) eliminates the routines that have to be executed to pack the field in storage. Reference to the documentation supporting the program (record layout form, for example) will

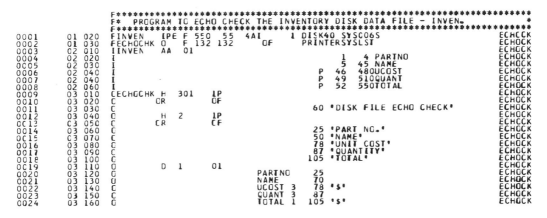

Fig. 11-9.   RPG II source listing for program to process an Indexed-Sequential disk file sequentially.

DISK FILE ECHO CHECK

PART NO.	NAME	UNIT COST	QUANTITY	TOTAL
1111	TABLE RADIOS	$35	242	$7,420
1112	CONSOLE RADIOS	$188	34	$6,392
1114	FM-AM RADIOS TABLE	$72	83	$5,976
1115	PORTABLE TELEVISIONS	$167	29	$4,843
1117	B/W PORT. TELEVISIONS	$183	18	$3,294
1118	B/W CONS. TELEVISIONS	$58	33	$1,914

Fig. 11-10.   Printer output for the sequentially processed (echo check) Indexed-Sequential disk file.

give the information regarding field sizes, location, and type. The need for documentation in addition to source program listings cannot be overemphasized and time should be spent to support all programs with the necessary forms, etc., for possible future reference.

The report generated by the program to process the ISAM file sequentially is shown in Figure 11-10.

FILE ADDITION (ISAM)

RPG II allows for the extension of an ISAM file by the addition of supplemental records after it is created. The addition feature is important because it eliminates the need to recreate a data file each time new records are added. For

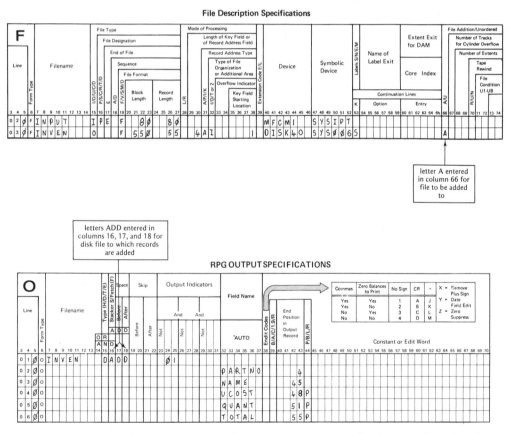

Fig. 11-11. File Description and Output-Format Specifications coding for the addition of records to an ISAM disk file.

example, if there were 80,000 inventory items in a file, the creation of the file each time a new record for a part was added would be an expensive and time-consuming task. All systems that support ISAM disk file organization provide for the addition of records to an existing file.

An RPG II source program to add data records to an ISAM file is identical to a program that created the file except for two additional entries. One entry is entered in the File Description form and the other on the output form. Figure 11-11 illustrates the new coding entries required to facilitate ISAM file addition. Notice the letter A is specified in column 66 of the File Description form for the disk file (INVEN) to which records will be added. The only other new coding requirement for file addition is in the Output-Format Specifications form. Refer to Figure 11-11 again and notice the word ADD is entered in columns 16, 17, and 18 of the output form on the same line as the file name. These are the only entries needed to modify an RPG II source program for the creation of a file for the addition of records.

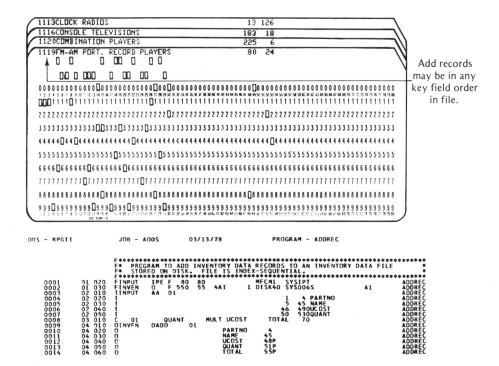

Fig. 11-12.   RPG II source listing for program to add data records to an existing Indexed-Sequential disk file.

Examination of the source program listing in Figure 11-12 indicates that no new coding entries for file addition are required in either Input or Calculation Specifications.

A comparison of the data file listings *before* addition and *after* two records have been added is illustrated in Figure 11-13. Notice the sorted sequence (ascending order by key field) has not been destroyed by the addition of data records. This is an advantage of ISAM file organization as compared to sequential. When records are added to a sequential disk file they are added at the end of the file (if enough disk room was provided) and destroy the sorted integrity of the records. If the sequential file was to be randomly processed by Matching Records or the READ operation (Chapter 10) it would have to be sorted in the required sequence before processing.

The processing logic of record addition was illustrated in Figure 11-4. *Add Records* are stored in the prime data area first and when it is full they are correspondingly stored in the Cylinder Overflow and then the Independent Overflow area if these areas are provided.

It was mentioned previously that duplicate key fields cannot exist in an ISAM file. Consequently, any add records that have key fields identical to a record already in the disk file will cause program execution to halt (cancel on some systems).

ISAM disk file *before* adds:

```
550   CHAR  1111TABLE RADIOS                                              *
      ZCNE  FFFFECCDC4DCCCDE444444444444444444444444444444440050220040
      NUMR  111131235091496200000000000000000000000000000003C01C072C
            1...5...10...15...20...25...30...35...40...45...50...55

      CHAR  1112CONSOLE RADIOS                                           <
      ZCNE  FFFFCDDEDDC4DCCCDE444444444444444444444444444444440180040032
      NUMR  111236526350914962000000000000000000000000000008C03C069C
            1...5...10...15...20...25...30...35...40...45...50...55

      CHAR  1114FM-AM RADIOS TABLE                                       ⅺ
      ZCNE  FFFFCD6CD4DCCCDE4ECCDC444444444444444444444444444440020030096
      NUMR  111464014091496203123500000000000000000000000007C08C057C
            1...5...10...15...20...25...30...35...40...45...50...55

      CHAR  1115PORTABLE TELEVISIONS                                    ⅾ
      ZONE  FFFFDDDECCDC4ECDCECECCDDE444444444444444444444444440170090083
      NUMR  11157693123503535592965200000000000000000000006C02C044C
            1...5...10...15...20...25...30...35...40...45...50...55

      CHAR  1117B/W PORT. TELEVISIONS                                    <
      ZCNE  FFFFC6E4DDDE44ECDCECECDDE444444444444444444444444440130080024
      NUMR  1117216076938035355929652000000000000000000008C01C039C
            1...5...10...15...20...25...30...35...40...45...50...55

      CHAR  1118B/W CONS. TELEVISIONS                                    <
      ZONE  FFFFC6E4CDDDF44ECDCECECDDE444444444444444444444444440080030094
      NUMR  111821603652B035355929652000000000000000000005C03C011C
            1...5...10...15...20...25...30...35...40...45...50...55
```

Fig. 11-13. Comparison of ISAM disk file *before* and *after* the addition of records. (continued on next page)

ISAM disk file *after adds:*

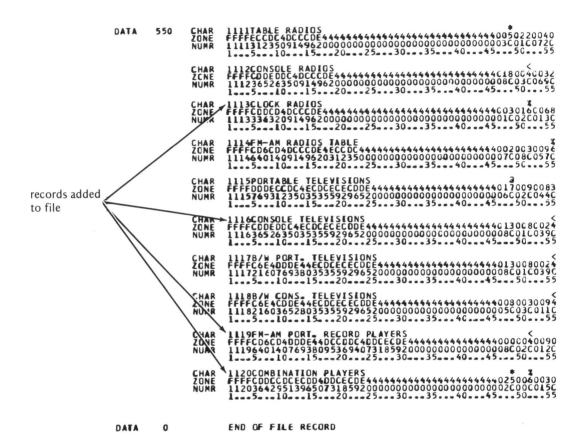

Fig. 11-13. (concluded)

PROCESSING BETWEEN LIMITS

Another processing feature available with ISAM disk files is *Processing Between Limits*. Limits processing refers to the access of groups of records at one time instead of individually, as done in *random processing*. Figure 11-14 illustrates the logic for processing an ISAM file between limits. The punch card in the figure contains two key fields: the first is the key for the low limit and the second the upper limit. When this record is processed, all the disk records from 1113 to 1117 will be extracted at one time. This single record is included in an input file called a *Record Address* file. In the example shown here the file is a card file,

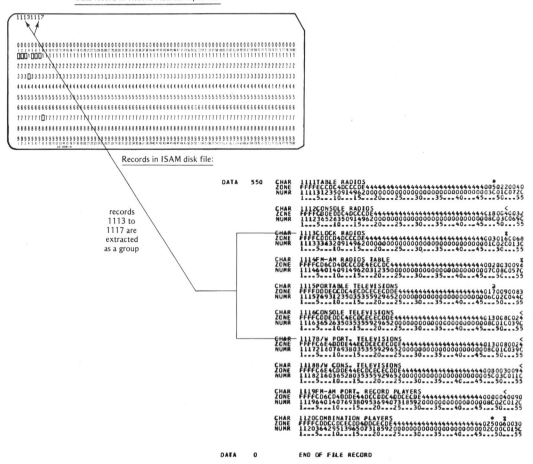

Fig. 11-14. Processing between limits logic.

but may be input from any input device supported by a computer system. An input file is defined as a *Record Address* file by entering the letter R in column 16 of the File Description form entry for the file (see Figure 11-15).

Furthermore, more than one group of records may be extracted from the file and the groups may overlap each other. However, each group to be processed requires a separate record, as only two key fields may be entered on a record. Consequently, if three groups were to be extracted from the ISAM file the Record Address file would have to contain three separate records.

The RPG II source program coding needed for limits processing requires the use of a new coding form called the Extension and Line Counter Specifications. Any source cards for this form are placed in the deck between the File

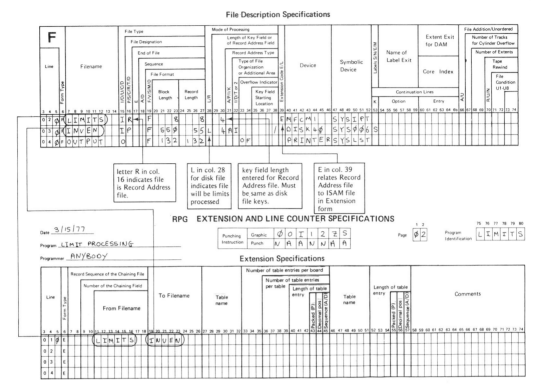

Fig. 11-15. File Description and Extension Specifications coding for the processing between limits program.

Description and Input Specifications cards. Before an explanation of the Extension form is presented, the File Description coding entries needed for limits processing will be discussed.

Examine the File Description form in Figure 11-15 and notice three files are used in this program: two input and one output. The disk file INVEN is the ISAM file that is to be limits processed. In addition to the standard coding entries in the File Description form to define an ISAM file, only one new entry is needed to facilitate limits processing. Look at Figure 11-15 again and notice the letter L is entered in column 28 for the Mode of Processing field.

Refer back to Figure 11-15 and notice the LIMITS file is an input card file but includes new entries not usually associated with an input card file. The new entries are entered in columns 16, 30, and 39. An explanation of the entries is given in Figure 11-15.

Note only two fields are used on the Extension form for limits processing. Other fields on the form have special purposes that will be discussed in subsequent chapters.

Form Type (Column 6).   The letter E must be entered in this field for every source program record of this form type.

From Filename (Columns 11–18).   The name of the Record Address file, LIMITS in the program example, must be left-justified in this field. Also, the name specified must be identical to the file defined as the Record Address file in the File Description form, which is the file with the R in column 16.

To Filename (Columns 19–26).   The file name specified in this field, INVEN in the example program, is left-justified in this field and must be identical to the ISAM file defined in the File Description form.

The preceding entries are the only ones that have to be included on the Extension type source program records for limits processing of an ISAM disk file.

Examination of the source listing in Figure 11-16 indicates the record and related fields for the Record Address file (LIMITS) are *not defined* on the input form. When a file is defined as a Record Address file (R in column 16) the Extension form *ties-in* the records from that file with the other sections of the program. Note, however, the record(s) and fields of the ISAM file are defined on input in the usual manner.

Further examination of Figure 11-16 reveals that standard coding procedures are used in calculations and output. Any calculations may be performed on the individual records included in the group as shown in the figure. Look at

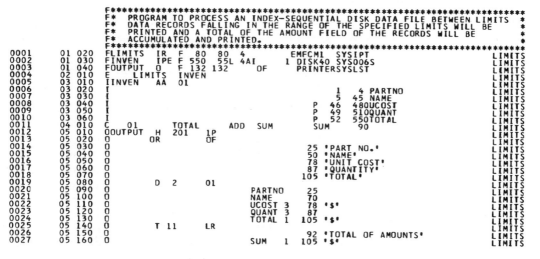

Fig. 11-16.   Source listing of program to limits process an ISAM disk file.

PART NO.	NAME	UNIT COST	QUANTITY	TOTAL
1113	CLOCK RADIOS	$13	126	$1,638
1114	FM-AM RADIOS TABLE	$72	83	$5,976
1115	PORTABLE TELEVISIONS	$167	29	$4,843
1116	CONSOLE TELEVISIONS	$183	18	$3,294
1117	B/W PORT. TELEVISIONS	$183	18	$3,294
			TOTAL OF AMOUNTS	$19,045

Fig. 11-17. Printed report of output from program to process an ISAM disk file within limits.

Figure 11-16 again and notice the TOTAL field values are added to an accumulator field (SUM) which is printed at LR time.

The printed report generated by the source program illustrated in Figure 11-16 is shown in Figure 11-17.

RANDOM PROCESSING INDEXED-SEQUENTIAL FILES BY THE CHAINING METHOD

An inherent advantage of indexed-sequential files is that they may be randomly processed faster and more efficiently than those that are sequentially organized. In other words, part of or the complete disk file does not have to be sequentially searched, record by record, for data information because the index of an indexed-sequential organized file provides immediate access to records stored on disk. Furthermore, the convenience of the random processing feature of these files is particularly suited to:

1. Master files which only have a proportionally small percentage of records accessed during a processing run. A part inventory and accounts receivable customer file are typical examples of files in which only a limited number of records are processed, and are referred to as having low activity.

2. Files that are in order by a different field. For example, assume that the results of daily charge sales are used to update an inventory file. The accounts receivable file would probably be in order by customer number and the inventory file by part number. Yet, because of the random processing feature of indexed-sequential files the part number from the customer's sales transactions card may be used to process the inventory file.

At least three files must be used in an RPG II program to random process an ISAM disk file, including two input and one output. One input file, commonly called the *transaction* file in random and update programs, contains, at the minimum, the key fields for the disk records to be accessed. The other input file is the ISAM disk file which is to be randomly processed by the records in the transaction file. Finally, the output file (printer, tape, disk, etc.) must be included in the program to provide for the required output.

Look at Figure 11-18 and notice the transaction file is called the *Chaining File* and the ISAM disk file containing inventory items, the *Chained File*. Chained files are normally master disk files containing permanent data as an accounts receivable file of charge customers or (as in the program example) an inventory file.

Figure 11-18 illustrates the relationship of the transaction *Chaining File* to the master disk *Chained* ISAM file for the program example used in this chapter. The Chaining File does not have to be an input card file but may be input from any suitable device. Notice in Figure 11-18 a field from the transaction record is used to access the related disk record information. The field from the *Chaining* File, which contains the key field value is called the *Chaining Field*. This field must have a value the same type and size as the keys stored in the index of the ISAM file and individual disk records. The key fields stored in the index and ISAM records are called the *Chained Field*.

In the example shown in Figure 11-18 the part number on the card record is the *Chaining Field* and the part number in the master disk record is referred to as the *Chained Field*.

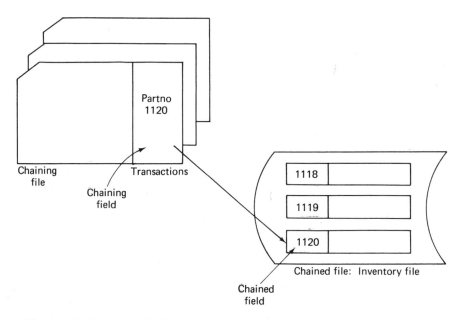

Fig. 11-18. Example of chaining a chaining field from a transaction card to an Indexed-Sequential chained file.

RPG II CODING TO RANDOM PROCESS AN ISAM DISK FILE

Only two forms, the File Description and Calculation Specifications are affected by the new entries required to random process an ISAM file by the CHAIN operation code. Standard coding techniques are used in the Input and Output-Format Specifications.

Reference to the File Description coding form, Figure 11-19, will show three files are used in the program. The input card file, INPUT, is the *Chaining File* which contains the Chaining Field, PARTNO, used to access the master disk file INVEN. This INVEN file is the *Chained File* which will be randomly

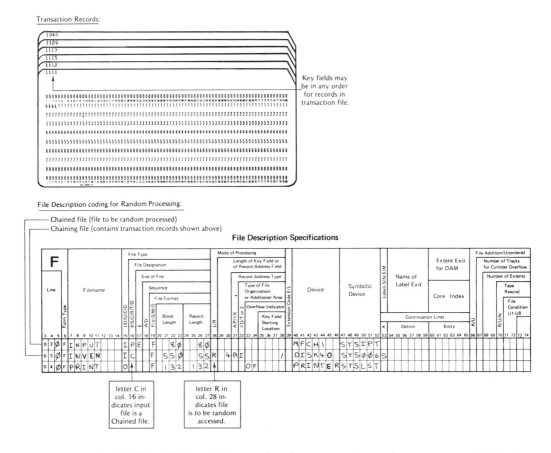

Fig. 11-19. File Description coding for program to random process an ISAM disk file by the CHAIN operation.

processed. Notice two new entries are specified in the coding for the indexed-sequential disk file (INVEN). The additional coding entries to facilitate random processing of ISAM files by the chaining method are required in the following fields of the Chained File:

File Designation (Column 16).   The letter C entered in this field indicates the INVEN disk file is a chained file.

Mode of Processing (Column 28).   The letter R must be specified in this field which informs the computer the file is to be randomly processed.

Except for the two new coding entries described above, the other entries in the File Description form for the random processing of indexed-sequential files are identical to those previously discussed.

The input form is shown in Figure 11-20 only to identify the relationship of this form to the Chaining File, Chained File, and Chaining Field.

The calculation coding for random processing an ISAM disk file is shown in Figure 11-21. Notice a new operation (CHAIN) is used in the operation field

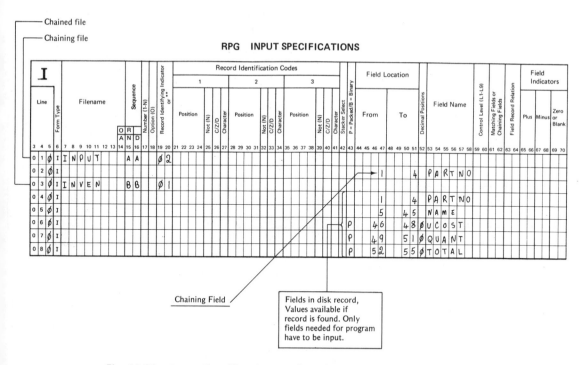

Fig. 11-20.   Input Specifications coding for program to random process an ISAM disk file.

(columns 28–32) which executes the chaining functions in the RPG II compiler. The coding for the CHAIN operation requires the use of Factor 1, Factor 2, Operation, and Resulting Indicator field for High (columns 54–55).

Observe in Figure 11-21 the chaining field PARTNO from the chaining file INPUT is entered in Factor 1; the operation code CHAIN in the Operation field; the ISAM file name INVEN in Factor 2; and the Resulting Indicator 99 in the High field (columns 54 and 55). The value in PARTNO will be used to search the index of the ISAM file, INVEN, and extract the related disk record information if the record is found in the file. The individual field values in the disk record are then available for calculations and/or output.

On the other hand, if the disk record is *not found*, indicator 99 will be turned on and any subsequent calculations and/or output may be conditioned by this indicator (see Figure 11-22). Note any acceptable RPG II indicator may be used in the High field. (columns 54 and 55).

In addition, the CHAIN operation coding line may be conditioned by indicator(s) entered in columns 7–17. Also notice in Figure 11-21 that the Result Field, Field Length, Decimal Position, Half-Adjust, Low, and Equal fields are *never* used with the CHAIN operation.

Figure 11-22 illustrates the output coding for the random processing program discussed in this chapter.

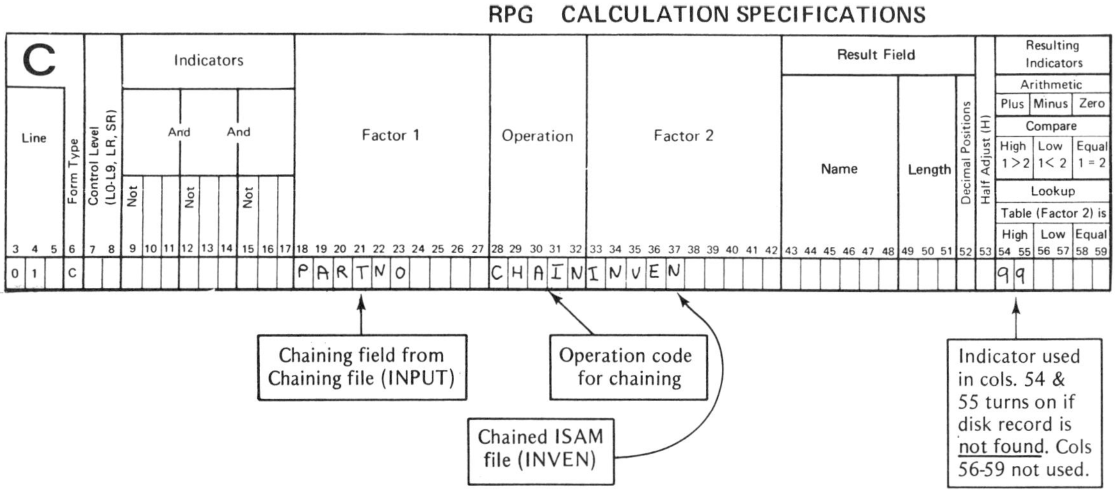

RPG CALCULATION SPECIFICATIONS

Fig. 11-21. Calculation coding for sample program for random processing an ISAM disk file by the Chaining Operation code.

RPG OUTPUT SPECIFICATIONS

Line	Form Type	Filename	Type (H/D/T/E)	Stacker S/Fetch (F)	Space Before	Space After	Skip Before	Skip After	Output Indicators			Field Name / *Auto	End Position in Output Record	Constant or Edit Word
010	O	PRINT	H			201			1P					
020	O	OR							0F					
030	O												25	'PART NO.'
040	O												50	'NAME'
050	O												78	'UNIT COST'
060	O												87	'QUANTITY'
070	O												105	'TOTAL'
080	O		D		3				02 99			PARTNO	25	
090	O												49	'NO MASTER RECORD'
100	O													
110	O		D		2				01					
120	O											PARTNO	26	
130	O											NAME	70	
140	O											UCOST 3	98	'$'
150	O											QUANT 3	87	
0 60	O											TOTAL 1	105	'$'

Zero Balances / edit word legend:

Commas	Zero Balances to Print	No Sign	CR	−	X = Remove Plus Sign
Yes	Yes	1	A	J	Y = Date
Yes	No	2	B	K	Field Edit
No	Yes	3	C	L	Z = Zero
No	No	4	D	M	Suppress

Error message will be printed when 99 is turned on in calculations if disk record not found. Record Identifying indicator for Chaining file record is used also.

Disk record fields will be printed if disk record is found.

Fig. 11-22. Output-Format Specifications coding for program to random process an ISAM disk file.

Locate line 080 (Figure 11-22) and notice an error message, NO MASTER RECORD, and the related part number are conditioned by the Record Identifying Indicator assigned to the chaining file records (INPUT) and the Resulting Indicator 99 entered in the High field (columns 54 and 55) of the calculation form. Remember the 99 indicator turns on only if the disk record is *not found*. The 02 indicator is used with 99 because 01 would not be on if the disk record was not found. Line 110, however, is conditioned by the Record Identifying Indicator 01 assigned to the disk records because that indicator is on when the ISAM record is found. All other coding on the output form is identical to concepts previously discussed.

The source listing and printed output for the random processing program are illustrated in Figure 11-23.

Source program listing:

```
0001   01 020   FINPUT    IPFAF  80   80              MFCM1  SYSIPT         CHAIN
0002   01 030   FINVEN    IC  F  550   55R 4AI      1 DISK40 SYS006S        CHAIN
0003   01 040   FPRINT    O   F  132  132      OF     PRINTERSYSLST         CHAIN
0004   02 010   IINPUT    AA   02                                           CHAIN
0005   02 020   I                                          1    4 PARTNO   CHAIN
0006   02 030   IINVEN    BB   01                                           CHAIN
0007   02 040   I                                          1    4 PARTNO   CHAIN
0008   02 050   I                                          5   45 NAME     CHAIN
0009   02 060   I                                        P 46  480UCOST    CHAIN
0010   02 070   I                                        P 49  510QUANT    CHAIN
0011   02 080   I                                        P 52  550TOTAL    CHAIN
0012   03 010   C         PARTNO       CHAININVEN                   99     CHAIN
0013   04 010   CPRINT    H  201   1P                                      CHAIN
0014   04 020   O         OR          OF                                   CHAIN
0015   04 040   O                                        25 'PART NO.'     CHAIN
0016   04 050   O                                        50 'NAME'         CHAIN
0017   04 060   O                                        78 'UNIT COST'    CHAIN
0018   04 070   O                                        87 'QUANTITY'     CHAIN
0019   04 080   O                                       105 'TOTAL'        CHAIN
0020   04 090   O         D  3      02 99                                  CHAIN
0021   04 100   O                        PARTNO         25                 CHAIN
0022   04 110   O                                       49 'NO MASTER RECORD'  CHAIN
0023   04 120   O         D  2      01                                     CHAIN
0024   04 130   O                        PARTNO         25                 CHAIN
0025   04 140   O                        NAME           70                 CHAIN
0026   04 150   O                        UCOST  3       78 '$'             CHAIN
0027   04 160   O                        QUANT  3       87 '$'             CHAIN
0028   04 170   O                        TOTAL  1      105 '$'             CHAIN
```

Printed report:

PART NO.	NAME	UNIT COST	QUANTITY	TOTAL
1111	TABLE RADIOS	$35	212	$7,420
1112	CONSOLE RADIOS	$188	34	$6,392
1115	PORTABLE TELEVISIONS	$167	29	$4,843
1119	FM-AM PORT. RECORD PLAYERS	$80	24	$1,920
1120	COMBINATION PLAYERS	$225	6	$1,350
1040	NO MASTER RECORD			

Fig. 11-23. Source listing and printed output of program to random process an ISAM disk file.

ADDITIONAL CHAINING CONCEPTS

The program explained in the preceding paragraphs illustrated the chaining method used to chain a field from a transaction card (chaining field) to an indexed-sequential file, the chained file. In addition, the chaining operation may be used to chain two indexed-sequential files at the same time from a transaction card. The example in Figure 11-24 shows that the transaction card contains two chaining fields. One of the chaining fields is used to chain to the inventory file and the other will be used to chain to the customer file for the retail price of the sale. Hence, each processed transaction card will access the two indexed-sequential files at the same time. The coding procedures required to accomplish the chaining of two files are identical to that previously discussed except that an additional chain operation is used in calculations. Reference to Figure 11-24 will show that the chaining field, PARTNO, is used to chain to the master inventory file, INVEN. The next operation on the following line links the chaining field for customer number, CUSTNO, to the accounts

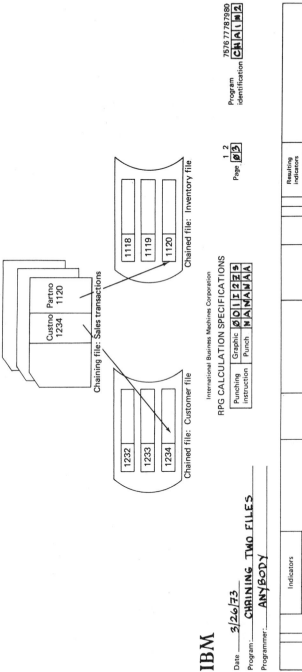

Fig. 11-24. Example of chaining to two indexed-sequential disk files at the same time with required calculation coding.

413

receivable file, ACCTRC. Of course, both of the disk files must be defined in the File Description Specifications as input chained files.

Another method available with the chaining process is the technique of using the chained file as a chaining file to retrieve data from another indexed-sequential file. An examination of Figure 11-25 will illustrate this processing technique. Notice that the part number, the chaining field, from the transaction card chains to the master inventory file, INVEN, and then a field from that file is used to chain to a general ledger account file, LEDGER.

Regardless of the chaining operation used, all of the indexed-sequential files defined in the program must be specified as chained files by the letter C specified in column 16 and an R in column 28 of the File Description Specifications form. Figure 11-25 also depicts the Calculation Specifications coding needed to use a chained file as a chaining file. Notice that the chaining field, PARTNO, is chained to the master inventory file, INVEN, and a field,

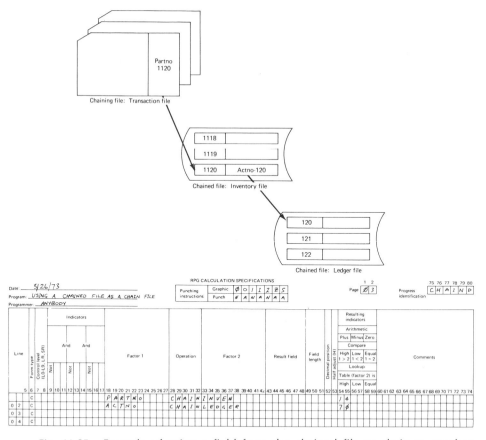

Fig. 11-25.   Example of using a field from the chained file to chain to another indexed-sequential file with required calculation coding.

ACCTNO, from that file, is used to chain the general ledger account file, LEDGER.

The chaining process may also be used with direct (Chapter 12) files in the same way except that instead of a key field the relative record number of the record's position in the file must be used. For example, if a part number of a direct inventory file had to be accessed and processed, the exact position of that record in the file would have to be known. In other words, if the record was in the first, tenth, hundredth, or thousandth position in the file, the numeric position of that record would be the contents of the chaining field used to chain the direct disk file.

Another important feature associated with file maintenance is updating. Practically all data information must be changed from time to time through the result of business transactions. For example, quantities and dollar amounts in an inventory file like the one used in this chapter will change when items are sold or received, and a file processing technique referred to as updating is used to maintain files when the data contents are changing.

RPG updating procedures will be used to reflect changes caused by purchases and sales of parts in the inventory file created in this chapter. However, before the source program coding is discussed, the accounting principles and practices of maintaining and costing merchandise inventory will be presented.

ACCOUNTING APPLICATION FOR UPDATING AN ISAM INVENTORY FILE

The data base used for the program examples presented in this chapter is an item inventory file for an appliance store. Inventories may be costed by many acceptable methods including FIFO, LIFO, Specific Identification, Weighted Average, and Moving Average. Because the Moving Average Method is particularly suited to a computerized system it will be used in the example program to illustrate the update of an ISAM disk file for purchases and sales of inventory items. Any first year accounting text should be referenced for a comprehensive discussion of the other inventory-costing methods.

A sequence of mathematical steps must be followed when a purchase is made if inventory is costed by the Moving Average Method: first, the total cost of the present inventory item is determined by multiplying quantity on hand by the unit cost; second, the total cost of the purchase is calculated by multiplying the unit purchase cost by the quantity purchased; third the original and purchased quantities are added together giving a total quantity available; fourth, the present inventory dollar amount, computed in step 1, is added to the purchase dollar amount computed in step 2, to give a total dollar amount; fifth, the total dollar amount (step 4) is divided by the total quantity (step 3) to determine the new unit cost. Figure 11-26 illustrates the mathematics of the

		Unit Cost	Quantity	Total
Step 1:	Compute present inventory amount	$ 11	10	$ 110
Step 2:	Compute dollar purchase amount	14	5	70
Step 3: and 4	Add present and purchase quantity and total dollar amounts together		15	$ 180
Step 5:	Compute new unit cost	$\dfrac{\$\ 180}{15\ \text{units}} = \$\ 12$ per unit		

Fig. 11-26. Mathematical steps to compute the new unit cost when a purchase is made if inventory is costed by the Moving Average Method.

Moving Average Method for costing inventory when a purchase is made which adds to an existing inventory amount.

Only two steps are required if an item is sold when inventory is costed by the Moving Average Method. First, the quantity sold (in units) is subtracted from the master inventory record amount. Second, the quantity sold is multiplied by the unit cost, which is stored in the disk record, to determine the total cost of the sale. Hence, the only disk record field changed is the quantity, as a sale does not affect the unit cost amount. The RPG II coding entries and procedures needed to update an ISAM disk file will be discussed in the following paragraphs.

RPG II CODING TO UPDATE AN ISAM DISK FILE

The ability to update a data file without deleting or reloading it is a very powerful and important feature. Obviously, card files cannot be updated unless new records are punched and physically placed into the proper order in the file. On the other hand, because of the nature of disk file organization and processing features, updating can be performed easily with either indexed-sequential or sequentially organized files.

Again the RPG source program coding rules are relatively simple for the updating procedure. In fact, the only new coding entry required is a letter U that must be specified in column 15 of the File Description Specifications form. The letter U replaces the I or O that is normally entered in the column because an update file functions as both an input and output file. During execution of the update procedure, the data record information from the disk file is loaded into core, processed according to the source program requirements, and then loaded back into the respective record location on disk.

Figure 11-27 illustrates the File Description Specifications coding needed for updating the sample inventory file (INVEN) used throughout this chapter.

File Description Specifications

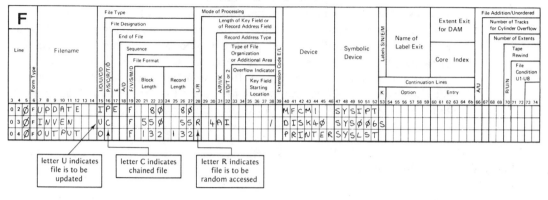

letter U indicates file is to be updated

letter C indicates chained file

letter R indicates file is to be random accessed

Fig. 11-27. File Description entries needed to update an ISAM file.

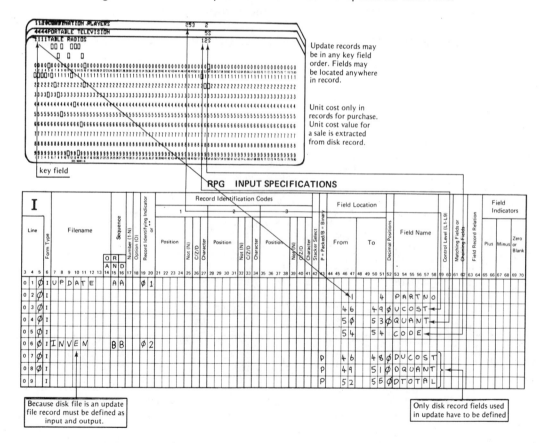

Update records may be in any key field order. Fields may be located anywhere in record.

Unit cost only in records for purchase. Unit cost value for a sale is extracted from disk record.

key field

RPG INPUT SPECIFICATIONS

Because disk file is an update file record must be defined as input and output.

Only disk record fields used in update have to be defined

Fig. 11-28. Input Specifications coding for update program and relationship of update records to input coding.

Except for the U in column 15, notice that all of the coding entries in the form are those typically used with an indexed-sequential disk file.

An examination of the Input Specifications form, Figure 11-28, will reveal that no new coding procedures are needed in the coding of this form for updating. Notice, however, that the fields of the update file (INVEN) are defined on input along with those of the transaction card file. However, all of the disk record fields from the update file do not have to be defined on output, but only those that are needed in the updating process.

RPG II CALCULATION CODING FOR THE MOVING AVERAGE METHOD

The calculation coding unique to the Moving Average Method of costing inventory is shown in Fig. 11-29. A line-by-line discussion of the calculation logic and purpose is presented in the following paragraphs.

Line 010. The part number field value (PARTNO) from the transaction

RPG CALCULATION SPECIFICATIONS

Line	Form Type	Control Level	Indicators And Not	And Not	Factor 1	Operation	Factor 2	Result Field	Field Length	Decimal Positions	Half Adjust (H)	Resulting Indicators Arithmetic Plus/Minus/Zero Compare High/Low/Equal Lookup	Comments
0 1	Ø	C			Ø1	PARTNO	CHAIN	INVEN		1Ø			
0 2	Ø	C*	IF	RECORD	NOT	FOUND	SKIP	ALL	CALCULATIONS.				
0 3	Ø	C		1Ø		GOTO	END						
0 4	Ø	C*	COMPARE	TO	DETERMINE	WHETHER	SALE	OR	PURCHASE.				
0 5	Ø	C		Ø1		CODE	COMP	'S'				2Ø	
0 6	Ø	C*	IF	CODE	=	S GOTO	SALE	CAL.,	OTHERWISE	DO	FOLLOWING	FOR	PURCHASE.
0 7	Ø	C		2Ø		GOTO	SALE						
0 8	Ø	C*	CALCULATIONS	FOR	A	PURCHASE.							
0 9	Ø	C		Ø1		UCOST	MULT	QUANT	TOTAL	7Ø			$ PURCHASE
1 0	Ø	C		Ø2		TOTAL	ADD	DTOTAL	DTOTAL				
1 1	Ø	C		Ø2		QUANT	ADD	DQUANT	DQUANT				
1 2	Ø	C*	COMPUTE	NEW	UNIT	COST.							
1 3	Ø	C		Ø2		DTOTAL	DIV	DQUANT	DUCOST				
1 4	Ø	C				SALE	TAG						
1 5	Ø	C*	CALCULATIONS	FOR	A	SALE.							
1 6	Ø	C		2Ø		QUANT	MULT	DUCOST	SALAMT	7Ø			$ SALES
1 7	Ø	C		2Ø		DTOTAL	SUB	SALAMT	DTOTAL				REDUCE DISK TOT
1 8	Ø	C		2Ø		DQUANT	SUB	QUANT	DQUANT				REDUCE DISK QTY
1 9	Ø	C				END	TAG						

Fig. 11-29. Calculation Specifications coding for sample program to update an ISAM organized inventory file for sales and purchases using the Moving Average Method of costing an inventory.

record is used to locate the corresponding record in the master inventory disk file (INVEN). If the disk record cannot be found, indicator 10 (columns 54 and 55) will turn on.

Line 020.   Comment.

Line 030.   If the disk record is not found in the CHAIN operation on line 010, indicator 10 will turn on and the GOTO operation on this line will execute, causing program control to skip over all calculations. If the GOTO operation was not provided for and a disk record was not found, every calculation line would be tested by program control. This would be both inefficient and could result in unwanted calculations.

Line 040.   Comment.

Line 050.   The value in the transaction record field, CODE, is compared with the letter S, and if equal, indicator 20 will turn on. Any transaction records coded with this letter indicates a sale, and those not coded, a purchase.

Line 060.   Comment.

Line 070.   If the compare operation on line 050 turned on resulting indicator 20 (a sale), program control will execute the GOTO operation here and skip to line 140, the entry point for the calculations needed for a sales transaction.

Line 080.   Comment.

Line 090.   If the compare on line 070 did not turn on indicator. 20, the calculations for a purchase (lines 090 to 110) will be executed. Line 090 multiplies the unit cost (UCOST) for the item purchased by the number of items purchased (QUANT) giving a total dollar amount of the purchase (TOTAL). Because both fields are included in the transaction record, the 01 record identifying indicator assigned to these records is used to condition the operation.

Line 100.   The total dollar purchase amount (TOTAL) computed on line 090 is added to the total dollar amount in the disk record field (DTOTAL) to give a new value for (DTOTAL). Record Identifying indicator 02, assigned on input to the disk records, is used to condition this operation because the related disk record must be in storage to perform this calculation.

Line 110.   The purchase quantity for the item (QUANT) is added to the disk record quantity (DQUANT) giving a new value for DQUANT. Again, anytime a disk record field is used in a calculation, the 02 indicator and not 01 must be used.

Line 120.   Comment.

Line 130.   The new unit cost value (DUCOST) to be stored in the updated disk record is calculated on this line by dividing the total dollar amount now on hand (DTOTAL) by the total quantity (DQUANT). The new value in DUCOST will be stored in the appropriate disk record. Any time a purchase is made of an item, a new unit cost must be determined for the Moving Average costing method.

Line 140. Entry point for sales calculations.

Line 150. Comment.

Line 160. The sale quantity (QUANT) is multiplied by the value stored in the disk record's unit cost field (DUCOST) to determine the dollar amount of the sale (SALAMT). Notice this line (and the other sales lines) is conditioned by the 02 indicator assigned to the disk records because a disk field is used in the operation.

Line 170. The sales dollar amount (SALAMT), computed on line 160 is subtracted from the disk record field for total dollar amount on hand (DTOTAL) giving a new value for DTOTAL which will be stored back on disk.

Line 180. The sales quantity (QUANT) is subtracted from the quantity stored in the disk record field (DQUANT) which gives a new value for DQUANT. This amount is stored back to the disk record.

Line 190. Entry point for the GOTO operation on line 030 which was executed if disk record was not found.

The sequence of the calculation steps given in Figure 11-29 are not to be considered absolute. As long as the mathematical logic of the Moving Average method of costing inventory is followed, the calculations may be arranged according to the programmer's preferences.

OUTPUT CODING

The output coding for the example update program is illustrated in Figure 11-30. Notice the disk file INVEN which was defined on input (Figure 11-28) is also defined on output. Any file designated as an update file (U in column 15) must be defined on input and output.

Locate line 010 in Figure 11-30 and notice it is a detail line (D in column 15) and conditioned by the 02 record identifying indicator assigned to the disk records on the input form (see Figure 11-28). It is important to understand that the 02 indicator is used here and not the 01 assigned to the transaction records, because the disk record must be found before it may be updated. If the wrong indicator was used, program control would try to update a disk record it has not retrieved which would cause the program execution to cancel (on some systems) or halt.

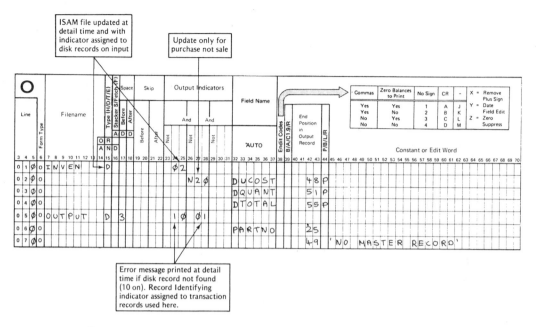

Fig. 11-30. Output-format specifications coding for example program to update an ISAM disk file.

The N20 indicator used to condition the DUCOST field indicates the field should not be updated if the transaction is a sale. Sales transactions do not change the item cost and there is no need to place the same value back on the disk record when it is already there. Extracting a field value does not destroy it. On the other hand, the DQUANT and DTOTAL fields are changed whether the transaction is a purchase or sale.

Line 050 conditions the printed output for a printed listing of transaction records for which there are no master records. Notice line 050 is conditioned by the 10 indicator which turned on in calculation line 010 (Figure 11-29) if a related disk record key could not be found. Furthermore, the 01 record identifying indicator is used because 02 would not be on if the disk record was not found. If 02 was incorrectly used, the error message and part number value would not print because the indicator would not be on for that condition.

Several disk file functions may be performed in one program. For example, the program to update an ISAM file could also include the add function. If a record was not found in the master disk file, the ADD entries could be included to add those records to the file. In any case, however, the key fields in the transaction or add records must be the same size and type as the ISAM record keys.

The source listing for the example program to update the ISAM disk file for inventory, costed by the moving average method, is shown in Figure 11-31. In addition, the error message generated when a disk record is not found is also included in the figure.

Figure 11-32 shows a utility program listing of the inventory file before and after two records are updated. Notice the effect on the DUCOST, DQUANT, and DTOTAL fields for a purchase and sale.

```
      F*****************************************************************************
      F*    PROGRAM TO UPDATE AN INDEX-SEQUENTIAL INVENTORY DISK DATA FILE.       *
      F*****************************************************************************
0001  01 020  FUPDATE   IPE F  80   80                  MFCM1  SYSIPT              UPDATE
0002  01 030  FINVEN    UC  F 550   55R 4AI     1 DISK40 SYS006S                   UPDATE
0003  01 040  FOUTPUT   O   F 132  132                  PRINTERSYSLST              UPDATE
0004  02 010  IUPDATE   AA  01                                                     UPDATE
0005  02 020  I                                          1    4 PARTNO             UPDATE
0006  02 040  I                                         46  490UCOST               UPDATE
0007  02 050  I                                         50  530QUANT               UPDATE
0008  02 055  I                                         54   54 CODE               UPDATE
0009  02 060  IINVEN    BB  02                                                     UPDATE
0010  02 090  I                                       P 46  480DUCOST              UPDATE
0011  02 100  I                                       P 49  510DQUANT              UPDATE
0012  02 110  I                                       P 52  550DTOTAL              UPDATE
0013  03 010  C     01      PARTNO      CHAININVEN                 10              UPDATE
      03 020  C* IF RECORD NOT FOUND SKIP ALL CALCULATIONS. . .                    UPDATE
0014  03 030  C     10                 GOTO END                                    UPDATE
      03 040  C* COMPARE TO DETERMINE WHETHER SALE OR PURCHASE. . .                UPDATE
0015  03 050  C     01      CODE        COMP 'S'                   20              UPDATE
      03 060  C* IF CODE = S GOTO SALE CAL., OTHERWISE DO FOLLOWING FOR PURCHASE. .UPDATE
0016  03 070  C     20                 GOTO SALE                                   UPDATE
      03 080  C* CALCULATIONS FOR A PURCHASE. . .                                  UPDATE
0017  03 090  C     01      UCOST       MULT QUANT      TOTAL    70   $ PURCHASES  UPDATE
0018  03 100  C     02      TOTAL       ADD  DTOTAL     DTOTAL                      UPDATE
0019  03 110  C     02      QUANT       ADD  DQUANT     DQUANT                      UPDATE
      03 120  C* COMPUTE NEW UNIT COST. . .                                        UPDATE
0020  03 130  C     02      DTOTAL      DIV  DQUANT     DUCOST                      UPDATE
0021  03 140  C                        SALE TAG                                    UPDATE
      03 150  C* CALCULATIONS FOR A SALE. . .                                      UPDATE
0022  04 010  C     20      QUANT       MULT DUCOST     SALAMT   70   $ SALES      UPDATE
0023  04 020  C     20      DTOTAL      SUB  SALAMT     DTOTAL        REDUCE DISK TOTUPDATE
0024  04 030  C     20      DQUANT      SUB  QUANT      DQUANT        REDUCE DISK QTYUPDATE
0025  04 040  C               END TAG                                              UPDATE
0026  05 010  OINVEN    D       02                                                 UPDATE
0027  05 020  O                        N20      DUCOST    48P                      UPDATE
0028  05 030  O                                 DQUANT    51P                      UPDATE
0029  05 040  O                                 DTOTAL    55P                      UPDATE
0030  05 050  OOUTPUT   D   3     10 01                                            UPDATE
0031  05 060  O                                 PARTNO    25                       UPDATE
0032  05 070  O                                           49 'NO MASTER RECORD'    UPDATE
```

Printed error message: (for transaction records for which no key exists in ISAM disk file)

```
4444        NO MASTER RECORD
```

Fig. 11-31. Source listing of example program to update an ISAM disk file with printed error listing of transaction records for which no ISAM disk record exists.

ISAM disk file before update:

```
DATA    550

CHAR         1111TABLE RADIOS
ZONE         FFFFECCDC4DCCCDE44444444444444444444444444444444400500230040
NUMR         11113123509149620000000000000000000000000000000003012C072C
             1...5...10...15...20...25...30...35...40...45...50...55

CHAR         1112CONSOLE RADIOS
ZONE         FFFFCDDCDDC4DCCCDE44444444444444444444444444444444C1800040036
NUMR         11123652635091496200000000000000000000000000008C03C069C
             1...5...10...15...20...25...30...35...40...45...50...55

CHAR         1113CLOCK RADIOS
ZONE         FFFFCDDDC4DCCCDE44444444444444444444444444444444400300160068
NUMR         11133432091496200000000000000000000000000001C02C01C
             1...5...10...15...20...25...30...35...40...45...50...55

CHAR         1114FM-AM RADIOS TABLE
ZONE         FFFFCD6CD4DCCCDE4ECCDC44444444444444444444444444002300096
NUMR         11146014091496203123500000000000000000007C08C057C
             1...5...10...15...20...25...30...35...40...45...50...55

CHAR         1115PORTABLE TELEVISIONS
ZONE         FFFFDDECCDC4ECDCECCDDE44444444444444444444444017009008
NUMR         11576931235035592965200000000000000006C02C044C
             1...5...10...15...20...25...30...35...40...45...50...55

CHAR         1116CONSOLE TELEVISIONS
ZONE         FFFFCDDCDDC4ECDCECCDDE4444444444444444444013008C027
NUMR         11636526350355929652000000000000008C01C039C
             1...5...10...15...20...25...30...35...40...45...50...55

CHAR         1117B/W PORT. TELEVISIONS
ZONE         FFFFC6C6E44DDDE44ECDCECCDDE44444444444013008024
NUMR         11721607693B035355929652000000008C01C039C
             1...5...10...15...20...25...30...35...40...45...50...55

CHAR         1118B/W CONS. TELEVISIONS
ZONE         FFFFC6C6E44CDDE44ECDCECCDDE4444444008000094
NUMR         11821603652B035355929652000000005C03C011C
             1...5...10...15...20...25...30...35...40...45...50...55

CHAR         1119FM-AM PORT. RECORD PLAYERS
ZONE         FFFFCD6CD4DDDE44DCCDDC4DDCECDE44444000000090
NUMR         11196014076933B09536940731859200008C02C012C
             1...5...10...15...20...25...30...35...40...45...50...55

CHAR         1120COMBINATION PLAYERS
ZONE         FFFFCDDCCDCECDD4DDCECDE4444444444400500040030
NUMR         11203642951396507318592000000002C00C015C
             1...5...10...15...20...25...30...35...40...45...50...55
```

DATA   0   END OF FILE RECORD

Values in DQUANT and DUCOST fields in records with key fields 1111 and 1120 after update.

Fig. 11-32.   Utility program listings of ISAM disk file *before* and *after* two records are updated.   (continued on next page)

ISAM disk file *after* update:

```
DATA    550     CHAR   1111TABLE RADIOS                                  *
                ZONE   FFFFECCDC4DCCCDE44444444444444444444444444444005020000
                NUMR   1111312350914962C000000C0C000000000000000003C00C070C
                       1...5...10...15...20...25...30...35...40...45...50...55

                CHAR   1112CCNSCLE RADICS                                   <
                ZCNE   FFFFCDDEDDC4DCCCDE44444444444444444444444444018004003
                NUMR   1112365263509149620000000CC000000000C0000000008C03C069C
                       1...5...10...15...20...25...30...35...40...45...50...55

                CHAR   1113CLCCK RADIOS                                      %
                ZONE   FFFFCDDCD4DCCCDE44444444444444444444444444440030160058
                NUMR   1113336320914962C000C0C0C0C0C000000000000000001C02C013C
                       1...5...10...15...20...25...30...35...40...45...50...55

                CHAR   1114FM-AM RADICS TABLE                                %
                ZONE   FFFFCD6CD4DCCCDE4ECCDC444444444444444444444440020030096
                NUMR   11146401409149620312350C0C0C00000C0C00000000007C08C057C
                       1...5...10...15...20...25...30...35...40...45...50...55

                CHAR   1115PCRTABLE TELEVISICNS                           @
                ZONE   FFFFDDDECCDC4ECDCECECDDE44444444444444444444017009008
                NUMR   1115769312350353559296520CC0000000000000000006C02C044C
                       1...5...10...15...20...25...30...35...40...45...50...55

                CHAR   1116CONSCLE TELEVISIONS                                <
                ZONE   FFFFCDDEDDC4ECDCECECDDE444444444444444444444013008002
                NUMR   111636526350353559296520C0C0C0C0C0C000000000008C01C039C
                       1...5...10...15...20...25...30...35...40...45...50...55

                CHAR   1117B/W PORT. TELEVISIONS                              <
                ZONE   FFFFC6E4DDDE44ECDCECECDDE4444444444444444444401300800024
                NUMR   1117216076938035355929652C0C00000000000000000008C01C039C
                       1...5...10...15...20...25...30...35...40...45...50...55

                CHAR   1118B/W CCNS. TELEVISIONS                              <
                ZONE   FFFFC6E4CDDE44ECDCECECDDE44444444444444444440080070094
                NUMR   11182160365280353559296520C0C00000C0C0000C0000005C03C011C
                       1...5...10...15...20...25...30...35...40...45...50...55

                CHAR   1119FM-AM PORT. RECORD PLAYERS                      <
                ZONE   FFFFCD6CD4DCDE44DCCDDC4DDCECDE4444444444444440000040090
                NUMR   1119640140769380953694073185920000C0C000000000008C02C012C
                       1...5...10...15...20...25...30...35...40...45...50...55

                CHAR   1120COMBINATICN PLAYERS                                %
                ZONE   FFFFCDDCCDCECDD4DDCECDE44444444444444444444444022008008
                NUMR   1120364295139650731859 2C0C000C0C0C00000000000003C00C015C
                       1...5...10...15...20...25...30...35...40...45...50...55

DATA      0            END OF FILE RECORD
```

Values in DQUANT and DUCOST fields in records with key field 1111 and 1120 before update.

Fig. 11-32. (Concluded)

QUESTIONS

1. Name some of the advantages of the indexed-sequential method of organizing a disk file.
2. What are a few disadvantages of ISAM disk file organization?
3. Name the logical areas of ISAM file organization. Which areas must be provided for when the file is created? What areas are optional?
4. Explain the function of each logical area named in Question 3.
5. Name and briefly explain the processing methods available with ISAM disk files.
6. How should the following disk files be organized (sequential or ISAM)?

PAYROLL	ACCOUNTS RECEIVABLE
INVENTORY	ACCOUNTS PAYABLE
GENERAL LEDGER	SUBSIDIARY LEDGERS
CHECKING ACCOUNTS	SAVINGS ACCOUNTS
STUDENT RECORDS	TOWNS'TAX RECORDS
BACKUP FILE	DAILY TRANSACTION FILE

7. What new coding entries are needed in the disk file coding to define it as an ISAM file when it is created?
8. Are there any restrictions concerning the data used to load an ISAM disk file? Explain.
9. Explain how data records are added to an existing ISAM file.
10. What are the new entries required in a program to add records to an existing ISAM file?
11. What is Limits Processing? What new coding form is needed in the program to facilitate Limits Processing?
12. Name the additional entries (and files) needed in the File Description Specifications to process an ISAM file between limits. What fields are used in the Extension Specifications form?
13. What is a Record Address file?
14. When an ISAM file is processed between limits, are the Record Address or the ISAM file's records defined on input?
15. If the key fields in an ISAM file are five bytes long, how is the Record Address file record formatted?
16. How does program control find a record in an ISAM file when the file is random processed?
17. Identify the additional File Description entries needed to random process an ISAM file.
18. Define the following terms:

CHAINING FILE	CHAINED FILE
CHAINING FIELD	CHAINED FIELD
RANDOM ACCESS	CHAIN (operation)

19. Name the fields and entries needed in the Calculation Specifications to random process an ISAM file. When does the indicator entered in the Resulting Indicator field turn on?

20. Do the transaction records in the file used to random process an ISAM file have to be in any sorted order?
21. What happens when a file is updated? What is unique about an update file in an RPG II source program?
22. Identify the new entries in the File Description form to update an ISAM file.
23. What entries are required in the calculation form to update an ISAM file?
24. May more than one processing function be included in a single ISAM disk file program? Give an example.

EXERCISES

11-1. An Indexed-Sequential disk file named MASTER is to be created as a master file for a parts inventory. The file is to be loaded from an input card file called PARTS. One record type is included in the card file with the following field format:

Part Number	Columns 1 to 5	(Alphanumeric)
Description	Columns 6 to 25	(Alphanumeric)
Quantity	Columns 26 to 30	(Numeric)

The disk record format must be the same as the card format, except the Quantity field must be in packed-decimal format. Part number is the key field.

Calculations. A count field is to be provided for the total number of records processed.

Printed report. A listing of the records loaded on disk is to be printed in the following format:

```
          0         1         2         3         4         5
    123456789012345678901234567890123456789012345678901234 5
H 1        RECORDS LOADED IN MASTER FILE   PAGE XX0X
H 2                           0X/XX/XX
  3
H 4     PART    DESCRIPTION                        QUANTITY
  5
D 6     XXXXX  X                        X          XX,X0X
D 7     XXXXX  X                        X          XX,X0X
  8
TLR 9                              RECORDS READ X,X0X
 10        NOTE:
 11
 12        HEADINGS ON TOP OF EVERY PAGE
 13
```

11-2. Write an RPG II program to process the ISAM file created in Exercise 11-1 sequentially. Use the same report format as in Exercise 11-1 for your printed output.

11-3. Write an RPG II program to *add records* to the ISAM file created in

Exercise 11-1. Use the same format for the add records as the card records to create the file (see Exercise 11-1). Records are only added if a disk record is not already in the disk file. Therefore, the chaining operation (CHAIN) must be used to search the index before any add is attempted. If the record is not found, the add function is executed. However, if the same record is found, it cannot be added. Any attempt to add a record already in the disk file would cause program execution to cancel or halt.

Provide for two count fields in the program: one for the number of records added and the other for the number of duplicate records.

A report is to be printed with the following design:

		0	1	2	3	4	5
H	1		DUPLICATE RECORDS & ADDS LISTING		PAGE XXØX		
H	2		FOR ØX/XX/XX				
	3						
H	4		PART	QUANTITY			
	5						
D	6		XXXXX	XX,XXX	RECORD ADDED TO FILE		
	7						
D	8		XXXXX	XX,XØX	DUPLICATE RECORD		
	9						
	10						
TLR	11		NUMBER RECORDS ADDED...X,XXØ				
	12						
TLR	13		NUMBER OF DUPLICATES...X,XXØ				
	14						
	15						
	16	NOTE:					
	17						
	18	HEADINGS ON TOP OF EVERY PAGE					

11-4. Write an RPG II program to process the ISAM file created in Exercise 11-1 Between Limits. The required printed report is given below:

		0	1	2	3	4
H	1	PARTIAL INVENTORY LISTING6		PAGE XXØX		
H	2	ØX/XX/XX				
	3					
H	4	PART NO. DESCRIPTION			AMOUNT	
	5					
D	6	XXXXX X————————X			XXØXX	
	7					
D	8	XXXXX X————————X			XXØXX	
	9					
	10					
TLR	11	TOTAL ITEMS		XXXXXØX		
	12					
TLR	13	RECORDS PROCESSED XXØX				
	14					

11-5. Write an RPG II program to Random Process the ISAM file created in Exercise 11-1. The transaction file is called SELECT and contains records with the following format:

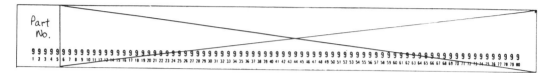

Use the same printed report format as given in Exercise 11-4.

11-6. Write an RPG II program to update the ISAM file created in Exercise 11-1. Include in the program the option to add to the file if the disk record is not found. Update records in the input card file UPDATES; include reductions and additions to the quantity stored on disk and have the following format:

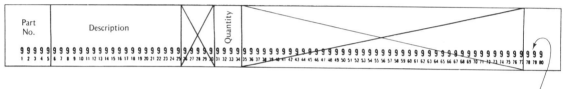

letters
ADD for add
RED for
reduction
to quantity

Calculations. Chain to the ISAM file and if a disk record is found, add additions in the update transaction records to the disk quantity and update the disk record. If the update transaction is a reduction of the quantity, subtract the transaction quantity from the disk record value and update the value stored on disk.

If the disk record is not found, add the transaction record to the ISAM file. Note that only transaction records that add to the quantity should be added not those which result in reductions.

Output. In addition to updating the ISAM disk file for changes in quantity and additions, the following printed report is to be generated:

		0	1	2	3	4	5
H	1	ØX/XX/XX	UPDATES & ADDS TO MASTER FILE			PAGE XXØX	
	2						
D	3	XXXXX X		X	XXXØ	AMOUNT ADDED	
	4						
D	5	XXXXX X		X	XXXØ	AMOUNT SUBTRACTED	
	6						
D	7	XXXXX X		X	XXXØ	NEW ACCOUNT	
	8						
	9						
	10	NOTE: HEADINGS ON EVERY PAGE					

LABORATORY ASSIGNMENTS

LABORATORY ASSIGNMENT 11-1:
CREATION OF ISAM DISK FILE FOR CHECKING ACCOUNT SYSTEM

This lab assignment and Laboratory Assignments 11-2, 11-3, 11-4, 11-5, 11-6, and 11-7 will complete all the programs used in a checking account system. The requirements for this laboratory assignment is to write an RPG II program to create an ISAM disk file from card input.

Format of Card Data Input:

Assign the L1 Control Level Indicator to the Customer Number field which will be used to condition output so no duplicate data records are loaded to disk file. Duplicate key fields sensed during the loading of an ISAM file will (depending on the computer system) cause program execution to cancel or halt.

Calculations. Provide for a record count of the data records loaded on the disk file and the number of duplicate records in the file. These fields will be printed on a report with the corresponding error messages.

Output. Pack the Zip Code and Account Balance field in the disk file. Load all fields next to each other without unused positions.

Format of Printed Report:

Data For Laboratory Assignment 11-1:

Cust. No.	Customer Name	Address	City & State	Zip	Account Balance
21345	JOHN DOE	212 ELM STREET	BPT, CT	06610	120000
31121	LOUISE LESSER	12 APPLES ROAD	BAHA, CA	92100	081299
48891	JUDY JOHNSON	114 EASY DRIVE	BEST, NC	44410	006017
48891	DAVE HOOTEN	8 STRIKE LANE	LOS ANGELES, CA	90000	064111
51540	MARIE BLAKE	GREEN PAST ROAD	HOLLY, NJ	07733	940013
63141	JOSEPH WELCH	110 DILL STREET	NEW YORK, NY	10000	077777
71510	JOHN HINES	220 HIGH DRIVE	KEENE, ND	58847	000940

Note: When an input data file is used to load an ISAM disk file, the records must be in ascending order by key field on an IBM 360 or 370 system. System/3, for example, allows records to be in any key field order (called unordered sequence).

If possible use the utility program on your system to check the disk to ascertain that your file is correctly loaded.

LABORATORY ASSIGNMENT 11-2:
SEQUENTIAL PROCESSING OF AN ISAM FILE (ECHO CHECK)

Write an RPG II source program to sequentially process (echo check) the ISAM file you created in Laboratory Assignment 11-1.

The format of your report is given below:

Note: Refer to the program to create the ISAM file (Laboratory Assignment 11-1) to determine the input field locations in the disk records.

LABORATORY ASSIGNMENT 11-3:
ADDING RECORDS TO AN ISAM DISK FILE

Write an RPG II source program to add the following data records to the ISAM disk file you created in Laboratory Assignment 11-1:

Add Records:

Cust. No. columns 1–5	Customer Name Columns 6–36	Address columns 37–52	City & State columns 53–68	Zip columns 69–73	Account Balance Columns 74–79
80000	LORRAINE FARRELL	4 TULIP LANE	NORWALK, CT	06854	020000
11111	DIANA COOPER	1 SPRING STREET	DARIEN, VT	05738	105000
49000	JAMES WHITTEN	15 BLOCK BLVD	NASHUA, NH	03060	094000

Use the echo check program you completed in Laboratory Assignment 11-2 to verify that the three add records *did add* to the existing ISAM disk file.

LABORATORY ASSIGNMENT 11-4:
PROCESSING AN ISAM DISK FILE BETWEEN LIMITS

Write an RPG II program to process the ISAM file you created in Laboratory Assignment 11-1 Between Limits. Records from key field 48891 to 63141 are to be accessed. Accumulate the Account Balance field and print a report with the following format:

LABORATORY ASSIGNMENT 11-5:
RANDOM PROCESSING OF AN ISAM FILE

Write an RPG II source program to process the ISAM disk file you created in Laboratory 11-1 randomly. An *inquiry* is often required to verify an account balance because of a customer complaint or credit check. Extract the following disk records from the ISAM file with key fields 21345, 51540, 71510, 31111, and 90000. Your report must be in the following format: (Note: an error message must be printed for any transaction records for which there is no related disk record.)

Notice in the Printer Spacing Chart shown below for this lab assignment that two count fields are to be printed with the related messages. Hence, two count fields must be created in calculations: one to accumulate the total number of records processed and another for the number of transaction records that do not have a related disk record.

		0	1	2	3	4
		1234567890	1234567890	1234567890	1234567890	1234567890
H	1	ØX/XX/XX	CUSTOMER INQUIRY	REPORT	PAGE	XXØX
	2					
H	3		CUSTOMER	ACCOUNT		
H	4		NUMBER	BALANCE		
	5					
D	6		XXXXX	X,XXØ.XX		
	7					
D	8		XXXXX	CUSTOMER NOT FOUND........		
	9					
TLR	10		TOTAL RECORDS PROCESSED XXØX			
	11					
TLR	12		RECORDS WITHOUT DISK RECORD XXØX			

LABORATORY ASSIGNMENT 11-6:
UPDATING AN ISAM FILE

Write an RPG II source program to update the ISAM file you created in Laboratory Assignment 11-1. Two record types are included in the input card file containing the update information. Record type coded with the letters SAL in columns 78–80 indicates a sales transaction. Notice this record type includes a field for customer number (chaining field), customer's maximum credit limit, and amount of the sale in dollars.

The card type coded with the letters CASH in columns 77–80 is for cash payments on account. If a customer's payment exceeds his or her account balance, the credit balance is indicated on the report by the letters CR after the new balance amount (see Printer Spacing Chart).

Card Record Formats (Updates):

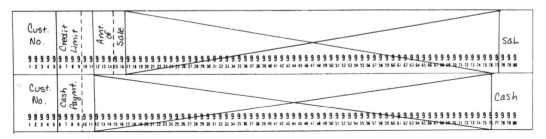

Calculations.   Chain the update records to the customer's master disk file. If the related disk record is found, add the sale amount to the account balance. Compare this total with the credit maximum. If it is greater, subtract the credit limit amount from the total to determine the amount the sale exceeds the credit maximum. If the total does exceed the credit maximum the sale will not be allowed and the customer's disk record will not be updated. On the other hand, if the total is not greater than the credit limit the customer's master disk record will be increased accordingly.

Other calculations related to sales transactions include:

1. Total number of sales transactions

2. Total dollar sales

3. Number of sales transactions that exceed credit limit

4. Dollar amount of sales transactions that exceed credit limit

If the transaction is a cash payment on account, subtract the amount of the payment from the account balance (stored in the disk record). The result of the subtraction must be checked for a negative balance which indicates an overpayment. Any overpayments (negative balances) are indicated in the report by the letters CR after the new balance amount.

Other calculations related to cash payments on account include:

1. Total dollar amount of cash payments

2. Total number of customers who paid on account

3. Total number of customers who overpaid

4. Total dollar amount of overpayments

In addition to the calculations given above a total must be included for all records processed.

Output. If the related disk record is found, update the account balance field for all sale amounts that do not exceed the credit limit and reduce the balance for all payments on account. Use your echo check program completed in Laboratory 11-2 to verify the accuracy of your update procedures. However, you may have to change the edit code in the Account Balance field to indicate negative balances in the printed report. Compare the updated printed output with a previous listing of the ISAM file before updating.

If possible, obtain a utility program listing of the updated file and note the change in the letter (last position in numeric field in NUMR row) for the packed Account Balance field when it has a negative balance.

Design of the Printed Report:

Update Data for Laboratory Assignment 11-6:

Sales transaction records:

Customer Number	Credit Limit	Amount of Sale
21345	150000	40000
48891	050000	10000
71510	200000	10160
80000	100000	20000

Cash Payment records:

Customer Number	Cash Payment
11111	110000
31121	081299
51540	200000

Note: The data records do not have to be sorted for updating.

LABORATORY ASSIGNMENT 11-7:
ADDING AND UPDATING AN ISAM DISK FILE IN ONE PROGRAM

Write an RPG II source program to add to and/or update the ISAM file you created in Laboratory Assignment 11-1. Laboratory Assignment 11-3 required you to write a program to add records to a file and Laboratory Assignment 11-6 required an update. These are both *stand-alone* programs. Sometimes it may be desirable to incorporate both of these processing functions into one program.

One input record format is included in the add/update file with the following fields:

Note: The format is identical to the records used to create the ISAM file [see Laboratory Assignment 11-1].

Calculations.   Use the CHAIN operation to locate a disk record. If the related disk record is found, add the sale amount to the existing balance and update the disk record accordingly. However, if the disk record is *not* found, add the complete update record to the ISAM file.

Three total fields are to be provided:

1. Total number of new customers
2. Total number of old customer sales
3. Total number of records processed

Output.   Depending on whether the disk record is found, information from the update records will either be used to update the account balance field in the disk records or add all of the field values to the disk file (new customer). Consequently, the ISAM disk file must be defined in the File Description form as an update/adds file.

Design of the printed report:

		0	1	2	3	4	5	6	7
H	1			SALES REPORT				PAGE XX0X	
H	2			FOR 0X/XX/XX					
	3								
H	4	CUSTOMER	CUSTOMER NAME			SALE			
H	5	NUMBER				AMOUNT			
	6								
D	7	XXXXX	X————————————X		X,XX0.XX NEW CUSTOMER				
	8								
D	9	XXXXX	X————————————X		X,XX0.XX CUSTOMER UPDATE				
	10								
	11								
TLR	12	TOTAL NUMBER OF NEW CUSTOMERS		XXX0					
TLR	13	TOTAL NUMBER OF OLD CUSTOMER SALE		XXX0					
	14								
TLR	15	TOTAL NUMBER OF RECORDS PROCESSED...		XX0X					
	16								
	17								
	18	NOTE:							
	19								
	20	HEADINGS ON TOP OF EVERY PAGE...							
	21								
	22								
	23								
	24								

Data for Laboratory Assignment 11-7:

Cust. No.	Customer Name	Address	City & State	Zip	Sale Amount
70000	SHIELA HAYES	10 OAK PLACE	LARSON, ND	58751	030000
48891	DAVE HOOTEN	8 STRIKE LANE	LOS ANGELES, CA	90000	100000
21345	JOHN DOE	212 ELM STREET	BPT, CT	06610	002500
90000	MARK PROKOP	44 PONDVIEW RD	COLBY, KA	67701	088800

Use the echo check program completed in Laboratory Assignment 11-2 to verify the updates and/or adds. In addition, if possible, use the computer system's utility program to check the results of this program.

12
DIRECT AND ADDROUT DISK FILE CONCEPTS

DIRECT DISK FILE LOGIC

Direct files, the third disk file organization type, are uniquely different from sequential or ISAM. A direct file may be compared to a football stadium. When the stadium is built, its size limitation provides for a maximum number of seats which are numbered from one to n (n = maximum seat number). As fans buy tickets they are assigned a prenumbered seat and occupy it for the event. People are usually assigned seats according to their specific request for a location, or randomly by the ticket agent, and not always in a consecutive order. The point is, the seats are already there and the people are assigned to them according to their ticket number.

A direct file parallels the same logic. When the file is created, the disk area (sectors, tracks, and cylinders) assigned to the direct file is automatically cleared to blanks by the system and the record numbers are assigned in ascending order to the positions for the records. This record number is called the *relative record number* and refers to the record's physical position in the file. For example, a record with a relative record number of one would be the first record in the file. One with a relative record number of 50 would refer to the fiftieth record in the file, and so forth.

Relative record numbers are assigned when the direct file is created *before* any data records are loaded. When the records are loaded they are stored in the position already created for them. Consequently, the control field (employee number, part number, etc.) in the logical data record must agree with a *relative record number*. This is an important consideration when numbers are assigned to records stored in a direct file. Frequently the control field is already established and the programmer must develop a conversion formula to convert the existing control field values to the *relative record numbers* assigned previously when the file was created.

Figure 12-1 illustrates the logic for direct file creation and load. Notice several features of direct file creation and processing. First, the disk area is

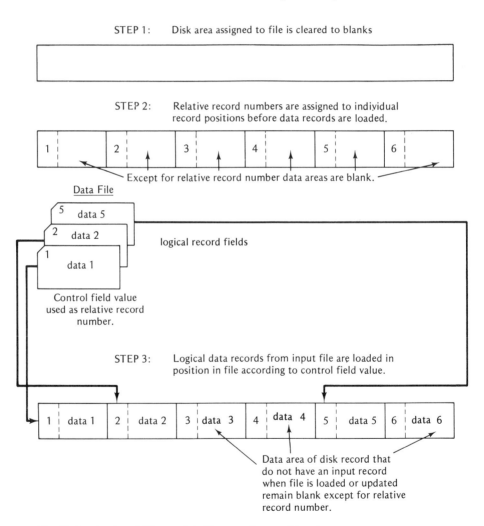

STEP 1:   Disk area assigned to file is cleared to blanks

STEP 2:   Relative record numbers are assigned to individual record positions before data records are loaded.

Except for relative record number data areas are blank.

Data File

data 5
data 2
data 1

logical record fields

Control field value used as relative record number.

STEP 3:   Logical data records from input file are loaded in position in file according to control field value.

| 1 | data 1 | 2 | data 2 | 3 | data 3 | 4 | data 4 | 5 | data 5 | 6 | data 6 |

Data area of disk record that do not have an input record when file is loaded or updated remain blank except for relative record number.

Fig. 12-1. Logic of Direct disk file creation and load.

cleared to blanks. Then, the *relative record numbers* are automatically assigned from one to *n* by the system. Finally, the data records are stored according to the value in their control field and related relative record number in the direct file.

Notice in step 3 (Figure 12-1) the direct file disk records that did not have a related input data record remain blank except for the system assigned relative record number. Further examination of the figure indicates the records are loaded in the disk file according to the value in the control field. The records with control field values one, two, and five, respectively, are loaded in the corresponding relative record position in the direct file.

Hence, the creation logic for a direct file is different than sequential or ISAM. When a sequential or ISAM file is initially loaded, the records are stored consecutively as they are processed and no blank record positions exist in either file organization type. Refer back to Figure 12-1 and notice that blank areas do exist in the direct file because the input data file used to load it did not include a related control field value equal to the relative record position already established. The figure shows relative record positions three, four, and six are blank except for the system-assigned number. In other words, if you relate back to the football stadium example, the numbered seats are there but are not occupied. Later, if a data record with a control field value of three, four, or six is processed the data information will be loaded in the relative record position.

Ideally, the control field values in data records should correspond to the relative record positions in the direct file. However, this is not always possible and a conversion procedure, written by the programmer and made part of the program, is often necessary to convert actual control field values to a relative record position. Examples of conversion techniques will be presented later in the chapter.

RPG II Coding to Create a Direct File

Figure 12-2 illustrates the source program coding needed to create a direct file on disk. Note IBM 360/370 systems do not provide for direct file creation with RPG II, but do allow for processing of the file type if it is created by COBOL or Assembler language. The method shown here is common to the System/3 computer series.

Examination of the figure shows that the direct file to be created, INVEN, is defined as an output chained file by the letter O in column 15 and C in column 16 in the File Description form. This coding informs the system to clear the designated disk area to blanks, and assign the relative record numbers before any data records are loaded.

File Description Specifications

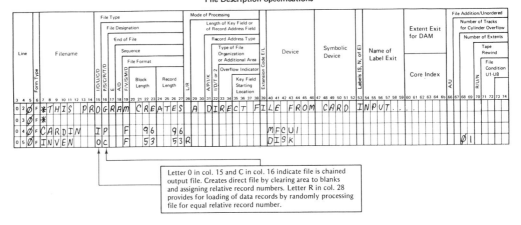

Letter 0 in col. 15 and C in col. 16 indicate file is chained output file. Creates direct file by clearing area to blanks and assigning relative record numbers. Letter R in col. 28 provides for loading of data records by randomly processing file for equal relative record number.

RPG INPUT SPECIFICATIONS

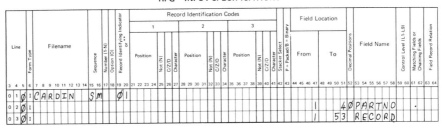

RPG CALCULATION SPECIFICATIONS

Records are loaded to direct file by chaining the Value in PARTNO to the file. If equal relative record number is found record is loaded in that position. If not found 99 turns on.

RPG OUTPUT SPECIFICATIONS

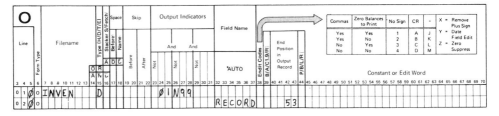

Fig. 12-2. Source coding for program to create a Direct File on disk.

The letter R is used because after the file is created it will be randomly searched by the CHAIN operation in calculations and load the input data record in the disk file position according to the control field value. Note the clearing of the disk, the assignment of relative record numbers, and the loading of the data records are executed in the same program by the coding indicated above.

Further examination of Figure 12-2 indicates that no new entries are required for direct file creation on the input form. The record is defined as one field because the disk format will be the same as the input record format. Note, however, the PARTNO field is defined separately as it is used as the Chaining Field in calculations. If any numeric fields were packed, or if a different disk record format was required, each field would have to be defined separately.

Examination of the calculation form shows the CHAIN operation (discussed in Chapter 11) chains the value in PARTNO to the direct file INVEN. The file is searched for a relative record number equal to the value in the input data record's control field. If found, the data record information is loaded into that disk record position. Again, this is similar to filling the seats in a stadium. The resulting indicator (99) is used in the same way it was used for ISAM files. If the disk record is found, the indicator does not turn on; but if not found it will turn on and may be used to condition subsequent calculations and/or output.

Output coding follows procedures discussed in previous chapters. Notice, however, data records are to be loaded to the direct file at detail time (D) and only when record identifying indicator 01 is on and 99 is not on. If the file was loaded at heading time, (H) and the line was not conditioned by an indicator, the first record in the file would be blank or contain zeros for any numeric fields.

This coding procedure may seem confusing to the reader, as sequential and ISAM disk files were created by defining them only as output files. The coding illustrated here is unique to direct files and is not used in the creation of other disk file types.

The source program listing for the program to create a direct file is illustrated in Figure 12-3. Because the job control language is unique to every

```
     01025F*THIS PROGRAM CREATES A DIRECT FILE FROM CARD INPUT....          DIRECT
     01030F*                                                                DIRECT
0001 01040FCARDIN  IP  F   96   96            MFCU1                         DIRECT
0002 01050FINVEN   UC  F   53   53R           DISK                     01   DIRECT
0003 02010ICARDIN  SM  01                                                  DIRECT
0004 020201                                          1   40PARTNO          DIRECT
0005 020301                                          1   53 RECORD         DIRECT
0006 03010C   01        PARTNO    CHAININVEN             99                DIRECT
0007 04010OINVEN   D          01N99                                       DIRECT
0008 040200                              RECORD    53                     DIRECT
```

Fig. 12-3. Source listing for program to create a Direct File on disk.

computer system, it is not shown. The programmer's manual for the system used should be referenced for job control requirements.

Figure 12-4 shows the relationship of the data records used to load the file to the contents of the direct file after it is loaded. Notice part numbers 0001, 0002, 0004, 0005, and 0007, included in the data input file, are loaded in the disk file in their related relative record positions. Other relative record positions between and at the end of the direct file remain blank except for the relative record number because a record for that position was not in the input file.

Again the football stadium example may be used to indicate the logic. People purchased seats with numbers 0001, 0002, 0004, 0005, and 0007 and occupied them, but the other seats, 0003, 0006, 0008, 0009, and so forth, are not sold yet and remain empty except for the seat numbers.

Notice in Figure 12-4 that unused positions exist between the logical records in the direct file. This is unique to direct file organization, as sequential and ISAM disk file load the records next to each other without any unused record positions.

Processing of Direct Files

Direct files may be processed sequentially or randomly, and may be added to and updated.

The sequential (consecutive) processing of a direct file is identical to that of a sequential file. Record locations are processed one after the other until the end-of-file record is sensed. Because unused record positions may exist between the records in a direct file, any output would have blank records for those records. For a printed report, a blank line would be printed and alter the spacing format of the report. The record position could be tested for blanks during processing and those records not printed.

RPG II source program coding is the same as that required for a sequential disk file (see Chapter 9). The file is defined as an input file and requires no special coding in the File Description, input, calculation, or output forms.

Additions to the direct file are different, however, than sequential or ISAM. Records are not always added at the end of the file, as with sequential organization, or placed in a sorted index order, as with ISAM, but are inserted in the relative record position already allocated for the control field value.

The coding entries, A in column 66 of File Description and letters ADD in the output form required for sequential and ISAM file adds, are not used for the addition of records to a direct file. Add records are not, in effect, added to the file but are placed in the relative record position allocated for the control field value. Consequently, adding records to a direct file is an update process in that the blanks existing in the record are replaced with the information in the

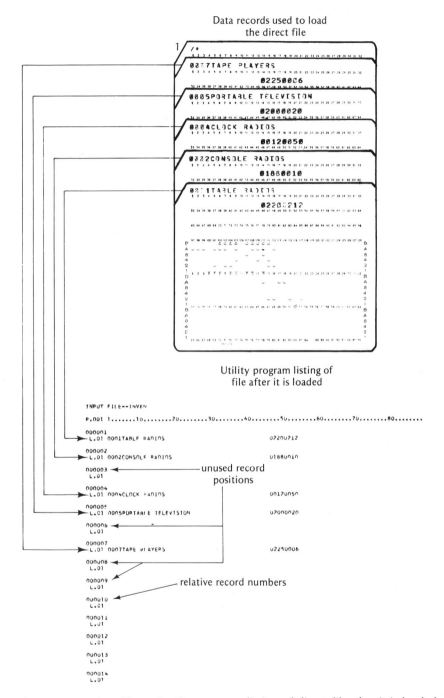

Fig. 12-4. Input data file and utility program listing of direct file after it is loaded with records.

add record(s). Therefore, no special coding is needed in RPG II programs to provide for record addition, as record addition is performed by a program that updates the direct file. What is discussed in the following paragraphs for the addition of records to a direct file also relates to the update function.

The complete source listing for the program to update and/or add records in a direct file is illustrated in Figure 12-9, and the coding for the individual coding forms is presented in Figures 12-5, 12-6, 12-7, and 12-8.

File Description coding for the update of the inventory file (INVEN) created in Figure 12-3 is shown in Figure 12-5. Notice the direct file, INVEN, is defined as an update file by the letter U in column 15 and a chained file by the C in column 16. This is the same coding used to update an ISAM file. In addition, the letter R is entered in column 28 to indicate random processing. No special entries are required in any input or output file to provide for updating.

The input coding for the program to update a direct file is shown in Figure 12-6. Because the direct file, INVEN, is defined as an update file in File Description (U in column 15), it is processed as both an input and output file by the system. The coding on lines 010 to 060 define the fields in the update records and lines 070 to 090 define the fields to be updated in the direct file. Notice the quantity field, QUANT, is conditioned by Field Indicator 60 entered in the Zero or Blank field (columns 69 and 70). The indicator is used to test the field for a blank or zero value and will be used to condition subsequent calculations and output. Only the fields used in the program have to be defined in the update disk file and any other fields included in the direct file records do not have to be included if they are not going to be used in the program.

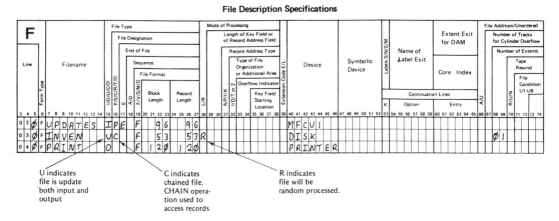

Fig. 12-5. File Description coding to update a Direct File stored on disk.

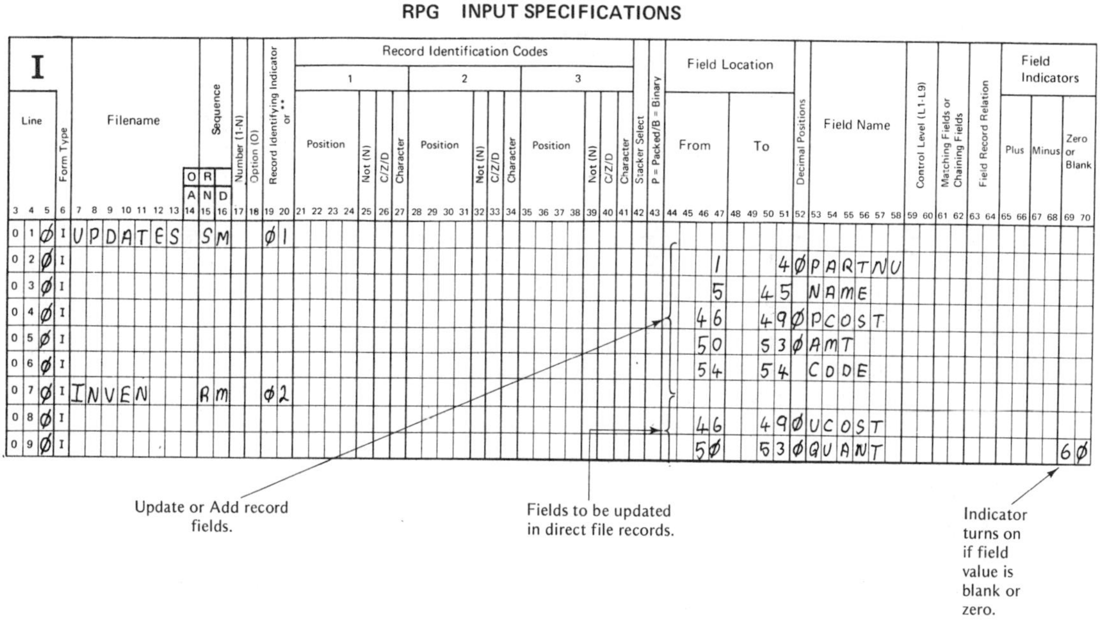

RPG   INPUT SPECIFICATIONS

Fig. 12-6.   Input Specifications coding for program to update or add to a Direct File stored on disk.

The logic of the calculation coding shown in Figure 12-7 is explained line by line in the following paragraphs:

Line 010.   The part number field, PARTNU, from the card input file is used to search the inventory file, INVEN, by the CHAIN operation. If the related disk record (relative record number) is not found, resulting indicator 90 will turn on which is used to condition calculations and a printed error message (see Figure 12-8). Reference to Chapter 11 will show this is exactly the same coding used for the update or random process of an ISAM file. The CHAIN operation may be used with direct or ISAM files but not with the sequential.

Line 020.   If the direct file relative record number is not found for the value in the PARTNU field, resulting indicator 90 will turn on and the GOTO operation on this line will execute, causing program control to skip over all calculations.

Line 030.   The value in the input field CODE is compared to the alphanumeric literal S and if equal, resulting indicator 80 is turned on and if less, 70 will turn on. The letter S indicates a sales transaction and a P, a purchase. Note that according to the collating sequence of the computer the letter P is less than S.

Programmer _____ RPG   CALCULATION SPECIFICATIONS

Line	Form Type	Control Level (L0-L9, LR, SR)	And (Not)	And (Not)	(Not)	Factor 1	Operation	Factor 2	Result Field	Field Length	Decimal Positions	Half Adjust (H)	Arithmetic Plus High 1>2	Minus Low 1<2	Zero Equal 1=2
01	C		Ø1			PARTNU	CHAIN	INVEN					9Ø		
02	C		9Ø				GOTO	END							
03	C		Ø1			CODE	COMP	'S'					7Ø	8Ø	
04	C		8ØN6Ø			QUANT	SUB	AMT	QUANT						
05	C		7ØN6Ø			UCOST	MULT	QUANT	TOCOST	8Ø					
06	C		7Ø			AMT	MULT	PCOST	TOPURH	8Ø					
07	C		7Ø			TOPURH	ADD	TOCOST	TOTAL	1ØØ					
08	C		7Ø			AMT	ADD	QUANT	QUANT						
09	C		7Ø			TOTAL	DIV	QUANT	UCOST						
10	C					END	TAG								

Fig. 12-7. Calculation Specifications coding for program to update or add records to a Direct File on disk.

Line 040. If the transaction is a sale (80 turned on by the COMP on line 030) and the QUANT field is not blank or zero (tested on input by the 60 indicator in columns 69 and 70) the sale amount, AMT, from the update record is subtracted from the direct file record field, QUANT, giving a new value for QUANT. The new value in QUANT will be stored back on the disk record (updated). This is the only calculation required for a sale as the unit cost, UCOST, would not change for a sale.

The coding entered on lines 050 to 090 relate to a purchase transaction and follow the Moving Average method of costing inventory discussed in Chapter 11. Hence, the arithmetic procedures for this method will not be repeated here as reference may be made to Chapter 11.

Line 050. If indicator 70 is on (transaction is a purchase) and the QUANT field is not blank (60 not on) the value in the disk record fields, UCOST and QUANT, will be multiplied to give a total dollar value for the inventory item (TOCOST).

Line 060. If indicator 70 is on (purchase), the values in AMT and PCOST from the update record (or add record) are multiplied to give the dollar amount of the purchase (TOPURH).

Line 070. The products, TOPURH and TOCOST, computed on lines 050 and 060 are added together to give a total dollar amount available (TOTAL).

Line 080. The purchase quantity from the update record field AMT is added to the amount on hand in the direct file record field QUANT to give the total quantity available or a new value for QUANT.

Line 090. The new unit cost for the inventory item (UCOST) is computed by dividing the total dollar amount available (TOTAL) by the total quantity available (QUANT). The new value for UCOST will be stored back on the disk record.

Line 100. Entry point for the GOTO operation on line 020.

If the transaction was the add of a new item to the inventory file, the relative record would be found as long as it was compatible to those created by the system and the instructions on lines 060 to 090 would be executed. The instruction on line 050 would not be executed because the QUANT field would be blank for any new item added to the direct file. Remember adds to a direct file are in effect an update of a relative record position established when the file was initially created.

The output coding is illustrated in Figure 12-8. Notice the INVEN file is updated at detail time (D in column 15) with the 02 record identifying indicator assigned to the direct file records and when 90 is not on. A separate coding line is not needed if the record is an *add* because, as indicated before, add records are considered update records in direct file processing. The UCOST field is conditioned by the 70 indicator because the value would only change for a purchase and not a sale.

An error message is printed when 90 is on and the relative record number is not found corresponding to the value in PARTNU. The complete source listing of the example program to update or add records to a direct file stored on disk is shown in Figure 12-9.

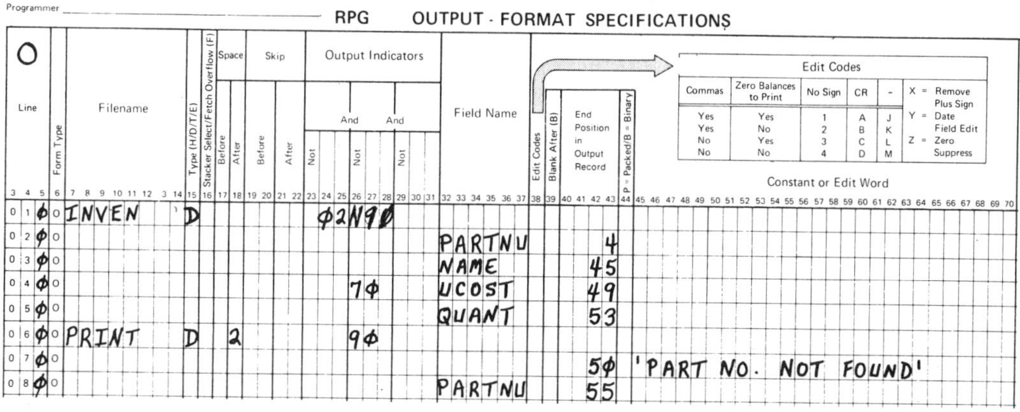

Fig. 12-8. Output-Format Specifications coding for program to update or add records to a Direct File stored on disk.

```
        01020F*THIS PROGRAM EITHER UPDATES A DIRECT FILE OR ADDS TO IT IF      UPDATE
        01030F*RECORD IS NOT FOUND....                                         UPDATE
        01040F*                                                                UPDATE
0001    01050FUPDATES IPE F  96  96                  MFCU1                     UPDATE
0002    01060FINVEN   UC  F  53  53R                 DISK                  01  UPDATE
0003    01070FPRINT   O   F 120 120                  PRINTER                   UPDATE
0004    02010IUPDATES SM  01                                                   UPDATE
0005    020201                                            1   40PARTNU        UPDATE
0006    020301                                            5   45 NAME         UPDATE
0007    020401                                           46   490PCOST        UPDATE
0008    020501                                           50   530AMT          UPDATE
0009    020601                                           54   54 CODE         UPDATE
0010    020701INVEN   RM  02                                                   UPDATE
0011    020801                                           46   490UCOST        UPDATE
0012    020901                                           50   530QUANT    60  UPDATE
0013    03010C     01      PARTNU    CHAININVEN                   90           UPDATE
0014    03020C     90                GOTO END                                 UPDATE
0015    03030C     01      CODE      COMP 'S'                         7080     UPDATE
0016    03040C     80N60   QUANT     SUB  AMT      QUANT                       UPDATE
0017    03050C     70N60   UCOST     MULT QUANT    TOCOST 80                   UPDATE
0018    03060C     70      AMT       MULT PCUST    TOPURH 80                   UPDATE
0019    03070C     70      TOPURH    ADD  TOCOST   TOTAL 100                   UPDATE
0020    03080C     70      AMT       ADD  QUANT    QUANT                       UPDATE
0021    03090C     70      TOTAL     DIV  QUANT    UCOST                       UPDATE
0022    03100C             END       TAG                                      UPDATE
0023    04010OINVEN   D       02N90                                           UPDATE
0024    040200                             PARTNU    4                        UPDATE
0025    040300                             NAME     45                        UPDATE
0026    040400                       70    UCOST    49                        UPDATE
0027    040500                             QUANT    53                        UPDATE
0028    04060OPRINT   D 2     02 90                                           UPDATE
0029    040700                                      50 'PART NO. NOT FOUND'   UPDATE
0030    040800                             PARTNU   55                        UPDATE
```

Fig. 12-9.   Source program listing of program to update or add records to a Direct File stored on disk.

The update/adds data file is shown in Figure 12-10 with a utility program listing of the direct file after the records have been added and the one has been updated.

Sequential processing of a file refers to the access of the records in a file consecutively or one after the other. The update mode of processing a file indicates that the file is both an input and output file and the original value of some of the records will be changed. Random processing of a file refers to the access of select records from a file not in a sequential order but at random.

RPG II coding to random process a direct file uses the CHAIN operation as in the update/adds program shown in Figure 12-7. The only other change in the program is to replace the U in column 15 with the letter I for an input file. Also, because the CHAIN operation is used in calculations to random process the direct file, INVEN, the letter C is specified in column 16. Input, output and other calculation coding follow procedures previously discussed.

In summary, the sequential, update, and random processing of a direct file follow the RPG II coding entries identical to those used for an ISAM file. Except, of course, the entries unique to an ISAM file in the File Description form are not used for a direct file.

Data records used to update
or add to the direct file

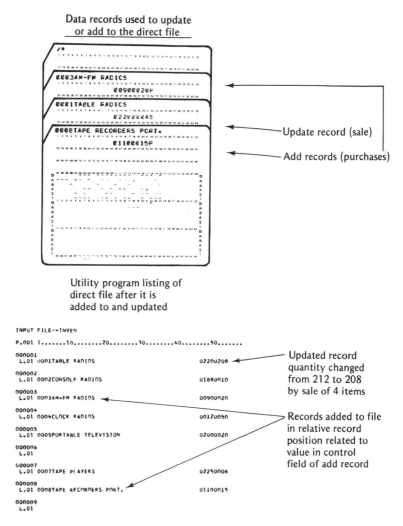

Update record (sale)

Add records (purchases)

Utility program listing of
direct file after it is
added to and updated

INPUT FILE--INVEN

P.001 1.......10.........20.........30.........40.........50.......

000001
L.01 0001TABLE RADIOS   0220U208

000002
L.01 0002CONSOLE RADIOS   0188O010

000003
L.01 0003AM-FM RADIOS   0090O020

000004
L.01 0004CLOCK RADIOS   00120050

000005
L.01 0005PORTABLE TELEVISION   02000020

000006
L.01

000007
L.01 0007TAPE PLAYERS   02250006

000008
L.01 0008TAPE RECORDERS PORT.   01100015

000009
L.01

Updated record
quantity changed
from 212 to 208
by sale of 4 items

Records added to file
in relative record
position related to
value in control
field of add record

Fig. 12-10.   Update/adds data file and utility program listing of direct file, INVEN, after one record is updated and two added.

CREATING RELATIVE RECORD NUMBERS FROM INPUT DATA

Relative record numbers may be compared to the key field of ISAM records, or the control field in the records of a sequential disk file. If the part, student, customer, or employee numbers were assigned in an ascending order, the control field values in the records would easily relate to relative record positions in the direct file.

For example, if a company has an inventory file of 1,000 items, more room may be provided in the file for up to 1,200 items to allow for expansion. Part numbers could be assigned from 0001 to 1200 and relate perfectly with the direct file logic for relative record numbers.

However, assume the inventory file was previously numbered from 0001 to 4000, but provision for only a maximum of 1,200 items should be made in the direct file. If the part numbering system was not adjusted, the direct file would be 2,800 records larger than necessary, which wastes disk space and increases processing time. Consequently, a conversion routine should be written to change existing part numbers to the parameters of the file size of 1,200 records.

One approach might be to divide the part numbers by three and drop any remainder. This would convert the largest number from 4000 to 1333, 3000 to 1000, and so forth. The file would still be 133 records larger than required, but 2667 less than required without the conversion. Figure 12-11 shows how the coding for the example program to create a direct file (Figure 12-2) could be modified to accommodate the conversion.

Things are not that simple, however. If 4,000 is divided by 3, a quotient of 1,333 results, and if 3,999 is divided by 3, the result is also 1333. This is called the *Synonym Concept* which refers to duplicate, relative record numbers created by a conversion routine. Obviously two records (or more) in a direct file cannot have the same relative record number; therefore, a conversion routine that produces no synonyms or the least number of synonyms should be used. In some applications they may be impossible to avoid and some provision must be included to accommodate them in the programs that use the direct file.

Many alternative methods are available to provide for synonyms that result from a conversion routine including the Chain Technique, Spill Method, and Separate Area. These are only suggested methods of handling synonyms and many other techniques may be devised. It is not within the scope of this text to discuss data-base management; therefore, a text on that subject should be referenced for a complete discussion of synonym-handling procedures.

The existing numbering system for a data file may make it very difficult if not impossible to convert a part, customer, or employee number to a compatible, relative record position in a direct file. Perhaps in applications of that type it may be more convenient to use ISAM or sequential file organization.

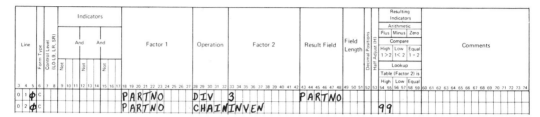

Fig. 12-11. Modified calculation coding to provide for a conversion routine to reduce a direct file size.

ADVANTAGES OF DIRECT FILE ORGANIZATION

Even with the synonym problem associated with direct files, the organization method offers flexibility and advantages not found in sequential or ISAM files. Some of the important advantages of direct files are listed below.

1. Direct files do not have to be sorted for processing. This is an important feature for small computer systems because the smaller the storage the longer the sort time.

2. Direct files take up less room than ISAM because an index area or overflow does not have to be provided.

3. Direct file may be loaded and records retrieved in the same program; something that cannot be done with sequential or ISAM.

4. Direct file may be processed consecutively more than once in same program.

5. Related records that are not stored next to each other but separated in the direct file can be retrieved as a group.

6. Arrays that are too large to be held in main storage may be stored in a direct file. The subscript of the array entry would become the related relative record number. See Chapter 14 for Array concepts.

7. Direct files may be used for the storing of messages in a telecommunication system (message queuing) and make them available at a later time.

Direct file organization has not been as widely used a sequential or ISAM because of the file maintenance problems inherent with it. However, when inquiry to the file (access) is low, direct files are faster to process.

WHICH FILE ORGANIZATION METHOD TO USE

Of the three file organization methods, Sequential, ISAM, and Direct, which one is the best? No absolute formula is available for choosing the organization method best suited to the job. However, the following concepts should be considered when selecting a file organization method:

1. Master or transaction file

2. Frequency of additions and deletions from file (volatility)

3. Activity of the file

4. Size of the file

A master file is usually a permanent file that contains information not subject to change. Some field information may be updated, but basic values as a part number or name would not be subject to changes.

A transaction file usually contains records less permanent in nature which are typically used to update a master file. For example, of the program examples presented in this chapter, the direct file, INVEN, is considered the master file, and the update card file, UPDATES, the transaction file. Master files that have a high incidence of updates or random access are more efficient if organized as ISAM or Direct.

If a file has a high percentage of additions and deletions (high volatility) the direct file method should not be used if too many synonym records are produced. Hence, in a file with that kind of activity it may be better organized as ISAM.

Additions also present a problem with sequential files. Because the records are added at the end of the file without regard to control field values, the file would have to be sorted before it was processed randomly by the Matching Record Method or by record groups. Direct or ISAM files do not have to be sorted and these may be the better organization methods when additions are frequent.

Activity of a file refers to the number of times it is accessed in a program. If a file has a low incidence of random access, it probably would be best organized as ISAM or Direct. On the other hand, a file with a high activity might be better organized as Sequential if sort time was not a consideration.

The size of a file is also a factor when deciding on the organization method to use. Because ISAM files consume more disk storage than sequential or direct, this may be an important consideration if storage is limited. Also, if the file has had a high volatility and a sort is needed before processing, the size of the work areas required for the sort, and sort time, are other considerations. The larger the file the longer the sort time and larger the work areas.

ADDROUT FILE CONCEPTS

Record address files were discussed in Chapter 11 for the limits processing of an ISAM file. Another record address type file is an ADDROUT (address out) file which is created from the output of a *Sort Utility Program*. Consequently, the sort program must be included in the system's software to create an ADDROUT file. Again, the programmer's manual for the system's sort utility must be referenced to identify the procedures needed for an ADDROUT sort.

An ADDROUT file is a separate file loaded with the relative record addresses of the records in a sequential, ISAM, or direct file. It is different from a regular "Tag-Along" sort in that the address of the record is loaded in the ADDROUT file and not the complete record. On some computer system utility sorts, the control field (field sorted) may be included with the record address.

ADDROUT files and processing offer the following advantages:

1. Use less disk storage because only the relative record number of the sorted records are stored and not the complete record.

2. Faster to sort.

3. Original sequence of file that is sorted is not destroyed and many small ADDROUT files may be created to process the master file in alternative record orders.

Figure 12-12 shows the logic related to ADDROUT sort and processing. Notice only two fields are included in each record and that the master inventory file is arranged in ascending sequence by part number. Assume that a report is needed of the file in ascending order by part name (fields with letters), but because disk room is limited and the file is large, a regular sort would be difficult. For an application of this type an ADDROUT sort would be both faster and use less disk and core storage.

The processing logic as detailed in Figure 12-12 is explained in the following paragraphs.

1. The sequential (ISAM or direct) resides on disk, arranged in ascending order by part number.

2. Sort utility program is executed with ADDROUT option to create an ADDROUT file in ascending record address order by part name.

3. ADDROUT file resides on disk in a separate storage area consisting only of the record addresses of the records in the master file.

4. RPG II source program is compiled and executed to process the master inventory file by the ADDROUT file. Record addresses in the ADDROUT file are used to random process the inventory file in part-name order.

5. Report is generated from RPG II ADDROUT program of inventory items in the same order ADDROUT file was sorted in step 2.

RPG II Coding for ADDROUT File Processing

After the ADDROUT file is created by the sort utility program, an RPG II program is required to process it against the file from which it was created. The record addresses in the ADDROUT file only relate to the sorted master file and cannot be used to process any other disk file.

Figure 12-13 shows a utility program listing of the master disk file used as input to the ADDROUT sort. Notice the records are arranged in the file in ascending order by part number (0001 to 0010). Also shown in the figure is the utility listing of the ADDROUT file created from the output of the sort. The contents of the records are the relative record addresses of the master records now sorted in ascending order by part name. On an IBM 370 system the record addresses in the ADDROUT file are a standard 10 bytes, but may differ for other systems.

Look at Figure 12-13 again and notice in the ADDROUT file listing the third character in from the low-order position represents the location of that

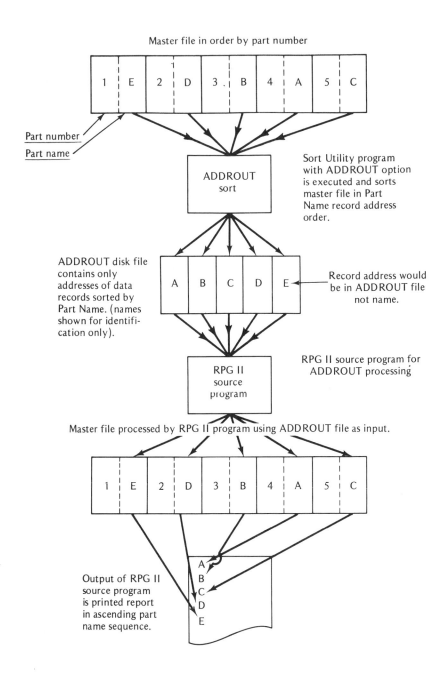

Fig. 12-12. ADDROUT file sort and processing logic.

Master disk file (MAISM) loaded in ascending order by part number

ADDROUT file sorted by utility sort program in ascending part name order

position of record in master file

Record address of master disk records

Part number

Fig. 12-13. Utility program listings of master file (MAISM) and ADDROUT file (created by utility sort program) loaded with record addresses of master records.

record in the master file. The number 8 in the first record in the ADDROUT file indicates this record is the eighth record in the master file; 7, the seventh; 3, the third, and A, the tenth. Note the letter A is the hexadecimal equivalent for the number 10. Some ADDROUT sort utilities will also allow the control field values to be stored with the record addresses. In practice there is little reason to read the output of an ADDROUT sort and it is shown here only for illustration.

The RPG II source program to process the master inventory file (MAISM) is shown in the listing in Figure 12-14.

New entries for the ADDROUT file processing program are detailed in the File Description form (Figure 12-15) and the Extension form (Figure 12-16). Because input, calculations, and output follow standard coding procedures previously discussed, and no special entries are required in the forms for ADDROUT processing, reference may be made to the source listing in Figure 12-14 for that coding.

Examine the File Description form in Figure 12-15 and notice that new entries are required which will be explained in the following paragraphs.

A minimum of three files have to be used in an ADDROUT processing program including the ADDROUT file, a disk file that was used to create the ADDROUT, and some output file. The coding requirements in the File Description form unique to the ADDROUT file are described below. Only the new entries on line 020 are defined and not the standard coding entries used for an input disk file.

File Designation (Column 16).   Letter R is entered in this column for the ADDROUT file to indicate it is a record address type file.

```
0001   01 030  FADDROUT IRE F  10   10 1C T     EDISK40 SYS008S              ADROUT
0002   01 040  FMAISM   IP F  51   51R ID        DISK40 SYS008S              ADRCUT
0003   01 050  FNAMES    O F  132  132    OF     PRINTERSYSLST               ADRCUT
0004   02 010  E         ADDROUT MAISM                                       ADRCUT
0005   03 010  IMAISM    SM  01                                              ADROUT
0006   03 020  I                                            1    4 PART      ADROUT
0007   03 030  I                                            5   45 NAME      ADROUT
0008   03 040  I                                        P  46  480COST       ADROUT
0009   03 050  I                                        P  49  510NUMBR      ADROUT
0010   04 010  C     01       COST      MULT NUMBR  TOTAL   70               ADROUT
0011   05 010  ONAMES   H      201    1P                                     ADROUT
0012   05 020  O        OR            OF                                     ADROUT
0013   05 030  O                        UDATE Y    8                         ADROUT
0014   05 040  O                                  32 'INVENTORY LISTING IN'  ADROUT
0015   05 050  O                                  48 'PART NAME ORDER'       ADRCUT
0016   05 060  O                                  53 'PAGE'                  ADROUT
0017   05 070  O                        PAGE  Z   58                         ADROUT
0018   05 080  O        H     2       1P                                     ADROUT
0019   05 090  O        OR            CF                                     ADROUT
0020   05 100  O                                  23 'PART NAME'             ADROUT
0021   05 110  O                                  63 'COST     QUANTITY'     ADROUT
0022   05 120  O                                  82 'TOTAL    PART NO'      ADROUT
0023   05 130  O        D     2       01                                     ADROUT
0024   05 140  O                        NAME      42                         ADROUT
0C25   05 150  O                        COST    1 51                         ADRCUT
0026   06 010  O                        NUMBR   1 61                         ADROUT
0027   06 020  O                        TOTAL   1 73                         ADROUT
0028   06 030  O                        PART      81                         ADROUT
```

Fig. 12-14. Source listing of program to process a disk file with the ADDROUT file created from it.

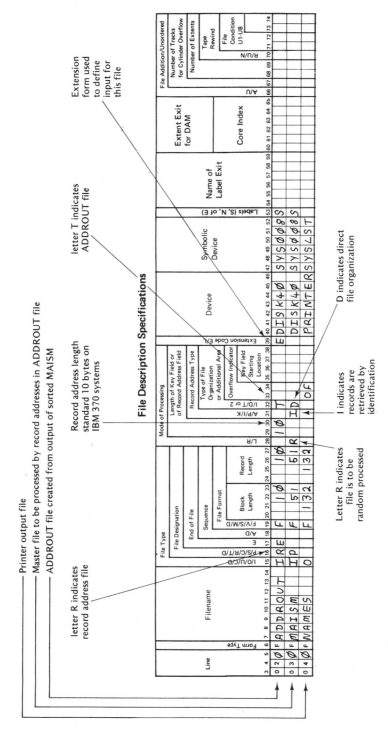

Fig. 12-15. File Description coding for ADDROUT file processing.

457

Length of Key Field or Record Address Field (Columns 29 and 30).   The standard record address length for an IBM 370 system is 10. This entry may be different for other systems. System/3, for example, is three bytes. This entry refers to the record length of the records in the ADDROUT file. The record length specified in columns 24–27 may include the control field value which would make the record length entry larger than the entry in this field. For example, if the control field was 41 bytes (part-name length in sample program) the entry in columns 29 and 30 would be 10 but the entry in columns 24–27 would be 51 if the control field value was to be stored with the record addresses in the ADDROUT file.

Type of File Organization (Column 32).   The letter T in this column informs the computer this is an ADDROUT file.

Extension Code (Column 39).   Letter E in this column indicates the extension form is used to define records in this file and not the input form. All record address files are defined in the extension form.

The entries required in the disk file used to create the ADDROUT file and then to be processed by it are entered on line 030 and are defined as follows:

Mode of Processing (Column 28).   The letter R indicates the file will be random processed.

Record Address Type (Column 31).   Letter I indicates that records in this file are retrieved by identification (record addresses).

Type of File Organization (Column 32).   Letter D indicates the file is considered a direct file for ADDROUT processing. Even if the file is organized as sequential or ISAM, it must be redefined as direct in the program for ADDROUT processing. Any job control coding must be changed accordingly to indicate the file is direct. Note that ISAM files cannot be sorted on an IBM 370 DOS system.

The Extension Specifications form for the ADDROUT processing program is illustrated in Figure 12-16.

The entries on the extension form are identical to those used to process an ISAM file within limits. Notice the addrout file name (ADDROUT) is entered in the From Filename field (columns 11–18) and the master file (MAISM) in the To Filename field (columns 19–26). No other entries are used in this form for addrout processing.

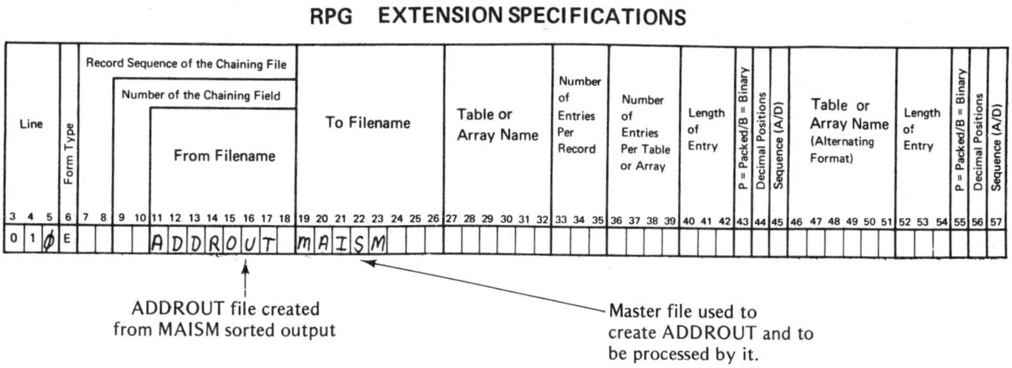

RPG   EXTENSION SPECIFICATIONS

Line	Form Type	Record Sequence of the Chaining File		To Filename	Table or Array Name	Number of Entries Per Record	Number of Entries Per Table or Array	Length of Entry	P = Packed/B = Binary	Decimal Positions	Sequence (A/D)	Table or Array Name (Alternating Format)	Length of Entry	P = Packed/B = Binary	Decimal Positions	Sequence (A/D)
		Number of the Chaining Field														
		From Filename														
3 4 5	6	7 8 9 10	11 12 13 14 15 16 17 18	19 20 21 22 23 24 25 26	27 28 29 30 31 32	33 34 35	36 37 38 39	40 41 42	43	44	45	46 47 48 49 50 51	52 53 54	55	56	57
0 1 Ø	E		A D D R O U T	M A I S M												

ADDROUT file created from MAISM sorted output

Master file used to create ADDROUT and to be processed by it.

Fig. 12-16. Extension Specifications coding for program to process a file by an ADDROUT file.

Look at Figure 12-14 again and notice the only fields defined on input are those for the master file, MAISM. Because the addrout file is a record address type, the extension form is used to define the records along with the record address field length (columns 29 and 30) entered in the File Description form for the file. Further examination of Figure 12-14 indicates that calculations and output coding follow normal coding procedures and are not affected by any new entries for ADDROUT processing.

Figure 12-17 shows the printed report generated from the ADDROUT processing program. Notice the report is in ascending part-name order and not by part number. The part numbers printed at the right-hand side of the report indicate how the original part number ascending order has been altered by the ADDROUT sort.

3/13/78	INVENTORY LISTING IN PART NAME ORDER PAGE	1			
	PART NAME	COST	QUANTITY	TOTAL	PART NO
B/W CONS. TELEVISIONS		58	33	1,914	0008
B/W PORT. TELEVISIONS		183	18	3,294	0007
CLOCK RADIOS		13	126	1,638	0003
COMBINATION PLAYERS		225	6	1,350	0010
CONSOLE RADIOS		188	34	6,392	0002
CONSOLE TELEVISIONS		183	18	3,294	0006
FM-AM PORT. RECORD PLAYERS		80	24	1,920	0009
FM-AM RADIOS TABLE		72	83	5,976	0004
PORTABLE TELEVISIONS		167	29	4,843	0005
TABLE RADIOS		35	212	7,420	0001

Fig. 12-17. Printed report generated from ADDROUT processing program.

QUESTIONS

1. Name the three file organization types.
2.. How do the file types named in Question 1 differ in organization?
3. What are the steps the computer follows when creating a direct file?
4. Define the term relative record number.
5. How is a direct file defined in the File Description Specifications when it is created? (System/3)
6. When a direct file is created, may blank record areas exist between the stored records? Explain.
7. May the file used to create a direct file be in an unordered sequence?
8. 'Name the processing functions available with direct files.
9. How are records added to a direct file? Where are the records added? How do adds to a direct file differ from sequential or ISAM?
10. Explain the Synonym Concept. What are some programming options to handle synonyms?
11. Name five advantages of direct file organization. What are some disadvantages?
12. What are some things to consider when selecting a file organization type?
13. Explain the purpose of an ADDROUT file(s).
14. How are ADDROUT files created? What are they used for?
15. What is stored in the records in an ADDROUT file?
16. Name the sequence of ADDROUT file processing.
17. When an ADDROUT file is defined on File Description, what type of file is it? Are the fields defined on input?
18. Name some advantages and disadvantages for ADDROUT file processing.

EXERCISES

12-1. Write the File Description and input coding to create a direct disk file. An input card file named NEWACTS contains the records to create the direct file NEWCUST. An output file (ERRORS) must be provided for an error listing for records that do not have a matching relative record number. The format of the records in NEWACTS is given below.

Cust. No.	Customer Name	Customer Address	Sale Amt.		ID Code N
99999	99999999999999999999	99999999999999999999999999999999999999999	999999	99999	99
1 2 3 4 5	6 7 8 9 10 11 12 13 14 15 16 17 18 19 20 21 22 23 24	25 26 27 28 29 30 31 32 33 34 35 36 37 38 39 40 41 42 43 44 45 46 47 48 49 50 51 52 53 54 55 56 57 58 59 60 61 62 63 64	65 66 67 68 69 70 71 72	73 74 75 76 77 78	79 80

Pack the sales amount field in the disk records and use a blocking factor of four.

12-2. Complete the calculation coding to create the file in Exercise 12-1.

12-3. Write the output coding for the information completed in Exercises 12-1 and 12-2. Provide for an error report with the following format:

		0	1	2	3	4	5
		1234567890	1234567890	1234567890	1234567890	1234567890	123456789
H	1	ERROR MESSAGES					
H	2	ØX/XX/XX					
	3						
D	4	XXXXX HAS INCORRECT RELATIVE NO.					
	5						
	6	NOTES:					
	7						
	8	① DETAIL LINES ARE SINGLE SPACED					
	9						
	10	② HEADINGS ON TOP OF EVERY PAGE					
	11						

12-4. Write an RPG II program to update or add records to the file created in Exercises 12-1, 12-2, and 12-3. Use UPADDS for the file containing the update and/or add records and increase the original sales amount balance for any sales for an existing account. New accounts should be identified by testing the name field for blanks. A printed report is required with the format given in the following printer spacing chart.

		0	1	2	3	4
		1234567890	1234567890	1234567890	1234567890	123456789
H	1	CUSTOMER ACTIVITY REPORT		PAGE XXØX		
H	2	AS OF ØX/XX/XX				
	3					
D	4	XXXXX NEW CUSTOMER				
	5					
D	6	XXXXX OLD CUSTOMER SALE				
	7					
D	8	XXXXX RECORD NOT FOUND				
	9					
TLR	10	TOTAL NEW CUSTOMER XXXØ				
TLR	11	OLD CUSTOMER SALE XXXØ				
TLR	12	TOTAL SALES XXXØ				

12-5. Assume an ADDROUT file was created by the sort utility program with the record addresses of the records in the direct file NEWCUST created in Exercise 12-1. The record addresses in the addrout file represent a sort of NEWCUST in ascending customer-name order.

Write an RPG II program to process NEWCUST by the ADDROUT file. Use the following format for your printed report:

Refer to the printer spacing chart for any calculations you may need in the program. Blocking factor of the ADDROUT file is one and the control field is not loaded with the record address.

LABORATORY ASSIGNMENTS

LABORATORY ASSIGNMENT 12-1:
CREATION OF A TOWN'S REAL PROPERTY TAX RECORDS
IN A DIRECT FILE ON DISK

A direct file is to be created for the real property tax assessment and quarterly payments information of a town's property owners. The format of the card records to create the file is given in the following card layout form:

Eight additional fields must be formatted in the disk records when the file is created. The description and length of these fields is given below:

Field Description	Length	Type
First quarter payment date	6	N
First quarter payment amount	6	N
Second quarter payment date	6	N
Second quarter payment amount	6	N
Third quarter payment date	6	N
Third quarter payment amount	6	N
Fourth quarter payment date	6	N
Fourth quarter payment amount	6	N

All fields are to be loaded next to each other in the disk records and all numeric fields must be stored as packed.

Calculations. Provide for a card count of the number of records processed and the number that do not have a related relative record number.

Format of printed report. In addition to creating the direct file, print a listing of the card records loaded on the disk file in the following format:

Data for Laboratory Assignment 12-1:

Tax Number	Taxpayer's Name	Taxpayer's Address	Assessment
00001	SEAN MAILLET	19 ROSEWOOD LANE	035000
00002	LAWRENCE FARRELL	1 LAUREL ROAD	027900
00005	PAUL GREGORY	7 PARK RIDGE ROAD	041012
00006	RICHARD SWANSON	40 WINDY RIDGE	067184
00008	MICHEAL DURGAS	8 TASHUA PLACE	082933
00000	SVEN ANDERSON	22 LAKEVIEW ROAD	110569

LABORATORY ASSIGNMENT 12-2:
CONSECUTIVE PROCESSING OF A DIRECT FILE

Write an RPG II program to consecutively process the direct file you created in Laboratory Assignment 12-1. Use the same report format for this assignment you used for the one in Laboratory Assignment 12-1.

LABORATORY ASSIGNMENT 12-3:
RANDOM PROCESSING A DIRECT FILE

Write a program to process the direct file you created in Laboratory Assignment 12-1 randomly. Access the record information for taxpayers with tax numbers 00001, 00003, and 00008. Use the same report format given in Laboratory Assignment 12-1 and your own random record format.

LABORATORY ASSIGNMENT 12-4:
UPDATE AND ADDS TO A DIRECT FILE

An input card file contains the information for quarterly tax payments and new taxpayers. Write a program to update the direct file for update and adds, processing from the following record formats:

Update record format:

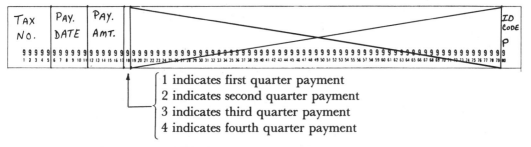

| TAX
NO. | PAY.
DATE | PAY.
AMT. | | ID
CODE
P |

{ 1 indicates first quarter payment
{ 2 indicates second quarter payment
{ 3 indicates third quarter payment
{ 4 indicates fourth quarter payment

Adds record format:

| TAX
NO. | TAXPAYER NAME | TAXPAYER ADDRESS | ASSESSMENT AMT. | | ID
CODE
T |

Calculations. Test the quarter payment field (1, 2, 3, or 4) and use an indicator to update the appropriate payment date and amount fields at detail time in output. The number of taxpayer accounts updated, total quarterly payments, and number of new taxpayer fields must be accumulated.

Output. Update or add to the direct file as the transaction indicates. Print a report with the following format:

```
                    0         1         2         3         4         5
           1234567890123456789012345678901234567890123456789012345678901
H    1                    PROPERTY TAX UPDATE/ADDS REPORT
H    2                            ØX/XX/XX                      PAGE XXØX
     3
H    4    TAX NO.          NAME              ASSESSMENT   PAYMENT
     5
D    6    XXXXX X--------------------X    $ XXX,XØX  $ XXX,XØX  UPDATE
     7                                                         (NEW)
D    8    XXXXX X--------------------X      XXX,XØX    XXX,XØX  UPDATE
     9                                                         (NEW)
    10
TLR 11    ACCOUNTS UPDATED.............XØX
TLR 12    NEW PROPERTY OWNERS.........XØX
    13
TLR 14    TOTAL QUARTERLY PAYMENTS RECEIVED  $ X,XXX,XXØ
    15
    16    NOTES:
    17
    18    ①HEADINGS ON EVERY PAGE.
    19
    20    ②PRINT EITHER WORD-UPDATE OR NEW-
    21       AS INDICATED IN FORMAT.
    22
    23    ③DOLLAR SIGNS ON FIRST DETAIL LINE.
    24
```

Data for Laboratory Assignment:

Tax Number	Payment Date	Payment Amount	Quarter	Letter P in column 80
00001	040479	000350	1	
00002	071079	000300	2	
00005	071879	000402	2	
00006	100579	000615	3	
00008	012280	001123	4	

Adds Records (ID code)

Tax Number	Taxpayer's Name	Taxpayer's Address	Assessment	Letter T in column 80
00003	JERRY FURMAN	18 EAGLE PASS LANE	0861111	
00007	ERIC FELDER	44 HAITIAN BLVD	0222100	
00009	THOMAS PARKER	8 MADISON STREET	019914	

Note: After this lab is completed and the file updated (or added to), use the program from Laboratory Assignment 12-2 to check the accuracy of the updating and adding procedures.

LABORATORY ASSIGNMENT 12-5:
CREATION OF ADDROUT FILE WITH RECORD ADDRESSES OF DIRECT FILE

Your instructor will advise you on the completion of this assignment because an addrout file cannot be created by an RPG II program. The system's sort utility program has to be used to create an Addrout file and may not be available for your use.

In any case, if you understand any may use the sort utility, create the addrout file from the record addresses of the direct file (created in Lab 12-1) sorted in ascending assessment amount order.

LABORATORY ASSIGNMENT 12-6:
PROCESSING OF A DIRECT FILE BY AN ADDROUT FILE

Write an RPG II program to process the direct file created, updated, and added to in Laboratory Assignments 12-1 and 12-4 by the addrout file created in Laboratory Assignment 12-5. Remember the addrout file must have been created to complete this assignment.

The format of the printed report is given below:

		0	1	2	3	4
		1234567890	1234567890	1234567890	1234567890	123456789
H	1	PROPERTY TAX REPORT IN ASCENDING				
H	2	ASSESSMENT AMOUNT ORDER				
	3					
H	4	ASSESSMENT TAX NO. TAXPAYER				
	5					
D	6	$ XXX,XØX XXXXX X————————————X				
	7					
D	8	XXX,XØX XXXXX X————————————X				
	9					
	10					
TLR	11	TOTAL NUMBER OF PROPERTY OWNERS XX,XØX				
	12					
TLR	13	GRAND TOTAL OF ASSESSMENTS $XXX,XXX,XXX				
	14					
	15	NOTES:				
	16					
	17	① HEADINGS ON EVERY PAGE				
	18					
	19	② DOLLAR SIGN ON FIRST DETAIL				
	20	LINE OF EVERY PAGE				
	21					
	22	③ LR TOTALS ON SEPARATE PAGE				
	23					
	24					

Note: Totals must be accumulated in calculations for total number of property owners and total assessed value of all property.

13
RPG II
TABLE CONCEPTS

Tables provide a convenient way of storing data that is not often subject to change or when information has to be looked up as, for example, telephone numbers of subscribers, a pay rate for an employee, or a sales tax based on a sale.

All tables used in RPG II programs may be defined as *Simple Tables* in that each entry in the tables contains only one item of logical information. Furthermore, simple tables are not commonly used alone, but with two or more *related* simple tables. Figure 13-1 shows examples of simple tables and how they are logically related to each other. In all cases the first entry, for example, is related to the first entry in the related table(s); the second entry to the second entry in the related table, and so forth.

Illustration 1 (Figure 13-1) shows how two simple tables relate to each other. The first entry (and so forth) in the Pay Code table relates to the first entry in the Pay Rate table. Consequently, the table entries must be arranged in the correct order so an entry from one table logically relates to an entry in another table(s). Also notice both simple tables are arranged in ascending sequence. Tables used in this manner do not have to be in any required sequence; however, a sorted arrangement of the table data does provide a convenient way to insure that table entries do relate to each other.

The simple tables shown in Illustration 2 are in an unordered sequence. As with all related tables, an entry in the Item Number table relates to the

Illustration 1

Pay Code	Rate of Pay
A	250
B	275
C	290
D	300
E	310
F	350

Simple tables related
to each other.

Illustration 2

Item Number	Price
1234	00056
5678	00188
9123	00239
8321	00751
1789	01051
4453	19899

Smaller numeric table entries
must be padded with zeros.

Illustration 3

Name	SS No.
DROPOUT A	040000009
FAIL Ybbb	222222222
HONORS HI	789665555
SUCCEED I b	020801234
TOPP ONbbb	534202601

Smaller alphabetic (or
alphanumeric) table
entries are padded with
blanks in table records
(the letter b denotes a blank[s]).

Illustration 4

Taxable Amount	Fixed Amount	Tax Percent
011	0000	14
035	0336	18
073	1020	21
202	3729	23
231	4396	27
269	5422	31
333	7406	35

Three simple tables
related to each other.

Note: Tables may be arranged in ascending, descending, or
unordered sequence. Decimal points are not entered
in table data, but indicated on the Extension form
entry for the table.

Fig. 13-1. Examples of related simple tables.

corresponding entry in the Price table. Note any entries in the Price table
smaller than the maximum length are padded with leading (high-order) zeros
because all table entries must be the same length. This is an important concept
to remember when table records are prepared.

Illustration 3 shows an alphabetic table in ascending sequence and a
numeric table in unordered sequence. Related simple tables do not have to be
in the same sequence as long as the entries relate logically to each other. Any
alphabetic (or alphanumeric) entries smaller than the longest table entry must
be padded with low-order blanks when the table records are created.

Illustration 4 shows how three simple tables relate to each other. The first
entry in the Taxable Amount table relates to the first entry in the Fixed
Amount and Tax Percent tables and so forth. Because the Taxable Amount
table indicates a minimum amount for a range of taxable income (discussed
later) it must be arranged in either ascending or descending order. The other
related tables, however, do not have to be sorted in any particular sequence but
do have to be logically arranged. In the example shown the three tables are
arranged in ascending sequence.

Some of the specific topics that will be discussed in this chapter for RPG II programs using tables include:

1. File Description Specifications coding to provide for table processing
2. Design of table records
3. Extension Specifications coding for table processing
4. Calculation Specifications coding for searching tables
5. Methods of handling the result of a table search
6. Time which tables are loaded in program cycle

EXAMPLE PROGRAM USING TWO SIMPLE TABLES

An example program will be discussed to illustrate the concepts and RPG II coding entries for programs using tables. Figure 13-2 lists the data for the two simple tables used in the program example. Examine the figure and notice two new terms are used to identify the table types, which are defined as follows:

Argument Table: Table initially searched by a transaction input field (called search word). Depending on information, may be an identical entry or the low or high value for a range.

Function Table: Table or tables in which entries relate to the corresponding entry in the argument table. First entry in the argument table relates to first entry in function table(s), and so forth. May logically be more than one function table in program.

The argument table, TAB1, in Figure 13-2 contains the labor grade code which will be searched by the value in a search word defined on input. If an

Argument table TAB1	Function table TAB2
1	125
2	150
3	175
4	200
5	225
6	250
7	275
8	300
9	325

Note: TAB2 has two decimal positions specified on the extension specifications form because decimals are never punched on data or table cards for numeric data.

Fig. 13-2.   Data for two tables used in sample related table program.

File Description Specifications

Line	Form Type	Filename	File Type	File Designation	End of File	Sequence	File Format	Block Length	Record Length	Mode of Processing	Device	Symbolic Device	Name of Label Exit	Overflow Indicator
0 2	F	FUNCT1	IT	F				27	27		EMFCM1	SYSIPT		
0 3	F	FUNCT2	IT	F				27	27		EMFCM1	SYSIPT		
0 4	F	PAYCARDS	IP	F				80	80		MFCM1	SYSIPT		
0 5	F	OUTPUT	O	F				120	120	OF	PRINTER	SYSLST		

RPG Extension Specifications

Line	Form Type	From Filename	To Filename	Table or Array Name	Number of Entries Per Record	Number of Entries Per Table or Array	Length of Entry	P / Decimal Positions / Sequence	Table or Array Name (Alternating Format)	Length of Entry	Comments
0 1	E	FUNCT1		TAB1	9	9	1	0A			
0 2	E	FUNCT2		TAB2	9	9	3	2A			

RPG INPUT SPECIFICATIONS

Line	Form Type	Filename	Sequence	Number (1/N)	Option (O)	Record Identifying Indicator	Position 1	C/Z/D	Character	Field Location From	Field Location To	Decimal Positions	Field Name	Control Level	Field Record Relation
0 1	I	PAYCARDS	AA			02	80	C	P						
0 2	I									1	50		EMPNO		
0 3	I									6	45		NAME		
0 4	I									46	460		LABGRD		
0 5	I									47	491		HOURS		

RPG CALCULATION SPECIFICATIONS

Line	Form Type	Control Level (L0-L9, LR, SR)	Indicators And (Not)	Factor 1	Operation	Factor 2	Result Field	Field Length	Decimal Positions	Half Adjust (H)	Resulting Indicators / Lookup High	Low	Equal	Comments
0 1	C		02	LABGRD	LOKUP	TAB1	TAB2						10	
0 2	C		10	HOURS	MULT	TAB2	GRSPAY	52	H					
0 3	C		10	GRSPAY	ADD	TOTPAY	TOTPAY	82						
0 4	C													
0 5	C													
0 6	C													
0 7	C													
0 8	C													
0 9	C													
1 0	C													
1 1	C													
1 2	C													
1 3	C													
1 4	C													
1 5	C													

Fig. 13-3. Source coding for example table program using an equal look-up.

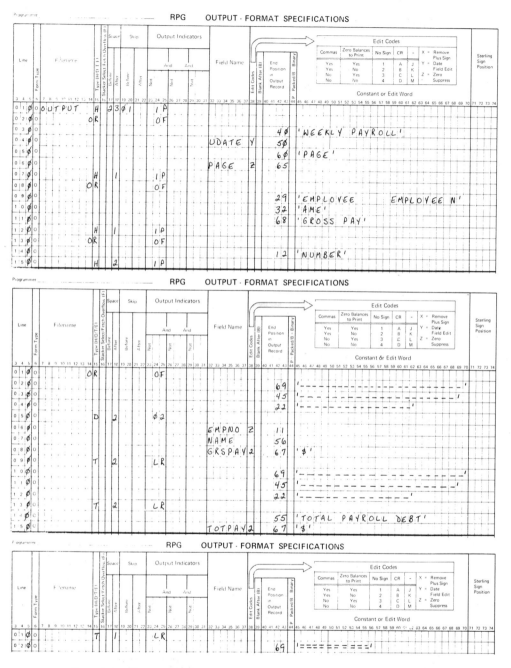

Fig. 13-3. Source coding for example table program using an equal look-up. (Concluded)

473

equal entry is found in the argument table, the corresponding entry in the function table, TAB2, may be extracted for processing. Notice both tables are in ascending order. Even though tables may be in an unordered sequence, a sorted order does speed processing. This may be significant when very large tables are used in a program. The RPG II coding entries and processing logic is presented in the following paragraphs.

RPG II Coding for the Example Table Program

The complete source program coding for the example table program using the tables illustrated in Figure 13-2 is shown in Figure 13-3. Each of the individual coding form entries and their relationship to table processing will be discussed separately.

File Description Coding for Tables

Figure 13-4 identifies the two new entries needed in the File Description form to specify an input file containing a table(s). The letter T must be entered in column 16 for the input table files and the letter E in column 39. All other entries on the form for input files are identical to those previously discussed. However, if the tables are arranged in sequential order, the appropriate letter, A or D, could be entered in column 18 to decrease processing time. Ascending or descending sequence must be specified if the low or high range of the

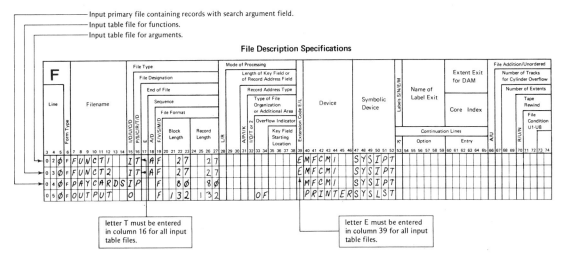

Fig. 13-4. File Description coding entries for example program using two simple related tables.

argument table entries were specified in the table records. This concept is covered in the application program presented later in this chapter.

Notice in Figure 13-4 three input files are specified. FUNCT1 contains the argument table, TAB1; FUNCT2, the function table, TAB2; and PAYCARDS includes the data records with the search field. Two considerations must be noted for table files: first, they should be specified on the File Description form in the order the tables are read and precede the primary and any secondary files; second, only one table may be specified per file unless the tables are arranged in alternating sequence on the records; then two tables may be included in one file (to be discussed later).

Tables which are entered from an input table file defined in the File Description form are called *Object Time* tables and are placed in the job stream like any input file. Note, however, tables may be an integral part of the program and do not have to be entered from an input file. These tables are called *Compile Tables* and in order not to confuse the reader, the discussion of the coding and concepts of this type will be presented in a later section. The tables discussed now are *object time* tables which may be stored on any input media and read in from any input device interfaced with the computer system.

Design of Table Records and Extension Specifications Coding

The manner in which table data is entered on the records may depend on the existing records or entirely on the programmer's preferences. Strict rules must be followed when entering table data on records including:

1. All entries in a simple table must have the same length. Smaller numeric table entries are padded with high-order zeros and alphanumeric entries are padded with low-order blanks.

2. The first table entry in a record must begin in position 1 of the record.

3. Numeric entries may be no longer than 15 digits and alphanumeric entries no longer than 256 characters.

4. All records for the table must contain the same number of entries except the last record which may have less.

5. Table entries may be sorted in ascending, descending, or no order. However, if a table range is used, tables must be in ascending or descending order.

6. No blanks may exist between table entries. Note, however, shorter table entries are padded with blanks so all entries are the same maximum table-entry size.

7. A table entry cannot be split between records but must be complete on each record.

8. Tables may be stored on a sequentially organized file.

9. When table data is arranged in alternating sequence, every record must begin with an entry from the first table.

Figures 13-5, 13-6, and 13-7 show a few typical arrangements of table data. Many other formats are available and the reader should be aware that as long as the preceding rules are followed, flexibility is provided in table record arrangement.

The Extension Specifications form is used to define the information for any tables used as a program. For example, the size, type, sequence, number of entries per table, and number of entries per table record are entered on this form. The input form is never used to define tables, but is needed for other input information including the *search word* which is used to "look up" table entries.

The manner in which the table entries are arranged on the records determines how the extension form is coded. Figure 13-5 shows the table records and related extension form for the program example discussed.

The fields on the Extension Specifications form shown in Figure 13-5, which are unique to table coding and related to the program example, are explained in the following paragraphs.

Form Type (Column 6). The letter E must be specified in this field for every extension card. Extension cards are placed in the source program immediately after the last File Description card and before the first Input Specifications card.

Columns 7–10. Not used for table coding.

From Filename (Columns 11–18). The filename for the table file defined in the File Description form is entered in this field. FUNCT1 contains the argument table (TAB1) and FUNCT2 the function table (TAB2). Both files were defined on the File Description form as table files by the letter T in column 16 and linked to the extension form by the E in column 39.

To Filename (Columns 19–26). This field is used only if a listing of the table records is required at the end of the report. If a listing was wanted in the program example, the name of the printer file (OUTPUT) would be entered left-justified in this field.

Table or Array Name (Columns 27–32). Observe the table names, TAB1 and TAB2, are entered left-justified in this field. All table names *must begin* with the word TAB and may be four, five, or a maximum of six characters in length. The other letters of a table name may be numeric or alphabetic providing the first three are TAB.

Number of Entries Per Record (Columns 33–35). The number 9 (Figure 13-5) entered in this field indicates the number of entries per table record. Alternative coding examples shown in Figures 13-6 and 13-7 show how this entry depends on the table record format.

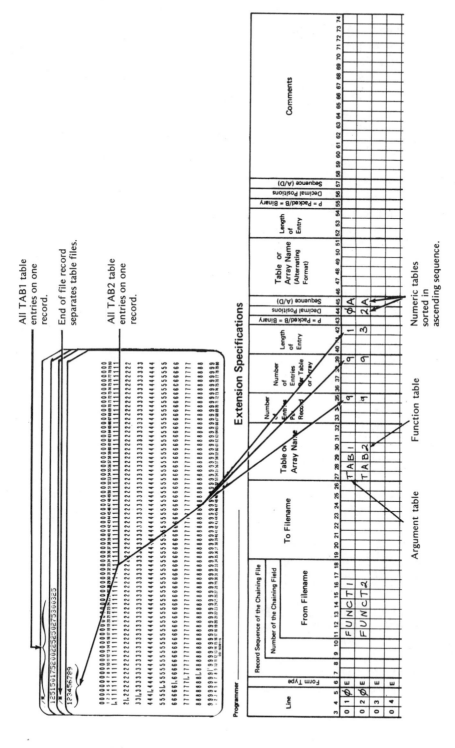

Fig. 13-5. Extension Specifications coding for example table program when table entries are included on one record.

477

Number of Entries Per Table or Array (Columns 36–39). The number 9 (Figure 13-5) indicates the exact number of table entries in the table. When two simple tables are related, both must have the same number of entries per table. Consequently, an exact count must be determined for any table used in a program.

Length of Entry (Columns 40–42). The longest entry in TAB1, which is 1, is entered right-justified in this field. Notice the entry length for TAB2 is 3. Remember every entry in the table must be the same length. Any shorter numeric entries must be padded with zeros and any alphanumeric entries padded with blanks to make every entry the same length.

P = Packed/B = Binary (Column 43). Numeric table entries may be in packed format in a tape, disk, or diskette file. If they are packed, the letter P must be entered in this field. In the program example the numeric entries are not packed so the field is blank. In addition, if the table data was in binary format (rarely found) the letter B would have to be used in this field to make the data compatible with the computer.

Decimal Positions (Column 44). The zero entered in this column for TAB1 (Figure 13-5) indicates the table entries are numeric but have no decimal positions. Entries for TAB2 are also numeric but have two decimal positions. Numeric table entries are the same as standard data fields in that no decimals are entered in the field value.

Sequence (A/D) Column 45. Because TAB1 and TAB2 are in sorted ascending order (Figure 13-5) the letter A is entered in this field. When an A or D is entered in this column, sequence checking is automatically performed and any table records out of order will cause program control to halt or cancel. For this program example the table records did not have to be in a sequence, providing an entry in TAB1 is related to the corresponding entry in TAB2. When the low or high range of a table is used, this field must be used (to be discussed later in this chapter).

Columns 46–57. The fields included in these columns are a repeat of the previous fields and are used to define a table arranged in alternating sequence on the table records with the table defined in columns 27–45.

Remember the table and entries are defined only on the Extension Specifications and not on the input form.

ALTERNATIVE CODING OF EXTENSION SPECIFICATIONS FOR PROGRAM EXAMPLE

Figures 13-6 and 13-7 show alternative arrangements of the entries on the table records and the related extension form coding. Figure 13-6 illustrates an example when the entries from TAB1 and TAB2 are entered on a table record

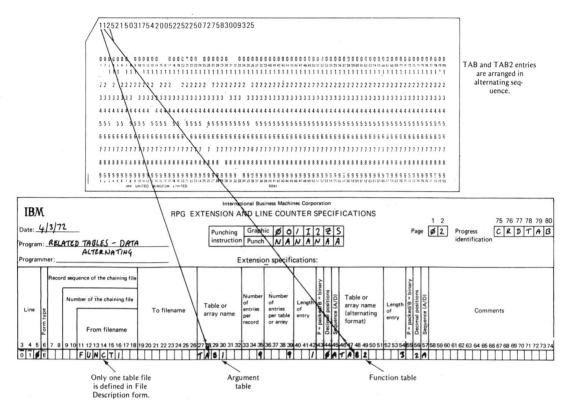

Fig. 13-6. Card format and Extension Specifications for alternating arrangement of table entries for example program.

in alternating sequence. Notice the first entry, 1, for the argument table (TAB1) is punched in column 1 followed by the related function table (TAB2), entry 125; then the second TAB1 entry, 2, followed by the second TAB2 entry, 150, and so forth.

The only coding changes needed to process tables arranged in alternating sequence are made in the extension form. In addition to the entries already discussed for the argument table, the alternating arrangement requires the use of columns 46–57 for the function table.

A re-examination of Figure 13-6 will indicate that instead of entering the coding for TAB2 on a separate extension form line, the table is defined by entering the table name in the Table Name Field (columns 46-51). The length of the table entry must be specified in columns 52 and 54 along with the decimal point in column 56 and the sequence in column 57.

An important point to consider when alternating arrangement of table entries is specified, is that pairs of entries (one argument and one function cannot be split on two different records, but must always be grouped together on a record.

A few other concepts concerning related simple tables should be mentioned. First, related tables do not have to be sorted in the same sequence providing the entries are logically related. Second, related tables do not have to be of the same type; one may be numeric and the other alphanumeric (or alphabetic).

Another alternative approach for coding table records is illustrated in Figure 13-7. In this example only one table entry is entered on a record.

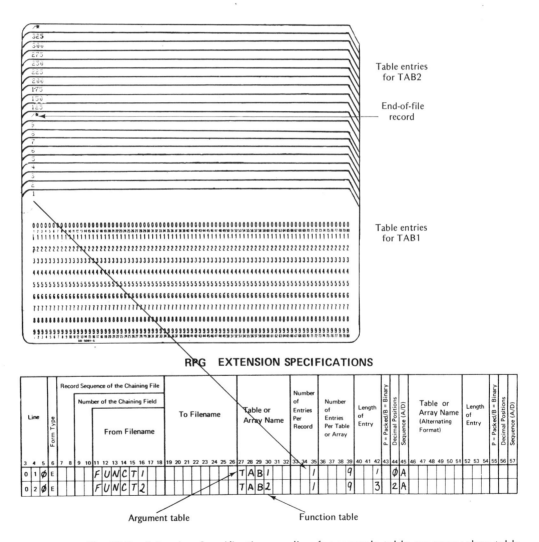

Fig. 13-7. Extension Specifications coding for example table program when table entries are included in separate records. Only one table entry per record.

RPG   INPUT SPECIFICATIONS

Line	Form Type	Filename	Sequence	Number (1-N)	Option (O)	Record Identifying Indicator or **	Record Identification Codes 1 Position	Not (N)	C/Z/D	Character	2 Position	Not (N)	C/Z/D	Character	3 Position	Not (N)	C/Z/D	Stacker Select	P = Packed/B = Binary	Field Location From	To	Decimal Positions	Field Name	Control Level (L1-L9)	Matching Fields or Chaining Fields	Field Record Relation	Field Indicators Plus	Minus	Zero or Blank	Sterling Sign Position
0 1	Ø	I PAYCARDSAA				Ø2	80		C	P																				
0 2	Ø	I																		1	50		EMPNO							
0 3	Ø	I																		6	45		NAME							
0 4	Ø	I																		46	460		LABGRD							
0 5	Ø	I																		47	491		HOURS							

search field (argument) value must
be same size and type as table
designated as argument table.

Fig. 13-8. Input Specifications coding for example table program. No special coding entries are required on this form for table coding.

Because each table is included in a separate file defined on the File Description form, an end-of-file record (/*) must separate the last table record in TAB1 from the first record in TAB2. The extension form coding is identical to that shown in Figure 13-5 except there is only one entry per record in this example as compared to nine in Figure 13-5.

An examination of the input form, Figure 13-8, will reveal that standard coding procedures are used and no special entries are required for table coding. Notice the input file (PAYCARDS), defined as the primary file in file description, includes one record type with fields for employee number (EMPNO), employee name (NAME), labor grade (LABGRD), and hours worked (HOURS). The LABGRD field is used as the search field (argument) in the program to "look up" the argument table (TAB1) entries. Any field value (or literal) used as the search argument *must be the same size and type* (numeric or alphanumeric) as the table designated as the argument table. If the preceding rule is not followed, an error will result during program execution that will cause a halt or cancellation.

Calculation Coding for Table Look-Up

The coding specified on the first line of the calculation form, Figure 13-9, causes the contents of the search argument field (LABGRD) to search the argument table, TAB1. A new RPG II operation name, LOKUP, is used to look up table (and array) entries. When the value in LABGRD equals the value in a TAB1 table entry, Resulting Indicator 10, specified in the equal field (columns 58 and 59) will turn on. If the table entry is not found, indicator 10 will not turn on and any calculations and/or output conditioned by the indicator would not be executed.

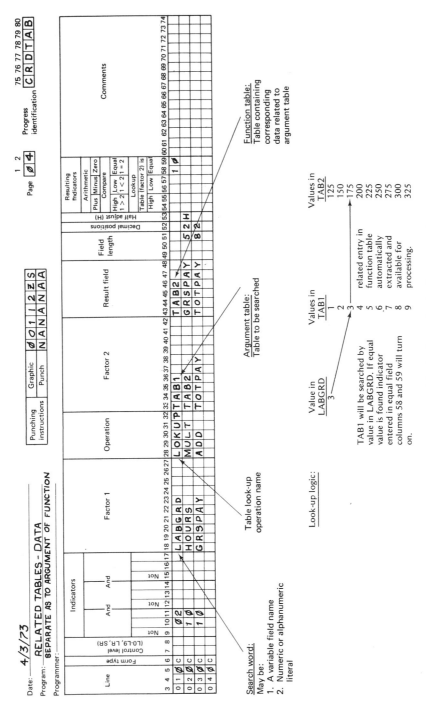

Fig. 13-9. Calculation Specifications coding and related table look-up logic for example program.

Furthermore, if the argument is found in TAB1, the corresponding function from TAB2, specified in the Result Field, will automatically be retrieved and become available for processing. Any table names entered in Factor 2 and the Result Field are considered variable fields and may be used in subsequent calculations and output as any variable field providing a successful look up took place. Figure 13-9 shows the logic related to a table look-up. The value in the search argument field searches TAB1; when an equal value is found in the table, the related value in TAB2 is also extracted.

When an equal condition results from the LOKUP operation, resulting indicator 10 will be on and the next two lines conditioned by 10 will be executed. The coding on line 020 multiplies the input field HOURS by the value in TAB2 (extracted by the LOKUP) to give a gross pay (GRSPAY) amount. Calculations on line 030 adds the gross pay for each employee to a total field (TOTPAY) which is printed at LR time.

The search argument entry in Factor 1 for the LOKUP operation does not have to be a variable field name but may be a numeric or alphanumeric literal or another table name. In all cases, however, the value in the Factor 1 entry must be the same size and type as the argument table specified in Factor 2.

Because output coding follows standard coding procedures it is not defined in a separate figure but may be referenced by an examination of the source program listing and corresponding printed output in Figure 13-10. In addition, the exact column locations used in the output form may be located by examining the output coding sheets in Figure 13-3.

Time Tables Are Loaded in Program Cycle

Tables may be loaded in the program cycle at *Object* or *Compile* time. The program presented in the preceding section used object time tables because the tables were loaded into core after the source program was compiled and stored in object code waiting for execution. Any tables loaded at object time must be defined in a table file in the File Description form and the related file name entered in columns 11-18 of the extension form. Hence, object time tables are processed like any other input file.

On the other hand, compile tables are an integral part of the program and are not entered by an input file defined in file description. In other words, they are considered an extension of the source program. In addition to omitting any table files in file description, the only other change is to leave the From Filename field (columns 11-18) blank on the extension form for all compile tables. Figure 13-11 illustrates how the extension form for the object time tables specified in Figure 13-5 would be modified to compile time tables. No other change is needed in source program coding to identify a table as a compile time table. The only restriction for compile time tables is that numeric table entries cannot be in packed or binary format.

Source Program Listing:

```
F***********************************************************************************
F*    PROGRAM TO PROCESS ONE CARD TABLE, SEPARATE .AS TO FUNCTION AND              *
F*    ARGUMENT.                                                                    *
F*    EMPLOYEE PAYROLL CARDS ARE THE TRANSACTION INPUT FILE.                       *
F*    THE ARGUMENT IS THE LABOR GRADE CODE USED TO ACCESS THE LABOR GRADE          *
F*    HOURLY RATE OF PAY WHICH IS THE FUNCTION.                                     *
F*    THE HOURLY RATE IS MULTIPLIED BY THE HOURS WORKED FOR THAT WEEK              *
F*    GIVING THE EMPLOYEE'S GROSS PAY.                                             *
F***********************************************************************************
0001   01 010  FFUNCT1   IT  F  27   27                EMFCM1  SYSIPT          CRDTAB
0002   01 020  FFUNCT2   IT  F  27   27                EMFCM1  SYSIPT          CRDTAB
0003   01 030  FPAYCARDSIP    F  80   80               MFCM1   SYSIPT          CRDTAB
0004   01 040  FOUTPUT   O   F      120    OF      PRINTERSYSLST               CRDTAB
0005   02 010  E    FUNCT1              TAB1   9   9  1 0A                      CRDTAB
0006   02 020  E    FUNCT2              TAB2   9   9  3 2A                      CRDTAB
0007   03 010  IPAYCARDSAA   02  80 CP                                         CRDTAB
0008   03 020  I                                        1    50EMPNO           CRDTAB
0009   03 030  I                                        6    45 NAME           CRDTAB
0010   03 040  I                                       46   460LABGRD          CRDTAB
0011   03 050  I                                       47   491HOURS           CRDTAB
0012   04 010  C    02        LABGRD    LOKUPTAB1   TAB2          10            CRDTAB
0013   04 020  C    10        HOURS     MULT TAB2   GRSPAY  52H                CRDTAB
0014   04 030  C    10        GRSPAY    ADD  TOTPAY  TOTPAY  82                 CRDTAB
0015   05 010  OOUTPUT   H 2301      1P                                        CRDTAB
0016   05 020  O         OR          OF                                        CRDTAB
0017   05 030  O                                   40 'WEEKLY PAYROLL'         CRDTAB
0018   05 040  O                         UDATE Y   50                          CRDTAB
0019   05 050  O                                   60 'PAGE'                   CRDTAB
0020   05 060  O                         PAGE  Z   65                          CRDTAB
0021   05 070  O         H 1         1P                                        CRDTAB
0022   05 080  O         OR          OF                                        CRDTAB
0023   05 090  O                                   29 'EMPLOYEE    EMPLOYEE N' CRDTAB
0024   05 100  O                                   32 'AME'                    CRDTAB
0025   05 110  O                                   68 'GROSS PAY'              CRDTAB
0026   05 120  O         H 1         1P                                        CRDTAB
0027   05 130  O         OR          OF                                        CRDTAB
0028   05 140  O                                   12 'NUMBER'                 CRDTAB
0029   05 150  O         H 2         1P                                        CRDTAB
0030   06 010  O         OR          OF                                        CRDTAB
0031   06 020  O                                   69 '------------------------'CRDTAB
0032   06 030  O                                   45 '------------------------'CRDTAB
0033   06 040  O                                   22 '------------------'     CRDTAB
0034   06 050  O         D 2         02                                        CRDTAB
0035   06 060  O                         EMPNO Z   11                          CRDTAB
0036   06 070  O                         NAME      56                          CRDTAB
0037   06 080  O                         GRSPAY2   67 '$'                      CRDTAB
0038   06 090  O         T 2         LR                                        CRDTAB
0039   06 100  O                                   69 '------------------------'CRDTAB
0040   06 110  O                                   45 '------------------------'CRDTAB
0041   06 120  O                                   22 '------------------'     CRDTAB
0042   06 130  O         T 2         LR                                        CRDTAB
0043   06 140  O                                   55 'TOTAL PAYROLL DEBT'     CRDTAB
0044   06 150  O                         TOTPAY2   67 '$'                      CRDTAB
0045   07 010  O         T 1         LR                                        CRDTAB
0046   07 020  O                                   69 '=========='            CRDTAB
```

Printed Report:

```
            WEEKLY PAYROLL    3/13/78        PAGE     1

EMPLOYEE      EMPLOYEE NAME                          GROSS PAY
NUMBER
-----------------------------------------------------------------------

12345      ALEXANDER PRIMADONNA                       $56.00

22222      MARIANNE HYPERBOLA                         $90.00

33333      WILIAM WORKHORSE                           $72.00

54545      ROBERT T. DOUGLAS                          $70.00

78945      JOHN PADAPODOLUS                          $113.75

89789      JUDY HOWDYDOYOU                            $45.00

-----------------------------------------------------------------------

               TOTAL PAYROLL DEBT      $446.75

                                       ==========
```

Fig. 13-10. Source listing and printed report for example table program for an equal look-up.

RPG   EXTENSION SPECIFICATIONS

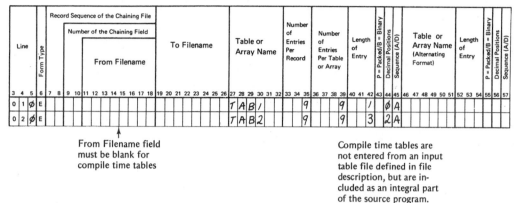

Fig. 13-11.   Extension Specifications coding for Compile Time Tables.

The job stream to include compile tables in a program varies for each manufacturer and computer system. Consequently, the manufacturer's supplied programmer's manual must be referenced for the control statements to specify a compile table(s). In an IBM 370 DOS system, compile tables are separated from the source program and each other by an ** control statement. The source program and compile tables are separated from any input files by the standard /* statement.

ACCOUNTING APPLICATION-DETERMINATION OF INCOME TAX LIABILITY BASED ON TAXABLE INCOME

Federal income tax liability is based on a taxable income amount determined from standard tax return forms and procedures. Reference should be made to any Internal Revenue booklet or tax text for the mechanics of determining taxable income. The application presented assumes taxable income has been previously determined and the only requirement is to calculate the dollar amount of the income tax liability.

In any case, once the taxable income is determined, standard tax tables are used to calculate the amount of federal tax liability for the current year. Figure 13-12 shows the tax tables for a single taxpayer and a married couple filing a joint return. These tables will be used for the table entries in the application program presented in this section. Two other schedules not shown are for a married couple filing separate returns and for an individual who qualifies as head of household.

The mathematical procedure used to compute a single taxpayer's income tax liability from the tax rate schedules is shown in Figure 13-13.

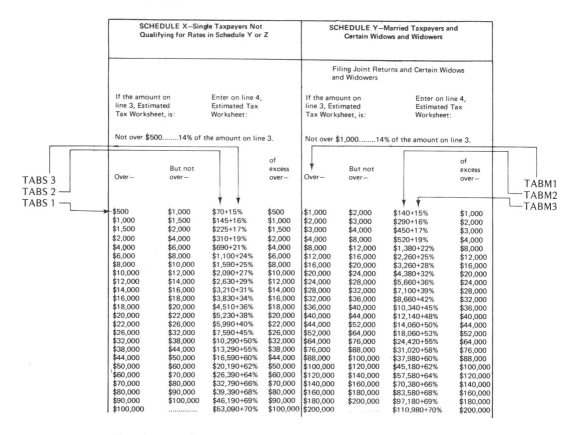

SCHEDULE X—Single Taxpayers Not Qualifying for Rates in Schedule Y or Z				SCHEDULE Y—Married Taxpayers and Certain Widows and Widowers			
				Filing Joint Returns and Certain Widows and Widowers			
If the amount on line 3, Estimated Tax Worksheet, is:		Enter on line 4, Estimated Tax Worksheet:		If the amount on line 3, Estimated Tax Worksheet, is:		Enter on line 4, Estimated Tax Worksheet:	
Not over $500........14% of the amount on line 3.				Not over $1,000........14% of the amount on line 3.			
Over—	But not over—		of excess over—	Over—	But not over—		of excess over—
$500	$1,000	$70+15%	$500	$1,000	$2,000	$140+15%	$1,000
$1,000	$1,500	$145+16%	$1,000	$2,000	$3,000	$290+16%	$2,000
$1,500	$2,000	$225+17%	$1,500	$3,000	$4,000	$450+17%	$3,000
$2,000	$4,000	$310+19%	$2,000	$4,000	$8,000	$520+19%	$4,000
$4,000	$6,000	$690+21%	$4,000	$8,000	$12,000	$1,380+22%	$8,000
$6,000	$8,000	$1,100+24%	$6,000	$12,000	$16,000	$2,260+25%	$12,000
$8,000	$10,000	$1,590+25%	$8,000	$16,000	$20,000	$3,260+28%	$16,000
$10,000	$12,000	$2,090+27%	$10,000	$20,000	$24,000	$4,380+32%	$20,000
$12,000	$14,000	$2,630+29%	$12,000	$24,000	$28,000	$5,660+36%	$24,000
$14,000	$16,000	$3,210+31%	$14,000	$28,000	$32,000	$7,100+39%	$28,000
$16,000	$18,000	$3,830+34%	$16,000	$32,000	$36,000	$8,660+42%	$32,000
$18,000	$20,000	$4,510+36%	$18,000	$36,000	$40,000	$10,340+45%	$36,000
$20,000	$22,000	$5,230+38%	$20,000	$40,000	$44,000	$12,140+48%	$40,000
$22,000	$26,000	$5,990+40%	$22,000	$44,000	$52,000	$14,060+50%	$44,000
$26,000	$32,000	$7,590+45%	$26,000	$52,000	$64,000	$18,060+53%	$52,000
$32,000	$38,000	$10,290+50%	$32,000	$64,000	$76,000	$24,420+55%	$64,000
$38,000	$44,000	$13,290+55%	$38,000	$76,000	$88,000	$31,020+58%	$76,000
$44,000	$50,000	$16,590+60%	$44,000	$88,000	$100,000	$37,980+60%	$88,000
$50,000	$60,000	$20,190+62%	$50,000	$100,000	$120,000	$45,180+62%	$100,000
$60,000	$70,000	$26,390+64%	$60,000	$120,000	$140,000	$57,580+64%	$120,000
$70,000	$80,000	$32,790+66%	$70,000	$140,000	$160,000	$70,380+66%	$140,000
$80,000	$90,000	$39,390+68%	$80,000	$160,000	$180,000	$83,580+68%	$160,000
$90,000	$100,000	$46,190+69%	$90,000	$180,000	$200,000	$97,180+69%	$180,000
$100,000	....	$53,090+70%	$100,000	$200,000	....	$110,980+70%	$200,000

TABS 3
TABS 2
TABS 1

TABM1
TABM2
TABM3

Fig. 13-12.   Federal income tax rate schedules.

Refer back to Figure 13-12 and notice the table names used in the application program are identified. Each rate schedule consists of three tables: TABS1, TABS2, and TABS3 for the single taxpayer, and TABM1, TABM2, and TABM3 for the married taxpayer filing jointly. TABS1 and TABM1 are loaded with the low amount of each bracket because the low amount is needed in the computation to determine any excess amount subject to the additional percent (see Figure 13-13). The fixed dollar amounts for the schedules are loaded in TABS2 and TABM2, and the bracket percents in TABS3 and TABM3.

The RPG II source program coding for this application follows the table rules previously discussed except the reader should be aware that a range is to be "looked up" and will not always be the exact table entry as in the previous program example. The only change needed in table coding is entered in the calculation form to accomodate a "range look-up." When the calculation coding for this program is introduced, the logic for this look-up procedure will be fully explored.

Taxable income: $9,000
Filing Status: Single

Procedure:

1. Locate the taxpayer's bracket in Schedule X. Taxable income is $9,000 so it falls in bracket, $8,000 to $10,000.
2. Subtract the low amount of the range from taxable income as follows:

$9,000	taxable income
8,000	low amount of bracket
$1,000	excess over $8,000

3. Multiply the excess determined in step 2 by the percent for the bracket as follows: $1,000 × .25 = $250.00.
4. Add the fixed dollar amount for the bracket to the excess computed in step 3 to determine total tax liability.

$1,590	fixed amount for bracket
250	excess computed in step 3
$1,840	total tax liability

Fig. 13-13. Mathematical procedure for computing federal income tax liability using rate schedules.

RPG II Coding For Federal Income Tax Application Program

Figure 13-14 shows the File Description coding for the application program. Notice four input table files are defined on the form. TABFIL1 contains tables TABS1 and TABS2 which are entered on the records in alternating sequence

File Description Specifications

Line	Form Type	Filename	File Type	File Designation	File Format	Block Length	Record Length	Overflow Indicator	Extension Code E/L	Device	Symbolic Device
02Ø	F	*PROGRAM TO CALCULATE FEDERAL INCOME TAX FOR SINGLE AND MARRIED									
03Ø	F	*STATUS. TABLES ARRANGED ON CARDS IN ALTERNATING FORMAT & SINGLE.									
04Ø	F	TABFIL1	I	T	F	8Ø	8Ø		E	MFCM1	SYSIPT
05Ø	F	TABFIL2	I	T	F	8Ø	8Ø		E	MFCM1	SYSIPT
06Ø	F	TABFIL3	I	T	F	8Ø	8Ø		E	MFCM1	SYSIPT
07Ø	F	TABFIL4	I	T	F	8Ø	8Ø		E	MFCM1	SYSIPT
08Ø	F	TAXINC	I	P	F	8Ø	8Ø			MFCM1	SYSIPT
09Ø	F	TAXDUE	O		F	132	132	OF		PRINTER	SYSLST

Fig. 13-14. File Description Specifications for example table program.

(see Figure 13-15). The percent table, TABS3, for the single taxpayer's schedule is included in TABFIL2. TABFIL3 contains TABM1 and TABM2 for the married taxpayer which are also entered in the table records in alternating sequence (see Figure 13-15), and TABFIL4 includes the bracket percent table, TABM3, for the married taxpayer.

The primary input file, TAXINC, contains data records with the search argument TAXINC (taxable income), the name of the taxpayer (NAME), and the taxpayer's filing status (STATUS). An output file, TAXDUE, is also defined for the required printed report.

Remember the arrangement of the table data determines the number of files required. If the tables were not arranged in alternating sequence, six files would be defined in the File Description form.

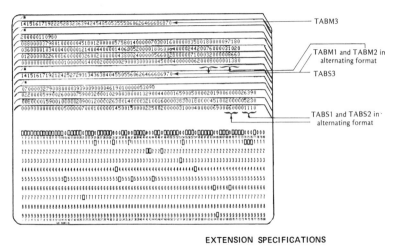

Fig. 13-15. Extension Specifications coding for example table program and format of table records.

Extension Specifications Coding
for Federal Income Tax Application
Program

A line-by-line discussion of the entries in the Extension form shown in Figure 13-15 is presented in the following paragraphs.

Line 010.   Comments.

Line 020.   Because the tables are loaded at "object time" the file name is entered left-justified in the From Filename field. The argument table name, TABS1, is entered in the table name field and the related information about the table in columns 33–45.

Examination of the records for this table indicates that seven entries are included on one table record. Therefore, the digit 7 is entered in the Number of Entries Per Record field. In addition, there are 25 entries per table and the entries are six digits in length. The appropriate values are entered in columns 36–39 and 40–42, respectively.

Furthermore, the table entries (TABS1) are defined as numeric and sorted in ascending sequence by the values in columns 44 and 45. Because a table range is searched, the argument table entries *must* be in either ascending or descending order. All function tables in the program, however, may be in any sequential order.

Look at Figure 13-15 again and notice the entries for TABS1 and TABS2 are arranged in alternating sequence in the table records. Consequently, columns 46–57 must be used to define this format. Notice only the table name (TABS2), the entry length (5), decimal positions (0), and sequence (A) are used to define the function table arranged in alternating sequence with the argument table. The number of entries per record and the number per table do not have to be mentioned again because all related simple tables must have the same number of entries. Note, however, the function table(s) does not have to be the same type, entry size, or be sorted in the same sequence as the argument table to which it relates.

Line 030.   Comments.

Line 040.   The tax bracket percent values (Figure 13-12) are read in from TABFIL2 and stored in table TABS3. All 25 table entries are included in one table record (Figure 13-15) which are defined as two digits in length with two decimal positions. Notice TABS3 is also defined as sorted in ascending sequence. Similar to any input data, decimal points (or other numeric field punctuation) are never included in the numeric input field.

Line 050.   Comments.

Line 060.   The input table file, TABFIL3, contains the low-range amount table (TABM1) and the fixed dollar amount table (TABM2) arranged in alternating sequence on the table records (see records in Figure 13-15). Remember because a table range is to be searched by a search argument field, the appropriate letter (A or D) must be entered in the sequence field (column 45).

Line 070.   Comments.

Line 080.   The tax bracket percent values (Figure 13-12) are read in from TABFIL4 and stored in TABM3 for the married taxpayer filing jointly. Again all 25 entries are included in one table record with each entry two positions in length with two decimal points.

The format of the table records and related extension form coding are not to be construed as the only methods of defining tables. Depending on the existing format of the table records or programmer's preference, many design alternatives are available.

Even though no special entries are required on the input form for table coding, it is shown in Figure 13-16 for reference. Note, however, the search

RPG INPUT SPECIFICATIONS

Line	Form Type	Filename	Sequence	Number (1-N)	Option (O)	Record Identifying Indicator or **	Position	Not (N)	C/Z/D	Character	Position	Not (N)	C/Z/D	Character	Position	Not (N)	C/Z/D	Character	Stacker Select P = Packed/B = Binary	From	To	Decimal Positions	Field Name	Control Level (L1-L9)	Matching Fields or Chaining Fields	Field Record Relation	Plus	Minus	Zero or Blank
0 1	Ø I	* D A T A R E C O R D S I N C L U D E I N F O R M A T I O N F O R T A X P A Y E R ' S N A M E , F I L I N G																											
0 2	Ø I	* S T A T U S , A N D T A X A B L E I N C O M E . . .																											
0 3	Ø I	*																											
0 4	Ø I	T A X I N C	S M	Ø /																								
0 5	Ø I																			1	2 5		N A M E						
0 6	Ø I																			2 6	3 1	Ø	T A X I N C						
0 7	Ø I																			3 2	3 3		S T A T U S						

search argument field
must be same size and
type as argument table

Fig. 13-16.   Input Specifications coding for federal income tax applications table program.

argument field, TAXINC, must be the same size and type as the table entries in the argument tables, TABS1 and TABM1. Furthermore, remember the value in TAXINC may not be equal to the value in TABS1 or TABM1, but may fall in the bracket range.

Calculation Specifications Coding
For Federal Income Tax Application
Program

A detailed discussion of the calculation coding for the federal tax application program is given in the following section. Reference should be made to Figure 13-17 for the coding entries relating to the logic discussed.

Line 04010.   Comments.

Line 04020.   The input field, STATUS, is compared to the alphanumeric literal MJ; if equal, resulting indicator 10 will turn on.

Lines 04030 and 04040.   Comments.

Line 04050.   If resulting indicator 10 turned on from the compare on line 04020 program control will branch to line 05060 where the computations for a married taxpayer filing jointly begin. If 10 is not turned on the normal sequence of instructions will be followed.

Line 04060 to 04090.   Comments.

Line 04100.   The search argument field, TAXINC, defined on input, looks up the entries in the argument table, TABS1. If an *equal to* or *less than* value is found in the table, the related value in the function table, TABS2, will be extracted.

Notice the 19 resulting indicator is entered in both the equal and less-than fields. When a table's low range of values are loaded in the argument table, the resulting indicators must be used in this manner. The processing logic of a *table low range* look-up is detailed in Figure 13-18.

Examination of Figure 13-18 indicates that when a higher-than table value is found, control *backs up* to the lower table entry.

If the higher amount of a table range was loaded, the resulting indicators would be entered in the High field (columns 54 and 55) and the Equal field. Then program control would extract the table entry one higher than the search argument value. This approach would not be logical for this application because the low range is subtracted from the taxable income amount to arrive at any excess subject to the additional percent.

The addition of the resulting indicator in the Low (or High) field is the only coding change in table coding to provide for a table range look-up instead of just an equal search.

RPG CALCULATION SPECIFICATIONS

International Business Machines Corporation

GX21-9093-1 U/M 050*
Printed in U.S.A.

Page 04 Program Identification TAXES

Line	Form Type	Control Level	And	Not	And	Not	Factor 1	Operation	Factor 2	Result Field	Field Length	Dec Pos	Half Adjust	Plus/High 1>2	Minus/Low 1<2	Zero/Equal 1 2	Comments
01	C						*COMPARE STATUS. ='MJ', MARRIED, GREATER THAN WOULD BE 'ST' FOR SINGLE										
02	C		01				STATUS	COMP	'MJ'							10	
03	C						*										
04	C						*IF = GOTO MARRIED COMPUTATION.										
05	C		10					GOTO	MARRIED								
06	C						*										
07	C						* SINGLE FILING STATUS COMPUTATION...										
08	C						*TAXABLE INCOME USED TO LOOK UP TABS1 WHICH INCLUDES LOW RANGE OF										
09	C						*SINGLE TAX TABLE...										
10	C						TAXINC	LOKUP	TABS1	TABS2				19	19		
11	C		19				TAXINC	LOKUP	TABS1	TABS3				20	20		
12	C						SUBTRACT TABS1 TABLE AMT FROM TAXABLE INCOME.GIVING AMT TO BE										
13	C						*MULTIPLIED BY PERCENT IN TABS3...										
14	C		20				TAXINC	SUB	TABS1	EXTRA	50						
15	C		20				EXTRA	MULT	TABS3	TAXEXT	50						

Line	Form Type	Control Level	And	Not	And	Not	Factor 1	Operation	Factor 2	Result Field	Field Length	Dec Pos	Half Adjust	High 1>2	Low 1<2	Equal 1 2	Comments
01	C						*										
02	C						*ADD EXTRA TAX AMT TO FIXED DOLLAR AMT FROM TABS2,GIVING TOTAL TAX..										
03	C		20				TAXEXT	ADD	TABS2	TAXDUE	60						
04	C							GOTO	END								
05	C						*COMPUTATIONS FOR MARRIED FILING STATUS...										
06	C						MARRIED	TAG									
07	C						*										
08	C						*TAXABLE INCOME USED TO LOOK UP TABM1 WHICH INCLUDES LOW RANGE OF										
09	C						*MARRIED TAX TABLE...										
10	C						TAXINC	LOKUP	TABM1	TABM2				29	29		
11	C		29				TAXINC	LOKUP	TABM1	TABM3				30	30		
12	C						*										
13	C						*SUBTRACT TABM1 TABLE AMT FROM TAXABLE INCOME GIVING AMT TO BE										
14	C						*MULTIPLIED BY PERCENT IN TABM3...										
15	C		30				TAXINC	SUB	TABM1	EXTRA							
16	C		30				EXTRA	MULT	TABM3	TAXEXT							

Line	Form Type	Control Level	And	Not	And	Not	Factor 1	Operation	Factor 2	Result Field	Field Length	Dec Pos	Half Adjust	High 1>2	Low 1<2	Equal 1 2	Comments
01	C						*										
02	C						*ADD EXTRA TAX AMT TO FIXED DOLLAR AMT FROM TABM2 GIVING TOTAL										
03	C		30				TAXEXT	ADD	TABM2	TAXDUE							
04	C						*										
05	C						END	TAG									

Fig. 13-17. Calculation Specifications coding for federal income tax application tables program.

Value in search argument field TAXINC	Values in argument table (TABS1) Entries
006171 ──────────────╮	000000
Value in TAXINC searches TABS1 until a higher table value is found. 008000 is higher than 006171, pro- gram control then "backs up" and extracts the 006000 table value and related function table value in TABS2.	000500 001000 002000 004000 006000 008000 (etc.)

Fig. 13-18.   Processing logic for table LOKUP when low amount of a table range is loaded in table entries.

Line 04110.   Another LOKUP operation is executed using the same processing logic as detailed for line 04100, only the percent table, TABS3, is now defined as the function table. Note the argument table, TABS1, relates to two function tables, TABS2 and TABS3. Resulting indicator 20 turns on if the table range is found.

Lines 04120 and 04130.   Comments.

Line 04140.   If a successful search resulted from the look-up on line 04110, the value in the low range amount table, TABS1, is subtracted from the taxable income amount (TAXINC) giving a remainder subject to additional tax. The mathematics of this operation is illustrated below:

Value in TAXINC		Value in TABS1		Value in EXTRA
006171	−	006000	=	00171

Line 04150.   The extra amount (EXTRA) determined in line 04140 is multiplied by the bracket percent from the function table, TABS3, to obtain the extra dollar amount as follows:

Value in EXTRA		Value in TABS3		Value in TAXEXT
00171	×	.24	=	00041

Lines 05010 and 05020.   Comments.

Line 05030.   The extra dollar amount (TAXEXT), computed on line 04150, is added to the fixed dollar amount from TABS2 to give total tax due

Source program listing:

```
           01 020 F*PROGRAM TO CALCULATE FEDERAL INCOME TAX FOR SINGLE AND MARRIED    TAXES
           01 030 F*STATUS. TABLES ARRANGED ON CARDS IN ALTERNATING FORMAT & SINGLE.  TAXES
0001       01 040 FTABFIL1 IT  F  80   80              EMFCM1   SYSIPT                 TAXES
0002       01 050 FTABFIL2 IT  F  80   80              EMFCM1   SYSIPT                 TAXES
0003       01 060 FTABFIL3 IT  F  80   80              EMFCM1   SYSIPT                 TAXES
0004       01 070 FTABFIL4 IT  F  80   80              EMFCM1   SYSIPT                 TAXES
0305       01 080 FTAXINC  IP  F  80   80              MFCM1    SYSIPT                 TAXES
0006       01 090 FTAXDUE  O   F 132  132        OF    PRINTERSYSLST                   TAXES
           02 010 E* LOW RANGE & FIXED AMT IN ALTERNATING FORMAT FOR SINGLE STATUS... TAXES
0007       02 020 E          TABFIL1       TABS1  7  25  6 0ATABS2   5 0A             TAXES
           02 030 E*PERCENT TABLE FOR SINGLE STATUS...                                TAXES
0008       02 040 E          TABFIL2       TABS3 25  25  2 2A                         TAXES
           02 050 E* LOW RANGE & FIXED AMT IN ALTERNATING FORMAT FOR MARRIED STATUS,,,TAXES
0009       02 060 E          TABFIL3       TABM1  6  25  6 0ATABM2   6 0A             TAXES
           02 070 E*PERCENT TABLE FOR MARRIED STATUS...                               TAXES
0010       02 080 E          TABFIL4       TABM3 25  25  2 2A                         TAXES
           03 010 I*DATA RECORDS INCLUDE INFCRMATICN FCR TAXPAYER'S NAME, FILING      TAXES
           03 020 I*STATUS, AND TAXABLE INCOME...                                     TAXES
           03 030 I*                                                                  TAXES
0011       03 040 ITAXINC  SM 01                                                      TAXES
0012       03 050 I                                        1   25 NAME               TAXES
0013       03 060 I                                       26   31 0TAXINC            TAXES
0014       03 070 I                                       32   33 STATUS             TAXES
           04 010 C*COMPARE STATUS,='MJ',MARRIED, GREATER THAN WOULD BE 'ST'FOR SINGLE TAXES
0015       04 020 C     01        STATUS    COMP 'MJ'                   10            TAXES
           04 030 C*                                                                  TAXES
           04 040 C*IF = GOTO MARRIED COMPUTATION.                                    TAXES
0016       04 050 C     10                  GOTO MARIED                               TAXES
           04 060 C*                                                                  TAXES
           04 070 C* SINGLE FILING STATUS COMPUTATION...                              TAXES
           04 080 C*TAXABLE INCOME USED TO LOOK UP TABS1 WHICH INCLUDES LOW RANGE OF  TAXES
           04 090 C*SINGLE TAX TABLE...                                               TAXES
0017       04 100 C          TAXINC    LOKUPTABS1    TABS2        1919                TAXES
0018       04 110 C     19   TAXINC    LCKUPTABS1    TABS3        2020                TAXES
           04 120 C*SUBTRACT TABS1 TABLE AMT FROM TAXABLE INCOME.GIVING AMT TO BE     TAXES
           04 130 C*MULTIPLIED BY PERCENT IN TABS3...                                 TAXES
0019       04 140 C     20   TAXINC    SUB  TABS1     EXTRA      50                   TAXES
0020       04 150 C     20   EXTRA     MULT TABS3     TAXEXT     50                   TAXES
           05 010 C*                                                                  TAXES
           05 020 C*ADD EXTRA TAX AMT TO FIXED DOLLAR AMT FROM TABS2.GIVING TOTAL TAX..TAXES
0021       05 030 C     20   TAXEXT    ADD  TABS2     TAXDUE     60                   TAXES
0022       05 040 C                    GOTO END                                       TAXES
           05 050 C*COMPUTATIONS FOR MARRIED FILING STATUS...                         TAXES
0023       05 060 C          MARIED    TAG                                            TAXES
           05 070 C*                                                                  TAXES
           05 080 C*TAXABLE INCOME USED TO LOOK UP TABM1 WHICH INCLUDES LOW RANGE OF  TAXES
           05 090 C*MARRIED TAX TABLE...                                              TAXES
0024       05 100 C          TAXINC    LOKUPTABM1    TABM2        2929                TAXES
0025       05 110 C     29   TAXINC    LCKUPTABM1    TABM3        3030                TAXES
           05 110 C*                                                                  TAXES
           05 120 C*SUBTRACT TABM1 TABLE AMT FROM TAXABLE INCOME GIVING AMT TO BE     TAXES
           05 130 C*MULTIPLIED BY PERCENT IN TABM3...                                 TAXES
0026       05 140 C     30   TAXINC    SUB  TABM1     EXTRA                           TAXES
0027       05 150 C     30   EXTRA     MULT TABM3     TAXEXT                          TAXES
           06 010 C*                                                                  TAXES
           06 020 C*ADD EXTRA TAX AMT TO FIXED DOLLAR AMT FROM TABM2 GIVING TOTAL TAX..TAXES
0028       06 030 C     30   TAXEXT    ADD  TABM2     TAXDUE                          TAXES
           06 040 C*                                                                  TAXES
0029       06 050 C          END       TAG                                           TAXES
0030       07 010 OTAXDUE  H  201       1P                                           TAXES
0031       07 020 O             OR               CF                                  TAXES
0032       07 030 O                          UDATE Y    8                            TAXES
0033       07 040 O                                     47 'FEDERAL INCOME TAX DUE'  TAXES
0034       07 050 O                                     77 'PAGE'                     TAXES
0035       07 060 O                          PAGE  Z    82                            TAXES
0036       07 070 O          H  1       1P                                           TAXES
0037       07 080 O             OR               CF                                  TAXES
0038       07 090 O                                     14 'NAME'                     TAXES
0039       07 100 O                                     50 'FILING        TAXABLE'    TAXES
0040       07 110 O                                     70 'FEDERAL INCOME'           TAXES
0041       07 120 O          H  2       1P                                           TAXES
0042       07 130 O             OR               OF                                  TAXES
0043       07 140 O                                     50 'STATUS         INCOME'    TAXES
0044       07 150 O                                     67 'TAX DUE'                   TAXES
0045       08 010 O          H  0       1P                                           TAXES
0046       08 020 O             OR               OF                                  TAXES
0047       08 030 O                                     40 '$'                        TAXES
0048       08 040 O                                     60 '$'                        TAXES
0049       08 050 O          D  2       01                                           TAXES
0050       08 060 O                          NAME       25                            TAXES
0051       08 070 O                          STATUS     32                            TAXES
0052       08 080 O                          TAXINC1    50                            TAXES
0053       08 090 O                          TAXDUE1    68                            TAXES
```

Fig. 13-19.   Source listing and printed report for federal income tax liability table program.

494

Printed report:

```
3/13/78                     FEDERAL INCOME TAX DUE                           PAGE    1
              NAME               FILING         TAXABLE        FEDERAL INCOME
                                 STATUS         INCOME           TAX DUE

ALFONSO ROBERTINA                  ST      $       6,171    $       1,151

ROBERT & MARY DOUGLAS              MJ             35,739           10,230

CAROLYN HENDERSON                  ST             13,826            3,159

ALEXANDER DUMAS                    ST            900,000           53,090

BARRY & HELEN BURPO                MJ             19,554            4,255

MICKEY & MINNIE MOUSE              MJ             77,991           32,174

JOE BEGINNER                       ST                877              126
```

Fig. 13-19. (Concluded)

(TAXDUE) which is the final answer. The values in the fields are shown below.

Value in TAXEXT		Value in TABS2		Value in TAXDUE
00041	+	01110	=	01151

Line 05040. The GOTO operation on this line allows program control to skip over all calculations for a married taxpayer filing jointly. There is no logical reason to pass through these calculations if the computations were made for a single taxpayer because individuals cannot file as both single and married.

Lines 05050 to 06040. The coding included in these lines is for a married taxpayer filing jointly and follows exactly the same logic discussed for the single taxpayer except the married taxpayer tables are used (TABM1, TABM2, and TABM3). Therefore, the computations will not be discussed. Remember the married taxpayer's tax computations were entered by the GOTO operation on line 04050 conditioned by the 10 indicator turned on if the value in STATUS equalled MJ.

Line 06050. Entry point for GOTO operation on line 05040.

Because the output coding is identical to procedures previously discussed, it is not shown in a separate figure, but may be examined in the source listing in Figure 13-19. The printed report generated from the federal income tax application program is also shown in Figure 13-19.

The tables in this program could be made an integral part of the source program and be loaded at compile time by omitting the file name in the From Filename field (columns 11–18) in the extension form. In addition, no table files would be defined in the File Description form. Compile tables are faster to process than object time tables and should be used when the table values are not often subject to change.

QUESTIONS

1. Explain the processing logic for related tables.
2. How many simple tables may be related to each other?
3. If the entries in a numeric table are not equal in length, how should the table data be entered on a record? If the entries in an alphanumeric table are not equal in length how should they be entered?
4. What changes are needed in the File Description Specifications to define an input file as a table file?
5. Shown below are two simple tables that relate to each other. Format the table entries in alternating format on a table record.

TABSTA	TABTAX
IDAHO	10.2%
CONNECTICUT	8.0%
FLORIDA	7.9%
OREGON	12.9%

Note: TABSTA must be sorted in ascending sequence.

6. Write the extension and calculation coding needed to process the tables in Question 5. Assume the search argument is STATE.
7. Examine the calculation coding below and define and explain the entries in Factor 1, Operation, Factor 2, and Resulting Indicator fields.

Factor 1	Operation	Factor 2	Result field	Field length	Decimal positions	Half adjust (H)	Plus	Minus	Zero or blank
							High 1 > 2	Low 1 < 2	Equal 1 = 2
18 19 20 21 22 23 24 25 26 27	28 29 30 31 32	33 34 35 36 37 38 39 40 41 42	43 44 45 46 47 48	49 50 51	52	53	54 55	56 57	58 59
EMPNO	LOKUP	TABNAM	TABRAT						40

8. Refer to Question 7. What are some of the rules that must be followed for the value in the field name included in Factor 1? May this entry be a numeric or alphanumeric literal?
9. What new entries are needed in the input form to process tables?
10. Given below are tables for a state's sales tax. Any sales above $1.07 are

subject to the standard seven percent tax rate. However, sales below that amount are taxed according to the range indicated.

Amount of Sale	Tax
.01–07	.00
.08–21	.01
.22–.35	.02
.36–.49	.03
.50–.64	.04
.65–.78	.05
.79–.92	.06
.93–1.07	.07

Format the table records so that all the entries for a table are included on one record. Use the low range for the amount-of-sale table.

11. Write the extension and calculation coding to process the tables in Question 10. How would you modify the calculation coding if the high range of the amount of sale was used instead of the low range?

12. Explain the processing logic of a low-range table look-up and a high-range look-up.

13. Do table entries have to be in any sorted order?

14. Define an object time table. A compile time table.

15. How does the coding in File Description, Input, Extension, and Calculations differ for object and compile time tables?

EXERCISES

13-1. The following tables are for a state's average county real property tax rates. The name of the county is included in one simple table and the average mill rate for a county in the other. Mill rate indicates the dollars per thousand dollars of assessed tax amount. For example, the tax liability on a dwelling assessed at $60,000 with a 40.6 mill rate would be computed as follows:

$$\text{Assessed value} \frac{\$60,000}{\$1,000} = 60 \text{ multiples of } \$1,000$$

Then:

$$60 \times 40.6 \text{ (mill rate per multiple)} = \$2,346 \text{ tax liability}$$

Table data is as follows:

TABCNT	TABMIL
FAIRFIELD	40.6
HARTFORD	46.2
LITCHFIELD	36.5
MIDDLESEX	44.4
NEW HAVEN	39.7
NEW LONDON	37.9
TOLLAND	35.1

Use COUNTIES for the table file name: NAMES for the primary file, and TAXREPT for the printer output file. The table names used for the program are indicated above.

Arrange the tables in alternating sequence on the table records with one Argument and one Function entry per record. Write the File Description and Extension Specification coding from the information given above.

13-2. From the information given above and your completed File Description and Extension Specifications write the input and calculation coding to process the tables and determine tax liability. The format of the data records in the NAMES file is shown below. Notice fields are included for county name (the search argument), assessed value, and veteran status.

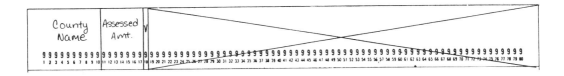

Veterans are eligible for a $1,000 tax exemption which is deducted before the tax liability is determined. Using the above example, the tax liability for a veteran would be computed as follows:

$$(60,000 - 1,000)/1,000 \times 40.6 = \$2,395.40.$$

Veteran status is determined by comparing the input field with the letter V; if equal, reduce the assessed value of the property before computing the tax liability. Following the mathematical procedures shown above, write the calculations to compute the taxpayer's tax liability. Use your own result field names and sizes.

13-3. Based upon the coding completed in Exercises 13-1 and 13-2, write the output coding for a report with the following format:

		0	1	2	3	4	5
		1234567890	1234567890	1234567890	1234567890	1234567890	1234567890
H	1	PAGE XXØX	STATE PRO	PERTY TAX S	TRUCTURE		
H	2		BY COUNTI	ES			
H	3		ØX/XX/XX				
	4						
H	5	COUNTY	ASSESSMENT	MILL RATE/	VETERAN	TAX	
H	6			THOUSAND		LIABILITY	
	7						
D	8	X X	ØX,XXX,XXØ	XX.X	YES	$ XXX,XXØ.XX	
	9				(NO)		
D	10	X X	X,XXX,XXØ	XX.X	YES	XXX,XXØ.XX	
	11				(NO)		
	12	NOTE:					
	13						
	14	HEADINGS ON EVERY PAGE					
	15						

13-4. Refer to Exercise 13-1 and modify the File Description form to load the table at *Compile Time* instead of *Object Time*. Also modify the extension form for a *Compile Time* table.

13-5. Refer to Exercise 13-1 and rewrite the extension form based on two other possible formats of the table data records.

13-6. A company offers quantity discounts based on a range of items purchased. The quantity range and discount percents are given in the following tables:

Not over 50—no discount

Over	Not over	Discount %
50 –	100	0.5%
100 –	200	1.0%
200 –	300	2.0%
300 –	500	2.25%
500 –	1000	2.50%
1000 –	any amount	3.00%

Write the File Description and Extension Specifications for the above tables to execute at object time. Create your own file and table names. You must also provide for a primary data file and a printer output file.

13-7. Write the input and calculation coding for the information included in Exercise 13-6. The format of the primary input data file records, which includes the search argument, is as follows:

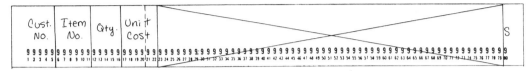

Use the quantity field in the input data file records to look up the range table to extract the discount from the quantity discount table. Determine the total cost of the sale and multiply it by the discount percent. Subtract the dollar amount of the discount from the total sales amount to determine the net amount of the sale. Accumulate totals for gross sales, discount amounts, and net sales. Refer to the Printer Spacing Chart in Exercise 13-8 for result field sizes.

13-8. The report for the program coded in Exercises 13-6 and 13-7 must be in the following format:

		0	1	2	3	4	5	6	7
H	1			CUSTOMER SALES REPORT					PAGE XXØX
H	2			AS OF ØX/XX/XX					
H	4	CUSTOMER	ITEM	QUANTITY	UNIT	TOTAL	DISCOUNT	NET	
H	5	NUMBER	NUMBER	PURCHASED	COST	COST	AMOUNT	AMOUNT	
D	7	XXXXX	XXXXXX	XX,XØX	X,XXØ.XX	XXX,XXØ.XX	XX,XXØ.XX	XXX,XXØ.XX	
D	9	XXXXX	XXXXXX	XX,XØX	X,XXØ.XX	XXX,XXØ.XX	XX,XXØ.XX	XXX,XXØ.XX	
TLR	11				TOTALS	X,XXX,XXØ.XX	XXX,XXØ.XX	XXX,XXØ.XX	
	13	NOTES:							
	15	① HEADINGS ON TOP OF QUERY PAGE							
	16	② TOTALS ON LAST PAGE ONLY							

LABORATORY ASSIGNMENTS

LABORATORY ASSIGNMENT 13-1:
DETERMINATION OF FACTORY OVERHEAD VARIANCES BASED ON FLEXIBLE BUDGET FORMULA

A company has a flexible budget formula for its factory overhead expenses. Each expense item has a fixed dollar amount plus a variable rate based on direct labor hours allowed for the level of production attained. The formula may be expressed as follows:

Budget for overhead expense = Fixed $ amt
+ (variable rate × direct labor hours allowed)

At the end of each accounting period the company wants to determine the flexible budget amount allowed and compare it with the actual dollar expense incurred for each overhead item to isolate any favorable or unfavorable variances. A favorable variance occurs when actual costs incurred are less than the budget allowance and unfavorable result when the actual costs are more than the budget allows.

Table data:

Account Number	Account Name	Fixed Amount in $	Variable rate per DL hour (2 dec. pos.)
600	INDIRECT LABOR	20000	015
601	FACTORY SUPPLIES	02000	100
602	FACTORY ELECTRICITY	03000	006
603	MACHINE REPAIRS	01000	010
604	PLANT MAINTENANCE	04000	020
605	FACTORY HEATING OIL	02700	004

Arrange the tables in any format you desire. (Hint: if the MOVE and MOVEL operations are used in calculations to separate table elements, only two tables would have to be specified.) The account name, fixed amount, and variable rate per direct labor hour table elements could be included in one table and separated by the move operations.

Data Record Format:

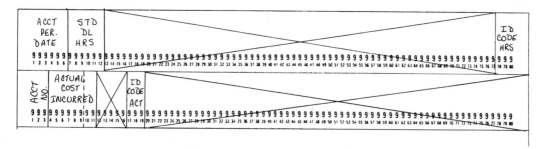

Calculations. After a successful table look-up, the direct labor hours allowed (field in data record coded with HRS) is multiplied by the value in the variable rate table to determine the total variable dollar budget amount. This amount is added to the fixed amount from the fixed amount table entry to obtain the total allowed budget amount allowed for the direct labor hours.

The favorable or unfavorable variance for each expense item is determined by subtracting the flexible budget amount from the actual costs incurred for the individual overhead expense item. If a negative answer results, the variance is favorable; if the answer is positive, the variance unfavorable.

Format of the Printed Report:

		0	1	2	3	4	5	6	7
H	1			VARIANCE ANALYSIS OF FACTORY OVERHEAD EXPENSES FOR						PAGE XXØX
D	2			XXX,XØX DIRECT LABOR HRS ENDING ØX/XX/XX						
	3									
D	4	ACCOUNT	ACCOUNT NAME		FIXED	VAR.RATE/	TOTAL	ACTUAL	VARIANCE	
D	5	NUMBER			AMOUNT	DL HR	BUDGET	COST	AMOUNT	
	6									
D	7	XXX	X————————X		XX,XXØ	X.XØ	XXX,XXØ.XX	XXX,XXØ.XX	XX,XXØ.XX	F
	8									U
D	9	XXX	X————————X		XX,XXØ	X.XØ	XXX,XXØ.XX	XXX,XXØ.XX	XX,XXØ.XX	F
	10									U
D	11	NOTES:								
	12									
	13		① HEADINGS ON EVERY PAGE.							
	14		② USE LETTER F AFTER VARIANCE IF FAVORABLE OR U IF UNFAVORABLE.							

Data for Laboratory Assignment:

Accounting Period Date	Standard Direct Labor Hours	
123179	050000	Record type coded with HRS in columns 78–80. (Only one card of this type in data file.)

Account Number	Actual Cost Incurred	
600	03000000	
601	05100000	Record type coded with ACT in columns 17–19.
602	00550000	
603	00840000	
604	.01500000	
605	00850000	

LABORATORY ASSIGNMENT 13-2:
WEEKLY PAYROLL CHECKS PROGRAM

This laboratory assignment requires you to complete individual payroll checks and stubs for the XYZ Company's employees. By federal law, all employee's wages are subject to two deductions: one for Federal Income Tax and the other

...he input information and calculation procedures

... record types are included in the data file. Only
...ayroll data followed by any number of employee
...record type. The format of the data records is as

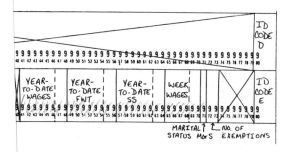

...acceptable methods of computing the federal
...eld under the pay-as-you-earn law of paying
...tage method is popular with a computerized
...use of tables.

...come tax withheld depends on the number of
...aims on the W-4 form and the payroll period.
..., biweekly, semimonthly, monthly, etc. The
...computation of the federal income tax to be
...ds.

...re to determine the federal income tax to be
... is as follows:

...iod the number of exemptions is multiplied by
...g a product that is subtracted from the week's
...ld the variable field name NET.

...used as the search field to search the ap-
...the corresponding functions.

...be created for the single employee category
...three for a married employee. The table information you will use

as table entries is listed below:

(a) SINGLE person—including head of household

If the amount of wages is:	The amount of income tax to be withheld shall be:

Not over $11 0

Over—	But not over—		of excess over—
$11	−$35	14%	−$11
$35	−$73	$3.36 plus 18%	−$35
$73	−$202	$10.20 plus 21%	−$73
$202	−$231	$37.29 plus 23%	−$202
$231	−$269	$43.96 plus 27%	−$231
$269	−$333	$54.22 plus 31%	−$269
$333	. . . .	$74.06 plus 35%	−$333

(b) MARRIED person—

If the amount of wages is:	The amount of income tax to be withheld shall be:

Not over $11 0

Over—	But not over—		of excess over—
$11	−$39	14%	−$11
$39	−$167	$3.92 plus 16%	−$39
$167	−$207	$24.40 plus 20%	−$167
$207	−$324	$32.40 plus 24%	−$207
$324	−$409	$60.48 plus 28%	−$324
$409	−$486	$84.28 plus 32%	−$409
$486	. . . .	$108.92 plus 36%	−$486

Refer to the creation and process techniques for the tables presented in the income tax application program in this chapter. A similar approach may be used for this laboratory assignment.

4. For the current year the Social Security tax (FICA) is computed at 5.85 percent of the first $16,500 of income. However, the percent and wage maximum subject to the Social Security tax is constantly changed by Congress and the student should be aware of any revisions in the tax structure.

Printed report. The printed report involves printing on a preprinted check form. Assume all of the literals shown in the printer spacing chart are already printed and the checks are attached together to form a continuous roll. You are only to fill in the areas identified by Xs and other punctuation with the variable input and calculated fields.

6 8 7 0

```
        0            1            2            3            4            5
   1234567890 1234567890 1234567890 1234567890 1234567890 1234567890
 1                          XYZ COMPANY                          8888
 2                          ALCATRAZ, CA
D 3                                         WEEK ENDING   0X/XX/XX
 4   PAY TO THE
D 5   ORDER OF        X                              X     EMP NO XXXX
 6
D 7      PAY EXACTLY                    ***$0.XX
 8
 9            ALWAYS ACCURATE BANK
10                 HOPE, CA
11                                            JOHN DIDIT, JR.
12                                            CONTROLLER
13
14   DO NOT CASH-CHECK STUB                       EMP NO XXXX
15
16   GROSS PAY   WITH.TAX   FICA    NET PAY    YTD EARNINGS
17
D 18  X,XX0.XX    X,XX0.XX   XX0.XX  X,XX0.XX   XX,XX0.XX
19
20              YTD WITH.TAX        YTD FICA
21
D 22            XX,XX0.XX          X,XX0.XX
23
24
```

Use the Following Data for Your Laboratory Assignment:

Employee Name	Stan Myers	Ken Hanson	Jim Walker	Sue Lynnely	Tony Deluz
Employee Number	2222	1111	3333	4444	6666
Social Security Number	030-21-6532	040-50-3871	020-31-5555	060-54-8754	050-63-5632
Earnings-to-Date	$10,500.00	$5,000.25	$17,500.00	$2,000.45	$7,992.10
Federal Income Tax to Date	$ 387.53	$ 385.75	$ 322.01	$ 98.50	$ 321.53
Social Security to Date	$ 614.25	$ 292.51	$ 965.25	$ 117.03	$ 467.54
Current Weekly Wages	$ 210.35	$ 358.66	$ 326.42	$ 98.32	$ 110.32
Number of Exemptions	3	4	2	1	2
Marital Status	M	S	M	S	S

14
RPG II
ARRAY CONCEPTS

COMPARISON OF ARRAYS TO TABLES

Because arrays and tables are so similar in nature, confusion may result as to when to use an array instead of a table or vice versa. Two broad considerations may help in determining whether to use an array or a table:

1. The method of loading the data in storage, and
2. How the stored data will be used.

Based on the first consideration, the criteria for using an array instead of a table may depend largely on the initial organization of the input data. For example, if a large amount of data is already arranged in table format, the table form should probably be used instead of repunching all of the data cards.

In addition, if each logical record included more than one physical record (a card) it is usually more efficient to use tables because the entries are automatically placed in the respective storage locations. However, when more than one card has to be used for each array entry, the data must be moved individually into the corresponding fields as it is processed.

More important in the choice between tables and arrays, however, is the consideration concerning how the data contained in the table or array is to be used in the program. Figure 14-1 compares some of the outstanding differences

Array Features	Table Features
1. A specific array entry may be referenced without searching the entire array. For example, if the 18th item in an array was needed it could be referenced immediately.	1. A table must be searched item by item until the appropriate entry is found. Hence, if the last entry in a 100 item table was needed the entire table would have to be searched until the 100th entry was located.
2. All of the data fields in an array may be referenced at one time. Consequently, only one set of coding specifications are required to accomplish the desired result. This feature is particularly useful in calculations using arrays.	2. All of the table entries cannot be referenced at one time. The table look-up specifications have to be repeated for every element contained in the table. Consequently, the complete program cycle would have to be repeated for every entry that is obtained.

Fig. 14-1.   Comparison of the features of arrays with tables.

between arrays and tables. An examination of the differences should reveal the advantages of arrays as compared to tables for a particular application.

It was stated in Chapter 13 that table data may be loaded in the program cycle at object or compile time. The difference arises when the table elements are loaded before processing. Object time table data is loaded from an input table file defined in File Description by the letter T in column 16 and the E in column 39. Compile time tables, however, are not defined as an input table file, but are an integral part of the source program (object after compilation) and are loaded with the program during execution.

Arrays may also be loaded at object or compile time; but, in addition, they may be loaded with data by the Input Specifications from any input file or as the result of calculations. The program examples discussed in this chapter will load the array data from input and calculations. Changes needed in the first program example to convert it from an input array to object and compile arrays will also be illustrated.

The first program example generates the report shown in Figure 14-2. If arrays were not used in the program a great deal more coding would have to be written to accomplish the same result. The advantage of arrays should become evident and appreciated by an examination and understanding of this report and the related RPG II source program coding to generate it.

An examination of the printed report in Figure 14-2 will help clarify an ideal application for arrays. The salesman amounts, 543.00, 570.00, 5,800.01, and so on, that are included on the line for week 1 represent the five field values in an array that will be defined in the Extension form. Each record in the input file includes the five salesman amounts for the related week number. As a record is read, the previous week's values are replaced with the next week. Hence, the five salesman values for week 1 will be replaced by the five for week 2, and so on. The important feature of arrays is that the five salesman values may be processed as one field (array) without defining each element separately.

BEST PRODUCTS INC.
WEEKLY ANALYSIS OF ORDERS RECEIVED BY SALESMAN
AS OF 3/13/78

WEEK NUMBER	SALESMAN 1	SALESMAN 2	SALESMAN 3	SALESMAN 4	SALESMAN 5	TOTAL ORDERS FOR WEEK
1	543.00	570.00	5,800.01	585.00	630.00	8,128.01
2	1,234.00	4,321.00	58.00	45,300.00	8,540.00	59,453.00
3	240.00	657.00	586.30	457.30	65.40	2,306.00
4	90.00	400.00	525.00	535.00	7,540.00	9,090.00
5	753.00	7,530.00	43.50	850.00	750.00	9,926.50
6	600.00	400.00	500.00	400.00	600.00	2,500.00
7	205.00	420.00	850.00	250.00	430.00	2,155.00
8	580.00	453.00	120.00	850.00	860.00	2,863.00
9	250.00	258.00	50.00	42.25	430.50	1,030.75
10	80.00	145.30	351.40	124.00	52.24	752.94
11	80.00	145.30	351.40	124.00	52.24	752.94
12	500.00	400.00	300.00	800.00	700.00	2,700.00
13	120.00	123.00	140.00	1,508.00	30.00	1,921.00
TOTAL	5,275.00	15,822.60	9,675.61	51,825.55	20,680.38	

TAL CO ORDERS 103,279.14

Fig. 14-2. Printed report generated from example array program.

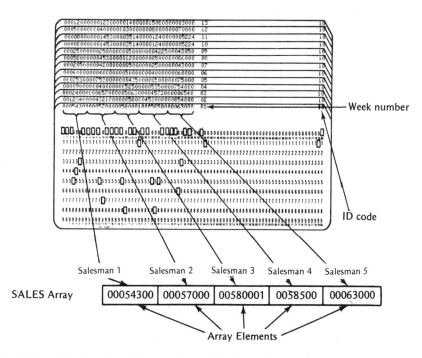

Fig. 14-3. Relationship of input data to loading of an array from input specifications.

Refer back to Figure 14-2 and locate the TOTAL line after the last salesman amount. This line of column totals represents another array loaded and accumulated in calculations from the weekly array.

Figure 14-3 shows the records in the input data file which are used to load the week's array. Notice that an individual record includes the values for the five salesmen; consequently, every record supplies the data to fill the array's elements. If the information for an array extended to more than one record, the array elements would have to be defined separately. This concept will be discussed later. The section at the bottom of Figure 14-3 shows how the five salesmen values are loaded as elements in the array.

RPG II CODING FOR ARRAYS LOADED FROM INPUT AND CALCULATIONS

An example program to process the data shown in Figure 14-3 will be used as the basis for discussing the coding concepts associated with arrays. Each coding form will be discussed separately to emphasize the entries used for arrays loaded from input and calculations. For an overall presentation of the program, refer to the source listing in Figure 14-9.

Figure 14-4 illustrates the File Description coding for the program example. Standard coding entries are used in this form with an input data and output printer file defined. Because the arrays are not loaded at object time, the data file containing the array values is defined as an ordinary input file without special coding.

Similar to the coding for tables, defining an array in a source program requires the use of the Extension Specifications form. An examination of Figure

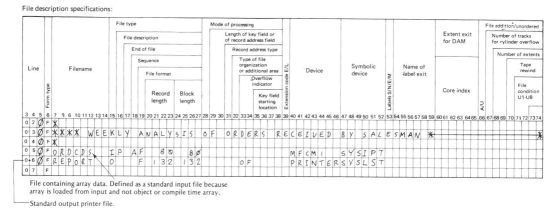

Fig. 14-4. File Description coding for example array program with array loaded from input.

Extension specifications:

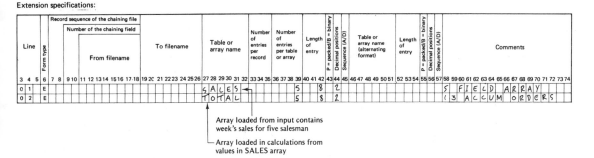

Line	Form type		Record sequence of the chaining file				To filename	Table or array name	Number of entries per record	Number of entries per table or array	Length of entry	P = packed/B = binary	Decimal positions	Sequence (A/D)	Table or array name (alternating format)	Length of entry	P = packed/B = binary	Decimal positions	Sequence (A/D)	Comments
			Number of the chaining field																		
				From filename																
3 4 5	6	7 8	9 10 11 12 13 14	15 16 17-18	19 20 21 22 23 24 25 26	27 28 29 30 31 32	33 34 35	36 37 38 39	40 41 42	43 44	45	46 47 48 49 50 51	52 53 54	55 56	57	58 59 60 61 62 63 64 65 66 67 68 69 70 71 72 73 74
0 1	E					SALES←		5	8	2							5 FIELD ARRAY
0 2	E					TOTAL		5	8	2							13 ACCUM ORDERS

Array loaded from input contains week's sales for five salesman
— Array loaded in calculations from values in SALES array

Fig. 14-5. Extension Specifications coding for arrays loaded from input and calculations.

14-5 shows the fields used for input and calculation time arrays. A discussion of the fields used for array processing is presented in the following paragraphs.

Form Type (Column 6).   Letter E must be used in column 6 for all source program extension cards which are placed in deck after File Description cards.

Columns 7 to 10.   Not used for Array coding.

From Filename (Columns 11-18.   Input file name entered in this column if array(s) is to be loaded at object time (to be discussed later in this chapter). Not used for input, calculation, or compile time arrays.

To Filename (Columns 19-26).   Printer output file name entered in this column if array is to be written out at end of job. Not used for arrays loaded from input or calculations.

Table or Array Name (Columns 27-32).   Name of all arrays used in programs must be entered on a separate line left-justified in this field. Array names *must not* begin with the letters TAB as they are reserved for table names only. All other rules for forming a field name must be followed. The two arrays used in the program example, SALES and TOTAL, are entered in the field. If individual elements of an array are to be accessed, the array name must be made shorter to accomodate a comma and the position of the element in the array.

Number of Entries Per Record (Columns 33-35).   Because SALES is loaded from input specifications and TOTAL loaded as a result of calculations, no entry is required in this field. If arrays were loaded at object or compile time, the corresponding value must be entered.

Number of Entries Per Table or Array (Columns 36-39).   Figure 14-5 shows a

5 is entered in this field which indicates the number of elements in an array. Number cannot exceed 9999.

Length of Entry (Columns 40-42). Notice in Figure 14-5 the number 8 is entered in this field indicating the length of the related array entries. Like table entries, every element in the array must be the same length. Numeric entries shorter than the maximum length must be padded with high-order zeros and alphanumeric with low-order blanks between the entries. Alphanumeric array elements may be a maximum of 256 characters and numeric, 15 digits. Any numeric data in binary format (rarely used) may only be nine long.

P = Packed/B = Binary (Column 43). Letter P is entered in this column if array elements are in packed format. Would not likely be from card input but tape disk, diskette, drum, or data cell stored file. B is entered if numeric data is in binary format.

Decimal Positions (Column 44). The 2 entered in this field for the SALES and TOTAL arrays (Figure 14-5) indicates two decimal positions are assigned to each array element in storage. This is identical to defining a numeric field as numeric in the input specifications (or calculations). Any number from zero to nine may be entered in this field to assign the required decimal positions.

Sequence (A/D) (Column 45). If the array elements are in ascending or descending sequence, the appropriate letter (A or D) may be entered in this field. Processing time will be decreased if the array is sorted and the sequence indicated. The only time sequence has to be specified, however, is if a High or Low array bracket look-up is used.

Columns 46-57. In this program example only one array is loaded from input (others in calculations). Therefore, it is not possible to have an alternating format for the elements. If two arrays were loaded from input (or object or compile) and the values were arranged in alternating format, the Array Name, Entry Length, Decimal Positions, and Sequence entries would be made for the alternating array.

Examine Figure 14-6 and observe how the SALES array is defined on the input form. Field Location fields (FROM and TO) contain the numbers 1 and 40 respectively, which represent the total length of the SALES array's records. Refer back to Figure 14-5 and notice each array element in SALES is eight digits long and there are five elements per array. Consequently, the length of the input field (array) defined on input corresponds to the length of the array records (8 × 5 = 40). The field name entered in columns 53-59 of the input form must be the same as the array defined in the extension form. Another field, WEEK, which is not part of the array contains the corresponding week number.

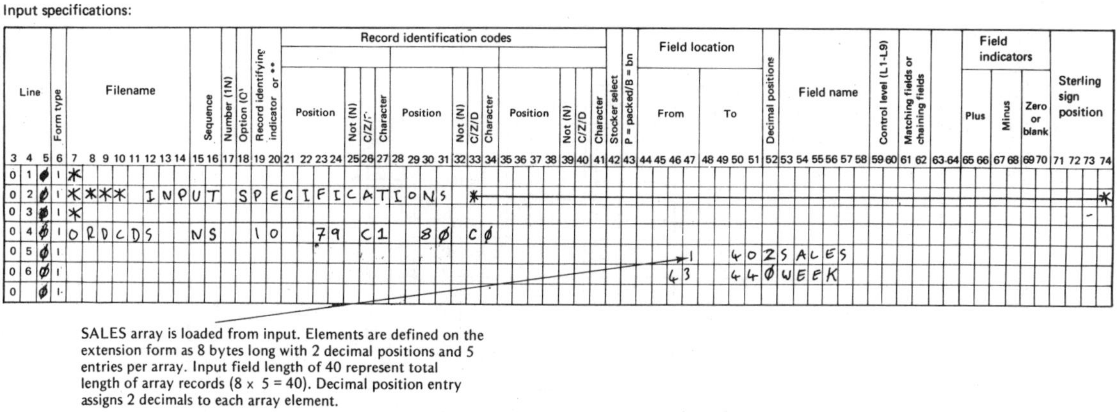

Input specifications:

Line	Form type	Filename	Sequence	Number (1N)	Option (O)	Record identifying indicator or **	Record identification codes Position	Not (N)	C/Z/␣	Character	Position	Not (N)	C/Z/D	Character	Position	Not (N)	C/Z/D	Character	Stacker select P = packed/B = bn	Field location From	To	Decimal positions	Field name	Control level (L1-L9)	Matching fields or chaining fields	Field indicators Plus	Minus	Zero or blank	Sterling sign position
0 1	␣	I	✳																										
0 2	␣	I	✳✳✳	INPUT SPECIFICATIONS											✳														✳
0 3	␣	I	✳																										—
0 4	␣	I	ORDCDS	NS	10		79		C1	80		C␣																	
0 5	␣	I															1	40	2	SALES						
0 6	␣	I															43	44	0	WEEK						
0	␣	I																								

SALES array is loaded from input. Elements are defined on the extension form as 8 bytes long with 2 decimal positions and 5 entries per array. Input field length of 40 represent total length of array records (8 × 5 = 40). Decimal position entry assigns 2 decimals to each array element.

Fig. 14-6. Input Specifications coding for SALES array loaded from input.

Regardless of when an array is loaded with elements (input, calculations, object, or compile) the Extension Specifications must define the array. Input Specifications is only used, however, to define arrays loaded directly from input coding as shown in this program example.

Refer to the Calculation Specifications form, Figure 14-7, and notice only three lines of calculations are needed to complete the totals required for the report in Figure 14-2. Locate line 060 and notice a new operation, XFOOT, is entered in the Operation Field (columns 28-32). The XFOOT operation automatically computes the sum of all the elements contained in the numeric array entered in Factor 2. Therefore, all the values of the elements in every record of the SALES array will be added and the sum stored in TSALES by only one calculation using the XFOOT operation. The result of the coding on line 060 for the first array record processed is shown at the bottom of Figure 14-7. Remember, however, the XFOOT operation is only for addition and not for any other arithmetic operation.

Examine line 100 of Figure 14-7 and notice the entire SALES array is added to the TOTAL array resulting in an accumulated amount in TOTAL. The TOTAL array was defined in the extension form and is loaded in calculations by the element values in SALES. After all the records for the SALES array are processed TOTAL will contain the totals for each array element. Look at the bottom of Figure 14-7 again and notice how the values in SALES are added to the TOTAL array for the first record processed.

Because output coding follows previously discussed coding procedures, reference may be made to the source listing in Figure 14-9 for an overall presentation. However, some discussion of output coding is needed because the printed output for arrays is unique. Remember an array is stored as one field without spaces in between the individual elements and when the array name is defined the complete array is accessed. This is ideal in calculations but on printed output requires other coding considerations. For example, if the array

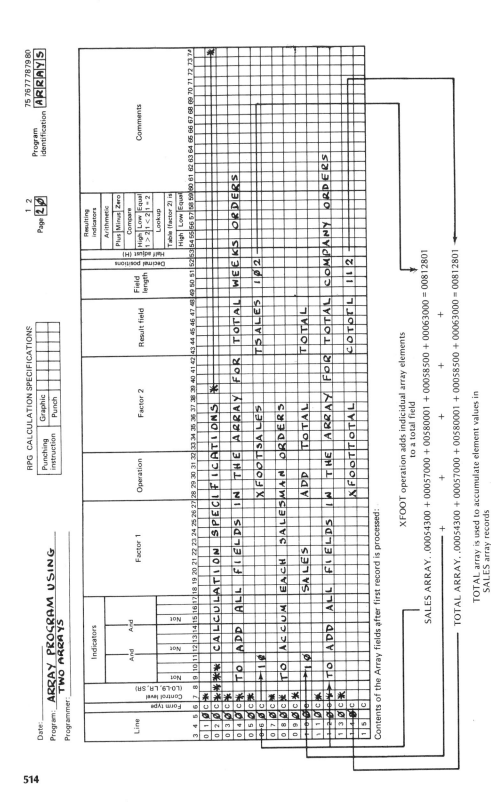

Fig. 14-7. Calculation Specifications coding for example program showing XFOOT operation and loading of an array (TOTAL) in calculations.

514

SALES was defined on output without editing, the elements would be printed next to each other without spaces separating them.

Three alternative coding procedures may be followed to control the spacing and editing of a numeric array. The first approach used in the example program uses an edit word formatted for the required spaces between entries. Locate lines 07060 and 07070 of the partial output coding in Figure 14-8. In order to format the required spacing between the SALES and TOTAL array elements, edit words are used with ampersands to control exact spacing requirements. Look at the bottom of Figure 14-8 and see how the edit word is used to edit the SALES array elements.

The ampersands used in the edit words in Figure 14-8 on lines 020 and 060 may be placed at the beginning of the word instead of the end. In addition, any number of spaces may be entered between elements, limited only by the width of the printer (and paper) used for the report. Edit word coding procedures were discussed in Chapter 3 (Figure 3-11) and a review of them might be timely for array editing. Obviously, any alphanumeric arrays cannot

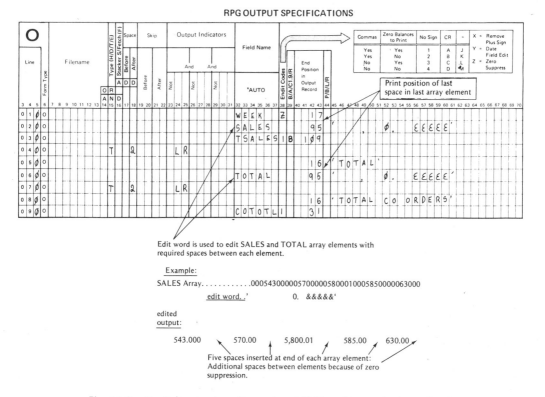

Fig. 14-8. Partial output coding using Edit Word to control spacing between array elements on printed output.

be edited and any spacing between elements has to be performed by identifying each element separately. This procedure will be discussed in one of the alternative editing and output procedures presented later.

Refer back to Figure 14-8 and notice 95 is entered as the end position for the SALES and TOTAL arrays on line 020 and 060. The print position represents the last blank position after the last array element, which is the fifth in this example. All other elements in the array are printed with the required spacing in relation to this position. Figure 14-9 illustrates the complete source listing for the array program discussed in this section. Comment cards are used to help the reader identify the logic of the program.

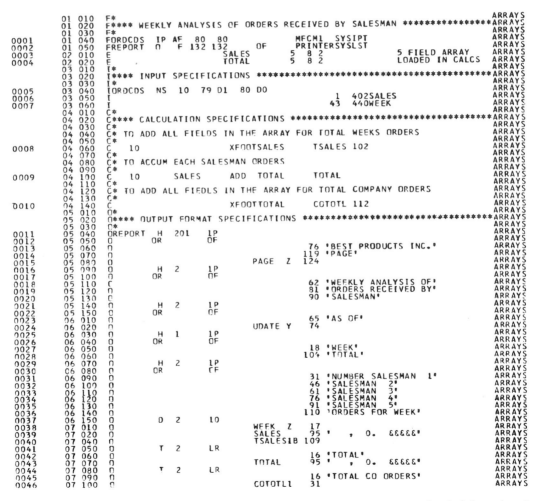

Fig. 14-9. Source listing of program using two arrays: one loaded from input specifications and the other in calculations.

ALTERNATIVE OUTPUT CODING
FOR THE EDITING
OF A PRINTED ARRAY

Figure 14-10 shows an alternative for the editing of the elements of a numeric array. In this example the SALES and TOTAL arrays (lines 020 and 060) are edited with an edit code instead of an edit word as in the program example. Two spaces are automatically inserted to the left of every array element. This is a fast and easy method of editing an array but does not give the programmer any flexibility in formatting printed output. Any of the available edit codes may be used with a numeric array; however, only two spaces will be entered between the array elements when they are printed. The edited result of the edit code 1 on the SALES array is shown at the bottom of Figure 14-10.

Another alternative for the printing of array is to define each element separately as shown in Figure 14-11. If individual array elements are to be accessed in this manner, the length of the array name must be considered when defined in the extension form because of the *required comma* and *element number*.

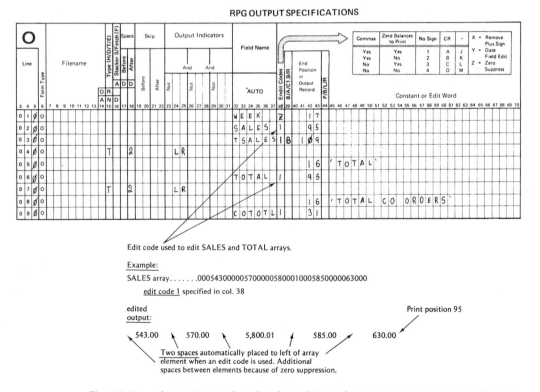

Fig. 14-10. Alternative coding for the editing of a numeric array using edit code.

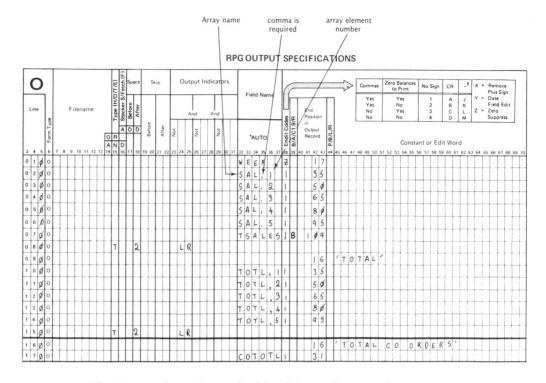

Fig. 14-11.   Alternative method for defining the printed output for an array. Array elements are defined individually.

Notice in the figure the array name has been changed from SALES to SAL which would, of course, require a change in the extension and input forms for the sample program. SAL,1 represents the first element of the SAL array; SAL,2, the second; SAL,3, the third, and so on.

This method must be used for alphanumeric arrays because edit words or codes are only applicable to numeric. However, if different editing is required for individual elements of a numeric array output, coding would have to be formatted this way. This method does provide flexibility in printed output, but requires more coding.

SOURCE PROGRAM CODING WHEN ARRAY FIELDS ARE SCATTERED WITHIN THE RECORD

Assume that the fields for the array contained in the data card for the previously discussed program were not arranged in consecutive order (one after the other), but as illustrated in the punched card shown in Figure 14-12 in the event that array fields are scattered throughout the card each field must be

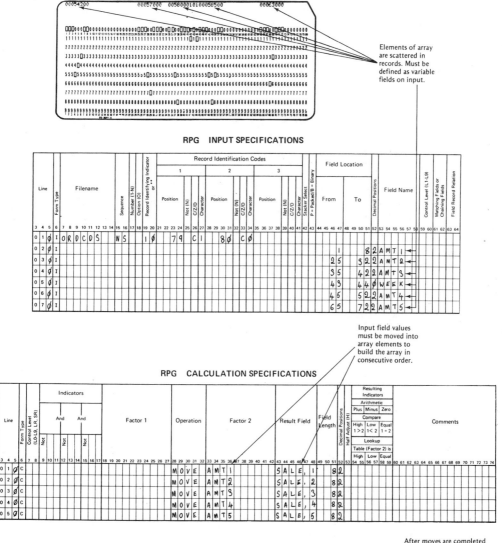

Fig. 14-12. Input and calculation coding when array fields are scattered within a record.

defined individually according to its location in the card. Figure 14-12 also shows the Input Specifications coding needed to define the fields in the card record. Notice that they are described according to standard coding procedures.

After the scattered fields are defined on input, every field that is to be included in the array must be moved into an individual storage area. Figure 14-12 also illustrates the Calculation Specifications coding to move the respective array field into its proper consecutive location in the array. Observe that each one of the scattered array fields defined in the Input Specifications is moved into a Result field that must include the name of the array specified in the Extension Specifications along with an index number that refers to its exact location in the array. This rearrangement of array entries must be done before any other calculations using array information are performed in the program.

File Description and Output-Format Specifications coding remain the same with one important exception. Because array names are limited to six characters, the array name SALES must be reduced to SALE as the complete array name, comma, and location number cannot exceed the six character limit. Otherwise, the coding entries are standard and are, therefore, not shown for the program revision.

CODING FOR AN ARRAY WHEN THE DATA IS INCLUDED ON MORE THAN ONE CARD

The coding for any array is considerably more complex when the data has to extend to more than one record. Therefore, when possible, all of the data for an array should be contained in one record or the use of tables should be considered as a possible alternative. However, the nature of the job may dictate that arrays are the best approach and the programmer should, therefore, be familiar with the coding procedures needed for arrays when the data is included on more than one record.

Assume for the example program previously presented, the array SALES consists of 12 elements instead of five. Because there are only 80 columns on the Hollerith card and the array element sizes are specified as eight long, the maximum number of array elements per record is 10. The array, however, consists of 12 elements which indicates that two must be included on another card with the week number. Even though the array elements are arranged in consecutive order on the cards, they cannot be included in the single input array, but must be specified individually as shown in Figure 14-13.

Because the array is loaded from input the SAL array name on line 020 (Figure 14-13) will provide the first 10 elements, and SAL,11 and SAL,12 will provide the other two, for a total of 12.

RPG EXTENSION SPECIFICATIONS

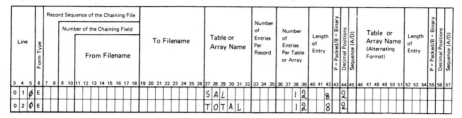

Line	Form Type	Record Sequence of the Chaining File / Number of the Chaining Field / From Filename	To Filename	Table or Array Name	Number of Entries Per Record	Number of Entries Per Table or Array	Length of Entry	P = Packed/B = Binary	Decimal Positions	Sequence (A/D)	Table or Array Name (Alternating Format)	Length of Entry	P = Packed/B = Binary	Decimal Positions	Sequence (A/D)
0 1	E			SAL		1 2	8		2						
0 2	E			TOTAL		1 2	8		2						

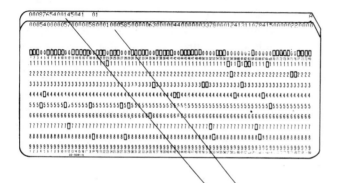

Array SAL includes 12 elements: 10 on one record and two on another.

RPG INPUT SPECIFICATIONS

Line	Form Type	Filename	Sequence	Number (1-N)	Option (O)	Record Identifying Indicator or **	Record Identification Codes 1 Position	Not (N)	C/Z/D	Character	2 Position	Not (N)	C/Z/D	Character	3 Position	Not (N)	C/Z/D	Character	Stacker Select	P = Packed/B = Binary	Field Location From	To	Decimal Positions	Field Name	Control Level (L1-L9)	Matching Fields or Chaining Fields	Field Record Relation
0 1	I	ORDCDS	NS			1 0															1	8 0 2	SAL			
0 2	I																									
0 3	I		SM	2 0		8 0		CA																		
0 4	I																			1	8 2	SAL, 1 1				
0 5	I																			q	1 6 2	SAL, 1 2				
0 6	I																			1 9	2 0 0	WEEK			

This record contains the two additional fields for the 12 field array. When the array fields span more than one card they must be defined individually on all other cards except the first one.

Fig. 14-13. Extension and Input Specifications when data for an array is included on more than one record.

521

INDIVIDUAL ARRAY ELEMENT LOOKUP

When a table entry is found in a lookup instruction the corresponding entry is available for further processing because the value is stored as a field. Array lookup logic differs in that arrays are searched only to determine if the element value is stored in the array. When the array value is found it is not retained as a storage value.

Figure 14-14 shows the coding for an array lookup. Similar to tables Factor 1 contains the search argument which may be a variable field or literal; the Operation Field, the operation code LOKUP; Factor 2, the name of the array; and a Resulting Indicator in the corresponding Resulting Indicator Field(s). If an equal search was required an indicator must be entered in columns 58 and 59 (Equal). However, if a low range was required columns 56 and 57 (Low) and 58 and 59 must be used and if a high range lookup columns 54 and 55 (High) along with columns 58 and 59. Any indicator turned on by the conditions that satisfy the array lookup may be used to condition subsequent calculations and/or output. Notice the Result Field is *not* used with array lookup as arrays can not relate to each other in the same way simple tables do.

In the example shown in Figure 14-14 the search field NUM, which must be the same type and size as the array elements values, is used to lookup the array SAL. If the same value is found in the array, indicator 44 will turn on which may be used to condition any subsequent calculations and/or output. Remember, however, the array element value cannot be retained or referenced when the array name (SAL) is used without indexing. This lookup procedure only determines whether the element value is in the array.

Indexing may be used to give additional flexibility and provide processing efficiency in array lookup. Figure 14-15 shows two examples of array lookup with indexing. The first example on lines 010 to 030 shows how indexing may be used to decrease array lookup time. The instruction on line 010 compares the value in NUM with the numeric constant 101. If equal to or higher than Resulting Indicator, 99 turns on, or if less than, 98 will turn on. If less than (98

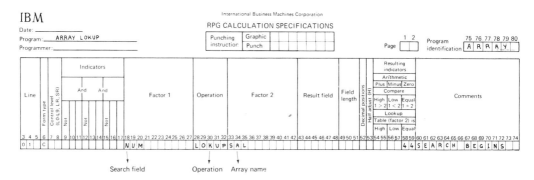

Fig. 14-14. Calculation specifications for array LOKUP.

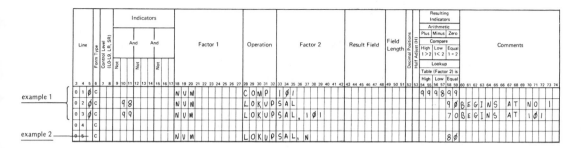

Fig. 14-15. Array lookup example using a numeric constant for the index and example using a variable numeric field for the index.

on) the instruction on line 020 will be executed which causes the array lookup to begin at the first element. On the other hand, if the value in NUM is equal to or greater than 101 the instruction on line 030 will execute and the array lookup will begin at the 101st element in the array. Notice the array name is used with the required comma and the corresponding numeric constant for the index. Because an equal condition is required, the result of the array lookup is tested by the indicator in the equal field (columns 58–59). As with the previous example in Figure 14-14, if the array element is found it is not retained and available for processing. Consequently, the lookup with a constant index is used only to determine if the element is present in the array.

The example on line 050 of Figure 14-15 shows array lookup with a variable numeric field index. The numeric index (N) may be defined as an input field or as a result field. The array search begins at the element specified as the value in the index N and if the conditions of the search are satisfied the location of the array element found may be referenced by specifying the array name and index. Again the actual element value is not retained from the lookup but may be referenced as indicated. If the array element is not found the index is automatically set to one before the next lookup. Because arrays are not related logically as tables; a lookup in one array, using the variable numeric field index method, may access the corresponding element in another array by indicating the array name and index from the lookup. By this procedure arrays may be processed as logically related arrays.

OTHER ARRAY CONCEPTS INCLUDING INDEXING AND THE MOVEA OPERATION

Two new concepts, indexing with a variable and the Move Array (MOVEA) operation, are introduced in this section. From the preceding discussion it has been established that individual array elements may be referenced by using the array name, comma, and the element number (position in array). In all other examples the element number was a constant (see Figure 14-12 or Figure 14-13); however, a variable field may be used instead.

For example, an array entry (AL,X) indicates an array element whose position in the AL array is based on the value in the variable field X. A looping operation may be used in calculations to index the value in X to test or extract an element based on value in the variable. This concept will be presented in the discussion of the example program; but before that, the logic of the Move Array (MOVEA) operation will be introduced.

The MOVEA operation provides for the movement of all or part of the data in an array to *another array or to a field*. Movement of data starts with the first element of the array if the array name is used or with the array element if indexing is specified. The movement of data from any array (or field) terminates when all of the elements have been moved or when the Result Field is filled. Figure 14-16 shows examples of the MOVEA operation coding and results of data movement.

A program example will be used to illustrate use of variable field indexing for an array and the MOVEA operation. The objective of the program is to reverse the first and last names of customers included in a name field. For example, customer names are stored in a name field in a last name first order as FOX DARRELL. The end result of the program is to reverse the name order and print DARRELL FOX on output. A separate field cannot be defined for the last and first names because the records are already formatted and the name lengths are not the same.

Because the two arrays used in the program are loaded from input and calculations respectively, File Description coding follows standard input file entries. Figure 14-17 illustrates the extension form coding for the two arrays used in the program.

Line 010 of the extension form defines the AL array as 15 bytes in length with each element one byte long. The AL array is loaded by the input form with the values in the data records (Figure 14-18). Line 040 defines the AF array which is loaded in calculations with the customer's first name separated from the AL array by a sequence of instructions.

The input form in Figure 14-18 defines the AL array because it is loaded on input. Notice the 15-byte length is identical to the multiple of the number of entries per table times the entry length in the extension form columns 36–39 and 40–42 respectively. Because the data is alphabetic, an entry is not needed in the decimal position field.

The separation of the last and first names in the AL array is identified by a blank between the names (Figure 14-19). Calculation instructions are needed to search the array for the blank and store the first name in the AF array and the last name in a field. Hence, every element in the AL array must be examined, starting with the first, until the blank is sensed. Once the blank is located, the appropriate instructions are executed to move array elements into the required field and AF array. These instructions and related logic are detailed below.

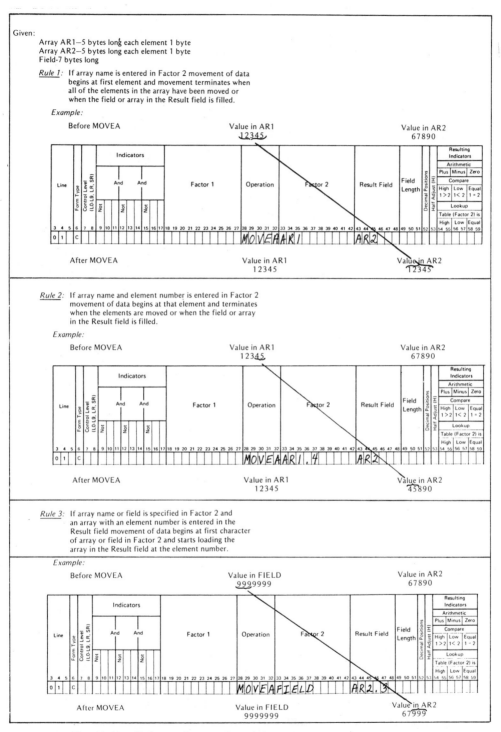

Given:

Array AR1—5 bytes long each element 1 byte
Array AR2—5 bytes long each element 1 byte
Field-7 bytes long

Rule 1: If array name is entered in Factor 2 movement of data begins at first element and movement terminates when all of the elements in the array have been moved or when the field or array in the Result field is filled.

Example:

Before MOVEA

Value in AR1
12345

Value in AR2
67890

After MOVEA

Value in AR1
12345

Value in AR2
12345

Rule 2: If array name and element number is entered in Factor 2 movement of data begins at that element and terminates when the elements are moved or when the field or array in the Result field is filled.

Example:

Before MOVEA

Value in AR1
12345

Value in AR2
67890

After MOVEA

Value in AR1
12345

Value in AR2
45890

Rule 3: If array name or field is specified in Factor 2 and an array with an element number is entered in the Result field movement of data begins at first character of array or field in Factor 2 and starts loading the array in the Result field at the element number.

Example:

Before MOVEA

Value in FIELD
9999999

Value in AR2
67890

After MOVEA

Value in FIELD
9999999

Value in AR2
67999

Fig. 14-16.   Rules and examples of the MOVEA (Move Array) operation.

Programmer _____   RPG Extension Specifications

Line	Form Type	From Filename	To Filename	Table or Array Name	Number of Entries Per Record	Number of Entries Per Table or Array	Length of Entry	Table or Array Name (Alternating Format)	Length of Entry	Comments
0 1	E			AL		5	1			
0 2	E*	ARRAY AL LOADED ON INPUT WITH LAST AND FIRST NAME								
0 3	E*	ARRAY AF LOADED IN CALCULATIONS WITH FIRST NAME..								
0 4	E			AF		1	1			

Fig. 14-17. Extension form coding for example program to separate the last and first names of an array loaded by input.

Programmer _____   RPG INPUT SPECIFICATIONS

Line	Form Type	Filename	Sequence	Number (1-N)	Option (O)	Record Identifying Indicator	Record Identification Codes Position 1	From	To	Decimal Positions	Field Name	Field Indicators
0 1	I	NAMFIL	AA			01						
0 2	I							1	15		AL	

Fig. 14-18. Input form coding for example program to separate the last and first names of an array loaded by input.

Line 04010.   The variable index (X) is created and defined.

Lines 04020 and 04030.   All resulting indicators used in calculations are set off to prevent any unwanted instructions from executing when a record is processed.

Line 04040.   Entry point for GOTO operation on line 04100.

Line 04050.   Comment.

Line 04060.   Index field X is incremented by one to identify array element to be examined.

Lines 04070 and 04080.   Comments.

Line 04090.   The array element, determined by the value in X, is compared to a blank. If equal to a blank, resulting indicator 20 will turn on; if higher (a character from A to Z) 30 will turn on.

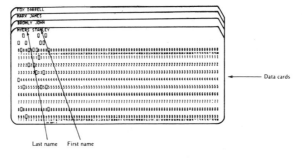

Last name   First name

Data cards

RPG CALCULATION SPECIFICATIONS

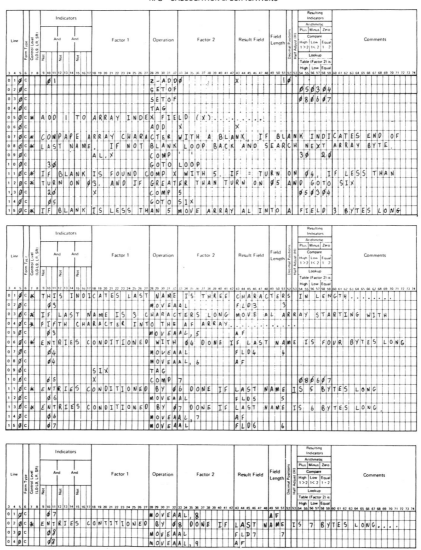

Line	Form Type	Control Level	Indicators	Factor 1	Operation	Factor 2	Result Field	Field Length	Dec	Resulting Indicators	Comments
01	C				Z-ADD	0	X	1 0			
02	C				SETOF					05 03 04	
03	C				SETOF					08 06 07	
04	C				TAG						
05	C*			ADD 1 TO ARRAY INDEX FIELD (X)........							
06	C				ADD		X				
07	C*			COMPARE ARRAY CHARACTER WITH A BLANK, IF BLANK INDICATES END OF							
08	C*			LAST NAME. IF NOT BLANK LOOP BACK AND SEARCH NEXT ARRAY BYTE.							
09	C			AL,X	COMP	' '				30 20	
10	C		30		GOTO	LOOP					
11	C*			IF BLANK IS FOUND COMP X WITH 5. IF = TURN ON 04, IF LESS THAN							
12	C*			TURN ON 03, AND IF GREATER THAN TURN ON 05 AND GOTO SIX							
13	C		20	X	COMP	5				05 03 04	
14	C		05		GOTO	SIX					
15	C*			IF BLANK IS LESS THAN 5 MOVE ARRAY AL INTO A FIELD 3 BYTES LONG							

Line	Form Type	Control Level	Indicators	Factor 1	Operation	Factor 2	Result Field	Field Length	Dec	Resulting Indicators	Comments
01	C*			THIS INDICATES LAST NAME IS THREE CHARACTERS IN LENGTH.........							
02	C		03		MOVEA	AL	FLD3	3			
03	C*			IF LAST NAME IS 3 CHARACTERS LONG MOVE AL ARRAY STARTING WITH							
04	C*			FIFTH CHARACTER INTO THE AF ARRAY..........							
05	C		03		MOVEA	AL,5	AF				
06	C*			ENTRIES CONDITIONED WITH 04 DONE IF LAST NAME IS FOUR BYTES LONG							
07	C		04		MOVEA	AL	FLD4	4			
08	C		04		MOVEA	AL,6	AF				
09	C			SIX	TAG						
10	C			X	COMP	7				08 06 07	
11	C*			ENTRIES CONDITIONED BY 06 DONE IF LAST NAME IS 5 BYTES LONG							
12	C		06		MOVEA	AL	FLD5	5			
13	C*			ENTRIES CONDITIONED BY 07 DONE IF LAST NAME IS 6 BYTES LONG							
14	C		06		MOVEA	AL,7	AF				
15	C		07		MOVEA	AL	FLD6	6			

Line	Form Type	Control Level	Indicators	Factor 1	Operation	Factor 2	Result Field	Field Length	Dec	Resulting Indicators	Comments
01	C		07		MOVEA	AL,8	AF				
02	C*			ENTRIES CONTITIONED BY 08 DONE IF LAST NAME IS 7 BYTES LONG....							
03	C		08		MOVEA	AL	FLD7	7			
04	C		08		MOVEA	AL,9	AF				

Fig. 14-19. Calculation form coding for example program to separate the last and first names of an array loaded by input. Indexing, looping, and the MOVEA operation are used.

527

Line 04100. If the value in array index X is greater than blank (A − Z), the GOTO operation on this line will transfer control back to line 04040 and the sequence of instructions will be repeated. Notice this operation is conditioned by the 30 indicator (turned on in line 04090 if X was greater than blank). If no indicator had been used here, perpetual looping would result because control could never exit from the loop.

Lines 04110 and 04120. Comments.

Line 04130. When a blank is sensed in the compare on line 04090, control is transferred out of the loop and the value in X is compared to five. The value in X indicates in what position the blank is located in the AL array. If value in X is less than five it indicates the last name is three bytes in length; if equal to, last name would be four bytes; and if greater than, it would be more than four bytes.

Line 04140. If value in X is greater than five, resulting indicator 05 turns on by compare on line 04130 and program control will branch to line 05090 followed by a sequence of instructions to separate the last and first name parts of the AL array.

Lines 04150 and 05010. Comments.

Line 05020. If the value in X is less than five, the last name is three bytes in length (assuming no last names are two bytes) and the MOVEA operation is used to move the first three AL elements into the variable field, FLD3, defined as three bytes in length. This operation has isolated the last name into a separate field.

Lines 05030 and 05040. Comments.

Line 05050. Because the last name is three bytes in length, the first name is moved (MOVEA operation) into the AF array beginning with the fifth byte in the AL array.

Line 05060. Comment.

Line 05070. Lines 05070–06040 follow the same logic as the discussion for lines 05020 and 05050 except the blank position is found in a higher location in the AL array. The corresponding MOVEA operations isolated the last and first names accordingly.

Examination of the output coding in Figure 14-20 shows that usual coding procedures are followed. The first name of a customer is contained in the AF array and the last name in the respective field size, identified by the

Source program listing:

```
          01 020  F*THIS PROGRAM USES TWO ARRAYS-ONE BUILT FROM INPUT RECORDS & THE    MOVEA
          01 030  F*OTHER FROM CALCULATIONS. MOVEA OPERATION CODE IS USED TO SEPARATE   MOVEA
          01 040  F*THE LAST & FIRST NAMES FROM THE INPUT ARRAY....                     MOVEA
          01 050  F*                                                                    MOVEA
0001      01 060  FNAMFIL IP F  15  15              MFCM1 SYSIPT                         MOVEA
0002      01 070  FNAMES  O  F 132 132     OF       PRINTERSYSLST                        MCVEA
0003      02 010  E                          AL      15  1                              MOVEA
          02 020  E* ARRAY AL LOADED ON INPUT WITH LAST AND FIRST NAMES.........        MCVEA
          02 030  E* ARRAY AF LOADED IN CALCULATIONS WITH FIRST NAME........            MOVEA
0004      02 040  E                          AF       1 11                              MOVEA
0005      03 010  INAMFIL AA  01                                                        MOVEA
0006      03 020  I                                          1  15 AL                   MOVEA
0007      04 010  C   01                 Z-ADDO         X       10                      MOVEA
0008      04 020  C                      SETOF                   050304                 MOVEA
0009      04 030  C                      SETOF                   080607                 MOVEA
0010      04 040  C          LOOP        TAG                                            MOVEA
          04 050  C* ADD 1 TO ARRAY INDEX FIELD (X).........                            MOVEA
0C11      04 060  C          1           ADD  X         X                              MCVEA
          04 070  C* COMPARE ARRAY CHARACTER WITH A BLANK, IF BLANK INDICATES END OF     MOVEA
          04 080  C* LAST NAME. IF NOT BLANK LOOP BACK AND SEARCH NEXT ARRAY BYTE..     MCVEA
0012      04 090  C          AL,X        COMP ' '                        30  20         MOVEA
0013      04 100  C          30          GOTO LOOP                                      MOVEA
          04 110  C* IF BLANK IS FOUND COMP X WITH 5. IF = TURN ON 04, IF LESS THAN      MCVEA
          04 120  C* TURN ON 03, AND IF GREATER THAN TURN ON 05 AND GOTO SIX            MOVEA
0014      04 130  C          20          COMP 5         X               050304         MOVEA
0015      04 140  C          05          GOTO SIX                                       MOVEA
          04 150  C* IF BLANK IS LESS THAN 5 MOVE ARRAY AL INTO A FIELD 3 BYTES LONG    MCVEA
          05 010  C* THIS INDICATES LAST NAME IS THREE CHARACTERS IN LENGTH........     MOVEA
0016      05 020  C          03          MOVEAAL        FLD3  3                         MOVEA
          05 030  C* IF LAST NAME IS 3 CHARACTERS LONG MOVE AL ARRAY STARTING WITH      MCVEA
          05 040  C* FIFTH CHARACTER INTO THE AF ARRAY............                      MOVEA
0C17      05 050  C          03          MOVEAAL,5      AF                              MOVEA
          05 060  C* ENTRIES CONDITIONED WITH 04 DONE IF LAST NAME IS FOUR BYTES LONG   MOVEA
0018      05 070  C          04          MOVEAAL        FLD4  4                         MCVEA
0019      05 080  C          04          MOVEAAL,6      AF                              MOVEA
0020      05 090  C          SIX         TAG                                            MOVEA
0021      05 100  C          05          COMP 7                          080607         MCVEA
          05 110  C* ENTRIES CONDITIONED BY 06 DONE IF LAST NAME IS 5 BYTES LONG...     MOVEA
0022      05 120  C          06          MOVEAAL        FLD5  5                         MOVEA
          05 130  C* ENTRIES CONDITIONED BY 07 DONE IF LAST NAME IS 6 BYTES LONG..      MOVEA
0023      05 140  C          06          MOVEAAL,7      AF                              MOVEA
0024      05 150  C          07          MOVEAAL        FLD6  6                         MOVEA
0025      06 010  C          07          MOVEAAL,8      AF                              MOVEA
          06 020  C* ENTRIES CONDITIONED BY 08 DONE IF LAST NAME IS 7 BYTES LONG....    MCVEA
0026      06 030  C          08          MOVEAAL        FLD7  7                         MOVEA
0027      06 040  C          08          MOVEAAL,9      AF                              MOVEA
0028      07 010  ONAMES  H  101          1P                                           MOVEA
0029      07 020  O       OR              OF                                           MOVEA
0030      07 030  O                                       22 'FIRST    LAST'            MCVEA
0031      07 040  O       H  2            1P                                           MOVEA
0032      07 050  O       OR              OF                                           MOVEA
0033      07 060  O                                       22 'NAME     NAME'            MOVEA
0034      07 070  O       D  2            01                                           MOVEA
0035      07 080  C                       03      AF       B  19                       MCVEA
0036      07 090  O                       03      FLD3        25                       MCVEA
0037      07 100  O                       04      AF       B  19                       MOVEA
0038      07 110  O                       04      FLD4        25                       MOVEA
0039      07 120  O                       06      AF       B  19                       MCVEA
0040      07 130  O                       06      FLD5        25                       MOVEA
0041      07 140  O                       07      AF       B  19                       MOVEA
0042      07 150  O                       07      FLD6        25                       MCVEA
0043      08 010  O                       08      AF          19                       MCVEA
0044      08 020  O                       08      FLD7     B  25                       MOVEA
```

Printed result:

FIRST NAME	LAST NAME
STANLEY	MYERS
JOHN	BROMLY
JAMES	MARX
DARRELL	FOX

Fig. 14-20. Source listing and printed output for program using the MOVEA operation and indexing with a variable field assigned to array elements.

number included in the field name (FLD3 indicates last name is three bytes in length.

The source listing and resultant output is illustrated in Figure 14-20. The first and last names are not separated by only one space because it would require a repeat of the preceding coding logic and it is not relevant for showing the use of the MOVEA operation or indexing with a variable field.

Other Time Arrays May Be Loaded In Program Cycle

Programs discussed previously in this chapter loaded arrays from input and calculations. In addition, arrays may be loaded at object or compile time similar to table processing. Any array loaded at object time must be defined as an input file in the File Description form. Figure 14-21 illustrates the File Description coding for an object time array. Notice the letter E is entered in column 39 of the input array file which informs the computer the array is

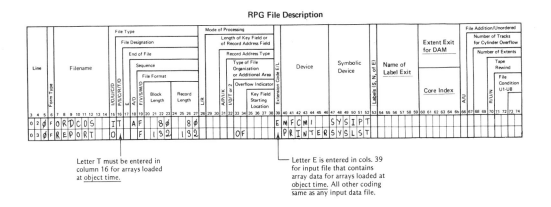

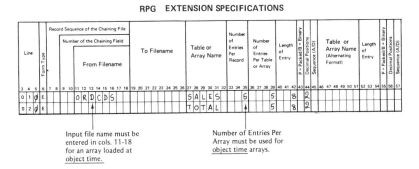

Fig. 14-21.   File Description and Extension coding for program shown in Figure 14-9 modified to load the array at *object time* instead of from Input Specifications.

defined in the extension form and not on input. The letter T must also be entered in column 16 for arrays loaded at object time.

An examination of the extension form in Figure 14-21 shows the additional fields used to define an object time array. The From Filename (columns 11–18) and Number of Entries Per Record, (columns 33–35) are required for arrays loaded at object time. These fields were not used for arrays loaded from the input form. Calculations and Output-Format coding are not affected when arrays are loaded in the program cycle.

Compile time arrays are an integral part and extension of the RPG II program. Arrays loaded at compile time are *not* defined in the File Description form, but are identified as compile time arrays by the control statements in the job stream. Job control differs for every manufacturer and computer system. Hence the respective manufacturer's programmer manuals must be referenced to specify a compile time array. In an IBM 370 DOS system, compile time arrays are separated from the source program and each other by an ** control statement. The source program and compile arrays are separated from any input file by the standard /* statement.

Figure 14-22 shows the extension form coding for a compile time array. Examination of the form indicates that the Filename field (columns 11–18) is *not* used for compile time arrays, but the Number of Entries Per Record is required. As with object time arrays, the input form is not used to define the compile arrays.

Determining when an array should be loaded in the program cycle usually depends on the storage status of the array data. If arrays are not subject to change, they may conveniently be included in the source program as compile time arrays, whereas if the array element values are variable, object or input time arrays would offer more flexibility. Arrays loaded in calculations are not subject to any coding changes whether input, object, or compile time loading is defined for other arrays in the program.

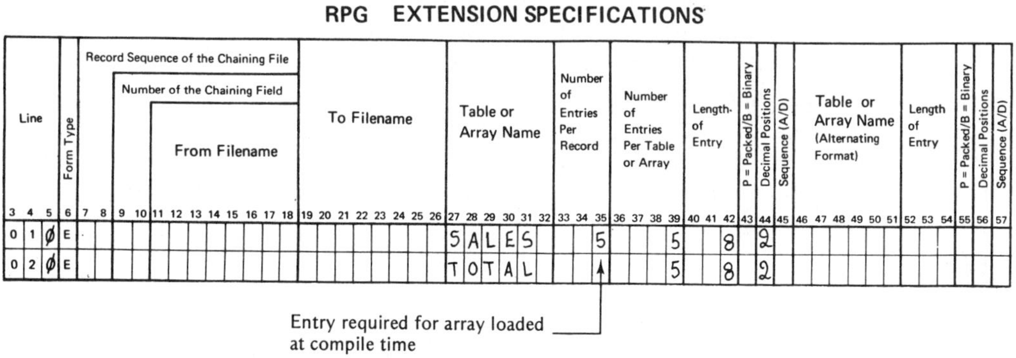

RPG   EXTENSION SPECIFICATIONS

Line	Form Type	Record Sequence of the Chaining File			To Filename	Table or Array Name	Number of Entries Per Record	Number of Entries Per Table or Array	Length of Entry	P = Packed/B = Binary	Decimal Positions	Sequence (A/D)	Table or Array Name (Alternating Format)	Length of Entry	P = Packed/B = Binary	Decimal Positions	Sequence (A/D)
			Number of the Chaining Field														
				From Filename													
3 4 5	6	7 8	9 10	11 12 13 14 15 16 17 18	19 20 21 22 23 24 25 26	27 28 29 30 31 32	33 34 35	36 37 38 39	40 41 42	43	44	45	46 47 48 49 50 51	52 53 54	55	56	57
0 1 0	E					S A L E S	5		5		8	2					
0 2 0	E					T O T A L	4		5		8	2					

Entry required for array loaded ____
at compile time

Fig. 14-22.   Extension coding for program shown in Figure 14-9, modified to load array at compile time.

QUESTIONS

1. What are some considerations in determining whether to use tables or arrays for an application?
2. Name advantages of using arrays in lieu of tables. Disadvantages.
3. How may array data be loaded in an RPG II program?
4. How does RPG II source program coding differ for the time an array may be loaded in the program cycle.
5. What are the limitations in the length of an array name? Also, what other factors should be considered when the array name is created?
6. If an array is named EMP how is the fortieth element specified in calculations or output?
7. What is the function of the XFOOT operation?
8. Explain the three coding methods of formatting the elements of an array on printed output.
9. The printed format of the elements in a numeric array is XXX,X$0CRbbbbbXXX,X$0CRbbbbbXXX,X$0CRbbbbbXXX,X$0CR (b's indicate blank positions). Write the edit word to obtain the required printed format.
10. How many spaces are automatically inserted between the elements of a numeric array if an edit code is used for editing?
11. How are alphanumeric arrays edited on output?
12. If the elements of an array are scattered within a record(s), what coding procedures are required to load the array?
13. How is an array loaded if the data is included in more than one record?
14. On a blank calculation form write the coding to lookup array elements. Array name is PT and search field name is PARTNO.
15. Refer to question 14. How would you modify the coding to reduce lookup time if the array was 200 elements long?
16. In what ways does array lookup differ from table lookup?
17. Explain the functions of the MOVEA operation.
18. How does the MOVEA operation differ from the MOVE and MOVEL operations?
19. What is meant by array indexing?
20. If the INV array is indexed, indicate how the array name would be written. How would the index value be changed in the program?

EXERCISES

14-1. Complete the File Description, Input, and Calculation coding for the following array information:

An input card file, CENSUS, consists of an array POP that includes 10 numeric elements, each nine characters in length, with no decimal positions. The array is to be crossfooted for a total of all the elements' values. Load the array from input specifications.

14-2. Modify the coding in Exercise 14-1 to load the array at object time.

14-3. Modify the coding in Exercise 14-1 to load the array at compile time.

14-4. Complete the output coding to print the array values with two spaces between the elements. Determine your own locations on the report.

14-5. Modify the output coding in Exercise 14-4 to print the array values with four spaces between the elements.

14-6. Complete the Calculation Specifications coding from the following information:

The array CY consists of 300 entries. Complete the calculation coding to LOKUP the 299th element, starting, not at the beginning of the array, but at the 201st position.

14-7. The array NAM consists of 25 bytes which includes information for city, state, and zip code. Values in the array elements vary in size. Consequently, the zip code will not always be in the same location in the element.

Write the calculation coding to extract the zip code from the field using indexing, looping, and the MOVEA operation.

LABORATORY ASSIGNMENTS

LABORATORY ASSIGNMENT 14-1:
FACTORY OVERHEAD BUDGET

Write an RPG II program using arrays from the following input and output formats. The quarterly values for each overhead expense account is loaded in an array from Input Specifications and the quarterly totals for all expense items is loaded to another array from calculations.

Format of the Data Records:

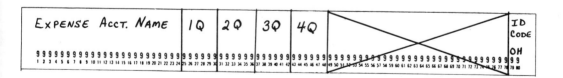

Calculations. Each individual expense account's quarterly totals are to be cross-footed to calculate the total yearly amount. In addition, the quarterly totals for all expense accounts are added to an array and cross-footed to give the grand total of all expenses. (see Printer Spacing Chart).

Design of Printed Report:

Data for Laboratory Assignment:

Account Name	1Q	2Q	3Q	4Q
INDIRECT LABOR	250000	190000	201910	186750
FACTORY SUPPLIES	086000	070000	103480	093100
HEAT, LIGHT, POWER	067440	079000	080500	071330
SUPERVISION	150000	150000	165000	167000
MAINTENANCE	090000	087000	089000	077900
TAXES AND INSURANCE	110000	110000	110000	110000
DEPRECIATION	125000	125000	125000	125000

LABORATORY ASSIGNMENT 14-2:
FACTORY OVERHEAD BUDGET (Arrays Loaded at Object Time)

Modify the array program completed in Lab 14-1 to load the overhead expenses array at object time.

LABORATORY ASSIGNMENT 14-3:
FACTORY OVERHEAD BUDGET (Arrays Loaded at Compile Time)

Modify the array program completed in Lab 14-1 to load the overhead expense array at compile time.

LABORATORY ASSIGNMENT 14-4:
FACTORY OVERHEAD BUDGET (Referencing a Single Array Element)

Refer to Lab 14-1 and use the overhead expense array data for this lab assignment. In addition to the array records, the following data card format will be included in a separate file:

Format of the Data Record (only one record is required of this format):

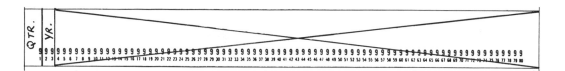

Use a 4 for the value in the quarter field (QTR) for the preceding record type and use an array index to access the required array expense account quarterly amounts. Notice in the report given below only the expense amounts for one quarter are printed.

Design of the Printed Report:

```
        0         1         2         3         4         5         6
   1234567890123456789012345678901234567890123456789012345678901234567890123456789
H  1                    PROJECTO MANUFACTURING COMPANY
H  2            BUDGETED FACTORY OVERHEAD COST FOR XXXXXX QUARTER
H  3                                 FOR 19XX
   4
   5
H  6                  EXPENSE ACCOUNT                    AMOUNT
   7
D  8            X------------------X              $  XXX,XX¢
   9
D  10           X------------------X                 XXX,XX¢
   11
   12
TLR 13                                TOTAL         $XX,XXX,XX¢
   14
   15          NOTES:
   16                 ① HEADINGS ON EVERY PAGE
   17
   18                 ② THE XXXXXX QUARTER ON 2ND HEADING LINE
   19                    WILL CONTAIN FIRST, SECOND, THIRD, OR
   20                    FOURTH DEPENDING ON VALUE IN QTR
   21                    INPUT FIELD.
   22
```

LABORATORY ASSIGNMENT 14-5:
INCOME STATEMENT BY QUARTERS

Write an RPG II source program for the quarterly Income Statement shown in the Printer Spacing Chart given. *Seven* arrays must be defined: one for Sales, Cost of Goods Sold, Gross Profit, Operating Expenses, Net Income, Decimal

Percent of Net Income to Sales, and the expressed Percent of Net Income to Sales. The arrays for Sales, Cost of Sales, and Operating Expenses are loaded from input specifications and the other arrays in calculations. In addition, the expressed Percent of Net Income to Sales is calculated by multiplying the decimal array by 100.

Format of the Data Records:

Calculations:. The elements of each array (quarterly amounts) are cross-footed to give the year's totals. Reference to the Printer Spacing Chart will indicate the mathematics used in the Income Statement to compute Net Income. Percent of Net Income to Sales is computed by dividing the Net Income array by the Sales array. The decimal answer stored in an array must be multiplied by 100 to give the expressed percent array. Notice, however, the percent for the total column cannot be calculated by cross-footing the percent array but must be determined by dividing total net income by total sales.

Design of the Printed Report:

Data for Laboratory Assignment:

Year	Sales	Cost of Goods sold	Operating Expenses	
79	200000	100000	070000	1st quarter amounts
79	175000	092000	052000	2nd quarter amounts
79	210000	120000	089000	3rd quarter amounts
79	309000	209000	105000	4th quarter amounts

LABORATORY ASSIGNMENT 14-6:
EXTRACTING THE STATE CODE FROM AN ARRAY ELEMENT

Write an RPG II source program using Indexing and the MOVEA operation to extract the two letter state code from an array element. The array used in the programs is loaded on input with the values in the City/State field within the data records. Each array element must be defined as one byte long with the size of the array equal to the City/State field length.

Format of Data Records:

NAME	STREET	CITY/STATE	ZIP	

Calculations.   Initalize an index field and create a loop so the City/State array elements may be searched to extract the state value from the city.

Design of Printed Report:

```
         0         1         2         3         4
    1234567890123456789012345678901234567890123456789
H  1        CUSTOMER REPORT LISTING BY    PAGE XXØX
H  2            STATE AS OF ØX/XX/XX
   3                     (UDATE)
   4
H  5                NAME              STATE
   6
D  7    X-                    X     XX
   8
D  9    X-                    X     XX
  10
  11  NOTE:
  12
  13    D HEADINGS ON TOP OF EVERY PAGE
  14
```

Data for Laboratory Assignment:

Name	Street	City/State	Zip
MICHAEL VANACORE	10 PASSAGEWAY PLACE	NEW YORK, NY	06854
ROBERT JORDAN	1040 AGOURA ROAD	CARMEL, CA	91301
ISSAC NEWTON	77 RESEDA BLVD	BULLRUN, SD	81134
BEN FRANKLIN	14 VAN OWEN STREET	COLUMBIAN, TN	77220

15
ADDITIONAL
RPG II FEATURES

Internal Subroutines, the *PLACE word, DEBUG operation, Look Ahead feature, DSPLY, and the FORCE operation provide additional flexibility in coding RPG II programs. The use and coding requirements for each of these concepts will be discussed in the following paragraphs.

INTERNAL SUBROUTINES

Internal Subroutines should be used in programs that require three or more repetitive calculations or when a sequence of calculations are to be executed only at select times. Coding for Internal Subroutines is entered in the calculation form. File Description, Extension (when used), Input, and Output-Format Specifications follow standard coding procedures and are not affected by Internal Subroutine entries. The calculation coding for Internal Subroutines is illustrated in Figure 15-1. Notice three new operations are used in the Operation field including EXSR, BEGSR, and ENDSR. An explanation of these operations is given below.

EXSR: Causes program control to branch to a following subroutine identified by the name (SUB1) entered in Factor 2. Subroutine name may be any acceptable RPG II field name not used anywhere else in the program.

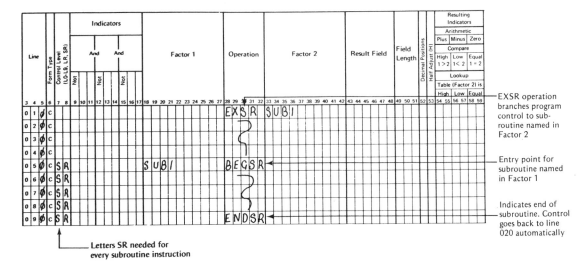

Fig. 15-1. Internal subroutine coding showing how EXSR, BEGSR, and ENDSR are used in calculations.

BEGSR: Identifies entry point for the subroutine named in Factor 2 of the EXSR operation. Name used in Factor 1 must be the same as the name used in the related EXSR operation.

ENDSR: Indicates end of the internal subroutine. When this instruction is executed, program control goes back to the calculation instruction following the related EXSR operation automatically.

Also notice the letters SR are entered in columns 7 and 8 for every instruction included in the internal subroutine. Any subroutines used in the program must be identified by these letters and follow all *detail and total time* calculations. If more than one subroutine is used in a program, the order they are entered on the calculation form does not matter as long as they follow all other calculations. In addition, if a subroutine is not branched to all instructions related to the subroutine are ignored as program control examines each calculation line in the RPG II processing cycle. Figure 15-2 summarizes the rules for internal subroutine coding.

Payroll Application Using An Internal Subroutine

A payroll application requiring a special sequence of calculations to compute overtime pay will be used to illustrate a typical application for internal subroutines. Because File Description, Input, and Output coding are not

---

INTERNAL SUBROUTINE RULES

1. Internal subroutine entries must follow all detail and total time calculations.

2. Every subroutine must have a name and no two subroutines may have the same name.

3. Three operation codes including EXSR, BEGSR, and ENDSR must be used with internal subroutine coding.

4. All instructions in the internal subroutine must be conditioned by the letters SR in columns 7 and 8.

5. Because columns 7 and 8 are used for the required SR entry, instructions in the subroutine cannot be conditioned by a level indicator.

6. All RPG II operation codes may be used in an internal subroutine.

7. Fields used in a subroutine may be defined in the routine or outside of it.

8. Any valid RPG II indicator may be entered in columns 9–17 (detail time) to condition a routine instruction(s).

9. The GOTO operation (branching and/or looping) may be used within subroutines. However, a GOTO operation outside the subroutine cannot be used to enter the routine. A GOTO operation within the subroutine may refer to a TAG operation outside the routine.

10. One subroutine may call another subroutine by use of the EXSR operation code.

11. If a name is entered in Factor 1 of the ENDSR operation code, it represents the entry point for a GOTO statement within the routine.

Fig. 15-2. Summary of RPG II internal subroutine rules.

affected by internal subroutine entries, reference may be made to the source listing in Figure 15-4 for that coding. The calculation form which is used for internal subroutine coding is illustrated in Figure 15-3 and explained in the paragraphs that follow.

Line 010. Comment.

Line 020. Input fields HRS and RATE are multiplied to compute a regular week's pay. If the employee worked 40 hours or less, WEKPAY would be the pay for the week.

Line 030. Comment.

Line 040. Hours are compared to 40, and if greater, Resulting Indicator 41 is

Programmer _____   RPG   CALCULATION SPECIFICATIONS

Line	Form Type	Control Level (L0-L9, LR, SR)	Indicators And Not	And Not	Factor 1	Operation	Factor 2	Result Field	Field Length	Decimal Positions	Half Adjust (H)	Resulting Indicators	Comments
010	C	*			COMPUTE GROSS PAY AT REGULAR RATE...								
020	C					HRS	MULT RATE	WEKPAY	62				
030	C	*			COMPARE HRS TO 40..								
040	C				HRS	COMP	40					41	
050	C	*			IF HRS GREATER THAN 40 EXIT TO SUBROUTINE TO COMPUTE O.T.PAY...								
060	C		41			EXSR	OTROUT						
070	C	*	ADD O.T.PAY COMPUTED IN ROUTINE TO WEEK PAY..										
080	C		41			OTPREM	ADD WEKPAY	WEKPAY					
090	C	*	ACCUMULATE DEPT & TOTAL FACTORY PAYROLL...										
100	C				DEPTPY	ADD	WEKPAY	DEPTPY	72				
110	C	L1			DEPTPY	ADD	FACTPY	FACTPY	92				
120	C	*	BEGIN SUBROUTINE FOR O.T. PAY...										
130	C	SR			OTROUT	BEGSR							
140	C	SR			HRS	SUB	40	OTHRS	20				
150	C	SR			RATE	DIV	2	OTRATE	53	H			
160	C	SR			OTHRS	MULT	OTRATE	OTPREM	52	H			
170	C	SR				ENDSR							
180	C	*	CONTROL GOES BACK TO LINE 070 AUTOMATICALLY...										

Fig. 15-3. Calculation coding for payroll application program using internal subroutines to compute overtime pay.

turned on which indicates overtime hours. If hours are 40 or less, instructions on lines 060–080 and 130–180 would not be executed because they related to overtime calculations.

Line 050.   Comment.

Line 060.   If HRS is greater than 40 (line 040) and indicator 41 turned on, the EXSR (exit to subroutine operation) will cause program control to branch to the OTROUT internal subroutine. Entry point for the routine is on line 130. However, if HRS is 40 or less, the exit to the subroutine will not be executed.

Line 070.   Comment.

Line 080.   The overtime premium pay (OTPREM) computed in the internal subroutine on lines 130–170 is added to the regular week's pay. Because this instruction is conditioned by resulting indicator 41, it will be executed only when HRS exceeds 40.

Line 090.   Comment.

Source program listing:

```
          01 020  F* THIS PROGRAM ILLUSTRATES THE USE OF INTERNAL SUBROUTINES...   SUBROU
          01 030  F*                                                               SUBROU
0001      01 040  FTIMECRDSIP  F  80  80              MFCM1 SYSIPT               SUBROU
0002      01 050  FWEEKPAYO    F 132 132      OF      PRINTERSYSLST              SUBROU
0003      02 010  ITIMECRDSSM  20  80 CT                                           SUBROU
0004      02 020  I                                      1    5 EMPNO              SUBROU
0005      02 030  I                                      6   30 NAME               SUBROU
0006      02 040  I                                     34   350DEPTNOL1           SUBROU
0007      02 050  I                                     39   40CHRS                SUBROU
0008      02 060  I                                     44   472RATE               SUBROU
          03 010  C* COMPUTE GROSS PAY AT REGULAR RATE...                          SUBROU
0009      03 020  C          HRS     MULT RATE       WEKPAY  52                    SUBROU
          03 030  C* COMPARE HRS TO 40...                                          SUBROU
0010      03 040  C          HRS     COMP 40                      41               SUBROU
          03 050  C* IF HRS GREATER THAN 40 EXIT TO SUBROUTINE TO COMPUTE O.T. PAY...  SUBROU
0011      03 060  C    41            EXSR OTROUT                                   SUBROU
          03 070  C* ADD O.T. PAY COMPUTED IN ROUTINE TO GROSS PAY...              SUBROU
0012      03 080  C    41    OTPREM  ADD  WEKPAY      WEKPAY  52                   SUBROU
          03 090  C* ACCUMULATE DEPT & TOTAL FACTORY PAYROLL...                    SUBROU
0013      03 100  C          DEPTPY  ADD  WEKPAY      DEPTPY  72                   SUBROU
0014      03 110  CL1        DEPTPY  ADD  FACTPY      FACTPY  92                   SUBROU
          03 120  C* BEGIN SUBROUTINE FOR O.T. PAY...                              SUBROU
0015      03 130  CSR        OTROUT  BEGSR                                        SUBROU
0016      03 140  CSR        HRS     SUB  40          OTHRS   20                   SUBROU
0017      03 150  CSR        RATE    DIV  2           OTRATE  53H                  SUBROU
0018      04 010  CSR        OTHRS   MULT OTRATE      OTPREM  52H                  SUBROU
0019      04 020  CSR                ENDSR                                        SUBROU
          04 030  C* CONTROL GOES BACK TO LINE 070 AUTOMATICALLY...               SUBROU
0020      05 010  OWEEKSPAYH     101     1P                                        SUBROU
0021      05 020  O           OR         OF                                        SUBROU
0022      05 030  O                                  29 'DEPARTMENTAL PAYROLL'     SUBROU
0023      05 040  O                                  36 'REPORT'                   SUBROU
0024      05 050  O                                  44 'PAGE'                     SUBROU
0025      05 060  O                           PAGE Z 49                            SUBROU
0026      05 070  O           H   2       1P                                       SUBROU
0027      05 080  O           OR          OF                                       SUBROU
0028      05 090  O                                  25 'FOR WEEK ENDING'          SUBROU
0029      05 100  O                           UDATE Y 34                           SUBROU
0030      05 110  O           H   2       1P                                       SUBROU
0031      05 120  O           OR          OF                                       SUBROU
0032      05 130  O                                   8 'EMP NO.'                  SUBROU
0033      05 140  O                                  27 'EMPLOYEE NAME'            SUBROU
0034      05 150  O                                  48 'WEEK PAY'                 SUBROU
0035      05 160  O           D   2       20                                       SUBROU
0036      05 170  O                           EMPNO   6                            SUBROU
0037      05 180  O                           NAME   35                            SUBROU
0038      05 190  O                           WEKPAY1 47                           SUBROU
0039      05 200  O                                  38 '$'                        SUBROU
0040      06 010  O           T  23       L1                                       SUBROU
0041      06 020  O                                  25 'DEPT'                     SUBROU
0042      06 030  O                           DEPTNOZ 28                           SUBROU
0043      06 040  O                                  34 'TOTAL'                    SUBROU
0044      06 050  O                                  38 '$'                        SUBROU
0045      06 060  O                           DEPTPY1B 47                          SUBROU
0046      06 070  O           T   3     01 LR                                      SUBROU
0047      06 080  O                                  15 'FACTORY TOTAL'            SUBROU
0048      06 090  O                                  17 '$'                        SUBROU
0049      06 100  O                           FACTPY1 30                           SUBROU
```

Printed report:

```
              DEPARTMENTAL PAYROLL REPORT      PAGE   1
              FOR WEEK ENDING  3/13/78

     EMP NO.      EMPLOYEE NAME            WEEK PAY

     12345    DAVID BLANCHARD          $   322.00

     23456    WAYNE BRACCIO            $   300.00

     34567    LORRAINE DOWNS           $   440.00



                   DEPT  1 TOTAL   $ 1,062.00


     45678    ANNE COOPER              $   381.80

     56789    SUE HAYES                $   580.00



                   DEPT  2 TOTAL   $   961.80



     FACTORY TOTAL $     2,023.80
```

Fig. 15-4. Source listing and printed report for payroll application program using an internal subroutine.

Line 100. The week's pay amount from line 020 or 080 is added to a department total pay field (DEPTPY). Hence, this instruction accumulates the total payroll for a department. The data must have been sorted by department groups before the payroll file is processed.

Line 110. When the department number changes and control level indicator L1 turned on (see input coding in Figure 15-4), the amount accumulated in the department total field, DEPTPY, is added to factory total field, FACTPY. Examine the printed report in Figure 15-4 to identify totals used in program.

Line 120. Comment.

Line 130. Entry point for the EXSR OTROUT on line 060. Internal subroutine name in Factor 1 must be identical to the name used in Factor 2 of the EXSR operation. BEGSR operation indicates beginning of the routine and must be conditioned by the letters SR entered in columns 7 and 8.

Line 140. The number 40 is subtracted from the value in HRS to compute overtime hours (OTHRS).

Line 150. The hourly rate, RATE, is divided by two to calculate the overtime rate (OTRATE). As with all subroutine calculations the instruction is conditioned by SR in columns 7 and 8.

Line 160. Overtime hours (OTHRS) is multiplied by the overtime rate (OTRATE) to compute overtime premium pay (OTPREM).

Line 170. The operation ENDSR indicates the end of the internal subroutine which causes program control to return to the instruction following the EXSR operation (line 070). Program control then follows the usual sequence of operations, but will ignore all SR lines as each instruction is examined.

Line 180. Comment.

The source listing and resulting printed report are illustrated in Figure 15-4.

External subroutines written in Assembler language may be used in RPG II programs on some systems. However, because of the uniqueness and restrictions of external subroutine coding, reference should be made to the manufacturer's programmer's manual for the system used. All computer systems do not provide for external subroutine coding.

THE *PLACE WORD

The reserved word *PLACE permits the duplication of fields on a line without repeating the field name on output. For example, assume a listing of customers similar to the one shown in Figure 15-5 is to be printed. Notice that the information for each customer is duplicated on every line. Because no changes in standard coding procedures are needed on the File Description Specifications form it will not be shown for the sample program that will be discussed. Also, no changes in normal coding are needed in the Input Specifications but the form is shown in Figure 15-6 as a reference for the field names used in the program.

If field names are to be printed twice on each line, standard coding would require that each field be specified twice on the Output-Format Specifications form, as illustrated in Figure 15-7. However, by use of the *PLACE word, the required coding for the duplication of field information on a line is minimized.

Reference to Figure 15-8 will show the coding entries needed to duplicate field information on a line by use of the *PLACE word. Notice that the word *PLACE is entered as a field with an appropriate end position which will cause all of the fields preceding it to be duplicated accordingly. Care must be exercised in assigning an end position to the *PLACE word to avoid any overlapping of data contained in the fields. When field information is duplicated by *PLACE, all of the spaces between fields are also considered on output. The end position that is specified with the *PLACE word refers to the end position of the last field duplicated.

In addition, if it is necessary to repeat field information three or more times on a line, another *PLACE word has to be entered for each time the information is to be printed with the corresponding end positions. For example, if the information for the above program was to be printed three times, another *PLACE word would have to be entered immediately after the first one. The only limitations on the number of times field information is to be printed is, of course, the width of the paper used. The source program listing and printed result is shown in Figure 15-9.

```
1111   ALEXANDER BELL     NEW YORK, N. Y.        1111 ALEXANDER BELL      NEW YORK, N. Y.

1112   WALTER BEADY       HARTFORD, CONN.        1112 WALTER BEADY        HARTFORD, CONN.

1113   HARRY CASE         ALBANY, N.Y.           1113 HARRY CASE          ALBANY, N.Y.
                  .                                            .
                  .                                            .
                  .                                            .
                  .                                            .
                  .                                            .
```

Fig. 15-5.   Sample output of duplicate printing.

Line (3–5)	Form type (6)	Filename (7–14)	Sequence (15–16)	Number (1-N) (17)	Option (O) (18)	Record identifying indicator or ** (19–20)	Record identification codes 1: Position (21–24)	1: Not (N) (25)	1: C/Z/D (26)	1: Character (27)	2: Position (28–31)	2: Not (N) (32)	2: C/Z/D (33)	2: Character (34)	3: Position (35–38)	3: Not (N) (39)	3: C/Z/D (40)	3: Character (41)	Stocker select (42)	P = packed/B = binary (43)	Field location From (44–47)	Field location To (48–51)	Decimal positions (52)	Field name (53–58)	Control level (L1-L9) (59–60)	Matching fields or chaining fields (61–62)	Field record relation (63–64)	Field indicators Plus (65–66)	Field indicators Minus (67–68)	Field indicators Zero or blank (69–70)	Sterling sign position (71–74)
01Ø	I	INPUT	AZ			Ø1	8Ø		C	R																					
02Ø	I																				1	4		CUSNUM							
03Ø	I																				5	24		CUNAME							
04Ø	I																				25	44		ADDRSS							

Fig. 15-6. Input specifications coding for example using the *PLACE word.

Line	Form type	Filename	Type (H/D/T/E)	Stacker select/fetch overflow (F)	Space Before	Space After	Skip Before	Skip After	Output indicators Not	And	Not	And	Not	Field name	Edit codes	Blank after (B)	End positions on output record	P = packed/B = binary	Sterling sign positions
3 4 5	6	7 8 9 10 11 12 13 14	15	16	17	18	19 20	21 22	23 24	25 26	27	28 29	30	32 33 34 35 36 37	38	39	40 41 42 43	44	71 72 73 74
Ø 1	O	O U T P U T	D			2			Ø 1					C U S T N O			6		
Ø 2	O													C U S T N A M E			3 1		
Ø 3	O													C U S T A D D R E S S			5 6		
Ø 4	O													C U S T N U M			8 Ø		
Ø 5	O													C U S T N A M E			1 Ø 5		
Ø 6	O													C U S T A D D R E S S			1 3 Ø		
Ø 7	O																		
Ø 8	O																		

Edit codes reference:

Commas	Zero balances to print	No sign	CR	−	
Yes	Yes	1	A	J	X = Remove plus sign
Yes	No	2	B	K	Y = Date field edit
No	Yes	3	C	L	Z = Zero suppress
No	No	4	D	M	

Fig. 15-7. Output-format specifications coding for duplicate printing *without* *PLACE word.

547

Fig. 15-8. Output-format specifications coding for duplicate printing *with* *PLACE word.

Line	Form type	Filename	Type (H/D/T/E)	Space After	Output indicators And	Field name	End position on output record
01	O	OUTPUT	D	2	01		
02	O					CUSNME	6
03	O					CUNAME	31
04	O					ADDRSS	56
05	O					*PLACE	130
06	O						

Edit codes reference:

	Commas	Zero balances to print	No sign	CR	−
	Yes	Yes	1	A	J
	Yes	No	2	B	K
	No	Yes	3	C	L
	No	No	4	D	M

X = Remove plus sign
Y = Date field edit
Z = Zero suppress

Source listing:

```
          01 020  F* EXAMPLE PROGRAM USING THE *PLACE WORD...                          *PLACE
0001      01 030  FINPUT     IP  F   80   80              MFCM1  SYSIPT                 *PLACE
0002      01 040  FOUTPUT    O   F  132  132              PRINTERSYSLST                 *PLACE
0003      02 010  IINPUT     AZ  01   80 CR                                             *PLACE
0004      02 020  I                                                   1    4 CUSNUM     *PLACE
0005      02 030  I                                                   5   24 CUNAME     *PLACE
0006      02 040  I                                                  25   44 ADDRSS     *PLACE
0007      03 010  OOUTPUT    D 2       01                                               *PLACE
0008      03 020  O                           CUSNUM      6                             *PLACE
0009      03 030  O                           CUNAME     31                             *PLACE
0010      03 040  O                           ADDRSS     56                             *PLACE
0011      03 050  O                           *PLACE    130                             *PLACE
```

Printed report:

```
1111    ALEXANDER BELL      NEW YORK, N.Y.              1111    ALEXANDER BELL      NEW YORK, N.Y.

1112    WALTER BEADY        HARTFORD, CONN.             1112    WALTER BEADY        HARTFORD, CONN.

1113    HARRY CASE          ALBANY, N.Y.                1113    HARRY CASE          ALBANY, N.Y.
```

Fig. 15-9. Source listing and printed output for example program using the *PLACE word to duplicate output.

THE DEBUG OPERATION

Because of errors made in source program coding, keypunch mistakes, or data errors, an RPG source program may not execute. Conveniently, RPG compilers provide for the listing of errors as part of the source program output. Included in these error messages are the sequence lines in which the errors appear, the code number of the error, and an explanation of the error in sentence form. Errors that are printed along with the source program listing typically fall into one of the following broad categories:

1. Incorrect coding entries on the forms as leaving out one of the letters, F, E, I, C, or O, in column 6; or right-justifying a field name instead of left-justifying it.

2. The use of the wrong calculation operation, incorrect result field size, multidefined field sizes, or attempting to divide by zero.

3. Specifying total time before detail time in calculations and/or output.

4. The improper formatting of input data as left-justifying numeric data fields instead of right-justifying; or including a decimal point in numeric fields.

Most of the error types mentioned above are easily found because they are listed and defined by the RPG compiler. However, even after all of the noted errors are corrected the program may still not execute. Errors that are not listed by the computer may be a program logic error or the use of an incorrect indicator. Some of the most common unlisted errors that are often frustrating to the RPG programmer are errors in the conditioning of calculations and/or output by Resulting, Record Identifying, Control Level, or Matching Record Indicators. Usually indicator errors are very difficult to locate, but RPG II offers an operation that expedites the location of errors caused by the misuse of an indicator. The special operation is called DEBUG and enables the RPG compiler to print a record that contains the indicators that are on for a particular line of calculations and, if desired, the data contained in a field.

The operation name DEBUG is obviously derived from the term debugging which refers to the process of eliminating errors in a program. Hence, to debug a program is to eliminate all the errors and make it executable.

Source program coding for the DEBUG operation involves an additional entry in the Control Card Specifications section of the File Description Specifications form (top part) and entries in the Calculation Specifications. Extension, Input, and Output Specifications are not affected by use of the DEBUG operation.

In addition to the normal coding entries in the Control Card Specifications (H in column 6, etc.), the number one must be specified in column 15. which indicates to the RPG compiler that the DEBUG operation is to be used in the program. If the DEBUG operation is used and the entry is not made in this column all of the DEBUG statements will be treated only as comments. Figure 15-10 shows the Control Card and File Description form and the respective entry for the DEBUG operation.

The DEBUG operation word may be placed anywhere in the calculation section providing it is entered in the operation field, columns 28–32. There is no limit to the number of DEBUG operations that may be specified in a program and when one is used the indicators that are on at that point in the program will be printed as an output record.

Depending on the information needed, there are several ways of using the DEBUG operation, as illustrated in Figure 15-11. The entry on line 050 includes the DEBUG word in the operation field, columns 28–32, and an entry left-justified in Factor 2. The name specified in Factor 2 refers to the printer output file name that was previously defined in the File Description Specifications form of the program. When the DEBUG operation is used in this manner only the indicators that are on at the point where the DEBUG is specified will be printed.

On the other hand, if the contents of a field are needed in addition to the indicators, the respective field name may be entered in the Result field. Line 090 shows the coding for printing both the indicators and field contents.

Furthermore, when several DEBUG operations are used it may be convenient to identify which one is being referenced. There, each DEBUG statement may be referred to by entering a literal left-justified in Factor 1, columns 18–27, as shown on line 150, Figure 15-11.

A computer executed program illustrating the actual use of the DEBUG operation will be discussed in the following paragraphs. The program calculates the annual depreciation, accumulated depreciation, and book value for each year of an asset's life by the Double-rate Declining Balance method of determining depreciation. Reference to source program listing in Figure 15-12

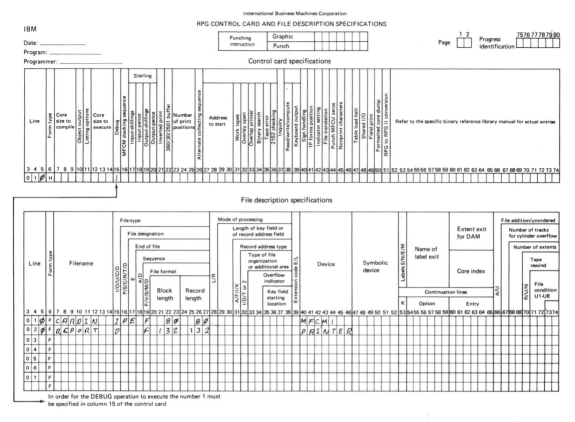

Fig. 15-10. Control card and file description specifications coding for DEBUG operation.

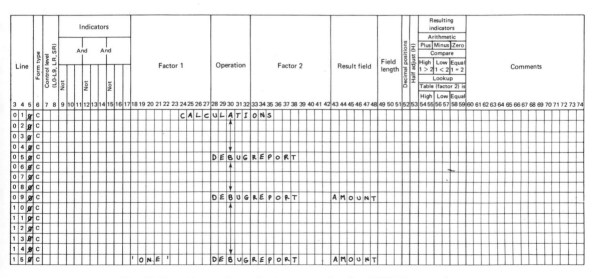

Fig. 15-11. Alternative calculation entries for DEBUG operation.

```
                 0101 H008   0091                                          DEBUG


                 0102 F*                                                   DEBUG
                 0103 F* PROGRAM TO CALCULATE DEPRECIATION                 DEBUG
                 0104 F*USEING THE DOUBLE-RATE DECLINING METHOD            DEBUG
                 0105 F****                                                DEBUG
                 0106 F*    FILE DESCRIPTION SPECIFICATIONS *************************************DEBUG
                 0107 F*                                                   DEBUG
            0001 0108 FINPUT   IPE F     96            MFCU1               DEBUG
            0002 0109 FOUTPUT  O   F     132           PRINTER             DEBUG


                 1001 I*                                                   DEBUG
                 1002 I**** INPUT SPECIFICATIONS ********************************************DEBUG
                 1003 I*                                                   DEBUG
            0003 1004 IINPUT   88  20   74 CB                              DEBUG
            0004 1005 I                                1  20 ASSET         DEBUG
            0005 1006 I                               21  260PDATE         DEBUG
            0006 1007 I                               27  320YEAR          DEBUG
            0007 1008 I                               33  56 VENDOR        DEBUG
            0008 1009 I                               57  642COST          DEBUG
            0009 1010 I                               65  712SVALUE        DEBUG
            0010 1011 I                               72  730LIFE          DEBUG


                 2001 C*                                                   DEBUG
                 2002 C**** CALCULATION SPECIFICATIONS *****************************************DEBUG
                 2003 C*                                                   DEBUG
            0011 2005 C                    SETON                    15     DEBUG
            0012 2006 C   15               EXCPT                           DEBUG
            0013 2007 C                    SETOF                    15     DEBUG
            0014 2008 C         'DEBUG1'   DEBUGOUTPUT                     *-*-*-
            0015 2009 C                    Z-ADDCOST     BOOKV  122        DEBUG
            0016 2010 C         1.00       DIV  LIFE     PERCNT  64        DEBUG
            0017 2011 C         PERCNT     MULT 2        RATE    64        DEBUG
            0018 2012 C         RATE       COMP .40               50       DEBUG
            0019 2013 C   50               Z-ADD.40      RATE              DEBUG
            0020 2014 C         YEAR       SUB  1        YEAR              DEBUG
            0021 2015 C         START      TAG                            DEBUG
            0022 2016 C         YEAR       ADD  1        YEAR              DEBUG
            0023 2017 C         LIFE       SUB  1        LIFE       25     DEBUG
            0024 2018 C   25               GOTO END                        DEBUG
            0025 2019 C         BOOKV      MULT RATE     ANNDEP 122H       DEBUG
            0026 2020 C         ANNDEP     ADD  ACCDEP   ACCDEP 122        DEBUG
            0027 20205C         'DEBUG2'   DEBUGOUTPUT   ACCDEP            *-*-*
            0028 2021 C         BOOKV      SUB  ANNDEP   BOOKV             DEBUG
            0029 2022 C         BOOKV      COMP SVALUE            4040     DEBUG
            0030 2023 C   40               GOTO END                        DEBUG
            0031 2024 C                    SETON                    45     DEBUG
```

DEBUG example that will print the identifying literal for the statement, indicators that are on, and field value.

DEBUG example that will print the identifying literal and only the indicators that are on at this point in the program.

Fig. 15-12.   Complete source program listing for program using DEBUG operation.

```
0032  2025  C    45              EXCPT                              DEBUG
0033  2026  C                    GOTO START                         DEBUG
0034  2027  C              END   TAG                                DEBUG


      3001  O*                                                      DEBUG
      3002  O**** OUTPUT FORMAT SPECIFICATIONS ********************************DEBUG
      3003  O*                                                      DEBUG
0035  3004  OOUTPUT E  103    15 20                                 DEBUG
0036  3005  O                                    67 'DOUBLE RATE DECLINING DEBUG
0037  3006  O                                    74 'BALANCE'        DEBUG
0038  3007  O        E  3      15                                   DEBUG
0039  3008  O                                    67 '**********************  DEBUG
0040  3009  O                                    74 '*******         DEBUG
0041  3010  O        E  2      15                                   DEBUG
0042  3011  O                                    24 'ASSET'          DEBUG
0043  3012  O                          ASSET     50                 DEBUG
0044  3013  O        E  2      15                                   DEBUG
0045  3014  O                                    32 'PURCHASE DATE'  DEBUG
0046  3015  O                          PDATE Y   45                 DEBUG
0047  3100  O      . E  2      15                                   DEBUG
0048  3101  O                                    27 'SUPPLIER'       DEBUG
0049  3102  O                          VENDOR    57                 DEBUG
0050  3103  O        E  2      15                                   DEBUG
0051  3104  O                                    23 'COST'           DEBUG
0052  3105  O                          COST  1   37 '$'             DEBUG
0053  3106  O        E  2      15                                   DEBUG
0054  3107  O                                    32 'SALVAGE VALUE'  DEBUG
0055  3108  O                          SVALUE1   45 '$'             DEBUG
0056  3109  O        E  2      15                                   DEBUG
0057  3110  O                                    23 'LIFE'           DEBUG
0058  3111  O                          LIFE  3   32                 DEBUG
0059  3112  O        E  2      15                                   DEBUG
0060  3113  O                                    44 '***********************' DEBUG
0061  3114  O                                    68 '***********************' DEBUG
0062  3115  O                                    92 '***********************' DEBUG
0063  3200  O                                    99 '*******'        DEBUG
0064  3201  O        E  1      15                                   DEBUG
0065  3202  O                                    31 'YEAR'           DEBUG
0066  3203  O                                    47 'ANNUAL'         DEBUG
0067  3204  O                                    70 'ACCUMULATED'    DEBUG
0068  3205  O                                    89 'BOOK VALUE'     DEBUG
0069  3206  O        E  2      15                                   DEBUG
0070  3207  O                                    51 'DEPRECIATION'   DEBUG
0071  3203  O                                    71 'DEPRECIATION'   DEBUG
0072  3209  O        E  2      15                                   DEBUG
0073  3210  O                                    44 '***********************' DEBUG
0074  3211  O                                    68 '***********************' DEBUG
0075  3212  O                                    92 '***********************' DEBUG
0076  3213  O                                    99 '*******'        DEBUG
0077  3214  O        E  2      45 20                                DEBUG
0078  3215  O                          YEAR  3   31                 DEBUG
0079  3216  O                          ANNDEP1   50 '$'             DEBUG
0080  3217  O                          ACCDEP1   70 '$'             DEBUG
0081  3218  O                                 1  89 '$'             DEBUG
```

Fig. 5.12.   (Concluded)

will reveal that File Description, Input, and Output-Format Specifications are not affected by the coding for the DEBUG operation. Consequently, the only entries, besides the number one in column 15 of the control card, are in the Calculation Specifications.

Examine Figure 15-12 and locate sequence line ∅∅14 of the calculation section; note the coding for the DEBUG operation. An alphanumeric literal DEBUG1 is specified in Factor 1, the word DEBUG in the operation field, and the output file name OUTPUT in Factor 2. Because a field name is not specified in the result field, only the indicators that are on at that point in the program will be printed and not the contents of any field.

Another DEBUG operation is used on sequence line ∅∅27 with a field name specified in the result field which will permit the contents of the named field to be printed as well as the indicators that are on at that point in the program. Notice that in both of the DEBUG statements the literal in Factor 1 is enclosed in apostrophes which is in accordance with the rules for forming alphanumeric literals.

Refer to the first printed output example in Figure 15-13 and notice that the first DEBUG record that is printed appears as follows:

DEBUG   DEBUG1   INDICATOR ON   20

The printed record shown above is divided into sections. First, the word DEBUG, which refers to the operation, is printed; second, DEBUG1 refers to the literal that was specified in Factor 1 of the DEBUG statement; and third, the phrase, INDICATORS ON, is automatically supplied by the RPG II compiler. The number 20 represents the indicator that is on at that particular point in the program.

The second DEBUG statement is identified as DEBUG2 and follows the same standard record format. However, because a field name was specified in the Result Field for the operation statement, the respective field value will be printed accordingly. The format of the DEBUG statement is as follows:

DEBUG   DEBUG2   INDICATORS ON   20
FIELD VALUE   000000400000

The phrase FIELD VALUE is supplied by the RPG compiler and the 000000400000 is the contents of the ACCDEP field at that point in the program. Reference to the accumulated depreciation field (ACCDEP) will reveal that it is 12 positions long with two decimals. Hence, after the field is edited on output it will appear as 4,000.00, as shown in Figure 15-13.

In order to show the value of using the DEBUG operation for finding indicator errors, the program has an intentional error built in. Refer to the second output listing, Figure 15-14, and observe that the 1969 output line is repeated twice along with the incorrect annual depreciation and accumulated depreciation amounts. An examination of the indicators that are on for the DEBUG operation entry reveals that indicator 45 has remained on, which has

```
                        DOUBLE RATE DECLINING BALANCE
                        *****************************

                ASSET      MACHINE

                PURCHASE DATE     1/27/71

                SUPPLIER     BRIDGEPORT MACHINE

                COST    $10,000.00

                SALVAGE VALUE     $700.00

                LIFE       5

        *************************************************************************
                        YEAR.          ANNUAL          ACCUMULATED       BOOK VALUE
                                    DEPRECIATION       DEPRECIATION
        *************************************************************************


  ── DEBUG       DEBUG1  INDICATORS ON  20

  ⎛ DEBUG       DEBUG2  INDICATORS ON  20
  ⎝ FIELD VALUE     000000400000
                        1971         $4,000.00         $4,000.00         $6,000.00


     DEBUG       DEBUG2  INDICATORS ON  20  45
     FIELD VALUE     000000640000
                        1972         $2,400.00         $6,400.00         $3,600.00


     DEBUG       DEBUG2  INDICATORS ON  20  45
     FIELD VALUE     000000784000
                        1973         $1,440.00         $7,840.00         $2,160.00


     DEBUG       DEBUG2  INDICATORS ON  20  45
     FIELD VALUE     000000870400
                        1974          $864.00         $8,704.00         $1,296.00


     DEBUG       DEBUG2  INDICATORS ON  20  45
     FIELD VALUE     000000922240
                        1975          $518.40         $9,222.40          $777.60
```

→ DEBUG output record *with* a field name specified in the
   result field of the Calculation Specifications form.

→ DEBUG output record *without* a field name specified in the
   result field of the Calculation Specifications form.

Fig. 15-13.   Printed program output showing DEBUG record form.

```
                    DOUBLE RATE DECLINING BALANCE
                    ••••••••••••••••••••••••••••••••


            ASSET      DELIVERY TRUCK

            PURCHASE DATE      3/29/69

            SUPPLIER     FORD MOTORS

            COST    $5,000.00

            SALVAGE VALUE      $900.00

            LIFE       7

••••••••••••••••••••••••••••••••••••••••••••••••••••••••••••••••••••••••

            YEAR        ANNUAL           ACCUMULATED      BOOK VALUE
                        DEPRECIATION     DEPRECIATION

            ••••••••••••••••••••••••••••••••••••••••••••••••••••••••••••


              1969         $518.40         $9,222.40        $777.60


DEBUG     DEBUG1  INDICATORS ON  20  25  45

DEBUG     DEBUG2  INDICATORS ON  20  45
FIELD VALUE    000001065040
              1969         $1,428.00       $10,650.40       $3,572.00


DEBUG     DEBUG2  INDICATORS ON  20  45
FIELD VALUE    000001167056
              1970         $1,020.16       $11,670.56       $2,551.84


DEBUG     DEBUG2  INDICATORS ON  20  45
FIELD VALUE    000001239937
              1971          $728.81        $12,399.37       $1,823.03


DEBUG     DEBUG2  INDICATORS ON  20  45
FIELD VALUE    000001292003
              1972          $520.66        $12,920.03       $1,302.37


DEBUG     DEBUG2  INDICATORS ON  20  45
FIELD VALUE    000001329199
              1973          $371.96        $13,291.95        $930.41


DEBUG     DEBUG2  INDICATORS ON  20  45
FIELD VALUE    000001355772
```

The year 1969 repeated twice because resulting indicator 45
was not SETOF. Notice also that annual depreciation,
accumulated depreciation, and book value are all wrong
because the amounts were picked up from the previous record
(see Fig. 13-12 and the depreciation figures for 1975).

Accumulated depreciation should also be set to zero before
the next record is processed to prevent the accumulation of
amounts.

Fig. 15-14.   Printed program output showing use of DEBUG in locating indicator
errors.

caused the error. Because the indicator has stayed on, it must be turned off which can be accomplished by inserting a SETOF 45 statement between sequence lines 0032 and 0033 of the source program.

In addition to the indicator message, the DEBUG2 statement provides for the contents of the accumulated depreciation field (ACCDEP) to be printed. An examination of the value contained in the field will reveal that it is incorrect because the field was not initialized to zero before computations.

Notice also that because the DEBUG2 statement is within the loop, it is repeated for every output line, whereas DEBUG1 is outside the loop and only printed once for each record.

The DEBUG operation offers another convenient way of locating troublesome and often hard to find errors in RPG source programs. An appreciation of this operation will be realized when a programmer experiences frustrating and seemingly unsolvable program errors.

LOOK AHEAD FEATURE

Every input record goes through the complete RPG cycle before another is processed and the computer does not know what is contained in the next record to be read until processing is completed on the one before it. A unique feature of RPG II, called Look Ahead, allows the programmer to make a slight change in the language's built-in logic. The significance of this feature can be best realized from a simple example. For instance, assume that a payroll transaction card file is to be processed which will update a master disk file and the programmer wants to insure that one and only one transaction record is included for each employee. The Look Ahead feature can conveniently provide this check and execute any procedures the programmer builds into the program. In other words, this feature actually permits the computer to examine and read another card while the one before it is still being processed.

A simple program example will be used to explain the coding requirements for the Look Ahead feature. Examine the Input Specification, (Figure 15-15) and notice that the coding for the first four lines follows standard coding procedures for an input record. However, line 05 shows that a double asterisk (**) is specified in the Record Identifying field, columns 19 and 20. The double asterisk (**) must be used in lieu of a Record Identifying indicator to inform the computer that the Look Ahead feature is to be used for this record type. Also, the field name entered on line 06 refers to the EMPNO field defined on line 02, but must be given a different field name. However, even though the actual field name must be different it must be defined exactly the same way as to field location, type, and size.

Furthermore, if a Record Identification code was used to identify the record type, a field must be created for it according to its location in the card. Reference to Figure 15-15 will show that the letter E was specified in column 96; therefore, a field must be created and the exact location indicated in the Look Ahead record, as shown on line 07.

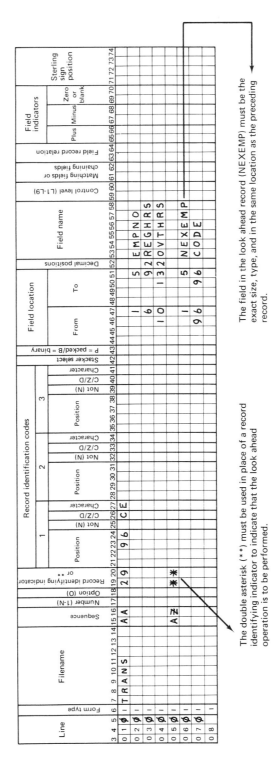

The field in the look ahead record (NEXEMP) must be the exact size, type, and in the same location as the preceding record.

The double asterisk (**) must be used in place of a record identifying indicator to indicate that the look ahead operation is to be performed.

Fig. 15-15. Input Specifications coding for Look Ahead feature.

558

Line (3–5)	Form type (6)	Control level (L0-L9, LR, SR) (7–8)	Indicators (9–17)	Factor 1 (18–27)	Operation (28–32)	Factor 2 (33–42)	Result field (43–48)	Field length (49–51)	Decimal positions (52)	Half adjust (H) (53)	Resulting indicators: High 1 > 2 (54–55)	Low 1 < 2 (56–57)	Equal 1 = 2 (58–59)	Comments (60–74)
01	C			EMPNO	COMP	NEXEMP							HI	
02	C													

→ The control field from the primary record is compared with the control field in the secondary record (NEXEMP). If equal a halt will result and the programmer or operator can intervene.

Fig. 15-16. Calculation Specifications coding for Look Ahead feature.

The Look Ahead feature by itself would have little value to the programmer. Therefore, subsequent operations will be conditioned accordingly. For example, assume that the programmer wants the computer to halt in order that any duplicate employee cards may be removed and updating errors avoided. The coding could be specified similar to that entered in the Calculation Specifications form, Figure 15-16. Halt indicators (H1 to H9) cause the computer to halt after sensing a condition and may be used to condition additional calculation and/or output.

THE FORCE OPERATION

When two or more input files are processed in a program, the records from the primary file will be processed before any of the records from the secondary file or files. We also know that this cycle may be altered by the matching record feature (Chapter 10) to allow processing to alternate between files according to a common matching field. However, if a common field was not included in the records of the files, the alternate processing of records between files would be impossible. RPG II offers the FORCE operation, which permits processing to alternate between files even though no common matching field is included. A simple program example will be used to explain the logic and coding concepts of the FORCE operation.

Examine Figure 15-17 and notice the organization of the two card files. The master file, PAYRTE, contains records with an employee name field and hourly rate, and the transaction card file, WEEKLY, includes the employee number and hours worked for the week. Notice that no common field is included in the records which can be used to match the two files and without the FORCE operation the processing of the two files alternately would be impossible.

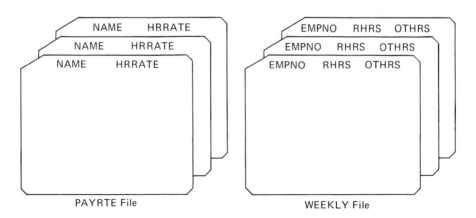

Fig. 15-17.   Arrangement of files when using FORCE operation.

However, in order to process the two files together by the FORCE operation, they must be physically arranged so that a record from the master file corresponds to a record in the same location in the transaction file.

Reference to the File Description Specifications form, Figure 15-18, indicates that the PAYRTE file is designated as primary and the transaction file, WEEKLY, as secondary. Ordinarily RPG program logic would process all of the records from the primary file first, followed by the records from the secondary; however, the FORCE operation can alter this logic.

An examination of the Input Specifications, Figure 15-18, shows that standard coding procedures are used to define the fields included in each of the records from the respective file. Obviously coding for the FORCE operation has no effect on File Description or Input Coding.

The only new coding entries needed for the FORCE operation are entered in the Calculation Specifications form. Examine Figure 15-18 and notice that the first four lines of routine coding are specified to compute total pay for an employee and each line is conditioned by the Ø2 record from the transaction file WEEKLY. The FORCE operation entered on line Ø5 causes a secondary record to be processed after each primary record. Notice that the coding requirements for this operation indicate that the word FORCE is entered into the operation field, columns 28–32, and the name of the secondary file, WEEKLY, is entered in Factor 2. In addition, also notice that the FORCE statement is conditioned with the Ø1 indicator from the master file PAYRTE. The conditioning of the statement with the primary file record indicator is very important for the execution of the FORCE operation.

Because of the FORCE operation each record from the primary file will be processed followed by the corresponding record from the secondary. It must be remembered, however, that the files must be arranged in the proper order or the wrong secondary record will be processed with the primary. The job will continue in this manner until both files are completely processed. In addition, if the programmer wants to insure that only one record is included in the file for each employee, the Look Ahead feature may be used in the program.

THE DSPLY OPERATION

The display (DSPLY) operation code allows input to and output from an operator's console during execution of a program. Only the File Description and Calculation forms are affected by coding for the DSPLY operation. An income statement application program presented in Chapter 5 will be modified to show how the DSPLY operation may be used practically.

Examination of the income statement in Figure 15-19 indicates a record is included in the input file for the statement date. All external and internal company reports require a date and are usually printed after the respective report date. Consequently, UDATE cannot often be used because it is usually

File description specifications:

Line	Form type	Filename	File type (I/O/U/C/D)	(E)	(A/D)	File format	Block length	Record length	Mode of processing / Device
0 2	F	PAYRTE	I P			F	96	96	MFCUI
0 3	F	WEEKLY	I S			F	96	96	MFCUI
0 4	F	REPORT	O			F		152	PRINTER
0 5	F								

Input specifications:

Line	Form type	Filename	Number (1N) / Option (O) / Record identifying indicator	Position 1	Not(N)/C/Z/D	Character	Field location From	Field location To	Decimal positions	Field name	Field indicators Plus
0 1	I	PAYRTE	C C 01	80		CR					
0 2	I						1	20		NAME	
0 3	I						21	24	2	HPRATE	
0 4	I	WEEKLY	F F 02	96		CT					
0 5	I						1	5		EMPNO	
0 6	I						10	12	2	HRS	
0 7	I						15	17	2	OTHRS	03
0 8	I										

Fig. 15-18. File description, input and calculation specifications coding for example program using FORCE operation.

Calculation specifications:

Line	Form type	Control level (L0-L9, LR, SR)	Indicators			Factor 1	Operation	Factor 2	Result field	Field length	Decimal positions	Half adjust (H)	Resulting indicators	Comments
			Not / And	And	Not / And								Arithmetic / Compare / Lookup	
01	C		Ø2			HRRATE	MULT	RHRS	RPAY	6	2	H		REGULAR PAY
02	C		Ø2	Ø3		HRRATE	MULT	15	OTRATE	4	2	H		OVERTIME RATE
03	C		Ø2	Ø3		OTRATE	MULT	OTHRS	OTPAY	5	2	H		OVERTIME PAY
04	C		Ø2	Ø1		RPAY	ADD	OTPAY	TOTPAY	6	2			TOTAL PAY
06	C						FORCE	WEEKLY						

Fig. 15-18. (Concluded)

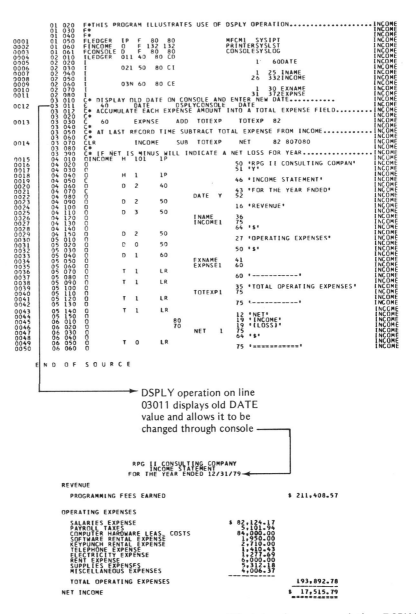

```
                01 020  F*THIS PROGRAM ILLUSTRATES USE OF DSPLY OPERATION..................INCOME
                01 030  F*                                                                  INCOME
                01 040  F*                                                                  INCOME
        0001    01 050  FLEDGER  IP  F  80  80           MFCM1 SYSIPT                        INCOME
        0002    01 060  FINCOME  O   F 132 132           PRINTERSYSLST                       INCOME
        0003    01 061  FCONSOLE D   F  80  80           CONSOLESYSLOG                       INCOME
        0004    02 010  ILEDGER   011 40  80 CD                                              INCOME
        0005    02 020  I                                           1  60DATE                INCOME
        0006    02 030  I        021 50  80 CI                                               INCOME
        0007    02 040  I                                        1  25 INAME                 INCOME
        0008    02 050  I                                       26  332INCOME               INCOME
        0009    02 060  I        03N 60  80 CE                                               INCOME
        0010    02 070  I                                        1  30 EXNAME               INCOME
        0011    02 080  I                                       31  372EXPNSE               INCOME
                03 010  C* DISPLAY OLD DATE ON CONSOLE AND ENTER NEW DATE...........         INCOME
        0C12    03 011  C      40          DATE    DSPLYCONSOLE    DATE                       INCOME
                03 012  C* ACCUMULATE EACH EXPENSE AMOUNT INTO A TOTAL EXPENSE FIELD........  INCOME
                03 020  C*                                                                   INCOME
        0013    03 030  C       60          EXPNSE   ADD  TOTEXP    TOTEXP 82                 INCOME
                03 040  C*                                                                   INCOME
                03 050  C* AT LAST RECORD TIME SUBTRACT TOTAL EXPENSE FROM INCOME...........  INCOME
                03 060  C*                                                                   INCOME
        0014    03 070  CLR         INCOME      SUB  TOTEXP    NET    82 807080              INCOME
                03 080  C*                                                                   INCOME
                03 390  C* IF NET IS MINUS WILL INDICATE A NET LOSS FOR YEAR................  INCOME
        0015    04 010  OINCOME  H  1O1    1P                                                 INCOME
        0016    04 020  O                                          50 *RPG II CONSULTING COMPAN*  INCOME
        0017    04 030  O                                          51 *Y*                     INCOME
        0018    04 040  O        H  1      1P                                                 INCOME
        0019    04 050  O                                          46 *INCOME STATEMENT*      INCOME
        0020    04 060  O        D  2      40                                                 INCOME
        0021    04 070  O                                          43 *FOR THE YEAR ENDED*    INCOME
        0022    04 080  O                              DATE  Y     52                         INCOME
        0023    04 090  O        D  2      50                                                 INCOME
        0024    04 100  O                                          16 *REVENUE*               INCOME
        0025    04 110  O        D  3      50                                                 INCOME
        0026    04 120  O                              INAME       36                         INCOME
        0027    04 130  O                              INCOME1     75                         INCOME
        0028    04 140  O                                          64 *$*                     INCOME
        0029    04 150  O        D  2      50                                                 INCOME
        0030    05 010  O                                          27 *OPERATING EXPENSES*    INCOME
        0031    05 020  O        D  O      50                                                 INCOME
        0032    05 030  O                                          50 *$*                     INCOME
        0033    05 040  O        D  1      60                                                 INCOME
        0034    05 050  O                              EXNAME      41                         INCOME
        0035    05 060  O                              EXPNSE1     60                         INCOME
        0036    05 070  O        T  1      LR                                                 INCOME
        0037    05 080  O                                          60 *-----------*           INCOME
        0038    05 090  O        T  1      LR                                                 INCOME
        0039    05 100  O                                          35 *TOTAL OPERATING EXPENSES*  INCOME
        0040    05 110  O                              TOTEXP1     75                         INCOME
        0041    05 120  O        T  1      LR                                                 INCOME
        0042    05 130  O                                          75 *-----------*           INCOME
        0043    05 140  O        T  1      LR                                                 INCOME
        0044    05 150  O                                          12 *NET*                   INCOME
        0045    06 010  O                                  80      19 *INCOME*                INCOME
        0046    06 020  O                                  70      19 *(LOSS)*                INCOME
        0047    06 030  O                              NET    1    75                         INCOME
        0048    06 040  O                                          64 *$*                     INCOME
        0049    06 050  O        T  O      LR                                                 INCOME
        0050    06 060  O                                          75 *===========*           INCOME
```

E N D O F S O U R C E

DSPLY operation on line
03011 displays old DATE
value and allows it to be
changed through console

```
        RPG II CONSULTING COMPANY
             INCOME STATEMENT
        FOR THE YEAR ENDED 12/31/79

REVENUE

    PROGRAMMING FEES EARNED                        $ 211,408.57

OPERATING EXPENSES

    SALARIES EXPENSE                  $ 82,124.17
    PAYROLL TAXES                        5,101.94
    COMPUTER HARDWARE LEAS_ COSTS       84,000.00
    SOFTWARE RENTAL EXPENSE              1,950.00
    KEYPUNCH RENTAL EXPENSE              2,710.00
    TELEPHONE EXPENSE                    1,410.43
    ELECTRICITY EXPENSE                  1,277.69
    RENT EXPENSE                         6,000.00
    SUPPLIES EXPENSES                    5,312.18
    MISCELLANEOUS EXPENSES               4,006.37
                                      -----------
    TOTAL OPERATING EXPENSES                         193,892.78

NET INCOME                                         $  17,515.79
                                                   ===========
```

Fig. 15-19. Income Statement program modified to show use of the DSPLY operation code.

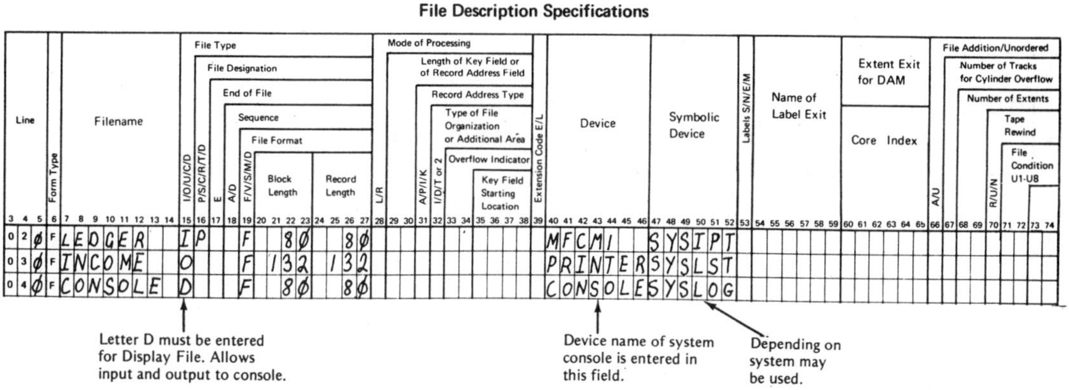

File Description Specifications

Line	Form Type	Filename	I/O/U/C/D	P/S/C/R/T/D	E	F/V/S/M/D	Block Length	Record Length	L/R	A/P/I/K	I/D/T or 2	Key Field Starting Location	Extension Code E/L	Device	Symbolic Device	Labels S/N/E/M	Name of Label Exit	Core Index	A/U	R/U/N	File Condition U1-U8
0 2 Ø	F	LEDGER	I	P		F	8 Ø	8 Ø						MFCM1	SYSIPT						
0 3 Ø	F	INCOME	O			F	1 3 2	1 3 2						PRINTER	SYSLST						
0 4 Ø	F	CONSOLE	D			F	8 Ø	8 Ø						CONSOLE	SYSLOG						

Letter D must be entered for Display File. Allows input and output to console.

Device name of system console is entered in this field.

Depending on system may be used.

Fig. 15-20. File Description entries required for DSPLY operation.

after the report date. In lieu of physically changing the value in the logical date record, which may be inconvenient if it is stored on disk or tape, it may be changed by using the DSPLY function. Figure 15-20 shows the new coding entries in the File Description form for the DSPLY operation. The entries are summarized below:

Filename (Columns 7–14). A file must be defined in the program which provides for input and output to the console. Any programmer-supplied file name may be used in this field.

File Type (Column 15). Letter D must be entered in this field to indicate a *display* file.

Device (Columns 40–46). The device name (usually CONSOLE) for the computer system's console is entered in this field.

Symbolic Device (Columns 47–52). Depending on the system, an entry may be required in this field. IBM 370 systems require that SYSLOG be used unless the console is assigned to another symbolic device in the job control.

Notice all other coding entries in the File Description form remain the same.

Figure 15-21 details the calculation form in three alternative coding examples available with the DSPLY operation. In all the examples the DSPLY operation code must be entered in the operation field (columns 28–32) and the file name, defined as the *display file* in File Description, has to be entered in Factor 2 (columns 33–42). Entries in Factor 1 and/or the Result Field depend on the DSPLY option required. The options are described below and illustrated in Figure 15-21.

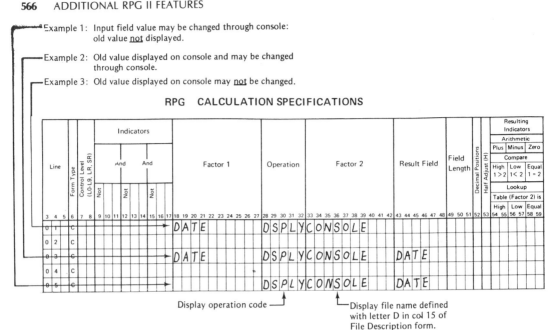

Example 1: Input field value may be changed through console: old value _not_ displayed.

Example 2: Old value displayed on console and may be changed through console.

Example 3: Old value displayed on console may _not_ be changed.

Fig. 15-21. Calculation coding alternatives for DSPLY operation code.

Example 1. If the input field value is to be displayed but not changed, the field name is entered in Factor 1. The Result field is not used for this display option.

Example 2. An input field value may be displayed and its value changed through the console by entering the field name in both Factor 1 and the Result Field. Note field names do not have to be the same.

Example 3. An input field value may be changed by entering the field name in the Result field. Factor 1 is not used if the previous value is not to be displayed.

The income statement application program in Figure 15-19 shows on calculation form line 03010 that the variable filed DATE is entered in both Factor 1 and the Result field. This coding option will display the value in DATE before the operator changes it and enters new date through the console. If the value was not to be changed, the ENTER key (on the console typewriter or keyboard), or other appropriate entry, would be pressed and the old date value would remain.

In summary, the DSPLY operation provides for additional input/output control of data often necessary for the processing of data files.

QUESTIONS

1. When should internal subroutines be used in a program?
2. What are the RPG II operations unique to internal subroutine coding?
3. Where in calculations are the instructions, included in the subroutine, located? How are they identified?
4. What is the function of the *PLACE word?
5. In what coding form and columns is the *PLACE word used?
6. What coding forms are used for the DEBUG operation?
7. Examine the Calculation Specifications for the DEBUG operation alternatives given below and explain the meaning of the entries in Factor 1, the Operation field, and the Result field.

Factor 1	Operation	Factor 2	Result field
18 19 20 21 22 23 24 25 26 27	28 29 30 31 32	33 34 35 36 37 38 39 40 41 42	43 44 45 46 47 48
	DEBUG	OUTPUT	
	DEBUG	OUTPUT	FIELDA
'ONE'	DEBUG	OUTPUT	
'TWO'	DEBUG	OUTPUT	FIELDT

8. Examine the DEBUG statements given above, and for each example write the format for the printed DEBUG record.
9. What is the function of the Look Ahead feature?
10. On a blank input form complete the following input coding to provide for the Look Ahead feature on the records in the data file.

Sequence	Number (1-N)	Option (O)	Record identifying indicator or **	Record identification codes 1 Position	Not (N)	C/Z/D	Character	2 Position	Not (N)	C/Z/D	Character	3 Position	Not (N)	C/Z/D	Character	Stacker select	P = packed/B = binary	Field location From	To	Decimal positions	Field name
15 16	17	18	19 20	21 22 23 24	25	26	27	28 29 30 31	32	33	34	35 36 37 38	39	40	41	42	43	44 45 46 47	48 49 50 51	52	53 54 55 56 57 58
C A			2 1	9 6		C	S														
																		1	4		SALNUM
																		5	1 2	2	SALES
																		1 3	1 6	4	COMRAT

11. Use the information from Question 10, and on a blank calculation form complete the coding needed to check for a duplicate record for the records assigned the 21-record identifying indicator. If a duplicate record is sensed halt processing.
12. What does the FORCE operation do? When should it be used?
13. What coding form and field entries are used for the FORCE operation?
14. What coding form(s) are used for the DSPLY operation?
15. What are the options available with the DSPLY operation code?
16. Explain applications where the DSPLY operation may be used.

EXERCISES

15-1. On a blank Output-Format Specifications coding form write the coding using the *PLACE word to print the fields given below twice on every line.

Fields to be included on line 1:

FIRST	(12 characters)
MIDDLE	(1 character)
LAST	(15 characters)
SSNUM	(11 characters)

Fields to be included on line 2:

STREET	(24 characters)

Fields to be included on line 3:

CITYST	(30 characters)
ZIP	(5 characters)

15-2. How would you modify the coding to print the fields three times on every line?
15-3. From the following flowchart complete the calculation coding for the internal subroutine CALROU.

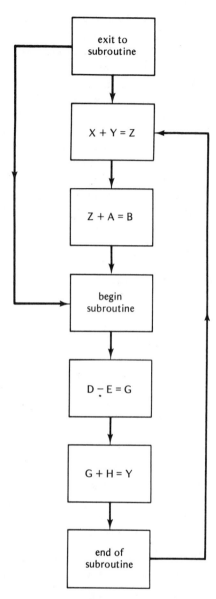

15-4. Assume that a primary file INPUT is in order by salesman name, and transaction file SALES is in order by the salesman number. The total sales to date for each salesman based on the total in INPUT and the current week's sales needs to be determined, but the files do not have any fields that permit a match and the subsequent multiprocessing.

Make the necessary Calculation Specifications coding so that the files may be processed and the corresponding records processed together.

Assign record identifying indicator 77 to the records from the INPUT file and 88 to the records from the SALES file. Assume that the first record in the INPUT file corresponds with the first record in the transaction file, SALES, and so on.

15-5. Write the File Description and Calculation coding using the DSPLY operation code based on the following information:

An input file named LEDGER consists of the general ledger account information for a company. The file is stored on disk and the first record type in the file is a data record for any statement date. Because of the inconvenience of updating this record value, the DSPLY operation code is to be used to change the value when processing the file. Define the output printer file as TRIBAL and the console file as CHANGE. Use 80 bytes for the input file with a blocking factor of one, and 132 for the output file. The console record size will depend on the system used.

LABORATORY ASSIGNMENTS

LABORATORY ASSIGNMENT 15-1:
ELECTRIC COMPANY BILLING FOR INDUSTRIAL AND HOME OWNERS

An electric company has different base and usage rates for industrial users and homeowners. The rate structure is as follows:

Rates for Homeowners:
Base amount = 1,000 kilowatt hours
Base rate = 5¢ per kilowatt hour
Usage rate over 1,000 kilowatt hours = 4.2¢ per kwh

Rates for Industrial Users:
Base amount = 5,000 kilowatt hours
Base rate = 4.5¢ per kilowatt hour
Usage rate over 5,000 kilowatt hours = 3.5¢ per kwh

Write an RPG II program using two subroutines: one for the homeowners' billing structure and the other for the industrial users.

Format of Data Records:

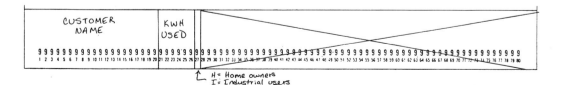

Calculations.   Compare the user field (H or I) to determine whether the routine for homeowners or industrial users is applicable for the record. Calculations in each subroutine requires that the base amount is multiplied by the base rate to give the base dollar amount. Any kilowatt hours over the base amount are multiplied by the usage rate to give an amount over the base. The base amount and excess are added to compute the customer's monthly bill.

Example calculation: Consumption: 1100 kwh (homeowner)

$$1{,}000 \text{ kwh} \times .05 = \$50$$
$$1{,}100 - 1000 = 100 \text{ usage kwh}$$
$$100 \times .042 = \$4.20$$
$$50 + 4.20 = 54.20 \text{ monthly bill}$$

All kwh usage is subject to a 1.5¢ per 100 kwh state tax, which is added to all customer bills.

Example calculation (Based on Example Given Above)

$$1{,}100 \text{ kwh} \div 100 = 11$$
$$11 \times .015 = .165$$
$$54.20 + .165 = 54.365 \text{ or } 54.37 \text{ total amount of bill}$$

Design of Printed Report:

Data for Laboratory Assignment:

Customer's Name	Kilowatt Hrs	User Type
IVAN PATZIK	000945	H
MANAGEMENT CO	011000	I
CHRIS LENTZ	001400	H
TAYCO INCORPORATED	004500	I
FRANZ ECKART	001050	H

LABORATORY ASSIGNMENT 15-2:
LOOK AHEAD FUNCTION

Modify a program you have previously completed so you may use the Look Ahead function. Check with your professor to insure that the look ahead function is practical with the program you select.

LABORATORY ASSIGNMENT 15-3:
DSPLY OPERATION

Modify a program you have previously completed so you may use the DSPLY operation. Check with your professor to insure that the display function is applicable to the program's logic.

Appendix I
MANUFACTURERS'
INPUT AND OUTPUT
DEVICE NAMES

IBM INPUT AND OUTPUT DEVICE NAMES:

Device Name	Related Hardware Unit
PRINTER	Line Printer
TAPE	Input or output for a tape unit
READ01	Input for an IBM 2501 card reader
READ05	Input for an IBM 3505 card reader
READ20	Input or output for an IBM 2520 Card Read/Punch unit
READ25	Input or output for an IBM 3525 Card Punch
READ40	Input or output for an IBM 2540 Card Read/Punch
READ42	Input or output for an IBM 1442 Card Read/Punch
MFCM1	Input or output for an IBM 2560 Multifunction Card Machine (primary input hopper)
MFCM2	Input or output for an IBM 2560 Multifunction Card Machine (secondary input hopper)
MFCU1	Input or output for an IBM 5425 Multifunction Card Device (primary input hopper)
MFCU2	Input or output for an IBM 5425 Multifunction Card Device (secondary input hopper)
DISKET	Input or output for an IBM 3540 Diskette input/output unit
DISK11	Input or output for an IBM 2311 Disk Storage Drive

DISK14	Input or output for an IBM 2314 or IBM 2319 Direct Access Storage device
DISK30	Input or output for an IBM 3330 Direct Access Storage device
DISK40	Input or output for an IBM 3340 Disk Facility device
CONSOLE	Output (and input) for a console typewriter or display unit
SPECIAL	Input or output to a device that is accessed by a user supplied routine. Programmer may use his own IOCS routine
BSCA	Input or output for a telecommunications device

BURROUGHS (B 1700 SYSTEMS):

Device Name	Related Hardware Unit
READER	80-column card reader
MFCU1	96-column card reader (primary hopper)
MFCU2	96-column card reader (secondary hopper)
PUNCH	80-column card reader
PRINTER or PRINTR2	Line printer
TAPE	Magnetic tape unit
DISK	Disk file
CONSOLE	Console unit
BSCA	Telecommunications file
DATACOM	Telecommunications file

The following additional Device Names (columns 40–46) are also acceptable on a B 1700 system:

READ01	PUNCH20
MFCM1	PUNCH42
MFCM2	PRINTUF
READ20	PRINTLF
READ40	DISK11
READ42	DISK11F
CRP	DISK45
CRP20	SPO
DATA96	

UNIVAC 9200/9300 SYSTEM DEVICE NAMES:

Device Name	Related Hardware Unit
READER	Univac 0716 or 0717 Card Reader Subsystem

PUNCH, or ROWPUNCH	Univac 0604 or 0605 Card Punch Subsystem
CRP, or RRP	Univac 0604 or 0605 Card Punch Subsystem with prepunch read feature
PRINT16,	Univac 0768, 0770, or 0773 Printer Subsystem
PRINT48, PRINT63, PRINTDR TAPE, TAPE6C, TAPE7	Uniservo VI-C, Uniservo 12/16, or Uniservo 20 Magnetic Tape Subsystem
DISC, DISC11, DISC14	Univac 8411, 8414, or 8430 Dic Sub

VARIAN SYSTEMS:

Device Name	Symbolic Device	Related Hardware Unit
DISK	30	Disk file
MFCU1	13	Card reader (hopper 1)
MFCU2	13	Card reader (hopper 2)
PRINTER	5	Line printer
PRINTER2	15	Line printer
CONSOLE	1(OC)	Cathode Ray Tube (console)
TAPE	18	Magnetic Tape Unit
READER	4	Card Reader
PUNCH	14	Punch unit

Note: Symbolic Device entries are right-justified.

DATA GENERAL SYSTEMS:

Device Name	Symbolic Device	Related Hardware Unit
PRINTER	$LPT	Line printer
CONSOLE	$TTI	Console input
CONSOLE	$TTO	Console output
TAPE	TAPE	Magnetic tape unit
DISK	file name entered in cols. 7–14 of file description is entered here	Disk file

Note: File description entry for line printer file requires that the letter D be entered in column 19 instead of an F.

Data General System is basically a cardless system.....

Appendix II
JOB STREAMS
AND JOB CONTROL
LANGUAGE (JCL)

IBM 370 DOS/VS SYSTEMS:

Example I.   Compile and execute an RPG II source program

```
// JOB XXXXXXXX        (first card of deck)
// OPTION LINK
// EXEC RPGII
   Source program here
/*
// EXEC LNKEDT
// EXEC
   Any card data here
/*
/&                     (last card of deck)
```

Example II.   Compile and execute an RPG II source program that includes Tables or Arrays stored on cards. OBJECT TIME TABLES OR ARRAYS.

```
// JOB XXXXXXXX
// OPTION LINK
// EXEC RPGII
```

```
      Source program here
/*
// EXEC LNKEDT
// EXEC
      Table or Array data here
/*
      Any card data here
/*
/&
```

Example III. Compile and execute an **RPG II** source program that includes Tables or Arrays stored on cards. For COMPILE TIME Tables or Arrays.

```
// JOB XXXXXXXX             (First card of deck)
// OPTION LINK
// EXEC RPGII
      Source program here
**
      Compile Table or Array here
/*
// EXEC LNKEDT
// EXEC
      Any card data here
/*
/&                          (last card of deck)
```

Note: All Compile Time Tables or Arrays must be preceded by a ** control card.

Example IV. Compile and execute an **RPG II** source program that either loads and/or processes a Sequential Disk file.

```
// JOB XXXXXXXX
// OPTION LINK
// EXEC RPGII
      Source program here
/*
// EXEC LNKEDT
// ASSGN SYSnnn,X'nnn'     (Note: n indicates appropriate numbers.)
// DLBL (operands)          See notes for format of DLBL control card.
```

```
// EXTENT operands)        See notes for format of EXTENT control card.
// EXEC
     Any card data here
/*
/&
```

Example V.   Compile and execute an RPG II source program that either loads and/or processes an Indexed-Sequential Disk File (ISAM).

```
// JOB XXXXXXXX            Note: X's indicate job name may be from
                          1 to 6 alphanumeric characters in length)

// OPTION LINK
// EXEC RPGII
     Source program here

// LBLTYP NSD(03)          number in parenthesis depends on EX-
                          TENT cards used
// EXEC LNKEDT
// ASSGN SYSnnn, X'nnn'    (n indicates appropriate numbers)
// DLBL (operands)         See notes for format of DLBL control card
// EXTENT (operands)       See notes for format of EXTENT control
                          card
// EXTENT (operands)       At least two EXTENT cards must be used
                          for an ISAM disk file.
// EXEC
     Any card data here
/*
/&
```

Example VI.   Compile a source program and catalog to the Core Image Library

```
// JOB XXXXXXXX
// OPTION CATAL
     PHASE name,*          (Note: name may be 1 to 6 characters in
                          length, first letter must be alphabetic.
// EXEC RPGII              Notice first letter of this card begins in
                          column 2.
     Source program here
/*
// EXEC LNKEDT
/&
```

Example VII. Execute a program cataloged in the Core Image Library to process an input card file

```
// JOB XXXXXXXX
// EXEC XXXXXXXX   (Name of Phase when program was cataloged)
    Card data here
/*
/&
```

Example VIII. Execute a program cataloged in the Core Image Library to process a sequential file stored on disk

```
// JOB XXXXXXXX
// ASSGN SYSnnn,X'nnn'
// DLBL (operands)
// EXTENT (operands)
// EXEC XXXXXXXX   (Name of Phase when program was cataloged)
/&
```

Note: The job stream to process an ISAM file is identical except the LBLTYP and additional EXTENT cards would be included.

Example IX. Catalog the JCL for a program in the Procedure Library. Program was previously cataloged in Core Image Library

```
// JOB XXXXXXXX
// EXEC MAINT
    CATALP XXXXXXXX      Name of procedure may be 1 to 6 char-
                         acters in length, first letter must be
                         alphabetic. Notice first letter of this card
                         begins in column 2.
// ASSGN SYSNNN,X'161'
// DLBL (operands)
// EXTENT (operands)
// EXEC XXXXXXXX     ⟵ Name of phase previously cataloged in
                        Core Image Library
/+
/*
/&
```

Note: ASSGN, DLBL, and EXTENT cards would be included as appropriate

Example X. Execute a cataloged procedure.

```
// JOB XXXXXXXX
// EXEC PROC = XXXXXXXX◄—Name of cataloged procedure
        Card data here      Would not be included if file on disk or
                            tape
/*
/&
```

EXPLANATION OF JOB CONTROL
LANGUAGE CONTROL CARDS
FOR IBM 370 DOS

// OPTION	(Variety of options may be used here separated by commas)
	Options include: LINK, LIST, NOLIST, DUMP, NODUMP, NOLINK, DECK, NODECK, CATAL
	(Use of option depends on job requirements and/or options in System Supervisor at SYSGEN (system generation) time.
// EXEC	(Name of program stored in Core Image Library to be executed)
	When RPGII is entered as program name the RPGII compiler is executed. User's program name entered executes a cataloged program. If no program name is used program previously link edited will be executed.
/*	Indicates end of program instructions and/or end of data files. Must be used at the end of data files or file *will not* be closed.
**	Separates source program from compile tables and compile tables from each other.
// ASSGN SYSnnn,X'nnn'	This control card assigns a symbolic device to a physical I/O device.
SYSnnn	Represents symbolic device name. Must be same as name entered in columns 47–52 of the File Description Specifications form.

X'*nnn*'	Indicates channel number of the device established when device was installed.
// LBLTYP NSD(nn) or TAPE	Defines amount of storage allocated for processing of a tape or ISAM file. The *n*'s contained in parenthesis indicate number of EXTENT cards used for file. Not used for sequential or direct disk files.
// DLBL filename, ['File-ID'], [date], [codes]	File identification name here', data, file type codes
Filename	Name used here may only be seven characters in length and be exactly the same as the name used in the File Description form columns 7-13.
'file-ID'	Name used here may be 1 to 44 alphanumeric characters in length. This name is stored in the Volume Table of Contents (VTOC). If file-ID is omitted from this control card the filename is used.
Date	May indicate expiration date in a yy/ddd format or retention period from 0 to 9999 days. If date is omitted in DLBL card an automatic 7-day retention period is assumed. If an earlier date is used than UDATE file area is written over without warning.
Codes	Entry here depends on file organization type as follows: SD-Sequential Disk Data File DA-Direct File ISC-Indexed-Sequential for creating a data file ISE-Indexed-Sequential for processing a data file. If this entry is omitted from DLBL card SD is assumed.
//EXTENT [symbolic unit], [serial-number], [type], [sequence-number], [relative track], [number of tracks]	Symbolic unit, serial number, type, sequence number, relative track, number of tracks
Symbolic unit	Name here must correspond with the one used in columns 47–52 of the File Description form for the related file.
Serial number	Six character entry indicating serial number of the disk pack used for the data file.

Type	Indicates type of EXTENT which include the following:
	1 prime data area
	2 independent overflow area (only for ISAM files)
	4 index area (only for ISAM files)
	8 data area for split cylinder
	If this entry omitted type 1 is assumed

Sequence number — Indicates sequence number of EXTENT cards in a multi-EXTENT file as an ISAM. ISAM files may include a maximum of 4 EXTENTS. One for a master index, another for the normal index, one for the prime data area, and one for an independent overflow area. At least the cylinder index and prime data areas must be provided for an ISAM file. Numbering begins with 0 for the master index; 1 for the cylinder index; 2 for the prime data area, and 3 for independent overflow area. Not used for SD (sequential) or DA (direct) disk files.

Relative track — Indicates the track on which the index, or prime data area, or independent overflow area begins. Entry may be 1 to 5 digits in length. If area began on track one hundred 100 would be entered. The prime data area of an ISAM file must begin on the first track of any cylinder.

Number of tracks — Indicates total number of tracks allocated to the data file. Number depends on size of data file in approximate total number of bytes. Additions to file must be considered.

For ISAM File Prime Date Area, number here must be multiple of whole cylinders.

Note: Brackets, [ ], indicate entry is optional.

IBM SYSTEM/3:

Note: JCL is called OCL for these systems . . . .

Example I. Compile and execute an RPG II source program.

// CALL RPG,F1

```
// RUN
    Source program here
/*
/&
// LOAD*
// FILE NAME-CUST, PACK, VOL1, UNIT F1, RECORDS 1000, RETAIN-P
    (needed for disk files)
// RUN
/*
    Any data cards here
/*
/&
```

Note: The // FILE NAME OCL cards are needed for every disk file referenced in program. Appropriate programmer's manual should be referred to for format options of this control card.

BURROUGHS B 1700 SYSTEMS:

Example I. Compile and execute an RPG II source program. Stores compiled program (object code) temporarily.

```
? COMPILE            (See below for options for this card)
? DATA RPG/CARD
    Source deck here
? END
? DATA RPG/CARD
    Any data cards here
? END
```

Options for ? COMPILE card

COMPILE TO LIBRARY: If source program compiles successfully will store object code on disk and enter program name into disk directory. Program would not be scheduled for execution.

COMPILE SAVE: If source program compiles successfully this option will store object code on disk and enter program name in directory. The program will also be scheduled for execution.

COMPILE FOR SYNTAX: This option provides for a diagnostic listing as the only output. Does not execute compiled program or store on disk.

Example II.   Compile and execute a source program containing tables:

```
?  COMPILE
?  DATA RPG/CARD
   Source deck here
?  END
?  DATA RPG/VECTOR
   Vector (table) data cards here
?  END
?  DATA RPG/VECTOR
                  Any data cards here
?  END
```

SPERRY   UNIVAC   OPERATING SYSTEM/3(OS/3)

Example I.   Compile, Link, and Execute an RPG II source program

```
// JOB jobname
// RPG
/$
   Source deck here
/*
// LINK your 6 character program name here
   (same name as that entered in cols. 75–80 of control card specifications form)
/*
// DVC 20
// LFD PRNTR
   device assignments as needed
// EXEC program name defined in // LINK card
   /$
   any data here
/*
/&
// FIN
```

Note: For a detailed explanation of control cards and options refer to programmer's manuals.

INDEX